The Best Book of:
WordStar®

The Best Book of:
WordStar®

Vincent Alfieri

HAYDEN BOOKS
A Division of Howard W. Sams & Company
4300 West 62nd Street
Indianapolis, Indiana 46268 USA

Also by Vincent Alfieri and published by Hayden Books:

Mastering WordStar

The Best Book of: WordPerfect®

Copyright © 1987 by Vincent Alfieri

FIRST EDITION
FIRST PRINTING—1987

International Standard Book Number: 0-672-48404-8
Library of Congress Catalog Card Number: 87-62224

The following people contributed to the publication of this book:

Acquisitions Editor: *James S. Hill*
Reviewer: *Peter Mierau*
Coordinating Editor: *Katherine S. Ewing*
Copy and Production Editor: *Brown Editorial Service*
Cover Photographer: *Lou Odor*
Compositor: *Impressions, Inc.*

To Ramón, who has the patience of a saint

Contents

Preface

Time, as you know, has a habit of flying, and the times are continually a-changin'. Both have caught up with and induced me to prepare a major revision of my book, *Mastering WordStar.* The appearance of a long awaited upgrade to WordStar has, however, made me alter my original plan. That is, because the newest WordStar is so different from older versions, I decided that a new WordStar book would signify a clean break with the past. Hence, *The Best Book of: WordStar.*

Be aware, then, that the new WordStar, officially known as *WordStar Professional Release 4,* or any release numbered greater than 4, is the "star" of this new book. If you have a previous release of WordStar, you can work with only a few of the exercises.

This book bears only a casual resemblance to its predecessor. Need I say (ahem!) that it's better? Oh, yes, the basic format is the same: it's still a hands-on, step-by-step tutorial. You'll see many examples from *Mastering WordStar,* and you'll still have to put up with my feeble attempts at humor. What's new is that I've restructured the material to present it in a more logical fashion, to make room for the new WordStar features, and to provide even more useful exercises and tips for working with WordStar. I think you'll like the results!

I've also incorporated in this new book many of the suggestions of readers who have taken the time to write to me about *Mastering WordStar.* From Indonesia to Kansas and from Sweden to Florida, the letters keep coming. My thanks to all!

Vincent Alfieri
Los Angeles, California

Acknowledgments

I wrote *Mastering WordStar* on an Osborne 1 computer, so I would again like to thank Thom Hogan and Mike Ianimico for their Osborne 1 tutorial manual: a good introduction to the mysteries of computers. Although I now own a "PC-compatible" Zenith computer, I am also obliged to the folks at Software Central in Pasadena, California, for letting me test the first version of the book on one of their IBM Personal Computers.

I am deeply grateful to the many people at the "new" MicroPro International Corporation for their help, guidance, and cooperation. Special thanks to Peter Mierau, programmer *extraordinaire,* for reviewing the final manuscript and providing extensive comments and clarifications, and to Lee Lensky for his good-natured support. It was also a great pleasure to be a member of the beta testing team for WordStar Professional Release 4. I even got a nifty paperweight!

What can I say about my editor, Lynn Brown, except that she's the best? What can I say about the entire staff at Howard W. Sams & Company, except that they're superb? Enough said!

For help over and above the call of duty, a tip of the hat to Lavon Collins at Hewlett-Packard's Boise Division. She came through for me, suffering as I was in the crunch of an imminent deadline, by providing the LaserJet soft fonts I needed to complete Chapter 26.

Thanks to my long-standing friend and former Columbia University colleague, Kirsten Grimstad, for her invaluable advice about the publishing world, and to Ramón Ramos, whose Libran level-headedness has always been a good antidote to this stubborn, impetuous, and at times grouchy Taurus.

Finally—last but not least—a sizable chunk of gratitude goes to Rosa Torge and her associates at the Word Processing Center of the law firm of Musick, Peeler & Garrett in Los Angeles, the benchmark by which to measure all other word processing departments.

Introduction

WordStar has been around almost since the beginning of the microcomputer era. For years anyone who wanted substantial word processing power on a microcomputer had no choice but to use WordStar. Now the number of word processing programs is legion, yet WordStar is still the favorite of millions.

There are good reasons for WordStar's continued popularity. WordStar is by far the most flexible word processing program on the market. Contrary to what you may have heard, WordStar is easy to learn and use for basic word processing, yet has all the power to accomplish more elaborate tasks. It won't "peak" before you do: the more you get to know it, the more versatile it becomes. It's fast and efficient, and you can customize it to work the way you want it to. Finally, it's consistent: after you learn WordStar on one computer, you know how to use it on any other computer.

Many people, once they've mastered the basics of WordStar, never go any further in exploring all its many features. That's unfortunate, because they miss learning ways to save themselves time and work, one of the reasons they probably bought a computer in the first place. A major goal of this book is to give you an awareness and understanding of the *entire range* of WordStar's power. I've organized the material as a series of graduated examples that you can study at your own pace. I have tried to provide realistic examples and to offer many tricks of the trade that experienced word processors use to save themselves time, work, and needless frustration.

I've arranged the exercises around standard word processing tasks, because that's how you'll normally work with WordStar. Right from the start you're learning WordStar in a realistic context. That is, you work with the program's features as they *interact* with each other to help you produce the best-looking results with the least amount of effort. The first few chapters jump around a bit from one type of feature to another, but I've found this to be the best way to learn WordStar.

Even if you already know the basics—and especially if you don't—I strongly urge you to study the chapters in order, because some examples build on and revise earlier ones (see Appendix A, "The Files Used in this Book"). To get the most out of this book, you should work your way through the examples at your computer and *learn by doing*. That way, you'll develop a solid set of good habits and reusable patterns that will pay you back continually in your real work.

After all, you didn't learn how to drive a car by sitting at home, did you? You need practice before you'll develop the patterns to use WordStar effectively. Of course you will make mistakes! But you will learn from them and maybe even have some fun along the way. At least I hope you'll get a kick out of some of the examples that I have chosen.

This book complements the excellent documentation that comes with WordStar. As a reference aid, I've provided a structured listing of all WordStar commands and features in Appendix B. If you're an experienced WordStar user, refer to this appendix to apprise yourself of the many new commands and in what chapter I discuss them. There's also a complete and cross-referenced index to help you find information easily.

So many novice computer users start off on the wrong foot. They read the documentation that comes with their new machines and fear that they'll never figure out what *bits* and *bytes* are. No wonder so many people have computer phobia! They are the victims of what I call the *terminology hassle*. I have tried to avoid "computerese" as much as possible. When I introduce a new term, I explain it in everyday language.

You'll be surprised at how quickly you can master the basics of WordStar and develop the confidence to explore the program in greater depth. After you have worked your way through this book, you should be able to answer with a resounding "yes!" the question that many people ask me: "Can I do such-and-such with WordStar?" Yes, more than likely you can! It may not be immediately obvious to you when you first begin using WordStar, but the capabilities are there for the finding. They help you get the most professional look for your work, and any experienced word processor will tell you that obtaining that professional look is always first priority.

This book is not meant to be the "last word" on WordStar. I want to teach you practical ways to make your life easier, but you're sure to come up with other, equally practical, methods of dealing with your own word processing needs. This book is as much a primer on word processing as it is a WordStar tutorial. After completing this book, you'll understand what it means to have an *active and creative* approach to word processing, an approach that takes full advantage of the power and versatility of WordStar.

Dear Reader, thanks a million for buying this book! I hope you enjoy using it as much as I've enjoyed writing it. Please drop me a line, care of the publisher, to tell me what you think.

Before You Begin

This section outlines some important information about computers, WordStar versions, and working with this book. Please take the time to read through the next few pages.

Hardware, Software, and Operating Systems

A computer is worthless without two things: (1) electricity, and (2) the instructions to run it. You must "feed" a computer its instructions whenever you use the machine. The instructions are the *program* (for instance, WordStar), and they come on floppy disks. When you give the machine its instructions you are *loading the program.*

If you prefer to think of your computer as a souped-up appliance, you should still realize that it's different from, say, a toaster. All the toaster's capabilities are built into the *hardware* of the toaster. A computer has hardware like a toaster, but it also needs the disk-based *software,* the programs to run it.

WordStar is actually a *sub*program that works under another (main) program of the computer. This main program is the *disk operating system,* which may be *CP/M, PC-DOS,* or *MS-DOS.* I'll refer to the disk operating system generically as *DOS.* **Note:** The discussion of DOS here and in Chapters 12, 13, and 28 applies only to PC-DOS or MS-DOS. Some differences may exist between DOS commands and those of the new *OS/2* operating system that will become available sometime in 1988. See also "A Note on CP/M" later in this Introduction.

DOS controls the flow of information between the various parts of the computer—the keyboard, central processing unit, disk drives, video display, printer, and so on. It acts very much like the hall monitor when you were in school, making sure that everyone moves along in the proper fashion and that order and decorum reign.

DOS is usually invisible to you, because you will spend most of your time working within WordStar. But, as sections of this book illustrate, learning how to use DOS in tandem with WordStar can be a great time-saver. I strongly urge you to familiarize yourself with at least the basic DOS operations before you get too far along in your apprenticeship.

Commands and Menus

Your computer doesn't know what to do until you tell it to do something. That's what *commands* are for. How you issue commands depends on what program you're using. When you see the DOS prompt on the screen, for instance, A> or C>, that means DOS is *waiting for a command.* You type the command next to the prompt and send it along to DOS by pressing the **RETURN** key. This DOS command:

```
C> dir a:
```

gives a directory listing of the A drive. Some DOS commands and other programs, such as WordStar, are in files whose names end with the extension .COM or .EXE. For example, the backup command (see below) is in the file BACKUP.EXE, but when you issue the command you don't type the extension. Similarly, WordStar is in a file called WS.EXE, but to start WordStar from DOS all you have to type is *ws* and press the RETURN key.

Every program has its own way of dealing with commands. For instance, when you first start working with WordStar you'll see the *Opening menu* (a long time ago, when we were all younger, its name was the No-File menu). Like its counterpart in a restaurant, a computer menu is a list of available choices, that is, available commands. You haven't started typing yet, so WordStar is merely waiting for a command. You need only press the letter representing that command, such as **D**, to open a document.

When you're typing in a file and the Opening menu isn't on the screen, however, WordStar has to distinguish between what is text (that is, your work!) and what might be a command. Because you can't speak to WordStar directly and expect it to understand you, you give it commands from the keyboard. Usually, you issue WordStar commands by holding down the *CTRL* ("control") key and pressing letter keys, or by pressing one of the *function keys* or one of the keys on the *numeric keypad*. The numeric keypad is generally on the right side of the keyboard, while the function keys are either on the left side or above the keyboard. A variety of *help menus* is always at your disposal to jog your memory of the many commands.

For example, when you *type* the letter A you insert an *A* into the file at the cursor location. However, when you *press and hold down* the CTRL key and then tap the letter A, you issue a command. If a command requires two letter keys for completion, such as a command with the prefix **K**, when you hold down the CTRL key and press the K key, a menu of completion commands appears to help you. If you issue the command quickly, the menu doesn't appear.

Formatting Floppy Disks

Make sure you understand how to *format,* or *initialize,* floppy disks before you start working. Unlike blank recording tapes, floppy disks don't come in a standard format. Each computer has its own disk format, although most MS-DOS or PC-DOS computers use the same format. On the IBM PC, the command to format floppy disks is in the file FORMAT.COM, and you'll find it on your DOS disk.

It's always a good idea to format all new disks when you get them. That way, you won't be caught without a prepared disk when you need one. Fortunately, you can now format a disk "on the fly" from within WordStar, but you'll save yourself needless hassle if you prepare all disks before using them. See Chapter 12 for more information about formatting floppy disks.

Documents, Nondocuments, Files, and File Names

In WordStar you create and edit either documents or nondocuments. A *document* can be, among other things, a letter, the chapter of a book, or a report. Besides containing text (typing), a document has a definite format that governs its appearance. This format includes margins, line spacing, and perhaps printing effects such as boldface or underlining. WordStar uses special codes for formatting.

Think of a WordStar document as a collection of related text that has a certain format and that you'll eventually print. Most of the time, and in most of the examples in this book, you'll be creating or editing WordStar documents with the **D** command from the Opening menu.

A WordStar *nondocument* contains text with no formatting or special codes. (Strictly speaking, WordStar nondocuments are *ASCII text files,* one of the subjects of Chapter 3.) Programmers use WordStar to create nondocuments containing computer program source files (Chapter 11), and later in this book you'll set up data files for merge printing operations in nondocuments (Chapter 19). You use the **N** choice from the Opening menu to create or edit nondocuments.

A file is the *container* in which to store a document or nondocument on the disk. Each file has a distinct name that reminds you of its contents. To avoid any confusion between WordStar's documents and nondocuments, I'll refer to whatever document or nondocument you're working on as *the file.*

The *disk,* either floppy or hard, is the storage location. Your office probably has filing cabinets with manila folders. On a computer, the file is the manila folder, the document (or nondocument) is the information in the folder, and the disk is the filing cabinet. You generally arrange the folders in your filing cabinet in some kind of order, usually alphabetic. When you want to pull a file, you can find it quickly by locating the correct drawer and looking at the little descriptive tags on the folders.

Because it makes finding your work easier, you should set up a different file for each different task. DOS, the computer's filing system, requires that each file have a unique name, just like the little tag that is on manila folders. Because you can't physically *see* the files on the disk, you would ask WordStar—via DOS—to *open* (retrieve) the file and show its contents on the monitor. WordStar is simultaneously loading this file into memory.

A computer can't read, so DOS can only look for a file by matching the letters of the name of the file, in the order that you type them, with the names of all the files on the disk. No two files can have the same name, because if they did, DOS would not be able to distinguish the two.

Computers are strictly *literal* beasts. As many others have pointed out, computers only do exactly what you tell them to do, not what you *mean.* DOS thus has no facility for guessing a file name. If you ask DOS to find and open a file named, say, TEST, but you type TEXT instead, DOS cannot intuit what you want. All it would do would be to match the letters T-E-X-T in that order and see if these four letters occur in the file directory on the disk.

DOS sees to it that each file has a distinct name, even if the names are as similar as CHAPTER.1 and CHAPTER1. Throughout this book, I give examples of naming files, but the final decision rests with you. Develop your own system and then *stick to it.* The DOS documentation covers in detail the few and easy rules for file names. These rules are, in brief:

- A file name can contain from one to eight characters, but no spaces.
- You can't include nonalphanumeric characters such as # or ? in file names. Some other characters, such as { or -, are acceptable.
- You don't have to use all eight characters.
- You can append a period and up to three more characters to any file name. This is the *file extension.*
- The file extension is optional.

A few typical and legal file names are: WORDSTAR.DOC, VERSION.1, SS.436, A, EXAMPLE, TT.A. (I list file names in uppercase, but you can type then in lowercase letters, too.) A few illegal names would be: CH#1, SS.5437, LOSANGELES, TWO BITS. *Question:* Why are these names "illegal"? *Answer:* The first contains an unacceptable character (#); the second has an extension that's too long; the third name is longer than eight characters; the fourth contains a space. DOS won't allow you to use these names.

File Management and Disk Space

WordStar works most efficiently with small files. It even warns you when a file is large. WordStar aficionados will tell you that the best way to maintain large writing projects is to break them up into smaller, *modular files.* For example, if you're writing a book, keep each chapter in a separate file. Develop a naming scheme that relates the files by name, such as CHAPTER.1, CHAP-TER.2, and so on. See Chapter 13 for more tips on organizing files and the modular approach.

Keeping track of your computer files is just as important as keeping track of the files in your filing cabinets. On floppy disks, files have a habit of multiplying like rabbits if you don't subject them to periodic *housekeeping* (again, Chapter 13). If you have a hard disk, you're well advised to learn how to divide your hard disk into *directories* to keep track of different programs and work files.

If the hard disk is your filing cabinet, then directories are like drawers, with the added plus that you can have drawers within drawers! A directory containing the WordStar program can have many *sub*directories, each holding different work files—one for letters, one for reports, and so on. The WordStar directory is the "parent," and the subdirectories are "children." The main directory on the disk—the "grandparent" of all—is the *root* directory. Figure 1 presents a graphic representation of a typical hard disk directory structure, with several children directories below the parent WordStar and Lotus 1-2-3 directories. See your DOS manual for more information about setting up directories.

Because no disk has an infinite storage capability, you should also keep daily tabs on the amount of *available disk space.* On a PC, DOS shows disk space in bytes. One of those nasty words that humbles beginners, a *byte* is merely the amount of space needed to store one character of information. Every character you type thus takes up one byte of storage. That includes spaces, too.

WordStar shows available disk space directly above the file listing under the Opening menu. WordStar measures disk space in *kilobytes.* For example, it may tell you that a file contains 23K (23 kilobytes). Those of you struggling to adjust to the metric system know that *kilo* means thousand, but you'll perhaps be chagrined to learn that a kilobyte is *not* 1000 bytes! It's technically 1024 bytes, but 1000 is close enough. (Like everything else in the computer world, there's a good reason to explain why a kilobyte is 1024 bytes, but you don't have to know it.)

I recommend that you start a new disk if there is less than ten percent of total disk space left on the current disk. That is, if you use floppy disks that can store 362,496 bytes (360K), start a new disk when WordStar tells you that there are 36K or less available. If you have a hard disk, delete unused files periodically, or archive them onto floppies to free up disk space. Again, see Chapter 13 for more information.

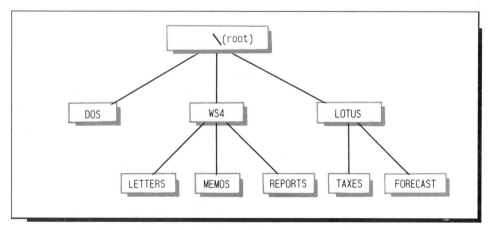

Figure 1   A Typical Hard Disk Directory Structure

Saving Your Work

When you open a document or nondocument with the **D** or **N** commands, respectively, from the Opening menu, you're making a copy of it from the disk, the storage location, and putting the copy into the computer's memory. The original *stays* on the disk, while WordStar works with the copy in memory.

After you've made your changes, you instruct WordStar to *save* the edited file back to the disk and in the process replace the original file with the revised version. By default, WordStar keeps the original in a separate *backup* file with the extension .BAK, although you can now instruct WordStar not to keep a backup file. This will be a welcome addition for many old-time users!

Caution: Never remove a disk from the drive until the current file is safely saved and the drive door light is no longer red.

Under normal conditions, you don't have to worry about losing your work, because the original is always on the disk. But that presupposes that you've stored it there in the first place. When you start a new writing project, the new work is not yet in a file at all. Any new typing is in memory and stays there until you save it to disk, you turn off or reset your computer, or the power goes off. It is therefore important for you to take the necessary precautions to save your new work.

One of my friends employs an interesting analogy to describe the difference between the work in memory and the file that you've saved to disk at least once. All work in memory is cash, and all files saved on the disk are traveler's checks. If you're on a trip and you lose cash, the cash is gone forever. But if you lose traveler's checks, you can get a refund. Save your work, and "don't leave your machine without doing it!"

If your cats, like mine, love to wander over computer keys when you're not looking or when you've decided to raid the refrigerator, heed my advice. Save your work *before* you leave your computer. Otherwise you'll be a victim of Meow's Laws!

A Word to the Wise About Backups

There is one *extremely important* procedure that you should know about before you work with any microcomputer: how to back up your work and program disks. Every computer book, every manual, stresses this operation, sometimes *ad nauseam*. But it *is* important! I'll bet dollars to donuts that each one of you out there has (or will have) a horror story to tell about backups, or what happened when there *weren't* any backups.

Determine from your work volume how often you should make backups, then schedule them as part of your normal routine. A good method to estimate how often to back up your files can be succinctly stated: *How much work would you care to lose?* Probably not too much!

I always recommend that people do backups at least *once a day*. This is the rule that I follow. You may find, however, that you may only need to back up files perhaps once a week, or once every two weeks. (Friday afternoons are a good time, when you come to think of it.)

If you use floppies, why not copy the DOS DISKCOPY.COM file, which lets you copy an entire disk easily, to the WordStar program disk? Then, whenever you want to make backups, you can go to DOS with the command ^KF from within WordStar (Chapter 12), and use the DISKCOPY command immediately. Or learn how to copy individual files quickly in WordStar (Chapter 13).

Hard disk users should make backups even more often than people with floppy disk-based systems. But they also have an easy way to do them with the special BACKUP utility, in the file BACKUP.EXE. The first backup session will take some time, because you will be copying your programs, too. But next time the BACKUP command lets you backup only those files that you've edited since the last backup session. Note that this command has nothing to do with DISKCOPY, which can only back up floppies.

Before You Finish for the Day

Always remove all floppy disks from your computer *before* you turn the power off. Never leave disks in the disk drives when the computer power is off. A power spike or "brownout" could cause an accidental loss of your valuable text.

A Short History Lesson

WordStar Professional Release 4 represents a major departure from previous manifestations of the product, so a short history lesson is in order. For a long time, "WordStar" was actually three separate products: *WordStar, MailMerge,* and *SpellStar.* MicroPro later replaced SpellStar, the spelling checker program, with *CorrectStar* (thank goodness!) and added an indexing program called *StarIndex* to what it then dubbed the *WordStar Professional* package. There was also *TelMerge,* a communications program for transferring WordStar files over the telephone lines.

In the meantime, another company began marketing a WordStar "clone," *NewWord,* that supplied features not available in WordStar. NewWord included a spelling checker and merge printing. In 1986, MicroPro bought the rights to NewWord, refurbished and enhanced the product with a faster version of CorrectStar and built-in table of contents and index generation to replace StarIndex. MicroPro issued this product in early 1987 as WordStar Professional Release 4. The package also included the *Word Finder* thesaurus program and computer-aided tutorials, but did not include TelMerge. (You can still send WordStar files over the telephone—see Chapter 28.)

Different Versions of WordStar

This book works well **only** with version 4.0 of WordStar, the afore-named *WordStar Professional Release 4.* Unless I note otherwise, the word *WordStar* always refers to the most current version of the product. If you're using any WordStar that's numbered less than 4.0, I strongly urge you to buy the upgrade. If you can't or don't want to buy the upgrade, I have only one suggestion: hunt down a copy of *Mastering WordStar!*

The "Demise" of MailMerge

Old-time WordStar users should be aware of a major change in how most *MailMerge* commands function in Release 4. Many features that were part of this separate merge printing program are now fully integrated into WordStar, and the term *MailMerge* has disappeared from the product. For instance, printing multiple copies of a file and inserting a file during printing are no longer strictly merge printing operations. See Chapter 16 to learn what MailMerge commands are now printing commands, and Chapters 19 through 24 for a discussion of merge printing.

Writer's Lament

Dear Reader: Continual software upgrades are the boon and bane of computer book writers! There will be new features in future releases of the product, and undoubtedly the wording of some prompts and messages will change, too. For example, WordStar Professional Release 5 will appear in early 1988—look for it.

Because of the inherent delays in the publishing world, this book might not include a discussion of every new feature as soon as it appears, and the messages and menus that you see here might not be exactly what you see on your screen. When in doubt, refer to the WordStar documentation for more help. Believe me, I'm trying to keep the book up-to-date, but it isn't easy!

A Note on CP/M

WordStar originally ran only under the CP/M operating system, but it now works with the more popular MS-DOS and PC-DOS, too. In discussions relating to operating system tasks, I list *only* the MS-DOS commands, which are for the most part identical to PC-DOS. Consult your CP/M documentation for more information about CP/M commands.

MicroPro has promised and delivered a CP/M version of WordStar Release 4. Most, but not all, features of the MS-DOS version are available in the CP/M version, so you can still use this book to learn WordStar Release

4 on your CP/M system. Because there is no standard keyboard setup for CP/M computers, check your manual for key variations.

Tips on Program and Printer Installation

Follow the instructions in the WordStar manual to install the program for your computer. Here are a few tips and guidelines to help you.

The Boot Disk. Always work with a *copy* of the WordStar program, *never the original!* Floppy disk users should first format a disk with the *DOS system files* before copying the Word Finder or WordStar files onto the disk. That way, they can use the same disk to "boot up"—start—their computers *and* load either Word Finder or WordStar. (You must load Word Finder *before* WordStar, so if you're using Word Finder, put the DOS system files on its disk.) With the DOS disk in the A drive and a blank disk in the B drive, type format b:/s and press **RETURN** to format a disk with the system files.

The WINSTALL Program. Then follow the instructions in the WordStar manual for copying the program files and using the WINSTALL program to set up the working program disks if you have a floppy disk system, or to install WordStar on a subdirectory if you own a hard disk. You can repeat the installation as many times as you want or cancel installation at any time by pressing ^C or ^**BREAK**. (The BREAK key is the SCROLL LOCK key.)

The CONFIG.SYS File. A DOS file called CONFIG.SYS *must* be on the floppy disk you use to start your computer, or in the root directory of your hard disk. It's likely that that file already exists, because other programs use it, too. If there is no CONFIG.SYS file, WINSTALL will create one for you. From the Main installation menu, press **C** [Computer] choice, then press **C** [Check CONFIG.SYS]. The CONFIG.SYS file must include the line FILES= 20, but it can contain other instructions, too. WINSTALL will change the FILES line if it's different (most of the time, if you have a CONFIG.SYS file on the disk, it already contains the line FILES=20.) **Note:** On a few computer systems the CONFIG.SYS file requires a FILES=30 line instead of FILES= 20. You can edit the CONFIG.SYS file yourself from within WordStar by opening the file as a nondocument (see Chapter 11).

Overlay Files. WordStar includes several *overlay* files. You can recognize these files because their file extension is .OVR. An overlay file is a section of the program that may not be necessary every day. WordStar's designers created overlays to keep the size of the program small and to make the program run fast. You should have the overlay files and the main program file, WS.EXE, on the same floppy disk or in the same hard disk directory.
WordStar "assumes" that its overlay files are on the A drive. If your hard disk is the default drive, you have to tell WordStar on what drive to find the overlay files. Suppose your hard disk is drive C. From the Main

installation menu, press **C** [Computer] and then **A** [Disk drives on your computer]. Type **Y** to change the defaults, then make sure that the default drive—in this example, C—is the *first* one you specify. An asterisk (∗) appears next to the drive name to show it as the default drive. Continue specifying any other drives on your computer, such as A and B. Press **RETURN** when you're finished.

If you own a hard disk, you'll probably set up the WordStar files in a directory called WS4. If you plan to rename this directory, you must tell WordStar what the new name is. See Chapter 27.

Networking WordStar. To set up WordStar for a *local area network (LAN)* environment, press **B** [Operating system choices] and then **B** [Shared file system]. WordStar will ask you if you want to give others the capability of simultaneously viewing (but not changing) a file that someone else on the network is editing. See Chapters 3 and 13 for more information about networking with WordStar.

The Spelling Checker. If you have a floppy disk system, make sure you change one setting for the spelling checker, CorrectStar. Press **D** [CorrectStar], then press **A** [Swap dictionary/program disk]. WordStar will ask you to change OFF to ON. You can then swap your WordStar program disk with the dictionary disk when you spell check a file. Hard disk users don't have to complete these steps.

Note: During installation, check how WordStar shows underlining on your monitor. Press **A** [Console] and then **B** [Example of underline text]. If you have a monochrome monitor and no color graphics card, WordStar should show the underlined example correctly. If you have a monochrome or color monitor with a *color graphics card,* you may have to change the default settings. I prefer the **C** [Use inverse video] choice to distinguish underlining from boldface print. Press **X** [Done with this menu] when you've chosen an underlining style, then continue with the installation.

Word Finder. Make sure you also install the Word Finder thesaurus program according to the instructions in the Word Finder section of the documentation. Word Finder is a *terminate and stay resident* program. You load it *before* you load WordStar, but Word Finder stays in memory ready when you need it. Chapter 8 discusses how to use this program.

Necessary Program Files. After you install WordStar and Word Finder on your computer, you should have a number of program, overlay, dictionary, and synonym files files on your WordStar program disks or in your WordStar directory (WS4). Table 1 lists the files that are necessary for running WordStar, CorrectStar (the spelling checker), and the Word Finder thesaurus properly. The table also lists the installation files that are not needed after you've set up the programs, unless you plan to customize the programs later. All other files, such as sample document files and WC.EXE, the word count program (see Chapter 8), are optional.

Table 1 WordStar and Word Finder Files

Files Necessary to Run WordStar and CorrectStar

WS.EXE	The WordStar Program
WSMSGS.OVR	Overlay File Containing Screen Messages
WSPRINT.OVR	Overlay File Containing Printer Drivers (see Chapters 3 and 27)
WSSHORT.OVR	Overlay File Containing Shorthand Definitions (see Chapter 7)
WSSPELL.OVR	Overlay File Containing CorrectStar ⎫
INTERNAL.DCT	Dictionary of Most Common Words ⎪ (see Chapter 8)
MAIN.DCT	Main Dictionary ⎬
PERSONAL.DCT	Personal Dictionary ⎭
WSINDEX.XCL	Exclusion List for Index Generation (see Chapter 25)

Files Necessary to Run Word Finder

WF.EXE	The Word Finder Program (see Chapter 8)
WFSM.SYM *or* WFBG.SYM	Small or Large Synonym File

Installation Files

WINSTALL.EXE	The WordStar Installation Program
WSCHANGE.EXE	The WSCHANGE Program (see Chapter 27)
WSCHANGE.OVR	Overlay File Containing Screen Messages for WSCHANGE
README.COM	Program to Display the README File
README.TXT	The README File
WFINSTAL.EXE	The Word Finder Installation Program
WFSCREEN.EXE	Program to Install Word Finder to Work with Certain Monitors

WordStar and Your Printer. The most difficult part about installing WordStar is setting it up to work with your printer or printers. To explain the ins and outs of printers would, alas, be beyond the scope of this book. However, here are a few points to consider. There are essentially two types of printers, *parallel* and *serial,* depending on how they're connected to your computer. Unless you tell it otherwise, DOS and WordStar both "assume" that you have a parallel printer connected to what it calls LPT1. This is a *port,* a connection in the back of your PC.

If you own a serial printer, you must override the LPT1 setting with the DOS MODE command. *Before* working with WordStar you use MODE to instruct DOS about (1) where the printer is connected (either COM1 or COM2), and (2) the printer's settings. For example, to redirect the output from the parallel printer port to the first serial port (COM1) and set up the settings for many serial laser printers, here are the instructions you'd issue from DOS before entering WordStar:

```
C> mode lpt1:=com1:
C> mode com1:9600,n,8,1,p
```

The first line redirects the printed output, while the second line tells COM1 that it's connected to a printer (p) running at 9600 bits per second, with no parity (n), 8 data bits, and 1 stop bit. You're no doubt already confused by the terminology! Here's a suggestion: just use whatever MODE settings are recommended by your printer manufacturer and don't worry about the terms at all!

If you work with a serial printer, you'll have to change the default port settings *within* WordStar, too. For instance, even though my printer was connected to the first serial port, COM1, and even though I had issued the correct MODE command from DOS, the printer wouldn't print. With the WSCHANGE program I had to set the port definition within WordStar to show the printer as attached to COM1. Success! (See Chapter 27 for more about WSCHANGE.) In addition, you can tell WordStar that you have two printers attached to your computer (also discussed in Chapter 27), or select a printer at another workstation on a local area network (Chapter 3).

Paper Position and Top-of-Form Setting. It may also take you a while to determine the exact paper position in non-laser printers. I offer this bit of advice: Determine where you'll put the paper in the printer and what the top-of-form setting should be, and use these settings consistently. The top-of-form is where the printer advances the top edge of the paper to align with the print head. Change the formats *within* WordStar when you need a different layout. That is, as much as possible, let WordStar handle the actual formatting. Don't change your printer switches willy-nilly.

Typestyles. WordStar "assumes" that your printer's typestyle prints 10 characters per horizontal inch (*pica*). If your printer prints 12 characters per horizontal inch (*elite*) you can still print the exercises, although they will be slightly smaller and more condensed looking on the page. Chapters 10 and 26 deal with different typestyle sizes.

You should be ready to go with program and printer before you begin studying this book. I'm assuming that you have either a hard disk or two floppy drives, and that in the latter case you're using the B (right or lower) drive for your work disk. See "The Daily Warm-Up" for more information. The instructions in this book work with either floppy disk or hard disk systems. When there is a difference between the two types of computers—for example, when you have to switch floppy disks—I'll instruct you accordingly.

Prelude: How to Use This Book

Dear Reader: Don't even *think* of starting until you've read this section! It shows you how to get the most of out this book. Don't worry! There aren't too many points to keep in mind.

Program Defaults

WordStar provides certain pre-established format settings, known as *defaults,* as a convenience to you. You thus don't have to think about margins, tab stops, line spacing, and other formatting when you begin. At first you'll work with the defaults and then gradually learn how to change them. Later, you might want to use the WSCHANGE program to configure the WordStar defaults to suit your own needs. See Chapter 27 for more information.

The Basic Instruction Set

To make your journey through the world of WordStar as uncomplicated as possible, I have limited my basic instruction set to a few words, notably, *Press* and *Type.* Each instruction appears on a separate line so you don't miss anything.

Press means to hit the key or key combination shown. For example,

Press   **RETURN**

means to press the **RETURN** key once. Many computers refer to the **RETURN** key as the *Enter* or *Send* key. WordStar shows it in some screen messages as a left-pointing arrow with a tag, like this: ↵.

Keys you should press right now are in **boldface** type, and I tell you when to press a key more than once. *Press* is thus always used to *issue a command* in WordStar. Do not *type* any "Press" instructions.

Most WordStar commands work with the **CTRL** ("control") key, and it's a tradition to represent this key with the *caret* symbol: ^. Who am I to buck tradition? The **CTRL** key is like the SHIFT key in that you must hold it down while you press the other keys shown with it. For example, this instruction—

Press   **^KS**

—means to hold down the **CTRL** key as you press *first* the shifted or unshifted K key and *then* the shifted or unshifted S key. (All commands are in uppercase for cosmetic purposes only.) Don't try to press the K and the S simultaneously; press K first and then S. If you have a heavy hand, your computer may repeat the ^K many times! So use quick and snappy strokes when you issue commands, and release the CTRL key when you're finished.

Note: The ^ symbol that represents the CTRL key in this book and other WordStar documentation has nothing to do with the caret symbol that you can type (SHIFT 6). The only place in this book where you'll see a typed caret is in Chapter 18, "Math Maneuvers," where the caret indicates exponentiation.

This command:

Press   **SHIFT F2**

means to hold down either the left or right **SHIFT** key as you press the **F2** function key. Then release both keys. The ALT key is also like the SHIFT or CTRL key: you hold it down as you press another key, then release both keys.

Sometimes you'll use the ESC ("escape") key with other keys, but you *don't* have to hold down the ESC key after you press it. For example, this instruction—

Press   **ESC @**

—tells you to press and release the **ESC** key and then press the @ key (SHIFT 2). Don't type the space between the two keys.

Just as the RETURN, CTRL, and ESC keys may have slightly different names on your computer, so, too, you may see different labels on the **TAB**, **INS** ("insert"), **DEL** ("delete"), and **BACKSPACE** ("rubout") keys. Identify these keys on your keyboard to make sure you know where they are.

Even though commands from the Opening menu are just letters, I still use the word *Press* to remind you that they're not text. I also include the menu's description in brackets:

Press   **D** [open a document]

HOWARD W. SAMS & COMPANY
Excellence In Publishing

DEAR VALUED CUSTOMER:

Howard W. Sams & Company is dedicated to bringing you timely and authoritative books for your personal and professional library. Our goal is to provide you with excellent technical books written by the most qualified authors. You can assist us in this endeavor by checking the box next to your particular areas of interest.

We appreciate your comments and will use the information to provide you with a more comprehensive selection of titles.

Thank you,

Vice President, Book Publishing
Howard W. Sams & Company

SUBJECT AREAS:

Computer Titles:
- ☐ Apple/Macintosh
- ☐ Commodore
- ☐ IBM & Compatibles
- ☐ Business Applications
- ☐ Communications
- ☐ Operating Systems
- ☐ Programming Languages

Electronics Titles:
- ☐ Amateur Radio
- ☐ Audio
- ☐ Basic Electronics
- ☐ Electronic Design
- ☐ Electronic Projects
- ☐ Satellites
- ☐ Troubleshooting & Repair

Other interests or comments:

_____

_____

Name _____
Title _____
Company _____
Address _____
City _____
State/Zip _____
Daytime Telephone No. _____

A Division of Macmillan, Inc.
4300 West 62nd Street
Indianapolis, Indiana 46268 USA

48404

Book Mark

ƒƒƒ
HOWARD W. SAMS
& COMPANY

Book Mark

BUSINESS REPLY CARD
FIRST CLASS   PERMIT NO. 1076   INDIANAPOLIS, IND.

POSTAGE WILL BE PAID BY ADDRESSEE

HOWARD W. SAMS & CO.
ATTN: Public Relations Department
P.O. BOX 7092
Indianapolis, IN 46206

NO POSTAGE
NECESSARY
IF MAILED
IN THE
UNITED STATES

HOWARD W. SAMS
& COMPANY

You don't have to use uppercase letters, and you shouldn't type the text in brackets. It's there merely as a reminder about what the command does.

I use the word *Type* when I want you to enter text from the keyboard. Thus:

Type   `Hello 'dere!`

means to type the phrase `Hello 'dere!` *exactly as you see it*. Make sure you type the spaces between the words. At times I'll admonish you not to miss a space by telling you to press the **SPACEBAR**.

Your entries that display on the screen appear in a boldfaced computer font, like `Hello 'dere!`, and messages displayed on the screen appear in a nonbold computer font, such as `this`.

The Cursor and the Keyboard

The *cursor* is the little blinking line that "runs" along as you type and shows your position in the file. (The word *cursor* comes from the Latin word "to run.") WordStar uses the *numeric keypad* on the right side of the PC keyboard as an alternative to some cursor-movement commands from the alphabet keys. I list alternate commands following their "traditional" WordStar equivalents, such as:

Press   **^R** or **PG UP**

Thus, even if your computer doesn't have a PG UP key, you can always press the original WordStar command, **^R**, instead. **Tip:** If you plan to use WordStar on different computers, always learn the CTRL key commands because they're the same on virtually all machines.

The ARROW keys move the cursor in the directions listed on the 2 (DOWN ARROW), 4 (LEFT ARROW), 6 (RIGHT ARROW) and 8 (UP ARROW) keys. Note also the HOME, END, PG UP and PG DN keys, whose meanings in WordStar you'll quickly learn. If you see *numbers* on the screen when you press a keypad key, press the **NUM LOCK** key once to toggle back to cursor mode.

Additionally, many of the *function keys* (**F1** through **F10**) issue popular WordStar commands. There are 40 function keys: the 10 keys used alone, and those 10 that you press with the ALT, SHIFT, and CTRL keys. At the bottom of the screen are *labels* to identify what commands the function keys (bottom row) and shifted function keys (top row) represent.

You can change the function key settings and labels as you wish, or remove the labels from the screen to make room (Chapter 27), but for the purposes of this book I'll list the default settings after their standard command equivalents. Here are two examples:

Press   ^U or **F2**

means to press either ^U or the **F2** function key.

Press   ^**QD** or ^**F10**

means to press either ^**QD** or hold down the **CTRL** key as you press the **F10** function key.

The WordStar documentation lists the function key settings. You can select the alternate commands interchangeably with the originals if your computer has the alternate keys. **Note:** These keyboard alternates are either different or nonexistent in earlier versions of WordStar. I show only Release 4 function key alternates in this book. WordStar does not yet work with the F11 and F12 function keys on the newer IBM (and compatible) computers.

On the keyboard template you received with the WordStar software, colors show when you press a key alone (black) or with the other keys: green for the ALT key, red for the SHIFT key, and blue for the CTRL key. The position of the commands on the template mimics the positions of the ALT, SHIFT, and CTRL keys on the keyboard, from bottom (ALT) to top (CTRL).

Beware the **CAPS LOCK** key! Not only is this key sometimes in the worst possible spot, but it doesn't allow you to access the characters above the numbers or punctuation marks (you must still use the SHIFT key). The CAPS LOCK key only enters uppercase *letters*. How many times have I inadvertently pressed the CAPS LOCK key when I intended to press the SHIFT key, only to find, generally much later, most of my text in uppercase! Fortunately, WordStar now has a way to help you correct this problem quickly, but try to keep your pinky as far away as possible from the CAPS LOCK key!

Icons

You'll see various icons in the left margin of the book. An *icon* is a pictorial representation of an important idea or point that I want to make. Here's a list of what these icons mean:

 This icon marks the beginning of an *example* that you are to type.

 This is a *tip* to help you.

 This is a *question*—no, it's not a quiz! It's just something for you to ponder, for which I *usually* supply an answer.

 This is a *caution* about something that could alter or damage your file. Disregard it at your own peril!

 This icon shows a *hint* to steer you toward a solution to something.

This is a *note* to suggest a feature or idea that you should keep in mind.

Warning and Error Messages

WordStar will present you with a warning or error message under certain conditions:

- When you attempt to do something that the program can't accommodate.
- When you're about to perform an action that may be hazardous to your sanity, such as deleting a large amount of text.
- When you don't complete a command correctly.

I'll discuss the most important messages, why they occur, and what to do about the problem. You'll find a list of error messages in the WordStar documentation.

Would that you never get a fatal error, but if you do you're in trouble! Fatal errors cause the program to "bomb," and you'll lose any work that's in the computer's memory. If a fatal error does occur, *run* to your WordStar dealer and *yell!*

The Files You'll Create

To save some typing work, you'll reuse files from previous chapters. That's why it's best to study the chapters in order. However, if you intend to skip around, take a look at Appendix A. It contains a listing of all files that you work with in this book, including in what chapter you created the file and in what other chapter(s) you used the file again. Make sure you complete all the examples relating to a particular file.

What Else You'll Need

If you have a hard disk computer, you can save all the examples in the same directory as your WordStar program files. If you're using a floppy disk system, you'll need one blank, *formatted* disk to store the examples (owners of some CP/M computers may need more than one storage disk). Label the storage disk *Book Work Disk*.

At times I refer you to the *WordStar Professional documentation,* so keep that handy, too. **Note:** Last-minute changes to WordStar may not appear in the documentation. MicroPro supplies a special README file that lists these changes, together with instructions on how to view this file. The README file also has important and late-breaking information about printers. Take a look at it sometime!

Two Good Tips

This is a step-by-step, "hands-on" book. I've tested it thoroughly to ensure that if you do all the steps in order everything will work. However, if you have problems keeping track of where you are in the instructions, here's a simple solution. Keep a *place marker*—a piece of paper or a bookmark—at the current instruction so you never miss a step.

In addition, save all scrap paper and use it instead of good paper for all the printing exercises. Do your part to conserve precious resources!

The Daily Warm-Up

At the beginning of each chapter, you'll see the following little sign:

> **DO WARM-UP**

The warm-up includes the steps to load the program and to begin using WordStar. Because you'll do this every day, I've put the steps here to avoid repeating them at the start of each chapter. Of course, if you continue from one chapter to the next, you don't have to warm up. But always make sure that you start each chapter with the *WordStar Opening menu on your screen*.

The warm-up steps are slightly different for floppy disk and hard disk computers, so I've listed them separately.

If You Have a Dual-Floppy System

Make sure that you've installed WordStar on a bootable DOS disk (see "Notes on Program Installation and Printers" in the Introduction) so you can start your computer with this disk alone. To begin using Word Finder and WordStar, insert the Word Finder program disk in the A (left or top) drive and close the drive door. Insert the work disk in the B (right or bottom) drive. Close the door for drive B.

If your computer isn't already on, turn it on now and type the date and time if DOS requests them, pressing **RETURN** after each. Remember to use the 24-hour clock for the time. For instance, 1:30 p.m. is 13:30. (Supplying the date and time helps you keep track of the editing history of your files.)

To load Word Finder:

Type   wf

Press   **RETURN**

Remove the Word Finder disk and insert the WordStar disk in the A drive. Then, switch over to the B drive and load WordStar from the A drive, like so:

Type   b:

(Don't forget the colon!)

Press   **RETURN**

Type   a:ws

Press   **RETURN**

You've loaded Word Finder and WordStar, the Opening menu appears, and you're ready to begin. All files you create or edit will be on the work disk in the B drive.

If You Have a Hard Disk System

Turn your computer on, if it isn't on already, and supply the time and date if DOS requests them. Make sure you use the 24-hour clock for the correct time. Then, move to the subdirectory containing the WordStar files. For example, if you're using the default WordStar subdirectory, WS4, do this:

Type   cd \ws4

Press   **RETURN**

Now, load the two programs:

Type   wf

Press   **RETURN**

to load Word Finder.

Type   ws

Press   **RETURN**

to load WordStar.

You've loaded Word Finder and WordStar, the Opening menu appears, and you're ready to begin.

Some Useful Tips

You can set up all warm-up steps in an *automatic executing file,* named AUTOEXEC.BAT (MS-DOS or PC-DOS), that will type the commands for you when you turn on your computer in the morning. These commands could include setting the MODE command for your printer and automatically loading WordStar. For instance, this AUTOEXEC.BAT file for a hard disk computer contains commands to request the time and date, set up a serial printer, switch to the WS4 directory, and then load Word Finder and WordStar:

```
DATE
TIME
MODE LPT1:=COM1:
MODE COM1:9600,N,7,1,P
CD \WS4
WF
WS
```

To learn more about how the AUTOEXEC.BAT file works, see your DOS manual and Chapter 28.

When you load WordStar and its sign-on screen appears, press the **SPACEBAR** once to display the Opening menu quickly. You can also change some of the *delays* in the program to make it run faster. See Chapter 27 for more information. That chapter also shows how to have the entire program, except help screens, resident in memory. That way, the program runs faster, or if you have only one floppy disk drive you can insert another work disk in the drive after you load WordStar.

As I previously mentioned, if you're working with a hard disk, you've probably set up WordStar in a directory called WS4. If your work files are in a different directory, however, there's a command to switch directories from within WordStar (see Chapter 12). Another way to go is to have WordStar automatically select any other directory when you load the program. See Chapter 27.

You can also load WordStar and immediately begin editing or printing a file, thus bypassing the Opening menu. Here are the options available to you. In each example, substitute the correct file name for <filename> below. You don't have to type in uppercase, but do make sure that there is a space between **WS** and the file name.

WS <filename>	Loads WordStar and opens <filename> as a document file
WS <filename> N	Loads WordStar and opens <filename> as a nondocument file
WS <filename> D	Loads WordStar and opens <filename> as a document file (only if the default file mode is nondocument)
WS <filename> P	Loads WordStar, prints <filename>, and then displays the Opening menu
WS <filename> PX	Loads WordStar, prints <filename>, and then exits back to the operating system

Dear Reader: You're *finally* ready to begin learning WordStar!

First Steps

In this chapter you will learn the following commands:

Opening Menu Commands

D	Open a document
J	Help for Opening menu commands
P	Print a file
X	Exit WordStar and return to DOS

Opening Menu and File Commands

^W (^PG UP)	Scroll up through the file listing
^Z (^PG DN)	Scroll down through the file listing

File Commands

^A (^LEFT ARROW)	Cursor to the previous word
^B	Align a paragraph (document mode)
^C (PG DN)	Scroll down through the file by screenful
^D (RIGHT ARROW)	Cursor right one character
^E (UP ARROW)	Cursor up one line
^F (^RIGHT ARROW)	Cursor to the next word
^G (DEL)	Delete the character at the cursor
^H (BACKSPACE)	Backspace the cursor and delete the previous character

more . . .

^I (TAB)	Tab
^J (F1)	Help
^KD (F10)	Save the file and return to the Opening menu
^KS (F9)	Save the file and stay at the same place in the file
^Q	Quick menu
^QC (^END)	Cursor to the end of the file
^QD (^F10)	Cursor to the right side of the line
^QE (HOME)	Cursor to the top left side of the current screen
^QP	Cursor to the previous position
^QR (^HOME)	Cursor to the beginning of the file
^QS (^F9)	Cursor to the left side of the line
^QX (END)	Cursor to the bottom line of the current screen
^R (PG UP)	Scroll up through the file by screenful
RETURN	End a paragraph *or* insert a blank line
^S (LEFT ARROW)	Cursor left one character
^T (F6)	Delete a word
^U (F2)	Cancel a command *or* "unerase" (restore) the previously deleted text
^V (INS)	Turn insert mode on/off
^W (^PG UP)	Scroll up through the file by line
^X (DOWN ARROW)	Cursor down one line
^Y (F5)	Delete a line
^Z (^PG DN)	Scroll down through the file by line

Other Feature

ESC	Repeat the last file name and complete a command

Note: The caret character, ^, stands for the CTRL (control) key.

You're probably thinking that I'm going to work your fingers to the bone, with so many commands to learn in the very first lesson. Relax! Here's a little secret: they're the most important WordStar commands, and they'll soon be second nature to you. What's more, you'll be using them in actual word processing situations—in other words, "on the job training."

Experienced WordStar users: the first three chapters go slowly in introducing the absolute basics of WordStar, but the pace picks up very quickly. Even if you're already comfortable with WordStar, take the time to do the examples. They provide good review, and you'll be using them in later chapters. What's more, this is a good way to learn many of the new WordStar features.

> ### *DO WARM-UP*

If you overlooked the daily warm-up instructions in the Prelude, read them now and perform a warm-up before you continue with this chapter.

The Opening Menu

You normally see a brief sign-on screen and then the Opening menu when you load WordStar. If you open or print a file when you load WordStar, you won't see the Opening menu until you save the file or select the print options.

Besides the menu itself, which takes up the top of the screen, you'll see a list of files on the current drive or in the current directory. There may be a few "sample" files in the directory listing: you copied them during the WordStar installation.

WordStar displays the current drive and directory and the amount of space left on the drive. It lists any "children" directories next, each one identified by a backslash (\) character. You'll also see the size, in bytes, of each file. If there are more files than can fit on the screen, WordStar tells you that you can press ^Z or ^PG DN to *scroll* down and bring more file names into view. Press ^W or ^PG UP to scroll the previous files up and back into view. Later in the chapter you'll learn more about scrolling.

Because WordStar doesn't normally show files that you can't edit (such as its own program files), even if no files appear below the Opening menu that doesn't mean that the drive or directory is empty. I find it a great convenience that program files don't clutter up the directory listing.

I reiterate what I mentioned in the Introduction: WordStar is waiting for you to issue a command, represented by one of the letter choices on the Opening menu. Novice users are often befuddled by the simplicity of the Opening menu setup. That is, they think that WordStar is more complicated than it looks. All you need do is press any letter choice on the Opening menu. You *don't* have to, and you shouldn't, press the RETURN key yet, nor do you have to use the SHIFT key. If you press a letter for which there is no choice, WordStar does nothing; it merely waits for you to enter a correct choice.

Canceling a Command

Say you've pressed **E** [rename a file] instead of **D** [open a document]. How do you correct this minor mistake? Merely press ^U or **F2** and start again. As you'll see, ^U (**F2**) often cancels another command. It's your *escape valve,* both at the Opening menu and in a file.

The only command in the Opening menu that doesn't react immediately to ^U is **F** [turn directory off]. If you pressed **F** instead of **D,** the file directory disappears instantly. Merely press **F** again and then press **RETURN** to reinstate the complete directory. (Chapter 12 discusses this command.)

Opening a Document File

The command you will use the most is the one to open a document file. You can't type or edit text until you've opened a file in which you'll save your work later.

Press   **D** [open a document]

WordStar prompts:

```
Type the name of the document to create or change.
Include drive and directory if they are different from current.

The directory, if on, displays the names of existing files you may
change. To create a new document, type a new name and press Enter.

Document to open?
```

 Note: Throughout this book, I'll show WordStar's response to a command only the *first* time you learn the command.

After a brief pause, the file directory listing and prompt lines appear. The two prompt lines show ways of editing the file name that you'll type. In later chapters you'll learn how to *select* a file name from the directory listing and open a file that's on another drive or in another directory. Here, because you want to create a new file named STORY, you must type in the new name on the edit line.

Type   **story**

If you make a mistake typing the file name, the easiest way to correct it is by pressing the **BACKSPACE** key to "rub out" the mistake. Type the correction. As the prompt lines tell you, you can also press ^Y to delete the entire file name and start again. To cancel the operation and return to the Opening menu, press ^U (**F2**).

One of the themes of this book is "saving keystrokes means saving work." Say you typed **stoy** instead of **story**. Don't retype the entire name! Press the **LEFT ARROW** key or ^S once, type the r (which you insert at the cursor location without deleting the *y*), and continue.

Press   **RETURN**

WordStar can't find this file name in the directory, so it asks you to confirm what you're doing:

Can't find that file. Create a new one (Y/N)?

If you type n, WordStar returns to the Opening menu. What you want to do here is:

Type   y

WordStar opens the blank, new file STORY.

What You See on the Screen

When you're editing a file, WordStar divides the screen into several distinct areas:

- At the top of the screen is the *status line.* It tells you the name of the file you're in, the page, line and column numbers (P01 L01 C01), and other information that I'll discuss shortly.

- Below that is the *Edit menu,* a helpful listing of the most important WordStar commands. Later, when you become familiar with the commands, you can remove this menu from the screen and make more space for viewing your work (Chapter 2).

- Under the Edit menu you'll see the *ruler line,* which shows the current left margin (with an L), the right margin (with an R), and tab stops (with exclamation points—!). The hyphens indicate column positions without tab stops. For the time being, you'll be using these default settings.

- Below the ruler line is the *text area* where you'll type in your work. The cursor is waiting for you at column 1 of line 1.

■ At the right side of the text area appear various symbols in the *flag character display*. Right now all you see is a caret (^). This symbol always shows the end of the file. I'll discuss the other flag characters in their turn.

■ Finally, at the bottom of the screen are two rows of *function key labels* to remind you what commands the normal and shifted function keys represent. The labels in the bottom row are for the normal function keys; those directly above are for the shifted function keys.

The Default Format Settings

Every document has a specific *format* that governs the look of the text. So that you don't have to worry about formatting when you're just starting out, WordStar provides certain default settings. For example, the left margin is at column 1 and the right margin at column 65, so you're working with a 65-character line. Even though the left margin is at column 1, when you print a file WordStar starts the margin eight columns from the left edge of the paper. You don't see this "page left margin" on your screen.

The other defaults that you'll eventually learn how to change are:

■ Tab stops at every fifth column, starting at column 6: 6, 11, 16, 21, 26, 31, 36, 41, 46, 51, and 56.

■ The document is single spaced.

■ There will be a top margin of three blank lines and a bottom margin of eight blank lines when you print the document.

■ WordStar prints a page number at column 28 in the bottom margin of every page.

■ There are 10 characters per column inch—what typists call *pica* size type.

■ Justification is on. That is, WordStar adds the necessary spaces between words to "fill in" the line so that each line is the same length. You'll see the right margin justification on the screen shortly.

■ Wordwrap and normal paragraph align are on, as the word Align on the status line tells you. You'll learn about these features in a moment.

Insert Mode and Overtype Mode

Normally WordStar operates in *insert mode:* everything you type goes into the file at the cursor position and pushes the cursor ahead. If the cursor is under existing text, the new text pushes the existing text forward on the line, too. The status line should say Insert to remind you that you're working in insert mode.

The opposite of insert mode is *overtype mode:* anything you type replaces the text at the cursor position. To switch to overtype mode:

Press   **INS** or **^V**

The word Insert disappears from the status line, and the Edit menu now says turn insert on next to ^V. Although at times it's beneficial to use overtype mode, you run the risk of overwriting text by mistake. What's more, on the PC keyboard, the INS key is easy to press when you don't mean to. *Always use insert mode when you work with the examples in this book, except in the rare instances when the instructions tell you to switch to overtype mode.*

Now, make sure you get back in insert mode:

Press   **INS** or **^V**

to turn insert mode on.

The word Insert reappears on the status line.

Entering Text and Correcting Typos

The file is blank, but you are now going to type some sentences into it.

Press   **TAB** or **^I**

You'd start a paragraph with a tab if you were typing on a typewriter, wouldn't you? There's no difference beginning a paragraph with WordStar. Even though you can use **^I** for the tab key, that requires two keystrokes, while pressing **TAB** is just one keystroke. Which would *you* rather use?

Type   It was one of those cleat

Oops! Your first mistake. No problem! The cursor should be directly after the *t.*

Press   **BACKSPACE** or **^H**

to delete the *t.*

The **BACKSPACE** key allows you to correct mistakes as you type. It *rubs out* the previous character and moves the cursor back, as if it contained a built-in eraser. If you hold it down, it will continue to delete backwards.

Go slowly through these examples and try to catch your typing mistakes as you proceed. Then what appears on your screen will be the same as in the examples. However, if you don't catch all your typos, don't worry. You can correct them later.

Caution: So that the examples work properly, make sure you follow the normal convention of typing *one* space—and one space only—between words and *two* spaces at the end of a sentence. As you'll see in a moment, WordStar supplies extra spaces between words to fill in the lines, but you should only type one space between each word.

Now type the rest of the example. Do *not* press the **RETURN** key at the end of each line, because WordStar automatically wraps text from one line to the next. This is *wordwrap,* and it's a convenience that you'll soon learn to appreciate. **Note:** If you're such a creature of habit that you *do* press the RETURN key inadvertently at the end of a line, just press **BACKSPACE** to delete your mistake and continue. When you're finished, the cursor should be at the end of the paragraph on line 7.

```
It  was one of those clear, blue days, the kind of days  one
only finds in Los Angeles at very rare moments of the year.   The
distant mountains, which for most of the time are nonexistent  to
normal  view,  appeared so clearly that they seemed  closer  than
they  really  are.  The scene was made even more unusual  by  the
presence  of  snow  on the mountains,  a  sight  that  contrasted
dramatically with the 80-degree weather in the city.
```

Making a Paragraph

WordStar would continue to wrap lines indefinitely if you didn't tell it where to end the paragraph and begin another. *Now* it's time to use the RETURN key!

Press   **RETURN**

You've inserted what WordStar calls a *hard return* to end the paragraph and position the cursor on the next line. The flag character display shows the hard return like this: <. At the moment there should only be one < symbol in the document.

When WordStar wraps words from one line to the next, it automatically inserts *soft returns* at the ends of lines. You don't see the codes for soft returns, but they're there. WordStar removes and repositions these soft returns when you edit a line, but any hard returns that you enter *stay in the document* and will affect the printout of your document. Many typists by habit press the RETURN key indiscriminately, a practice that they soon learn to change. In a moment you'll see how to get rid of unwanted hard returns.

Press   **RETURN**

This time, you've used the RETURN key to add a *blank line* between paragraphs. Now there are two < symbols in the flag character display and the cursor is on line 9. So you normally use the RETURN key either (1) to end paragraphs, or (2) to add blank lines between paragraphs. Later, you'll see that you also use the RETURN key to create short lines, that is, lines that don't extend to the right margin.

Just Keep Typing!

Type the next two paragraphs, remembering to start each with a tab and to press **RETURN** *twice* at the end of each. WordStar will *scroll* part of the file up and out of view to make room for new text. Don't worry: you haven't lost anything!

    For sure, it was one of those days when being inside would have been a total waste of time! So I decided to hop on my motorcycle and take a leisurely jaunt through the mountains -- those delightful, snow-capped mountains -- that enticed me from the near distance. Before I knew it, I was speeding along towards the Angeles Crest Highway.

    I had so many things planned for the day, routine chores that had to be done, or so I thought. But when I opened the door in the morning to let the cats out and pick up the paper from the doorstep, I knew that this was not going to be the day for chores.

When you're finished, the cursor should be on line 22.

Save Your Work

Because this is new typing, you haven't saved your work to the disk yet. Although it would hardly be a horrendous problem if your computer went "down" and you lost three paragraphs, get into the habit *right now* of saving your work often. That way, if Mr. Murphy with his infamous laws comes to call you'll be ready for him!

You can save your work, *stay* in the file, and resume where you left off quickly. All saving commands start with the prefix ^K. The command to save a file and stay in it is ^**KS** (**F9**):

Press   ^**KS** or **F9**

WordStar says, briefly, Saving... as it saves the STORY file to disk. Now you're safe! Experienced WordStar users rely on **^KS (F9)** to save their work every few pages or so. A good rule of thumb is: Never assume that *anything* is safe until you've saved it to disk. Use the **^KS (F9)** command a lot. Remember the habits of cats and Meow's Laws, too!

Moving the Cursor Around in the File

The cursor always shows your *current position* in the file, but often you'll want to move it somewhere else—for instance, when you need to edit your work. WordStar has many cursor commands. Learning how to move the cursor quickly through a file will save you time and is one of the first operations any novice word processor should master.

Single Moves

Look at the keyboard for a moment. The four keys—D, S, E and X—form a diamond pattern on the keyboard. Think of the diamond as WordStar's "compass." It helps you remember how the keys move the cursor: **^D** one column to the right, **^S** one column to the left, **^E** up one line, and **^X** down one line. These keys also appear under the CURSOR column on the Edit menu. Many touch typists don't like to stray off the letter keys, so they use this cursor diamond instead of the ARROW keys. They press the CTRL key with their pinky and the letter key with another finger of the left hand.

However, I find it just as easy—and it involves fewer keystrokes—to use the ARROW keys. All cursor movement commands have equivalents on the numeric keypad, but I'll continue to list both arrangements in the instructions. At this point, the cursor is at the end of the file.

Press   **^E** or **UP ARROW** *twice*

to move the cursor up into a line of text.

Press   **^D** or **RIGHT ARROW** a few times

to move the cursor to the right.

Press   **^S** or **LEFT ARROW** a few times

to move the cursor to the left.

Press   **^X** or **DOWN ARROW** once or twice

to move the cursor down by line.

Press ^E or **UP ARROW** four times

to get ready for the next example.
    The keys will repeat if you hold them down, but make sure you also hold down the CTRL key.

Moving by Word

On the keyboard, the A key is to the left of the cursor diamond, and the F key to the right. *Hint:* Think of A as "aft" and F as "forward." So, the commands ^A and ^F move the cursor backward or forward, respectively, by word. There are keypad alternates to these commands, too.

Press ^F or ^**RIGHT ARROW**

to move the cursor to the beginning letter of the next word.

Press ^A or ^**LEFT ARROW**

to move the cursor to the beginning letter of the previous word.
    Repeat the commands to become familiar with them.

Scrolling

You've seen that parts of your file are out of view off the screen. You can *scroll* them back into view. Think of the screen as a window past which the file, like a parchment roll, moves. To see parts of the file *above* the screen, you scroll the file *down*. To see parts of the file *below* the screen, you scroll the file *up*. Note the scrolling commands on the Edit menu. They, too, have keypad alternates.

Press ^W or ^**PG UP** a few times

to scroll up through the file by line.

Press ^Z or ^**PG DN** a few times

to scroll down through the file by line.
    If you wish, repeat these commands to get the hang of them. The cursor doesn't move when you scroll the file by line, unless the line that has the cursor scrolls off the screen. In that case, the cursor stays at the top or bottom line of the screen.

Press   ^R or **PG UP**

to scroll up through the file by screenful.

Press   ^C or **PG DN**

to scroll down through the file by screenful.

These two commands, ^R (**PG UP**) and ^C (**PG DN**), are useful for leisurely viewing your file in "chunks." To remind you how the four scrolling commands work, take a look at the location of the W, Z, R, and C keys on the keyboard.

Wholesale Moves and the Quick Menu

Saving keystrokes means saving work. You'll often want to move the cursor in a more "wholesale" fashion. Why use the ARROW keys when WordStar has a better—that is, faster—way?

All "wholesale" moves use double-letter commands with the prefix ^Q for *Quick*. Take a look at the listing of other MENUS on the right side of the Edit menu. There are only five prefixes that require an additional letter to complete a command, ^K, ^O, ^P, ^Q, and ESC.

If you forget the completion letter of a command, just press the **CTRL** key and the letter prefix (you don't use the CTRL key with the ESC key—see Chapter 7). WordStar then shows you a menu that lists the most common commands for that prefix. So, to see the Quick menu:

Press   ^Q

WordStar displays the Quick menu and waits for you to type the second letter to complete the command. Just look at the commands now. You'll learn them all in due time! When you're finished:

Press   **SPACEBAR** or **ESC**

to leave the Quick menu without issuing any "quick" command.

So, pressing the **SPACEBAR** or the **ESC** key while a menu is on the screen just takes you back to the text area.

You can use two quick cursor movement commands to zip the cursor to the *beginning* or *end* of the file.

Press   ^QR or ^**HOME**

to move the cursor to the beginning of the file.

Tip: You could have pressed ^Q, waited for the Quick menu to appear, and then *typed* the r. This is the easiest way to learn the WordStar double commands. Experienced WordStar users just quickly press both keys of the command to bypass the menu altogether.

Press   ^QC or ^END

to move the cursor to the end of the file.

When you move the cursor to the end of the file, it always goes to the *last entered character* in the file—here, that hard return on line 21—so it's now on line 22 again. As you'll see, often when you open a file you'll want to move the cursor quickly to the end to start typing in new text. Now you know how!

Press   ^QR or ^HOME

to move the cursor to the beginning of the file.

Press   ^QP

This command moves the cursor to whatever was its *previous position.*

Press   ^QR or ^HOME

to move the cursor to the beginning of the file.

Two other commands that experienced word processors use a great deal move the cursor to the *right side of the line* and to the *left side of the line.*

Press   ^QD or ^F10

to move the cursor to the right side of line 1.

Press   ^QS or ^F9

to move the cursor to the left side of line 1, that is, the left margin.

Just as the ^D and ^S commands move the cursor right and left one character, respectively, ^QD (^F10) and ^QS (^F9) make the move "wholesale" to the right side of the line and the left side of the line.

Tip: These two commands help you correct typing mistakes at the other side of the line. Most typists instinctively know when they've made a mistake, but they may not stop typing immediately because their fingers are faster than their thoughts! So, they move back to the left side of the line with ^QS (^F9), use ^D or the **RIGHT ARROW** key to move the cursor to the mistake, and correct it. Then they press ^QD (^F10) to return to where they left off. This command positions the cursor past the *last entered character* on the line. However, it cannot move the cursor past a hard or soft carriage return at the end of the line.

Press   **^QX or END**

to move the cursor to the bottom line of the *current* screen.

Press   **^QE or HOME**

to move the cursor to the top left side of the *current* screen. Old timers refer to this as the "home" position.

Question: Given the cursor diamond, what is the "logic" of these two commands? *Hint:* What does the single-letter command do? Right! These **^Q** commands are wholesale moves up and down in the same general direction as the single-letter commands. WordStar gurus will notice that the **^QE** command has changed slightly: no longer do you have to press **^QE** and then **^QS** to move the cursor to the home position.

Tip: You may find, as I did, that you use **^QS** and **^QD** much more often than **^QE** and **^QX** but you find pressing **^F9** and **^F10** slightly awkward. Using a *keyboard enhancer program,* you can set up the **HOME** and **END** keys for these commands (Chapter 28). There's also a way to reconfigure these keys with the WSCHANGE program (Chapter 27).

There you have the most important cursor movement commands. Take the time to learn them now, because you'll be using them a great deal. Figure 1–1 presents a diagram of the basic cursor movement commands; you'll learn about the ones in the figure that you haven't yet studied, as well as others, in later chapters.

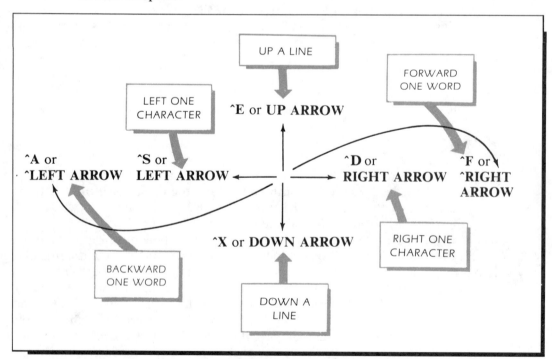

Figure 1–1   Cursor Movements and Scrolling

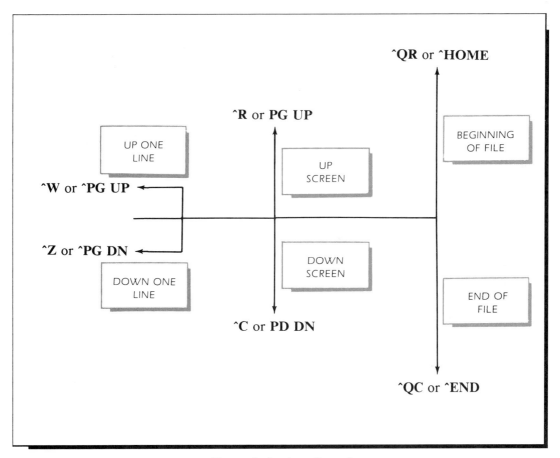

Figure 1-1 (continued)

Deleting and Inserting Text

It's time to put your knowledge of the cursor movement commands to work. Most of the time you'll move the cursor to mistakes in the file so that you can then make corrections, or to locations in the file where you want to delete or insert text. In either case, the cursor must be where you want it before you can make your changes.

Press   ^QR or ^HOME

to position the cursor at the beginning of the file.

Press   ^F or ^RIGHT ARROW three times

to position the cursor under the *o* of *one*.

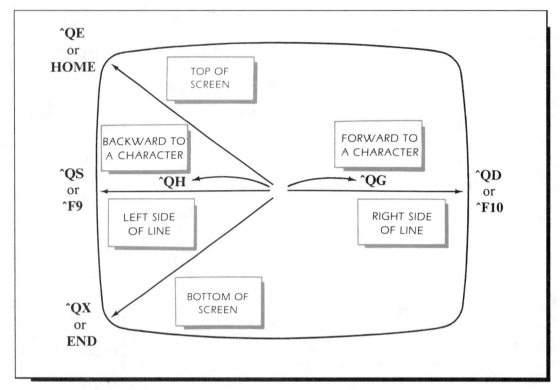

Figure 1-1   (continued)

Deleting One Character at a Time

Just as you can delete the *previous* character by pressing the **BACKSPACE** key (^H), you can also delete the character at the cursor location.

Press   ^G or **DEL** three times

to delete the word *one.*
    The cursor doesn't move, but the text past the deletion does move back to fill in the hole left by the deletion. When you delete individual characters, whether you use **BACKSPACE** (^H) or **DEL** (^G) depends on where the cursor is. Figure 1-2 shows the difference.

    Tip: Get in the habit of using **BACKSPACE** (^H) to delete mistakes as you type in new text. That way, you'll catch most mistakes when they occur. Use **DEL** (^G) to delete and correct mistakes later. Make sure you position the cursor under the mistake first.
    Notice that you didn't delete the *space* after the word *one,* because you're going to insert another word here. Your sentence now doesn't make any *grammatical sense,* which brings me to . . .

In this example, the cursor is under the space at the end of the line:

    I'm definitely not going to stay at home todd_

When you press **BACKSPACE (^H)** once, the space moves back as you delete the *d*, but you *don't* delete the space:

    I'm definitely not going to stay at home tod_

In this example, the cursor is directly under the mistake:

    I'm definitely not going to stay at home todday.

When you press **DEL (^G)**, you delete the *d* and fill in the rest of the line:

    I'm definitely not going to stay at home today.

Figure 1–2   Deleting by Character

Inserting Text

Always make sure the cursor is where you want it to be before you insert text. It should be under the character *in front of which* you plan to insert text. Here, you decide to replace the word *one,* which you've already deleted, with another word.

Type   **another**

Caution: Whenever you delete text and insert new text, make sure that the spacing *between* words is correct. The cursor should be under the space after *another.*

Press   **^F** or **^RIGHT ARROW** three times

to move the cursor under the *c* of *clear.*
    Deleting by character is useful, but what's even more useful is making "wholesale" deletions.

Deleting by Word

Often when you edit a file you'll want to substitute one word for another. The easiest way to do so is to use **^F** (**^RIGHT ARROW**) or **^A** (**^LEFT**

ARROW) to move the cursor to the beginning of the word, and then press the *word delete* command.

Press   ^T or **F6**

to delete the word *clear.*

A nice touch is that WordStar doesn't delete the comma after *clear.* Normally, the word delete command, **^T,** deletes the word *up to and including the space* following the word, except when there's a punctuation mark in the way. You can now substitute the word you want:

Type   `bright`

Note: If the cursor is in the *middle* of a word and you press **^T (F6)**, WordStar deletes only the rest of the word starting at the cursor. Always make sure the cursor is under the beginning letter of a word to delete the entire word with **^T (F6)**.

Whenever you delete or insert text, WordStar doesn't automatically fix *(align)* the line endings, although the next release of the product will probably have an automatic align feature. Right now, the first line of the paragraph isn't correct. You'll adjust that in a moment. First, learn about one more way to delete.

Deleting by Line

Suppose you want to delete this entire line and start over. Do it quickly like this:

Press   ^Y or **F5**

to delete the entire line.

Whereas it's a small matter to retype a word that you may have accidentally deleted, it's much more frustrating when you delete an entire line by mistake. Not to worry: WordStar now has a way to *restore* text that you've removed with any "wholesale" deletion command, such as **^T (F6)** or **^Y (F5)**. Leave the cursor where it is.

The "Unerase" Feature

Besides canceling any command in progress, **^U** is the *undo* or *unerase* command. WordStar only "remembers" whatever is the *last* deletion you made, so it's important to "undelete" text as soon as you delete it by mistake. To restore the deleted line:

Press   ^U or **F2**

Voilà! The line is back. Now, delete a word and then restore it:

Press   ^F or ^RIGHT ARROW five times

to position the cursor under the word *those*.

Press   ^T or **F6**

to delete the word and the space following it.

Press   ^U or **F2**

to restore the deletion. WordStar also restores the space.

How does this unerase feature work? Whenever you delete text with ^T (**F6**) or ^Y (**F5**), and certain other deleting commands discussed in other chapters, WordStar keeps the deleted text in a holding zone called a *buffer*. When you press ^U (**F2**), WordStar brings the text in the buffer back into the file. WordStar can only retain the *last* deletion, so always use ^U (**F2**) as soon as you can to restore your mistake. (Later releases of the program may have multiple restores.)

The unerase command doesn't normally work with *individual* characters that you've deleted with **DEL** (^G) or **BACKSPACE** (^H), because it's easier just to type in the characters again (although you could configure WordStar to "undelete" individual deletions if you wish).

Tip: The unerase feature lets you *experiment* with different words. If you don't like a word, just delete it and try another. Want to change your mind and go back to the first word? Undo! As Chapter 5 will show you, you can also use the unerase feature to move or copy text quickly.

Note: The function key label at the bottom of the screen shows the unerase command as Undo.

Aligning Paragraphs

You'll continue editing this file in the next chapter. After editing a file you'd want to fix the line endings so that they are correctly within the margins. WordStar calls this *aligning,* or *reforming,* the paragraphs. WordStar Release 4 does *not* align edited paragraphs automatically for you.

As I just mentioned, it's possible that by the time you read this book WordStar *will* automatically align edited paragraphs. In that case, you don't have to do the following examples and those in other chapters that specifically align paragraphs after editing.

Whenever you want to align an edited paragraph, make sure the cursor is on the *first* line that contains editing changes. It should still be on line 1.

Press   **^B**

to align the first paragraph.

Notice that the cursor is now on the blank line (line 8) between the first and second paragraphs, because WordStar has gone through and aligned the first paragraph.

How does the align feature work? It readjusts the lines in the paragraph to the margins until it finds a hard return, which should only be at the end of the paragraph. That's why it's so important *not* to press the RETURN key until you want to end the paragraph. If there are superfluous hard returns in the middle of paragraphs, they would "hang up" the align command (ending lines in unwanted places), and the text won't print correctly. See the next section to learn how to delete hard returns.

Note: Most of the time, you'll be working with text in paragraphs that you'll *want* to be able to align. Sometimes, however, you'll have tables or other text that you don't want to align. You can turn the align feature off, in which case the word Align disappears from the status line. You'll learn about this in Chapter 9.

Just keep in mind a standard WordStar Release 4 rule of thumb: *Whenever you make any corrections or revisions to a file by deleting or inserting text, you must align the edited paragraphs.*

Deleting Hard Returns

Well, then, if you *did* mistakenly insert hard returns in the middle of a paragraph, how do you delete them? How can you tell they're there in the first place? You should already know the answer to the second question: the flag character display will show a < wherever there's a hard return in the file. Check your file to make sure that there are hard returns only at the ends of the paragraphs.

Now for the answer to question number one. *A hard return is just like any other character, and you can delete it like any other.* The trick is knowing where to position the cursor.

Press   **^E or UP ARROW**

to position the cursor on the last line of the first paragraph, line 7.

Press   **^QD or ^F10**

to position the cursor at the right side of the line.

The cursor is now directly under the hard return, although it's not obvious from the screen display. Now you can delete the hard return:

Press   ^G or **DEL**

to delete the hard return.

It's as simple as that! **Caution:** Because you really *do* want a hard return here, put it back in:

Press   **RETURN**

So much for the mysterious hard return! Now, check your typing and, using the cursor movement and deletion commands you've just learned, correct any mistakes in the text. Make sure you use the ^B command to align any edited paragraphs.

Getting Help

Besides the menus, there's an extensive help feature in WordStar.

Press   ^J or **F1**

WordStar responds with basic information about getting help:

```
To get help with the Edit Menu above, press one of the keys that are
shown to the left of each description in the menu at the top of the
screen.  (Remember that ^ means you should use the control key.)

For a general explanation of the screen, press question mark (?).
For help with dot commands, press dot (.).
For help with saving your work, press ^KD.

If you would like to change the help level, press ^J again.
```

At this point WordStar is waiting for you to press any command to give you help about the command. You'll learn about dot commands and changing the help level in other chapters. The only way to get out of help here is by pressing the **SPACEBAR**. Take a look at help for ^U:

Press   ^U or **F2**

WordStar shows information about the unerase command.

You can get help by pressing the function key equivalent of a command, too! This feature also "jogs" your memory about what command a function key does if you forget, or if you lose the keyboard template.

Press   **ESC**

to leave help.

Now press **^J (F1)** and then press **^Q.** WordStar presents the Quick menu. You then press any command letter to get help for that command, such as **C** for help with **^QC.** As WordStar mentions, press **ESC** when you're finished looking at the help screen. Or press **^U, ESC,** or the **SPACEBAR** to leave help.

Note: Say you want help for the **^F** command. You press **^J (F1)** and then *type* an *f,* forgetting to hold down the CTRL key. WordStar tells you that the letter is not a command:

```
(Any character not a command)

You typed a character that was not a command.  To get help for a command,
hold down the Ctrl key (abbreviated to ^ on the menu) while you press the
letter of the command you want.

For example, if you want help with ^E, hold down Ctrl and press E.

Press Esc to continue.
```

Press **ESC** to leave help and try again. This time, press **^F** after you press **^J (F1)** for help. When you've returned to the text area, press **^J (F1)** and type a question mark (?) to see extensive help about the screen, ruler line, flag characters, and so on. Make sure you have left help and are back in the text area before continuing the lesson.

Note: From the Opening menu, use the J [help] command or F1 in the same fashion. Press **J (F1)** and then an Opening menu command letter to get information about that command.

Closing the File and Returning to the Opening Menu

Here's one final and important habit to get accustomed to. Always save your file and return to the Opening menu *before* you turn off your machine or remove the disk from the drive. If you wanted to work on another file, you'd have no choice *but* to close this file—in the future WordStar may let you edit two files at the same time. In either case, the command is:

Press   **^KD or F10**

All file commands from within a file use the prefix **^K.** When you open a document file, you use **D** from the Opening Menu. When you close and save the file the command is **^KD.**

Tip: I always try to impress upon my students this general rule: If you don't see the Opening menu on the screen, then you aren't finished yet! If you *do* see the Opening menu, then you know that you've properly saved the file.

So Now, Print!

What good is all your work if you can't get a *hard copy* version of it? Here's a fast way to print the STORY file. First, turn on your printer and insert a piece of paper (or move to the top of a form if you have continuous-form paper). Then:

Press   **P** [print a file]

WordStar prompts:

```
To skip further questions, press the Esc key at any point. Press ↵
at any question to use the default answer.

Document to print?
```

You'll learn the ins and outs of printing in Chapter 3. Instead of typing in the name, use a *shortcut:*

Press   **ESC**

The **ESC** key often acts as a *keystroke saver.* When you press **ESC** in response to WordStar's request for a file name, WordStar presents the *last file you were working on,* which is exactly the one you want! It also *completes* the command, so you don't have to press RETURN. WordStar begins printing immediately, and the message Printing appears above the Opening menu.

After the file prints, determine on what line of the paper the printing starts and how the left and right margins look. If WordStar didn't center the text on the page, adjust the position of the paper in the printer and use that position in the future. Reprint the STORY file, if you wish, to see the results.

Exiting WordStar

As long as the Opening menu is on the screen, you can safely remove all floppy disks from the drives and turn off your computer. However, if you want to begin working with another computer program you can *exit* WordStar and return to DOS:

Press   **X** [exit WordStar]

You soon see the DOS prompt, which is probably either B> or C>. **Note:** If you attempt to exit WordStar while it's printing a file, you'll either have to cancel the print job or wait until printing is completed. See Chapter 3.

I've now introduced you to most of the important day-to-day word processing commands in WordStar—commands that you'll use continually. If you feel unsure of yourself, go back and work through this chapter again. Create another file (say, STORY2) and repeat the examples. Or better yet, do some typing on your own to practice the deleting, inserting, cursor movement, and saving commands.

When you're ready to start learning how to edit files, go on to Chapter 2. You will be surprised how quickly and effortlessly you will learn WordStar's many features. It is my intention to make you a "dedicated word processor" by the time you finish this book!

Revisions, Revisions

In this chapter you will learn the following new commands:

Opening Menu Command

Y	Delete a file

File Commands

ESC P	Cursor to the previous paragraph
ESC T	Transpose the word at the cursor with the next word
^JJ	Change the help level
^KQ	Quit the current edit without saving any changes
^M	Insert a carriage return
^N	Insert a blank line without moving the cursor
^O	Onscreen Format menu (document mode)
^OB	Turn the soft space display on/off
^OC (SHIFT F2) (ESC C)	Center a line
^OT	Turn the ruler line on/off
^Q DEL	Delete from the cursor to the left side of the line
^QG	Cursor forward to a character
^QH	Cursor backward to a character

more . . .

^QI (^F4)   Cursor to a page number (document mode)

^QT   Delete forward to a character

^QU   Quick align the entire file (document mode)

^QY   Delete from the cursor to the right side of the line

Other Features

^R   Repeat the last file name

F7   Align a paragraph (^B) and return the cursor to the previous position (^QP)

Typing in new text is the most strenuous part of word processing, because most of the time WordStar can't help you do that! But it *can* help you edit your files quickly and easily. This chapter presents the basic editing patterns you'll use continually and some other useful WordStar features. (In Chapter 7, you'll learn how WordStar can even help you type at times!)

DO WARM-UP

The Opening menu appears. From now on, I'll not mention this fact . . . it's obvious.

Selecting a File by Name

You'll begin by opening the STORY file from last time. Remember that your computer can't intuit what file you want to open, so you have to type its name *exactly as it appears* in the file listing. If you make even the slightest mistake, WordStar won't be able to locate the file and will tell you, in no uncertain terms:

```
Can't find that file. It may be misspelled or on a different disk or directory.

Press Esc to continue.
```

You have no recourse but to press **ESC** and try again. One way to get around the possibility of a typing error is to *select* the file name from the directory listing. That way, you don't have to type at all!

Press   **D** [open a document]

When the directory listing appears:

Press   **^X or DOWN ARROW**

to move the cursor into the directory.

Now, using the **^D, ^S, ^E,** and **^X** commands—or the ARROW keys for fewer keystrokes—position the cursor on the STORY file (*not* STORY.BAK— you'll learn about that later). Then:

Press   **RETURN**

to open the file.

WordStar says briefly:

```
Reading from disk...
```

Soon you see the STORY file on your screen. WordStar always positions the cursor at the beginning of the file you open. (See Chapters 12 and 13 for more information on working with files.)

Adding Text to a File

One type of revision that you'll do often is to add more text to the end of the file. **Caution:** Make sure insert mode is on: the word Insert should appear on the status line. This is the last time I shall remind you that insert mode should always be on whenever you begin a new section of this book. But what do you have to do first? Right! Move the cursor to the end of the file quickly:

Press   **^QC or ^END**

to position the cursor at the end of the file.

Press **TAB** (**^I**) to begin each paragraph, then type them as you see them below. Press **RETURN** twice to end each. The cursor should be on line 33 when you're finished. Use one space before and after the dash, two hyphens.

```
        Angeles  Crest -- why even the name sounds romantic.  And  I
was  ready  for  anything today!  I had left  all  responsibilities
behind  me and was heading for the Great Unknown, far into  those
beautiful, and mysterious, mountains.  What would I find?

        Probably  nothing at all, if I didn't get past  the  traffic
jam  that  was backing up the freeway  for  miles.   Fortunately,
```

```
motorcycles are easier to manipulate than cars.  To the  disgust
of  all those envious drivers, I slowly rode between the  stalled
cars and was soon in the clear.
```

Pretend that you've typed in more text than just two paragraphs. What should you do now? Right! Save your work:

Press   ^KS or **F9**

to save the file and resume where you left off.

Paragraph Practices

Often you'll want to insert paragraphs in existing text, add text in the middle of or at the ends of paragraphs, split paragraphs, or join paragraphs together. Use the following patterns as the models for these operations.

Inserting a Paragraph

First, position the cursor at the *left margin* of the line where the new paragraph is to go:

Press   ^**R** or **PG UP**

to scroll the file up.

Press   ^**E** or **UP ARROW**

to position the cursor on line 22.

Then you must make space for the new paragraph by adding blank lines. The command to add a blank line is ^**N**. Here you'll add two blank lines, one for the end of the new paragraph and one for the spacing between paragraphs. **Caution:** When adding blank lines, you should always make sure the cursor is at the left margin. Otherwise, you'll split the lines at the cursor location.

Press   ^**N** twice

You've added the blank lines and pushed the text down. ^**N** always inserts one blank line but doesn't move the cursor. The command ^**M**, which you'll probably not use too much, inserts a hard return just like the **RETURN** key. **Tip:** WordStar gives you a close *visual approximation* on the screen of how your file will eventually print, so be careful that you always have the correct spacing between paragraphs.

Now, press **TAB** (^I) to begin the paragraph and type it as you see it below. Stop! Don't add any returns to the end of the paragraph because you've already put in the correct number of returns with the ^N command.

```
        Even Pato, my oldest and wisest cat, seemed to intuit that I
wasn't in a working mood.  He looked at me as if to say, "I
thought you were going to clean my litter box today," and gave a
disapproving meow.
```

Inserting Text in the Middle of a Paragraph

Again, move the cursor to the spot in the file where you want to insert the text. You'll add a sentence to the first paragraph.

Press   **^R or PG UP** twice

to scroll the file up. The cursor is on line 5.

Press   **^F or ^RIGHT ARROW** four times

to position the cursor under the *T* of *The*.
        Type the following sentence (WordStar will wrap part of it to the next line as you type):

```
In fact, it was almost as if you could reach out and touch them.
```

        Stop! Take a look at the end of the sentence. What do you have to do now?

Press   **SPACEBAR** twice

to separate the new sentence from the next one.
        You've changed the paragraph, so now you must align it back to the margins.

Press   **^B**

to align the paragraph. The cursor is on line 9.

Splitting a Paragraph

To split a paragraph into two paragraphs, first position the cursor at the beginning character of the section you want to split:

Press   **^E or UP ARROW** three times

to position the cursor on line 6.

Press   **^F or ^RIGHT ARROW** five times

to position the cursor again under the *T* of *The*.

According to the Edit menu, you can use ^N to split the line, but that leaves the cursor at its present position. Because in this example you want to construct a new paragraph from the split section, use the RETURN key to move the cursor as you split the paragraph.

Press   **RETURN** twice

Now what? Insert a tab to begin the new paragraph:

Press   **TAB or ^I**

Align the new paragraph:

Press   **^B**

Leave the cursor where it is.

Joining Paragraphs

There are several ways to join paragraphs depending on where the cursor is located, but the process generally requires removing the hard returns and tabs between the paragraphs and tidying up the results. For example, you now want to join the next paragraph with the preceding one.

Press   **^T or F6** twice

to delete the carriage return and the tab at the beginning of the next paragraph.

Even though ^T (**F6**) is the word delete command, you can use it to delete other things. It's especially useful for deleting the five spaces that WordStar inserts when you press **TAB** (^I) to begin a paragraph. That's because besides deleting any text in a word, it deletes all spaces from the cursor position to the next nonspace character.

Press   **BACKSPACE or ^H**

to bring the line up and join it with the previous line.

Stop! Are the sentences spaced apart correctly? Probably not.

Press   **SPACEBAR** twice

to separate the sentences correctly.

Press   ^**B**

to align the edited paragraph.

Press   ^**KS** or **F9**

to save the file and resume where you left off.

There are other ways to join paragraphs. If the cursor is at the beginning character of the text you want to join to the preceding paragraph, press **BACK-SPACE** (^**H**) enough times to delete the tab spaces and hard returns and move the text back. If the cursor is at the end of the paragraph and you want to join it with the next paragraph, press **DEL** (^**G**) enough times to remove the intervening hard returns and tab spaces.

The End-of-Paragraph Trick

Experienced word processors know that they often have to add more text to the ends of paragraphs when they later edit a file. If your boss is a lawyer you know what I mean! A trick we used at the law firm where I worked was to include two spaces after the last sentence in each paragraph. Then when we needed to add text to the end of the paragraph, we positioned the cursor on the line, pressed ^**QD** (^**F10**) to move to the end quickly, and we were ready to go!

A Special Function Key

Say you've done some "heavy" editing to a paragraph and you want to align the paragraph to see how it looks, but you also want to leave the cursor where it is to continue editing. Use the special function key, **F7**. This key combines *two* WordStar commands. It aligns the paragraph (^**B**) and then returns the cursor to the previous position (^**QP**).

Moving to the Beginning of the Paragraph

The cursor must be on at least the first edited line before you align the paragraph. Otherwise, you'll miss aligning any previous lines. One way to ensure that you don't miss anything is to move the cursor to the beginning of the paragraph before pressing ^**B**, and an easy way to do that is to press **ESC P.** When I discuss *macros* in Chapter 7, you'll understand how this "shortcut" works. At this point all you need know is that it takes the cursor to the *previous paragraph,* that is, to the first previous hard return it finds.

Aligning an Entire File

Many people don't bother aligning paragraphs individually when they edit a file because that's a waste of time. They wait until they're finished, move the cursor to the beginning of the file with ^QR (^HOME), and then use the ^QU command. This command aligns the rest of the file from the cursor location. You can stop it at any time by pressing ^U (F2).

Later you'll see that you wouldn't want WordStar to align certain sections of text, such as a table or chart. You can instruct WordStar to *bypass* these sections when you use ^QU to align an entire file. See Chapter 9 for more information.

The Center Command

To center a line on a typewriter you have to find the approximate center of the page, then press BACKSPACE once for every *two* characters in the line. WordStar has a much better way to center a line between the margins. You want to add a title to the file and center this title.

Press   ^QR or ^HOME

to position the cursor at the beginning of the file.

Press   ^N three times

to add three blank lines without moving the cursor.

Press   CAPS LOCK

to turn on uppercase.

Type   ANGELES CREST ADVENTURE

Press   CAPS LOCK

to turn off uppercase.

Centering is part of the *onscreen formatting* of the file. All onscreen formatting commands use the prefix ^O (Chapter 4). The command for centering is ^OC. The cursor can be anywhere on the line you want to center (it should still be on line 1 now). Take a look at the Onscreen Format menu before you center the title:

Press   ^O

The Onscreen Format menu appears. To center the line:

Press   C or ^C

to complete the command, **^OC.**

WordStar centers the line and moves the cursor down to the next line. (You can also use **SHIFT F2.**) Whenever you change the margins of a file (but you haven't learned how to do that yet!) or edit a centered line, you must *re-center* the line. Here's an example.

Press   **^E or UP ARROW**

Press   **^F or ^RIGHT ARROW** three times

to position the cursor under the *A* of *ADVENTURE.*

Press   **^T or F6**

to delete that word.

Type   ROMANCE

Press   **^OC or SHIFT F2**

to recenter the edited line.

Press   **^KS or F9**

to save the file and resume where you left off.

Another one of the ESC key shortcuts is **ESC C** to center a line. Use it instead of ^OC to save a keystroke!

Note: Programmers who write and edit computer programs must use non-document mode (covered in Chapter 11). When you work with nondocuments, the ^O command has another function, and all other onscreen commands that begin with the ^O prefix don't apply. That's because nondocuments have no onscreen formatting like documents.

The Logic of WordStar's Commands

The design of WordStar makes it *machine independent.* WordStar's basic command structure uses only those keys that are on all computers: the alphanumeric keys, the CTRL (^) key, RETURN (ENTER) key, and the ESC key. That's why, for example, pressing ^I is the same as pressing the TAB key: not all computers have a TAB key. On the IBM PC, there are additional keys, and you've seen that WordStar uses these keys as shortcuts for many commands.

Many CTRL ("control" or ^) key commands are single-letter commands. As the "diamond" arrangement illustrates, there's a logic to how these commands work—for instance, to move the cursor or scroll the file. All double-letter commands work with one of four prefixes: **K, O, P,** and **Q.** (The **ESC** key commands are a recent addition that I'll discuss separately in Chapter 7.)

The Edit menu shows the single-letter commands and the command prefixes. When you press one of the prefixes, you see another menu that covers its commands. Although you haven't learned everything yet, here is the basic setup for the prefixes:

- ■ **^K** is for manipulating text within a file using *blocks* (Chapter 5), for saving files, and for file maintenance within a file (Chapters 12 and 13). WordStar refers to the **^K** menu as the Block & Save menu.
- ■ **^O** is for onscreen formatting and displays in document mode only.
- ■ **^P** is for special print features, such as underlining and **boldface** print.
- ■ **^Q** is for quick operations (moving the cursor, certain deletions, aligning an entire file, and quick math) and the spelling checker.

If you wish, press each prefix key and look at its menu. Press the **SPACE-BAR** to leave each menu.

Changing the Help Level and Making Screen Space

One frequent cause of frustration to novice WordStar users is the amount of screen space that the program appropriates for menus and messages. After learning the WordStar basics, many people would rather have more space for their work but don't know whether that's possible! It is, Dear Reader, and here's how you do it.

There are several ways to increase the size of the text area on the screen. The two fastest ways are to remove the display of the Edit menu and ruler line while you're working. To remove the Edit menu, you change the *help level,* that is, the amount of help WordStar provides:

Press   **^JJ** or **F1 ^J**

WordStar prompts:

```
The four levels of help that can be in effect during your session are:

    3  All menus are always on. Some descriptions are simplified.
```

2 Except when editing a document, all menus are on.
1 Very few menus are on.
0 No menus are on. The status line is off.

The current help level is 3.
What help level do you want?

Type   2

Press   **RETURN**

You can also change the help level from the Opening menu by pressing **JJ.**

I suggest keeping the help level at 2, because then the **^K, ^O, ^P,** and **^Q** menus appear if you need them. If you set the help level to 1, you get very little help. Level 0 gives you *no help* and even removes the status line from the screen. It's only for real WordStar pros and other crazies! You can always turn the Edit menu back on by resetting the help level to 3, or turn the status line on by resetting the help level to 1, 2, or 3.

Caution: At help levels 0 or 1, WordStar won't ask you to type **y** to accept the creation of a new file from the Opening menu. Nor will it ask you for confirmation when you delete a file. Be careful!

You can get an extra screen line for the text area if you turn off the ruler line:

Press   **^OT**

This is a *toggle switch,* something you'll see a lot of in WordStar. You issue the same command to turn a feature off when it's on, or on when it's off. *Question:* What toggle switch have you already learned? *Answer:* **INS (^V)** to turn insert mode on and off. To toggle the ruler line back on, repeat the command. Do it now for practice!

Tip: You may also want to customize WordStar so that the help level is automatically 2 (my preference) when you load the program, or to turn off the ruler line or function key labels from the bottom of the screen, thus giving you even more text area. Use the WSCHANGE program to change the default setup. See Chapter 27.

Computer Limbo and Garbage

Even though the screen may show a lot of blank space, that space may not be readily available to you.

Press   ^QC or ^END

to position the cursor at the end of the file.

Press   **^D or RIGHT ARROW**

What happened? Nothing! Because this is the end of the file, the cursor can't go past it even though there's plenty of screen space! The flag character display indicates the end of the file with a caret (^). The area past this is "computer limbo." The cursor cannot go into this area until you have typed more text or added blank lines to the file.

Be careful about "garbage" characters when you do the examples. If you accidentally press the **SPACEBAR** or the **TAB** key, you will insert superfluous spaces or tabs into the file. You may not see these characters, but WordStar "remembers" them! This is a problem when insert mode is on, as it is usually, and something that first-time word processors often have trouble with. If the cursor isn't *exactly* where I mention it should be and you suspect that there are some extra spaces in the file, press **BACKSPACE** (^H) to delete the extra spaces and move the cursor back.

Soft Spaces

You've probably noticed that even though you type one space between words and two spaces at the ends of sentences, WordStar inserts additional spaces to fill in the lines when right margin justification is on (the default setting). These are *soft spaces.* When you edit your file and align the paragraphs, WordStar readjusts the lines with new soft spaces where necessary.

Note: WordStar *never* removes the spaces that you typed by pressing the SPACEBAR or TAB. They're *hard spaces,* just like the hard returns you put in at the ends of paragraphs.

I feel that, with justification on, it's easier to delete all the spaces between words when you delete the words and then type in a new space between words. However, at rare times what appears to be a hard space between two words on the screen doesn't print as a space. That's because it's a soft space, and if there's no regular (hard) space between the two words WordStar doesn't print just the soft space. There's a way to determine where the soft and hard spaces are:

Press   **^OB**

This toggle command turns on the display of soft spaces. They appear as little ovals, although you can customize WordStar to show soft spaces as any character you want (Chapter 27). To turn off the soft space display:

Press   **^OB**

Later, you'll learn how to turn justification off to make your text look "ragged." WordStar does not insert soft spaces into unjustified text.

Press   **^KD** or **F10**

to save the file and return to the Opening menu.

Other Ways to Delete Text

You're back at the Opening menu for a reason. The next examples show you how to delete text in a variety of ways. You'll use the STORY file but then you'll *abandon* the edit so that you don't save the changes. Make sure you *are* at the Opening menu now!

Press   **D** [open a document]

Stop! Here's a shortcut: When you're opening the same file as the one you just edited, do this:

Press   **ESC**

 Note: You can also press **^R** to *repeat* the file name, and then **RETURN** to open the file, but that means more keystrokes!

Deleting Forward to a Character

You can delete text from the cursor location to the next occurrence of a character you specify. Two useful applications of this features are to *delete a sentence* and *delete a paragraph* (there are other ways to do "wholesale" deletions: with blocks—see Chapter 5). The cursor is at the beginning of the file.

Press   **^X** or **DOWN ARROW** three times

Press   **^F** or **^RIGHT ARROW**

to position the cursor under the first word of the paragraph.
    To delete a sentence, you tell WordStar to delete to the *next period* character, provided that this particular sentence ends with a period! Mercifully, it does.

Press   **^QT**

WordStar prompts:

`Delete forward to what character?`

Stop! You can only type *one* character:

Type   .

(that's a period).

    WordStar deletes the first sentence. Unfortunately, it doesn't delete the spaces between this sentence and the next, but it's a piece of cake just to press **DEL (^G)** as many times as necessary. You can use **^U (F2)** to "undelete" the sentence, but don't worry about that right now. If this sentence ended with a question mark or exclamation point, just use the correct character to delete the sentence.

    Question: To delete a paragraph, what character do you delete to? *Hint:* What character ends a paragraph? Right! A hard return. Do one for practice:

Press   **^QT**

Press   **RETURN**

    You can delete to any character, but this feature only works *forward* through the file. See what happens when you delete to the next occurrence of *t,* for instance. I'll let you do this one yourself. There is a way to delete backward, with a block (Chapter 5).

Deleting Parts of Lines

Two useful commands delete only part of a line from the cursor location, either to the right side or to the left side of the line.

Press   **^QC** or **^END**

to position the cursor at the end of the file.

Press   **^E** or **UP ARROW** five times

Press   **^F** or **^RIGHT ARROW** five times

to position the cursor under the *t* of *the.*
    To delete from the cursor to the right side of the line:

Press   **^QY**

Unlike **^Y (F5)**, which deletes *everything* on the line including a soft or hard return at the end of the line, **^QY** does not delete a soft or hard return. Just for practice, restore the deletion:

Press   **^U** or **F2**

To delete to the left side of the line from the cursor location:

Press   **^Q DEL**

When you delete to the right side of the line with **^QY**, the cursor doesn't move. When you delete to the left side of the line with **^Q DEL**, the cursor *and* text move back to the beginning of the line. Don't forget to use **^B** to align the paragraph when you delete text.

Tip: You can use these two commands to delete an entire line *without* deleting the hard or soft return at the end of the line. Just make sure that the cursor is at the left or right side of the line before pressing **^QY** or **^Q DEL**, respectively.

You now know all the basic deletion commands in WordStar. Table 2–1 summarizes these commands.

Transposing Words

One final editing shortcut lets you *transpose* two words. It switches the word at the cursor with the next word.

Press   **ESC T**

In Chapter 7 I'll explain how this feature works. Just make sure the cursor is at the *beginning* of the first word when you want to transpose it with the next word.

Table 2–1   Basic Deletion Commands

Key	Action
^H (BACKSPACE)	Delete Previous Character
^G (DEL)	Delete Character at Cursor
^QT	Delete Forward to a Character
^T (F6)	Delete Word Right
^Y (F5)	Delete Entire Line
^QY	Delete from Cursor to Right Side of Line
^Q DEL	Delete from Cursor to Left Side of Line

Abandoning an Edit

You've made deletions to your file that you don't want to save. You can *abandon* the current version and return to the file as it was before you began the editing session. This is one great way to overcome writer's block, when every change you make to your text is not acceptable to you and you'd rather just go back to the original version of a file.

Press   ^KQ

WordStar warns you that it will cancel your changes:

Modifications have just been made.

Are you sure you want to abandon them (Y/N)?

You would type n for no if you wanted to continue editing without losing the changes. Here, however, you do want to abandon the edit, so

Type   y

to abandon the edit and return to the Opening menu.

This quit without saving command, ^KQ, is helpful not only for a writer's block but also for any time when you revise a file but decide to go back to the file as it was *before* your revisions. **Note:** This command reverts to the *last saved version* of the file. If you had saved the file with ^KS and then later pressed ^KQ to quit without saving, WordStar would revert to the version you saved with ^KS.

The ^KQ command can be a lifesaver when you do something really horrendous to the file, such as inadvertently deleting a huge chunk of text or messing up the file in some other way. **Caution:** The command can only work with an *established* file. If you just started a new, unsaved file and then tried to use ^KQ with it, you would delete the entire file. That's because there's no file to go "back" to. Watch out!

Backup Files

The reason ^KQ works at all has to do with how WordStar keeps versions of your file. After you've created a new file and saved it once, every time you save the file again WordStar keeps the *last saved version* in a separate backup file. This file has the extension .BAK, so if your file's name is TEST, its backup is TEST.BAK. When you abandon an edit session with **^KQ,** WordStar uses the backup file for the regular file.

There are thus usually *two* versions of a file on the disk: the most current version and the last version (the backup file). Fortunately for everyone concerned, WordStar doesn't make a backup of the backup!

Note: WordStar's backup files have nothing to do with the backups ("copies") of files that you periodically create on separate disks as a safeguard for your work. See Chapter 13 for more information about backing up your files.

Look at the directory listing a moment to see the STORY.BAK file. WordStar won't let you edit this file unless you *rename* the file first with the **E** command. WordStar *will* let you open a .BAK file, but only in protected mode (see Chapter 13). Normally, you *wouldn't* want to open a backup file because you'd be working with the original. However, suppose you accidentally delete the original? You could then rename the backup and use it, saving yourself at least a bit of work!

Deleting Files

Sometimes you'll need to make space on the disk for other files, so you can safely delete the backup files. As an example and because you'll soon create another backup for the STORY file, learn how to delete a file from the Opening menu.

Press   **Y** [delete a file]

WordStar prompts:

```
Specify the document that you wish to be permanently erased from disk.

If you do not specify a drive in the document name, it will be
erased from drive B.

You can stop any erasure from occurring by typing ^U (press the U
key while holding down the CTRL control key).

Document to be erased?
```

Note: Your disk drive letter may be different.

Type   story.bak

or select STORY.BAK from the file directory.

Press   **RETURN**

Just to make doubly sure you know what you're doing, WordStar prompts:

Are you sure (Y/N)?

You could type n or press ^U to abandon the operation. Here:

Type   y

 Caution: Always be careful when you delete a file with **Y**, because it's then gone (almost) forever. The only way you could reclaim it is if you buy a disk utility program with a file unerase feature, and only if the file hasn't been written over by another file at a later time. See Chapter 28 for more information about restoring deleted files.

More Editing Practice

Just to give you a bit more exposure to editing with WordStar, here's another editing lesson. You'll even use some of the new commands you learned in this chapter. Make sure you complete this section and the next before going on to Chapter 3.

Press   **D** [open a document]

Press   **ESC**

to reopen the STORY file.

Press   **^C** or **PG DN**

to scroll to line 20.

Press   **^X** or **DOWN ARROW** twice

to position the cursor on line 22.

Press   **^F** or **^RIGHT ARROW** ten times

to position the cursor under the *w* of *when.*

Press   **^T** or **F6** ten times

and watch the screen as you delete all the words from *when* up to the word *let.*

Type   after

Press   **SPACEBAR**

for the correct spacing between words.

Press   **^D** or **RIGHT ARROW** three times

to position the cursor under the space after the word *let.*

Type   ting

Press   **^F** or **^RIGHT ARROW** five times

to position the cursor under the *p* of *pick.*

Press   **^D** or **RIGHT ARROW** four times

to position the cursor under the space after the word *pick.*

Type   ing

and notice that WordStar wrapped the lines as you typed because the cursor reached the right margin.

Press   **^X** or **DOWN ARROW**

Press   **^F** or **^RIGHT ARROW** twice

to position the cursor under the *t* of *this.*

Press   **^QY**

to delete the rest of the line.

Type   I would not be able to do any

Press   **SPACEBAR**

for the correct spacing between words.

Press   **^X** or **DOWN ARROW**

to position the cursor on the last line of the paragraph, directly after the period.

Press   ^S or **LEFT ARROW**

to position the cursor under the period.

Press   **SPACEBAR**

Type   today

Press   **ESC P**

to position the cursor at the beginning of the paragraph.

    Tip: Always make sure that the text in your file makes *grammatical* sense and that there is one space between words when you delete words and insert new ones. As in this example, you may have to insert the space yourself.

    Now, align the paragraph:

Press   **^B**

to align the paragraph.

Introducing Page Two!

As your final lesson today, you'll add more text to the end of the file and see what happens when WordStar starts a new page.

Press   **^QC or ^END**

to position the cursor at the end of the file on line 42.

    Type the following new paragraphs. When you get to the last paragraph, watch what happens as you type it.

```
        Eventually  the  freeway ends and the road  narrows  to  two
        lanes as it gradually ascends to several thousand feet above L.A.
        As its name implies, the Angeles Crest Highway follows the  crest
        of  the  mountains, and it's by no means an easy road  to  drive.
        For  a motorcyclist, it's something of a challenge,  because  the
        frequent hairpin turns call for nerves of steel.

        As  I  started  negotiating  the first  of  those  turns,  I
        wondered if I hadn't made a mistake.  Was I correctly heeding the
        Call  of  Nature?  Maybe she had really meant for me to  mow  the
        lawn!  I imagined the smirk on Pato's face when I returned, tired
        and irritable after a long day's grueling driving.  His  "I-told-
        you-so" meow chanted in my ears.
```

> Needless to say, I was definitely ready for adventure, or romance, or something, the longer I drove that blasted road. "I'll show that smart-alecky cat," I repeated as I honked my horn at yet another car that veered perilously close to my side of the line. "Litter box indeed!" echoed for the 100th time in the silent canyons around me.

Press   ^KS or F9

to save the file and resume where you left off.

Because it couldn't fit the entire paragraph on the first page, WordStar started a new page. The line of hyphens and P in the flag character column show the *page break display,* which is there as a convenience to you. It doesn't print. WordStar starts a new page according to the following settings:

- The top margin has 3 blank lines and the bottom margin 8 blank lines, for a total of 11 blank lines on the page.
- Standard paper is 11 inches long with 6 lines per inch, so there are 66 total lines on the page.
- Subtract 11 from 66, and you get 55 lines on the page.

So when WordStar reaches what would be text line 56 on page 1, it starts a new page. The status line shows the page where the cursor is. You can change these page defaults like all other format settings (Chapters 4, 14, and 15).

Moving the Cursor to a Page

It's a little silly talking about multiple-page files when yours is only slightly more than one page long! But get to know an important cursor movement command, cursor to page number. As you can imagine, it's a quick command, ^QI (or ^F4). First, position the cursor at the beginning of the file:

Press   ^QR or ^HOME

Then:

Press   ^QI or ^F4

WordStar prompts:

Find what page?

Type   2

Press   **RETURN**

When you position the cursor *forward* to a specific page number, WordStar moves the cursor to column 1 of line 1 on the page. If the page number doesn't exist, WordStar goes to the end of the file. Now go *backward* to a previous page to see what happens. First, position the cursor at the end of the file:

Press   ^QC or ^END

Press   ^QI or ^F4

Type   1

Press   **RETURN**

What happened? WordStar positions the cursor on the *last line* of page 1 instead of the first line! (In Chapter 11, you'll see that this command works differently in nondocuments.)

Moving the Cursor to a Character

Two other useful commands take the cursor to the *next occurrence of a character,* either forward or backward through the file. The cursor should be on the last line of page 1.

Press   ^X or **DOWN ARROW**

to position the cursor on line 1 of page 2.

Press   ^QG

WordStar prompts:

Find what?

Now, the *next* character you type is what WordStar will find, just as it deletes to the next character when you press ^QT.

Press   **RETURN**

to position the cursor at the end of the paragraph. That is, it found the next hard return.

To find a character backward:

Press   **^QH**

WordStar presents the same response.

Type   t

to find the first occurrence of the letter *t* backward from the cursor location.
    Question: Can you now intuit how **ESC P** finds the previous paragraph? In Chapter 7 you'll learn for sure. (You'll see other ways to find text in Chapter 6.)

Finishing for the Day

Dear Reader, I think you've had enough work for today, so:

Press   **^KD** or **F10**

to save the file and return to the Opening menu.
    Now that you've edited and saved the file again, WordStar creates another backup file. Print the file if you wish: press **P** and then **ESC** after preparing your printer and paper. Or wait until the next chapter, because it discusses printing at greater length.

Print Effects and Printing

In this chapter you will learn the following new commands:

File Commands

^KP	Print a file from within a file
^OD (SHIFT F1)	Turn the print controls display on/off
^PRT SC	Save and print a file
^P	Print Controls menu
^PB (F4)	Turn boldface print on/off
^PC	Pause the printer from within a file
^PD	Turn doublestrike print on/off
^PO	Binding (nonbreak) space
^PS (F3)	Turn underlining on/off
^PX	Turn strikeout on/off
^PY	Turn italics on/off *or* change the ribbon color

DOS Command

SHIFT PRT SC	Print a "screen dump"

Other Features

Print options

ASCII and PRVIEW printer drivers

more . . .

>>   Redirect the output to another
      printer on a local area network

WordStar supports a variety of *special print effects,* such as underlining and boldface print. You'll learn about other important print effects in this chapter, including one special feature that can help you produce the best-quality print-outs. (Chapter 17 continues the discussion of print effects.) Then you'll take a close look at printing and WordStar's many print options.

DO WARM-UP

Special Print Effects

All special printing effects depend on *codes* that you insert and save in a file. Most of the special effects that you'll learn in this chapter require *two* codes, one to turn the special printing on, and another to turn it off. Remember that WordStar refers to these on/off codes as *toggle switches* or *toggles.* You've already seen several toggle switches, for instance ^OT to turn the ruler line on and off.

Directions to the Printer

A printer, like a computer, is a dumb machine that will do everything you tell it to do and will *continue* to do so until you tell it to stop. If you instruct it to begin underlining but forget to tell it to stop underlining, then it will duly underline the rest of your file. Figure 3–1 illustrates toggle switches that begin and end underlining.

WordStar shows the text you want to print with a special effect in high-lighting, shading, or a different color on the screen. What you see may depend on your monitor. Monochrome monitors display true underlining, but monochrome monitors with graphics cards show underlining as shading or intense video. Color monitors show underlining as a separate color.

So if you look up and see WordStar underlining the entire file before your very eyes, that means you forgot to turn off the underlining. It's a simple procedure to right this minor wrong at any time.

 Note: Although WordStar supports many print effects, your printer may not be able to handle all these features. For instance, dot-matrix printers generally can print italics, but daisy wheel printers cannot unless you change the typewheel in the printer.

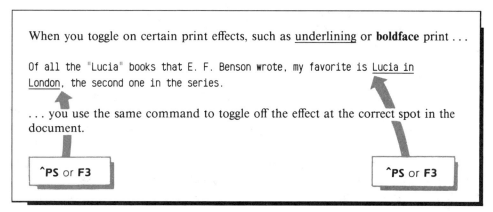

When you toggle on certain print effects, such as <u>underlining</u> or **boldface** print . . .

Of all the "Lucia" books that E. F. Benson wrote, my favorite is <u>Lucia in London</u>, the second one in the series.

. . . you use the same command to toggle off the effect at the correct spot in the document.

^PS or F3

^PS or F3

Figure 3-1   Printer Toggle Switches

The Print Controls Menu

The print controls are commands that start with the prefix **^P.** Sure there's a menu for them!

Press   **D** [open a document]

Type   story

or select the STORY file from the directory listing.

Press   **RETURN**

Press   **^P**

The Print Controls menu appears. When you're finished looking at this menu,

Press   **SPACEBAR**

(Dear Reader: WordStar has so many features. You're learning about them little by little. Rome wasn't built in a day, you know!)

Underlining as You Type

Most of the time you'll insert print codes as you type new text. The trick is to turn the effect on *just before* you type the text with the special effect, and then to turn the effect off *directly after* the text and before you type any "normal" text. You'll work with underlining in this section, but the procedure is the same for all print toggles.

Press   ^QC or ^END

to position the cursor at the end of the file, on line 8 of page 2.

Start typing the following new paragraph (remember to begin the paragraph with a tab), but when you get to the word *No,* stop!

```
       I guess I must have taken a wrong  turn  somewhere,  because
all  of  a sudden a sign loomed directly ahead.  It said,  in  no
uncertain  terms,  No Outlet.  I had just enough time to  make  a
fast stop to miss crashing into it.  A close call!
```

Now, to start underlining:

Press   ^PS or F3

WordStar inserts an ^S code here. All print effects start with the prefix ^P, but WordStar only inserts the second letter of the command in the file. Now, type the underlined phrase:

Type   No Outlet

Stop! Always turn a printing effect off at the correct spot. Here, you don't want to underline the period, so:

Press   ^PS or F3

to insert the ending ^S code into the file.

Type the period and finish the rest of the paragraph. Make sure you press **RETURN** twice to end the paragraph and position the cursor on line 13.

What's this? The line containing the print effects extends *past* the right margin. The entire paragraph looks like this on the screen:

```
       I  guess I must have taken a wrong  turn  somewhere,  because
all  of  a sudden a sign loomed directly ahead.  It said,  in  no
uncertain  terms,  ^SNo Outlet^S.  I had just enough time to  make  a
fast stop to miss crashing into it.  A close call!
```

Previous versions of WordStar didn't show print effects with underlining, shading, or highlighting. You only saw the codes, such as ^S for underlining, and as a reminder WordStar extended the lines with codes past the right margin to make them stand out. This brings the discussion to . . .

Turning Off the Print Codes Display

Because WordStar shows print effects on the screen, you don't have to display the print codes if you don't want to. You can turn off the codes but still see the special effects. That way, the codes won't distract you as you type.

Press   **^OD** or **SHIFT F1**

The codes "disappear" and WordStar now shows the line correctly within the margins. The **^OD** (**SHIFT F1**) command toggles the print code display on or off. In a minute you'll learn how to delete the codes, but for the time being leave the display off. **Tip:** You can set up WordStar to have the print codes display off by default. I think that's a better way to go. (See Chapter 27.)

Underlining Existing Text

You can insert print toggles around existing text just as you can insert any other character anywhere in the file. But make sure the cursor is where you want it to be first. In this example, you'll underline the word *something* in the second-to-last paragraph.

Press   **^R** or **PG UP**

Press   **^E** or **UP ARROW**

to position the cursor on line 2 of page 2.

Press   **^F** or **^RIGHT ARROW** twice

to position the cursor under the *s* of *something.*

Press   **^PS** or **F3**

Whoa! The entire file past this point appears underlined! That's WordStar's gentle reminder that you haven't turned underlining off yet. Move the cursor to the end of the word quickly, like this:

Press   **^QG**

Type   ,

(that's a comma).

Again, you don't want to underline the comma, but the cursor is in the correct spot because when you insert the end underline code it pushes the comma ahead.

Press ^PS or **F3**

to end underlining.

Press ^KS or **F9**

to save the file and resume where you left off.

Underlining Spaces

By default WordStar does *not* underline the spaces between words in a phrase. If you prefer to underline the spaces, too, you can change WordStar's defaults (again, see Chapter 27). There's another way to do the same thing, and you'll learn about it in Chapter 4 when you investigate dot commands. In either case, when you set up WordStar to underline the spaces between words, it still won't show you the spaces as underlined on the screen.

Question: If you do choose to have WordStar underline the spaces between words normally, how would you occasionally underline individual words for emphasis? Right! Just put begin and end underline codes around each word separately. For example, to underline the words *No Outlet* individually, set up the codes so that the result would look like this on the screen:

^SNo^S ^SOutlet^S

Boldface Print

Most printers, except laser printers, print in boldface by printing over a character several times. Some printers even move the printhead slightly to produce a "filled in" look. Laser printers generally print in boldface by selecting a boldface *font* (Chapter 26). Inserting boldface print codes is the same as inserting underline codes, only the command is different. You'll put the title of your story in boldface.

Press ^QR or ^HOME

to position the cursor at the beginning of the file.

Stop! Is the cursor where you want it to be? Not yet. Although you *could* put the beginning boldface code here at the left margin, I always recommend that you insert the codes as close as possible to the text. That way you'll be able to find and delete the codes easily later.

Press ^F or ^RIGHT ARROW

to position the cursor under the *A* of *ANGELES.*

Press   ^PB or **F4**

WordStar shows the entire file in boldface (highlighting) because you haven't turned off the print effect yet.

Press   ^QD or **^F10**

to position the cursor at the end of the line.

Press   ^PB or **F4**

to turn boldface print off.

Press   ^OD or **SHIFT F1**

to display the print codes.
        As you would expect, the boldface codes appear as ^B on the screen. Leave the codes on.

Doublestrike Print

On some printers you can print over each character twice to get a result that approximates boldface print. This is *doublestrike,* and its command is **^PD.** **Tip:** A great use for doublestrike print is to get more "mileage" out of faded ribbons. Be aware, though, that when you print in doublestrike your document may take a while to complete!
        To print text in doublestrike (the cursor should be at the end of line 1):

Press   ^X or **DOWN ARROW** three times

to position the cursor at the left margin of line 4.

Press   **^PD**

WordStar puts a ^D code in the file but shows doublestrike as highlighting, just like boldface.

Press   **^QG**

Press   **RETURN**

to move the cursor to the end of the paragraph.

Press   ^PD

to turn off doublestrike.

    Note: On laser printers, WordStar may print doublestrike as boldface, depending on the font you're using (Chapter 26).

Strikeout with Hyphens

The strikeout command prints hyphens over text to show that you're considering deleting this text from the next edit of the file. Strikeout does *not* delete the text. The command for strikeout is **^PX** and it, too, is a toggle switch.

    Suppose you're intending to delete a sentence from the file, and you want your editor to approve the move. The cursor should be at the end of the first paragraph.

Press   ^QG

Type   B

and make sure you type the *B* in uppercase!

    The cursor moves to the sentence beginning with the word *Before* in the next paragraph.

Press   ^PX

Press   ^QG

Press   **RETURN**

to position the cursor at the end of the paragraph.

Press   ^PX

to insert the end strikeout code.

Press   ^KS or **F9**

to save the file and resume where you left off.

    If you want WordStar to use another character, such as the slash (/) for strikeout, you can change the default (Chapter 27). WordStar does not print the strikeout character over spaces, nor does it show the strikeout character on the screen. On my monitor, strikeout text appears as highlighting.

    Leave the cursor where it is for a moment, please!

Italics and Ribbon Color

Most laser printers, and some dot-matrix ones, let you print text in *italics*. WordStar can handle italics, too. **Note:** Italics aren't the same as underlining! On laser printers, you have to have an italic font available.

WordStar has always had a command, **^PY,** to switch ribbon colors on printers with dual or multicolor ribbons. Now WordStar uses the *same* command for italics because there are virtually no printers that support both features simultaneously (or so the folks at MicroPro International tell me). As with the other print toggles, the **^PY** command requires a beginning and an ending code.

Deleting Print Codes

Whenever you delete a print effect, make sure you delete *both* codes, because if you leave in a code WordStar uses it as the "begin" code. There should always be an even number of toggles. The next example shows you how to put a code somewhere else by deleting one of the codes. (The cursor should be at the end of the paragraph on line 18.)

Press	**^QG**

Type	t

to position the cursor under the word *things* in the next paragraph.

Press	**^PS** or **F3**

Press	**^F** or **^RIGHT ARROW**

Press	**^S** or **LEFT ARROW**

Press	**^PS** or **F3**

to end underlining.

You decide that you want to underline the phrase *so many things* instead of just the word *things.*

Press	**^A** or **^LEFT ARROW**

The cursor is at the beginning of the "word," which now includes the ^S code.

Press	**DEL** or **^G**

to delete the code.

Press   ^A or ^**LEFT ARROW** twice

Press   ^**PS** or **F3**

to insert the beginning code here.

      Note: Once you get to be an experienced WordStar user, you'll even be able to delete print codes with the code display off! For the time being, however, always turn on the code display with ^**OD (SHIFT F1)** before you attempt to delete codes.

Press   ^**KD** or **F10**

to save the file and return to the Opening menu.
      Later in the chapter you'll print the file to see the results. For the time being, take a look at another interesting "printing" feature.

The Binding Space

Psst! When is a space not a space? When it's a *binding space!* And what, pray tell, is *that?* It's a way to overcome an inherent limitation to wordwrap: where WordStar ends each line. First, start a new file.

Press   **D** [open a document]

Type   space

Press   **RETURN**

Type   y

because this is a new file.
      Look at the following example, but *don't* type it. What's "wrong" with it?

      We hereby acknowledge receipt of your letter postmarked June 15, 1987. Our records indicate that an order was placed for 200 Disposable Dipsy Diapers on May 16, 1987, by someone named Sylvia Q. Roper of your company. Therefore, our invoice postmarked May 19, 1987, is correct. We at Dapper Dandy Diaper Delivery feel that there is no cause to contest that invoice. If, however, you wish to contact our attorneys, send all correspondence to Smudge & Smudge, Solicitors, at 15 Barristers Court, San Francisco, CA 91405. Thank you.

      WordStar doesn't know what a word is, but it can recognize the spaces between words to determine where one "word" ends and another begins. The space, like every other character you type, has a *code number* (more about this at the end of the chapter), and WordStar looks for the code number of the space character when it uses wordwrap to form the lines.

So WordStar forms the lines to fit within the margins without regard to what the words mean. Any editor, lawyer, supervisor, or even a client would have a conniption about this example because certain phrases aren't kept together. It just does not look good when a first name (*Sylvia*) is not on the same line as its middle initial (*Q.*), or when the month is not together with the day (*June 15*).

WordStar has a command to avoid this problem, but *you* have to remember to use this command. *Instead* of a regular space, you enter a print code at those spots where you do not want WordStar to split two words or any two terms at the end of a line—ever. That code is the *binding space*. Previous versions of WordStar referred to it as the "nonbreak" space. The binding space will still print as a space. Oh, yes, there is such a thing as a "printable" character called the space. It's an instruction to the printer to move over one character position.

Unlike the other print codes you've learned so far, the binding space code is not a toggle switch. You only use one code. WordStar never breaks a line at the binding space. If both words don't fit on a line, WordStar brings them down to start the next line. Like all print codes, the binding space *stays* in the file and still works if you edit the lines later.

Now type the example using the binding space in certain spots. Here's how. Start typing, but when you get to the word *June* on the first line, type it and then stop. The cursor should now be directly after the word *June*. Do this:

Press   **^PO**

Type the date (*15*), but *do not type an extra space.* When you do type the 15, WordStar finds that it cannot fit the entire phrase *June 15* on one line, so it begins another line. With the print codes on, as they should be now, the phrase appears as June^O15 on the screen and the line extends past the right margin. If you turn the print codes off, all you see is what looks like a space.

Continue typing, but make sure that you insert binding spaces instead of regular spaces between *Sylvia* and *Q.*, between *May* and *16* and *May* and *19*, and between the first *Smudge* and the ampersand. (There are three other spots which could use a binding space. Can you figure out where?) Now, compare the two examples: the original one and yours.

The other spots are between *15* and *Barristers,* between *San* and *Francisco,* and between *CA* and the zip code (use two binding spaces here). Now that you have inserted binding space codes, WordStar forms the lines differently and consequently some of the phrases are in the middle of the line.

Here are examples of the most important places to use a binding space—shown by an underline—instead of a regular space:

- Between a title and a name—Dr._Einstein, Miss_Lizzie Borden
- Between a first name and middle initial—John_F. Kennedy
- Between a street number and street name—507_Sycamore Street
- Between a month and day—April_26, 1947
- Between the words of a multiword name—Santa_Fe, van_Beethoven, de_Gaulle
- Between a state and zip code—CA__90065
- Between an ampersand and the word preceding it—Harry_& David

Other places where you would perhaps wish to consider using binding spaces might be

- Between the parts of mathematical formulas—$a^2\_+\_b^3\_=\_c$
- Between section numbers or letters and the first word of the text—(a)_when it is necessary
- Between such words as *section* or *page* and the number following these words—Section_II or Chapter_6 or pp._254–256
- Any time and for any reason that you do not want two words or phrases to separate over lines

Can you think of situations in your own work where the binding space might come in handy? You can insert and delete binding space codes in your file like any other character. It takes a while to get into the habit of using the binding space command, because it's probably totally new to you. But it can greatly improve the look of your work.

Here's another example of where the binding space can come in handy. The cursor should be on the blank line after the end of the previous example.

Press   **^KS** or **F9**

to save the file and resume where you left off.

Press   **RETURN** two or three times

to space down for the next example.

Type the following example, but be careful to use a **TAB** (**^I**) to begin each numbered section and then *two regular spaces* after the numbers. You'll soon understand the method behind my madness.

I have reached the following conclusions about the patient:

1.   The patient suffers from a decided lack of the ability
to make normal decisions in life situations ("lose the name of
action," and so on).

2.   He often wants to go off into his own world of
speculation as an escape from reality ("to be or not to be," and
so on).

3. He seems to have little grasp of the exigencies of human
destiny as perceived by his superiors (cf. Claudius as King).

Look at the example to see how the three sections don't align underneath each other correctly. That's because WordStar inserts soft spaces where it can to fill out a line, but it has no way of knowing or caring how the text looks. *You,* however, can prevent this unsightly printout by using binding spaces.

Instead of adding normal spaces after each section number, you would use *two* binding spaces by pressing ^PO twice. So, go back and delete the regular spaces—including the soft spaces that WordStar inserted to fill out the line—between each number and the beginning word of the sentence. For instance, with the cursor on the *t* of *The,* press **BACKSPACE (^H)** three times to delete the spaces. Then insert *two* binding spaces instead. Do the other two lines, and the beginning of each numbered line will look like this on the screen:

Section 1.^O^OThe patient ...

Section 2.^O^OHe often ...

Section 3.^O^OHe seems ...

Go back to the first paragraph and align the edited file with ^QU. Using binding spaces, you have instructed WordStar *not* to add any superfluous spaces at the beginning of the line. The beginning word of each section will print out beautifully aligned, one under the next. (There's another way to accomplish the same effect, but you'll have to wait until you get to Chapter 17 to learn it.)

Press   ^KD or F10

to save the file and return to the Opening menu.
Such attention to detail is up to you, but these little things do add up and can impress even the most demanding boss!

The Basics of Printing

So much for some standard print effects. Chapter 17 continues the discussion when it introduces superscripts, subscripts, condensed and expanded printing, and other print features. Now turn your attention from special print effects to printing files.

Up till now you've just pressed the ESC key to start printing immediately without bothering with the print options. This time, follow along to learn what these options can do for you. I'm assuming that you just edited the file called SPACE. First, prepare your printer and paper. Then:

Press   **P** [print a file]

Press   **^R**

to repeat the file name, SPACE.

(If you didn't just edit this file, type **space** instead.)

Press   **RETURN**

to bring up the print options questions (if you want to cancel at any time, press **^U** or **F2**).

The Print Options

Most of the time you don't have to answer the print options individually, because you'll accept the standard defaults and print the entire file. You can also answer only one or two options and then press **ESC** to bypass the rest, if they're the ones you want.

Tip: Set up WordStar's print options so that the defaults are those you use the most, so that you can bypass them often. For example, if your printer accepts individual sheets of paper, you would want to change WordStar's default of continuous paper to have your printer stop at the end of each page and let you insert another sheet of paper (Chapter 27).

Multiple Copies. The first option is a useful one:

Number of copies?

Normally WordStar prints one copy of each page. You can print any number of copies. Press **RETURN** to continue after typing the number you want, or **RETURN** alone to accept the default of one copy.

Pausing Between Pages. The next option is important if your printer has to stop between pages to let you insert the next sheet of paper:

Pause between pages (Y/N)?

The default is no pause, so if you press **RETURN** WordStar "assumes" that your printer accepts continuous form paper.

Form Feeds. The next question—

Use form feeds (Y/N)?

—generally need concern you only if you have a laser printer. Press **RETURN** to answer no to this question or type y if you have a laser printer.

Printing Specific Pages. The next two questions work together to request the *page ranges* you want to print. You have several choices here, so pay close attention. You'll see this question first:

Starting page?

WordStar considers the *first* page of the file to be the starting page, and the *last* page of the file to be the ending page, no matter what page numbers the file contains (in Chapter 14 you'll see how to change the pagination of a file). Normally, you'd want to start at the beginning of the file, so you'd just press **RETURN** to see the next question:

Ending page?

To print to the last page of file, press **RETURN.** What if you only want to print certain pages? If the page range is *unbroken*—say, pages 2 through 7—type in the beginning page number and press **RETURN.** Then type the ending page number and press **RETURN.** For example, if you wanted to start at the beginning of the file and print up to and including page five, press **RETURN** to answer the Starting page? question, then type **5** and press **RETURN** to answer the Ending page? question.

Suppose you want to start printing at page two and end at page six. You'd type **2** and press **RETURN** after the Starting page? question, then type **6** and press **RETURN** after the Ending page? request.

What about *noncontinuous* pages? Supply *all* page numbers you want after the Starting page? question, and WordStar doesn't even ask you about the ending page. For example, you want to print pages 1 through 5, then page 7, and finally page 10. You'd type **1-5,7,10.** Use hyphens for ranges (beginning and ending pages) and commas between individual page numbers. *Do not* type any spaces between the numbers.

Here's another example. You want to print pages 2, 8, and 9 through 12: **2,8,9-12** is what you'd type.

Finally, you can specify that only *even* or *odd* numbered pages print. Supply the letter **E** or **O** after the beginning page number. For instance, to start at page three and print only odd numbered pages, you'd type **3o**. *Question: What happens if you specify the page range as 3e?* Go ahead, try it!

Note: There's a limit to the number of different pages you can specify, so you may have to divide the printing request into batches to print all the individual pages you want. For instance, WordStar won't let you enter all these page numbers at once: **1,3,6-10,12,14,15,20-24**. Just break the job into two jobs.

Nondocument Formatting. After you determine the pages you want to print, WordStar then asks:

```
Nondocument (Y/N)?
```

As I mentioned in the Introduction, nondocuments don't have document-type formatting. If you answer **y** to this question, WordStar will "pretty print" a nondocument file with the default *document* format. Normally, you'd press **RETURN** to accept the default of no, because most of the time you'll be printing documents. (In Chapter 4 you'll learn that you can use this option to print the *dot commands* in a file, but you don't know what dot commands are yet!)

Selecting the Printer Driver. Finally, WordStar asks—

```
Name of printer?
```

—and provides a list of printer drivers from which you can choose. A *printer driver* contains the instructions for how to work with a specific printer. You'll note that WordStar shows the primary printer that you installed at the top of the list. It's in parentheses. Again, you'll usually accept the primary printer, so just press **RETURN**. To print with another printer driver, use the arrow keys to select it from the list or type its name on the edit line. Then press **RETURN**. Later in this chapter you'll learn about the types of special printer drivers available to you.

Once you've answered or bypassed the print options, WordStar flashes the message `Printing` at the top right corner of the screen until it's finished printing the file.

Note: You can't backtrack once you've answered a print option. If you supplied incorrect information for an option and pressed RETURN, press **^U (F2)** to cancel and start again. Press **P** [print a file], then **^R** and **RETURN** to use the same file name.

Controlling the Print Job

You have complete control over the print job, which means you can pause printing or cancel it altogether. Just press **P** while WordStar is printing, and you'll see the Printing menu. Once this menu is on the screen you have several options:

- Press **P** again to pause the print job. However, it may take your printer several seconds to stop, because it has to clear its buffer of characters waiting to print.

- Press **C** to continue printing after a pause.

- Press **^U (F2)** to cancel the print job entirely and return to the Opening menu or to the text area of a file if you're printing while editing (a method I'll describe in a moment).

- Press **F** to print at *full speed,* which means WordStar stays in the Printing menu and you can't edit another file until printing finishes, until you change the print job to background printing by pressing **B,** or until you cancel the print job. This command only works if you've used the WSCHANGE program to alter your printer's default speed to be less than full speed (Chapter 27).

- Press **B** to print in the *background* (the default) and return to the Opening menu so you can open another file and edit while printing. **Note:** WordStar may slow down a little or a lot while it's printing and editing at the same time. That depends on the type of printer you have. You'll need a certain amount of extra memory for background printing while editing. You can turn off background printing altogether (Chapter 27) and print only in the foreground—the faster method.

By the way, if you press **X** from the Opening menu or **^KX** from within a file to end WordStar while it's printing a file, WordStar brings up the Printing menu. Either press **^U (F2)** to cancel the print job or wait until the printing has finished.

Problems?

You've seen that for each printer WordStar works with a set of instructions in what it calls a *printer driver.* No two printer manufacturers use the same codes, so there are many different printer drivers. WordStar keeps all the printer drivers in a separate file called WSPRINT.OVR. If the printer doesn't start printing right away, look at the top right of the screen. Has the word Printing changed to Print Wait ? If so, press **P** to see the Printing menu. If WordStar is showing this error message:

Can't print unless WSPRINT.OVR is on the disk.

```
Press Esc to continue.
```

That means you haven't copied this file onto the WordStar disk or into the WordStar directory. Press **ESC,** exit WordStar, and copy that file to your WordStar disk or directory. Make sure you run the WINSTALL program to set up your printer.

If you get this message:

```
Can't use that printer. Incorrect name or not enough memory.

Press Esc to continue.
```

your system probably doesn't have enough memory to hold the printer driver file. If the entire WSPRINT.OVR file can't fit on your program disk, you can reduce the size of WSPRINT.OVR with the WSCHANGE program so that only the printer drivers you need are in the file (Chapter 27).

Another problem you may encounter comes in the form of this message:

```
Printer may not be ready. Press C to continue.
```

WordStar could be receiving a stop or pause code from the printer because the printer may not have any paper, the ribbon might need changing, or the cover is up. If none of these problems is the culprit, check that the printer is *on* and *on-line* and that the connections are tight. Then press **C** to continue. If you're still having problems, maybe you didn't tell DOS the correct printer settings with the MODE command before you loaded WordStar. See the Introduction for more help.

Finally, you may get this message after you press ^KP to print a file while you're editing another:

```
Insufficient memory for print while editing.

Press Esc to continue.
```

That means your system doesn't have enough memory to print in the background *and* let you edit a file simultaneously. Finish editing first, then save the file with ^KD **(F10)** and print from the Opening menu.

Inserting Paper During Printing

If you answered **y** for yes to the question, Pause between pages (Y/N)?, or if you set up the defaults to answer yes to this question, WordStar stops after printing the first page and flashes the prompt Print Wait in the top right corner of the screen. Press **P** to see the Printing menu and WordStar's message:

Pausing at top of page. Press C to continue.

Insert another sheet of paper into the printer, then press **C** to continue. If you stay in the Printing menu, just press **C** to restart printing for each new page. Notice that WordStar displays the page it's printing at the top of the Printing menu.

Saving and Printing in One Fell Swoop

One nifty command lets you cut down on unnecessary keystrokes by saving your file and printing it, too. Instead of pressing ^KD (F10) and then **P** from the Opening menu, just press ^PRT SC within the file. Answer the print options as usual, or press **ESC** to bypass them. (Later I'll cover another use of the PRT SC key.)

Printing from Within a File

Just as you can edit one file while printing another, you can also start a print job from within a file. You can print either the current file you're editing or another file, but in the former case be careful! First, open the STORY file, because it's time you printed it anyway to see the special effects.

Press   **D** [open a document]

Type   story

Press   **RETURN**

The command to print a file from within a file is ^KP, and it has a couple of peculiarities. (You can't use P from within a file, because that's just a letter!) First, prepare your printer and paper; then start the printing:

Press   **^KP**

Here's peculiarity number one! From the Opening menu there are two printing commands, **P** and **M** (merge printing). From within a file there's only ^KP, so WordStar first has to ask whether you want standard printing or merge printing:

You can print your file using either standard printing or merge printing.

Merge print (Y/N)?

Well, you won't learn about merge printing until Chapter 19, so:

Type   n

If you type any letter except y or n, WordStar honors you with this message:

Please press Y for yes, or N for no.

After typing n because you don't want to merge print, WordStar asks for the file name to print. Type it in, select it from the directory listing, or press **ESC** for the current file. *However,* this brings up peculiarity number two. If you want to print the same file you're editing, WordStar can only print the *last saved version* of this file. **Tip:** Always press ^KS to save the file just before you print it with ^KP. Otherwise, WordStar asks you to confirm what you're doing:

You are printing the file you have been editing, but modifications have been made since you last saved it. Print it anyway (Y/N)?

Either type y to continue or n to stop now and give yourself a chance to save the file first. When you continue, answer or bypass the print options as usual. To pause or cancel printing while you're working in a file, you'd press ^KP instead of **P** to bring up the Printing menu. So you control printing with **P** from the Opening menu or ^KP from within a file.

WordStar starts printing the file. Suppose you try to save the file now and return to the Opening menu before the printing is completed. Here comes peculiarity number three! When you press ^KD to save the file that's also printing, WordStar honors you with *another* message:

Cannot save file until printing is finished.

Press Esc to continue.

Just press **ESC**, be patient, and wait until printing finishes, or press ^KP and then ^U (**F2**) to cancel the print job if you're so much in a hurry to get to the Opening menu. By the way, how did the various print effects come out? In another chapter, you'll learn how to remove the print codes quickly.

Inserting Printer Pauses in a File

Suppose you want to print part of a file in another typestyle and you have to change the daisy wheel or thimble in your printer. Or maybe you have to switch paper trays in your laser printer. You can insert a *pause* instruction in the file to make WordStar stop at the exact location necessary. The command is **^PC.** Make sure you put in another pause at the point where you want to change back to the original typewheel or cartridge. (You'd have to turn the print controls on with **^OD (SHIFT F1)** to see the ^C codes in the file.)

During printing, WordStar stops at the location of the print pause and flashes the message Print Wait at the top of the screen. Press **P** (from the Opening menu) or **^KP** (from within a file) to see the Printing menu, change the typewheel, and press **C** to continue.

Selecting a Different Printer Port

When you installed WordStar you set it up to work with a primary printer and possibly a secondary printer, too. WordStar uses the primary printer unless you answer the final print option, Name of printer?, by typing the name of—or selecting from the directory listing—another printer driver. WordStar then automatically sends the output to the alternate port, because it "assumes" that both printers are connected to the computer through different ports.

Note: You must install the alternate port. For instance, you have a dot-matrix printer connected to LPT1, the parallel port, and a laser printer connected to COM1, the serial port. During installation you install the dot-matrix printer, but you also tell WordStar what the alternate port is. During printing when you choose a printer driver that isn't the default printer, WordStar sends the output to the serial port.

If you're working on a local area network, see the information later in the chapter on how to select printers.

"Printing" to Disk

As strange as it may seem, you can "print" a file or part of the file to a disk file. There are *four* different ways to print to disk.

Printing with Printer Codes. The first way is to have WordStar print the file to a disk file just as if it were sending the information to your printer. That is, the file contains the text and all printer formatting codes for the printer you select. Why use this feature? When your printer is not available and you're in a rush, you can print the file at another computer that doesn't have WordStar. You'd use the DOS COPY command to copy the file to the printer port and thus to the printer itself.

When you see the question, Name of printer?, type the printer driver name, then a right-pointing chevron or greater than sign (>), and the name of the disk file. **Caution:** Make sure you choose a *new* name for the disk file. If you don't supply a printer driver name, WordStar "assumes" the primary printer you've installed. For example, to send the file you're printing to a disk file named TEST using the primary printer, you'd type > **test** . To send it to the same file but in the form recognized by a Hewlett-Packard LaserJet, type **hpljet > test** . Later, to print the TEST file on a LaserJet connected to the parallel port (LPT1), you could type at the DOS prompt **copy test lpt1** .

The other three ways to print to disk let you *preview* the printing, *extract* certain information, or *filter out* unwanted characters. You select one of three special printer drivers supplied with WordStar in answer to the Name of printer? prompt. The three special printer drivers are PRVIEW, XTRACT, and ASCII.

The Preview Printer Driver. The "preview" driver, PRVIEW, is especially helpful when you want to check the results of merge printing *before* you merge print (Chapter 19), but you can also use it whenever you want to determine how a file will print before actually printing it.

If you choose PRVIEW as the printer driver, WordStar prints to a file called PRVIEW.WS, which you can then open with the **D** command from the Opening menu. You'll see a funny line at the top of the file that says .PL. This is a special WordStar command to make sure that the pages—as you view them on the screen—"break" exactly as they would in the printout so you can check page breaks.

You can also supply a different file name, a much better way to go, because the next time you print to disk with the PRVIEW driver WordStar would overwrite the previous PRVIEW.WS file. (The same holds true for the ASCII and XTRACT drivers.) For example, to "preview print" to the file name TEST.2, you would type this in response to the Name of printer? question: **prview>test.2** (notice that you don't have to put spaces between the driver, right-pointing chevron, and file name).

The Extract Printer Driver. The "extract" driver, XTRACT, sets up another file with only certain information from the original file. Because it's most useful with merge printing information, you'll learn about it in Chapter 20.

The ASCII Printer Driver. The ASCII print driver brings up a different—and important—issue. The American Standards Committee for Information Interchange (ASCII) has standardized the codes representing printable characters. There are 256 possible codes on IBM type computers, but only the first 128 are "standard ASCII" or "straight ASCII." (By the way, the ASCII code for a space is 32.) WordStar uses the other 128 in ways that would "confuse" other programs, for instance, to insert soft carriage returns or print effects in a file.

You print to the ASCII driver when you want to convert WordStar documents for use by other programs (Chapter 28) or when you want to convert a WordStar document to a WordStar nondocument. If you don't supply a file name, WordStar uses the file ASCII.WS. WordStar filters out any nonstandard codes when it prints to the new file so that other programs can then read the resulting "ASCII text file." Using the ASCII driver is also helpful when you want to convert a WordStar file to transmit it over telephone lines. You'll learn more about ASCII codes in Chapter 17. To convert an ASCII file to WordStar document format, see Chapter 28.

If there's no room on the disk to store the file, WordStar gives you this message:

```
Can't create output file.
```

```
Press Esc to continue.
```

You may have to delete a few files or try printing to a different disk or directory. See Chapter 13 for more information about deleting files. **Caution:** It makes no sense to print a file to a disk file with the same name. WordStar will just cancel a print job without further ado if you try to print, say, a file called TEST to a disk file called TEST. Don't do it!

Accessing Network Printers

One of the nicest features of *local area networks (LANs)* is that they let many people share the same expensive machines such as laser printers or plotters. If you're on a LAN, there's a little more to learn about printing files with WordStar.

Unless you set it up differently, WordStar normally "assumes" that you want to print at the printer attached to your network workstation, also called a *node*. That printer may be an inexpensive dot-matrix printer that you use for drafts. When you want to print on another printer elsewhere on the network, you *redirect* the output by typing a special instruction after the Name of printer? question.

To redirect the printed output, type the printer driver name, then *two* right-pointing chevrons, >>, and finally the *port* through which this printer connects to the network. For example, if you were redirecting the output to a Hewlett-Packard LaserJet that's attached to the network through the standard parallel port (LPT1), you would type hpljet >> lpt1 or hpljet>>lpt1. You can install a network printer as your default printer using WSCHANGE (Chapter 27).

Note: The two chevrons serve to redirect printed output to a *device*. If you're a DOS guru, you understand what this means. If you're not a DOS guru, don't worry about it.

A "Quick-and-Dirty" Printout

As long as you're exploring printing, learn about a DOS command that you can use within WordStar for a "quick-and-dirty" printout with just two keystrokes. First, make sure that the screen displays the text that you want to print. Then, after you've turned on your printer and prepared the paper:

Press   **SHIFT PRT SC**

Note: Laser printer owners may have to press the manual form feed button after the screen has printed to eject the paper.

There are several disadvantages to using **SHIFT PRT SC.** First, it gives you a printout of the *entire* screen—including the status line, ruler line, Edit menu, and function key labels! Second, some printers can't print all the graphics elements on the screen, so you might see other characters—or blank spaces—on the paper. Third, you would have to repeat the operation for additional screens of text. Finally, the command won't format the lines exactly as they appear when you print the file with WordStar. For instance, it won't show special print effects. I *told* you it was quick-and-dirty!

But one nifty use of SHIFT PRT SC is to print specific WordStar help screens or menus that you want to refer to without stopping your work or fumbling through the manual. Keep these visual aides near your computer or in a notebook. By the way, if you press **PRT SC** by itself, it will insert an asterisk (*****). The official computerese for what **SHIFT PRT SC** does is the inelegant but descriptive term, *screen dump*—you're dumping the current contents of the screen to the printer.

Tip: Before pressing SHIFT PRT SC, use ^OT to toggle off the ruler line, then change the help level to 0, 1, or 2 to remove the Edit menu. That way, you'll be able to print more text in the screen dump.

More to Come!

See Chapters 17 and 26 for more information about printers, such as how to change sheet feeder bins, how to turn bidirectional printing on or off, letter-quality and proportionally spaced print, and working with laser printers. For the time being, however, you now know the basic ins and outs of printing with WordStar.

Dear Reader, the pace is going to pick up very quickly, because you're about to explore the real nitty-gritty of working with WordStar. Now would be an excellent time to review what you've learned and make sure you feel comfortable with the program before you take the big plunge into formatting, block operations, and much more.

Chapter

4

Formatting Essentials

In this chapter you will learn the following new commands:

File Commands

ESC @	Insert today's date
.. (.IG)	Nonprinting comment line
.LM (^F5)	Set the left margin
.LS	Set the line spacing
.MB	Set the bottom margin
.MT	Set the top margin
^OF	Set the ruler line from a file line
^OI	Set a tab
^OJ	Turn right margin justification on/off
.OJ ON/OFF	Turn right margin justification on/off
^OL	Set the left margin
^OO (F8)	Insert the current ruler line in the file
.OP	Omit printing of page numbers
^OP	Turn preview on/off
^OR	Set the right margin
^OS	Set the line spacing
^ON	Clear a tab or all tabs
.PO	Set the page offset

more . . .

.RM (^F6)	Set the right margin
.RR	Insert a ruler line
.UL ON/OFF	Turn the underlining of spaces in a phrase on/off

By far the most complicated aspect of working with a word processor like WordStar is *formatting.* You and I are going to spend a lot of time learning how to format your documents the way you want to. Because everyone has different format requirements, the examples illustrate only a few popular format types. You can use them as models from which to *customize* formats for your own needs. This chapter provides the essential information about formatting documents with WordStar. *Read this chapter carefully,* because the information here forms the foundation for virtually all your future work.

> ### *DO WARM-UP*

Formats in a Nutshell

WordStar allows you almost unlimited freedom in determining formats, but there are several general points to consider. They apply to *all* format changes:

- A format change represents an instruction to WordStar to change one of the default formats or a previous format change.

- Most, *but not all,* format changes use *dot commands* that you insert and save in a file. You'll learn about dot commands in a moment.

- All other format changes are part of the onscreen commands, which begin with the prefix **^O.** There are now dot command equivalents for most onscreen formatting changes. This is a new and welcome development for users of previous versions of WordStar.

- Any dot command starts from its position in the file and affects *only* the text following the change, while onscreen format commands affect whatever text you add or edit after you issue the command.

- Format changes represented by dot commands remain in effect until you change the format somewhere else—by inserting another dot command or issuing an onscreen command—or delete the original dot command from the file.

- WordStar doesn't save onscreen format changes (^O commands) with the file, although there are ways to get around this restriction for some onscreen commands. You must repeat the onscreen command the next time you open the file. That's why it makes sense to use dot commands whenever you can.

■ WordStar always honors the *last* formatting command, whether it be a dot command or an onscreen command. However, WordStar only *saves* dot commands in the file.

■ WordStar ignores incorrect or incomplete dot commands. (See "Changing a Dot Command" in this chapter.)

■ Unlike in previous versions of WordStar, when you change onscreen formatting and save a file, WordStar now reverts to the *default* formatting when you open another file during the same work session. If the next file you open has dot commands, WordStar uses them for formatting.

With these points in mind, follow these four easy rules when you change formats:

1. Whenever possible, insert formatting dot commands at the *beginning* of your file. Not only will this eliminate the chance of missing text you want to reformat, but it also lets you find the dot commands easily if you want to check them or change them.

2. Don't insert formatting dot commands in the *middle* of a paragraph. They might throw off paragraph alignment.

3. Issue onscreen formatting commands *before* you add new text or edit existing text in the file. That way, any new text appears in the correct format, and when you align edited text with ^B, the edited text appears in the correct format, too. You'll also learn that there's a way to save certain onscreen commands with a special ruler line.

4. *The best rule of all:* Whenever you can, use dot commands instead of onscreen formatting commands because the commands stay in the file and work whenever you open the file again. There are very few onscreen commands that don't have dot command equivalents.

One great advantage of word processing is its capability to let you change formats at any time. Many people don't worry about the fine points of formatting until they get the text correct, that is, when the file reaches its final stages. Chapter 15 discusses a typical *document history.*

Now that you're probably *thoroughly confused,* take a look at all these points and learn formatting in the best possible way: by practice!

Dot Commands, Part 1

Using dot commands is by far the best way to change formats. In this first example you'll create a *letter* with a nondefault format. The letter will have different left and right margins. Justification will be off, so the lines will print "ragged" to make the letter appear typed. You'll also turn the default page numbering off.

Press   **D** [open a document]

Type   jones.ltr

Press   **RETURN**

Type   y

because this is a new file.

You want to change the format for the entire file, so put the dot commands at the *beginning* of the file before any text. As its name implies, a dot command begins with a period ("dot"), which must be in column 1. Normally, periods either end sentences or appear as decimal points in numbers, but a period would not appear in column 1. So whenever WordStar sees a period in column 1, it assumes that this line contains a dot command.

The only time there will be confusion between a period as the beginning of a dot command line and its use as something else occurs when you have an *ellipsis* (. . .) in your paragraph that happens to fall at the beginning of the line. Later you'll see how to avoid this confusion.

Besides starting with a dot in column 1, dot commands must be on their own lines, one line per command. **Caution:** Do not separate the dot from the command name with a space. WordStar would just ignore any text on the line past the dot command. After all this rigmarole, you're *finally* ready to use dot commands!

Changing the Left Margin

To change the left margin, use the **.LM** dot command. This command requires an integer number representing the new left margin. You don't have to type a space between the **.LM** and the number, but I find it visually more appealing and easier to read on the screen. **Note:** Although I'll show dot commands in uppercase, you can type them in lowercase to save keystrokes.

The cursor should be at column 1 of line 1.

Type   .LM 10 or .lm 10

(You could press ^F5 first to issue the .lm part.)

Press   **RETURN**

If you typed a *space* between the dot and the command, WordStar would show a question mark in the flag display column. The question mark tells you something's amiss. This is wrong:

. LM 10

Take a look at the status line—it still says L01 for line one! That's because a dot command line never counts as part of the *actual* line count in the document. Now look at the ruler line—the left margin marker (L) has changed to show the new left margin at column 10. **Note:** Column 1 is the lowest possible left margin setting.

Changing the Right Margin

To change the right margin, use the **.RM** dot command, but watch the screen as you do to learn something else about these commands.

Type   .R or .r

but don't type anything else yet!

WordStar displays a ? in the flag character column because you haven't completed the dot command. If the command is incorrect or incomplete, you'll see this ? as a sign that WordStar can't "understand" the command.

Type   M 60 or m 60

to complete the command so that it reads .RM 60 or .rm 60 .

Press   **RETURN**

(You could press ^F6 first to issue the .rm part.)

Now the ruler line shows the new right margin at column 60. The largest possible right margin is at column 255. The left and right margin settings determine the total *line length,* that is, the length of the printed line. Keep in mind that WordStar still maintains blank left and right margins on the printed page.

Turning Justification Off

Right margin justification can be either *on* or *off,* so the dot command to change this feature, **.OJ,** must contain either the directive **ON** or **OFF.** Alternately, you could use the number **1** for "on" and the zero (**0**) for "off," but I think it's easier to read with the words.

Type   .OJ OFF or .oj off

Press   **RETURN**

When you type the letter, WordStar won't insert any soft spaces to fill in the lines.

Turning Off Page Numbers

Finally, because this is a letter you wouldn't want WordStar to print a page number at the bottom of the page. As Chapter 14 will show you, there are many ways to control page numbering. Here, all you want to do is *turn off* the default page numbering. The dot command for this is **.OP**, for "omit pagination":

Type   .OP or .op

Press   **RETURN**

The entire set of dot commands should look like this (or in their lowercase equivalents):

```
.LM 10
.RM 60
.OJ OFF
.OP
```

One final point before you begin the actual letter: although you've changed the margins, you haven't changed the default tab stops. Notice the tab at column 11, but don't worry about it because it won't get in the way when you type the first example. In another section you'll learn how to change tab stops, too.

Letters, We Get Letters . . .

I'm going to step you through the first part of the letter because there are some other important points to learn. Take a look at the entire letter, which will begin directly below the dot command lines, but don't type it yet.

4118 Hollywood Boulevard
Hollywood, CA 90028
<today's date>

Ms. Penelope Jones
101 Pomander Walk
Los Gatos, CA 94205

Dear Ms. Jones:

Thank you for your kind letter and for the numerous
photographs of your impressive cat, "Cozy Toes."
We are returning the photos herewith.

Although we share your enthusiasm for your pet, our
Reviewing Committee has decided that "Cozy Toes"
is, unfortunately, not exactly what we are looking
for. As you know, our newest advertising campaign
will include the "Moist Munchies Marvelous Pet of
the Year." Our Committee feels that "Cozy Toes" is
perhaps a bit -- shall we say? -- too large for the
campaign.

Thanks again, and keep munching!

                    Sincerely,

                    Pepe Lephew
                    Director of Advertising
                    Moist Munchies, Inc.

     encl.

    For the return address lines you'd still have to tab over to where you
want the cursor to be, just as if you were using a typewriter.

Press	**TAB** or **^I** six times
Type	4118 Hollywood Boulevard
Press	**RETURN**
Press	**TAB** or **^I** six times

Type   `Hollywood, CA  90028`

Press   **RETURN**

The cursor is on line 3. Now for something really nifty!

Inserting Today's Date

The third line says `<today's date>`, but don't type that! Here's how to have WordStar insert the date for you. This feature only works correctly if you set the date when you turned on your computer. Otherwise, you'll see DOS's default date (January 1, 1980).

Press   **TAB** or **^I** six times

Press   **ESC @**

(that's **ESC SHIFT 2**). Don't hold the ESC key down as you press SHIFT 2.

WordStar inserts today's date in the standard format of the month name, day, and year. You can change the format with the WSCHANGE program (Chapter 27). If you didn't enter today's date correctly, there's even a way to change it while you're working in WordStar (Chapter 12).

Press   **RETURN** four times

for spacing.

Where's the Left Margin?

You're now ready to type the interior address lines, but notice where the cursor is. It's at column 1, even though that's not the new left margin. **Caution:** You *don't* have to tab over to start each line. In fact, you shouldn't. Just follow these instructions.

Type   `Ms. Penelope Jones`

As soon as you start typing, WordStar jumps to the new left margin at column 10. That's why you don't press the TAB key.

Press   **RETURN**

to end the line.

Because this is a "short" line, you must end it with a hard return, just as you would on a typewriter.

Type   `101 Pomander Walk`

Press   **RETURN**

Type   `Los Gatos, CA  94205`

Press   **RETURN** twice

for spacing.

Type   `Dear Ms. Jones:`

Press   **RETURN** twice

for spacing.

You're On Your Own Now

You're now ready to type the rest of the letter on your own! Let WordStar wrap the lines for each paragraph, but press **RETURN** twice to end each paragraph and space down. Do *not* start each paragraph with a tab! When you finish typing the final paragraph, press **TAB** (**^I**) six times, type `Sincerely,` then press **RETURN** four times for spacing and continue. When you're finished:

Press   **^KS** or **F9**

to save the file and resume where you left off.

Press   **^QR** or **^HOME**

to position the cursor at the beginning of the file.
    Cursor through the file and make any necessary editing corrections. Don't align the paragraphs individually! When you're finished:

Press   **^QR** or **^HOME**

to position the cursor at the beginning of the file.

Press   **^QU**

to align the entire file.

Press   **^KD** or **F10**

to save the file and return to the Opening menu.

Dot Commands, Part 2

The previous example showed you how to change the format of a new file before you typed anything into the file. Now you'll take a look at what happens when you change the format of an existing file; in the process you'll learn some other important dot commands.

Changing Line Spacing

By default WordStar uses single spacing, but you can change line spacing to any integer number from 1 to 9. The dot command is **.LS**.

Press   **D** [open a document]

Type   story

Press   **RETURN**

You'll change line spacing from single to double. Remember that every dot command has to be on its own separate line, so you must *insert a line* at the beginning of the file.

Press   **^N**

to insert a line but leave the cursor where it is.

Type   .LS 2 or .ls 2

Caution: Do *not* press RETURN, because that would add an extra hard return to the file. Why not two? After all, you just changed line spacing from single to double with the **.LS 2** command. However, WordStar always inserts just one hard return when you press RETURN *at the end of a dot command line,* no matter what the line spacing setting is. At the end of text lines, when you press RETURN you enter the same number of returns as the line spacing setting.

The status line now says Spacing-2.

What Happens When You Change Formats?

In the first example, the dot commands governed the formatting of the new text that you typed. When you change the format of an existing file, WordStar doesn't automatically readjust the format of any affected text. You must do that yourself. How? Right! Use either **^B** to align paragraphs individually, or better still, **^QU** to align the entire file. (When WordStar has automatic paragraph align, you won't have to perform the next step.)

Press   ^QU

to align the entire file.

Notice that WordStar substituted two soft returns for each one soft return within paragraphs, but only added one extra return between paragraphs. Now, even though the paragraphs are in double spacing, they're still visually separated from each other with the extra return between paragraphs.

Tip: Old-time WordStar users might not like the way WordStar Release 4 handles multiple line spacing (with its combination of soft and hard returns). Using the WSCHANGE program (Chapter 27), you can revert to "WordStar 3.3 compatibility" in dealing with line spacing. WordStar will then insert only hard returns.

Caution: If you're realigning individual paragraphs from one spacing to another, make sure the cursor is on the *first* line of the paragraph before you press ^**B.** Otherwise, WordStar won't realign the entire paragraph, and you'll have to repeat the command.

Changing a Dot Command Setting

Dot commands are just like any other text in that you can edit or delete them. Suppose you want the file in triple spacing?

Press   ^**QR** or ^**HOME**

to position the cursor at the beginning of the file.

Press   ^**QD** or ^**F10**

to position the cursor at the end of the dot command line.

Press   **BACKSPACE** or ^**H**

to delete the *2.*

Type   3

You've changed the format again, so:

Press   ^**QU**

to realign the entire file.

Deleting a Dot Command

The easiest way to delete a dot command is with ^**Y** (**F5**), which deletes the entire line. Make sure the cursor is on the line you want to delete. If you delete a dot command that governs onscreen formatting, you must then re-align the text.

Press   **^QR** or **^HOME**

to position the cursor at the beginning of the file.

Press   **^Y** or **F5**

to delete the dot command line.

Press   **^QU**

to align the entire file back to single spacing.

Underlining the Spaces Between Words

In the previous chapter I promised to tell you how to have WordStar underline the spaces between words in a phrase. If you don't want to set this as one of the program defaults, you can use a dot command, **.UL,** instead. It, too, requires an "on" or "off" specification.

Press   **^QR** or **^HOME**

to position the cursor at the beginning of the file.

Press   **^N**

to insert a line but leave the cursor where it is.

Type   .UL ON or .ul on

This dot command doesn't change the lines, so you don't have to align the file with **^QU.** Even though you've now told WordStar to underline the spaces, WordStar doesn't show the spaces as underlined on the screen. To turn underlining of spaces off, use **.UL OFF.**

Note: On some dot-matrix printers .UL ON might throw off alignment of right-justified text. Experiment with this command to see that it works properly on your printer. If you can't use the **.UL ON** command, the only other way to underline the spaces between words in a phrase is to insert the underline character (SHIFT HYPHEN) yourself *instead of* a space.

Tip: You can have some sections of a file with underlining of spaces and other sections without. Just insert the desired **.UL ON** and **.UL OFF** dot commands where you need them.

If you wish, print the file to see the difference. Prepare your printer and paper, then press **^PRT SC** and answer the print options as necessary.

Or:

Press   ^KD or F10

to save the file and return to the Opening menu.

    Note: Now that you know how to print your files, I won't bother to tell you to do it. Whenever you want to, just print the examples!

Changing Top and Bottom Margins

WordStar's default top margin is three blank lines, and the bottom margin, eight blank lines. You can change these settings with the **.MT** and **.MB** dot commands, respectively. Because when you change the top or bottom margin the number of text lines on a page could change, WordStar's uses the new settings to show the correct page breaks in the file.

Press   **D** [open a document]

Type   jones.ltr

Press   **RETURN**

    Suppose you want to start the letter farther down on the page, say, at line 10. Why add blank lines to the file? It's easier just to change the top margin.

Press   **^N**

to insert a line but leave the cursor where it is.
    Notice that the ruler line shows the default left and right margins and tab stops, because the cursor is ahead of the dot commands.

Type   .MT 10 or .mt 10

Press   **RETURN**

to add a new blank line.
    You also want a bottom margin of seven lines. This is just for practice because the file never reaches the bottom of the first page anyway!

Type   .MB 7 or .mb 7

    If you press RETURN, you'd add an extra blank line here. Just leave the cursor at the end of the line for the moment.

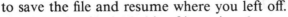

Press   ^KS or F9

to save the file and resume where you left off.

Tip: Get in the habit of inserting the top and bottom margin dot commands at the beginning of the file. The flag character column shows a 1. This means that these two commands work best if they're at the *top* of the page. In Chapter 14 you'll return to the page formatting issue.

Note: WordStar doesn't show the blank top and bottom margins on the screen. That is, even though the top margin of your printout will have 10 blank lines, on the screen the first line of each page will *still* be L01. Get used to this difference between screen numbering and actual printout. Laser printer users: See Chapter 26 for more information about top margins and paper length.

Changing the Page Offset

You changed the left margin in the letter to learn about the **.LM** command. There's another way to go, one that I prefer because you don't have to change the left margin at all! That is, you can use the default left margin of 1 for most files and just change where this left margin prints on the page. WordStar calls this feature the *page offset,* and the dot command for it is **.PO** followed by an integer number.

The default page offset is eight characters from the edge of the paper, which leaves just slightly less than a one-inch blank margin on the page. **Note:** The left margin on the screen is thus not the blank left margin on the page. It's where the *printed* left margin starts. You may also have to experiment with the paper position in your printer to see where the default page offset starts printing the left margin. Most laser printers can't print starting from the exact left edge of the paper (Chapter 26).

As an example of using the page offset command, suppose you wanted to offset the printing 15 spaces instead of the default of eight. Press ^N to add a blank line and include this command in the file:

.PO 15

Tips: On my printer, the default page offset of eight characters prints too far to the left, according to where I position the paper. I changed the default page offset from 8 to 13 using WSCHANGE (Chapter 27). That way, I don't have to type a **.PO** command in each file, and I can always work with the same paper position in the printer. If your printer paper has tractor feed holes, you can avoid printing over those holes by setting a different page offset. In other chapters, you'll see many more uses for the **.PO** command.

Note: In many of the examples in this book, you'll see a **.PO** setting. Just use the one that works best for your printer, or none at all to accept the default.

Press   ^KS or F9

to save the file and resume where you left off.

Using Onscreen Formatting Commands

I reiterate: when you can, always insert dot commands in your files because the commands stay with the file and govern the formatting whenever you edit the file. However, at this point in the ever-changing development of WordStar there are some onscreen formatting commands that don't (yet!) have dot command equivalents. You've already learned one: ^OC (SHIFT F2) to center a line. Other onscreen formatting commands are "temporary" toggles that don't require corresponding dot commands, such as ^OD to turn the print controls on or off.

In this section you'll learn about the most important onscreen formatting commands and how to save what seems like some "nonsavable" formats! A contradiction? Perhaps not! First, however, learn a very useful onscreen command.

Temporarily Hiding the Dot Commands

Dear Reader: there are a lot of dot commands! Sometimes you'll find that the *blank lines between text sections* in your file don't print correctly, most likely because you put dot commands on blank lines that should have been part of the actual file. **Tip:** Always use ^N to add a new blank line for every dot command that you insert in a file.

One easy way to check the actual file lines is to *turn off* the dot commands temporarily. Use what WordStar calls the *preview* command, the toggle switch ^OP. Not only does this command turn off dot command lines, it also turns off print codes (you'll still see the screen representation of the print effects) and soft spaces.

(Experienced WordStar users: This command has changed from previous versions. To approximate the *old* ^OP command, use either the new ^Q? command for a character count, or a .PL 0 setting at the top of the file for a line count. See Chapter 13.)

The JONES.LTR file should still be open.

Press   ^OP

The status line now says Prtect Preview to remind you that you've "protected" the file. That means you can move through it with any cursor command, but you *cannot* edit the file. WordStar will *beep* at you if you type something or press a command that's not allowed! The Edit menu is now the Protected menu.

If you press the ^K, ^O, or ^Q prefix keys, you'll see other protected menus that show only those commands that WordStar *does* allow in preview mode. The ^P commands are not available at all, but you can still press ^J to get help. Go ahead: Take a look at the three protected menus! Press the **SPACEBAR** to remove each menu from the screen when you're finished looking at it. Make sure to turn the preview off when you're finished, too:

Press   **^OP**

to turn the preview off and continue editing.

Press   **^KD** or **F10**

to save the file and return to the Opening menu.

There's more about protecting files from accidental editing changes or deletions in Chapters 13 and 28.

Clearing and Setting Tabs

The other important onscreen commands that don't have *direct* dot command equivalents are the commands to clear and set tab stops. As you'll soon see, however, it's possible to save tab stops along with margin settings so that you don't have to enter the onscreen commands the next time you edit a file. First, you must learn the commands!

Press   **D** [open a document]

Type   perkins.ltr

Press   **RETURN**

Type   y

because this is a new file.

You'll take a different approach to typing a letter in this example. To save repeated use of the TAB key, you'll clear all default tabs and set only two new tabs, one to indent each paragraph, and one to indent to the middle of the line for the return address.

The command to *clear a tab* is **^ON**. You can clear a tab in three different ways after pressing this command:

- Type the *column number* of a tab and press **RETURN** to clear one tab only.
- Press **ESC** to clear one tab at the *present cursor location*.
- Type the letter **a** and press **RETURN** to clear *all* tabs quickly.

You'll clear all tabs:

Press   ^ON

WordStar's prompt tells you what *I* just said:

```
Current tabs: 6 11 16 21 26 31 36 41 46 51 56
Decimal tabs: None

You may clear one tab stop by specifying its column. All tab stops
can be cleared at once if you enter an "A" instead of a number.
For decimal tabs, precede the column number with a "#" (for example,
#15). Press the escape (Esc) key if the cursor column in the text
should be used.

Enter a tab stop to be cleared.
```

In Chapter 9 you'll learn about decimal tabs. For the time being, do this:

Type   a

Press   **RETURN**

to clear all tabs from the ruler line.

Now, you want new tabs at columns 10 and 30 only. The command to *set a tab* is **^OI.** You have two ways to set a tab after pressing this command:

- Type the column number and press **RETURN.**
- Press **ESC** to set a tab at the *present cursor location.*

Press   **^OI**

WordStar prompts:

```
Current tabs: None
Decimal tabs: None

Tab stops can be put at any column from 2 through 254.
For decimal tabs, precede the column number with a "#" (for example,
#15). Press the escape (Esc) key if the cursor column in the text
should be used.

Enter new tab stop.
```

Type   10

Press   **RETURN**

Press   **^OI**

Type   30

Press   **RETURN**

to set tabs at columns 10 and 30 only.

The new tab stops appear as ! at columns 10 and 30 on the ruler line.

Changing the Left and Right Margins

There are similar onscreen commands for changing the left and right margins: ^OL and ^OR, respectively. After issuing each command, either type a new margin column number and press **RETURN,** or press **ESC** to set the margin at the current cursor location.

Why not use the dot commands **.LM** and **.RM**? Dear Reader, have patience! You'll see in a moment. Although you won't change the left margin, you *do* want to change the right margin to 60:

Press   **^OR**

WordStar prompts:

```
Right margin currently at column 65

Enter a new margin either by typing a column number, or by typing
the escape (Esc) key if the current column in the text should be
used.

New right margin?
```

(You'd get a similar message if you used ^OL to change the left margin.)

Type   60

Press   **RETURN**

to change the right margin to column 60.

(An aside: It makes no sense to put the right margin *in front of* the left margin, so if you attempt to do this WordStar gives you a cybernetic Bronx cheer in the form of an error message.)

Inserting a Ruler Line

Now you get to see the method behind my madness. Once you've set tabs and left and right margins the way you want them, you can *save* these settings by inserting a *ruler line* into the file! The ruler line then governs the formatting of all text past it.

Here's how to create a savable ruler line. First, make sure the cursor is where you want the ruler to be (it's at the beginning of the file), just as if you were inserting any text. Then:

Press   **^OO or F8**

WordStar inserts a *dot command* with a ruler line attached to it! The dot command, **.RR,** begins a ruler line. The **^OO** command always creates a ruler line from the *current settings.* **Caution:** Make sure the cursor is at column 1 *before* you insert a ruler line with the **^OO** command. Otherwise, WordStar inserts the dot at the cursor location, which invalidates the entire dot command. Interestingly, the F8 key is set up to issue the **^QS** command—to position the cursor at the left side of the line—before the **^OO** command, so the cursor can be anywhere on the line when you press F8.

The ruler line doesn't show the left margin, but it's still at column 1. The **.RR** part of the command is hiding it. The ruler line display at the top of the screen always shows the correct left margin position. In another chapter, I'll show you how to *construct* a ruler line from scratch by typing it in, but the easiest way to set up a saved ruler line is to follow this pattern:

1. Change the tab and margin settings with the onscreen commands.

2. Position the cursor where you want the ruler line to go.

3. Press **^OO (F8)** to insert the ruler line in the file.

The cursor is right on the dot command line, because you can *edit* or even *delete* the ruler line if you wish. *Question:* What would happen if you inserted a **.RM** dot command line with a different right margin setting *below* the ruler line? *Answer:* The dot command would take precedence over the ruler line setting.

In other chapters you'll use *several* ruler lines to change the format of text within a file. Every time you insert a new ruler line, the new line governs the formatting of text following it until you issue other formatting commands.

Press   **^N**

to insert a line but leave the cursor where it is.

Now, type the following dot commands into the file. Press **RETURN** after the first four but not after the fifth, and remember to start each command at column 1:

```
.MT 12
.MB 6
.OJ OFF
.OP
.PO 15
```

(Dear Reader: In another chapter you'll learn how to save only the dot commands in a special *format file* and then copy the format whenever you want to start a new letter.)

Just to make sure you don't have to go through these steps again,

Press   ^KS or F9

to save the file and resume where you left off.

Now that you have your format the way you want it, time for some work.

Press   ^QC or ^END

to position the cursor directly past the dot commands on line 1 of the file.

Type the following letter as you see it. Press **TAB (^I)** twice to enter the return address lines and use **ESC @** to insert today's date. Insert four blank lines between the date line and the recipient's address, use one **TAB (^I)** to begin each paragraph, and two blank lines between paragraphs.

```
                              101 Pomander Walk
                              Los Gatos, CA  94205
                              <today's date>
```

```
Jeremy F. Perkins, President
Moist Munchies, Inc.
4118 Hollywood Boulevard
Hollywood, CA  90028
```

```
Dear Mr. Perkins,
```

```
        I have received a most ungracious letter from your
Director of Advertising, Mr. Pepe Lephew, regarding the
entry of my cat, "Cozy Toes," in your current promotional
campaign.
```

```
        You are missing an extraordinary opportunity.
"Cozy Toes" is an exceptional animal in every way.  I am
deeply distressed at the decision of your Reviewing
Committee.
```

```
        I'm afraid that you have left me no alternative but
to stop purchasing Moist Munchies.  I intend to advise my
friends and fellow members of the Los Gatos Feline Fanciers
Club to do the same.

                        Yours truly,



                        Penelope Jones
```

When you're finished:

Press   ^KS or F9

to save the file and resume where you left off.

Other Onscreen Commands

Just for the sake of completeness, I'll mention *en passant,* as it were, other onscreen commands that you shouldn't use if you can help it. Always work with the dot command equivalents so that the format stays with the file. The only advantage to using these onscreen commands occurs when you *know* you only need the file once and want to change formats "on the fly."

The first command is ^OS to change line spacing. WordStar asks you to supply a number from 1 to 9 and press **RETURN**. This is the same as .LS, except if you type an incorrect number you get an error message.

Another command is ^OJ, a toggle switch to turn justification on or off. It's like .OJ but it reverses the current setting. The default is on, so if you press ^OJ you turn justification off.

Finally, the command ^OF is almost totally useless now that WordStar has savable formats. This command creates a ruler line from a line of text in the file, but it involves a rigmarole that you don't have to bother with anymore. The .RR dot command and ^OO command have taken care of that! As you can imagine, I am *no longer* a fan of the ^OF command!

How About Envelopes?

So now you have two letters for which you need envelopes. You could easily create a file that prints an envelope, now that you know about the .MT, .MB, .OP and .PO commands. For example, here is a typical legal-size envelope setup for the second letter. Look at it, but don't take the time to create a new file like this one now.

```
.MT 1
.PO 4
.OP
Penelope Jones
101 Pomander Walk
Los Gatos, CA  94205
```

```
                        Jeremy F. Perkins, President
                        Moist Munchies, Inc.
                        4118 Hollywood Boulevard
                        Hollywood, CA  90028
```

I used 12 blank lines from the last line of the return address to the first line of the recipient's address, which starts at column 35. *Question:* An envelope is smaller than a piece of letter paper, so how would you change the paper length? *Answer:* Although there's a command to accomplish this, here you're just "fooling" WordStar, because it never reaches the bottom of the paper anyway.

In this example the page offset setting differs, depending on where you want your printer to print the return address of the envelope and where you insert the envelope in the printer. The top margin setting is **.MT 1** because presumably you'd would want to start the return address almost at the top of the envelope. The **.OP** command is also necessary.

Although it's possible to reuse this envelope file by merely typing over the address lines, WordStar has a better way. You can set up a "stock" envelope document *once* and then, each time you need an envelope with a new recipient's name and address, you merely supply the information from the keyboard to the stock envelope format just before it prints (Chapter 21). *That's* why I said you don't have to do this example!

Note: If you have a laser printer, you may have to change the *paper orientation* to print envelopes (Chapter 26).

Character, Line, and Page Formats

Most word processing programs, including WordStar, make a distinction between the formatting commands that govern *character* formatting, those commands that govern *line* formatting, and the ones that govern *page* formatting.

Character formatting commands are the print commands, such as ^PS (F3) to turn underlining on and off. You've already seen some of these commands in action. In this chapter you learned about the .UL ON/OFF command to determine how WordStar underlines the spaces between words.

Think of line formatting commands as those that affect the way lines form into paragraphs. Most line formatting commands work with ^B or ^QU: whenever you issue one of these commands, you use ^B or ^QU to realign the affected paragraphs. In this chapter you learned the following line formatting commands: ^OL and .LM, ^OR and .RM, ^OS and .LS, ^OJ and .OJ ON/OFF.

Certain line formatting commands don't work yet with ^B or ^QU, but that may change in future versions of WordStar. These commands are those that clear and set tabs (^ON and ^OI) and the center command (^OC).

Page formatting commands are the topic of other chapters, but you should know now that they control the entire *printed* page. The top and bottom margin commands, .MT and .MB, and the omit pagination command .OP are page formatting commands.

Unfortunately, some commands are neither "fish nor fowl," as it were. A prime example is .PO, which appears to be a page formatting command because it determines the page offset for the screen left margin. You can use it with individual lines, too. Most of the time, however, you'll have one page offset setting for the entire file. Other commands, like ^OF and ^OO, are just setup commands. Sheesh!

Dot Commands, Part 3

Dear Reader: You're almost finished for today! There are a few other important points to learn about dot commands, and then you can take a break.

Writing a Note to Yourself

One of the most useful dot commands inserts a *nonprinting comment line* in your file. This is a way to write a note to yourself to remind you about something. The command can be either .IG (for "ignore this line"), or *two* dots (..). I prefer the latter because it involves less typing.

Press   **^QR or ^HOME**

to position the cursor at the beginning of the file.

Press   **^N**

to insert a line but leave the cursor where it is.

Type the following dot command line at column 1:

```
.. check to see if the name is correct!
```

The next time Ms. Jones opens this file, the nonprinting comment line reminds her to check the recipient's name. You'll see many uses for comment lines in the examples in this book.

Press   ^KD or F10

to save the file and return to the Opening menu.

Ellipses and Dot Commands

If you use dots for *ellipses* in your files, take care with them! Say you're typing away and wordwrap causes the ellipses to start a new line. WordStar then "thinks" this line contains dot commands, and it won't align the line or the paragraph correctly.

There's an easy way to avoid this problem: just insert *two* print toggles directly in front of each ellipsis when you type it. For example, the following short section of text shows an ellipsis preceded by two underline codes:

```
As you can see, I'm typing away, but when I get to  an  ellipsis
^S^S... well, you get the message!
```

Because you're inserting beginning and ending codes at the same spot, there *is* no print effect. WordStar disregards the underline codes, and you've successfully "hidden" the ellipsis. WordStar treats it as text. Neat!

Suppressing Dot Commands in a Printout

Occasionally you might want to include the dot command lines in a printout to check the commands in a hard copy version of the document. You can *suppress* the dot commands during printing by answering y to the print option, Nondocument (Y/N)?. Treating a document temporarily as a nondocument in this manner means that the dot commands don't change the default formatting. They just print as text lines. When you've verified the dot commands, print the file as a normal document to see the results.

Note: This feature may not seem terribly useful to you at this point, but it can come in handy when you learn about merge printing in Chapters 19 through 24.

And there you have it: the most important formatting capabilities in WordStar and the essentials of working with dot commands. When you continue, you'll learn about blocks, another important WordStar feature, and other formatting tricks.

Chapter 5

Moving, Copying, and Deleting Blocks

In this chapter you will learn the following new commands:

Opening Menu Commands

E	Rename a file
O	Copy a file

File Commands

^K	Block & Save menu
^KB (SHIFT F9)	Mark the beginning of a block
^KC (SHIFT F8)	Copy a block
^KH (SHIFT F6)	Hide a block
^KK (SHIFT F10)	Mark the end of a block
^KR	Read (insert) a file into the current file
^KV (SHIFT F7)	Move a block
^KW	Write a block to a file
^KX	Save the file and exit to DOS
^KY (SHIFT F5)	Delete a block
^QB	Cursor to the beginning of a block
^QK	Cursor to the end of a block
^QV	Cursor to the previous block location

Two of the most useful word processing features involve moving or copying text, either within a file or from one file to another. Moving and copying are related operations, and this chapter shows just how much work they can save you. You'll also learn how to delete large sections of text quickly, what boiler-plates are, and how to save a lot of boring typing work.

DO WARM-UP

More Opening Menu Commands

In preparation for the rest of the chapter, you'll learn and use two other commands from the Opening menu: the **E** command to *rename* a file, and the **O** command to *copy* a file. Chapters 12 and 13 discuss all file operations in full.

It turns out that you write many stories, so you want to distinguish "Angeles Crest Romance" from other story files. You'll give the file a more informative name.

Press   E [rename a file]

WordStar prompts:

Specify the name of the document that you wish to rename.

Document to be renamed?

As usual, you can type the name of the existing file or select it from the directory listing.

Type   story

Press   **RETURN**

WordStar then asks:

What do you want its new name to be?

You must type in a new name.

Type   story.la

Press   **RETURN**

When you rename a file, that doesn't alter the *contents* of the file. It just supplies a new name for the directory. Now, copy the STORY.LA file to a new file. As you would expect, when you copy a file the original stays on the disk and you create an exact duplicate file with a new name.

Press   **O** [copy a file]

WordStar prompts:

```
Specify the name of the document that you wish to copy.

Document to be copied?
```

Type   `story.la`

Press   **RETURN**

WordStar then prompts:

```
Name a document to hold the new copy.
```

Type   **temp**

Press   **RETURN**

WordStar starts copying and displays a dot for every 4000 characters it copies. However, if you don't put a disk in the drive or if you forget to close the drive door, WordStar says:

```
Can't create a file. The disk may be full, or there was a disk write error,
or CONFIG.SYS on your boot (system) disk lacks the line FILES=20.

Press Esc to continue.
```

This rather confusing message is meant to cover several sins, most likely a disk write error. Press **ESC,** rectify the problem, and try again.
    Now, open the TEMP file:

Press   **D** [open a document]

Press   **ESC**

because WordStar "remembers" the *last file name* when you press the ESC key in response to a prompt.

Introducing Blocks

Whenever you want to move, copy, or delete a large amount of text, use the block technique. A *block* is any continuous section of text, whether a word, a phrase, a line, a sentence, a paragraph, a page, or even the entire document.

Before you can use a block, WordStar has to know the limits of the block. To *delimit* a block, you position the cursor at the beginning character in the block and then *mark* its beginning with a special code. Then you position the cursor at the end of the block and mark its end.

The Block & Save Menu

All block commands use the ^K prefix. As you know, the saving commands (such as ^KS) also use this prefix. When you press ^K alone, you see the Block & Save menu. If you wish, press ^K to display the menu, then press the **SPACEBAR** when you're finished looking at it.

Marking the Beginning of a Block

For all block operations—moving, copying, or deleting—you start in the same manner. That is, you set up the block as outlined here. First, position the cursor at the beginning character of the block. You want to block out a sentence in preparation for moving it.

Press   ^X or **DOWN ARROW** eight times

to position the cursor on line 8 (there should be a .UL ON dot command line at the top of the file).

Press   ^F or **^RIGHT ARROW** four times

to position the cursor under the *I* of *In*.

The command to begin a block is **^KB (SHIFT F9)**.

Press   ^KB or **SHIFT F9**

to begin the block here.

WordStar inserts a begin block marker here. It looks like this: <B>. The line extends past the right margin, but that won't affect the printout.

Marking the End of the Block

Now, quickly position the cursor at the end of the sentence. Do you remember how?

Press   **^QG**

Type   .

(that's a period).

Are you *really* at the end of the sentence? No! You want to include the period, too.

Press   **^D** or **RIGHT ARROW**

to position the cursor past the period.

Stop! Are there two spaces at the end of the sentence? Probably not, so add them first:

Press   **SPACEBAR** twice

(Dear Reader: This is an example of why you'd want to use the end-of-paragraph trick from Chapter 2.)

Question: Won't the ^D be part of the block? *Answer:* No! Watch when you mark the end of the block with the command **^KK (SHIFT F10)**.

Press   **^KK** or **SHIFT F10**

WordStar inserts the block end marker (<K>), although you don't see it because the entire block is now highlighted, shaded, or in another color, depending on your monitor. Always make sure you define the *entire* block you want. You can position the beginning or ending markers elsewhere by moving the cursor where you want to be and repeating the **^KB (SHIFT F9)** or **^KK (SHIFT F10)** commands. That's the subject of a later example.

Note: You can only have one marked block at a time, and the beginning block marker must be somewhere in front of the end block marker. The flag character display shows a B on the line containing the beginning block marker and a K on the line that has the end marker. If the entire block is on one line, the flag character display shows just the K.

Tip: Old-time WordStar users might not like the way WordStar Release 4 moves the cursor when you block out a line beginning at column 1. After pressing **^KB (SHIFT F9)** to begin the block, you press **^X (DOWN ARROW)** only to discover that WordStar doesn't position the cursor at column 1 of the next line. All is not lost! With the WSCHANGE program (Chapter 27), you can revert to "WordStar 3.3 compatibility" in marking blocks.

Moving a Block

When you move a block, you're physically "cutting" it from its present location in the file and "pasting" it somewhere else. Why, it's almost as if you had electronic scissors! You must, however, position the cursor exactly where you want the block to go, just as if you were inserting text into the file.

Press   ^QH

Type   T

(make sure it's an uppercase *T*) to position the cursor at the beginning of this sentence.
There are actually two ways to move a block. You'll learn the standard way first—the ^KV (**SHIFT F7**) command.

Press   ^KV or **SHIFT F7**

to move the block here.
Because you've deleted and inserted text, you must now align the paragraph from the cursor position.

Press   ^B

The cursor is now on the line directly below the paragraph.

Deleting a Block

Another way to move a block is to delete it from one location and then restore it at another. Remember that ^U (**F2**) only remembers the last deletion, so issue this command immediately after you delete the block! The command to delete a block is ^KY (**SHIFT F5**).

Press   ^KY or **SHIFT F5**

You've deleted the block even though the cursor is not even *near* the block. Did you notice that when you moved the block it was still highlighted? Now, position the cursor where the sentence was originally.

Press   ^QG

Press   **RETURN**

to position the cursor at the end of the paragraph.

Press   ^S or **LEFT ARROW** twice

to position the cursor in front of the ^D print code.

Press   ^U or **F2**

to restore the block here.

Press   **ESC P**

to position the cursor at the beginning of the paragraph.

Press   **^B**

to align the paragraph.

　　When you unerase a block, WordStar doesn't restore the beginning and ending block markers. However, if you had moved the block with ^KV (**SHIFT F7**) instead of deleting and restoring it, the block highlighting would still display. It's up to you!

　　Tip: You can block out and move, copy, or delete dot command lines. For instance, say you want to copy a ruler line and several other formatting dot commands somewhere else in the file. Just block them out, but make sure the end of the block is at column 1 of the *next* line to include the hard return that ends the dot command line. Or use ^Y (**F5**) to delete an individual dot command line, then ^U (**F2**) to restore it somewhere else.

Deleting Large Blocks

Although you can *theoretically* restore any major deletion, there's a limit to the size of WordStar's unerase buffer. The default limit is 500 characters. If you block out a section of text that's bigger than the buffer and then press ^KY (**SHIFT F5**), WordStar warns you before deleting it:

The block is too large to unerase later.

Erase anyway (Y/N)?

　　Type **y** to delete the block or **n** to abandon the operation. If you want to delete a block with the possibility of restoring it (say, to move the block elsewhere), break up the block into miniblocks. You can also change the size of the unerase buffer with the WSCHANGE program (Chapter 27), but then you reduce the maximum characters in the file that WordStar can have in memory at one time.

Another way to go would be to copy the large block to a separate file, then insert the block elsewhere. See the discussion of the ^**KW** and ^**KR** commands later in the chapter.

Moving a Paragraph

When you move or copy a paragraph, make sure you include the *entire* paragraph. That means the five spaces for the tab at the beginning of the paragraph and the hard return or returns that end the paragraph. That way, the text is intact when you move it, and the spacing is still correct.

Press   ^X or **DOWN ARROW**

to position the cursor at the left margin of line 11.
    This is the beginning of the paragraph.

Press   ^**KB** or **SHIFT F9**

to mark the beginning of the block.

Press   ^**QG**

Press   **RETURN**

    Wait! You aren't at the end of the block yet. It should include *both* hard returns, because they belong to the paragraph.

Press   ^X or **DOWN ARROW** twice

to position the cursor at the left margin of line 21.
    Even though it looks as if you've gone too far, you haven't. That's because you want to include both hard returns, so you have to position the cursor *directly past* the second return before you end the block.

Press   ^**KK** or **SHIFT F10**

to end the block.
    Now you're ready to move the block.

Press   ^**QC** or ^**END**

to position the cursor at the end of the file.
    Are there two hard returns at the end of the file? The cursor should be at the left margin of line 13 on page 2. If not, add the hard returns first before moving the paragraph.

Then:

Press   **^KV or SHIFT F7**

to move the paragraph here.

Cursor Movement with Blocks

Will writers ever be satisfied? You decide you don't like how the story now reads (indeed, it makes no sense!), so you're going to move the paragraph back. First, learn a nifty cursor movement command, **^QV,** which positions the cursor at the *previous location* of a block that you've moved or copied.

Press   **^QV**

If you look at this command in the Quick menu, it says that the command moves the cursor to the last find. You'll learn about the find command in the next chapter, but **^QV** also goes to the last block location.

Using **^QV** is a fast and easy way to check the original block location to see if the spacing between paragraphs is correct (it should be). Now you can move the block back.

Press   **^KV or SHIFT F7**

to move the block back.

Here are two other useful cursor movement commands. **^QB** moves the cursor to the beginning of the block, and **^QK** to the end. These commands are especially helpful when the cursor is somewhere else in the file and you want to go back to the block quickly. Experiment with these commands now to see how they work:

Press   **^QK**

to position the cursor at the end of the block.

Press   **^QB**

to position the cursor at the beginning of the block.

Make sure the cursor is at the beginning of the block before you continue with the next example.

Changing a Block Definition

You can change a block by resetting its beginning or ending markers. Say you want to *extend* this block to include the next paragraph. You just change the end of the block.

Press   **^C** or **PG DN**

Press   **^X** or **DOWN ARROW** five times

Press   **^KK** or **SHIFT F10**

to extend the end of the block.

Now, for practice, change the beginning of the block:

Press   **^E** or **UP ARROW** five times

to position the cursor on line 21.

Press   **^KB** or **SHIFT F9**

to begin the block here.

Question: What if you want to set up another block somewhere else in the file? *Answer:* Just move the cursor to the new location and repeat the steps for beginning and ending the block. The old block is no longer active. **Tip:** You can set the end of the block before setting the beginning of the block, too.

"Hiding" a Block

Say you don't want the highlighted block to distract you, but you *do* want to keep the block as you marked it. You can "hide" the block with the command **^KH (SHIFT F6)**.

Press   **^KH** or **SHIFT F6**

The block highlighting disappears. This is a toggle command, so if you press it again—

Press   **^KH** or **SHIFT F6**

—the block reappears.

Tip: What if you press **^KB (SHIFT F9)** or **^KK (SHIFT F10)** by mistake and you don't want to see the beginning or ending block marker on the screen? Just leave the cursor where it is, then press the command again to remove the marker.

Note: You can't move or copy a block when it's hidden, unless the help level is 0 or 1. For help levels 2 or 3, the block must be showing first. Otherwise, you get this message:

```
Can't do block operations on a hidden block. Press ^KH and try again.
```

```
Press Esc to continue.
```

Just press **Esc, ^KH (SHIFT F6)** to "unhide" the block, then continue. Even if the block is hidden, if you press **^QB** or **^QK** to move the cursor to the beginning or end of the block, respectively, that automatically redisplays the block.

Here are two other block error messages. If you attempt to move or copy a block that you haven't set up yet, WordStar says:

```
You have not yet defined a block. Use ^KB and ^KK.
```

```
Press Esc to continue.
```

If you insert an end block marker before a beginning block marker and try a block operation, WordStar admonishes:

```
The end of the block is at or before the start of the block.
```

```
Press Esc to continue.
```

Last but not least, WordStar doesn't save block markers when you save the file.

Press   **^KD or F10**

to save the file and return to the Opening menu.

(You could have just quit without saving with **^KQ,** too. Type y to abandon the edit.) If you wish, delete the TEMP file with the **Y** [delete a file] command in the Opening menu.

Copying a Block

When you copy a block WordStar leaves the original where it is, then inserts one or more copies where you want them. Here's where you'll learn how to save boring and repetitive typing work.

Press   **D** [open a document]

Type   **siglines**

Press   **RETURN**

Type   y

because this is a new file.

Dear Reader: It's bad enough having to work in the first place, but now you have to type the following series of signature lines. What could be more boring? *Don't* type them yet.

Signed_____Dated_____

Signed_____Dated_____

Signed_____Dated_____

Signed_____Dated_____

Signed_____Dated_____

One way to do these signature lines is to type only *one* line and then let the copy block command set up the others for you!

Type   **Signed**

Type   _

(that's **SHIFT HYPHEN**) thirty-five times for the first underline.

Type   **Dated**

Type   _

(that's **SHIFT HYPHEN**) fifteen times for the second underline.

Press   **RETURN** three times

for spacing.

Press   **^QR** or **^HOME**

to position the cursor at the beginning of the file.

Press   **^KB** or **SHIFT F9**

to begin the block.

Press   **^QC** or **^END**

to position the cursor at the end of the file, past the three hard returns.

Press   ^KK or **SHIFT F10**

to end the block.
      The command to copy a block is ^KC (**SHIFT F8**):

Press   ^KC or **SHIFT F8**

to copy the signature line and the three hard returns.
      WordStar leaves the *first* block highlighted no matter how many times you copy it.

Press   ^QC or ^END

to position the cursor at the end of the file.

Press   ^KC or **SHIFT F8**

to copy the block again.
      Repeat the same steps of positioning the cursor at the end of the file and copying the block as many times as you need signature lines. As you can see, not only can the copy block command save you unnecessary and boring typing, it can also ensure that the file is *consistent*. Each signature line will be the same, and you can maintain a quality appearance in your work.

Press   ^KD or **F10**

to save the file and return to the Opening menu.

A More Elaborate Example

The copy command can save you a lot of work! Here's another example of how to use it, and some good word processing practice to boot.

Press   **D** [open a document]

Type   int

Press   **RETURN**

Type   y

because this is a new file.
      (Dear Reader: Have you realized yet that you can *get ahead* of WordStar by following the above instructions quickly and letting WordStar catch up?)

A set of *interrogatories* is a series of questions that one party in a law suit asks the opposing party. Now, before any smart lawyer objects, let me add that the example is not in the correct format. It's just an example! Gentle Reader: I must also beg your indulgence about the subject matter of the following interrogatories. If you don't like cats, so be it. If you love cats you'll perhaps understand how such unfortunate events might occur! In either case, please remember that all is in fun.

Read the following interrogatories, but don't type them yet. How could you finish this example with a minimum of hassle and boredom?

INTERROGATORY NO. 1:

With respect to Plaintiff's allegation that you willfully killed her cat by pushing it into your swimming pool and keeping it under water until it was drowned, on November 12, 1987, did you, or did you not, call Plaintiff and threaten to "strangle the beast" if it were not removed from your premises immediately?

INTERROGATORY NO. 2:

With respect to Plaintiff's allegation that you willfully killed her cat by pushing it into your swimming pool and keeping it under water until it was drowned, on November 12, 1987, did you, or did you not, deliberately and with malice aforethought attempt to lure said cat into your house?

INTERROGATORY NO. 3:

With respect to Plaintiff's allegation that you willfully killed her cat by pushing it into your swimming pool and keeping it under water until it was drowned, on November 12, 1987, did you, or did you not, when said cat refused to be enticed into your house, put its favorite food, Moist Munchies, on the very rim of your swimming pool, at the deep end?

INTERROGATORY NO. 4:

With respect to Plaintiff's allegation that you willfully killed her cat by pushing it into your swimming pool and keeping it under water until it was drowned, on November 12, 1987, did you, or did you not, hide in a bush located near the spot where the cat food was placed and wait for said cat to approach the food?

```
INTERROGATORY NO. 5:

     With  respect to Plaintiff's allegation that  you  willfully
killed her cat by pushing it into your swimming pool and  keeping
it  under water until it was drowned, on November 12,  1987,  did
you,  or did you not, force said cat into the pool and,  when  it
attempted to jump out of the pool, physically hold it down  until
it had drowned?
```

Each interrogatory is virtually the same up to a specific point, so you can create the first interrogatory. Then, after blocking it out correctly, copy it for each successive interrogatory and then finish the interrogatory. Here's how.

Type   INTERROGATORY No. 1:

Press   **RETURN** twice

Type the paragraph, starting it with a **TAB** (**^I**) and ending it with three hard returns. The cursor should be on line 10 when you're finished.

Tip: Because you're going to copy a part of this interrogatory, it makes sense to be careful that there are no *typing mistakes* in it! Otherwise, you'll just copy the mistakes and have to correct them many times later—a drag! So make sure your typing is correct now. When you're ready to continue:

Press   **^QE** or **HOME**

to position the cursor at the home position, which also happens to be the beginning of the file.

Press   **^KB** or **SHIFT F9**

to begin the block.

Press   **^X** or **DOWN ARROW** five times

Press   **^F** or **^RIGHT ARROW** five times

to position the cursor under the *c* of *call.*
     This part of each interrogatory (except the number) is the same.

Press   **^KK** or **SHIFT F10**

to end the block here.

Press   **^QC** or **^END**

to position the cursor at the end of the file.

Press   **^KC** or **SHIFT F8**

to copy the block.

Press   **^QD** or **^F10**

to position the cursor at the end of the line.

Press   **^S** or **LEFT ARROW**

Press   **BACKSPACE** or **^H**

to delete the *1*.

Type   2

Press   **^QC** or **^END**

to position the cursor at the end of the file.

Note this very important use of the cursor to end of file command, ^QC (^END). It takes the cursor to the *last entered character* in the file, and you are ready to fill in the second interrogatory. Type the rest of the interrogatory, press **RETURN** three times for spacing, and continue copying the block and finishing each interrogatory.

You don't even have to be anywhere near the original block when you move or copy it so long as you didn't hide the block with **^KH (SHIFT F6)**. What *is* important, though, is that you have the cursor exactly where you want to move or copy the block. When you're finished:

Press   **^KD** or **F10**

to save the file and return to the Opening menu.

Writing a Block to a File

Just as you can move or copy a block somewhere else in the current file, you can *write* the block to another file. That is, you're copying the block to this new file. The command to write a block to a file is **^KW,** and it can also save you a lot of work.

Press   **D** [open a document]

Type   perkins.ltr

Press   **RETURN**

Suppose you want to use the formatting dot commands, including the ruler line, again for another letter? Instead of setting up the commands again—surely a waste of time and energy—just block them out and write them to a file. In a moment, you'll see how to use this new file.

The cursor is at the beginning of the file.

Press   ^X or **DOWN ARROW**

because you don't want the nonprinting comment line in the block.

Press   **^KB or SHIFT F9**

to begin the block.

Press   **^X or DOWN ARROW** six times

to position the cursor directly below the ruler line.

Stop! First, the cursor should be at the left margin before you end the block (it's in the middle of the line now). Second, if you always need your return address when you create a new letter, why not include that in the block, too? Finally, you should delete the date and leave that line blank so whenever you start a new letter you don't have to delete the date.

Press   **^X or DOWN ARROW** twice

to position the cursor on line 3.

Press   **^F or ^RIGHT ARROW**

to position the cursor on the date (you *do* want to keep the tabs).

Press   **^QY**

to delete the rest of the line.

Now, include the four blank lines in the block, too.

Press   **^QG**

Type   J

(make sure it's uppercase).

You've included the extra blank lines between your return address and the recipient's name and address, so you don't have to add them either.

Press   **^KK or SHIFT F10**

to end the block.

Press   **^KW**

WordStar prompts:

```
Specify a file name where the marked block is to be stored on disk.

Name?
```

Supply a *new* file name, then press **RETURN.** If a file by that name is on the current drive or in the current directory, WordStar tells you:

```
That file already exists. Overwrite (Y/N)?
```

Either type **y** to overwrite the existing file name, or type **n** (or press ^U [F2]) to cancel the operation. (Dear Reader: One item on my current "WordStar Wish List" would be the ability to *append* a block to an existing file with ^KW. Perhaps a future release of the program will have this feature.)

Tip: Because you'll be using this block a lot, why not give it a *short, yet descriptive* file name, so you don't have to type too much? Because this block contains the formatting for your letters, call it LET.

Type   **let**

Press   **RETURN**

Press   **^KQ**

Type   **y**

to quit this file and return to the Opening menu.

Caution: Don't try to write a marked block to a file with the same name as the one you're editing. If you do, WordStar presents an inexplicable message:

```
Can't rename that file. The name you chose is already in use.

Press Esc to continue.
```

I don't know what this message has to do with your booboo either, but forewarned is forearmed!

Introducing Boilerplates and Format Files

Dear Reader, you've just created a *boilerplate* that you can use as a *format file!* Years ago, syndicated newspapers would make one set of typeset copy on printer's *plates* for an article and then send these plates around to their syndications for publication. This process became known as boilerplating. Now, a boilerplate in word processing terminology is any text that you use over and over.

Word processing means you never have to retype. You'll find boilerplates one of the most hard-working word processing tools. This boilerplate sets the format for your next letter and includes your return address. That's why I call it a format file. In Chapter 16, you'll learn more about boilerplates and format files.

Tip: Make sure the typing and formatting are correct before you create a boilerplate, because you'll be copying the boilerplate many times later.

"Reading" a File

Once you've created a boilerplate, either by writing a block to another file or typing the boilerplate from scratch, here's how to use it. First, create a new file. Say you're planning to send a letter to a Ms. Calhoun, so you create a file called CALHOUN.LTR:

Press	**D** [open a document]
Type	`calhoun.ltr`
Press	**RETURN**
Type	`y`

because this is a new file.

Now, use the *read a file* command, **^KR.** Think of this command as the *read in* command. It inserts a file into the current file at the cursor location, so always make sure the cursor is where you want it first before issuing the command.

Press   **^KR**

WordStar prompts:

`Specify the name of the document that you wish to insert into the file` being edited. If no drive is specified, the logged drive will be used.

Document?

You can type the file name or select it from the directory listing. **Caution:** Don't press **ESC** the *first* time you run the ^**KR** command each day. (Old-time WordStar users, beware!) WordStar would insert a copy of the entire file into itself! However, after you've just used the ^**KR** command during the current session, WordStar "remembers" the last file you inserted. So if you then press **ESC** for the file name, WordStar will insert another copy of the file. You can cancel the command before selecting a file by pressing ^**U** (**F2**) or **RETURN**.

Type   **let**

Press   **RETURN**

Now, all you have to do is press ^**X** (**DOWN ARROW**) seven times, then ^**QD** (^**F10**) to go to the end of the line, where the date should be, press **ESC** @ to enter today's date, and press ^**QC** (^**END**) to position the cursor in preparation for finishing the rest of the letter. You never have to worry about setting the format or creating the same ruler line again. Hooray for WordStar!

Leave the file open for a moment. If you type an incorrect or nonexistent file name after pressing ^**KR,** WordStar honors you with this message:

WordStar cannot find that document.

Press Esc to continue.

Press **ESC** and try again. Perhaps you didn't put in the drive designator, or the full directory path? See Chapters 12 and 13 for more information about file management.

Tips: Using ^**KW** together with ^**KR** is the best way to move or copy a block in a large file. WordStar slows down considerably when you move or copy a block over many pages. Instead, write the block to another file with ^**KW**, delete the block, position the cursor where you want the block to go, and read in the block with ^**KR**. This same technique is the best way to delete a large block and still give you the option to restore it if necessary. Remember that the default unerase buffer is only 500 characters.

Saving and Exiting to DOS

To round out this discussion of the block and save commands, here's a final save command that you'll find handy. The command is ^**KX,** and it does two operations in one: it saves the file (^KD) and exits WordStar (X), thus by-passing the Opening menu.

Press   ^KX

In a moment you see the DOS prompt on your screen. You may want to delete the unnecessary CALHOUN.LTR file now:

Type   `del calhoun.ltr` or `erase calhoun.ltr`

Press   **RETURN**

(This is just a prelude to Chapters 12 and 13, which discuss file management in greater detail.)

Final Notes on Boilerplates

You may have noticed that when you write a block to file with ^KW you are writing the block only, *not* the entire file (unless, of course, you block out the entire file!). But when you read a block with ^KR you are copying the entire file into the current file. You can't read *part* of another file into the current file with ^KR. This brings me to other tips . . .

 Tip: Set up your boilerplates to allow for as *flexible* a use as possible. That is, only include in the boilerplate those dot commands and text that go together. If necessary, create *several* boilerplates for different uses. To keep track of your boilerplate files, have a *crib sheet* handy near your computer. Include on it the name of each file and what it contains. After a while you'll know all your boilerplates by heart because you'll use them repeatedly.

^KR merely copies the file but does not change its contents or destroy the boilerplate file. At the risk of sounding like a broken record, I repeat: "saving keystrokes means saving work."

Once you've mastered the block technique, you will find yourself using blocks a great deal. Lawyers and other writers especially will be ecstatic about being able to move lines or paragraphs at will ("cut and paste"), either within a file with ^KV (**SHIFT F7**) or between files with ^KW and ^KR. And if you do a lot of repetitious typing, you can use the copy block command, ^KC (**SHIFT F8**), to your advantage. In Chapter 11, you'll learn other block commands that work with *text arranged in columns.*

Finding and Replacing

In this chapter you will learn the following new commands:

File Commands

^L (^F3)	Repeat the last find or find and replace
^QA (^F2)	Find and replace
^QF (^F1)	Find
^QV	Cursor to the last find location

Other Features

B, G, U, W, ?, n	Find options
A, B, G, N, R, U, W, ?, n	Find and replace options

You've already learned many ways to move the cursor through your files quickly. This chapter shows you how to zero in on specific text by using WordStar's find command. No experienced word processor would be without this command. You'll also learn about find's companion, find and replace, a most helpful work-saving feature.

DO WARM-UP

Groan!

Dear Reader, before you take a look at find, I'm going to have to ask you to do a little typing work. As a consolation, you'll use the same example in other chapters, so you won't have to type it again.

Press   **D** [open a document]

Type   contract

Press   **RETURN**

Type   y

because this is a new file.

First, Set the Format

Whenever possible, set up the format for a new file *before* you begin typing. That way, you won't have to realign the text later. This example also comes from the legal world. It's a fictitious contract between two parties. (Would-be lawyers, please take note: this is not a legally correct contract!)

You'll use the standard left and right margins, but you want to turn right margin justification off and put the text in double spacing. Additionally, have WordStar underline the spaces between words in a phrase. Do you remember the dot commands you'll need?

Type   .OJ OFF or .oj off

Press   **RETURN**

Type   .LS 2 or .ls 2

Press   **RETURN**

Type   .UL ON or .ul on

Press   **RETURN**

Get the Typing Done

The next step is to type the text. Try to correct mistakes as you go along, but don't fret if you can't catch them all. In another chapter you'll have WordStar check the spelling of this file, so you can just concentrate on the typing now. Later, you'll also learn how to *hyphenate* words to fill in the lines.

The first part of the contract follows. Take a look at the title. *Question:* How do you type it? *Answer:* First, press the **CAPS LOCK** key, then type each letter separated by a space. Release the CAPS LOCK key. Then press **^OC** or **ESC C** to center the title. Press **RETURN** twice to put in four blank lines—a "double-double space"—because line spacing is now double.

Use *two* tabs to begin each paragraph. (Patient Reader: There's a nifty way of avoiding having to press even the TAB key. It's called the *paragraph margin,* and you'll learn about it in Chapter 9. For the time being, however, stick to the old way.) When you're finished, the cursor should be at the end of the paragraph on line 31.

```
.OJ OFF
.LS 2
.UL ON
```

A G R E E M E N T

        The following Agreement has been entered into this 18th

day of January, 1988, between Janet ("Red") Smith, dba LITTLE RED

RIDING HOOD ENTERPRISES, INC. (hereinafter "Red"), and FRANK

WOLFE, an individual (hereinafter "Wolfe").

        WHEREAS, Red maintains a delivery service for indigent

and bedridden elderly people in the City of San Diego,

California; and

        WHEREAS, Wolfe is the owner and operator of a pickup

truck with a certain load capacity; and

        WHEREAS, Red desires to contract with Wolfe for various

pickup and delivery services, and Wolfe has agreed to perform

those services;

        IT IS NOW HEREBY RESOLVED, that the following

conditions have been agreed upon by both Red and Wolfe:

Next, you want a "double-double" between this section and the next:

Press   **RETURN** twice

Underline and type the first heading like this:

Press   ^PS or **F3**

to turn on underlining.

Type   Compensation

Press   ^PS or **F3**

to turn off underlining.

Press   **RETURN**

for spacing.

Type the rest of the example, using the pattern above. That is, separate each section from the next with a double-double, but use only one press of the RETURN key between a heading and the paragraph following it. For the underlines in the last paragraph, press SHIFT HYPHEN seven times for the first and twelve times for the second. Here's the rest of the contract:

<u>Compensation</u>

Red agrees to pay Wolfe an hourly rate of $12.50 an hour for all delivery services performed by Wolfe for Red. This hourly rate shall be computed from the time Wolfe leaves Red's business establishment, located at 145 Cedar Street, San Diego, California, until such time as all deliveries contracted by Red for that business day are made. Furthermore, Wolfe agrees to telephone Red at her place of business (619-555-0010) to inform Red of the exact time that he completed deliveries for that business day.

<u>Description of Services to Be Performed</u>

The services covered in this Agreement include pick-up and delivery of articles designated by Red to Wolfe to such of Red's clients as are specified on each delivery day. Wolfe is to take care that such articles are delivered promptly by the time requested by the client and are to arrive in perfect condition. Red agrees not to entrust Wolfe with delivery of any items or articles that Wolfe would be unable to transport in his vehicle because of space limitations.

Overtime

For the purposes of this Agreement, a normal business day is understood to be between the hours of 8 a.m. and 4 p.m., Monday through Friday, except legal holidays. For any services rendered to Red by Wolfe at any other time, including Sundays and holidays, Red agrees to pay Wolfe the overtime rate of $18.75 per hour.

Gasoline Expenses

Wolfe agrees that any gasoline, oil or other maintenance expenses incurred during his performance of pick-up and delivery services for Red will be borne by him and not charged to Red at any time.

Liability

Red assumes no liability for injuries or accidents suffered by Wolfe during the time when he is performing the services described in this Agreement.

<u>Miscellaneous</u>

This contract is governed by the laws of the State of

California.

EXECUTED this _____ day of _____, 1988, in San

Diego, California.

When you're finished the cursor should be at the end of the paragraph on line 13 of page 3. Before continuing, what should you do? Right!

Press   ^KS or F9

to save the file and resume where you left off.

Press   **RETURN** twice

for spacing.

You now want to type in signature lines that will be single spaced, so enter the **.LS 1** dot command on its own line, as shown below. Make sure you press **RETURN** to end the dot command line. Then press **TAB (^I)** 6 times to indent and type 30 underscores for each line. Press **RETURN** four times, because spacing is now single, at the end of the Enterprises, Inc. line.

.LS 1

_____

Janet Smith

Little Red Riding Hood
Enterprises, Inc.

_____

Frank Wolfe

When you're finished:

Press   ^KS or F9

to save the file and resume where you left off.

Press   **^QR** or **^HOME**

to position the cursor at the beginning of the file.

Now you're ready to learn about the find command.

Using Find for Quick Cursor Movement

Assume that this contract is much longer and you want to edit the section on overtime. You don't know what page number it's on, so you can't use **^QI** (**^F4**). How could you get to it quickly without having to scroll through the file? Use find, another one of the quick commands. It's **^QF or ^F1**.

Press   **^QF or ^F1**

WordStar asks:

Find what?

Recall that WordStar presents the same message when you press **^QG** or **^QH.**

Type   **Overtime**

(make sure to type an uppercase *o*).

As you type the word you want to find, it appears on the screen above the ruler line. If you make a mistake, use the standard editing keys to correct it. As usual, you can cancel by pressing **^U** (**F2**).

Note: The longest word or group of words you can find is 65 characters.

Stop! If you press RETURN after typing **Overtime**, WordStar presents a variety of *find options*. You'll learn about them in a moment, but there's an easy way to *bypass* the options.

Press   **ESC**

The status line flashes a Wait message, and soon WordStar positions the cursor at the beginning of the word **Overtime**.

Tip: If you know that the first few letters of the word you're looking for are unique, you don't have to type the entire word. In this example, you could have typed **Over** instead of **Overtime** to save keystrokes.

Computers Are Literal Beasts

Suppose you typed *Overtime* as **Ovrtime** but didn't catch your mistake. WordStar can't intuit what you want, so it won't be able to find the word. It tells you, in no uncertain terms:

```
Could not find: Ovrtime

Press Esc to continue.
```

A computer is a strictly literal beast. WordStar can't read, so what it's doing when you use the find command is matching each letter that you type against the words in the file, starting at the present cursor location. Although *you* see your work as a series of lines and paragraphs on the screen, WordStar "sees" text as an uninterrupted string of characters.

If WordStar can't find the characters you type—in the order you type them—somewhere in the file, the find command "fails." That is, WordStar reaches the end of the file before making a complete match and gives you the error message. You'd press **ESC** and then the cursor to previous position command, **^QP,** to try again.

Repeating the Last Find

Assuming, then, that you typed *Overtime* correctly and WordStar finds the first occurrence of that word, you now want to locate the next occurrence. You don't have to type the word again or even press **^QF (^F1).** There's the *repeat find* command, **^L (^F3).** It "remembers" whatever was the *last* word you were trying to find.

Press   **^L or ^F3**

This time, WordStar didn't find any more occurrences of the word and told you so:

```
End of search for: Overtime

Press Esc to continue.
```

An aside: You can press **^QF (^F1)** and then **ESC** to repeat the last find command, too, but pressing **^L (^F3)** is faster.

Press   **ESC**

to continue.

The cursor is now at the end of the file. Leave it there for the moment.
Question: Why didn't WordStar find the word *overtime* in the paragraph? *Answer:* The two words don't match, because the case of first letter in each instance is different. Later, you'll see how to overcome this problem when you want to find all occurrences of a word, regardless of case differences.

A Good Tip

When you work with a long file, if you don't know the page number you need, pick a unique or unusual word to find. That is, don't use a common word like *the* unless you are looking for a specific occurrence of that word. Even if the particular word or sentence you wish to find is not unusual in any way, there may be a word *close by* that you can find and thus position the cursor close to where you really want to be.

Finding Backwards

Find works in either direction, forward or backward, through the file. However, WordStar "assumes" that you want to find forward unless you tell it to find backwards. Here's where you have to use one of the *find options*. The cursor should be at the end of the file.

Press   **^QF or ^F1**

Type   Agreement

This time, *don't* press ESC. Instead:

Press   **RETURN**

WordStar now prompts:

```
Option(s)?
W whole words    U ignore case    B look backwards    ? wildcards
G start from beginning or end
```

You'll learn the other options in a moment. You want to find backwards, so:

Type   b

Press   **RETURN**

Because you can choose more than one option, you must press **RETURN** to "send" the options on to WordStar and start the find operation.

WordStar stops at the first occurrence of *Agreement,* working from the end of the file backwards. To repeat the find,

Press   **^L or ^F3**

The ^L (^F3) command "remembers" the word you want to find *and* any find options you specified the last time you used the find command. So, WordStar stops at the next occurrence of *Agreement,* again working backwards through the file.

Oops! You want to return to the *previous* occurrence of the word to check something. Don't forget a useful command:

Press   **^QP**

to position the cursor at the previous position.

Press   **^L** or **^F3**

to continue finding *Agreement* backwards.

Eventually WordStar would reach the beginning of the file, and find would "fail." Instead of continuing, do this:

Press   **^QR** or **^HOME**

to position the cursor at the beginning of the file.

Question: If you type a letter, such as **S,** that isn't one of the correct find options, guess what happens? Right! WordStar gives you an error message:

```
S is not a valid option.

Press Esc to continue.
```

Press **ESC** to remove this message from the screen. As your punishment, you must start the find again!

Repeating the Word

You now want to find the word *Agreement* again, but this time you'll go forward through the file. WordStar still "remembers" the last word you typed.

Press   **^QF** or **^F1**

Press   **^R**

This command, as you saw in Chapter 1, *repeats* a file name. Now you know that it also repeats the last word or string of characters you want to find.

Disregarding Case

Instead of finding just *Agreement,* you decide to find any occurrence of the word, regardless of case: *agreement, Agreement,* or even *AGREEMENT.* Find is still waiting for you to continue.

Press   **RETURN**

to see the options.

Type   u

Press   **RETURN**

This is the *ignore case* option. (The *u* stood for uppercase in previous WordStars.) Now WordStar will find the word in any form. When WordStar stops at the first occurrence of the word, do this:

Press   **^QF or ^F1**

Press   **^R**

to repeat the word.

Press   **RETURN**

to see the options.

Type   bu or ub

Press   **RETURN**

You can mix and match the find options. WordStar now looks for the word backward, and it ignores case, too. What happens? It doesn't find any occurrence of the word. *Question:* What about the title? Why didn't WordStar find it? *Hint:* Is it *exactly* like the word you typed? No! Why not? *Answer:* There are spaces between the letters, so WordStar doesn't "understand" this to be the same word as *Agreement.* There's your literal computer again!

Press   **ESC**

as WordStar prompts.

When a Word Isn't a Word

I've used the term *word* to refer to what you're finding, but it needn't be a real word. It can be any *string of characters*. That includes numbers, punctuation marks, spaces, or whatever. For example, you could find the date *1988* or the string *18th* in this file. Just make sure you type in the string exactly as you think it appears in the file, and that it doesn't exceed 65 characters.

Tips: You can find print controls by using the command as normal. For example, to find boldface print codes, press ^PB (F4) after pressing ^QF (^F1). To find hard or soft returns, press ^N as the string to find. WordStar shows this as ^M^J on the find edit line.

Using Wildcards

A *wildcard*, as you poker fans know, can substitute for any other card. WordStar has a wildcard find option, the **?,** that lets you "broaden" the search in two different ways, but using it is slightly tricky. Pay close attention!

One way to use the wildcard is as a substitute for any *one* character in the string you're finding. Say you want to find the string *t?e*, where the question mark means any character in the second position of the string.

Press   **^QF** or **^F1**

Type   t?e

Press   **RETURN**

Stop! You *must* include the ? option, because if you don't WordStar "assumes" you're looking for the *real* question mark in the string!

Type   ?

Press   **RETURN**

WordStar first stops at the word *between* because it contains the string *twe*. Press ^L (^F3) a few more times, and WordStar stops at *the, Street,* and *Furthermore,* because they all meet the wildcard match. You can also use the **?** wildcard as the *first* character, say, in the string *?he*. WordStar then matches any character in the first position, and would find words such as *the* and *The*.

Now do this:

Press   **^QC** or **^END**

to position the cursor at the end of the file.

This time you'll learn the other way to use the **?** wildcard. When it's at the *end* of a string, it substitutes for *all* remaining characters.

Press	^QF or ^F1
Type	th?
Press	**RETURN**
Type	b? or ?b

to find backwards with the wildcard.

This time, WordStar first stops at the word *this*. Use ^L (^F3) a few more times to see WordStar stop at *the, other,* and *that*. The wildcard can be a very powerful find tool!

Finding Whole Words

Suppose you're looking for the word *his*. If you're not careful, WordStar may stop at words like *this* or *his*tory or *hiss*. That's because normally it finds any occurrence of the string you type, within other words or not. If you want only the *real* word *his*, use the whole word option.

This option only finds the string when it's a word. *Question:* If WordStar can't read, how does it "know" what a word is? It doesn't; it merely looks for the spaces, punctuation marks, or any other character that isn't alphabetic on both sides of the word.

Press	^QR or ^HOME

to position the cursor at the beginning of the file.

Press	^QF or ^F1
Type	his
Press	**RETURN**
Type	w
Press	**RETURN**

This time WordStar didn't stop at *this*, because that doesn't fulfill the whole word criterion.

Starting at the Beginning or End of the File

The find command works from the *present cursor position* either forward by default or backward when you use the **B** option. Suppose the cursor is at the top of page six and you try to find a word. WordStar says it can't find it, but you *know* it's in the file somewhere. Assuming you typed the word correctly, it's undoubtedly *before* page six.

So, note where the cursor is before you start find. Or use the **G** find option to start at the beginning of the file automatically. If you use the **B** and **G** options together, WordStar starts at the end of the file and finds backwards. Another way would be to press **^QR** (**^HOME**) or **^QC** (**^END**) just before starting a find.

Cursor to the Last Find

In the previous chapter you learned about the **^QV** command to position the cursor at the original block location. Officially, its name is the "cursor to the last find" command. So if you press **^L** (**^F3**) to continue find, you can go back to the previous find with **^QV**. The difference between **^QV** and **^QP** is that with **^QV** you can move the cursor around first before returning to the previous find location. **^QP** just returns to the previous *cursor* location.

A "Secret" Find Option

There's one find option that's not on the list. It's your secret! If you type an integer number, WordStar finds the occurrence of the word matching the number. For example, specify the word to find and press **RETURN.** Then type **6** and press **RETURN** to find the sixth occurrence of the word.

Thus, to find the 200th line in the file (that is, the 200th carriage return, either hard or soft), press **^QF** (**^F1**), press **^N,** press **RETURN,** type 200, and press **RETURN.**

Canceling Find

Suppose you start finding a string in a large file only to realize that you typed the string incorrectly. Instead of waiting for WordStar to reach the end of the file and tell you the obvious, you can cancel find at any time by pressing **^U** (**F2**). WordStar tells you:

```
Find or replace interrupted.

Press Esc to continue.
```

Press **ESC** and then **^QP** to return to where you started.

Help for Find

In previous releases of WordStar, typing **?** for an option brought up a help screen describing the find options. Now because that's an option itself, you can't get help while working with find. Just return to the text and press **^J**, followed by **^QF** (**^F1**), for help. You'll see two help screens, on one of which is the secret **n** (integer number) option. Oh, well, it isn't much of a secret, I guess!

Soft Spaces and Split Strings

In previous releases of WordStar, what looked like the simplest operation could turn out to be a nightmare. Usually the nightmare occurred when you were working with right-justified text. Suppose you have the STORY.LA file open and you want to find the phrase *Angeles Crest*. WordStar would not have found this phrase if there were soft spaces between *Angeles* and *Crest*. This problem no longer occurs: WordStar *will* find the string, no matter how many soft returns are in it. Hooray!

Another problem that is a thing of the past involves a phrase that WordStar splits over two lines. Formerly, WordStar wouldn't catch such occurrences, but now it does. Hooray again!

A Find Miscellany

Because you can find any character that you've typed from the keyboard, there are many ways to use find. For example, you might want to find all *dot commands* in a file. Say you want to find the nonprinting comment lines. That's an easy one: just type .. as the string to find.

Question: What if you wanted to find *all* dot commands? It wouldn't make sense to find the period (.), because then WordStar would stop at the ends of sentences, too. Think, Dear Reader, think! A dot command has to begin a line, so what's immediately in front of it? Right! A return. *Answer:* To find all dot commands, press **^QF** (**^F1**), then press **^N** (WordStar shows this as **^M^J**), and type a . character. Try it! What you're doing is finding the carriage return that's immediately in front of the dot command, along with the dot.

Another use of find is to go quickly through a file and make sure that all open quotation marks have corresponding close quotes. Find can even help you improve your writing style. For instance, if you fear you have a tendency to use a word—say, *accordingly*—too much, just use find and repeat find to locate each occurrence of that word in your file. In a moment, you'll see how to find and replace words.

Dear Reader: Maybe it's time for a break? I could use a cup of coffee, so:

Press   ^KD or F10

to save the file and return to the Opening menu.

Finding and Replacing

Just as you can find text, print codes, or dot commands, you can also find strings and replace them with something else. This feature is one of the all-time best word processing work savers!

Press   D [open a document]

If you took a break and left WordStar running:

Press   ESC

If you turned off your machine and are resuming the lesson now:

Type   contract

Press   RETURN

Assume you've printed the contract and now want to use the same file to create a contract for another agreement between Red and a second pickup truck owner named Badd. You could easily ask WordStar to find all occurrences of the name *Wolfe* and replace them with the new name. If you wish, WordStar even *aligns* the paragraphs as you go, because you may be replacing the word with a longer or shorter word, so the line endings might change.

One Time Only

The command for find and replace is ^QA (^F2). WordStar first acts as if you are just finding text.

Press   ^QA or ^F2

WordStar asks:

Find what?

Type   Wolfe

Make sure you type it correctly as shown.

Press   **RETURN**

Now, WordStar has to know what you want to replace the word with:

Replace with?

Type   **Badd**

Just for practice, bypass the find and replace options:

Press   **ESC**

WordStar stops at the first occurrence of the word *Wolfe* and flashes this message on the top right corner of the status line:

Replace Y/N

The cursor is blinking at the message and also at the word in the text. WordStar is telling you that find and replace won't continue until you type either y or n, or press ^U (**F2**) to cancel.

Type   n

The reason I told you to type n is that using find and replace one time only doesn't make much sense here, because there are other occurrences of the word in the file. What's more, WordStar won't realign the paragraph when you replace *Wolfe* with *Badd,* and you'd have to do this yourself later. A much better way to go—because it takes less time and means less work—is to use the *global* option, **G,** the *nonstop* option, **N,** and the *align* option, **A.** First, do this:

Press   **^QR** or **^HOME**

to position the cursor at the beginning of the file.

Keep in mind that the limit for any find or replacing string is 65 characters.

Replacing All Occurrences Quickly

Here's how to find and replace one word with another quickly when you are certain you want to replace all occurrences of the word.

Press   **^QA** or **^F2**

Here you can repeat the previous word:

Press   **^R**

Press   **RETURN**

Press   **^R**

to repeat the previous replacing word.

Press   **RETURN**

to bring up the find and replace options.
This is what you see:

```
Option(s)?
W whole words    U ignore case    B look backwards    ? wildcards    A align
G start from beginning or end    N replace without asking    R rest
```

There are three additional options when you use find and replace instead of find. You already know about the **G** option, which starts at the beginning or end of the file. The **G** option also *continues* the find and replace after you type **y** or **n** to replace the word. However, the best way to use it is with the **N** option to replace all occurrences of a word with another word without stopping. That is, WordStar won't request a yes or no answer before replacing the word. Also type the **A** option to have WordStar realign any changed paragraphs. Keep in mind that one word is more than likely longer or shorter than the other.

Type   **gna**

in any order.

Press   **RETURN**

Now watch as, before your very eyes, WordStar finds and replaces. Eventually it reaches the end of the file and tells you:

```
All replacements complete of: Wolfe
```

```
Press Esc to continue.
```

Press   **ESC**

If you typed *Wolfe* incorrectly, say, as *wolfe,* WordStar would honor you with this message instead:

```
Could not find: wolfe
```

```
Press Esc to continue.
```

Later you'll see how to disregard case.

What's "Wrong" with the File?

Find and replace is a great feature, but it has its limitations. It turns out that Mr. Badd's first name is Joseph, so you now have to replace *Frank* with *Joseph* on the last signature line. Don't worry about it now, because this is just an example. Instead, do this:

Press   **^QR** or **^HOME**

to position the cursor at the beginning of the file.

Scroll down through the first paragraph. Because the first occurrence of Frank Wolfe's name is *FRANK WOLFE,* WordStar doesn't catch this either. The moral here, again, is that computers are literal beasts. You still might have to "clean up" parts of the file manually. But think of the time you've saved!

A Nifty Trick

Here's another way to save even more time. Suppose this contract were much longer. Every time WordStar found the word *Wolfe* and replaced it with *Badd,* it stopped and "refreshed" the screen. Here's a trick to speed up find and replace by halting the screen refresh. Say you want to change *Badd* back to *Wolfe:*

Press   **^QR** or **^HOME**

to position the cursor at the beginning of the file.

Press   **^QA** or **^F2**

Type   Badd

Press   **RETURN**

Type   Wolfe

Press   **RETURN**

Press   **^R**

to repeat the same **G, N,** and **A** options.

Press   **RETURN**

to begin, but *immediately after WordStar starts finding and replacing,* do this:

Press   **^E or UP ARROW**

Actually, you can press *any* arrow key to stop the screen refreshing. WordStar freezes the screen as it completes the find and replace. Nifty! In a jiff, it's at the end of the file.

Press   **ESC**

when WordStar has finished.

Press   **^QR or ^HOME**

to position the cursor at the beginning of the file.

Finding and Replacing Backwards

You won't stop to practice the **B** option, but you can use it if the cursor is at or near the end of the file. You might then want to type the four options gnba in any order.

Replacing Part of the File

No matter where the cursor is, if you use the **G** option WordStar always starts the find and replace at the beginning or (with the **B** option) at the end of the file. This may take time. If you only want to replace the *rest* of the file starting at the cursor location, use the **R** option. It's like the **G** option, but it works only from the cursor position forward. However, do *not* use the **G** option and the **R** option together. If you do, WordStar honors *only* the **G** option and disregards **R.** They're mutually exclusive.

Replacing Selectively

If you use the **G** option without the **N** option, WordStar finds every occurrence of a word and prompts you to type y or n. That way, you can replace some occurrences of the word, but not all. Thus you could replace, say, *Accordingly* with *Therefore,* but not all the time.

Replacing Whole Words

Use the **W** option when you want to avoid the possibility of replacing parts of words. Say this contract was set up between Red and Lucille Brown. You'd want to find all occurrences of *his* and replace them with *her,* but you don't want to replace *this* with *ther.* The **W** option is there to help you. See the end of the chapter for more about this option.

Disregarding Case

Be careful when you use the **U** option! It can be helpful at times, but at other times it can wreak havoc. For example, say you're replacing *Wolfe* with *Badd* and you include the **U** option. WordStar doesn't honor case, so it would have replaced *WOLFE* (uppercase) in the first paragraph with *Badd* (mixed case)! I'm hoping that a future version of the product *will* honor the exact case of the found word.

Replacing with Wildcards

It's one of those days. You're not on your toes—maybe it was a rough weekend— and you don't type a name consistently. Say at times you type *Wolfe* and at other times you type *Wolf.* Use the **?** option as a wildcard so WordStar catches all occurrences. The string you'd want to find would be `Wolf?`. Don't forget to type **?** as one of the options; otherwise, WordStar would look for the **?** as part of the word.

Or maybe you typed *Smythe* and *Smithe* indiscriminately for *Smith.* To replace your mistakes with the correction, enter `Sm?th?` or `Sm?the` as the word to find. Make sure you type **?** as one of the options.

The "Secret" Option Again

Okay, so it isn't a secret! You can find and replace only a certain number of words by typing an integer as the option. Say you know that you only want to replace a word five times, and you want to do it nonstop and have WordStar realign the paragraphs. The options you'd type, in any order, would be **an5.**

Repeating and Canceling Find and Replace

The **^L** (**^F3**) command repeats the last find and replace operation, including whatever options you used. Even when you close one file and open another during the same work session, WordStar "remembers" the last find or find and replace. Say you're replacing the same string in several files. After you've finished one file and saved it, open the other and press ^L (^F3) to continue.

As usual, press ^U (F2) to cancel and find and replace. Then press ESC as WordStar prompts.

A Tricky Example

Always be careful to type what you want correctly and make sure to include spaces and punctuation as needed. Here's what I mean. The cursor should be at the end of the file.

Press   ^QA or ^F2

Type   WHEREAS,

(make sure you type the comma).

Press   **RETURN**

Type   WHEREFORE:

(make sure you type the colon).

Stop! Although only one space generally follows a comma, after a colon many people use *two* spaces. You have to add an extra space to the one already in the file wherever the string *WHEREAS,* occurs.

Press   **SPACEBAR**

to add a space to the find string.

Press   **RETURN**

Type   gnba

in any order.

Press   **RETURN**

WordStar goes through the file and finds each occurrence of *WHEREAS,* and replaces it with *WHEREFORE:* plus an additional space. As it replaces, it realigns the paragraphs.

Press   **ESC**

when WordStar has finished.

Replacing Print Codes

You can find and replace print codes just like any text. Suppose you want to change the underlining in the headings to boldface and underlining. The cursor is now at the beginning of the file.

Press	^QA or ^F2
Press	^PS or F3
Press	RETURN
Press	^PS or F3
Press	^PB or F4
Press	RETURN
Type	gn
Press	RETURN

Voilà! (Press ESC when WordStar has finished.)

Finding and Deleting

Now for a very useful application of find and replace. You can find something and delete it by replacing it with *nothing!* Suppose you want to remove the boldface and underlining codes in this file. The cursor should be at the end of the file.

Press	^QA or ^F2
Press	^PS or F3
Press	^PB or F4

Note: Make sure you enter the codes in the order they appear.

Press   RETURN

As the replacement string, nothing, just do this:

Press   RETURN

Continue with the options:

Type   gnb

Press   **RETURN**

Press   **ESC**

when WordStar has finished.
　　You don't want to save the editing changes in the file, so:

Press   **^KQ**

Type   y

to abandon the edit.

A Brief Interlude—Do This, Please!

Before you learn more about how to use find and replace, delete the print codes in the STORY.LA file. **Note:** Make sure you do this now because you'll use the file—without print codes—in other chapters.
　　Open the STORY.LA file and, using the find and delete technique that you just learned, delete all **^PS** (underline), **^PB** (boldface), **^PD** (doublestrike), and **^PX** (strikeout) codes from the file. Save the file with **^KD** (**F10**) when you're finished.

Dealing with the Boredom Factor

I'm sure you already realize some of the time and work saving benefits of find and replace. One great benefit is the way find and replace can help you avoid boring and repetitious typing.

Press   **D** [open a document]

Type   huntpeck

Press   **RETURN**

Type   y

because this is a new file. WordStar reverts to the default format settings.
　　Once again, picture yourself in a law office. You are preparing a partnership agreement and getting bored typing in all those words *Partner, Partners,* or *Partnership.* There's an easier way! Type the following sample *exactly*

as you see it. Use one space between "words" as normal and let WordStar fill in the lines with soft spaces. Notice the asterisks. What do they represent?

```
        This is a limited *ship Agreement between two *s, MAUREEN T.
HUNT  and  RICHARD J. PECK, who will henceforth  be  collectively
referred to as the *s.  It is understood that the *s have  agreed
to  abide  fully by all the provisions of this  *ship  Agreement.
Each  *  has  further agreed that he or she  has  not  previously
entered into a similar *ship agreement with any other *, nor will
do so during the term of this present *ship Agreement.
```

Press   **^KS** or **F9**

to save the file and resume where you left off after you've typed the paragraph.

This could go on for pages and pages, but you get the picture. Now do the following with the cursor at the end of the file.

Press   **^QA** or **^F2**

Type   *

Press   **RETURN**

Type   Partner

(use an uppercase *p*).

Press   **RETURN**

Type   abgn

in any order.

Press   **RETURN**

What happened? Of course! Good old find and replace did exactly what you told it to do. Remember *not* to use the asterisk for anything else in this file—such as its normal use as an asterisk!—because WordStar will replace it, too, with *Partner*. Another limitation of find and replace: make sure you use characters from the keyboard that you don't need to type!

Why did I use **s* and **ship?* Because the "common" word for each of the three words is *Partner*. When find and replace substitutes the word *Partner* for each ***, this takes care of the other two possible words, *Partners* and *Partnership*.

Press   **ESC**

when find and replace is finished.

Press   ^KD or F10

to save the file and return to the Opening menu.

Although you don't have to stop and type this next example, take a look at it for a moment. You decide you like the replacement method as a way to save typing work so you decide to use it in another file.

    p objects to contention by d regarding the merit of this
particular witness, because p has not had, nor ever has had, in
p's knowledge, any relationship with the witness in question.   p
furthermore attests that d is trying to slander p's good name
because d has no other competent and acceptable witness to have
appear before this Court.

You'll eventually replace each *p* with the word *Plaintiff* and each *d* with the word *Defendant*. To avoid wrecking your sanity, however, what do you have to remember to include? Right! The **W** (whole word) option, because if you don't, WordStar replaces *every* occurrence of the letter *p* with *Plaintiff*! The **W** ensures that WordStar will only look for the letter *p* when it has spaces or other nonalphabetic characters on either side of it.

Tip: Always be *very* careful how you set up a find and replace! If you're trying to replace a common word, like *his,* that could occur in other words, use the **W** option.

The substitution of one character by many is also helpful when you're doing repetitive mailing lists in which certain cities occur often. For instance, you could use an ampersand (**&**) for *Los Angeles, CA* and a percent sign (**%**) for *San Francisco, CA* in a list. When you replace these characters, include the two spaces that normally separate the state from the zip code. Typical entries in your mailing list file would then look like this:

&90027
&90004
%94107
&90049
%94114

When you're finished typing the list, use find and replace to find the character and replace it with the appropriate city and state.

Finally, say you've written a book that takes place in Albuquerque, and the main character's name is Fanny. Your publisher likes the book, but insists that the story take place in Abilene and that Fanny should be Frieda. Instead of missing all those royalties, movie rights, and spin-offs, and *definitely* instead of retyping, just use find and replace!

Dear Reader: another long chapter! I haven't exhausted all the possibilities of using find or find and replace. You'll see find again in the next chapter. But give yourself another break before you continue.

Keyboard Macros and Other Shortcuts

In this chapter you will learn the following new commands:

Opening Menu and File Command

      ESC   Shorthand menu

Opening Menu Command

      L   Change the current drive or directory

File Commands

  ESC ^J   Display help for shorthand

  ESC ?   Display the shorthand definitions screen

  ESC !   Insert the current time

  ^K0–9   Set a place marker

  ^Q0–9   Cursor to a place marker

  ^QQ   Repeat the next command or keystroke

  ^QW   Scroll continuously up

  ^QZ   Scroll continuously down

Other Features

  0–9   Change the repetition speed for **^QQ**

  ^P   Prefix for all commands in macros

WordStar has many features that save you time and work. For example, there are ways to move the cursor quickly through a file, there's the **^R** command to repeat a file name or find string, and there's find and replace to help you avoid retyping. Now you'll learn how WordStar can help you type!

In my own sneaky way, I've already introduced the subject of this chapter—WordStar's *shorthand* feature. Remember **ESC P, ESC C, ESC T,** and **ESC @?** Now you'll learn what they mean. I'll also show you other useful word processing shortcuts, such as the repeat command and place markers.

> ### DO WARM-UP

Introducing Macros

Say you work for The Society for the Prevention of Cruelty to Cats. Think about how many times you type that name in a day—boring! And how often do you type your *own* name? Instead of doing all that work yourself, let WordStar do it! Maybe you also find that you press the same commands over and over in a certain order. WordStar can help you issue them, too. Remember Alfieri's motto: saving keystrokes means saving work.

What I'm talking about here is using macros. A *macro* is simply a collection of many keystrokes that you can issue with a few keystrokes—usually two. For instance, you can have a macro that inserts many dot commands, all with two keystrokes. A macro can contain text, commands, or a combination of both.

How does WordStar do it? It *stores* the macro instructions in a special file, WSSHORT.OVR, or in another file that you specify (Chapter 27). When you load WordStar, you're also loading this file into memory, so your macros are always ready when you need them. You can also have temporary macros for the current work session only. These macros don't become part of the WSSHORT.OVR file. You can add, delete, or change macros at any time and save your changes back to WSSHORT.OVR.

The Shorthand Key

Although I prefer the term *macro,* WordStar uses the word *shorthand* to refer to its keystroke-saving feature and to remind you about what it does. You've seen all along that the **ESC** key provides certain shortcuts in your work, such as repeating the last file name. You use the **ESC** key to issue macros, too. You can create as many as 36 different macros, one for each letter of the alphabet and the digits 0 through 9. In addition, WordStar provides five useful macros that work with certain other key combinations.

To investigate macros, first start a new file (later you'll learn some macros that work at the Opening menu, too).

Press   **D** [open a document]

Type   `mactest`

Press   **RETURN**

Type   `y`

because this is a new file.

Here's how to set up a shorthand macro.

Press   **ESC**

In a second or two, the Shorthand menu appears.

The Predefined and Sample Macros

The Shorthand menu displays the five special, predefined macros: **ESC =**, **ESC ?**, **ESC #**, **ESC @**, and **ESC !**. You've already used one of these, **ESC @**, to insert the current date. This chapter discusses the **ESC !** macro. Chapter 18, which introduces math features, covers the other three. You cannot edit or change these special macros, except to change the format of what they type (Chapter 27).

Below the Shorthand menu is a list of predefined sample macros. In other chapters you learned about three of the predefined macros: **ESC P** to position the cursor at the beginning of the paragraph, **ESC C** to center a line (**^OC**), and **ESC T** to transpose one word with the next. Notice that each one has a *description,* such as `Previous Paragraph`, to remind you about what the macro does. You can delete or change these sample macros if you wish. **Caution:** If you change the **ESC C**, **ESC P**, or **ESC T** macros, some of the examples in previous chapters won't work! Wait until you're finished studying the entire book before changing these keys. Thanks!

Getting Help

With the Shorthand menu on the screen you can press **^J** (**F1**) to see help about the shorthand feature. Press **ESC** after you've finished reading the help screen. There's more help coming momentarily.

Adding a Macro Definition

 As your first example you'll create a new macro that types your name. You'll assign it to the **N** key to remind you that it stands for "name." **Tip:** Whenever possible, use *mnemonics* in your macro definitions. After all, assigning your name to the **Q** key doesn't make sense, unless of course your name begins with a *Q!* Mnemonics help jog your memory!

As the Shorthand menu suggests, to display and/or change definitions, do this:

Type   ?

Another version of the Shorthand menu appears. This time you see more help with setting up macros. You also see the five predefined macros. Below each are the actual keystrokes the macros perform. WordStar is asking you:

Character to be defined?

WordStar wants to know the letter or digit you want to assign a macro to, which means defining a new macro or changing an existing macro (you'll do that later).

Type   n

(you don't have to use uppercase).

(Once you start defining a macro, you can cancel by pressing ^U (**F2**) twice, once to cancel the definition, and then again to leave the shorthand menu.)

WordStar now asks:

Description for Esc menu?

This means the name you'll give the macro to remind you about what it does. Type the label exactly as you want it to appear when WordStar shows it below the Shorthand menu.

Type   My Name

(use upper and lowercase as you wish).

Press   **RETURN**

Finally, WordStar asks for the

Definition?

This means the actual keystrokes the macro is to perform.

Type   <your first and last names>

(make sure you type the space between the two names).
      If you make a mistake, just press **BACKSPACE (^H)** and continue. When you're finished,

Press   **RETURN**

WordStar displays your new macro in the list along with its description and keystrokes.

Saving the Macro Definitions

You could continue adding other macros, but for the time being assume you're finished.

Press   **RETURN**

WordStar asks:

Store changes onto disk (Y/N)?

If you type n, your new macro is only good for the current work session until you exit WordStar. You want to save the new macro, along with the others, into the WSSHORT.OVR file.

Type   y

WordStar updates the shorthand file and returns you to the text area.
      Tip: You can create macros "on the fly" for the current work session without bothering to save them. Suppose today you're typing a long name repeatedly in a file, so you set up a shorthand for it. In the future you won't need this shorthand, so when you exit WordStar today you can forget about it. Later I'll describe other tips on customizing WordStar for your own needs.

Using a Macro

Whenever you want to insert your name in a file, do this instead of typing it:

Press   **ESC N**

(you don't have to use uppercase).
      Voilà! Press **RETURN** once or twice in preparation for the next macro.

Changing a Macro Definition

Oops! You decide that the **N** macro should also type out your middle initial, so you'll have to edit the definition.

Press   **ESC**

Type   ?

Find the definition in the list if you've forgotten which one you want to change. If you can't see all definitions, use ^Z and ^W to scroll through the list. Then:

Type   n

to change the current definition for N.
      Now for a nifty feature.

Press   **^R**

to *repeat* the previous description.

Press   **RETURN**

Press   **^R**

to *repeat* the previous definition.
      Once you've repeated the previous definition, just use any cursor movement and editing key to make your changes. For example:

Press   **^F or ^RIGHT ARROW**

to position the cursor at the beginning of your last name.

Type   ⟨your middle initial including the period⟩

Press   **SPACEBAR**

for correct spacing between the middle initial and last name.

Press   **RETURN** twice

to complete the definition and leave the Shorthand menu.

Type   y

to save the changes to the disk.

Press   **ESC N**

to test the macro.

Using Commands in Macros

This next macro combines text and WordStar commands. The macro definition must include *all* keystrokes you want the macro to issue in the *exact* order. **Caution:** Don't add any superfluous characters, such as spaces, in a macro definition. Suppose you often type *and underline* the phrase *ad nauseam*. Here's how to set it up in a macro. Use the **A** key to hold the macro.

Press   **ESC**

Type   ?

Type   a

Type   Ad

Press   **RETURN**

for the description.
    As the menu notes, to issue a standard WordStar control-key command you press **^P** *before* the CTRL (^) keystroke:

Press   **^P^P**

Type   s

to begin underlining.

    You don't have to issue a **^P** before the *second* part of a two-letter command. **Caution:** Don't use the function key equivalents of the commands. Use the actual commands, but remember to press **^P** first.

Type   ad nauseam

Press   **^P^P**

Type   s

to end underlining.

The entire definition now looks like this on the screen:

^Psad nauseam^Ps

Notice that no spaces separate the underline commands from the text. Even though the definition looks weird, it'll work correctly, just as if you had entered the keystrokes yourself from the keyboard.

Press   **RETURN** twice

Type   n

This time you won't save the new macro to disk because it's just for illustration's sake. You'll delete it in a moment. Go ahead! Press **ESC A** to see your new macro.

Note: You can also set up two-letter commands by pressing **^P** before each letter, but make sure you also press the **CTRL** key with the letter. That is, you could have set up **^PS** in the previous macro by pressing these keys: **^P^P^P^S.** WordStar would have displayed the command as ^P^S on the screen. To enter a **TAB** in a macro, press **^P^I.** The macro definition showing on the screen should thus look like the *keystrokes* you would normally be entering yourself.

Using the RETURN Key in a Macro

Take a look at the sample macro for **S.** It types the ending of a letter, that is, the phrase *Sincerely,* and then inserts three carriage returns for spacing. To include a hard return in your macro definition, press **^P^M** (or **^P RE-TURN**) for each hard return. You'll only see an ^M on the screen. In a moment I'll show you how to insert other keys in macros.

Deleting a Macro Definition

To remove a macro definition, merely pretend you're changing the definition but replace its description and definition with nothing. Here's how:

Press   **ESC**

Type   ?

Type   a

Press   **RETURN**

to "blank out" the description.

Press   **RETURN**

to blank out the definition.

Press   **RETURN**

Type   n

to finish.

    If you had saved the macro and then wanted to delete it from the disk, you would have typed **y** to save your changes after deleting the macro from the Shorthand menu. You can also *temporarily* delete a macro by not saving the changes to disk. The next time you load WordStar, the macro will reappear.

Aha!

Now take a look at the predefined macro for **T** that transposes a word. How does it work? It merely deletes the word (^T), then positions the cursor at the beginning of the next word (^F), and finally unerases the word (^U). It's as simple as that!

    The **P** macro is a bit more complicated. Can you figure it out? The **^QH** part is easy: it tells WordStar to move the cursor backwards to the first carriage return (^M) it finds, which presumably ends the previous paragraph, and then to position the cursor at the beginning of the next paragraph with ^F. But why did the WordStar people include the ^A? Simple: They assumed that you would have pressed **RETURN** to end the current paragraph, so ^A just moves the cursor back in front of that return before looking for the previous one. Sneaky!

Limitations

A shorthand definition can only be at most 50 characters long. That includes text and WordStar commands. You'll note that you can't type past the right side of the Shorthand menu box when you define a macro. WordStar will cut off any superfluous characters in the shorthand definition, that is, characters past the limit of 50.

    You may have also noticed that when you create or change a macro definition, WordStar shows the number of bytes available to you. Every character, including a command, takes up one byte of storage. By default, WordStar sets aside a total of 512 bytes for the shorthand definitions. However, this total includes the bytes required to store the *names and descriptions,* too.

    That means that the **C** macro requires extra bytes of storage for the name (**C**) and the description (*Center*), as well as for the actual keystrokes (^OC). Although a macro can be as long as 50 characters, use as short a descriptive label as possible to allow more room for definitions. You can change the default size of the shorthand feature or the name of the shorthand file with the WSCHANGE program (Chapter 27).

Tip: You can have even more macro definitions if you avoid using any descriptions at all. One way to have your cake and eat it, too—that is, to have as many macros as possible *and* keep track of what they do—is to maintain a crib sheet of macro definitions. Don't type in a description on the shorthand definitions screen when you create a new macro. Instead, set up a separate file with this information, print the file, and keep this printout near your computer. Eventually, you'll know instinctively what your macros do anyway.

Some Useful Macros

Throughout the rest of this book I'll suggest some nifty macros, but even now I bet you've already started to think about the ones you want to set up. Below are a few typical macros and some other useful pointers.

Tip: Before you create a new macro, to avoid missing a step when defining a macro jot down the steps you want to include in the macro definition. Do a "dry run" of the steps if necessary. For example, you want to set up a macro that inserts certain dot commands in a file. Jot down the exact sequence of keystrokes you'll need or issue the keystrokes in any file, or try the steps by hand. Write ^M each time you have to press the **RETURN** key. Use **^KQ** to abandon the file when you're finished.

Press   **^KQ**

Type   y

to quit without saving the MACTEST file.

A Macro to Change the Drive or Directory

Although you'll use macros most often within a file, you can have macros that work at the Opening menu. Again, you press the **ESC** key to define or issue a macro. If you have a hard disk and you've set up several subdirectories to store your work, you can have a macro change directories for you quickly. A similar macro could switch between disk drives.

The next example is another one of my sneaky introductions to a new command! From the Opening menu, the **L** command changes drives or directories. Suppose you have a subdirectory called LETTERS under the WS4 directory that contains all your letter files. When you start with WordStar, the default directory is WS4. Here's a macro called **ESC L** to change to the LETTERS directory.

Press   **ESC**

Type   ?

Type   l

(that's a lowercase *L*).

Type   `Chng Sub`

Press   **RETURN**

for the description.

Type   `lletters`

(that's two *L's*).
    You can substitute another subdirectory name for LETTERS.

Press   **^P^M**

for a hard return.
    The entire definition looks like this on the screen:

`lletters^M`

Press   **RETURN** twice

Type   y

to store your changes to disk.
    See Chapter 12 for more information about directories: how to create them, use them, and remove them.

A Macro to Type Dot Commands

To experiment with the new few macros, open a new file again called MAC-TEST before you continue to the next example. Perhaps you don't want to bother yourself with creating format files. Instead, you want to set up a macro that inserts the dot commands you'll need. Here are the dot commands:

```
.MT 6
.MB 6
.PO 13
.OJ OFF
.OP
```

As usual, press **ESC** and type **?** to define the macro. Assign it a letter and, if you wish, a description. Here's how the entire definition line would look when you're finished:

```
.MT 6^M.MB 6^M.PO 13^M.OJ OFF^M.OP^M
```

Go ahead, try creating this macro! Make sure you press **^P^M** for each hard return. Then see if the macro works correctly. If it doesn't, edit it until it does!

A Macro to Insert a Boilerplate

Suppose you *do* like format files and you've set up a file called FORMAT with the same dot commands listed in the previous example. Whenever you start a new file with this format, you want to have a macro call up the format file boilerplate into your document. Additionally, the macro then positions the cursor at the end of the file, that is, directly after the dot commands you've just inserted.

Once again, press **ESC** and type **?** to define the macro. Give it a letter and, if you wish, a description. Here's how the entire definition line would look when you're finished:

```
^Krformat^M^Qc
```

Can you figure this macro out?

A Macro to Enter a Log

Together with the @ macro, the ! macro is useful for keeping a *log* of your activity. The ! macro inserts the current time into a file, provided you entered the time when you started today. The default time format shows the hour in standard 12-hour notation, followed by a colon and a two-digit minute, followed by AM or PM (example: *9:32 PM*).

But what if you want to have WordStar enter your log like this?

```
Date: <today's date>
Time: <current time>
```

Well, you can set up a macro that calls other macros. Use **D** for "date and time." First, press **ESC** and type ? to define the macro. Use **D** for the assignment letter and type in a description, if you wish. When you get to the definition line, follow these steps:

Type   **Date:**

Press   **SPACEBAR**

Press   **^P ESC**

Note: Don't hold down the CTRL key when you press the ESC key. When you insert the ESC key in a macro, WordStar shows it as **^[**. If you don't see **^[** right now, you didn't do it correctly.

Type   **@**

for the date macro.

Press   **^P^M**

to insert a hard return.

Type   **Time:**

Press   **SPACEBAR**

Press   **^P ESC**

Type   **!**

for the time macro.

Press   **^P^M**

for another return.

The entire definition looks like this on the screen:

```
Date: ^[@^MTime: ^[!^M
```

Press   **RETURN** twice

Type   y

to save the definition.

Press   **ESC D**

to check your results.

Keep in mind that **^M** inserts whatever number of returns are set with the line spacing command. **Question:** If you always wanted just one return between lines, how would you define the macro? *Answer:* Instead of inserting **^M** in the macro, issue a **^N** to add a blank line and then a **^X** to move the cursor down. Remember you would press **^P^N** and **^P^X** for these commands, respectively. The complete definition would then look like this on the screen:
Date: ^[@^N^XTime: ^[!^N^X.

Tip: You can change the way WordStar displays the date and time (Chapter 27).

Chaining Macros

Dear Reader: you just set up a *macro chain!* That is, one macro called two others. There are many ways to chain macros together. For example, you may have several different macros that insert different boilerplates into a file. You could have another macro that calls the others when you want to insert *all* the boilerplates quickly.

Recursive (Repeating) Macros

A macro can even call itself! In the computer world, the term for this phenomenon is *recursion.* Suppose you want a macro that repeatedly deletes a line. (There's another way to do this in WordStar, but just bear with me.) The macro, assigned to **Y**, issues the **^Y** command to delete a line and then calls itself to delete the next line, and so on.

Once again press **ESC** and type ? to define the macro. Assign it to **Y** and give it a description, if you wish. When you get to the definition line, follow these steps:

Press   **^P^Y**

Press   **^P ESC**

Type   y

The entire definition looks like this:

^Y^[y

Press **RETURN** twice and type y to store the changes to disk. **Caution:** Read the next instructions carefully! To test this macro, go to the top of the MACTEST file and press **ESC Y.** Or, better yet, exit the MACTEST file with **^KQ,** open any long file, and press **ESC Y.**

What happens is known as an *endless loop* in computer terminology. WordStar would continue to issue the macro endlessly until it reaches the end of the file or you cancel the macro. To stop a recursive macro, press **^U (F2).**

Caution: Because you've deleted text that you want to keep, don't forget to abandon the edit with **^KQ** when you're finished testing this most dangerous of macros! That is:

Press   **^KQ**

Type   y

to abandon the edit.

A Macro to Delete Print Codes

The next macro definition deletes all underline codes from a file. Substitute another print code for **^PS** if you wish. The macro uses the various find and replace options. Here's how the entire definition looks on the Shorthand menu when it's finished:

^Qa^P^S^M^Mgn^M

Make sure you understand the definition and how to set it up.

A Macro to Block a Paragraph

Finally, here's a macro that blocks out the paragraph where the cursor is in preparation for whatever else you want to do: copy, move, or delete. The cursor can be anywhere in the paragraph. The macro works with paragraphs that begin with one tab and end with *one* hard return. You can customize the macro to work with other types of paragraphs.

I assume you have a file—any file (such as STORY.LA)—open and that the cursor is in the middle of any paragraph. Then, press **ESC** and type ? to define the macro. Assign it to a letter and give it a description, if you wish. When you get to the definition line, follow these steps:

Press   **^P ESC**

Type   p

to position the cursor at the beginning of the paragraph.

Press   ^P^Q

Type   s

to position the cursor at the left margin.

Press   ^P^K

Type   b

to begin the block.

Press   ^P^Q

Type   g

Press   ^P^M

to position the cursor past the next return.

Press   ^P^K

Type   k to end the block.

The entire definition looks like this:

```
^[p^Qs^Kb^Qg^M^Kk.
```

Try it! Then abandon the edit by pressing ^KQ and typing y. Make sure you're at the Opening menu before you continue.

Use Boilerplates for Lengthy Text "Macros"

When you have lengthy sections of text that you want to copy repeatedly, it's a good idea to set these up in boilerplates instead of using a shorthand key. That way, you can have more macros for other frequent keystroke combinations. Recall that the limit to a shorthand macro is 50 characters. Setting up boilerplate files is thus a way to maintain *glossaries* of frequently used text.

Tip: *Modularity* is the key. Divide your boilerplate text into the least significant unit to make working with boilerplates more efficient. That is, decide how you want to use your boilerplates, then save each in its own separate file. Make sure of the spacing, such as blank lines, that you want to include in the boilerplate, too. Use the ^KR command to read the file whenever you need the text, or create a macro to read in the file. See Chapter 16 for other boilerplate tips.

A Prelude to Coming Attractions

I've already mentioned scores of times that you can change most of WordStar's default settings to reflect the way you want to work. That's the subject of Chapter 27, but now that you've learned about macros, pause and consider ways to customize WordStar efficiently.

You'll probably want to set up the function keys to perform the WordStar commands you use the most. That way, you cut down on a lot of keystrokes. And you'll have shorthand setups for typing short lines of text, or for temporary macros. Finally, use boilerplate files for inserting long sections of text.

Place Markers

You're moving right along! The rest of the chapter covers new commands that also provide helpful shortcuts. Sometimes you'll want to *mark* the location of a specific text in a file so that you can return the cursor to it quickly. Of course, you could use the find command, but what if the section contains words that occur elsewhere in the file? It would take find a while to locate the section you want each time you were looking for it.

Instead, use any of 10 place markers. A *place marker* is a temporary stamp that stays in the file during the current editing session only, although there is a way to save a *pseudomarker* with the file. Once you set a place marker you can move the cursor to it quickly, no matter where the cursor is in the file. That is, WordStar moves the cursor forwards or backwards depending on where the marker is.

Press   **D** [open a document]

Type   contract

Press   **RETURN**

Suppose you later want to refer to how much Red is paying Wolfe per hour (your memory for figures is bad!), so you'll mark the location of this amount. Fortunately, *I* remember how much it is. First, get there quickly:

Press   ^QF or ^F1

Type   12

Press   **ESC**

to bypass the find options.

Setting a Place Marker

You can use any of the nine numeric keys (1–9) at the top of the keyboard and the zero key (0) for place markers. You don't have to set markers in any numerical order, but you *do* have to be a little careful. The command to set a place marker is ^K followed by the number, but do *not* hold down the CTRL key after you've pressed ^K.

So, to set place marker 1 here:

Press   ^K

and release the CTRL key.

Type   1

A 1 appears. It may display with highlighting, in reverse video, or in a different color, depending on your monitor. Notice that the marker is between the dollar sign and the 1. The marker doesn't change the printout, but it may make the line extend past the right margin on the screen. In previous versions of WordStar the marker was enclosed in angle brackets, like this: <1>.

To set another place marker with the same number elsewhere, position the cursor at the new location and repeat the steps. To remove a place marker from the screen, make sure the cursor is at the marker, press ^K, and type the appropriate number. To hide a place marker temporarily, press ^KH (**SHIFT F6**). Then press ^KH again to unhide it. If you have a hidden block in the file, when you press ^KH WordStar unhides both the block and any hidden place markers.

Moving to a Place Marker

Just as you set a place marker with ^K, to move the cursor to a place marker use ^Q plus the number of the marker. Again, don't hold down the CTRL key after you've pressed ^Q. First, position the cursor at the end of the file to learn about this command:

Press   ^QC or ^END

Now, to move to the marker:

Press ^Q

and release the CTRL key.

Type 1

(On some computers, the keystroke sequence ^1 inserts a foreign language character. If you see something funny on the screen and if WordStar didn't move the cursor to the place marker, delete the superfluous character and try again!)
If you attempt to move to a place marker that you haven't identified, WordStar gives you this message:

`Cannot move to a marker that has not yet been defined.`

`Press Esc to continue.`

You can move the cursor to a hidden place marker, but WordStar won't unhide the marker until you press ^KH (**SHIFT F6**).

Saving Place Markers

Although place markers disappear when you save the file and return to the Opening menu with ^KD—not, by the way, when you save the file and continue working with ^KS—you can use an easy trick to save pseudomarkers with the file. For instance, use a savable place marker as a *bookmark* to show where you left off the last time, if that location isn't the end of the file.
For each pseudomarker that you want to save, just go to the place in your file that you want to mark and type an unusual string of characters, such as ## or ??. Then, the next time you open the file, use the find command to find these characters. Remember to delete these markers before you print the file.

The Repeat Command

Another shortcut and work saver is the repeat command, ^QQ. This command repeats the next *single* keystroke, whether it be another command or a character. To stop the repetition, press any alpha or arrow key or ^U (**F2**). I use the **SPACEBAR** because it's the easiest to press. You can even adjust the speed at which the repetition occurs, but be careful how you issue the command.

Continuous Scrolling

Probably the most helpful way to use the repeat command is to scroll continuously through a file to view it leisurely. The cursor should be at the place marker from the last example.

Press   **^QQC** or **^QQ PG DN**

Careful! Make sure you're still holding down the CTRL key when you press the **C.** Otherwise, WordStar starts inserting a string of *c's* into the file! If you issued the command correctly, WordStar scrolls the file down by screen.

Press   **SPACEBAR** or any other alpha or arrow key

to stop.

Press   **^QQR** or **^QQ PG UP**

to scroll continuously up by screen.

Press   **SPACEBAR** or any other alpha or arrow key

to stop.
To scroll continuously by line, you *could* use **^QQW** or **^QQZ,** as you might expect. However, shortcuts to these commands are **^QW** and **^QZ,** respectively. Go ahead, try them! When you're finished,

Press   **^QR** or **^HOME**

to position the cursor at the beginning of the file.

Changing the Repetition Speed

After you issue the repeat command, you can vary the speed at which it works by pressing one of the number keys at the top of the keyboard. Zero (0) is fastest, 9 is slowest. The default speed is 3, 4, or 5, but I haven't been able to pin MicroPro down on this one! In any case, try these instructions:

Press   **^QZ**

to begin continuous scrolling down.

Type   **9**

to slow it down.

Press   **SPACEBAR** or any other alpha or arrow key

to stop.

Press   **^QC or ^END**

to position the cursor at the end of the file.

Press   **^QW**

to begin continuous scrolling up.
       Notice that WordStar "remembers" the last speed and uses it.

Type   5

to speed it up a bit.

Type   0

to speed it up a lot!

Type   3

to slow it down a bit.

Press   **SPACEBAR** or any other alpha or arrow key

to stop.

Press   **^QC or ^END**

to position the cursor at the end of the file.

Repeating Text

If you press **^QQ** and then release the CTRL key, WordStar will repeat the next character you type until you stop the repeat command. Suppose you want a string of hyphens. Make sure the cursor is on a blank line before continuing.

Press   **^QQ**

and release the CTRL key.

Type   -

(that's a hyphen).

You can vary the speed, too. When you have enough hyphens, press any alpha or number key to stop. Because you don't want to save this edited file:

Press   **^KQ**

Type   y

to quit without saving the file.

A *^QQ Miscellany*

What do you think **^QQB** does? Right! It realigns the file from the cursor location. It's essentially the same as **^QU**. The only difference between **^QQB** and **^QU** is that you must press **^U (F2)** to cancel the latter command.

Now for something totally bizarre! If you press **^QQU,** what will happen? No, you *won't* cancel the **^QQ** command. Instead, WordStar starts repeating the last deleted text, that is, whatever is in the unerase buffer! Hey, that might be an easy way to repeat text: just delete it once and use **^QQU** to restore it as many times as you want. Chapter 21 shows you a nifty way to use this feature when you set up forms.

Tip: Earlier in the chapter, you created a superfast, repeating macro to delete lines. Another way to delete many lines at once, but one that works at *your* speed, is to issue the command **^QQY.** Make sure you position the cursor on the *first* line you want to delete. After issuing the command, vary the speed if it's too fast or slow. Be ready to press the **SPACEBAR** when WordStar reaches the last line you want to delete.

To cancel the **^QQ** command before you press another key or command, press **ESC** *twice.*

Dear Reader: I'll make it "short" and sweet. Use the shortcuts you've learned in this chapter to save yourself work. Enough said!

Chapter 8

Watch Your Words!

In this chapter you will learn the following new commands:

Opening Menu Command

N	Open a nondocument

File Commands

^OE	Enter a soft hyphen from the keyboard
^OH	Turn hyphen help on/off
^QL (SHIFT F3)	Check the spelling of the rest of the file
^QN (SHIFT F4)	Check the spelling of the word at the cursor
^QO	Check the spelling of the next word you type

Other Features

A, B, E, G, I, M, T	CorrectStar options
ALT 1	Look up the word at the cursor in the Word Finder thesaurus
^P SHIFT ^-	Find or find and replace code for a soft hyphen at end of the line
^P SHIFT ^6	Find or find and replace code for a soft hyphen in middle of the line

Even if you don't have a way with words, WordStar can help you. This chapter introduces *CorrectStar,* WordStar's built-in spelling program that checks your files for misspellings and typographical errors. Later in the chapter, you'll also learn how WordStar's hyphenation feature works. As a bonus, I'm throwing in—free of charge—a discussion of the Word Finder thesaurus. Such a deal!

DO WARM-UP

How CorrectStar Works

With a short file on the screen, you can easily see your mistakes. But that's unrealistic! With longer files, you won't be able to see everything at once, and even if you scroll through the file your eye can overlook misspellings. CorrectStar checks your files for possible mistakes. Note the word *possible*. Like everything else in this world, computers are not perfect, and spelling checkers aren't either.

CorrectStar has a dictionary of many common—and not so common—English words. When you ask the program to check the spelling in a file, it matches each word in the file against the words in its dictionary. If it finds an *exact match,* it considers the word correct. (It will disregard upper- and lowercase, by the way.) If not, it stops and shows you the "offending" word in context and even suggests possible corrections.

There are two limitations to all spelling checkers like CorrectStar. First, they can't possibly have all words in their dictionaries. Sometimes, a word *is* correct, but the program can't find it so it flags it as an "error." *You,* as the captain of your fate, must make the final decision about the correctness of a word. The other limitation is that CorrectStar can't read a word for its meaning in the file. For example, if you typed *from* instead of *form,* CorrectStar won't flag either of these words, because they're both spelled correctly.

When I first started using CorrectStar, it stopped at *Alfieri.* Of course, *I* know that it's a correctly spelled name, but the program didn't. It would be a hassle if CorrectStar stopped every time it came to your name, so you can customize the dictionary by adding your own specialized words to it.

Actually, CorrectStar works with *three* dictionaries at once. There's the *internal* dictionary, in the file INTERNAL.DCT. It contains the most common English words. CorrectStar checks this dictionary first. The *main* dictionary, MAIN.DCT, contains all others. The *personal* dictionary, PERSONAL.DCT, stores the words you instruct CorrectStar to add. When you first begin using CorrectStar, the personal dictionary is empty except for one entry: the word *WordStar!* I'll refer to all three dictionaries collectively as "the dictionary."

 Tips: Every so often, make a copy of the PERSONAL.DCT file as a backup so you don't lose those "personal" words if something happens to the master file. If you have enough system memory, you might be able to load the entire MAIN.DCT file into memory to make CorrectStar *fly* (Chapter 27).

If *there, their,* and *they're,* or *its* and *it's,* confuse you, CorrectStar can't help you—it doesn't correct your grammar. It can, however, suggest possible sound-alike words to jog your memory. CorrectStar also flags a word containing a digit (such as *thi9s*). CorrectStar can check an individual word, part of a file, or an entire file. You can even check a word that isn't in the file! When it flags a word, CorrectStar gives you a variety of options:

- You can *ignore* the word if its spelling is correct.

- You can *enter* the correction manually.

- You can have CorrectStar *bypass* the word once or *ignore* the word throughout the rest of the file.

- You can *substitute* with one of the alternates that CorrectStar supplies for an incorrect spelling or ask CorrectStar to show more alternates.

- You can *add* the word to your personal dictionary so that CorrectStar doesn't stop at the word again.

CorrectStar automatically realigns a paragraph when you correct a word. You have the option to turn this feature off if you wish.

Checking a File

There are different commands for checking a file or a word. They're all part of the "quick" prefix, **^Q.** The first command you'll learn, and the one you'll probably use the most, is **^QL (SHIFT F3)** to check the rest of the file. You must open the file before you can check its spelling.

Press   **D** [open a document]

Type   contract

Press   **RETURN**

Checking the Entire File

The command **^QL (SHIFT F3)** checks the *rest* of the file starting at the cursor location. To check an entire file, position the cursor at the beginning of the file first (it should be there now). CorrectStar can only work forward through a file.

Checking Part of a File

To check part of a file, position the cursor where you want CorrectStar to begin. Suppose you want to check only pages 3 through 10 of a large file. Go to the top of page 3 with ^QI (^F4) and start CorrectStar. When CorrectStar finishes checking page 10, press ^U (F2) to cancel. Of course, you can cancel the spelling check at any other time, too.

Tip: WordStar "remembers" the cursor position when you begin spell checking a file. To return to where you left off after the spelling check, press ^QP.

Time to Begin

Start checking this file:

Press   **^QL or SHIFT F3**

If you have a dual-floppy system, WordStar tells you:

```
Please replace WordStar program diskette with dictionary diskette.

Press Esc to continue.
```

Remove the WordStar program disk from the A drive and insert the dictionary disk. Close the drive door and press **ESC.** If you have a hard disk, the dictionary should already be in the WordStar directory, WS4, so CorrectStar begins immediately. If you insert the wrong disk or if for any reason WordStar can't find the dictionary, you see this message:

```
Cannot find B:\INTERNAL.DCT

Press Esc to continue.
```

(The drive letter may be different.)

On a dual-floppy system, you have to remove the WordStar program disk to replace it with the dictionary disk. If you were printing a file in the background and then tried to start a spelling check, WordStar couldn't continue printing because it needs the program disk for its printing instructions. It would tell you this:

```
Spell checking temporarily disabled. Cannot change diskettes while
background printing is in progress.

Press Esc to continue.
```

Press **ESC** and wait until you finish printing before running the spelling check.

 Note: If you continue to have problems getting CorrectStar to work correctly, check the way you installed WordStar. If you have a hard disk, perhaps you didn't specify the correct subdirectory. If you have a dual-floppy system, you must tell WordStar that it's to swap disks. See the Introduction for more help.

Bypassing a Correct Word

If all systems are go, CorrectStar begins scanning the file and tells you:

```
Checking spelling..

^U to quit.
```

Unless you made a typing mistake before the "word" *18th,* the *th* is the first unknown word, so CorrectStar stops there. It also presents the Spelling Check menu, which shows these options:

```
I ignore, check next word      E enter correction              ^U quit
A add to personal dictionary   T turn auto-align off
B bypass this time only        G global replacement is off
```

Additionally, CorrectStar is checking the dictionary to see if it can find sound-alike words. (Dear Reader: Don't ask me how it does it, but it really *can* sound out a word!) This is CorrectStar's "guessing game." If it finds any sound-alikes or what it considers possible corrections, it displays them. It doesn't find any for *th,* so it tells you None. (It bypasses the *18* and looks up *th.*)

Because you know that this "word" is correct, and you don't want to add it to your personal dictionary, you have three options:

- Press **I** [ignore, check next word] to bypass this and all further occurrences of the word in the file. This is usually the option you'd want.

- Press **B** [bypass this time only] to ignore the word, but if it occurs again CorrectStar will flag it. Don't use this option unless you really want to.

■ Press **G** [global replacement is off] to turn global replacement on. Later you'll learn more about this option.

Because you want to bypass the word for the rest of the file (it does occur again), do this:

Press   **I** [ignore, check next word]

CorrectStar continues checking. Again, unless you've made a mistake, it next stops at *Janet.*

(An aside: Did you notice that CorrectStar doesn't check dot command lines? Also, how did it handle the title? It bypassed it because it "saw" spaces between the letters. To CorrectStar this was not just one word, but many single-letter words. By default, CorrectStar doesn't check single-letter words.)

Adding a Word to the Dictionary

Dear Reader: If your name is Janet, you're in luck! If not, follow along anyway. CorrectStar presents alternate spellings for what it considers an incorrect word:

```
   Word: "Janet"
Suggestions: 1 Jennet  2 Jaunt  3 Joint  4 Gannet  5 Genet  6 Giant
```

(Another aside: Why CorrectStar would "know" *Gannet* and *Genet,* two highly uncommon words, but not know *Janet* is beyond me!)

Notice that CorrectStar honors the *case* of the word, so it would replace *Janet* with the correct word and initial cap here. If the word were incorrect, you could type the *number* next to the correction. Instead, if your name is Janet and *if the word is correctly spelled already,* you would:

Press   **A** [add to personal dictionary]

If your name is *not* Janet,

Press   **I** [ignore, check next word]

 Tip: If a word is correctly spelled, you can speed CorrectStar up by immediately pressing **I** [ignore, check next word] *before* it shows you any alternate spellings.

Correcting the Word Yourself

Next, CorrectStar stops at *dba* but doesn't suggest any alternates. For the sake of example, you decide to type in a correction from the keyboard.

Press   **E** [enter correction]

CorrectStar says:

```
    Word: dba
Replace with:
```

Normally, you'd type the word, but *make sure it's correct and in the correct case!* Use the editing keys to correct any mistakes. Then press **RETURN.** CorrectStar checks your correction. If it still doesn't find the word in the dictionary, it stops and waits for you to accept the word. Provided the word you entered is typed correctly, you'd press **I** [ignore, check next word] to continue.

Tip: If most of the word is correct, why retype the entire word should you have to edit it? Just press **^R** to insert the word on the edit line and use any cursor movement and editing keys to make your corrections.

In this example, however, just do this:

Press   **^U** or **F2**

to cancel the edit.

Press   **I** [ignore, check next word]

to continue.

Seeing More Alternates

As a bit of comic relief, CorrectStar flags *WOLFE* and suggests either *WOLF* or *WELL-OFF* (notice the case). For the time being, however, cancel the spelling check altogether:

Press   **^U** or **F2**

Suppose that you typed *hee* instead of *he*. CorrectStar would flag the error and show you this:

```
    Word: "hee"
Suggestions: 1 hen  2 her  3 hey  4 fee  5 see  6 wee  7 he  8 heel
             M display more suggestions
```

The **M** [display more suggestions] option only appears when there *are* more alternates. If you pressed **M,** this is what you'd see:

```
       Word: "hee"
Suggestions: 1 here  2 thee  3 hi  4 hie  5 ho  6 hoe  7 who  8 hoar
             M display more suggestions
```

Finally, if you pressed **M** again, this appears:

```
       Word: "hee"
Suggestions: 1 hoer  2 hour  3 whore
             M redisplay first suggestions
```

You can cycle through the suggestions again, or press **M** to see the first screen and then type the correct choice, **7**.

Globally Replacing a Word

If a word is correct and just not in CorrectStar's dictionary, you'd press **I** [ignore, check next word] to instruct CorrectStar not to stop at the word again.

If a word is incorrectly spelled, you can choose the correction *and* tell CorrectStar to replace this correct word whenever it finds the incorrect word again in the file. This is useful if you've misspelled, say, a name many times.

When CorrectStar flags at the word, do this *first*:

Press   **G** [global replacement is off]

The Spelling Check menu now says [global replacement is on] . Global replacement uses the *current* word only, so when you've selected or typed in the correction global replacement returns to off for the next word.

Caution: Don't cancel the spelling check if you're using the global replacement option. When you cancel the spelling, CorrectStar stops, *period*. Always check the entire file if you want correct global replacement.

A Note on Paragraph Alignment

Although it's a convenience to have CorrectStar automatically realign paragraphs during a spelling check, there are times when you might not want this to happen. For example, CorrectStar won't *hyphenate* words when it realigns a paragraph. (You'll soon learn about hyphenation.)

So whenever CorrectStar flags a word, you can press **T** [turn auto-align off]. The Spelling Check menu changes to [turn auto-align on] . Unlike the **G** option, the **T** option remains in effect during the session until you change it. You can change the CorrectStar defaults to have auto-align off automatically (Chapter 27).

Try It Again

If you wanted to check this file to the end, press **^QR (^HOME)** to position the cursor at the beginning of the file, then **^QL (SHIFT F3)**. What do you think happens? CorrectStar "remembers" the words you told it to ignore the last time, provided you haven't exited WordStar for the day. It won't stop at the words again. Go ahead, try it if you don't believe me! It's good practice, too.

When you're finished:

Press   **^KD** or **F10**

to save the file and return to the Opening menu.

Checking One Word

Sometimes you're merrily typing away and for some reason you have a mental block—is the word spelled *occurrence* or *occurence?* You can check an individual word, either one that you've already typed or one that you haven't typed yet!

The Word at the Cursor

If you've typed the word already, make sure the cursor is anywhere under the word. If you've *just* typed the word and the cursor is directly *past* the word, that's okay, too (the manual is wrong here, by the way). Floppy disk users: Make sure the dictionary disk is in the A drive. To check the word at the cursor,

Press   **^QN** or **SHIFT F4**

CorrectStar presents the same Spelling Check menu. Use the options exactly as you would if you were checking the file, *with these two exceptions:*

- If you accept one of CorrectStar's alternates by number or enter one yourself by first pressing **E** [enter correction], CorrectStar checks your entry and returns to the file without further ado.

- If you press **I** [ignore, check next word] *or* **B** [bypass this time only], CorrectStar skips the word and checks the next word in the file. You can continue checking individual words. You must press **^U (F2)** to cancel if the word is correctly spelled and you don't want to check the next word.

Tip: Use the ^QN (SHIFT F4) command to check words in dot command lines. Make sure the cursor is under the word you want to check. When you learn about headers, footers, and indexing, you'll understand how useful this is.

The Next Word You Type

The last CorrectStar command is ^QO to check the next word you type. It's like checking a dictionary, but much faster because of CorrectStar's ability to sound out a word. The cursor can be anywhere in the file, but it's handy to have the cursor at the location where you *might* want the word to go. Here's what I mean (floppy disk users: make sure the dictionary disk is in the A drive):

Press   **^QO**

CorrectStar asks:

```
Check the spelling of what word?
```

Type the word and press **RETURN.** This time, CorrectStar presents a modified Spelling Check menu. The **A** [add to personal dictionary] and **T** [turn auto-align off] options work exactly as you'd expect. Here are your other options:

- Press **^U (F2)** to cancel at any time.
- Press **I** [ignore, check next word] to clear the first word and enter another one.
- Press **E** [enter word into text] to insert the word into the file at the cursor location if it's correctly spelled. If not, type the number of the correct alternate.

Dealing with Dictionaries

—You've learned how to add words to your personal dictionary when CorrectStar is working. Your personal dictionary is in a file called PERSONAL.DCT. Suppose you want to check what words are in the PERSONAL.DCT file? Or maybe you want to delete some words that you no longer need. For instance, one of your bosses leaves the firm and you want to remove her name from the dictionary. Perhaps you'd like to add words without running a spelling check. You can easily accomplish all these goals.

PERSONAL.DCT: Your First Nondocument!

Although WordStar won't let you look at or change the INTERNAL.DCT or MAIN.DCT files, you have total control over the PERSONAL.DCT file. That is, you can edit, add, or delete words without using CorrectStar.

The single most important point to remember when you change the personal dictionary yourself is to open the PERSONAL.DCT file as a *nondocument*. **Caution:** Never, I repeat, *never* open this file with the **D** command from the Opening menu! (If you mistakenly open the file as a document, press **^KQ** to quit the file *immediately*.) So here's your first nondocument:

Press   **N** [open a nondocument]

WordStar prompts:

Nondocument to open?

Type   `personal.dct`

or select it from the directory listing.

Press   **RETURN**

Notice that the Edit menu has become the *Nondocument Edit menu* and the status line doesn't show page numbers. Chapter 11 contains information about commands that only work in nondocuments. Unless you're a programmer, probably the only other time you'll work with nondocuments happens when you want to use WordStar's merge printing capability (Chapter 19).

If you've already added a few words to your personal dictionary during a spelling check, the file contains these words, each on a separate line ending with a hard return. Otherwise, your PERSONAL.DCT file will only contain the word *WordStar*. Here are a few entries in my personal dictionary:

```
WordStar
WordStar's
Vincent
Vince
Alfieri
CorrectStar
ctrl
esc
```

To *add* words to the dictionary, press **^QC** (**^END**) to position the cursor at the end of the file. Then type each word you want on its own line, but for heaven's sake make sure the word is correctly spelled! Use upper or lowercase as you wish (CorrectStar honors case differences anyway). Do *not* type any extra spaces after the word, but *do* press **RETURN** at the end of each line. **Note:** Make sure the *last* line in the file ends with a hard return. Otherwise, CorrectStar will skip the word on this line.

Suppose you don't know whether the other two dictionaries already contain the word you want to add. After all, it would make no sense to add a word that is already in the dictionary. To see, press ^QO and type the word to check. (Oh, yes, you can still use CorrectStar in a nondocument file!) If CorrectStar tells you the word is correctly spelled, then you know that you don't have to add it to the personal dictionary.

Tip: If you add any personal names, add the possessive version of those names, too, if you plan to use the possessive in your files. For example, your name is *Constance,* so you add this name to the dictionary. On another line, add *Constance's.* You may also want to add your nickname, such as *Connie.*

To *delete* a word, position the cursor on the line containing the word and press ^Y (F5). To *edit* a word, correct it as you would any other text.

Caution: There's a limit of about *1500* words that you can add to your personal dictionary. Every so often, check the PERSONAL.DCT file and delete any unnecessary words. When you're finished:

Press   ^KD or F10

to save the PERSONAL.DCT file.

Tips: Make a backup copy of the new PERSONAL.DCT file *now* before you forget! Although you don't have to *sort* the words in your personal dictionary to put them in alphabetical order, CorrectStar works a little faster if you do. See the discussion of the DOS SORT command in Chapter 28.

Working with Several Personal Dictionaries

You can have different personal dictionaries, each with a different set of personal words. This is one way to overcome the limit to the size of the PERSONAL.DCT file. What you do is configure WordStar to request the personal dictionary file name when you start the first spelling check for the day. See Chapter 27 for instructions on how to use WSCHANGE to set up WordStar in this fashion.

When you start the first spelling check, WordStar then asks you to supply the personal dictionary name. It suggests the default name (your drive or directory may be different):

```
The default personal dictionary is: C:\WS4\PERSONAL.DCT

Press Esc to use default, or enter personal dictionary file to use.

Personal dictionary?
```

Press **ESC** to accept the PERSONAL.DCT file or type a new name—including drive and directory path—and press **RETURN. Note:** If you press ^U (**F2**) to cancel at this point, WordStar starts the spelling check without a personal dictionary. Just press ^U (**F2**) *again* to cancel for good.

If you have the different personal dictionaries on the same drive or in the same directory, you must give each one a different name. I suggest you name the one you use most often as PERSONAL.DCT. You could also keep different PERSONAL.DCT files, each with the name PERSONAL.DCT, on different drives or in different directories. In either case, you can use only one personal dictionary at a time.

Specialized Dictionaries

It's possible that your work requires the use of jargon or other industry-specific words. You may wish to investigate the different *specialized dictionaries* available from MicroPro International Corporation for WordStar. There are specialized dictionaries for the legal, medical, and business and financial professions. There's also a dictionary with British spellings, such as *favour* instead of *favor.*

The legal, medical, and business dictionaries are *supersets* of the main dictionary. That is, they include all the words in the MAIN.DCT file *plus* a host of specialized words for the profession you choose. Each specialized dictionary contains substitute files for the MAIN.DCT and INTERNAL.DCT files that come with WordStar.

To set up a specialized dictionary, follow the instructions enclosed with the disk to (1) delete the default MAIN.DCT and INTERNAL.DCT files, (2) copy the specialized dictionary files to your working disk or directory, and (3) rename the files to be MAIN.DCT and INTERNAL.DCT. Then whenever you use CorrectStar, it works with the specialized dictionary.

Caution: If you don't have a hard disk or a high-capacity disk drive, you can't use the medical dictionary. It's far too big to fit on a normal floppy disk. What's more, you can't load the entire dictionary into random access memory (RAM).

A Big Hype for Hyphenation

Dear Reader: Do you consider yourself a professional? I hope so! A professional wants to get the best results for his or her efforts. After all, your work reflects on *you!* Don't be a "lah-dee-dah" person, that is, someone who is mainly interested in getting the job done and not how to make that job look its best.

The topic of this section is hyphenating words. A lah-dee-dah type of person might not take the time to learn how to "break" words so that the file, when you print it, looks as professional as possible. Wouldn't you rather take the professional approach? Read on then.

Think for a moment about what is was like in the dark ages of the typewriter. Whenever you reached the end of a line, the bell would ring, reminding you that the end of the line was near. Sometimes you also had to think about hyphenating a long word by splitting it over two lines.

Using a word processing program like WordStar you never have to worry about breaking the lines, because WordStar does that for you. All you have to do is put in a hard return at the end of the paragraph or other short line. You don't have to stop and look up to see where to break a line or fiddle with hyphenating words. So when *do* you hyphenate words? Glad you asked. In a few pages you'll know. But first a little discussion about hyphenation and its relationship to wordwrap.

How WordStar Breaks the Lines

How does WordStar "know" where to break each line when you type text into a file? It's not magic—after all, a computer cannot read. But it *can* distinguish letters and numbers from spaces because everything you type in from the keyboard has a code number. That is why the spaces are so important: they have their own code number. Every time you press the SPACEBAR, you enter the code for a space in the file.

Whenever you type a new word you also separate it from the next word with a space. WordStar normally breaks lines *only* at the spaces and won't extend the line past the right margin setting. That is why it won't split up a word at the end of a line. If the word is too long to fit in the present line, WordStar brings it down in its entirety to begin a new line.

A computer can only follow its instructions to the letter and will *never* break them on its own initiative. Computers are very much different from human beings in this respect, because a computer doesn't know that "rules were made to be broken." A computer will never even *bend* the rules. By the way, WordStar does not eliminate the spaces between words at the end of the line. If you edit the line later and move the words around, the spaces are still there, as long as you didn't delete them yourself.

To justify right margins, WordStar fills some lines with extra soft spaces. You have probably seen files with such "spaced-out" lines, and I bet you knew that a computer was the culprit here. Using a good word processor like WordStar, you could have avoided this unsightly mess if you had hyphenated longer words to close up the extra spaces. When you take the trouble (and it isn't much trouble at all) to hyphenate a word, you put part of it on one line and part on the next. The printout looks more professional.

Two Kinds of Hyphens

WordStar distinguishes between *two* kinds of hyphens, just as it uses two types of carriage returns. These hyphens both look the same in the printout, but they are decidedly different in the file itself.

The first kind of hyphen is the normal one that you type whenever a word always contains a hyphen. WordStar refers to it as a hard hyphen, but you can also think of it as a *necessary* hyphen. Such terms as *twenty-five* or *research-related* contain hard hyphens. You instinctively type these hyphens with the HYPHEN key. That is exactly how you should treat hyphenated words: as you always have. WordStar will break lines at hard hyphens if the first part of the hyphenated word can fit on the line, but the second part can't.

You insert the other kind of hyphen when you check to see if you could *possibly* hyphenate words at the ends of lines to fill up these lines. You need not do this at the time you enter the text. Do it later when you've finished typing and editing.

As you would expect, WordStar calls this second type of hyphen a *soft hyphen.* A soft hyphen is a conditional hyphen that only appears at a syllable break if the word is at the end of the line and if the word won't fit entirely on one line. Some word processors like to think of soft hyphens as *discretionary;* that is, they appear only at the discretion of the line breaks.

If you edit the file later and a word containing a soft hyphen appears in the middle of a line, WordStar won't print the soft hyphen or show it on the screen if the print codes are off. The soft hyphen is still there, ready to work again if necessary. You can see soft hyphens in the middle of lines by turning the print codes on with ^OD (SHIFT F1).

How WordStar Hyphenates

WordStar gives hyphenation the name *hyphen help.* By default, hyphen help is off in WordStar (in previous versions it was on). When you want to check which words could possibly be split at line endings, you must turn hyphen help on and then instruct WordStar to find the possible hyphenation spots. That is, you use ^B or ^QU to realign each paragraph. Even with hyphen help on, WordStar won't ask you to hyphenate words when you're typing in *new* text. You must realign the paragraph. (This feature may change in the next version of the product, so check the manual.)

When it finds a possible hyphenation spot, WordStar stops and asks you to make a decision. You can choose (1) to hyphenate the word at a specific syllable break, (2) not to hyphenate the word at all, thus bringing the entire word down to the next line, or (3) to cancel hyphenation for the rest of the paragraph and go on to the next. You don't have to hyphenate all paragraphs.

At this point you may be remonstrating that these extra steps mean extra time. That's true, of course, but the time you save *not* having to consider hyphenation during typing and editing is more than compensated by the little bit of time it takes to hyphenate later.

During hyphenation, WordStar considers a paragraph a distinct entity because it ends with a hard return. WordStar thus hyphenates to maintain the flow of the entire paragraph. That is why it is so important *not* to press RETURN when you are typing in normal paragraphs until you get to the end of the paragraph. WordStar would "hang up"—that is, prematurely end the paragraph—at any misplaced hard return codes. It does, however, readjust all the soft returns and soft spaces and puts in new ones for the newly adjusted lines.

Turning Hyphen Help On

You'll use the STORY.LA file to learn about hyphenation, so open that file now:

Press   **D** [open a document]

Type   `story.la`

Press   **RETURN**

Stop! Did you delete all the print codes in this file? If not, follow the instructions in the section "A Brief Interlude" in Chapter 6 before you continue.

The command to turn hyphen help on is **^OH**. It's another toggle switch.

Press   **^OH**

Nothing seems to have happened, but if you press **^O** you'll see that the Onscreen Format menu now says `turn hyphen help off` next to the H entry, because hyphen help is now on. Press the **SPACEBAR** to leave the Onscreen Format menu.

Hyphenating a Paragraph

The easiest way to hyphenate an entire file quickly is to position the cursor at the beginning of the file and press **^QU** to realign the entire file. However, for the sake of argument, you'll use **^B** to realign just the first paragraph, because I want to teach you hyphenation slowly.

You don't want to start with the title, but here's a trick. You can press **^B** to move the cursor down to the beginning of the next paragraph. When there isn't a paragraph in the way, **^B** acts just like **^X (DOWN ARROW)**.

Press   **^B** four times

to position the cursor at the beginning of the paragraph.

When you want to hyphenate an entire paragraph, make sure the cursor is at the beginning of the paragraph. Then:

Press   **^B**

There are no words to be hyphenated in the first paragraph. Try the second! Position the cursor at the beginning of the paragraph and press ^B.

WordStar stops at the word *leisurely* and positions the cursor under the *r*. At the top of the screen you see the Hyphen Help menu. Take a look at the help provided in this menu. Here's what it all means:

- WordStar doesn't "know" where a correct syllable break occurs. It just stops at the *last letter in a long word that fits on the line*. WordStar stops at words that are at least five characters long, but you can change this "zone" setting (Chapter 27).

- If the cursor location isn't a correct syllable break, you have to decide where to hyphenate the word by *first* positioning the cursor. Use ^S (**LEFT ARROW**) as normal. The cursor must be under the letter that is to begin the next line, because you'll *insert* a soft hyphen at this spot.

- Often WordStar by chance stops at a correct syllable break. You can accept it or position the cursor at another break.

- To hyphenate at the syllable break you choose, press the **HYPHEN** key.

- If you don't want to hyphenate the word at all, press ^B to continue to the next long word in the paragraph, if any.

- To cancel hyphenation for the rest of the paragraph, press ^U (**F2**).

It turns out that the *r* is not a correct syllable break. Try to hyphenate *leisurely* at the *l*:

Press   **^D or RIGHT ARROW**

What happened? No go! Why not? WordStar stops at the last possible character in the word that will fit on this line. It's telling you that there isn't enough room on the line to hyphenate at the spot you selected. You must choose a character before this spot to break the word.

Here's where your sense of aesthetics comes into play. The only other syllable break is at the *s*, but that doesn't look aesthetically pleasing on the screen. So, after all this rigmarole, you decide not to hyphenate the word at all:

Press   **^B**

to bypass hyphenation of this word and continue.

WordStar stops at *distance*. This time:

Press   **^S or LEFT ARROW** three times

to position the cursor under the *t*.

Press   -

to hyphenate the word here.

A Very Useful Purchase

If you're as bad at hyphenating as I am, how do you quickly find the correct hyphenation spot for a word? Get yourself one of those paperback *speller/ divider* books and keep it next to your computer. These books are one of the best $3 investments you could make.

Hyphenating an Entire File

Now that you know how to hyphenate, you can quickly hyphenate the rest of the file:

Press   **^QU**

If you typed the example correctly, there should be no other words to hyphenate. When you're finished:

Press   **^KS** or **F9**

to save the file and resume where you left off.

Hyphenating Part of a File

To hyphenate just part of a file, position the cursor at the beginning of the section you want to check and turn hyphen help on. Use **^B** to realign individual paragraphs or **^QU** to realign the rest of the file.

The Soft Hyphens

The soft hyphens that you just inserted look like regular hyphens when they're at the ends of line. If you turn the print code display off with **^OD** (**SHIFT F1**), you'll see exactly how the lines will print. Later, if you edit a line that ends in a soft hyphen, WordStar may position the word in the middle of the line. It doesn't delete the soft hyphen, but the display of this hyphen changes to an equals sign: =. You'll only see these soft hyphens when you turn the print codes on. They do not print, so you never have to delete them.

It's to your advantage to leave soft hyphens in the file. If you edit the same line again and the word is at the end of the line, WordStar will honor the syllable break if necessary. That's why some people call soft hyphens *ghosts:* they're there, but they don't appear all the time. You don't have to remove soft hyphens if you rearrange the lines. They're friendly ghosts!

Deleting a Soft Hyphen. If you later decide to change the hyphenation spot for a word, you must delete the soft hyphen and pick another word break. Position the cursor on the soft hyphen and delete it with ^G (DEL). (If the soft hyphen is in the middle of a line, make sure the print codes are on.) Then turn hyphen help on and realign the paragraph to choose a different syllable break, or enter the soft hyphen yourself. . . .

Manually Inserting a Soft Hyphen. Occasionally you may want to insert a soft hyphen yourself without going through the entire hyphenation rigmarole. First position the cursor on a correct syllable break, then press ^OE. You won't see the soft hyphen symbol (the =) unless you turn on the print codes, but it will be there. And it will stay in the word and work at the end of a line. (Old timers: This command has changed in WordStar Professional Release 4 from previous versions.)

Finding Soft Hyphens. You can use the find command to locate soft hyphens, but WordStar maintains *two* special codes to distinguish the soft hyphens that are at the ends of lines and those that are hidden in the middle of lines.

To find soft hyphens at the ends of lines, press ^QF (^F1) as usual, then press ^P SHIFT ^- and continue the find command. (That is, press ^P, then hold down the SHIFT and CTRL keys as you press the HYPHEN key.) To find soft hyphens that may be hidden in the middle of lines (the = symbols), press ^QF (^F1), then press ^P SHIFT ^6 and continue the find command. (That is, press ^P, then hold down the SHIFT and CTRL keys as you press the 6 key on the top row of the keyboard.)

To find hard hyphens, press ^QF (^F1), then *type* a hyphen and continue the find command. Of course, you can find and replace soft hyphens, too. For example, you may want to find and delete all soft hyphens using the technique you learned in Chapter 6.

Hyphenating a Word with a Hard Hyphen

Some words that already have required hyphens in them are long. Think, for example, of *hard-to-find* or *down-to-earth.* At times WordStar might stop at such a word and ask you if you want to hyphenate it. Every book on style will tell you the same thing: it's not "proper form" to hyphenate a word other than at the hyphen itself.

So when WordStar stops at a word with a required hyphen, press ^B to continue. If the cursor is under the second half of the word, WordStar will still break the word at the hard hyphen. (Another aside: Again, good form dictates that you shouldn't hyphenate proper nouns, such as *Hollywood,* but that decision is also up to you. If you can, avoid ending a paragraph with a line that contains only the second half of a hyphenated word.)

Press   ^KD or F10

to save the file and return to the Opening menu.

(You may also wish to print it to see the results of your hyphenation decisions.)

By the way, if you open another file now, hyphen help is again off.

Dashes and Minus Signs

You've already used a double hyphen for a dash (--), and you'd type a single hyphen before an amount for a minus sign (-9.09). WordStar may break a line at these special hyphens. A future release of the product will have a nonbreak hyphen, like a binding space. Stay tuned for it!

The Hyphenation Zone

How does WordStar determine where to stop and request hyphenation? It has a *zone* setting at the end of the line. The default setting is five characters. If a word extends into the right margin and the word contains five or more characters, WordStar stops and asks about hyphenation. Otherwise, it moves the word down to the next line. Using the WSCHANGE program, you can change the zone (Chapter 27).

Note: Earlier versions of WordStar used a formula known as an *algorithm* to instruct the program when to stop for hyphenation by trying to determine correct syllable breaks. Now WordStar stops only if the word at the end of the line has five or more characters. A more sophisticated algorithm that determines correct syllable breaks might appear in a future release.

The Word Finder Thesaurus

Another way to "watch your words" is to use the *Word Finder thesaurus.* While you're working in WordStar you can ask Word Finder to give you a synonym for the word at the cursor location. You can also use the thesaurus to help you find what the French call *le mot juste,* the correctly chosen word according to its use in the sentence, and to offer some help if you have problems with homonyms (words that sound alike).

What "TSR" Means

Word Finder is a *terminate and stay resident* program, a TSR. You may hear others refer to it as a *memory-resident* program. Here's how it works. Because it's a completely separate program, you load Word Finder before you load

WordStar or other programs. After it loads into memory, it "terminates"—that is, returns to the DOS prompt—but stays in memory, ready at your beck and call. (I'll mention other popular TSRs in Chapter 28.)

As you work with WordStar or another program, Word Finder monitors your keystrokes to see if you press **ALT 1,** its command key. If you press anything else, it just passes the keystroke on to WordStar. When you press **ALT 1,** however, Word Finder tries to give you a list of synonyms for the word at the cursor. Unfortunately, it doesn't have synonyms for every word!

Finding Synonyms

If you've installed Word Finder, take a look at how to use it. First, open a file:

Press   **D** [open a document]

Type   contract

Press   **RETURN**

Position the cursor on the word you want to check. Suppose you don't like the word *maintains* in the second paragraph and you want to substitute a synonym for it. First, position the cursor at the word:

Press   **^QF** or **^F1**

Type   maint

Press   **ESC**

Now, start Word Finder:

Press   **ALT 1**

Word Finder highlights *maintains* and tells you in a window that takes up part of the screen:

Just a moment...while I look up: maintain

Soon an enormous list of synonyms for *maintain* appears. Word Finder tells you what part of speech the word is and arranges the synonyms by related meanings:

maintain:
    verb egg on, encourage, lead on, string;

```
assist, keep up, provide, support, sustain, uphold;
argue, assert, believe, claim, contend, defend, justify, know, state,
think, vindicate, warrant;
conserve, preserve, protect, save;
adapt, adjust, balance, fit, fix, inspect, overhaul, recondition,
refurbish, regulate, repair, service, support, tune up;
allege, assert, avow, claim, say, state;
commit, continue, extend, perpetuate, prolong, pull.
```

Now, a thesaurus is a great writer's tool, but you have to know how to use it. What meaning of *maintain* are you looking for? Certainly not one like *egg on* or *overhaul!* Word Finder just lists words for you; it does little more than jog your memory.

Once you see a list of synonyms you have several options:

- Choose a synonym by moving the cursor to it with the arrow keys. (**Note:** ^E and ^X work to move the cursor up or down instead of **UP ARROW** and **DOWN ARROW,** respectively, but ^D and ^S don't. To move the cursor right or left, press the **RIGHT ARROW** or **LEFT ARROW** keys, or ^F or ^A, respectively.)
- Press **RETURN** to substitute the word in the file with the word you've selected from Word Finder's list.
- Press the Word Finder command key, **ALT 1,** to see synonyms for any word you choose. You can continue to press **ALT 1** to look up other words, or ^**PG UP** to see the last word.
- Press **PG DN** when Word Finder tells you that there are even *more* synonyms. Press **PG UP** to return to the first screen.
- Press **ESC** to cancel Word Finder without changing the file.
- If Word Finder can't find the word, it shows an alphabetical list of words that appear near that word in its thesaurus.

Suppose you want to substitute *provides* for *maintains*:

Press   ^X or **DOWN ARROW**

Press   **RIGHT ARROW** or ^F three times
(you can't use ^D or ^**RIGHT ARROW**).

to position the cursor under *provide.*

Press   **RETURN**

to insert this word in the file.

Stop! Look at the word! Word Finder substituted *provide* for *maintains!* It can't determine the proper *ending* of a verb or the plural of a noun. You must type that in yourself. You'd also have to realign the paragraph after changing it. To give Word Finder its due, it *will* honor the case of a word. What Word Finder is doing is just *deleting* the original word and inserting its substitute.

This time, take a look at the other features. The cursor should be directly past *provide:*

Press   **ALT 1**

to see synonyms for *provide.*

Press   **PG DN**

to see more synonyms.

Press   **PG UP**

to see the first screen.

Press   **ALT 1**

to see synonyms for *endow.*

Press   **^PG UP**

to return to the first screen.

Press   **ESC**

to exit Word Finder.

When you're finished experimenting with the Word Finder thesaurus, make sure you abandon any changes:

Press   **^KQ**

Type   **y**

to quit without saving the file.

Now that you know ways to work with words in WordStar, you can use the features you've learned in this chapter as you work through the rest of this book. After taking a well-earned break, continue to the wonderful world of tabs. . . .

Adventures with Tab Stops

In this chapter you will learn the following new commands:

File Commands

.AW ON/OFF	Turn paragraph align on/off
^OG	Paragraph tab
^OW	Turn wordwrap on/off
^OX	Turn margin release on/off
.PM	Set the paragraph margin

Other Feature

#	Set or clear a decimal tab stop

Dear Reader: What could be more boring than tab stops? Well, you may not think of tabs as exciting, because on a typewriter there's not much to them. But you'll soon learn otherwise. This chapter takes you on a little safari through the world of tabs, covering related items as well: regular indents, "hanging" indents, simple columns of figures and text, outlines, and WordStar's new paragraph margin feature.

DO WARM-UP

Using Decimal Tabs

Normal tabs are *left-justified*. That is, when you type text at a tab stop, you insert the text to the right of the tab stop. In contrast, a *decimal* tab automatically aligns numbers underneath the decimal point at the tab stop. The numbers you type before the decimal point move *left* until you type the decimal point. The numbers after the decimal point move *right*. If you frequently type columns of figures with decimal points, you'll appreciate this feature.

As an example of using decimal tabs, you'll create a simple table of text and figures. In Chapter 18 you'll learn how to use WordStar's math feature to *total* figures.

Press	**D** [open a document]
Type	expenses.jan
Press	**RETURN**
Type	y

because this is a new file.

First, determine the overall page formatting of the file. Type at *column 1* the following dot commands, each command on a separate line ending in a hard return:

```
.MT 12
.OP
.PO 12 [or whatever page offset your printer uses]
```

The cursor should be on blank line 1 below the dot commands. Take a look at the example, but don't type it yet. Notice how the figures align under the decimal points.

MONTHLY EXPENDITURES

January

Rent	$350.77
Groceries	185.22
Utilities	77.34
Automobile	85.23
Insurance	114.86
Clothing	47.30

```
Entertainment          52.95
Cats                   12.00
Medical                92.50
Home Upkeep           250.82
                    _____

           Total
```

Setting Decimal Tabs

Now, create a ruler line and save it with the file so that the next time you use this file you don't have to worry about the tab settings. Because you only want a regular (left-justified) tab stop at column 20 and a decimal tab stop at column 45, first clear all tabs:

Press   **^ON**

Type   **a**

Press   **RETURN**

to clear all tabs.
     Set a regular tab at column 20:

Press   **^OI**

Type   **20**

Press   **RETURN**

    To set a decimal tab, follow the same procedure as setting a regular tab but type the number or pound sign (#, SHIFT 3) *before* the column number. You want a decimal tab at column 45, so:

Press   **^OI**

Type   **#45**

Press   **RETURN**

     WordStar shows regular tab stops with an exclamation point (!) on the ruler line and decimal tab stops with a number sign (#) on the ruler line. **Note:** You can have any combination of regular and decimal tabs, but the greatest number of tab stops you can set in one file is 30.

To set a decimal tab at the current cursor location, press ^OI, type #, and press **ESC. Caution:** WordStar then "assumes" that the next time you press **ESC** to set a tab at another cursor column, it will be a decimal tab. To get around this, set a regular tab by typing in the column number.

Clearing Decimal Tabs

To clear a decimal tab you must type the number sign before the column number, too. Press ^ON, type # followed by the column number of the decimal tab, and press **RETURN.** If you don't type the number sign or if you type a column number at which there is no tab stop, WordStar tells you:

```
Could not find that tab.

Press Esc to continue.
```

This message appears if you're clearing a regular tab that doesn't exist, too. To clear a decimal tab at the current cursor location, press ^ON, type #, and press **ESC. Caution:** WordStar then "assumes" that the next time you press **ESC** to clear a tab at another cursor column, it will be a decimal tab. To get around this, clear a regular tab by typing in the column number.

Continue . . .

Now that you have your ruler line the way you want it, save it with the file:

Press   **^OO** or **F8**

to insert the ruler line in the file.

Press   **^X** or **DOWN ARROW**

to move the cursor to the first text line.
      Type the title lines:

Press   **CAPS LOCK**

Type   MONTHLY EXPENDITURES

Press   **CAPS LOCK**

to release this key.

Press   **^OC** or **ESC C** or **SHIFT F2**

to center the title.

Press   **RETURN** twice

for spacing.
    Type and center January and press **RETURN** four times for spacing. Here's how to do the first line of the table:

Press   **TAB** or ^I

to move the cursor to column 20.

Type   Rent

Press   **TAB** or ^I

to move the cursor to column 45.
    The status line says Decimal to note that the cursor is at a decimal tab stop. Now, watch the screen as you type the amount:

Type $350.77

(don't forget the dollar sign).
    As you type, WordStar moves the dollar sign and figures left until you type the decimal point! (It moves *anything that's not a decimal point* left, something that will soon prove most helpful.)

Press   **RETURN**

to end the line.
    Continue typing the other lines, following the same pattern. After the last figure (250.82), press **RETURN** twice. Then, with the **SPACEBAR,** move the cursor across the page to column 39. You have to "eye-ball" where you want the line to go. Type an underline (SHIFT HYPHEN) eleven times and press **RETURN** twice. To do the last line, press **TAB** (^I) once and then the **SPACEBAR** twice. Type Total. When you're finished:

Press   ^**KD** or **F10**

to save the file and return to the Opening menu.

Right-Justified Text Columns

Because WordStar moves *any* text that's not a decimal point to the left of a decimal tab stop until you type a decimal point, you can fool WordStar to do right-justified columns of text. There's just one little trick to know when using decimal tab in this manner.

Press   **D** [open a document]

Type   `pies`

Press   **RETURN**

Type   `y`

because this is a new file.

Here's the example you'll type:

```
              United Bakeries of Santa Barbara County

                   Welcome to the Friendly Pies

                     Seasonal Availability

              Apple      All year
             Cherry      May-September
          Blueberry      June-July
              Peach      June-October
              Pecan      All year
            Pumpkin      All year
            Rhubarb      July-August
         Strawberry      May-September
```

This time, the *first* tab stop is a decimal tab and the second is a regular tab. However, set the decimal tab one column *more* than where you want the text to end. In this example, the *e* of *Apple* is at column 29, so the decimal tab stop has to be at column 30. When you tab over to the first stop and type each pie name, WordStar right-justifies the name! That's because you never get around to typing a decimal point.

I won't step you through the entire example, but here are the general directions. First, insert the same dot commands as in the first example. Then clear all tabs with **^ON a RETURN** and set a decimal tab at column 30 (**^OI #30 RETURN**) and a regular tab at column 35 (**^OI 35 RETURN**). Press **^OO** (**F8**) to insert the new ruler line and **^X** (**DOWN ARROW**) to begin. Type and center each title line, but remember to underline the second title. Press **RETURN** twice for spacing between lines.

To type each pie name, press **TAB** (**^I**) once, type the name, and without typing a space after the name, press **TAB** again. Type the second column information and press **RETURN** to continue. When you're finished:

Press   ^KD or F10

to save the file and return to the Opening menu.

Right-Justified Lines

You can apply your knowledge of decimal tabs to right justify entire lines of text. Some word processors refer to this as *flush right* text. Although there's no specific example to study, here are the steps you'd take:

1. Set the right margin *two* columns past the real right margin. That's because you need one extra column for the decimal tab stop, but WordStar won't let you tab to a tab stop at the right margin. So, if you want the lines right-justified at column 65, set the right margin at column 67.

2. Clear all tabs and set one decimal tab at the column past the one you want (here, column 66).

3. Press **TAB** (^I) once and type each line. Make sure you press **RE-TURN** to end each line and avoid wordwrap. You'll have to watch the screen to determine where you'll want the lines to break.

4. Reset the right margin after you've typed the text that you want to justify.

What Happens When You Change the Tab Stops?

When you press the **TAB** key (^I), WordStar doesn't insert a special code for a tab in the file. It merely inserts spaces up to the next tab stop. If you decide to change a tab stop later, there's no easy way to realign the current text in the file. Perhaps a future version of WordStar will provide a feature that automatically readjusts tabular text. See Chapter 11 for an example that shows you how to edit a ruler line and for information about the "nondocument fixed tab," also known as the "variable tab."

Indented Text

There are many types of indentations and many ways to do them in WordStar. Often you'll indent text at tab stops. That's why I'm discussing indents in this chapter. I also feel it's high time you learned about a truly nifty feature, WordStar's *paragraph margin,* which is the best way to do indents.

The Paragraph Margin Command

A very useful command new to this release of WordStar, the paragraph margin is a setting that works with the *first line* and *only* the first line of each paragraph. Because it's a dot command, **.PM,** you save it with the file and it takes effect from its location in the file.

The **.PM** command requires an integer number representing the column number at which to begin the first line of each paragraph. The paragraph margin can be greater than, less than, or the same as the left margin setting. If it's greater than the left margin, it creates a regular indent; if it's less than the left margin, it creates a hanging indent; if it's the same as the left margin or 0, the default setting, it does nothing.

There is only one possible paragraph margin setting at any one time, so the paragraph margin works best with just single indents. Below are examples illustrating the paragraph margin.

Automatic Indenting!

Perhaps the niftiest use of the paragraph margin is to bypass the TAB key at the beginnings of paragraphs (in Chapter 6 I mentioned this to whet your curiosity). I call this "automatic indenting," but you must take care when using this feature. To see what I mean, open the CONTRACT file again:

Press   **D** [open a document]

Type   contract

Press   **RETURN**

When you typed this file you had to press **TAB** (^I) twice to begin each paragraph at the second default tab stop, column 11. If you had instead set the paragraph margin to 11, each time you began a new paragraph WordStar would indent the paragraph automatically. You wouldn't have to press TAB at all! To see this feature in action you'll set up the paragraph margin and add a short paragraph to the file.

Press   ^N

to add a blank line at the top of the file.

Type   .PM 11 or .pm 11

The ruler line shows a P in column 11 to indicate that the paragraph margin is set for that column. Now, position the cursor at the spot where you want the new paragraph to go:

Press   **^C** or **PG DN** twice

to position the cursor on line 17.

Press   **^QD** or **^F10**

to position the cursor at the end of the line.

Press   **RETURN**

for spacing.

Type the following paragraph, but *do not* press the TAB key to begin. When you type the first character, WordStar jumps to the paragraph margin.

> WHEREAS, Red's business obligations require her to
>
> increase the size and capability of her delivery staff; and

Stop! Don't press RETURN at the end of the paragraph, because you already have the correct spacing. Before you continue, however:

Press   **^KS** or **F9**

to save the file and resume where you left off.

As you can see, if you type mostly paragraphs the paragraph margin can be a great keystroke saver. (It will take you a while to get out of the old typing habit of pressing the TAB key to begin each paragraph, though.) If you indent one standard tab stop (to column 6), you can press **^F7** to insert the **.pm6** command into a file.

However, what happens when you *don't* want to indent a line? For example, say you're adding a new section and you want to type a heading. How do you disable the paragraph margin? Simple—use the *margin release!*

The Margin Release

Like its counterpart on the typewriter, WordStar's margin release command, **^OX,** lets you bypass the margins. It's most useful in temporarily disabling the paragraph margin. Pretend you're adding an addendum to this contract:

Press   **^QC** or **^END**

to position the cursor at the end of the file. It should be on a blank line at column 1. If it isn't, press **RETURN** once.

To bypass the paragraph margin, *before* typing the text, do this:

Press   **^OX**

The status line says Mar-Rel. The margin release stays in effect until you move the cursor past the paragraph margin or off the *current* line, or if you press **^OX** again.

Type   Addendum

The text starts at the left margin, thus avoiding the automatic indent.

Press   **RETURN**

to disable the margin release.

Question: What about lines that you want to center? *Answer:* You don't have to use the margin release, because even if the line indents to the paragraph margin, as soon as you center the line everything's "jake" again. The margin release disables the current left and right margins, too. For example, if the left margin were at column 5, the margin release would let you type in columns 1 through 4. However, you can't go in front of column 1. Similarly, you could type past the right margin—say, to insert a note to yourself on this line—by first turning on the margin release. Then use the SPACEBAR to move the cursor past the right margin.

Caution: After you've used the margin release, don't realign that section of text with **^B** or the entire file with **^QU**, because WordStar would align the "released" section back into the margins.

Disabling the Paragraph Margin

If you now realigned the CONTRACT file with **^QU**, every heading would appear at column 11 because the **.PM 11** command affects the first line of each "paragraph" in the entire file. WordStar considers the headings and subheadings as *very* short paragraphs!

The best way to get around this is to turn off the paragraph margin before each heading and turn it back on after the heading. You may want to set up two boilerplate files or macros with the necessary dot commands to do this.

To turn off the paragraph margin, use either **.PM 0** or just **.PM**. So, each heading line would look something like the first:

```
.PM
Compensation
.PM 11
```

Caution: Make sure that each dot command line doesn't interfere with the *actual* blank lines between sections. Remember to press **^N** to add blank lines for dot commands.

Press   **^KQ**

Type   **y**

to quit without saving the file.

Indenting an Entire Paragraph

The easiest way to indent a paragraph is just to change the left margin setting. For example, take a look at the following memo, especially the dot command lines:

```
.MT 10
.OP
Memo to: All Employees
From:    J.R.
Re:      Peanuts

     It  has  come  to my attention that there  are  an  enormous
amount of peanut shells littering the office.  This situation  is
intolerable and must cease immediately.

.LM 6
     AS  YOU WELL KNOW, OUR COMPUTER EQUIPMENT IS VERY  EXPENSIVE
     AND  VERY  SENSITIVE.  YOU HAVE ALL BEEN INSTRUCTED TO  KEEP
     ALL FOOD, DRINK AND SMOKING MATERIALS AWAY FROM THE AREA  OF
     THE EQUIPMENT.

.LM 1
     In  addition,  if  anyone  has  any  information  about  the
elephant  in  the  storeroom, please  contact  my  administrative
assistant, Ms. Board, at once.
```

This memo is in the default format, but the indented paragraph has a left margin setting of 6. There's no paragraph margin at all. If you wish, create a new file called MEMO.1 and type this example exactly as you see it. Save it with ^KD (**F10**) when you're finished. In another chapter you'll do an example that illustrates how to type text that's indented from *both* margins.

The Paragraph Tab Command

In *Mastering WordStar,* the predecessor to this book, I used the previous memo file to illustrate the *paragraph tab* command, **^OG.** This command offers a temporary indentation of the left margin to the next tab stop. The temporary indentation remains in effect until you press **^B** to reform the paragraph or **RETURN** at the end of the paragraph.

Although still useful if you're typing a file on the fly or doing outlines (see below), paragraph tab is again one of those onscreen formatting commands that you must repeat each time you edit the file. To see how the paragraph tab command works, create a file called MEMO.2. Type the same memo as you see it up to, but *not* including the **.LM 6** command. Instead of inserting that command, do this before typing the indented section:

Press   **^OG**

A V appears on the ruler line at the first tab stop, column 6. For every press of **^OG,** the V moves over one tab stop to the right. That will be the temporary indentation. (In earlier versions of WordStar, the tab stop displayed in intense video.)

Type   ⟨the indented paragraph⟩

Notice that WordStar wraps the lines to the temporary indentation instead of to the real left margin at column 1. To disengage the paragraph tab, merely press **RETURN** at the end of the paragraph. But you'd do that *anyway!* The V disappears from the ruler line. Press **RETURN** again and continue typing the memo, but don't type the **.LM 1** dot command.

Suppose you saved the MEMO.2 file and wanted to edit the indented paragraph during another session. *Before* realigning that paragraph with **^B,** you must press **^OG** to turn paragraph tab on. I think you now see how much better it is to have savable formats in the file!

 Note: The paragraph tab command works on individual paragraphs only. You'll get unpredictable results if you attempt to realign an entire file using **^QU** with a paragraph tab setting also in effect. Don't do it!

"Hanging" Indents

A hanging indent has a long first line and indented subsequent lines. There are several different ways to produce hanging indents in WordStar.

By now you've probably figured out that the best way is to use the paragraph margin, because you can save the format with the file. This time, the paragraph margin setting will be *less than* the left margin setting.

Press   **D** [open a document]

Type   pecan.pie

Press   **RETURN**

Type   y

because this is a new file.

Dear Reader: Little did you realize what a *bargain* this book really is! Not only is it a tour through WordStar, but it even includes a free recipe for you to try. I've baked this pie many times, always to great acclaim. It came to me from someone who grew up in the South, so I guess it's authentic enough. And even if you're not a gourmet cook, at least you'll learn about hanging indents!

```
.OJ OFF
.PM 1
.LM 5
.RM 45
```

DEEP SOUTH PECAN PIE

Prepare a 9-inch pie crust in the usual
    manner and set aside. Preheat the oven
    to 350 degrees.

Melt 1/4 cup butter and cook it until it
    begins to brown. Let it cool for 5 to 10
    minutes. Stir in 1 cup granulated sugar
    and 4 eggs, one at a time, beating after
    each addition until the mixture is
    smooth.

Add 1/2 cup light corn syrup, 1 teaspoon
    vanilla, and 1 cup diced pecans. The
    pecans will rise to the top during
    baking.

Pour the mixture into the pie crust and bake
    for 45 to 60 minutes, until the pie is
    completely firm. Serve warm or cold.

Variations: Use 1/2 cup brown sugar and 1/2
    cup granulated sugar instead of 1 cup
    granulated; add 1/2 to 1 cup dark rum.

Notice the dot command lines: they do all the formatting work. Watch how the ruler line shows the left margin and paragraph margin after you type the dot commands. Center and type the title. Press **RETURN** three times for spacing. Then just type each paragraph as you see it, letting WordStar form the hanging indents. When you're finished, save the file with **^KD (F10)**. Bon appétit!

Here are two other ways to do hanging indents, but they mean more work, and you can't save the entire format with the file:

1. Leave out the **.PM 1** dot command line. At the beginning of each paragraph, press **^OX** to bypass the left margin so that the line starts at column 1. Too much work!

2. Leave out both the **.PM 1** and **.LM 5** dot command lines. Type the text with the left margin at column 1. Set a new tab at column 5. Then go back to the *second* line of each paragraph, press **^OG** to turn paragraph tab on, and press **^B** to realign the paragraph. Repeat for each paragraph. Sheesh! (By the way, microjustification wouldn't be exactly right either if you used this method.)

Outlines

Combine your knowledge of the paragraph margin and the paragraph tab to create an outline. (An aside: WordStar doesn't have a true *outline processor* feature that will automatically number outlines for you or let you "collapse" and "expand" outline sections, but you can buy a program called PC-Outline that works very well with WordStar. See Chapter 28.)

Press   **D** [open a document]

Type   `meeting.apr`

Press   **RETURN**

Type   `y`

because this is a new file.

    The entire outline follows. Take a look at it before you start. *Questions:* What do the dot commands do? When will you have to use the paragraph tab command? While you're pondering these questions, type the dot commands and then type and center each title line. Press **RETURN** twice for spacing after the first two, three times after the third line.

```
.OP
.OJ OFF
.PM 1
.LM 6
                 The ABCXYZ Company

           Board of Directors Monthly Meeting

                    April 1988


I.   Call the meeting to order at 8:00 p.m. sharp (even if Joe
     and Laura aren't there yet)
```

```
II.  Old Business
     A.   Reading of minutes of March meeting-remember to ask
          Shirley to read President's letter
     B.   Corrections or revisions of minutes
     C.   Any additional old business that has not been resolved
          and is still pressing
     D.   Acceptance of minutes

III. New Business
     A.   New equipment report: what progress?
     B.   Worker discipline: Case of S. N.
          1.   New information?
          2.   Supervisor's recommendation -- he's o.k.
          3.   N.'s statement (read it)
     C.   Building & grounds expenditures
          1.   Costs escalating
          2.   No efficiency seen
          3.   Consolidation of services & personnel for all six
               plants probably the wisest move
```

Answers: The **.PM 1** and **.LM 6** commands set up the *first level* indent. That is, to prepare the first level entries, type the Roman numeral, for example **I.**, press **TAB** (**^I**) once, and type the rest of the entry. WordStar indents the second line automatically. Press **RETURN** twice for spacing and type the **II.** entry.

You can use the paragraph tab command, **^OG,** for further indentation levels. For instance, to type the second level entry, the **A.** line, press **TAB** (**^I**) once and type **A**. Then press **^OG**. WordStar shows the temporary indent at column 11. Type the rest of the entry, and WordStar automatically indents the lines. Continue with the other entries but *stop* at number **3.** in the last section. To do this one, press **TAB** (**^I**) *twice* and type **3**. Then press **^OG** *twice* to indent to column 16, and type the rest of the entry. Press **RETURN** once to turn off paragraph tab.

You could also use different **.PM** and **.LM** commands for the different levels. For example, here's how to accomplish the second level indents in section II:

```
II.  Old Business
.PM 6
.LM 11
     A.   Reading of minutes of March meeting-remember to ask
          Shirley to read President's letter
     B.   Corrections or revisions of minutes      and so on
```

Make sure you adjust the **.PM** and **.LM** commands when the levels change. I'll let you try the rest of the outline on your own. **Tip:** If you work with outlines a lot, set up shorthand macros to establish the different outline levels for you!

When you're finished typing the entire outline:

Press   ^KD or F10

to save the file and return to the Opening menu.

You can use the paragraph tab command, ^OG, repeatedly to indent as many tab stops as you wish, but it will always follow the *one farthest right*. Notice that you can also combine regular tabs and paragraph tabs, as in this example. If you later edit the sections that you originally indented with paragraph tabs, remember to turn on the temporary indentation before realigning the lines. However, if you're working with a justified right margin, it's best to use the .PM and .LM commands instead of ^OG. That way, you won't have any potential problems with microjustification.

A More Elaborate Example

The next example combines the decimal tab with the paragraph tab command to create a table of dates for a book you're writing on Ludwig van Beethoven. Later in the chapter you'll learn some important points about how to avoid potential catastrophes when files contain tables or other unusual formatting.

Press   D [open a document]

Type   dates

Press   RETURN

Type   y

because this is a new file.

The table of dates uses a decimal tab to right justify the dates and two regular tab stops for the other columns. First, create the necessary ruler line by following these steps:

Press   ^ON

Type   a

Press   RETURN

to clear all tabs.

Press   ^OI

Type   #23

Press   RETURN

to set a decimal tab at column 23.

Press   **^OI**

Type   **26**

Press   **RETURN**

Press   **^OI**

Type   **30**

Press   **RETURN**

to set regular tabs at columns 26 and 30.

Press   **^OO** or **F8**

to insert the new ruler line into the file.

Press   **^X** or **DOWN ARROW**

Type   **.OJ OFF** or **.oj off**

Press   **RETURN**

to insert the dot command line.

The entire table, including dot commands, is shown next. Here's how to type the first line. Follow the same pattern for typing the others.

Press   **TAB** or **^I**

Type   **10 June 1813**

Press   **TAB** or **^I**

Type   **-**

(that's a hyphen).

Press   **^OG** twice

for the paragraph tab.

Type   **Letter to Grump**

and so on (let WordStar form the lines as you type).

Press   **RETURN**

for spacing and to turn off the paragraph tab.

Continue typing the entire table. Make sure you include beginning and ending underline codes for *Sachertorte Sonata*.

```
.RR-----------------#--!---!----------------------------R
.OJ OFF
        10 June 1813   -   Letter to Grump and sketches begun
                           for what would appear as the
                           Sachertorte Sonata
        8 August 1813  -   Beethoven stops all work because of
                           intestinal problems caused by eating
                           a rotten sausage at the Opera
       11 October 1813 -   Beethoven resumes writing and
                           composing
       15 October 1813 -   Composer shows sketches for "first
                           movement" of something to landlady,
                           Gertrude Kram, who is not impressed
        5 January 1814 -   Dispute with landlady forces
                           composer to move, disrupting all
                           work in progress; Beethoven spends a
                           great deal of time at the Sacher
                           Hotel, devouring pastries
       2 February 1814 -   Last mention of sketches
         13 March 1814 -   Beethoven complains to Grump of
                           gastric problems
         26 April 1814 -   Beethoven performs the premiere of
                           the Sachertorte Sonata
```

When you're finished,

Press   **^KS** or **F9**

to save the file and resume where you left off.

Avoiding Align Catastrophes

Now that you've typed your table, suppose you want to run it through WordStar's spelling checker? You'll be in a pretty pickle indeed if you don't think before you start. Why?

Using CorrectStar with a Table

Remember that CorrectStar usually *realigns* paragraphs every time it corrects a word. You certainly don't want this to happen here! Here's what to do:

Press   **^QR** or **^HOME**

to position the cursor at the beginning of the file.

Press   **^QL** or **SHIFT F3**

to begin the spelling check.
    (Insert the dictionary disk if you have a dual-floppy system.)
    When CorrectStar stops at the first "unknown" word, probably *Sacher-torte,* and *before* you decide about this word,

Press   **T** [turn auto-align off]

    Then press **I** [ignore, check next word] if the word's correct and continue as normal.

Realigning the Table

Say you've made a few typing mistakes in the third column and you've corrected them. To realign the affected sections of the table, position the cursor on the first line of the text in the third column, press **^OG** twice to turn the paragraph tab on, and then press **^B** to realign the text. Continue with any other lines as necessary.
    When you're completely finished,

Press   **^KD** or **F10**

to save the file and return to the Opening menu.

Turning Alignment Off

You'll now insert your table into the file that contains the text for Chapter 27 of your "Beethoven book." First, create the new file:

Press   **D** [open a document]

Type   ch.27

Press   **RETURN**

Type   y

because this is a new file.
    Type the dot command lines in the example that follows. Then type and center the title lines. Press **RETURN** once between title lines and twice for spacing

after the second line. Underline and type the heading (don't forget to turn underlining off), and press **RETURN** twice for spacing. Type the first paragraph and again press **RETURN** twice for spacing. Repeat the steps for the second section. The cursor should be on line 37 when you're finished.

```
.LS 2
.OJ ON
.UL ON
```

                            Chapter 27

                    Beethoven's "Tenth Symphony"

Background

    All evidence seems to point to the year 1813 as the first

time Beethoven contemplated writing a tenth symphony.   Most

scholars base their conclusions on a letter dated 10 June 1813 to

Beethoven's friend, Johann Friedrich Grump.   One researcher,

Claudia Trelawny, even thinks that the sketches that would

eventually become the Sachertorte Sonata were originally intended

as part of the "Tenth Symphony."

Chronology

    As far as we can gather from what scant evidence exits, here

is a list of dates that pertain to the "Tenth Symphony":

    Now, insert the table into the file at this location:

Press   **^KR**

Type   dates

Press   **RETURN**

    Leave the cursor on line 37.

    Stop! There's a potential problem here. When you originally created the DATES file, you used the default single line spacing. You've now inserted the file into another file that's in double spacing. What do you do? Right! Add the correct dot command to govern this section:

Press   **^N**

to add a blank line.

Type   .LS 1 or .ls 1

    In the next chapter you'll add more text to this file. Suppose, however, that every so often after a "heavy" editing session you want to realign the entire file with ^QU? Just as you have to tell CorrectStar not to align paragraphs, you must also tell WordStar to *skip* the table when it aligns the rest of the file.

    The command to turn paragraph alignment off is **.AW OFF.** Always insert this command directly in front of sections that you don't want WordStar to re-align later. So:

Press   **RETURN**

Type   .AW OFF or .aw off

    Notice that Align has disappeared from the status line. Now you must instruct WordStar where to turn alignment back on.

Press   **^QC or ^END**

to position the cursor at the end of the file. It should be on the blank line below the table.

Type   .AW ON or .aw on

Press   **RETURN**

    Alignment is now on again and the word Align reappears on the status line. The **.AW** command is such an important one that you'll see it many times in this book. Learn to use it! If you wish, position the cursor within the table and press **^B** or **^QU**. What happened? Exactly as you'd expect: *nothing!* Your table is safe and protected from accidental realignment.

    Even though you inserted the ruler line that governs the table, WordStar now won't realign the text between the **.AW** commands if you change this text. *Question:* What if you have to edit the table? *Answer:* You have two options. You can delete the **.AW OFF** command line temporarily and reinsert it later after you've made your changes and realigned the lines. Or you can edit the original DATES file, delete the table from the CH.27 file, and insert the new version. Don't delete the **.AW** lines!

Press   **^KD** or **F10**

to save the file and return to the Opening menu.

If you want to align text in tables and charts yourself as you type, insert an **.AW OFF** command directly before the table and an **.AW ON** command after it. With alignment off, any text you type won't wrap until you press RETURN to end each line. You can even extend text past the right margin with this technique.

Tip: If you hate to type as much as I do, you can type . AW OF without the final *F*. You can also type just . AW to turn alignment back on, instead of . AW ON . Well, that's at least a little bit of work saving!

WordStar the Typewriter!

In previous versions of WordStar the only way to turn paragraph alignment off was to turn wordwrap off. The command is **^OW,** and it's a toggle switch. Using **.AW OFF** is normally the better way, however, because you save the command with the file. When you realign the entire file with **^QU,** you don't have to skip the unaligned sections of text manually.

With wordwrap off, WordStar acts like a typewriter. That is, when the cursor reaches the right margin WordStar *beeps* at you! WordStar won't start a new line until you press RETURN. This feature can be useful when you're typing columns of text. The **.AW OFF** command doesn't cause WordStar to beep at the end of the line: the cursor just keeps moving past the right margin until you press RETURN.

Dear Reader: Your little trip through the world of tabs is over. In the next chapter you'll continue learning about the many formatting possibilities at your disposal.

Chapter 10

Fun with Multiple Formats

In this chapter you will learn the following new command:

File Command

.CW   Change the horizontal character width

"Fun indeed!" you're probably thinking, "Who is he trying to kid?" Well, at least I got your attention! Working with multiple formats in a file *can* be fun, if you follow the tips and patterns in this chapter. At least you don't have to memorize too many new commands!

In the previous chapter you inserted a table with special formatting into another file. In my own sneaky fashion I was giving you a taste of this chapter's topic. You'll now continue to learn about working with files that contain sections with different formatting requirements.

DO WARM-UP

Primary and Secondary Formats

Always determine what the *primary* format for the file is to be—that is, the format for the bulk of the file. Insert the necessary dot commands at the beginning of the file before any text. That way, the dot commands govern all new text you type. When you began the CH.27 file, that's exactly what you did.

When you reach a section that requires another format, this new format is a *secondary* one. For example, the table of dates is in a secondary format. The most important point to remember when you're working with multiple formats is to be aware of exactly what format is "current." Remember that a format change stays in effect until you change it.

Ways to Change Formats

Depending on the actual format you need, you'll use dot commands, ruler lines, or a combination of both, when you change formats. Here are some patterns to follow.

Returning to the Primary Format

You'll add more text to the CH.27 file and learn a fast way to return to the primary format. First, open the file:

Press   **D** [open a document]

Type   ch.27

Press   **RETURN**

Press   **^C** or **PG DN** three times

The cursor is on line 28, and at the bottom of the screen you see the beginning of the table setup. When you inserted the date table, you also inserted a different ruler line into the file and other dot commands that govern formatting. Suppose you now want to add more text to the end of the file, but this text has to be in the primary format. The easiest way to revert to the primary format is to *copy* its ruler line where you want the format to change back. First, however, you need the ruler line itself.

Tip: The cursor can be on any blank line in that portion of your file with the format you want. The present cursor location is fine, as long as it's in front of the table.

Press   **^OO** or **F8**

to insert the ruler line into the text.

Now that you've inserted the ruler line into the file, just delete the ruler line and restore it where you want it. You could leave it here, but that's not necessary:

Press   **^Y** or **F5**

to delete the ruler line.

Press   ^QC or ^END

to position the cursor at the end of the file. It should be on the line below the **.AW ON** dot command.

Press   **RETURN** three times

for spacing.

Question: Why three times? *Answer:* Because the file at this point is in single spacing and you want four blank lines between the table and the next section of text. You already pressed RETURN once at the end of the table, so to get four blank lines you press RETURN three more times. When the file was in double spacing, you pressed RETURN twice for a "double double."

Always be careful about the spacing settings when you add blank lines to a file. **Tip:** If you're not sure of how many *real* blank lines are in the file when the dot command lines may throw you off, turn the preview on with ^OP and *count* the lines. Then turn preview off to continue working.

Press   ^U or **F2**

to restore the ruler line here.

Stop! What else do you have to do? Right! Turn right margin justification back on and return line spacing to double:

Press   ^X or **DOWN ARROW**

Type   .OJ ON or .oj on

Press   **RETURN**

Type   .LS 2 or .ls 2

Press   **RETURN**

Now, type the new text, shown below. Press **RETURN** twice after the heading but only *once* at the end of the paragraph.

The Extant Material

Aside from the completed sonata, there are several other

sketches in Beethoven's notebooks for the years 1813-1814 that

point to a tenth symphony. For example, page 28 of Notebook 7

contains a theme that is definitely "symphonic." It is already scored for most of the orchestra. Page 13 of Note book 8

contains a heading, "Second Movement," but no music of any kind.

The rest of the page is blank, although there does appear to be a

chocolate stain in the lower right corner.

Press   ^KS or F9

to save the file and resume where you left off.

A Boilerplate Ruler Line

 Another way to revert to the primary format is merely to save its ruler line to a separate boilerplate file. Then whenever you need it, copy the file with ^KR. That way, you don't have to finagle with creating a new ruler line each time you need it. **Tip:** Set up boilerplate files with the ruler lines you use the most, one ruler line per file.

Press   ^QF or ^F1

to begin find.

Type   .RR

Press   **RETURN**

Type   **b**

Press   **RETURN**

for a backwards find.

Press   ^KB or **SHIFT F9**

to mark the beginning of the block.

     Stop! Suppose you always use double spacing and right margin justification with the default format, too. Why not include those dot commands in the same boilerplate file as the ruler line? You'll add them to the block.

Press   ^X or **DOWN ARROW** three times

to move the cursor to the line below the **.LS 2** line.

Press   **^QS or ^F9**

to position the cursor at the left margin.

Press   **^KK or SHIFT F10**

to end the block here.

Press   **^KW**

Type   **df**

Press   **RETURN**

to write the block to the new DF file.

Tip: Use *short file names* for your boilerplate files. This is yet another way to save keystrokes when you insert the boilerplates with the **^KR** command. Keep a "crib sheet" list of your boilerplates and what each contains.

Indenting from Both Margins

In a moment you'll create another secondary format, but this time you'll use dot commands.

Press   **^QC or ^END**

to position the cursor at the end of the file.

The cursor should be on line 26 of page 2. Type the next paragraph and press **RETURN** twice at the end of it:

```
    In  the aforementioned letter to Grump, Beethoven  seems  to

indicate that he was working on a symphony at the time:
```

The cursor is on line 32. You now want to insert an indented section. This time, the indentation will be from *both* margins. What's more, it will be in single spacing. Type the following dot commands at column 1 and press **RETURN** after each:

```
.LS 1
.LM 6
.RM 60
```

Now, type the indented section and then press **RETURN** four times for spacing.

```
Ach!  My stomach hurts and my feet ache!  Frau Kram  is
the  world's worst cook.  Indeed, her midday meals  are
not  fit for human consumption.  I've had to eat out  a
lot, but the nearest Gasthaus is leagues away.  I can't
afford  a  carriage,  so my  shoes  are  wearing  thin.
Needless  to  say, all this is affecting my  work.   My
current  project, especially the scoring, is not  going
well  at all.  Don't ask me what it will be, because  I
don't know yet.  Just have pity on my plight.
```

Using the Boilerplate

The cursor should be on line 44 of page 2. Once again you want to revert to the primary format. This time, why not use your boilerplate?

Press   **^KR**

Type   df

Press   **RETURN**

Although you won't type any more text into the file, the next time you open the file you're ready to go. Just press **^QC** (**^END**) to position the cursor at the end of the file and start typing.

Press   **^KD** or **F10**

to save the file and return to the Opening menu.

Tip: If you plan to type indented sections often, set up the dot commands in another boilerplate file and read in the file with **^KR** whenever you need it. Of course, you can also put the commands in a macro and have a macro insert the commands or boilerplate. It's up to you!

Watch Those Tabs!

The next example shows you what happens when you're not on your toes. It illustrates a potential problem with tab stops.

Press   **D** [open a document]

Type   computer

Press   **RETURN**

Type   y

because this is a new file.

Type the dot commands and the first paragraph. Remember to press **^PS (F3)** to turn underlining on and off when you type the book title. At the end of the paragraph, press **RETURN** twice for spacing.

```
.LS 2
.OJ OFF
.UL ON
     As far as learning about exactly what a computer is and can

do, I offer what I have found to be a highly understandable

explanation.  It's from a book entitled Elementary BASIC.  In

this clever book, the figures of Sherlock Holmes and his sidekick

Dr. Watson explain the BASIC programming language to computer

users.  This is how Holmes in part describes the computer, which

he calls the "Analytical Engine":
```

You are now going to type in an indented quote, single spaced, as in the previous example. This time, however, you decide to set the left margin to 5 and the right margin 60, but watch what happens when you do. Type the following dot command lines at column 1, pressing **RETURN** after each:

```
.LM 5
.RM 60
.LS 1
```

Here's where the potential problem raises it nasty head. Take a look at the ruler line. There's still a tab stop at column 6. That tab stop is going to get in your way if you don't remove it. You should also set a new tab stop for the paragraph indentation, or use the **.PM** command, to indent the first line five spaces. Here, you'll set a new tab.

Because you plan to use the formatting again later, set up a ruler line that you can copy. You have two options:

1. Clear and set the tabs correctly with the **^ON** and **^OI** commands, respectively, and then insert the ruler line.
2. Edit the ruler line after you insert it.

I'll discuss the second option in the next chapter. First, remove the tab stop and set another:

Press   **^ON**

Type   6

Press   **RETURN**

to remove the tab stop at column 6.

Press   **^OI**

Type   10

Press   **RETURN**

to set a new tab at column 10.

Press   **^OO or F8**

to insert the new ruler line.

Press   **^X or DOWN ARROW**

to position the cursor before typing the text.

Don't worry about the tab stop at column 11 because it won't get in your way. Now you're ready for the indented section. (Don't type the asterisk.)

```
        "The major problem in communicating with the
    Engine is that one must use the utmost care and
    precision in giving it instructions, for it has no
    imagination whatsoever and cannot correct even trivial
    errors in spelling or punctuation.  It is, after all,
    like other machines in that it has no awareness of the
    tasks that it performs; therefore it will obey the most
    unreasonable of instructions.  For example, if it is
    told to print the number zero ad infinitum, it will
    continue to do so for hours on end, until a human being
    finally causes it to stop." *
```

*From *Elementary BASIC* by Henry Ledgard and Andrew Singer (New York: Vintage Books, 1982,) p. 4. Copyright 1982 by Henry Ledgard. Reprinted by permission of Random House, Inc.

After you have typed the indented paragraph:

Press   **RETURN** four times

for spacing.

Now you have *another* problem. You want to revert to the original format, but what about the tab stops? Because you need the default tabs, you should create a ruler line and copy the ruler line before typing the next section. I think you're beginning to see what happens if you're not careful when you work with different formats!

Press   **^QR** or **^HOME**

to position the cursor at the beginning of the file.

Press   **^OO** or **F8**

to insert a ruler line here.

Press   **^KB** or **SHIFT F9**

to begin the block.

Press   **^X** or **DOWN ARROW** twice

Press   **^QS** or **^F9**

to position the cursor at column 1.

Press   **^KK** or **SHIFT F10**

to end the block here.

You've included the **.LS 2** line in the block that you'll now copy to reset the format.

Press   **^QC** or **^END**

to position the cursor at the end of the file.

Press   **^KC** or **SHIFT F8**

to copy the block.

Press   ^X or **DOWN ARROW** twice

to position the cursor before typing.
    Finish typing the rest of the example:

This is a very important point about computers. Because

they are machines, they have no knowledge or discretion about

what they're doing. They merely follow the instructions given to

them. And they will follow these instructions continuously until

someone stops them or changes the instructions.

Press   ^KS or **F9**

to save the file and resume where you left off.

Press   ^QR or ^HOME

to position the cursor at the beginning of the file.

Hyphenation Again

After my "big hype" about hyphenation in Chapter 8, I think it's time for
another little example in hyphenating text in a file. If you've typed the example
correctly, here's what happens when you hyphenate the words in this file.

Press   ^OH

to turn hyphen help on.

Press   ^QU

to realign the file.
    WordStar first stops at the word *explanation*. Using the patterns you
already know, position the cursor on the *p* and press the HYPHEN key to
hyphenate the word at that syllable break. It turns out there are no other
words to hyphenate, so

Press   ^KD or **F10**

to save the file and return to the Opening menu.

Getting Along with Long Lines

All the files you've worked with so far have used either the default right margin at column 65 or one that was less than that setting. This next section shows you how to edit files with longer lines.

Using an Elite Typesize

WordStar "assumes" that your printer prints 10 characters per horizontal inch. Typists will know the word *pica,* which refers to type of this size. The other popular typesize is *elite.* It prints 12 characters per horizontal inch. (When you study laser printers in Chapter 26, you'll learn about other typesizes.)

WordStar can accommodate the elite typesize, but you must adjust the format accordingly. That is, the *more* characters you want to print per horizontal inch, the *longer* the length of the text line should be. You also have to tell WordStar when you want to use a different typesize.

If you printed a file with a 65-character line but used an elite typesize, the lines would only extend about five inches across the page. That much blank right margin space would look ugly! In fact, the standard line length for elite is about 80 characters, which fills out the page nicely.

To learn about working with long text lines and different typesizes, you'll use a copy of the STORY.LA file. (Make sure you've deleted the print codes from this file; see "A Brief Interlude" in Chapter 6 if you haven't.)

Press	**O** [copy a file]
Type	`story.la`
Press	**RETURN**
Type	`story.elt`
Press	**RETURN**

The file extension .ELT reminds you that this file is, or will be, in an elite typesize. When the copying has finished:

Press	**D** [open a document]
Press	**ESC**

to open the last file, that is, STORY.ELT.

Leave the left margin settings as is, but change the right margin to 80.

Press	**^N**

to insert a blank line.

Type   .RM 80 or .rm 80

Press   **RETURN**

to add another blank line.

Changing Horizontal Character Width

The dot command to change the horizontal character width is **.CW**, followed by an integer number. Here's where things get a little tricky, so bear with me. The number you type for the width represents the *divisor of 120*. The figure 120 (that is, 120th of an inch) represents the smallest distance WordStar can tell your printer to advance horizontally on the line. For instance, the default 10 characters per inch computes as $120/12 = 10$, so this setting is **.CW 12**, *not* **.CW 10** as you might think.

To get 12 characters per horizontal inch, think what number, when divided into 120, equals 12. Right! The answer is 10. So, on the blank line type this dot command:

Type   .CW 10 or .cw 10

Press   **RETURN**

Most letter-quality and laser printers can deal with these minute spaces, but some dot-matrix printers cannot. WordStar uses this minute spacing to set up the extra spaces on right-justified lines, a term known as *microjustification*. Often, WordStar will insert microspaces between letters to fill in lines. With some dot-matrix printers WordStar will add spaces between words only. That's why right-justified output produced on these printers may not be as visually pleasing as output produced on a letter-quality or laser printer.

Tip: Refer to the WordStar manual under Character Width for a handy table of the common settings and recommended right margins. That way, you don't have to wrack your brains with division!

Note: If you have a laser printer, you will use the **.CW** command not only to change horizontal character width, but also to choose different *fonts* (Chapter 26).

As a nice touch, you'll insert a message to remind you about the typesize:

Type   .. Change typewheel to elite!

(Make sure the dot command starts at column 1.)

Now that you've changed the margin, you must realign the file. Stop! What else must you do? Right! Recenter the title line:

Press   **^X** or **DOWN ARROW** twice

because there is still a .UL ON line in the file.

Press   ^OC or ESC C or SHIFT F2

to recenter the title.

Press   ^QU

to realign the file.
      (You could have turned hyphen help on, but for the moment don't bother
with hyphenation.)

Press   ^KS or F9   ·

to save the file and resume where you left off.

Scrolling Long Lines into View

Your computer screen can only show 80 characters at a time, but in WordStar
you can have lines that are up to 255 characters long. The flag character
display shows a long line with a +. To see that portion of the line that isn't
on the screen, you *scroll* the file left or right.
      As you type new text in a long line, WordStar automatically scrolls the
screen so you always see what you're typing. When you want to look at the
text later, here's how. First, position the cursor in any paragraph.
      To scroll the right side of the line into view,

Press   ^QD or ^F10

to position the cursor at the right end of the line.
      To scroll the left side of the line into view,

Press   ^QS or ^F9

to position the cursor at the left end of the line.
      The ends of long lines also scroll into view when you're moving the
cursor through the line with ^D (RIGHT ARROW) or ^F (^RIGHT ARROW).
Notice that WordStar can't show a smaller typesize on the screen—no matter
what typesize you print, the screen appearance of the text doesn't change.

Printing with an Elite Typesize

Before printing this file, change your typewheel and prepare the printer and
paper. If you don't have an elite typestyle, try printing the file anyway. WordStar
should still print 12 characters per horizontal inch. To start printing:

Press   ^PRT SC

Press   **ESC**

to save the file and print it.

How does it look? Is the text *centered* between the blank left and right margin space? If not, you might want to add a **.PO** command in the file to adjust where the left margin of the file starts printing on the page. Where's the page number? It's still at column 23. Dear Reader, soon enough you'll learn about how to control pagination in WordStar.

Note: The page offset dot command, **.PO,** works with the *current* horizontal character width. Normally, that would be **.CW 12** for 10 characters per horizontal inch, so a **.PO 5** setting offsets the left margin one-half inch (5/10). However, if you're using an elite typesize (**.CW 10**) and you insert a **.PO 5** command, the printer offsets the left margin slightly less than one-half inch (5/12).

Compressed and Expanded Printing

Using the **.CW** command is the best way to accomplish compressed or expanded printing on dot-matrix printers that support these features. Taking a look at the table in the WordStar manual, you'll notice that a **.CW 24** setting, for instance, prints five characters per inch. Again, you'd have to adjust the line length, but this time make the margins smaller to accommodate fewer characters per inch.

Tip: The README file contains **.CW** settings for the available types of compressed and expanded printing on each dot-matrix printer. Check this file for the settings you need. See Chapter 17 for other ways to do compressed or expanded printing.

Editing Format Changes

In a fit of temporary insanity, you decide to print the COMPUTER file with an elite typesize. Careful! The file has several format changes, so you have to change each one. This last section shows you how to edit the format settings in a file and how to change a ruler line quickly.

Press   **D** [open a document]

Type   computer

Press   **RETURN**

In general, when editing existing formatting dot commands keep two things in mind:

1. Make sure you edit all affected dot commands throughout the file.

2. Realign the file after you've made the changes.

Your first order of business is to change the horizontal character width:

Press   ^N

to insert a blank line.

Type   .CW 10 or .cw 10

Next, you have to delete the primary ruler line and insert another one showing the new right margin. Because you need the ruler line elsewhere, you'll also block it out.

Press   ^X or **DOWN ARROW**

Press   ^Y or **F5**

to delete the current ruler line.

Press   **^OR**

Type   80

Press   **RETURN**

to set the right margin to 80.

Press   **^OO** or **F8**

to insert the new ruler line.

Press   **^KB** or **SHIFT F9**

to begin the block.

Press   **^X** or **DOWN ARROW**

Press   **^QS** or **^F9**

to position the cursor at the left margin.

Press   **^KK** or **SHIFT F10**

to end the block.
Next, find and delete the .RM 60 dot command line:

Press   ^QF or ^F1

Type   60

Press   ESC

Press   ^Y or F5

to delete the line.

You now want to change the ruler line for the indented section, but you don't want to have to reset the tab stops. How would you make the change? Easy! Copy the ruler line, but first change the right margin to whatever you want. You must position the cursor past the current ruler line, which sets the right margin to 60. I used 75 for the new right margin.

Press   ^X or DOWN ARROW twice

to position the cursor on the line past the ruler line.

Press   ^OR

Type   75

Press   RETURN

to set the right margin at column 75.

Remember that WordStar always honors the *last* formatting command, whether it be a dot command or an onscreen command. However, WordStar only saves dot commands with the file. Right now the new right margin of 75 takes precedence over the ruler line setting.

Stop! Make sure the cursor is at the left margin before you insert another ruler line. If it isn't, move it there now. Then insert the new ruler, which takes its tab settings from the previous ruler:

Press   ^OO or F8

You could, if you wish, delete the old ruler line now (press ^E [UP ARROW] and then ^Y [F5]). Next, position the cursor on the last ruler line on line 31, which reverts to the primary format. Delete the line with ^Y (F5), then use ^KC (SHIFT F8) to copy the new primary format ruler line here. Finally, press ^QR (^HOME) to position the cursor at the beginning of the file, then ^QU to realign the file. A lot of work!

Dear Reader: An ounce of prevention is worth a pound of cure. When you can, determine the formatting you'll need *before* you start. But if you have to, you can always change a format later. Just make sure you change all affected dot commands and realign the file when you're finished.

Press   ^**KD** or **F10**

to save the file and return to the Opening menu.

Because there are endless formatting possibilities, I could only show you a few in this chapter and point out some general guidelines for making in-file format changes. In other chapters, including the next, you'll learn much more about formatting.

A Mixed Bag of Editing Features

In this chapter you will learn the following new commands:

Opening Menu and File Command

^\   Clear the screen

File Commands

^6 (SHIFT ^6)   Change a hard return to a soft return (document mode)

Turn auto indent on (nondocument mode)

^B   Turn the eighth bits off in all words on a line (nondocument mode)

^K'   Change a block to lowercase

^K"   Change a block to uppercase

^KI   Turn column replace mode on/off

^O   Set the fixed tab interval (nondocument mode)

^KN   Turn column mode on/off

^PM (^P RETURN)   Overprint a line with the next line

^QI (^F4)   Cursor to a line number (nondocument mode)

^QU   Turn the eighth bits off in an entire file (nondocument mode)

This chapter presents a variety of other editing techniques that will come in handy when you work with WordStar. You'll learn more about positioning text over columns, how to use the overtype mode to your advantage, and how to construct or edit a ruler line. Other topics include how to get rid of hard returns in the middle of paragraphs, how to work with WordStar as a program editor, how to convert WordStar documents to nondocuments, how to move or copy columns, what to do if WordStar prints blank pages, and what "screen garbage" is.

DO WARM-UP

Positioning Titles over Columns

In Chapter 9 you created a file with two columns set at tab stops. Suppose you want to "pretty up" the file a bit by adding some descriptive titles over the columns.

Press	**D** [open a document]
Type	expenses.jan
Press	**RETURN**
Press	**^X** or **DOWN ARROW** ten times

to position the cursor on line 6.

Press	**^N**

to add a blank line.

Although you can position the cursor over the columns by pressing the TAB key, you still have to "eye-ball" the titles to center them over the columns. Here's where your own personal sense of aesthetics comes into play.

Press	**TAB** or **^I**
Type	Type of Expense

Well, that doesn't look too good because it's too far over! Move the title a bit to the left:

Press	**^A** or **^LEFT ARROW** three times

to position the cursor under the *T* of *Type*.

Press   **BACKSPACE** or **^H** four times

to move the entire title back.

For the second title you'll bypass the TAB key altogether because the next tab stop is a decimal tab.

Press   **^QD** or **^F10**

to position the cursor at the end of the line.

Press   **SPACEBAR**

until you reach column 42.

Type   `Amount`

Press   **^KS** or **F9**

to save the file and resume where you left off.

Leave the cursor at the end of the line, directly past the word *Amount*.

Underlining Titles

Suppose you now want to underline both titles, including the spaces between them. Easy! With the cursor directly after the word *Amount*:

Press   **^PS** or **F3**

This will be the *end* underline toggle. Now for the beginning one.

Press   **^A** or **^LEFT ARROW** four times

to position the cursor under the *T* of *Type*.

Press   **^PS** or **F3**

Wait! What else do you have to do? Right! Tell WordStar to underline the spaces between words. First, move to the beginning of the line:

Press   **^QS** or **^F9**

Then insert the correct dot command:

Press   ^N

to add a blank line.

Type   .UL ON or .ul on

Prepare your printer and paper, then:

Press   ^PRT SC

Press   ESC

to save the file and print it.

The Overtype Trick

As I mentioned back in Chapter 1, when you turn insert mode off you run the risk of typing over text that you really want to keep. Some times, however, using overtype mode can come in handy.

Press   D [open a document]

Type   expenses.feb

Press   RETURN

Type   y

because this is a new file.
    As the basis for your February expenses, you'll copy the EXPENSES.JAN file and then make the necessary changes. This time instead of using the O [copy a file] command from the Opening menu, you'll use ^KR in the new file.

Press   ^KR

Type   expenses.jan

Press   RETURN

to copy in the EXPENSES.JAN file.
    All you have to do is change the month name and the figures, because the categories remain the same.

Press   ^V or INS

to turn insert mode off. The word Insert disappears from the status line.
Change the title:

Press   ^X or **DOWN ARROW** six times

Press   ^F or ^**RIGHT ARROW**

to position the cursor under the *J* of *January.*

Type   February

Press   ^**OC** or **SHIFT F2** or **ESC C**

to recenter the heading.

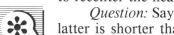

Question: Say you were typing over *February* with *March.* Because the latter is shorter than the former, how would you get rid of the extraneous characters *ary? Answer:* Either use spaces or press ^**QY** to delete the rest of the line.

To insert February's figures, position the cursor correctly and type over the January data with the February amounts.

Press   ^X or **DOWN ARROW** six times

Press   ^F or ^**RIGHT ARROW** twice

to position the cursor under the figure for Groceries, 185.22.

The assumption—an optimistic one!—is that your rent is the same for each month, so you would skip that figure. Now type in the new figures *over* the old ones (I've listed the categories, but you don't need to retype *them*).

Groceries	177.15
Utilities	52.90
Automobile	66.00
Clothing	24.80
Entertainment	45.00
Cats	13.50
Medical	112.75
Home Upkeep	322.14

I confess that I threw you a little curve. The insurance figure is also the same for each month, and I deliberately omitted it to make sure that you're on your toes!

(An aside: What happens when you press the **TAB [^I]** or **RETURN** key with the insert mode *off?* Try them!)

Press   ^**KD** or **F10**

to save the file and return to the Opening menu.

When you save the file and open another, insert mode is again on.

Creating and Editing Ruler Lines from Scratch

All along I've taken what I consider the "easy route" to inserting ruler lines in a file. You first determine the left and right margin and tab settings, then press ^OO (F8) to insert the ruler line. You can also type in a ruler line yourself, but I find this a tedious procedure. Of more use is the ability to edit an existing ruler line.

Press   **D** [open a document]

Type   ruler

Press   **RETURN**

Type   y

because this is a new file.

A Simple Ruler Line

I'll bypass for a moment the more difficult part of creating your own ruler line, that is, how to do a left margin that interferes with the **.RR** dot command on the screen. Suppose you want the left margin at column 10, the right margin at column 50, regular tab stops at columns 16 and 21, and a decimal tab at column 35. First, start the dot command:

Type   .RR or .rr

(make sure it's at column 1).

For your ruler line, you type the same characters you would see on the ruler line at the top of the screen:

- Type an L for the left margin and an R for the right margin.
- Type a hyphen (-) for other columns without tab stops.
- Type an exclamation point (!) for regular tab stops.
- Type a number sign (#) for decimal tab stops.
- You can edit the line as any other text with the editing commands you already know.

So, to set up the left margin:

Press **SPACEBAR** six times

to position the cursor at column 10.

Type   L or l

for the left margin.
  Notice how WordStar shows your ruler line at the top of the screen as you construct it.

Type   -

(that's a hyphen) five times to position the cursor at column 16.

Type   !

for the first tab stop.

Type   - four times

to set up the columns to column 21.

Type   !

for the second tab stop.

Type   - thirteen times

to set up the columns to column 35.

Type   #

for the decimal tab stop.

Type   - fourteen times

to set up the columns to column 50.

Type   R or r for the right margin.

Press **RETURN**

And there's your new ruler line! For the sake of experiment, press ^E (**UP ARROW**) to move up to the ruler line. Then press ^F (**^RIGHT ARROW**) a few times and then ^A (**^LEFT ARROW**) to see how you can move the cursor through the ruler line. WordStar doesn't stop at the decimal tab, but it does stop at the regular tab stops.

Editing a Ruler Line

It turns out that you don't like the tab stop at column 16, so you want to put it at column 15 instead. With any cursor key, first position the cursor directly under the ! at column 16. Then:

Press   **BACKSPACE** or **^H**

to delete the previous hyphen.

Better! Now what do you have to do? Right! Because you just reduced the length of the ruler line by one column, adjust the right margin:

Press   **^QD** or **^F10**

to position the cursor at the end of the line.

Press   **^S** or **LEFT ARROW**

to position the cursor under the right margin marker.

Type   -

to add a column.

Press   **^KS** or **F9**

to save the file and resume where you left off.

Press   **^X** or **DOWN ARROW**

to position the cursor on the next line.

A More Complicated Example

How do you construct a ruler line with the left margin in one of the first three columns of the line? What happens to the **.RR** part of the command? Here's where you must use a new command, **^PM** (**^P RETURN**) to *overprint one line with the next.* Take a look at this ruler line:

```
.RR
L----!----!----!---------------------------R
```

Notice that the **.RR** part of the command *seems* to be on a separate line, but it really isn't. Here's how to set up this line:

Type   .RR or .rr

Press   **^PM or ^P RETURN**

The flag character display shows a hyphen (-) to remind you that WordStar will "print" the *next* line over this one. Here it doesn't print anything, because dot command lines don't print anyway. But this is how you get a left margin in the same space at the **.RR** command. (If there *isn't* a hyphen in the flag column, press **BACKSPACE** to delete the hard return and try again.)

Now, type the ruler line as you know how (there are tab stops at columns 6, 11, and 16, and the right margin is at column 45). Press **RETURN** at the end of the line.

A Ruler Line with a Paragraph Margin

To include a paragraph margin in a ruler line that you construct, type a P at the paragraph margin location. Suppose you want to change the ruler line you just created so that it creates a hanging indent. First, position the cursor under the left margin marker. Then:

Press   **^G or DEL**

to delete the left margin marker.

Type   P or p

to set up the paragraph margin at column 1.

Press   **^D or RIGHT ARROW** five times

to position the cursor under the first tab stop.

Press   **^G or DEL**

to delete the !.

Type   L or l

to set the left margin here.

Press   **^KD or F10**

to save the file and return to the Opening menu.

I hope you now see that it's much easier to insert ruler lines *my* way! You'll see other uses of the overprint line command, **^PM (^P RETURN)** in later chapters. **Note:** When constructing a ruler line, you *don't* have to use the **^PM (^P RETURN)** command at all if the left margin or paragraph margin settings aren't in columns 1, 2, or 3.

Changing Hard Returns to Soft Returns

Now for something completely different! Suppose someone hands you a file that's in ASCII format. (Do you remember my discussion of ASCII in Chapter 3?) An ASCII file is not in WordStar document format because there are hard returns at the ends of all lines. An ASCII file also contains no other special formatting, such as soft spaces. It's a "straight text file."

You want to convert most of the hard returns to soft returns so you can then align the paragraphs with WordStar. (In Chapter 28 I discuss at greater length using WordStar files in other programs.) Or perhaps you inadvertently inserted a few hard returns in the middle of paragraphs and you want to get rid of them quickly.

WordStar has a command, **^6,** to convert a hard return at the end of the line to a soft return. The cursor can be anywhere on the line containing a hard return when you issue the command. This command only works in document files because there's no such thing as a soft return in nondocuments. In nondocument mode the **^6** command does something else, as you'll see later.

Dear Reader, I'm going to have to beg your patience and indulgence. You first need a file with which you can experiment with this command, so why not practice a little more with the nondocument mode? In nondocument mode there is no wordwrap, and every line must end with a hard return.

Press **N** [open a nondocument]

Type paris

Press **RETURN**

Type y

because this is a new file.

Type the following example but press **RETURN** at the end of *each* line, including the last. Notice the < symbols in the flag character display.

```
Our reports from various cities indicate growing anti-American
sentiment in certain segments of the population, especially those of
college age.  In Paris alone there occurred seventy-seven
arrests last week for rioting and disturbing the peace around the
```

```
American Embassy and also in front of the American Express office
near the Opera.  The most recent non-proliferation talks were
the major object of the demonstrations.
```

When you're finished:

Press   **^KD or F10**

to save the file and return to the Opening menu.

Pretend this report came over the wire services to you, so it's not yet in WordStar document format. To turn it into a WordStar document, first open the file as a document:

Press   **D** [open a document]

Press   **ESC**

to open the same file name, even though it's now in document mode instead of nondocument mode.

For every line ending with a hard return *except the last line,* you press **^6.** (On some computers, you may have to press **SHIFT ^6** instead.) *Question:* Why not the last line? *Answer:* You want to keep the return there so that WordStar "knows" where the end of the paragraph is. The cursor is at the beginning of the file.

Press   **^6** six times

to change the hard returns to soft returns.

Notice that the < symbols disappear from the flag character column and that the cursor moves down to the next line as you change the return on each line. Make sure you didn't convert the last hard return. (If you did, you'd have to position the cursor at the end of the line and insert a new hard return manually.) Now all you need do is "pretty up" the file at bit.

Press   **^QR or ^HOME**

to position the cursor at the beginning of the file.

Press   **TAB or ^I**

to insert a tab at the beginning of the paragraph.

Press   **^B**

to align the paragraph.

Voilà! WordStar even adjusted the spaces between words when it aligned the paragraph. **Tip:** If this were a longer file, you could have used ^QU to realign the file, but always make sure to leave hard returns at the ends of paragraphs.

Press   **^KD** or **F10**

to save the file and return to the Opening menu.

There is another way to convert a file with hard returns at the ends of lines to WordStar document format; it's described in Chapter 28. **Caution:** When you use the ^6 command, keep your pinky away from that potentially dangerous ^Y directly below it!

(An aside: If you turned hyphen help on with ^OH and then realigned the paragraph, you'd have a good example in hyphenating words that contain hard hyphens. Try it!)

Dealing with Nondocuments

Working a little with a nondocument, as you just did, leads into this section. If you're not a programmer or you don't plan to convert WordStar document files for use by other programs, your experience working with nondocuments may be limited to an occasional edit of your personal dictionary file (Chapter 8) or performing merge printing operations (Chapter 19). Refer to this section when you have to deal with nondocuments, especially when you find that you need to convert a document to a nondocument.

WordStar's Infamous Eighth Bit

The next two chapters cover how to use various DOS commands in WordStar for file management. You may have already experimented with the DOS TYPE command, which displays a file's contents on the screen, only to see what appear to be a lot of "garbage" characters when you TYPE a WordStar document file. Take heart: there's nothing wrong with your file!

The reason a WordStar document file appears with "garbage" characters when you TYPE the file from DOS has to do with bits and bytes, the ASCII codes, and the history of microcomputers. Here is a simplified explanation of what this means to you.

Although there are eight bits in a byte, early microcomputers used only the first *seven* bits to represent characters. A bit can be one of two states: either on or off. Thus, the highest possible number of seven on or off bits strung together is 2^7, or 128. The original ASCII coding scheme contained 128 different items, more than enough for the uppercase and lowercase letters, the nine digits and zero, punctuation marks, and other control characters. No one used the eighth bit at all: it was "off."

WordStar's designers decided to employ a trick with that unused eighth bit—also known as the *high order bit*—in document files. They set this bit "on" in the last character of each word within the left and right margins to help determine where to microjustify when printing. However, when IBM introduced its microcomputers, it used the "on" eighth bit to add 128 more characters to what it called the *extended ASCII character set.* That is, there are now 2^8, or 256 possible characters.

A dual problem arose out of all this. Because to WordStar the eighth bit meant formatting, it originally couldn't display the extra 128 ASCII characters. (This is now possible, as you'll see in Chapter 17.) And when you TYPE a WordStar file from DOS, DOS displays the ASCII character when the eighth bit is on. That's why you see a variety of graphics, foreign language, and other symbols in WordStar document files. All this brings me to . . .

Converting Documents to Nondocuments

Nondocument files don't have special formatting, so the eighth bit of every byte in these files is automatically off. Programmers refer to this as "straight ASCII" format. You'll also hear the term "ASCII text file" for this type of file. You can convert a document to a nondocument with one of two very simple operations. The first method involves opening the original document as a nondocument with the **N** [open a nondocument] command from the Opening menu. Then press ^QU at the beginning of the file to turn off all eighth bits in the file.

As you know, ^QU in a normal WordStar document realigns the entire file. In nondocument mode the command merely turns off all high order bits. You can also use ^B to turn off high order bits per line, but this means many more keystrokes. Most of the time you'll want to do the conversion quickly, so ^QU is a better bet.

Using the ^QU or ^B commands to convert a document to a nondocument won't automatically delete all dot command lines and print codes. This brings me to the other way to convert a document to a nondocument that *will* remove dot commands and print codes. To wit: "print" the file to a disk file with the special ASCII printer driver. Remember to supply a file name at the Name of printer? prompt like this: ascii > filename . Otherwise, WordStar "prints" to a disk file called ASCII.WS. **Note:** Using this printer driver has the added advantage of changing the "extended ASCII" codes to "straight ASCII" (Chapter 17).

Changing Nondocument Tab Stops

When you press the **TAB** key or ^I in a nondocument, WordStar inserts a fixed tab code instead of spaces. By default, fixed tabs in nondocuments move the cursor to the next column that is an even multiple of eight, and there are no changing tab stops. You can, however, alter the fixed tab setting with the

^O command. Recall that in document mode this command brings up the Onscreen Format menu. In nondocument mode when you press ^O, WordStar says:

```
Tab characters are now 8    columns wide.

Enter new width (2, 4, 8, 16).
```

You can change the tab interval to a *binary* number only, that is, one that's a multiple of 2. The tab setting also affects the next new command, auto indent.

Auto Indent

Programmers often indent sections of program code for readability. That is, the indentations make relationships between certain lines of code more immediately obvious. In nondocument mode, WordStar now has a nifty *auto indent* feature. When you press RETURN at the end of a line, WordStar positions the cursor at the column where the indent occurs on the line directly above, instead of at the left margin.

So when you're typing in many indented lines, you don't have to press the TAB key to begin each indentation. WordStar "remembers" the indent from the previous line. To turn auto indent on, press ^6. You'll see the message Auto-In on the status line. Toggle auto indent off by pressing ^6 again. If you like this feature, and I think you will, you can configure WordStar to turn auto indent on automatically (Chapter 27).

Remember that you can change the tab interval with the ^O command or set it up as a default. For example, when I write programs, I prefer an automatic indentation of two columns instead of eight, so I've configured WordStar accordingly.

Different Defaults for Different Languages

Most programming languages use file extensions to identify files. For example, if you write programs in Pascal you append the .PAS extension to files, while the C language uses the extension .C. You can have different default formats for each extension. That is, for .PAS files the indentation may be four columns, while for .C files the indentation could be two columns. Chapter 27 gives more information.

Going to a Line

The ^QI (^F4) command used in a nondocument moves the cursor to a specific line number instead of to a specific page. There *are* no page breaks in a nondocument! When you press ^QI or ^F4, WordStar prompts:

Find what line?

Type the line number and press **RETURN.** The **^QI (^F4)** command always positions the cursor at the beginning of the line.

Printing Nondocuments

Answer y for "yes" to the print option, Nondocument?, if you want WordStar to format a nondocument as a document during printing. WordStar uses whatever are the default document page formats. You'll then get an aesthetically pleasing page layout, including margins and pagination, for your nondocument printout. If you answer "no" to the same print option, WordStar just prints the nondocument without any formatting.

Tip: When you print a nondocument as a document, WordStar won't change the line endings. If your nondocument is a program source file with very long lines, change the default page offset if the lines print too far to the right.

Changing Case

The rest of the chapter deals with new commands on the Block & Save menu. All these commands begin with the prefix **^K.** Programmers and nonprogrammers alike will like two new WordStar commands that change the *case* of a marked block. The first command, **^K',** changes an entire marked block into lowercase letters, while the second command, **^K",** changes a block into uppercase letters. These two commands do nothing to nonalphabetic characters, such as numbers or punctuation marks.

Whereas going from lowercase or mixed case to uppercase characters is easy, moving in the opposite direction can present a problem. WordStar doesn't honor mixed case; it just changes all letters to lowercase. This may not always be exactly what you want.

As an experiment, open the EXPENSES.FEB file:

Press   **D** [open a document]

Type   expenses.feb

Press   **RETURN**

Press   **^X** or **DOWN ARROW** eleven times

to position the cursor at the beginning of the *Type of Expense* line.

Press   **^KB** or **SHIFT F9**

to begin the block.

Press   **^QD** or **^F10**

to position the cursor at the end of the line.

Press   **^KK** or **SHIFT F10**

to end the block here.

Press   **^K"**

(that's **^K SHIFT'**) but *don't* hold down the CTRL key as you press the double quotes.

You've changed the block to uppercase. What happens when you change the block to lowercase? You get all lowercase letters, even though that's not the way the block was when you started, because WordStar can't "remember" whether part of a block was originally in uppercase.

Press   **^K'**

but *don't* hold down the CTRL key as you press the single quote. You've just changed the block to lowercase. The moral to this example is to be careful and know what you're doing when you change the case of a block. (Perhaps in a future release at least WordStar will be able to change a block to mixed case, with initial caps.)

Press   **^KQ**

Type   **y**

to abandon the edit.

Moving or Copying Columns

When you set up a block to move or copy, WordStar blocks each line of the text *horizontally* from the beginning block marker to the end marker. That means everything on each line within the block markers is part of the block. That's fine for moving or copying lines and paragraphs, but it won't work for columns because columns are *vertical*. This section shows you how to deal with columnar blocks. You'll first use the EXPENSES.JAN to experiment with this type of block.

Press   **D** [open a document]

Type   expenses.jan

Press   **RETURN**

Note: The next examples show you how to move a column, but the same procedures apply to copying a column, except you'd use the ^KC (**SHIFT F8**) command instead of ^KV (**SHIFT F7**) after blocking out the column you want. You can also press ^KY (**SHIFT F5**) to delete a column block.

Using Column Mode

The first rule of thumb when you work with columns is to turn on what WordStar calls *column mode,* the command for which is ^KN. Suppose you want to move the column of figures—the second column—over a bit to the right. First, position the cursor on the *A* of the word *Amount* directly above the column of figures on line 7 because you want to include the title in the column block.

Press   **^KN**

to turn column mode on.

The word Column appears on the status line. Column mode stays on until you turn it off. The ^KN command is a toggle switch, so when you're finished moving a column you'd turn column mode off by pressing ^KN again (don't do it yet, though!). **Note:** As you'll see in a moment, when column mode is on the flag character display shows a K on *each* line of a marked block. When column mode is off, the flag character display shows a K only on the line containing the ending block marker.

Care with Rectangular Blocks

Are you ready to begin? No! When column mode is on, you must be careful about how you set the beginning and ending block markers. You're about to delimit a vertical, rectangular block, which must include both the *leftmost* character you need in the block and the *rightmost* character.

Cursor down and take a look at the dividing line below the figures on line 18. It extends a bit to the left and right of the figures, so you must position the cursor carefully when delimiting the block. As it turns out, the line starts at column 39 and ends and column 49, so those are the left and right limits of the rectangular block you want to move.

Return the cursor to line 7 under the letter *A* of *Amount,* then follow the instructions. Turn the print codes off with **^OD** (**SHIFT F1**) to see the exact location of this word. Because *Amount* starts at column 42, move the cursor left to include the first part of the divider line in the block:

Press   ^S or **LEFT ARROW** three times

to position the cursor at column 39.

Press   **^KB or SHIFT F9**

to begin the block here.

Press   **^C or PG DN**

Press   **^X or DOWN ARROW**

to position the cursor on line 18, which contains the underlines.

Press   **^QD or ^F10**

to position the cursor at the end of the line at column 50.

Press   **^KK or SHIFT F10**

to end the block here.
    Now, take a look at the rectangular block:

Press   **^R or PG UP**

On some monitors, the underlined word *Amount* may not appear to be in the block because WordStar uses the same highlighting for both underlining and blocks, but don't worry. Before continuing, you should position the cursor under the *A* of *Amount* on line 7 again, then follow the next instructions. You want to move the block over a bit to the right so that it starts at column 45.

Press   **^D or RIGHT ARROW** three times

to position the cursor under the *u* of *Amount*.

Press   **^KV or SHIFT F7**

to move the block.
    What happened? Nothing! WordStar didn't move the block. Why not? Normally, you can't move or copy a block *into itself*. You could have moved the block somewhere else in the file, but not in the same columns that the block presently occupies. This brings me to . . .

Column Replace Mode

All is not lost, Dear Reader! You *can* move a block into itself, but you must tell WordStar that this is what you intend. Use the *column replace* command, **^KI,** to turn column replace mode on:

Press   **^KI**

The status line now says ColRepl. Like **^KN,** the column replace command, **^KI,** is a toggle switch and remains in effect until you turn it off. It works only in tandem with **^KN.** With the cursor still at column 45 of line 7, you're now ready to move the block into itself:

Press   **^KV or SHIFT F7**

It worked! *Question:* What's "wrong" with the file now? First, because you've moved the column over, you'd have to adjust the ruler line to show the decimal tab stop at column 45 if you planned to enter more text in the file. Second, the titles at the top of the file aren't centered nicely over the columns.

Switching Columns

If you wanted to move column 1 so that its position switches with that of column 2, be careful! With column replace mode on if you move one column into the space of *another* column, you'll *overwrite* the second column. As an example, press **^KI** to turn column replace mode off (leaving just column mode on), block out the first column, and move it over past the second column.

When you're finished experimenting:

Press   **^KQ**

Type   y

to quit without saving the file.

A Column Miscellany

Here are other points to keep in mind about column operations. First, if there is a print code such as **^S** at the end of the column, WordStar won't move or copy it with the column. You'd have to reinsert the code manually, so always check the codes after a column move.

Second, if with column mode on you attempt to insert a file with the ^KR command, WordStar checks to see if the file contains column formatting. If it doesn't, or if only part of the file contains columns, you see this message:

```
The file to insert is NOT a column document (line lengths vary).

You can...

 - Press N to insert the entire file.

 - Press Y to insert the file up to the point where it ceases to be a column
   document, and highlight the insertion (for easy deletion).

 - Press ^U to insert the file up to the point where it ceases to be a column
   document.

Press N or Y or ^U.
```

If you want to cancel altogether, press **Y,** then delete any portions of the file that WordStar may have inserted. Otherwise, choose **N** or **^U** as the message instructs.

Finally, to move or copy dot commands with a column, open the document in *nondocument* mode and perform the operation. Make sure you then save the file and reopen it with the **D** [open a document] command before making any other changes.

Newspaper Columns

WordStar doesn't handle multiple columns of text that "snake" from one column to the next, as in newsletters. That is, even though you can set up these columns, if you edit one column WordStar can't adjust the lines in other columns. Eventually, MicroPro will provide this feature in WordStar. Until then, here's a short example that shows how to move text columns.

Copy the STORY.LA file to a new file called STORY.COL, then open the file:

Press	**O** [copy a file]
Type	story.la
Press	**RETURN**
Type	story.col
Press	**RETURN**

Press   **D** [open a document]

Press   **ESC**

     Suppose you want two columns of text, with each column being 30 characters wide. First, realign the entire file into one smaller column.

Press   **^Y or F5**

to delete the .UL ON line.

Press   **^X or DOWN ARROW**

to bypass the title.

Press   **^OR**

Type   30

Press   **RETURN**

to set the right margin at column 30.

Press   **^QU**

to realign the rest of the file.

Press   **^QR or ^HOME**

to position the cursor at the beginning of the file.

Press   **^OR**

Type   65

Press   **RETURN**

to reset the right margin at column 65.
     You'll now move page 2 of the file so that it becomes a second column on page 1. Stop! Because the title ("ANGELES CREST ROMANCE") takes up three lines on page 1, you would not include all of page 2 in the block you want to move. That is, you leave out three lines on the page.

Press   **^QI**

Type   2

Press   **RETURN**

to position the cursor at the top of page 2.
    Now, block out the page as a column:

Press   **^X or DOWN ARROW**

to bypass the blank line at the top of the page.

Press   **^KN**

to turn column mode on.

Press   **^KB or SHIFT F9**

to begin the block.

Press   **^QI**

Type   **3**

Press   **RETURN**

to position the cursor at the top of page 3.

Press   **^E or UP ARROW** five times

to position the cursor on line 51 of page 2.
    After a bit of experimentation, I discovered that only the first line of the paragraph that begins *Needless to say* would fit on page 1 when I moved the block. A single line "stranded" at the bottom of a page is a *widow,* an unfortunate entity that you'll want to avoid. You'll learn about widows in Chapter 15. Here, you decide to end the block with the previous paragraph.

Press   **^KK or SHIFT F10**

to end the block.
    What happened? You didn't block the entire column! Remember you must include the *rightmost* column position. So:

Press   **^QD or ^F10**

to position the cursor at the end of the line.
    You still aren't there yet! You must move the cursor over so that it is past the left margin of the line above the last line.

Press   **SPACEBAR**

repeatedly until the cursor is at column 31.

Press   ^KK or **SHIFT F10**

to end the block here.
    Now, move the block into page 1:

Press   **^QR or ^HOME**

to position the cursor at the beginning of the file.

Press   **^X or DOWN ARROW** three times

Press   **^QD or ^F10**

to position the cursor at the end of the line.
    You aren't there yet! You must use the **SPACEBAR** to position the cursor
where you want the second column to start. Use column 36:

Press   **SPACEBAR**

until the cursor is at column 36 of line 4.

Press   **^KV or SHIFT F7**

to move the column here.
    Are you finished? No! Why not?

Press   **^QI**

Type   2

Press   **RETURN**

New page 2 contains a whole slew of blank lines! That's because WordStar
didn't move the soft and hard returns when you moved the column. To bring
up the existing text from old page 3 to new page 2, delete the blank lines
quickly:

Press   **^QQY**

Caution: Watch the screen as WordStar deletes the blank lines. When
the first text line reaches the top of the page, press the **SPACEBAR** to stop
the continuous line deleting.
    Now your file is correctly formatted in two columns. If you scroll through
the file, you'll notice some soft hyphen codes (=) in the middle of lines. When
you realigned the file most of the hyphenated words shifted to the middle of
the lines. Just press **^OD (SHIFT F1)** to turn off these codes and see the
correct line endings. When you're finished:

Press   **^KD** or **F10**

to save the file and return to the Opening menu.

I think you can see that you wouldn't want to do this all the time!

Note: You may also have to turn off microjustification with the **.UJ OFF** command when you're working with text columns. See Chapter 17.

When WordStar Prints Blank Pages

Do you remember my discussion of "garbage" in Chapter 2? Here's one final editing point to learn. If your printout contains one or more blank pages, check the end of the file. Often superfluous carriage returns force WordStar to start a new page, but there's no text on the page. WordStar "assumes" that this blank page is still part of the file and thus prints it.

You can tell if there's a blank page if you see a page break display at the end of the file but no text after the page break. To overcome this problem, position the cursor on a blank line at the end of the last page but *before* the page break. Then press **^QQY** to delete the extra blank lines. When WordStar's finished it should not show you a new page break.

Another Kind of "Garbage"

Here's another kind of garbage: screen garbage. Once in a while a power surge or other hardware problem may cause extraneous characters to appear on the screen, although they aren't part of any file, nor will they affect WordStar's operation. They're just visually annoying. To clear the screen of these characters, press **^\\.** This is one command that works both at the Opening menu and in a file.

Dear Reader: Enough editing and formatting for a while! The next two chapters change the pace a bit. They discuss some very important features: working with DOS, file maintenance, and housekeeping.

Chapter 12

Working with DOS and File Management, Part 1

In this chapter you will learn the following new commands:

Opening Menu Commands

F	Turn the file display on/off, restrict the file listing
R	Run a DOS command

File Commands

^KE	Rename a file
^KF	Run a DOS command
^KJ	Delete a file
^KL	Change the current drive or directory
^KO	Copy a file

DOS Commands

^NUM LOCK (^S)	Stop scrolling temporarily (resident)
^PRT SC (^P)	Send the screen display to the printer (resident)
^BREAK (^C)	Cancel a DOS command (resident)
CD *or* **CHDIR**	Change the current directory (resident)
COMMAND	Run the DOS command processor (resident)
DATE	View or change the current date (resident)

more . . .

DIR	Display the files on a drive or in a directory (resident)
EXIT	Return to the previous level (resident)
FIND	Search files for a text string (transient)
FORMAT	Format (initialize) a disk (transient)
LABEL	Create or change the volume label (DOS 3.0 and higher, transient)
MD *or* **MKDIR**	Make a new directory (resident)
RD *or* **RMDIR**	Remove (delete) an empty directory (resident)
SEARCH	Locate specific files (transient)
TIME	View or change the current time (resident)
TREE	Display all directories (transient)
TYPE	Display the contents of a text file (resident)
VOL	Display the volume label (resident)

Other Features

..	Parent directory
****	Path designator
/	Switch designator
*	Wildcard to match any characters
?	Wildcard to match one character

Dear Reader: lest you totally "freak out" because there seem to be so many new commands to learn, relax! You probably know most of the DOS commands already. What's more, many of the commands are duplicates, even triplicates. That is, there are three different ways to copy, delete, or rename files, but the procedure for each is about the same.

This chapter and the next discuss how to work with DOS from within WordStar and the essential file operations you should master for your day-to-day activities. You'll learn what file management is, how to maintain a housekeeping schedule for keeping track of your files, and how to work with disks and directories. I suggest that you study both chapters together.

Note: The DOS commands discussed in this chapter may be different from those of the new operating system, OS/2, that will become available sometime in 1988. When in doubt, check your operating system manual.

$$\boxed{\textit{DO WARM-UP}}$$

Running a DOS Command

Because DOS is your computer's file manager, take a look at an important feature that you'll use often: running a DOS command from within WordStar. This feature *goes out to DOS* and then returns to where you left off in WordStar, that is, to the Opening menu or into the file you were editing. The WordStar command is **R** [run a DOS command] from the Opening menu or **^KF** from within a file.

There are two ways to run a DOS command. WordStar expects you to run only *one* DOS command and then return immediately to WordStar. But you can also tell WordStar that you want to *stay* in DOS for a while, for example, to issue several DOS commands in succession.

When you run a DOS command, WordStar loads a temporary version of DOS's *command processor.* This is in a file called COMMAND.COM on your boot disk or in the root directory of your hard disk. It "processes," that is, *interprets* all DOS commands. After running the DOS command, you press a key to return to WordStar and WordStar releases the temporary command processor from memory. If you want to stay in DOS, WordStar doesn't release the command processor until you tell it. You can run normal DOS commands and even an entirely separate program—for example, Lotus 1-2-3—from within WordStar.

Note: Your system has to have enough memory to accommodate WordStar's requirements, the DOS command processor, and the other program you want to run. Depending on your version of DOS, the command processor may take up as much as 23K of memory (for DOS 3.1), and WordStar requires at least 256K. The size of the COMMAND.COM file tells you how much memory it requires (mine contains 23322 bytes). See "Looking at Memory" in Chapter 13 for ways to check your system's memory.

Caution: Don't try to load any terminate and stay resident programs, such as Word Finder, from *within* WordStar. You run the risk of "hanging" your computer. DOS programs that you also shouldn't run from within WordStar are MODE and PRINT, unless you've already issued these commands from DOS at least once before loading WordStar. (See the Introduction for information about the MODE command. You probably wouldn't use the PRINT command anyway, because it doesn't work well with WordStar document files.) As a general rule, then, always load TSR programs *before* you load WordStar.

One DOS Command: Viewing the File Directory

As an example of the "one shot deal," suppose you want to view the file directory to display the date and time when you last edited a file. WordStar doesn't show this information in its directory display, so you'll go to DOS. If you wish, open any file or do the following steps from the Opening menu.

Caution: Whenever you run a DOS command from within a file with the ^**KF** command, *save your work first!* In fact, you might want to create a macro that issues the ^**KS** command as a precaution and *then* the ^**KF** command. Also, don't turn your machine off until you've properly returned to WordStar, saved your file, and exited to DOS.

Press   **R** [run a DOS command] from the Opening menu or ^**KF** from within a file

WordStar prompts—

```
Enter the DOS command that you wish to use. WordStar will remain in
memory while it is being used.
```

—and you see the DOS prompt on the screen. It will probably be B> if you have a floppy disk system or C> if you have a hard disk.

Type   dir

Press   **RETURN**

The DOS command DIR shows the file listing of the current drive or directory, including file names, the size of each file in bytes, the date and time you last edited or created each file, how many files are on the drive, and how much disk space is available. **Note:** To stop the scrolling of a long directory listing, press ^**NUM LOCK** or ^**S.** Then press any key to start again.

After the DIR command has finished, at the bottom of the screen WordStar tells you:

```
Press any key to return to WordStar.
```

Press   <any key>

If you were working in a file when you tried the previous example, you may have noticed two files with funny names in the directory. These are *temporary* files that WordStar uses to keep track of the editing. They end in the extensions .A and .B. I'll discuss them at more length in the next chapter. Should your computer system not have sufficient memory to run a DOS command from within WordStar, you'll see this message:

```
Can't execute command. Your computer may not have enough memory.
Press any key to return to WordStar.
```

Press a key. To eliminate this problem, you have two options: (1) purchase more memory, or (2) exit WordStar, remove any terminate and stay resident programs (such as the Word Finder thesaurus) from memory, and load WordStar again.

One DOS Command: Formatting a New Floppy Disk

As another example of going to DOS once, suppose you discover that you need a new, formatted floppy disk before you can save the file you're editing but you don't have any formatted disks ready. You can format a new disk "on the fly" by going out to DOS temporarily. In Chapter 13 I'll discuss ways to avoid this situation altogether, but it's a useful procedure to know!

The DOS FORMAT command is a *transient* command. That is, it's not part of the basic DOS command set—the *resident* commands—but instead is in its own separate file called FORMAT.COM. Notice that I list the DOS commands as resident or transient at the beginning of the chapter. You can issue DOS resident commands, such as DIR, any time you see the DOS prompt. To issue a transient command, you need access to its command file.

Note: If the file containing a transient DOS command is on another drive or in another directory, you must include the drive designator or the directory path in the command. See the examples below. In Chapter 28, I'll show you how to set up a file search path for file names.

Tip: Copy the file FORMAT.COM to your WordStar program disk so that it's always ready when you need it. See "Copying Files" in the next chapter if you want to copy FORMAT.COM now without leaving WordStar.

Here, then, are the steps for formatting a new floppy disk from within WordStar:

Press   **R** [run a DOS command] from the Opening menu or ^**KF** from within a file

Stop! If FORMAT.COM is on a disk in the A drive and the DOS B> prompt appears, you have to tell DOS where to find that file. If you have a hard disk, FORMAT.COM should be either in your root directory or in a separate DOS directory. If FORMAT.COM *isn't* on your WordStar program disk, you must replace the WordStar disk in the A drive with the DOS disk *before continuing*. You should also tell DOS where the new disk you want to format is. Assume you'll put it in the B drive.

You're now ready to choose *one* of the options below:

Type   a:format b:

(notice the colons!) if FORMAT.COM is on a disk in the A drive

    or

Type   \format b:

if FORMAT.COM is in the root directory of the hard disk

  or

Type   \dos\format b:

if FORMAT.COM is in the DOS directory of the hard disk (if it's in another directory, substitute the correct name for DOS above, but don't forget the \).

Press   **RETURN**

DOS tells you to put the new disk in drive B before continuing. Remember to replace the WordStar program disk in the A drive and the work disk in the B drive before you press any key to return to WordStar. You can return to WordStar first, but it's a good habit to learn to replace the disks as soon as you can. WordStar will need to access the disk at some point, so it's a dangerous situation not to have the disk in the drive!

You can also append a *volume name* to the newly formatted disk if you use the /V switch with the FORMAT command. You would type a:format b:/v to include the switch in the first example above. After it formats the disk, DOS will ask you for a volume label that can be up to 11 characters long. *Don't* use nonalphanumeric characters like # or -. In DOS 2.0, you can't add or change a volume label later; you must do it at the time of formatting (or purchase a separate utility). DOS versions beginning with 3.0 include the utility for changing volume names.

Note: Switch characters for some MS-DOS commands are different in PC-DOS. Check your documentation if a switch doesn't work correctly.

How to Stay in DOS: Changing the Date and Time

Suppose you forgot to enter today's date and the correct time when you turned on your computer. You later press **ESC @** or **ESC !** to insert the date or time in a file only to see DOS's default date, January 1, 1980, or a time that's a few minutes past midnight! You can go to DOS and change the date and time. In the process you'll learn how to *stay* in DOS until you want to return to WordStar.

Press   **R** [run a DOS command] from the Opening menu or **^KF** from within a file

Type   command

Press   **RETURN**

This resident DOS command loads the command processor and retains it in memory. You don't have to tell DOS the drive designator because DOS keeps track of the location of COMMAND.COM. You'll now stay at the DOS prompt until you tell DOS to *exit* back to WordStar. Suppose today is April 26, 1987. To set this date:

Type   **date 4/26/87**

Press   **RETURN**

If it's now 1:32 p.m., to set this time:

Type   **time 13:32**

(remember the time must be in 24-hour format).

Press   **RETURN**

You could now issue other DOS commands, such as DIR. When you're finished working in DOS and you want to return to WordStar:

Type   **exit**

Press   **RETURN**

Press   ⟨any key⟩

in response to WordStar's prompt.

   The DOS EXIT command returns to the previous command level, that is, the program that called DOS. Here, the previous command level is WordStar itself. **Caution:** Always issue the EXIT command when you're finished working in DOS, return to WordStar, and exit WordStar correctly.
   One nifty use of the run a DOS command is to run an entirely separate version of WordStar. If you have enough memory, you could try it! But don't edit the same file you're already working on unless you've installed WordStar in a shared environment (Chapter 13). *Now* you're ready to learn about file management.

File Management

As its name implies, *file management* or *file maintenance* simply means keeping track of your files. Some typical file management operations include displaying the file directory, deleting files, renaming files, copying files, finding files, checking disk space, and making backups. In the previous section you were working with file management while learning about the run a DOS command.

DOS Versus WordStar

You can perform *basic* file operations from the Opening menu or from within a file in WordStar. By "basic" I mean working with one file at a time. However, at times you might want to use DOS for file management because DOS is much more flexible at this operation than WordStar is. One of DOS's primary jobs is to keep track of files (but, then again, DOS is a *terrible* word processor!). This brings me to . . .

Wildcards

DOS really shines over WordStar in the file management arena when you want to copy, delete, or rename groups of related files. By *related* I mean files with similar names or extensions. (DOS doesn't "know" or "care" about the contents of files.) For example, the two files CH.1 and CH.2 both have the same name but different extensions. The files JONES.LTR, SMITH.LTR, and WOOD.LTR all have the same extension.

What Wildcards Do. You can use DOS's *wildcards* to restrict the copying, deleting, and renaming operations to act with certain files. You've already learned what the find and find and replace wildcards are when you looked at those two commands in Chapter 6. In DOS, wildcards act as *templates,* that is, patterns for working with related files. There are two DOS wildcards.

Match Any Character. The ? wildcard matches *any single character.* For example, using TE?T as the file name would tell DOS to work with all file names that begin with TE and end with T, no matter what the third letter is. DOS would use files such as TEXT or TENT or TEST, but *not* TEXT.2, because you didn't include a file extension.

Match All Characters. The * wildcard is more useful. It tells DOS to match *all* characters starting from the position of the * in the file name you type. For example, TE?T.* tells DOS to find all files with the previous restriction, but to include files with extensions, too. If you use *.LTR, this instructs DOS to find all files with the extension .LTR.

Suppose you want all "letter" files but you named some with the extension .LTR and some with .LET. You can issue the command as *.L*. The wildcard to use all files is *.*. In the examples below, you'll see many other examples of working with the DOS wildcards. There are, unfortunately, only a couple WordStar file management commands that can accept wildcards.

File Names

As you can imagine, a crucial point to keep in mind about file management is to name your files logically. Use file extensions to identify those files that contain similar documents, such as .LET or .LTR for "letters." You can then use wildcards to filter out nonapplicable files. When I was writing this book, I kept each chapter in a file called CH.1, CH.2, and so on. I could then do a variety of file management tasks with just these files, and leave the others alone.

The Modular Approach, Again

As I suggested in the Introduction, use the modular approach to keep the size of files small. Why? Because if you break your longer files into small modules, they're easier to work with. What's more, if something goes wrong with a large file you run the risk of losing more of your efforts. And small files have small backup files. As crazy as it may seem, you can get *more* of a project on a floppy disk if you break up the project into small files instead of leaving it as one large file.

In the case of a book, for instance, it's sheer madness to have the entire book in one file. I suggest restricting file size to no more than 20 to 25 pages. You can combine the files later or *chain* them together when you print them, as Chapter 16 describes.

WordStar's File Management Commands

You've already learned how to delete, copy, and rename files from the Opening menu with the **Y, O,** and **E** commands. Most Opening menu commands have ^K equivalents when you're working in a file. Table 12–1 shows an alphabetical listing of these commands and their in-file and DOS equivalents where applicable. Other sections in this chapter and the next explain most of the new commands and show you other ways to delete, copy, and rename files.

 Tip: Whenever you issue any WordStar file management command, you can type the file name yourself or select the file by name from the file listing. Position the cursor on the file name and press **RETURN.** In DOS, you must always type the file name.

Disks and Directories

Both WordStar and DOS "assume" you want to work with files on the current floppy drive or in the current directory of your hard disk. This is the *default drive.* During warm-up, you set the default drive to B for a floppy disk computer or to the directory WS4 for a hard disk system. You can *change* the

Table 12–1 WordStar's File Management Commands

Opening Menu	In a File	DOS Equivalent	Operation
C	None		Protect a file*
E	^KE	REN	Rename a file
F	None†	DIR	File directory
J	^J		Help
L	^KL	CD	Change drive/directory
M	^KP		Merge print‡
O	^KO	COPY	Copy a file
P	^KP		Print a file§
R	^KF		Run a DOS command
X	^KX		Exit to DOS
Y	^KJ	DEL	Delete a file
None	^KR		Insert a file
None	^KW		Write a block to a file

*The ^OP command protects a file temporarily. It's not a real equivalent of the C command. There *is* a DOS equivalent, but it's an advanced topic that you'll investigate in Chapter 28.

†To display the file directory listing from within a file, issue any file command, such as ^KJ. Press ^U (F2) or RETURN to cancel the command after you've looked at the directory.

‡See Chapters 19 through 24.

§There is a PRINT command in DOS, but it's not terribly useful for printing WordStar document files. What's more, because it's a terminate and stay resident program you shouldn't work with it from within WordStar.

default drive or work with files on other drives or in other directories whenever you wish.

Paths

If you have a floppy disk system, you can probably skip this section. Hard disk users know that the best way to keep track of files is to set up separate directories for their work. Figure 12–1 shows a typical directory structure that I'll use in the examples.

DOS views each directory as a *path* that starts at the root directory and works its way down through the disk. Think of the directory structure as an inverted tree with the root at the top and "branches" below it. All directories are thus *sub*directories that branch from the root.

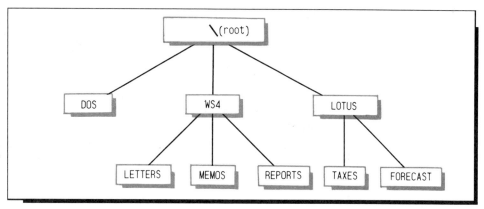

Figure 12–1 A Typical Hard Disk Directory Structure

Thus, the directory structure in Figure 12-1 contains three directories—DOS, WS4, and LOTUS—that branch from the root directory. The WS4 directory contains subdirectories LETTERS, MEMOS, and REPORTS, while LOTUS contains subdirectories TAXES and FORECAST. WS4 and LOTUS are the *parent* directories for their respective subdirectories, which in turn are the *children*. The root directory is the *grandparent* of them all.

Opening Files in Other Drives or Directories

To open a file on another drive, append the drive name plus colon to the file name. If you're on the B drive and you want to open the file CH.22 on the A drive, you'd type **a:ch.22** after pressing **D** [open a file] from the Opening menu.

For directories, separate paths with a backslash (\). There are two ways to identify files. Normally, DOS looks for files starting at the *current* directory and working downward through the path. That is, if you're in the WS4 directory and you want to open the MEMO.2 file in the MEMOS subdirectory without switching directories, you identify the file as \MEMOS\MEMO.2 after pressing **D** [open a document].

However, if you want to open a file in another directory that's at the same or higher level, or in a child directory of another directory, you must designate its path starting at the root directory. For example, you're in the WS4 directory and you want to open the file REPORT.1 in the TAXES subdirectory that's a child of the LOTUS directory. You would identify it as \LOTUS\TAXES\REPORT.1. The first backslash designates the root directory.

Use these techniques whenever you want to access a file on a different drive or in a different directory. In all cases, WordStar saves the file back to its current location, not to the logged directory.

Changing the Drive or Directory

You've already briefly investigated the **L** [change logged drive/directory] command at the Opening menu (Chapter 7). Its counterpart in a file is **^KL**. When you change the default drive or directory, any *subsequent* file operations occur on the new default drive or in the new directory unless you specify otherwise. That is, when you attempt to open a new file, WordStar looks in the new default drive or directory.

However, if you change drives or directories while you're working in a file, WordStar still saves the file—and that file only—to the drive/directory where it was originally located. That's because it makes a note of the file's location when you *open* the file.

When you press **L** from the Opening menu or **^KL** from within a file, WordStar gives you an abundance of information:

```
The logged disk drive is where WordStar will get a document if you
do not specify a drive letter as you enter a document name.

The logged disk drive is currently: C

You may also specify a directory path name. For example, if you
wanted to log onto the directory TESTDIR on drive C, you would
type C:\TESTDIR here.

Legal drives are: C A B

What would you like the new logged drive to be?
```

Your current logged drive may be different, as will the "legal drives." Recall that these are the drives you designated when you installed WordStar. Although DOS expects a colon at the end of the drive name, in WordStar you don't have to type the colon. **Caution:** You must have the legal drives set up correctly for WordStar to "recognize" them. So, to change the default drive from C to B,

Type   **b**

Press   **RETURN**

To switch to a subdirectory that is *lower* than the current directory, merely supply the subdirectory name and the rest of the path. That is, if you're in the WS4 directory and you want to change to the LETTERS subdirectory, you would type **letters** and press **RETURN**. **Tip:** Select the child directory from the file listing by moving the cursor to the directory name and pressing **RETURN**.

Note: WordStar shows the children subdirectories with a backslash in the directory listing to remind you that they're directories and not files. You don't type the \ when you move from a parent to its children.

To switch to a directory that is *higher* or at the *same level* as the current directory, supply the complete path name. For example, to move from the WS4 directory to the TAXES subdirectory, you'd press **L** from the Opening menu or **^KL** from within a file, then type \lotus\taxes and press **RETURN**.

Tip: If you're moving from a child back up the path to its parent, you can type .. (that's two dots) to signify the parent. You can't, however, combine the .. with another path name or use the .. at the root directory.

Suppose you are in \WS4\LETTERS and you want to move to \WS4\REPORTS. Because both subdirectories are at the same level, you can't access them by just typing \reports. WordStar would give you this message:

```
Can't find that directory path. It may be misspelled, incomplete, or
doesn't exist.

Press Esc to continue.
```

You would have to type \ws4\reports to move to a directory that's at the same level as \WS4\LETTERS. **Tip:** Set up macros to move between directories. For example, this macro definition moves from the current directory to a subdirectory called LETTERS: lletters^M (notice the two L's and the RETURN key at the end). A macro to move from \WS4\LETTERS to \LOTUS\TAXES would be: l\lotus\taxes^M.

WordStar's L [change logged drive/directory] and ^KL commands issue two DOS tasks. One is just to change the disk drive. For example, at the DOS B> prompt, if you type a: you switch to the A drive. The other task mimics the DOS CD (or CHDIR) command to change directories. For example, if you are in \WS4\LETTERS and you want to move to \LOTUS\TAXES, from the DOS prompt (that is, after issuing the run a DOS command) you could type cd \lotus\taxes and press **RETURN**.

Creating and Removing Directories

You can't create or remove a directory with a WordStar command. Instead, go out to DOS with **R** [run a DOS command] from the Opening menu or **^KF** from within a file. Then use the correct DOS commands.

To create ("make") a *new* directory that will be a child of the *current* directory, issue the MD (or MKDIR) command. For example, to create a new child directory called ARTICLES under the current directory, WS4, after going to the DOS prompt, type md articles and press **RETURN**. Once you've created a new directory, remember to change to that directory if you want it to be the default.

To *delete* ("remove") a directory, you must first delete *all* files from the directory. Use the *.* wildcard as explained in Chapter 13 under "Deleting Files," then go to the DOS prompt. The command to remove a directory is RD (or RMDIR). You must be in the parent directory to remove a child directory. Suppose you're in the WS4 directory and you want to remove the empty WS4\ARTICLES directory. At the DOS prompt, type rd articles and press **RETURN.**

Viewing All Directories: The TREE Command

Once you change to a different drive or directory, WordStar shows the file listing for the new default drive (see the next section for more information about the file listing). Suppose, however, you'd like a listing of all the directories on the disk.

First, issue the run a DOS command, followed by the TREE command. This transient command, in a file called TREE.COM, lists all subdirectories of the *current* disk drive. In this example, the TREE.COM file is in the root directory of the current drive (C).

Press   **R** [run a DOS command] from the Opening menu or **^KF** from within a file

Type   \tree

Press   **RETURN**

Supply another drive designator (such as b:) to see the directories on a different disk. If you type \tree/f, DOS presents a list of the files in each subdirectory on the drive, along with the subdirectory name. To get help with the TREE command, type \tree ? . To stop the scrolling temporarily, press ^S (^NUM LOCK) then press any key to continue, or ^C (^BREAK) to cancel the command. (The BREAK key is the SCROLL LOCK key.)

Viewing and Changing the Volume Label

When you format a new disk you have the option to supply a *volume label* to identify the disk. Then whenever you display the disk directory, DOS shows the volume label, too. Using labels is a great way to keep track of a disk's contents. For example, you may have a disk for MEMOS and one for LET-TERS.

To view just the volume label, at the DOS prompt type the resident command VOL, followed by the drive designator. To see the volume label for drive B:

Type   vol b:

Press   **RETURN**

If you have DOS 3.0 or higher, you can change or delete the volume label at any time with the transient command LABEL, in the file LABEL.COM. Suppose LABEL.COM is on the A drive and the current drive is B. To change the label for the B drive,

Type   `a:label`

Press   **RETURN**

DOS shows you the present label and prompts:

```
Volume label (11 characters, ENTER for none)?
```

Type the label and press **RETURN.** If you press **RETURN** alone, DOS asks:

```
Delete current volume label (Y/N)?
```

Type **y** and press **RETURN** to delete the label, or type **n** and press **RETURN** to retain the current label.

The File Listing

As you know, WordStar shows the *file directory*—the list of files on the current drive or in the current directory—directly beneath the Opening menu. You can also view the file directory from within a file by pressing any file command, such as ^**KR** to read a file or ^**KW** to write a block to a file.

    Tip: You can use this method to view a file directory while editing even if you don't actually want to read or write a file. Just press **RETURN** when WordStar asks for the document to read or write. This method approximates the *old* ^**KF** command in previous versions of WordStar.
    Here are other ways to work with the file directory.

Filtering Out Files

The **F** [turn directory off] command in the Opening menu has two tasks. Normally, WordStar shows the file directory, but if you press **F**, the directory disappears. Do that now! To make the directory reappear, press **F** [turn directory on]. WordStar prompts:

You have just turned on the file directory. File names that are now
displayed use the directory match name: ????????.???

(Question marks are used where any file name character is permissible).

New directory match name?

WordStar is telling you that you can use wildcards to *restrict* or *filter out*
file names from the directory listing. That is, suppose you only want to see
your "letter" files, those files with the extension .LTR.

Type   `*.ltr`

Press   **RETURN**

Now only files that match the wildcard template appear in the directory
listing. However, you can still open any file, even if its name isn't showing.
Use other wildcards as discussed previously. To make the entire directory
appear again after you've filtered the directory listing:

Press   **F** [turn directory off]

Press   **F** [turn directory on]

Type   `*.*`

Press   **RETURN**

to show all files.
     Recall that WordStar by default doesn't show .COM, .EXE, or .OVR
files in the directory display, because you can't edit those files anyway. You
can change this setup with WSCHANGE (Chapter 27).
     To turn the directory display on when you've turned it off without fil-
tering files, press **F**, then press **RETURN**. There is no equivalent of the **F**
command from within a file (for users of earlier WordStar releases who remember **^KF**), but you can see a directory by issuing any command that
requires a file name, such as **^KR**.

Other Ways to Display Files

Earlier in the chapter you used the DIR command from DOS to display all
the information that DOS maintains for your files. There are many ways to
use DIR to your advantage. First, go to DOS for a while:

Press	**R** [run a DOS command] from the Opening menu or **^KF** from within a file
Type	command
Press	**RETURN**

You can display the directory in a *wide* fashion, similar to WordStar's display, but without showing the file's size:

Type	dir/w
Press	**RETURN**

If your disk or directory has a lot of files, you can *page* through the listing, one screenful at a time:

Type	dir/p
Press	**RETURN**
Press	⟨any key⟩

at the end of each screenful until you see the DOS prompt again.

To view the file listing of another directory, supply the correct path. For example,

Type	dir \lotus\taxes
Press	**RETURN**

to see the directory of \LOTUS\TAXES.

Type	dir ..
Press	**RETURN**

to see the file directory of the parent directory.

In Chapter 28, you'll learn how to *sort* the file listing in any number of ways. Stay at the DOS prompt for the next examples.

Finding Files by Name

Use the DIR command to locate files that you know are on the default drive or in the default directory. You can look at certain files, or determine if a file exists on the current drive or in the current directory. For example, suppose you're looking for the file PERKINS.LTR.

Type   `dir perkins.ltr`

Press   **RETURN**

You can also work with the DOS wildcards when you aren't sure what the exact file name is. For example, you know the file begins with M, so to display all files that begin with M:

Type   `dir m*`

Press   **RETURN**

To display all files that begin with MEMO in the directory \WS4\MISC when you're in the WS4 directory:

Type   `dir misc\memo*`

Press   **RETURN**

Sometimes you can't find a file that you want. Where is it? Use the DOS SEARCH command, a transient command that's in the file SEARCH.COM. This example "assumes" that SEARCH.COM is in the DOS directory of the hard disk, that you're in the WS4 directory, and that the DOS prompt is on the screen.

SEARCH always looks for files starting in the default directory and working down through the path. For example, to search for all files that begin with M in WS4 and its children directories:

Type   `\dos\search m*`

Press   **RETURN**

Use any combination of the following switches with SEARCH. The /C switch tells SEARCH *not* to look in subdirectories, but just to look in the current directory. The /D switch tells SEARCH to list all directories while searching. The /T switch tells SEARCH to list all directories in a "tree" structure to show their relationships. Try these switches to see how they work.

To search *all* directories on a disk, first change to the root directory:

Type   `cd \`

Press   **RETURN**

Then use the SEARCH command. Don't forget to change back to the default directory when you're finished:

Type   cd \ws4

Press   **RETURN**

You can also use the **L** command at the Opening menu or ^**KL** while editing to change the logged directory.

Finding Files by Content

To see if a file is the one you want, the easiest method is to open it with the **D** or **N** commands from the Opening menu, depending on whether the file contains a WordStar document or nondocument. Then press ^**KQ** to abandon the file if it's not the one you want. See also "Creating a Document Summary" in the next chapter.

You can also use the resident DOS command TYPE to view a file, but if the file is a WordStar document you will see what looks like "garbage" on the screen. That's because of the way WordStar uses the eighth bit (Chapter 11). Because WordStar nondocuments contain no formatting, when you TYPE a nondocument from DOS you won't see any "garbage."

However, even with the apparent "garbage" characters in document files, you may still be able to determine if a certain file is the one you want. For example, to display the STORY.LA file from the DOS prompt:

Type   type story.la

Press   **RETURN**

Remember that you can stop the scrolling with ^**S** or ^**NUM LOCK**. Sometimes, however, it might be easier to search through files for a specific *text string* to locate the file that you want. In this case, use the FIND command . . .

The DOS FIND Command

The transient DOS command FIND is in the file FIND.EXE. This command searches the files you name for a specific word or string. Like SEARCH, FIND works from the current directory.

Unfortunately, there are several restrictions to using FIND. First, it can't accept wildcards. You must specify the exact file name you want to search. You can, however, type more than one file name with each name separated from the previous one with a space. Second, you must enclose the actual string in double quotation marks. Third, unless you instruct it otherwise,

FIND is "case-sensitive," so be careful how you type the string. Finally, type any switch *before* the text string.

However, the main restriction to working with FIND involves that funny WordStar eighth bit, as you'll see below. As an example of how to use FIND, suppose you forgot in which chapter of your Beethoven book you mentioned his friend *Grump,* but you remember that it was either in Chapter 27 or Chapter 28. Here's how to find the string at the DOS prompt. These examples use a copy of FIND.EXE on the current drive or in the current directory.

Type   `find "Grump" ch.27 ch.28`

[note the uppercase *G*].

Press   **RETURN**

In this example, because there *is* no CH.28 file, FIND tells you so. It then shows you the occurrences of *Grump* in the CH.27 file.

Wait! It appears that *Grump* occurs only twice in the file, but you *know* it's in there more times than that. Here's where WordStar's eighth bit comes into play. Even though you see the last letter in the word as *p,* recall that WordStar sets the eight bit high, so DOS "assumes" that the character is really a ≡. **Note:** The ASCII code for the "garbage" character at the end of each word is always 128 higher than the ASCII code for the "normal" character. Thus, the ASCII code for *p* is 112, while the ASCII code for what you see when you type the file is 240.

So, DOS won't find all occurrences of *Grump.* It only finds those occurrences that end in a punctuation mark, which to WordStar is still part of the "word." The eighth bit for the punctuation mark, instead of the *p,* is thus set on in WordStar.

Here's a trick, then, for using the DOS FIND command with WordStar document files. Don't type the *entire* word you're looking for. Merely type as much of the word as necessary to distinguish what you want. *In all cases, leave out the last character of the word.* So to find the word *Beethoven* in the same file, this is what to do:

Type   `find "Beeth" ch.27`

Press   **RETURN**

You could have typed *Beethove,* too, but I wanted to show you that you can save keystrokes by typing only as many characters as make the word unique.

You might also want to investigate the helpful FIND switches. For example, the /C switch counts the number of lines in which the string occurs. The /I switch ignores case distinctions, while the /N switch displays the line numbers for each line in which the string appears. So, to display which line numbers in the CH.27 the string "Grump" occurs and to tell FIND to ignore case:

Type   find /i/c "grum" ch.27

Press   **RETURN**

You can type the switches in any order, but you must include the / before each switch. In Chapter 28 I'll discuss some separate programs that can help you view WordStar documents and find text quickly. See "Housekeeping" in the next chapter for more tips on finding files by content.

Printing the File Directory

One way to keep track of files is to print the file directory and keep the printout in a convenient place. There are two ways to print the file directory from DOS. Make sure the printer is on and that you've inserted paper. The first way is to issue the correct DIR command and then, when DOS has finished listing the directory, to press **SHIFT PRT SC** to "dump" the contents of the screen to the printer.

However, you may not get a complete directory printout if the entire directory is not on the screen. That's because **SHIFT PRT SC** only prints the current screen. A better way to go, and one that lets you print the entire directory, is to press **^PRT SC** (or **^P**) *before* you type DIR. Then, whatever you type and whatever DOS displays also prints. Because **^PRT SC** is a toggle switch, remember to turn it off when you're finished. **Caution:** The **^PRT SC** command has a different meaning within WordStar: it saves and prints a file (Chapter 3).

In Chapter 28, you'll learn how to redirect the directory listing to a disk file and then print the file.

Dear Reader: You may want to take a break before continuing. However, do study the next chapter as soon as you can after finishing this one, because there's a lot more to learn about day-to-day file management.

Chapter 13

Working with DOS and File Management, Part 2

In this chapter you will learn the following new commands:

Opening Menu Commands

?	Check WordStar's memory allocation
C	Protect a file

File Command

^Q?	Display the character count from the beginning of file to the cursor location

DOS Commands

BACKUP	Back up files for archive purposes (transient)
CHKDSK	Check the disk space and available memory (transient)
COPY	Copy files (resident)
DEL *or* **ERASE**	Delete files (resident)
DISKCOPY	Copy an entire floppy disk (transient)
REN *or* **RENAME**	Rename files (resident)
RESTORE	Restore files archived with BACKUP (transient)
VERIFY	Verify a copy (resident)

Other Feature

WC	Display the character, word, and line count of selected files

This chapter continues the discussion of working with DOS and file management from WordStar, so make sure to study the previous chapter before this one. You'll learn how to check for available disk space; protect, copy, delete, and rename files; copy entire disks; and back up your hard disk. There's even discussion of a nifty way to move files!

You'll also discover how to track WordStar's use of memory; create a document summary; get a character, word, and line count of your files; and set up a housekeeping schedule. The end of this chapter covers how to run two versions of WordStar simultaneously or use WordStar in a shared (local area network) environment.

Note: The DOS commands discussed in this chapter may be different from those of the new OS/2 operating system that will be available sometime in 1988. When in doubt, check your operating system manual.

> ### DO WARM-UP

Checking Available Disk Space

As I mentioned in the Introduction, always keep track of available disk space. A good habit to pursue is to check disk space when you begin working in the morning (or whenever you begin!). As you know, WordStar shows the available space directly below the Opening menu and above the file listing.

From within a file use any WordStar file management command (such as ^KR) to bring up the file listing and the amount of available disk space. Press **RETURN** or ^U (**F2**) to cancel the command once you've noted the disk space.

Note: As a handy safeguard, WordStar now opens a file in *protected* mode when there's not enough disk space to save another version of the file. The word Prtect appears on the status line, and if you attempt to edit the file, WordStar beeps at you. Press ^KQ to abandon the edit, then copy the file to a new disk. See the sections "Deleting Files" and "Looking at Memory" later in the chapter for more help when you run out of disk space and you're attempting to save a file.

Protecting Files

You've already learned how to turn the preview mode on from within a file by using the ^OP command. In preview mode, you can't edit the file: it's "protected." When you save the file, however, WordStar removes the protected status from the file.

From the Opening menu, use the **C** command to protect a file from editing. This command is helpful when you're working on a local area network (LAN) and you don't want others to change the file willy-nilly. When you protect a file, you can't delete it either. As an example, suppose you want to protect the CH.27 file:

Press   **C** [protect a file]

WordStar prompts:

```
You can protect a document so that it can't be modified or deleted.
You can also remove any existing protections if it is necessary to
make changes.

What document?
```

Type   ch.27

Press   **RETURN**

WordStar tells you:

```
The document is currently not protected.
Change it (Y/N)?
```

Type   y

You can open the protected file but you can't edit it. If you press **^OP** in the file, you just turn off dot commands, print codes, and soft hyphens, but you don't take the protected status off the file. To "unprotect" the file, repeat the above steps from the Opening menu. Do it now before continuing!

What's really happening here? Normally, files are *read-write,* that is, you can look at and edit them. What WordStar is doing here is changing the *file attribute* to make the file *read only* and prevent editing changes. Protecting a file also prevents *you* from making inadvertent changes, even with a DOS command! See Chapter 28 for more information about the file attribute.

Note: Even if you protect the file, other users on the network could "unprotect" it. A good way to avoid this potentially hazardous situation is to have your network administrator maintain separate directories for each person on the network (see "Sharing WordStar with Others"). Only those with the correct access information, such as a password, would have permission to edit files in a directory.

Copying Files

You've already learned the **O** [copy a file] command from the Opening menu. Its in-file counterpart, **^KO,** works in the same way. You can't use wildcards with these two commands. Below I'll show you some ways to copy files from the DOS prompt.

Keep in mind that copying a file makes an exact copy, either to a different file name on the current drive or in the current directory, or to the same file name on a different drive or in a different directory. The original file is still there. See also "Moving Files."

Making a Quick Backup

Always *back up your work* regularly. That way, you never have a problem with full disks. An ounce of prevention now is worth a pound of headaches later. If you only work on a few documents each day, the easiest way to back up your work is to copy each file to a backup disk as soon as you finish editing the file.

Suppose you're editing one particular file. Why not set up a macro to save the file and do an automatic backup? In this example, the file name is CH.27 and you want to copy the file from the C drive to the B drive after saving any changes. The macro definition would look like this: ^Kdo^[b:ch.27^My. Remember to use **^P** before each command when you set up this macro. The macro works correctly only if a copy of CH.27 is already on the B drive.

The macro saves the file (**^KD**), starts the copy command (**O**), uses the same file name (**^[**, the ESC key), types the copied file name (B:CH.27, followed by RETURN), and types **y** for "yes" to overwrite the file. When the file already exists on the drive, WordStar always asks you to confirm overwriting the file:

```
That file already exists. Overwrite? (Y/N)
```

That's why you include the **y** in the macro definition. **Tip:** When copying a file with the same name to a different drive, you can save keystrokes by using the **ESC** command. For example, to copy TEST.1 to A:TEST.1, start the copy command and type the file name. Press **RETURN.** For the copied file name, type **a:**, then press **ESC** to use the same file name on the A drive and complete the command.

If the disk to which you want to copy files is full, if you didn't put a disk in the drive, or the drive door isn't closed, you get that bizarre message:

```
Can't create a file. The disk may be full, or there was a disk write error,
or CONFIG.SYS on your boot (system) disk lacks the line FILES=20.

Press Esc to continue.
```

Press **ESC,** then determine what the problem is. If there *is* a disk in the drive and the drive door is closed, do a directory listing of the disk to see if it's full. Then delete any superfluous files on the disk (see "Deleting Files"), and try again. Here's another error message you may encounter if you're not careful:

```
The logged drive is protected.

Press Esc to continue.
```

This warning generally means that you have a *write-protect tab* on the disk to which you want to copy. Remove the write-protect tab or insert another disk without a tab. The message may also mean that the entire drive or directory is protected from change on a local area network. Choose another drive or directory, or contact your network administrator.

Note: When you copy a *protected* file in WordStar *or* DOS, the new file does not receive the protected status of the original file.

Copying Related Files with DOS

Just as you can display related files from DOS, you can also copy files in a batch using the resident DOS COPY command and wildcards. Here are a few examples you would try after first issuing the **R** [run a DOS command] or **^KF** command, typing `command`, and pressing **RETURN** to stay at the DOS prompt. **Caution:** DOS, unlike WordStar, *doesn't* ask you to confirm the overwriting of existing files! These are just examples to look at and learn; you don't have to enter them at your computer.

Type   `copy *.ltr a:/v`

Press   **RETURN**

This command copies all files on the current drive or in the current directory with the extension .LTR to the A drive. The /V switch *verifies* the copy. It's a good option to use. You may want to include in your "automatic executing file" (AUTOEXEC.BAT) the line `VERIFY ON`, which also ensures that DOS will always verify the accuracy of the copy. Normally, VERIFY is "off." You can override this default with the /V switch.

Type   `copy *.ltr \ws4\letters\*.let`

Press   **RETURN**

This command copies all files on the current drive or in the current directory that have the extension .LTR to the LETTERS subdirectory of the WS4 directory and in the process changes the extension to .LET.

Type   `copy a:te?t.*`

Press   **RETURN**

This command copies all files on the A drive that begin with TE and have T as the fourth letter in their name—no matter what the third letter or extension—to the current drive or directory (which is not the A drive).

Type   `copy *.* a:/v`

Press   **RETURN**

This command copies all files on the current drive or in the current directory to the A drive and verifies the copy. Use this command *after* you've deleted any .BAK files (see "Deleting Files," below) to make sure that you don't copy unnecessary files. In Chapter 28, I'll show you how to *concatenate—* join—files together with the COPY command.

DOS is not as generous with error messages as WordStar. If there's no disk in, say, the A drive, the drive door isn't closed, or the disk contains bad sectors (parts of the disk that are unusable), you'll see this infamous warning:

```
Not ready error reading drive A
Abort, Retry, Ignore?
```

If the problem is no disk or an open drive door, rectify the problem and type r to retry. If the problem is bad sectors, type a and then run the CHKDSK program. See "How Much System Memory Do You Have Left?".

"Cleaning Up" the Disk with the COPY Command

Here's something to mull over in your mind: when you edit an existing file and then save the file to disk, DOS may not store the entire file in the same place on the disk! DOS puts the new parts where it can and then keeps track of where all the separate parts of a file are located.

This may seem strange to you, but it is a good way to use the disk space *dynamically.* Think of the alternative. DOS would have to rearrange *all* the files on the disk each time you saved a file. This would be ridiculously time-consuming because DOS would have to read each file into memory first and then write it back to disk.

Even the dynamic storage method can waste some disk space at times, so once in a while it's a good idea to copy the file to a new disk or a new file name. By copying the file, you are also compressing its disparate parts back together. If you have a large file that has gone through many heavy editing sessions, it's a good idea to do this periodically using the techniques outlined above.

Copying an Entire Floppy Disk

The COPY command only copies the file you specify. It doesn't touch the other files on the disk. If you work with floppy disks, you can copy the entire disk quickly with DOS's transient DISKCOPY command. Unlike COPY, however, DISKCOPY copies *over* all files on the disk to which you're copying. It makes a "mirror-image" of the original disk.

This example "assumes" that DISKCOPY.COM is in the A drive, you're working in the B drive, and you want to copy the disk in drive A. **Caution:** Don't perform these steps unless you really *do* want to copy the disk in the A drive. Make sure that the disk in the B drive doesn't contain any files that you want to keep! From the DOS prompt:

Type   `a:diskcopy a: b:`

Press   **RETURN**

This command copies the contents of the disk in the A drive (the "source" disk) to the disk in the B drive (the "target" disk). DOS will ask you to insert the correct disks before pressing **RETURN** to continue.

Backing Up and Restoring Hard Disk Files

The DISKCOPY command doesn't copy entire hard disks. Instead, use the transient DOS command, BACKUP, when you want to copy large sections of your hard disk, or the entire disk, to floppies. Unlike COPY, the BACKUP command squeezes as many files as possible on each floppy and prompts you to insert more floppies when necessary. **Tip:** Before you back up a hard disk or directory, delete unnecessary files, such as WordStar .BAK files, to save time and disk space.

Caution: Don't attempt to back up a file that you're currently editing in WordStar. It's best to issue the BACKUP command from the DOS prompt, or use the **R** [run a DOS command] from the Opening menu, when you want to back up an entire hard disk or directory.

Assume, then, that the current directory is \WS4\LETTERS and you want to back up all files in this directory to the A drive. The BACKUP.COM file is in the root directory. Here's what you'd do:

Type   \backup *.* a:

Press   **RETURN**

Investigate the various BACKUP switches. For example, the first time you back up your hard disk, you may want to copy all files to floppies. First, change to the root directory with the **L** [change logged drive/directory] command from the Opening menu. Then issue the BACKUP command with the /G (or /S) switch to include all files in all subdirectories. Here's a typical command:

Type   \backup *.* a:/g

Press   **RETURN**

This command backs up all files in all directories to the A drive. After you've backed up the entire hard disk, it makes no sense to back up program files that don't change. You can save time with other switches that govern the backup of selected files.

For instance, the /T switch backs up files that you edited today only. The /B switch backs up only those files edited *on or before* a date you specify. The /D switch copies files edited *on or after* a designated date. You must type the date with hyphens separating the month, day, and year (MM-DD-YY), and separate the date from the BACKUP switch with a colon (:). Suppose you want to back up all .LTR files that you edited on or after April 26, 1988. Here's how:

Type   \backup *.ltr a:/d:04-26-88

Press   **RETURN**

The /Q switch *queries* you about whether to back up each file: you type y to back up the file, n to skip it. The /N switch bypasses the normal formatting of the floppy disks holding the backups. The useful /A switch *appends* files to an existing backup disk. See your DOS manual for more information about other BACKUP switches.

After you have backups of your hard disk files on floppies, you may occasionally need to copy all or some of the files back onto the hard disk. That's why you backed them up in the first place! Because BACKUP squeezes as many files together as possible, you can't COPY them. Use the transient RESTORE command instead. RESTORE, as you can imagine, reverses the backup procedure. **Note:** Make sure you're in the directory you want to hold the files before starting the RESTORE command.

Suppose your hard disk "dies" and you have to reformat it. Luckily, you've backed up all files to the A drive, as a previous example illustrated. Now you want to restore the files from the A drive:

Type   \restore a: *.*

Press   **RETURN**

The RESTORE switches are similar to their BACKUP counterparts. For instance, you can restore only files edited on or before, or on or after, a certain date. Again, refer to your DOS manual for complete information.

Deleting Files

WordStar's **Y** [delete a file] command from the Opening menu and **^KJ** command from within a file are the only other file management commands besides **F** [turn file directory off/on] that can take wildcards. These commands mimic the resident DOS command DEL (or ERASE), but ask you to confirm what you're doing.

 You already know how to delete individual files. **Note:** WordStar won't let you delete the last file name by pressing **Y ESC** from the Opening menu. If you try to delete a protected file, WordStar says:

That document is protected.

Press Esc to continue.

You must remove the protected status from a file before you can delete it. Here are other points to consider about deleting files.

The "Disk Full" Nightmare

I can't reiterate enough: Please do periodic and *frequent* checks of your disks to determine available space! This is one of the cardinal rules for working with computers. How much time or energy does it take to glance at the amount of free space when you're at the Opening menu?

Sometimes, however, you have one of those days. You forget to check available disk space, and you're forced to make room on the disk to save your work. Say you're attempting to save a file, but WordStar tells you in no uncertain terms:

Can't continue--disk full or disk error.
If full, use ^KJ to erase files to make room.
Someone else may be using that file. Try again later.

Press Esc to continue.

Press **ESC** to cancel the save command. [The third line in the message about someone else using the file only appears if you're working on a local area network (LAN). Normally, only one person can edit a file at any one time.]

The first files you should consider deleting are any WordStar .BAK files. Here's how to delete the .BAK files and make disk space:

Press   **^KJ**

Type   *.bak

Press   **RETURN**

Type   y

to confirm your decision.

As you see, you can use a DOS wildcard with the **Y** [delete a file] and **^KJ** commands. Here are other ways to save a file when there's no room on the disk:

- Insert another formatted disk with enough space into the drive before you attempt to save the file a second time or before you follow one of the next steps.

- Use the **^KO** command to copy one or two files to the A drive. Then use **^KJ** to delete the files from the B drive. Try saving the current file again. **Tip:** Always leave a certain amount of free space on the A drive for such emergencies. Later, exit WordStar and copy the files from the A drive back to a disk in the B drive.

- If the file fits entirely in memory, block the entire file out and then use **^KW** to write the block to another file. Otherwise, divide the file into smaller blocks and write each block to a separate file with **^KW**. Then use **^KY** to delete each block after you've written it to a file.

The DOS DEL Command

Here is one command that I suggest you *don't* use unless you're very careful. At least WordStar gives you a warning to type y to confirm the deletion of many files, but DOS does not. Otherwise, follow the same patterns when you work with DOS's resident DEL (or ERASE) command. For example,

Type   del te?t.*

Press   **RETURN**

to delete files that begin with TE, have T as the fourth letter in their name, no matter what the third letter or extension.

 Caution: Don't use the DOS DEL command to delete the file you're currently editing in WordStar. The same caveat applies to renaming files in DOS: don't rename any file that's open. If you attempt to delete a protected file, you get a cryptic message: Access denied . Remove the protected status from the file before deleting it.

"Undeleting" Files

Suppose you aren't totally awake yet and you delete a file that you really wanted to keep. Neither WordStar nor DOS lets you "undelete" a deleted file. However, there are utility programs that can help you out of this particular jam. See Chapter 28.

Renaming Files

Again, you've already learned the basics of working with the **E** [rename a file] command from the Opening menu. Its counterpart within a file, **^KE,** works in the same fashion. WordStar first requests the original name, then the new name. You can only rename one file at a time with these commands.

There are two important new points to learn about renaming files. First, you can't rename a file that you're currently editing. You'll see this message:

```
Cannot rename document being edited.

Press Esc to continue.
```

Second, WordStar won't let you rename a file with a name that already exists on the default drive or in the default directory. WordStar presents this message if you try:

```
Can't rename that file. The name you chose is already in use.

Press Esc to continue.
```

Remember, too, that you can copy files and rename them in the process with the COPY command.

Renaming .BAK Files

One good use of the rename commands you'll discover is to open a .BAK file when the original file doesn't exist or has been damaged. Suppose you've inadvertently deleted the CH.27 file, and it's gone into computer heaven for good. You can still save most of your work by using the .BAK file. That's what it's there for! However, WordStar won't let you edit a .BAK file until you rename it. If you open a .BAK file, WordStar puts it into protected mode. Just follow the steps to rename the file and remove the .BAK extension.

Moving Files

Here's something that not even the DOS RENAME command (described in a moment) can do: *move* a file from one place to another. If you "rename" a file in WordStar by including a different drive or directory, WordStar physically takes it from its current location and moves it to the new place. For example, to move the file TEST.LTR from the current directory, \WS4, to the subdirectory \WS4\LETTERS:

Press   **E** [rename a file] from the Opening menu or **^KE** from within a file

Type   `test.ltr`

Press   **RETURN**

Type   `letters\test.ltr`

Press   **RETURN**

Notice that you must type the same file name as the "new name" to move a file correctly. To accomplish the same thing in DOS requires two steps: copying the file to its new location, and deleting the file from its original location.

The DOS REN Command

DOS provides you with more flexibility than WordStar because you can use wildcards with its resident command, REN (or RENAME). At the DOS prompt, for instance, you can rename groups of files. DOS, however, won't step you through the process. You must type the command, the original file name, and then the new name (separated by a space).

Here's an example to look at, but don't type it because you want to leave the file names as they are:

Type   `ren *.ltr *.let`

Press   **RETURN**

This command renames all files with the extension .LTR to have the extension .LET instead. Here's an example of renaming a single file, here CH.BAK:

Type   `ren ch.bak ch.27`

Press   **RETURN**

If the name already exists, or if you don't supply both original and new names, DOS will give you an error message.

Looking at Memory

As I mentioned at the beginning of the chapter, it may behoove you to check the amount of memory on your computer system before attempting to run a DOS command. There are two ways to check memory: check WordStar's memory usage, and check how much memory is available from the DOS prompt.

WordStar's Use of Memory

From the Opening menu, there's a "hidden" command not listed on the menu that lets you see how much memory WordStar needs. Do this:

Press   ?

This is what you see (the figures may be slightly different):

```
Memory Usage...

WordStar        74k

Text and data   64k

Messages        17k

Printing        22k
```

```
CorrectStar        84k

TOTAL             261k
```

Press Esc to continue.

You can change memory usage with the WSCHANGE program (Chapter 28), but attempt this only if you know what you're doing!

Press   **ESC**

when you're finished looking at this screen.

How Much System Memory Do You Have Left?

WordStar's display of memory usage doesn't tell you how much memory is available for your computer system as a whole. To ascertain this figure from within WordStar, go to DOS with the **R** command from the Opening menu or the **^KF** command from within a file. Then issue the transient DOS command CHKDSK. Assume, then, that CHKDSK.COM is on the A drive. To look at the amount of available memory from the DOS prompt,

Type   a:chkdsk

Press   **RETURN**

Press   ⟨any key⟩

to return to WordStar when you're finished.

There are two switches, /F and /V, that you can use with the CHKDSK command. **Caution:** Do *not* use the /F switch from within WordStar. This switch fixes file errors, but it may get in the way of WordStar's use of temporary files (explained later). You can, however, safely use the /V switch, which shows all file names. Try it:

Type   a:chkdsk/v

Press   **RETURN**

Press   ⟨any key⟩

to return to WordStar when you're finished.

If CHKDSK tells you that there are a lot of bad sectors on the disk, insert a new, blank, formatted disk before copying any more files.

Other File Maintenance Features

Dear Reader, you're almost finished learning the basics of good file management. Here are a couple of other ways to keep track of your files.

Adding a Document Summary

You may have several current versions of a document floating around. You'll probably develop a system for keeping track of these files, but even the most organized person runs amok at times. One way to reduce the frustration of having to figure out which file contains which document version is include a *document summary* in each file.

Recall that you can use the .. (or **.IG**) dot command to insert nonprinting comment lines anywhere you want. If you use this command to insert a document summary at the beginning of each file, you can quickly see what the file contains by either opening the file or using the DOS TYPE command. Because dot command lines contain no justification, the eighth bit is off and TYPE will show the lines correctly. **Tip:** As soon as you TYPE a file, press **^NUM LOCK** (or **^S**) to stop the scrolling and view the document summary.

Here's an imaginary document summary for the CH.27 file that you can imitate or modify for your own files:

```
.. File:          CH.27
.. Description:    Chapter 27 of "Beethoven" book
.. Author:        Ramon Ramos
.. Typist:        Vincent Alfieri, Ph.D.
.. Created on:     March 1, 1987
.. Last edited on: April 26, 1987
.. Notes:         There is a table on page 10
..                Check footnote reference on page 25
```

Of course, you can make the summary as long or as short, as complicated or as simple, as you wish. **Tip:** Make a "document summary template" that contains the information on the left side of the example. Whenever you start a new file, use **^KR** to insert the template, then just fill in the blanks on the right side!

Getting a Character, Word, and Line Count

One of a writer's biggest problems is keeping track of how big a writing project is. Often writers must conform to strict size guidelines. That is, an editor might have a heart attack if an article is larger than, say, 5,000 words. Sometimes writers don't have *enough* words, so they must "pad" things a bit.

From within a file, WordStar can give you a *character count* only. The command is ^Q?. (Notice that you must press the **SHIFT** key to issue the question mark.) WordStar counts every byte in the file from the beginning of the file up to the current cursor location. So, to get a character count for an entire file, open the file and press ^QC (^END) before you press ^Q?. Finish the command by pressing **ESC** to return to your work.

Tip: Experienced WordStar users who want to approximate the *old* ^OP command to get a *line count* can insert a **.PL 0** dot command at the beginning of the file. The status line then shows the line count. Continue to use ^Q? for a character count. Novices: See Chapter 15 for a discussion of the **.PL** command.

Well, a character or line count alone isn't much help at times. An alternative feature comes with WordStar. It's the separate program WC, in the file WC.EXE, and it stands for "word count." This nifty program not only counts characters, but also words and lines. Unlike ^Q? from within a file, however, WC can only work with the entire file.

Suppose you've issued the run a DOS command and you now want to get a character, word, and line count of the CH.27 file. If WC.EXE is on the A drive and CH.27 is on the current drive, at the DOS prompt:

Type   `a:wc ch.27`

Press   **RETURN**

You can't use wildcards to get character, word, and line counts for related files, but you can specify several file names on the command line. WC will even *total* the characters, words, and lines for you. Just separate each name with a space. For example:

Type   `a:wc ch.26 ch.27 ch.28`

Press   **RETURN**

This example gives a character, word, and line count for three files: CH.26, CH.27, and CH.28 (of course, there *is* no CH.26 or CH.28 file—this is just an example!). **Note:** To obtain an accurate count with WC.EXE of the file you're currently editing, save the file first with ^KS. If the file or files are not on the current drive or in the current directory, supply the correct drive designator or path for *each* file listed. To get a word count for part of a file, block out the part you need and use ^KW to write the block to a new file. Then issue the WC command with that file.

Housekeeping

Patient Reader, you probably have one of them in your house, too. It's that closet into which you throw things that you don't want to deal with at the moment. I call mine "Siberia." You should see all the junk in there! Every few months or so, of course, things come to such a pass that I can't find anything in Siberia, so I have to clean it out—one of my least-favorite tasks.

When you work with computers, you run the risk of creating "mini-Siberias" on all your disks. Files seem to multiply like rabbits, and disk space is at a premium. If you don't check your directory often, you'll tend to overlook superfluous files, unless you include in your work routine a very important operation known, aptly enough, as *housekeeping.*

Housekeeping means cleaning up your act and, as with cleaning closets, it need not be done (thank goodness) on a daily basis. But you would be well advised to set up a housekeeping schedule for your work disks and to stick to this schedule. If you have a hard disk system, consider file maintenance on a frequent basis as essential. A hard disk can store many files, and you must develop a way of keeping track of them. But even with floppy disk-based computers, you will find that you are wasting disk space if you don't clean house every so often.

Active and Inactive Files

A standard practice in many professional word processing centers is to maintain the difference between the documents that are *active,* that is, on-going, and those that are *inactive,* finished and no longer needed on a daily basis. Inactive files are the ones you wish to keep and perhaps reuse later, but they don't have to clutter up your day-to-day work disks.

It's a good idea to spread out your active files over many disks to allow enough space for multiple editions. Once you're finished with a document, you can then free up this space by archiving its inactive file.

Experienced word processors store their inactive files on specially marked storage disks. They also give their files descriptive names and perhaps even insert a printout of the disk directory in its jacket for quick reference. What file names you eventually use is up to you, but short file names mean fewer keystrokes. For day-to-day word processing activity, this is a work saver. But rename your files with more descriptive names later when they become inactive and you plan to store them.

Organizing Work Disks

Everyone has a preferred way to organize his or her work. I have found that if I divide my files by subject or type, I have less trouble finding things. For instance, I have a "letters" directory and a "memos" directory. If I were using a dual-floppy computer, I probably would have used a different disk for each chapter of this book. I could then grab the disk I needed quickly without having to fumble, because I usually work on the book by chapter.

Of course, I label each disk to know exactly what it contains. Instead of using stick-on labels, I insert a piece of paper in the disk sleeve. This allows me to change the labels quickly and also to thumb through the disks almost as if they were manila file folders. When I archive files, *then* I use a "permanent" label.

A Housekeeping Schedule

For your own sanity, Dear Reader, I suggest a frequent computer house-cleaning arrangement. Set up a schedule that makes you feel comfortable. A good rule of thumb is this: How much work do you care to lose? Probably not much. So, determine a time to do backups and "closet cleaning" of disks—perhaps once a day or once a week.

Because I use a hard disk and generally work on one project at a time, I find it most convenient to back up my work as I save it. That is, when I was writing this book I would save the current chapter and exit WordStar with ^**KX,** then *immediately* copy the file to a backup disk. I used a DOS *batch file* to type the appropriate commands for me (see Chapter 28). That way, I never had to worry about *not* saving my work. It's a good habit to learn.

I also check disk space *daily* before working with WordStar. If less than 20 percent is still available, I consider archiving files that I haven't used or edited for a while. Then, every so often when it's a rainy day (which doesn't happen too often in Los Angeles!), I clean house thoroughly.

Working with Multiple Copies of WordStar

Now that you know about how to work with DOS, perform file maintenance, and keep a housekeeping schedule, it's time to delve more deeply into learning how to use WordStar to your advantage. You'll also discover more about WordStar's own internal file maintenance procedures.

As you may have gathered from the discussion of running a DOS command, it's entirely possible to run two versions of WordStar, one within the other. Although not the same as having multiple *windows,* it can be helpful at times, especially when you have to refer to two documents simultaneously.

 Note: Make sure your computer system has enough memory for both WordStars before you begin. Press **R** [run a DOS command] from the Opening menu or ^**KF** from within a file, then type the appropriate command to load WordStar. To wit:

Type   `a:WS`

if you have a floppy disk

or

Type   **WS**

if you have a hard disk.

Press   **RETURN**

Once you've loaded the second version of WordStar you can open another file and edit it. However, see the next section for a very important caveat about file names. **Caution:** Don't forget to save your work, exit the second WordStar, return to the first WordStar, and save your work *there* before you quit for the day!

WordStar's Temporary Files

Now that you know how to work with two versions of WordStar, and as an introduction to the final section of this chapter, it's time to understand what WordStar is doing behind the scenes as you edit a file. Every time you open a file, WordStar opens two *temporary* files, with the extensions .A and .B, as "spillovers."

The temporary files, among other things, keep track of that portion of long files that don't fit entirely into memory. WordStar "spills" the file over into the temporary files. By the way, if you move or copy any blocks with the ^KV or ^KC commands, respectively, WordStar sets up a third temporary file with the extension .C.

Thus, if you're working on the file called CH.27, WordStar uses CH.A and CH.B, too. Remember, too, that WordStar renames the original CH.27 file to be CH.BAK when you save the file. That's why you need a certain amount of free disk space—enough space for all *four* files. When you save the file, WordStar puts everything back together and deletes the two temporary files. Normally, you're not even aware that the temporary files exist.

A potential problem arises, however, when you run two versions of WordStar simultaneously and when you open two files with the same name. That is, suppose you have CH.27 open, you run another version of WordStar, and you then open CH.26. Both files have the same name, CH, although their extensions are different.

Because WordStar only maintains *one* set of temporary files, it will then "assume" that the temporary files belong to CH.26, the last file you opened and then saved. What's more, because there now are no longer any temporary files for CH.27, when you attempt to save this file WordStar tells you that the disk is full! This isn't the case at all, but you're stuck anyway.

Tip: A way to get out of this "felonious disk full" situation is to block out the entire file, if you can, and then use ^KW to write the block to another file.

To avoid this problem altogether, configure WordStar to be in a *shared environment,* that is, a local area network. See Chapter 27. So, even if you're not working on a local area network, you can "fool" WordStar into thinking so. Then, if you have one file open in the *first* version of WordStar running and you attempt to open another file with the same name—or another copy of the same file—in the *second* version of WordStar, here's what you see:

```
That file is already being edited. Temporary files with the same name
exist. Try editing a file with a different name.

You can look at the file (but not change it), or you can return to the
Opening Menu. (You can only look at the first part of very large files.)

Look at the protected file (Y/N)?
```

Type **y** to view the protected file, if you wish. What if you find it necessary to edit a file with the same name as the first file? Merely *rename* the file before you try to open it, or copy it to another drive or directory. For example, in the scenario above, use **E** [rename a file] from the Opening menu or **^KE** from within a file to rename CH.26 to something else (such as CHAP.26). You can then open the file in the second version of WordStar with no problem. Remember to change the name back when you're finished.

Sharing WordStar Files with Others

I've already mentioned certain problems that may crop up when you're working in a shared environment. However, there's usually a network administrator who knows how to take care of problems that occur when two or more people are attempting to work with the same program or file.

The network administrator should set up your directory space so that only those who have access to this space can look at or edit files. Even so, when two people are attempting to edit the same file only the person who opened the file first can make changes. When that person has finished, the next person can edit the file. You can also configure WordStar to *lock* a file and thus prevent others from viewing the file at the same time as you're editing it (Chapter 27).

Dear Reader: So much for file management! You've had a long enough break from the nitty-gritty of word processing. It's time to conquer greater heights: pagination and page formatting.

Chapter 14

Headers, Footers, and Page Numbering

In this chapter you will learn the following new commands:

File Commands

.F1 (.FO)	First footer line
.F2	Second footer line
.F3	Third footer line
.FM	Footer margin
.H1 (.HE)	First header line
.H2	Second header line
.H3	Third header line
.HM	Header margin
.PC	Page number column position
.PG	Restore page numbers
^PK	Suppress blanks in the header or footer text (for alternating text) on odd-numbered pages
.PN	Change the page number

Other Features

#	Page number in a header or footer
****	Print the next character literally in a header or footer

Dear Reader, word processing is great, but please don't be chagrined if I tell you you're still working too hard! Little do you perhaps realize just how much unnecessary labor WordStar can save you. For instance, WordStar can print incremented page numbers or any other "running" text at the top or bottom of each page. These *headers* and *footers,* as word processors know them, are the subject of this chapter.

> ## DO WARM-UP

Page Formatting

Pagination, headers, and footers are part of the *page format* of a WordStar document. Study this chapter with the next one, which completes the discussion of page formatting. Unlike most of the commands you've learned so far—ones that govern the appearance of characters, words, and lines—page formatting commands determine how an entire page prints. Most page formatting commands are dot commands.

You might not be able to view the complete results of the page formatting until you print the file. For some page formatting dot commands you'll see a : in the flag character display to remind you that the command works during printing only.

Rules of the Page

Generally, you set up page formatting at the beginning of the file. You've already used some page formatting commands, such as **.MT** (top margin), **.MB** (bottom margin), and **.OP** (omit page numbering). The first two commands govern the page break display, but you don't see the blank top and bottom margins on the screen. As you might expect, you can change the page formatting at any time with the correct dot commands.

Tip: The "WordStar Examples and Tips" section of the WordStar documentation contains a visual diagram of the page formatting dot commands.

As you may also expect, there is a rule of thumb to observe when working with page formatting commands, and it's fortunately a simple one. Always put the commands at the *top* of the page where you want them to take effect. By this I mean before any *printed text lines* on the page. That includes, by the way, any blank lines that "print," too. WordStar shows a 1 in the flag character display to remind you that page formatting dot commands work best when they're "first on the page."

You might get some unwelcome results if you don't follow this easy rule. WordStar will honor a page formatting command as soon as it can, but it may not be as soon as you expect. For example, you want a header to start printing on a specific page, but you don't insert the instruction to accomplish this at the very top of the page in the file. So WordStar dutifully starts printing the header at the top of the *next* page. Be careful!

Because a footer doesn't print until the bottom of the page, it's possible to put a footer instruction anywhere on the page you want it to start. Well, almost anywhere. I've found that WordStar won't *let* you insert any footer instruction on the last line of a page. (It will insert a blank line at the bottom of the page.) Still, you're well advised to keep *all* page formatting commands at the top of pages for consistency's sake.

Introducing Headers and Footers

As the names imply, a *header* prints at the top of a page and a *footer* prints at the bottom. The only real difference between a header and a footer, then, is where each appears in the printout. The setup for both is basically the same. The standard page numbering that WordStar provides by default is actually a simple footer.

You decide about headers and footers once, usually at the beginning of the file, and WordStar takes care of printing them on each page for you. Of course, you don't have to use any headers or footers at all if you don't want to, or you can have any combination of up to three header lines and three footer lines. You can also create *alternating* headers and footers, that is, different setups for odd-numbered and even-numbered pages.

In deference to the podiatrists of this world, I feel compelled to mention that footers have merely a casual relationship to *footnotes* (Chapter 25), and both in turn have only a semantic relationship to *feet*. By the way, a footer appears below everything else on the page, including footnotes.

WordStar prints headers and footers in the top and bottom margin space, respectively. That means you have to make sure that there's a large enough top or bottom margin to accommodate the header or footer lines. By default, headers or footers print two lines above or below the regular text, but you can change this *header or footer margin,* too. The examples will help you determine the correct amount of margin space you'll need.

You can have WordStar print headers or footers—or both—on all pages, or on selected pages. As a convenience to you, WordStar has special setups for page numbering alone, or you can create your own customized headers and footers with text and page numbering.

Like all format changes, any page numbering, header, or footer instruction stays in effect in the rest of the file forward from the location of the instruction. Except for the page number, if any, a header or footer text doesn't change. WordStar just prints the same header or footer on each page and continues to do so until or unless you tell it otherwise.

If you want to turn off a header or footer or change it at a specific point in the file, you must give WordStar the correct instructions at the correct location. It's easy to change a header or footer in the middle of a file. But remember the rule of thumb for page formatting: If you insert a header change in the middle of a page, the new header won't take effect until the *next* page.

Page Numbering

The simplest kind of footer is WordStar's default page numbering. As you know, WordStar numbers pages for you unless you use the **.OP** command or change the defaults (Chapter 27). If you do let WordStar paginate, you don't have to worry about the numbers. WordStar increments the page number for each page and prints the number in the bottom margin.

Note: WordStar only "knows" about Arabic numerals. To print Roman numerals for tables of contents pages, you have to be a bit of a contortionist. See Chapter 25.

You may have noticed that WordStar Professional Release 4 doesn't print the page numbers in the exact center of the page. The default *page number column position* is column 28. Don't ask me why WordStar's designers changed this setting from previous versions, which *did* print centered page numbers for the standard 65-character line. Soon, you'll learn how to adjust the page number column position.

Default page numbering is of the "vanilla" type only: an unadorned number at the bottom of each page. Although you can control the column position of this number and what number to begin pagination, if you want anything fancier you have to use a header or footer setup. You'll explore fancy pagination later in the chapter.

So, the rule of thumb when you work with page numbering is: use either (1) the default setup or (2) a header or footer. (You wouldn't want page numbers in both a header and a footer, would you?) You might get some strange results, such as *two* page numbers on a page, if you're not careful!

Default Page Numbering

You'll use the CONTRACT file to experiment with page numbering, headers, and footers. You've probably printed this file once, so you should get your printout to compare it with the examples in this chapter. If you haven't printed the file yet, do so now before continuing. Prepare your printer and paper, then:

Press   **P** [print a file]

Type   contract

At this point, if you've set up WordStar to bypass all the print options, press **ESC;** if not, press **RETURN** and proceed to answer the print options questions. You must press **C** after you insert each new page to continue printing. (See Chapter 27 for information on how to set the printing defaults.)

Changing the Page Number Column Position

To print default page numbers at a different column, use the **.PC** command. You must supply a valid integer number representing the text column. The column numbers are the same as those on the ruler line, *not* on the page as a whole.

For example, with a standard 65-character line the center of the page is at column 33.

Press   **D** [open a document]

Type   `contract`

Press   **RETURN**

(or press **ESC** instead of typing the name if you printed the CONTRACT file.)

Although there are other dot commands in this file, the **.PC** command doesn't affect them, so you can put it at the beginning of the file.

Press   **^N**

to insert a line but leave the cursor where it is.

Type   `.PC 33` or `.pc 33`

starting at column 1 of the line.

Print the first page to see the difference. You'll print from within the file, but remember that WordStar only prints the *last saved version* of the file. I'll present the printing instructions once; follow them whenever you want to print pages in the other examples. Prepare the printer and paper, then:

Press   **^KS** or **F9**

to save the file and resume where you left off.

Press   **^KP**

Type   `n`

because you don't want to merge print.

Press   **^R**

to accept the last file name.

Press   **RETURN**

Answer the print options as normal, but type 1 as the "ending page." Continue answering the other options. Compare this page 1 with that of your original printout.

Using the correct **.PC** setting, you can print the page numbers at the left margin, the right margin, or anywhere between. **Note:** WordStar doesn't change the page number column position when you change the left and right margins. You should determine the column depending on the line length. For example, if the left margin is at 5 and the right margin is at 75, the center of this 70-character line is at column 40 (70/2 = 35 + 5 = 40).

Tip: If you're printing the page numbers flush with the right margin and justification is on, you'll have to change the page number column after page 9. Suppose the right margin is at column 65, so you use **.PC 65.** The first 9 pages will print at the right margin, but page number 10 will print one character into the right margin space. Ugly! At the top of page 10, insert a new command, **.PC 64,** to accommodate the two-digit page numbers. (Chapter 25 shows you another way to accomplish the same objective.) See also the discussion under "A Header and Footer Miscellany."

Skipping Page One

Suppose you don't want a page number to print on the first page, but you *do* want numbers for all other pages. This setup requires two dot commands: an **.OP** command at the beginning of the file, and a **.PG** command at the top of page 2. This command instructs WordStar to restart the *printing* of page numbers beginning with whatever page contains the command. The **.PG** command does not take an integer number.

(Although the **.PG** instruction could be anywhere on page 2 except on the last line, I'll continue to emphasize putting it at the top of the page.)

The cursor should be at the end of line 1. Leave the **.PC 33** line in the file. Follow these instructions:

Press   **RETURN**

to add a blank line.

Even though spacing is double, when you press **RETURN** at the end of a dot command line, WordStar inserts just one hard return.

Type   .OP or .op

starting at column 1 of the line.

Press   **^QI** or **^F4**

Type   2

Press   **RETURN**

to position the cursor at the top of page 2.

Type

Tip: Always make sure that dot command lines are on their own lines, ones that don't number in the actual text lines.

Press   **^N**

to insert a line but leave the cursor where it is.

Type   .PG or .pg

Now, save the file with **^KS** again, then print the file with **^KP,** but this time print both pages 1 and 2. Notice that the **.OP** command overrides the **.PC 33** command, but when you reinstate page numbers with **.PG** on page 2. WordStar still honors the page number column position that you originally specified.

Changing or Skipping a Page Number

By default WordStar begins page numbering with page 1. In the previous example you turned off numbering of the first page, but WordStar was "smart" enough to know that it should print page 2 as 2 and not 1. WordStar always increments page numbers according to the page breaks in a file.

Suppose, however, that one file is the *continuation* of another file. You've divided the document into two separate, easy-to-work-with module files. If you want consecutive page numbering from the first file to the second, you must supply the correct beginning page number in the second file. That is, if the first file ends with page 11, then set the first page of the "continuation" file to be page 12 with a **.PN 12** command at the top of the file.

So, wherever you want to override the default page numbering, insert a **.PN** command. Include the correct page number with which you want to start pagination. WordStar shows the correct page number on the status line and continues pagination with the new number.

Suppose this file is the continuation of another, and page numbering should start with page 10. The cursor should still be on the **.PG** command line at the top of page 2.

Press   **^Y or F5**

to delete the line.

Press   **^QR or ^HOME**

to position the cursor at the beginning of the file.

Press   **^X or DOWN ARROW**

to position the cursor on the **.OP** line.

Press   **^QY**

to delete the text to the hard return.

Type   .PN 10 or .pn 10

Notice the page number display on the status line now shows P10. *Question:* What if you wanted to go to page 2? *Answer:* There *is* no page 2 now! The next page in the file is page 11. Be careful when you use different page numbers that you specify the correct numbers according to the setup in the file. That is, ^QI (^F4) works with whatever is the *current* setup. See also "A Note on Printing Specific Pages" later in the chapter.

Suppose you wanted to begin printing page numbers on page 11. You could insert an **.OP** command on page 10, leaving the **.PN 10** command line. **Caution:** Make sure the **.OP** command comes *after* the **.PN** command. Then, at the top of page 11, insert a **.PG** line. WordStar still "remembers" the beginning page number, but reinstates the printing of numbers with page 11.

(Old-time WordStar users: be careful! If you supply just the command **.PN** without an integer number, WordStar starts numbering with page 0! Formerly, you could reinstate page numbering to 1 with a "blank" **.PN** command. No longer!)

Use the same command *within* a file to skip a page number. For example, you don't want a printed number on the first page of the file because it's a title page, and you want page number 1 to start with current page 2. Make sure there's an **.OP** command on page 1. Then go to the top of page 2 and insert a **.PN 1** command. Technically, you have two page 1's, but only the second one will print with a page number.

Here's another example. Say you're inserting a nonpaginated chart of accounts between pages 1 and 2 of the CONTRACT file, so page 2 of the file should be page 3 instead. Merely go to the top of current page 2 and insert a **.PN 3** dot command line. See the next chapter for a way to have a blank page for an illustration, but one that still prints with a page number.

Note: The *order* of some page formatting commands is important. The *last* command in the file takes precedence over previous ones when WordStar reaches that command. Thus, if you have the commands in this order—

.PN 5
.OP

—WordStar won't print page numbers at all, but it will show you the correct page numbers on the status line. If the commands are in this order—

```
.OP
.PN 5
```

—WordStar does print page numbers, because the **.PN** command overrides the **.OP** command.

Press   **^KD** or **F10**

to save the file and return to the Opening menu.

A Note on Printing Specific Pages

In Chapter 3 you learned how to print selected pages of a file. Be cautious when your file contains nondefault page numbering to give WordStar the correct page numbers *according to the file's pagination.*

That is, if the file begins with page 10 and you want to print the first five pages, supply 10 as the beginning page and 14 as the ending page. If you typed 1 and 5, WordStar wouldn't print any pages at all. To print an entire file, no matter what the pagination, just press **RETURN** in answer to the beginning and ending page questions. In the example just mentioned, you could press **RETURN** to start printing on the first page of the file (page 10), but you'd still have to type 14 and press **RETURN** to print only the first five pages.

Customized Page Numbering

Suppose you want a more elaborate page number, say, one enclosed in hyphens, like this: - 3 -. Here's where you must forego the predefined setup and use a footer (or, for the top of the page, a header). You'll create a footer in the lesson that follows, but setting up a header is for the most part the same as creating a footer. I'll note any differences later.

There are four footer commands, depending on how many footer lines you want. Originally, WordStar only allowed one footer line, and the command was **.FO.** Now you can have up to three lines, which you set up with the **.F1, .F2,** and **.F3** commands, respectively. **Note:** The **.FO** and **.F1** commands are identical; you can use either one, but not both, in a file.

A nice touch in WordStar Release 4 is that a footer setup automatically turns off the default pagination. In previous versions, you'd have to insert an **.OP** command in the file or you'd get a printout with two page numbers at the foot of the page. Footers also override a **.PC** dot command, but *not* a **.PN** command. That's because you still may need to begin pagination with a number that's not 1.

Here's how to create page numbering with page numbers centered on the line and enclosed in hyphens. First, open a file:

Press   **D** [open a document]

Type   `computer`

Press   **RETURN**

I deliberately chose this file because of its formatting. You may recall that the file prints with 12 characters per inch, so the line length is 80 characters. Because you want page numbers centered within the correct margins and printed in elite typestyle, set up the footer instruction *below* the **.CW 10** dot command and the ruler line. That way, WordStar knows what settings to use.

Press   **^X** or **DOWN ARROW** twice

to position the cursor below the `.RR` line.

Press   **^N**

to insert a line but leave the cursor where it is.

The footer instruction, **.FO,** takes up *four* column positions at the beginning of the line: three columns for the **.FO,** and one space. So here's a trick to center the page numbering in the footer. Set up the numbering *first,* then add the footer instruction later.

Type   -

(that's a hyphen).

Press   **SPACEBAR**

In a footer or header, you designate incremented page numbers with a number sign (#).

Type   #

(that's **SHIFT 3**).

Now, finish the rest of the setup:

Press   **SPACEBAR**

Type   -

(again, a hyphen).

Press   **^OC** or **SHIFT F2** or **ESC C**

to center the line.

Press   **^E** or **UP ARROW**

to position the cursor on the centered line. It should be at column 1 of the line.

Now, make sure insert mode is on (it should be) before you add the footer instruction:

Type   .F0 or .fo

(you could also use .F1 or .f1, but make sure that's a number 1 and not a lowercase L).

Press   **SPACEBAR**

to add the space separating the footer instruction from the actual footer text.
The entire setup for all dot commands now looks like this:

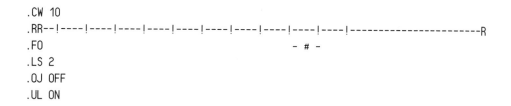

If you press **^F** (**^RIGHT ARROW**) to position the cursor under the first hyphen, you'll note that it's at column 42. But it will print correctly at column 38. Later you'll see how to have a *real* number sign in a header or footer, that is, one that doesn't mean page numbering.

Print the file now with **^KP**, but remember to save it with **^KS** (**F9**) first. Stay in the file for the next example.

Question: How would you print this page numbering setup starting at page 2 of a file? *Answer:* Insert an **.OP** command on page one, and move the footer line to the top of page 2.

Custom Page Numbers at the Top of the Page

As an introduction to headers, suppose you want to print page numbers at the top of each page instead of the bottom. All you need do is change the footer line to a header line. The four header commands are similar to their footer counterparts: **.H1** or **.HE** for the first header line, **.H2** for the second, and **.H3** for the third.

However, because WordStar normally prints page numbers in a footer, if you want custom numbering in a header, you *must* use **.OP** to turn off the default setup. Otherwise, you'd have two sets of page numbers!

The cursor should still be on the footer line.

Press   **^QS** or **^F9**

to position the cursor at the left side of the line.

Press   **^D** or **RIGHT ARROW**

to position the cursor under the *F*.

Press   **^V** or **INS**

to turn insert mode off.

Type   HE or he

to change the footer line into a header line (if you used **.F1,** you need only change the *F* to an *H*).

Press   **^V** or **INS**

to turn insert mode back on.

Press   **^QS** or **^F9**

to position the cursor at the left side of the line.

Press   **^N**

to insert a line but leave the cursor where it is.

Type   .OP

to turn off default pagination.

The **.OP** line can come before or after the header line.

Press   **^KD** or **F10**

to save the file and return to the Opening menu.

Print the file to see the difference, if you wish.

More Headers and Footers

By far the most frequent use of headers and footers includes page numbering, but there's no restriction to what you can include as "running" text at the top or bottom of the page. You can also change the *position* of the header or footer text in the margin space. You'll use yet another file to experiment:

Press   **D** [open a document]

Type   story.la

Press   **RETURN**

          Tip: Keep in mind that the following examples apply to either headers or footers.

A Composite Footer

In this example you'll set up page numbers preceded by the word *Page* and centered in a footer, which will also include other text at the left margin.

Press   **^N**

to insert a line but leave the cursor where it is.

Type   Page #

for the page numbering instruction.

Press   **^OC** or **SHIFT F2** or **ESC C**

to center the *Page* # string.

Press   **^E** or **UP ARROW**

to return to the same line.
     Now, you don't want to throw off the centered page number, so what do you do? Right!

Press   **^V** or **INS**

to turn off insert mode.

Type   "Romance"

Caution: If you make a mistake, *don't* use the BACKSPACE key! You'd bring the other text back, too. Press ^S (**LEFT ARROW**) instead to make any corrections. When you're finished:

Press   **^A or ^LEFT ARROW**

to position the cursor at the beginning of the "word" (the open quote mark). Now add the footer instruction:

Press   **^V or INS**

to turn insert mode back on.

Type   .F0 or .F1

Press   **SPACEBAR**

Make sure there's the added space between the instruction and the actual text of the footer, which should now look like this:

```
.FO "Romance"                    Page #
```

A Header and a Footer

Leave the footer as it is and add a header instruction to the file so that you'll print a header and a footer. Press ^QS (^F9) to position the cursor at the left side of the line, then press ^N to add a blank line. As long as *all* page formatting dot commands are at the very beginning of the file and before any actual text lines, you can have the footer instruction before the header instruction.

For the header type this as you see it, but make sure you start at column 1. The backslash (\) tells WordStar that it should read the *next* character—and only the next character—literally, that is, as a # instead of the pagination symbol. The backslash doesn't print. By the way, I used **ESC @** to enter the date:

```
.HE Draft \#3 - April 9, 1987
```

When you're finished, press ^KS (F9) to save the file, and use ^KP to print just page 1. Stay in the file for the next example.

Note: If you want to print a backslash in a header or footer, use *two* backslashes in a row: \\. If you want to print the page number like this—*Page #3*—here's how it would look in the dot command line: Page \##.

Starting with a Different Page Number

Suppose this story starts on page 10. You can include a **.PN** dot command line either above or directly below the footer. Because page numbers print in the footer, WordStar follows both the footer and page number commands when it reaches the bottom of the page.

The only time you have to be careful about changing page numbers occurs when you set up pagination in a header. Remember that a **.PN** command also *turns default pagination back on.* Here's what I mean: assume you have the following setup:

```
.OP
.HE Page #
```

You think that it's okay to change page numbering to start at page 10 like this:

```
.OP
.HE Page #
.PN 10
```

What you get is not what you want: page numbers in the header *and* default page numbers at the bottom of the page! What you want to do is change the page number *first,* then set up the header, and *then* turn off default pagination, like this:

```
.PN 10
.HE Page #
.OP
```

That will work just fine!

Multiline Headers and Footers

When you want multiline headers or footers, be careful that you have enough room in the margin space to accommodate the extra lines. Recall that WordStar uses a default top margin of three blank lines, and a bottom margin of eight blank lines. Recall also that WordStar wants to have two blank lines between the header or footer and the regular text.

As an experiment, remove the footer instruction in the STORY.LA file. First, make sure the cursor is on the line. Then:

Press   ^Y or **F5**

to delete the footer line.

Press   **^N**

to insert a line but leave the cursor where it is.

Type the first footer line, shown below, and press **RETURN** at the end
to do the next line. Type it, then press **RETURN.** Type the third line, but
don't press **RETURN** because then you'd add an extra blank line to the file.
To insert today's date instead of the date shown on the second line, press
ESC @.

```
.F1 "Romance"
.F2 April 9, 1987
.F3 Page #
```

Because there's enough bottom margin space to fit all three footer lines,
the file will print correctly. However, what happens if you want a three-line
header? Try it! Change the header instructions for this file so that they read:

```
.H1 <your name>
.H2 <your telephone number>
.H3 Draft \#3
```

When you print the file now, WordStar inserts the three header lines,
but there aren't any blank lines between the headers and the text. How would
you rectify this problem? Right! Increase the size of the top margin with the
.MT command, but make sure it's at the top of the file. This discussion leads
me to . . .

The Header and Footer Margins

The blank lines *within* the top or bottom margins that separate a header or
footer from the main text are the *header margin* and *footer margin,* respectively. The default is two lines, but you can change the header or footer margin
with the **.HM** and **.FM** commands. Supply an integer number following the
command. The higher the number, the farther from the text the header or
footer will print.

For example, try this setup in the STORY.LA file:

```
.MT 6
.HM 1
.H1 <your name>
.H2 <your telephone number>
.H3 Draft \#3
```

Of course, it makes no sense to have a header or footer margin that's larger than the entire margin! That is, if the top margin setting is 4 (.MT 4) and the header margin is 5 (.HM 5), you're in trouble. Fortunately, whenever possible WordStar will do its best to print the header or footer *somewhere* within the margin, but don't try to defeat the program. If you want a header or footer to print directly above or below the text with no header or footer margin, use the dot commands **.HM 0** or **.FM 0,** respectively.

Blank Header or Footer Lines

If you want three header or footer lines, but you want the middle line to be blank, you must include *two* spaces after the **.H2** or **.F2** instruction. One space represents the normal separation between the command and the actual text of the line, while the other space is the "text." For example, delete the footer lines from the STORY.LA file and insert these lines, but note that you must type two spaces on the **.F2** line:

```
.F1 "Romance" - April 9, 1987          Two spaces here, cursor is
.F2                                     under the R when you're
.F3 Page #                              finished
```

If you neglect to add the extra space, WordStar just disregards the line entirely and prints the first and third lines only. Save and print the file to see the results.

(An aside: If you include a **.F3** instruction but no **.F1** or **.F2** lines, WordStar prints just one footer line.)

Using Print Codes in Headers and Footers

You can print header or footer text, including page numbers, with special printing (underlining, boldface, and so on). Just insert the correct print codes where you want them. WordStar doesn't show the *effect* of the codes on the screen, so when in doubt press **^OD (SHIFT F1)** to turn the code display on. **Note:** Always make sure that you insert the end code to turn the print effect off at the correct spot in the header or footer.

If you wish, try printing the phrase *"Romance"* in boldface.

Suppose you want an entire file, including headers and footers, to print in a special effect, such as doublestrike. If you insert one **^PD** instruction at the beginning of the file past any dot commands, it won't work with the header or footer text. Set up beginning *and* ending **^PD** codes within *each* header and footer instruction, too.

In a previous example, you inserted a footer instruction *after* a **.CW** dot command line so that the footer would print in the same typesize. If you change the horizontal character width elsewhere in a file, insert a copy of any header or footer lines *after* the new **.CW** line. That way, the header or footer lines will print in the new typesize.

Turning Off a Header or Footer

You can delete header or footer instructions if you want to start with a clean slate. But if you want to stop printing a header or footer somewhere in the *middle* of a file, position the cursor on the correct page. Then insert *blank* instructions on that page. Make sure the instructions are at the top of the page. You must include blank lines for *each* header and footer instruction line. Otherwise, WordStar only turns off the lines you instruct it to.

For example, if you've been following the examples you have three header lines and three footer lines in the STORY.LA file. Turn them off on page 2:

Press   ^QI or ^F4

Type   2

Press   **RETURN**

Type the following lines as you see them, each on a new line (use ^N to insert the first new line). Make sure there are *no* spaces after each instruction.

.H1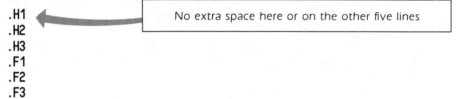
.H2
.H3
.F1
.F2
.F3

No extra space here or on the other five lines

Save the file and print it to see the results. **Tip:** You can search for header and footer lines by searching for the instruction, such as **.F1**.

Reinstating a Header or Footer

Once you turn them off, the only way to reinstate headers or footers is to reinsert the instruction lines at the top of the page where you want them to start. The easiest way to accomplish this is to copy the original instructions where you need them. Just block them out, go to the top of the desired page, and press ^KC to copy the block of dot command lines.

Alternating Headers and Footers

The text in a header or footer can *alternate* from one side to the next, depending on the page number. That is, on odd-numbered pages the text prints at the right side of the page, while on even-numbered pages the text appears at the left side. The idea is to approximate the look of a printed book.

To set up alternating text, you determine how many extra spaces you want to "push" the text over on the odd-numbered pages. You then insert a special print command, ^PK, to *suppress* the printing of the spaces on even-numbered pages.

Tip: Make sure the text for odd-numbered pages extends as far to the right as you want. The best way to determine exactly where the header or footer text will print is to set up the text first before inserting the dot command and the ^PK command.

For the sake of simplicity, just try an alternating one-line footer. Later, when you become a WordStar guru, you can experiment with more complicated setups. Here's an example. Your file has the standard, 65-character line, and justification is on. You want to print the word *Page* and the page number flush to the right margin (column 65) on odd-numbered pages, but at the left margin on even-numbered pages.

First, open the file you want to use and position the cursor where the dot command is to go. Then:

Press   ^N

to insert a line but leave the cursor where it is.

Press   **SPACEBAR** but *hold it down* until the cursor is at column *60.*

If you go too far, use the **BACKSPACE** key to erase the extra spaces.

Type   **Page**

Press   **SPACEBAR** once

Type   **#**

for the page numbering.

Now, set up the footer and alternating instructions:

Press   **^QS** or **^F9**

to position the cursor at the left end of the line.

Make sure insert mode is on!

Type   .F0 or .fo

Press   **SPACEBAR**

Press   **^PK**

A ^K appears here (if the print code display is on). The entire footer looks like this:

```
.FO ^K                                                      Page #
```

Save the file and print at least two pages of it to see the results. For the first nine pages of the file, the page number will print flush with the right margin on odd-numbered pages. On page 11, insert a new footer instruction to make the word *Page* start printing at column 59 to accommodate the two-digit page numbers. In Chapter 25, you'll see another use for the **^PK** command.

"Fooling" WordStar to Begin a Header on Page Two

Because WordStar won't honor a header instruction on the current page if the instruction isn't at the top of the page, you can fool WordStar when you want to set up different header formats for the first page and all succeeding pages. Here's what I mean.

Suppose you have special letterhead stationery for the first page of your letters, but no stationery for the other pages. You don't need or want a header on the printed stationery, but you'd like one to begin on page 2. Suppose further that the top margin setting for the first page should be set to 12 to allow room for the letterhead, but 6 for all other pages.

You can set up *both* first page and subsequent page header instructions at the top of the file! The trick is to include at least one blank "text" line between the first page and other page instructions. The blank line will "print" on the first page, so take it into consideration when determining the top margin. Here, then, is the finished example:

```
.MT 11
.MB 6
.OP
```
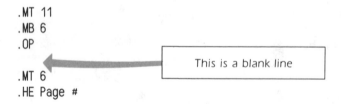
This is a blank line
```
.MT 6
.HE Page #
```

Because the blank line between the dot commands will print on page 1, I've reduced the top margin setting for the first page by one line. The last two lines then don't take effect until the top of page 2, because both affect the *top* of the page, and WordStar has already received and processed its instructions for formatting the first page.

The nice thing about this arrangement is that you can use it as a format for *all* letters, even those that are only one page long. WordStar would just disregard the subsequent page instructions altogether.

Note: This trick, alas, won't work with different footers, because WordStar honors a footer instruction on the same page where the instruction occurs.

A Header and Footer Miscellany

To change the footer margin for default pagination, use the **.FM** command. If you're printing with a nondefault character width setting, which may also be a different *font,* WordStar won't print page numbers in the new width or font unless you tell it. For instance, suppose you're using a **.CW 5** setting and default pagination. To print default page numbers in this character width, insert these commands in the file:

```
.CW 5
.FO
```

The "dummy" footer line establishes the correct character width for default pagination. To print customized headers and footers in another character width, insert the header and footer dot commands *below* the **.CW** command line.

Note: The total text in any one header or footer line can't exceed 100 characters—more than enough for most cases. Each character, including print codes and the carriage return at the end of the line, counts as one character. "Extended" characters, the topic of Chapter 17, count as three characters each. WordStar will print an asterisk (∗) at the right edge of a header or footer if it's too long. If you need a longer header or footer line, you can change WordStar's defaults with the WSCHANGE program (Chapter 27).

The setup for headers and footers is independent of the left and right margins. So it's entirely possible to have headers or footers print *outside* the normal margins of the text as a way of emphasizing them. For example, suppose the file's left margin is at column 5, and the right margin at column 60. You can have an "outdented" header at column 1 and an outdented footer that ends at column 65. However, so that WordStar doesn't wrap the line when you set up the footer text past the right margin, insert the footer instruction (**.FO**) before you type the text.

Using Caution with Dot Commands

Be careful to make sure you place all dot commands properly. If you should edit the file later, the number of lines on each page may very well change, and WordStar will automatically readjust the page breaks. Dot commands, such as header and footer instructions in the middle of the file, may then not be at the top of the page.

I have emphasized the tricky aspects of printing page numbers, headers, and footers so you're well prepared when you do your own. Most of the time, you'll have standard setups—say, default page numbering or a simple header on all but the first page. When your needs become more complicated, however, WordStar is at your disposal.

Controlling the Page

In this chapter you will learn the following new commands:

File Commands

.CP	Conditional page break
.LH	Set the vertical line height
.PA (^F8)	Unconditional page break
.PL	Set the page length

Dear Reader, WordStar has many built-in features, but ultimately you have to be the one "in control." For example, you might want to fine-tune the look of your printed pages by controlling the page breaks yourself or determining how many lines should print in each vertical inch.

Now that you know about page numbering, headers, and footers, you're ready to look more closely at overall page formatting and how to control the appearance of the printed page in WordStar. In this chapter you'll encounter some sad entities known as widows and orphans, and you'll learn a wealth of nifty WordStar tricks for page formatting.

DO WARM-UP

Drafts Versus Final Printouts

Before you begin, however, I'd like to teach you a practice, current in many word processing centers, that can save you time and frustration. Make a distinction between the *draft* stages of a document and its *final* form.

A document generally goes through any number of drafts until it reaches that stage of *semi*perfection (nothing's perfect in this imperfect world, after all), at which point you're ready to send it out into the world. All the many versions of a WordStar document make up the *document history.* You should only know how many drafts I did of this book before I was able to pass it on to the publisher!

During the draft stage you type in new text and make editing changes, while during the final stage you're more concerned with formatting—hyphenating words and making sure that each page breaks properly to produce the final product in its best-looking form. The point here is that you don't want to spend a lot of time worrying about page formatting that most likely will change in the next draft of a document anyway.

For example, in the law firm where I worked the lawyers insisted that draft versions of files be in double spacing, sometimes even in triple spacing, to give them enough room to pencil in corrections and changes. Later, we changed the spacing back to single where necessary. We used cheap paper for drafts and the expensive stuff only for final printouts.

I firmly believe that one's work is a reflection of oneself. Getting your final document to be of the highest quality takes a bit of extra time and effort, but it's worth it. If you did the extra "prettying-up" steps each time you printed a draft, you'd be wasting time. So, many word processing operators, including yours truly, choose not to delve too deeply into elaborate page formatting until a document reaches the final stage.

More About How WordStar Makes Page Breaks

I've already outlined the basic "computing" that WordStar does to figure out where page break are to occur. You'll recall that WordStar takes the total number of line on the pages—by default, 66—that is, the length of the entire page. It then subtracts whatever are the top and bottom margin settings to reach the number of *possible printed text lines.* If you don't change the top and bottom margins, the defaults of three and eight blank lines apply, so WordStar calculates $66 - 3 - 8 = 55$ total printed lines.

There's another factor that comes into play: the number of lines per *vertical inch.* By default, WordStar "assumes" you want six lines per inch, but you can change this setting, too. (Six lines per inch times 11 inches is 6 $\times$ 11 = 66.) If you do, the new setting will also affect how the pages break. In any case, WordStar *never* breaks a page *before* the last printed text line unless you tell it to do so.

Thus there are four essential page formatting factors:

- The page length
- The top margin
- The bottom margin
- The number of lines per vertical inch

Because it's a *line-oriented* word processor, WordStar automatically adjusts the page breaks according to these factors. That is, whenever you edit a file and the line count changes, the page breaks will change, too. During the draft stage, it's not terribly important where page breaks occur, because all you want are fast printouts for review or editing. But when the document reaches the final stage you may want to check page breaks yourself.

WordStar can't read, after all, so it doesn't "know" what's on a line. Sometimes you won't want pages to break in the middle of a table, or you'll decide to keep certain lines together on a page. You may also have to break a page "early" to leave blank space for an illustration or graph.

Top and Bottom Margins Reviewed

In many of the examples I've used nondefault top and bottom margin settings. Because these two page elements are so important to page formatting, do one more example that changes the default settings. (There's a method to my madness, as you'll see in a moment.)

Press   **D** [open a document]

Type   ch.27

Press   **RETURN**

It's back to Beethoven! You originally used the default top and bottom margins for this file, but now you'll supply other settings. Keep in mind that it's always a good idea to insert these changes at the top of the file, so that they govern the formatting of the entire file. (There are three other dot commands in the file, and the cursor should be on the first dot command line.)

Press   ^N

to insert a line but leave the cursor where it is.

Type   .MT 4 or .mt 4

Press   **RETURN**

Type   .MB 6 or .mb 6

Don't press RETURN after the second dot command because then you'd have an extra blank line. Whenever you change the top or bottom margin settings, WordStar recomputes the number of possible printed text lines and changes the page breaks accordingly.

Note: It's entirely possible to have *no* top or bottom margins. Just insert **.MT 0** and **.MB 0** commands.

Forcing Page Breaks

At any time, and definitely during the final stage of a document, you can check the page breaks and adjust any breaks that you don't like. Most often, WordStar will have set up acceptable page breaks, but there are occasions when you'll want to determine the breaks yourself. This means forcing the page break before WordStar expects it, or telling WordStar to break the page given a certain condition.

The Unconditional Page Break Command

Whenever you want to insert a page break yourself, position the cursor at the desired line and use the *unconditional page break* dot command, **.PA.** This command instructs WordStar to break a page wherever it sees the command. No ifs, ands, or buts about this command—it's unconditional!

Suppose this file were longer than two pages. Now that you've changed the top and bottom margins, you might want to see where WordStar begins page 2 and adjust the page break if necessary.

Press   ^C or **PG DN** six times

to see the page break between pages 1 and 2.

This is how the file looks at the page break:

```
   2 February 1814  -  Last mention of sketches
      13 March 1814  -  Beethoven complains to Grump of
                        gastric problems
      26 April 1814  -  Beethoven performs the premiere of
-------------------------------------------------------------------P
                        the ^SSachertorte Sonata^S
```

It turns out that WordStar broke the pages in the middle of the table of dates. What's more, it divided an entry from one page to the next. Now, where you decide to put the page break is a matter of your own *personal aesthetics.* At the very least, you should break the page one line up so that the entire *26 April 1814* entry is on the same page. However, that means there is only one entry in the table at the top of page 2. I suggest instead, then, that you break the page so that the *last two* entries in the table appear on page 2.

Position the cursor at the left margin of line 54.

Type   .PA or .pa

or

Press   ^F8

Stop! WordStar inserted a new page break, but you aren't finished yet! Remember that no other text should be on the same line as the dot command.

Press   **RETURN**

to end the dot command line.

Now the last two entries begin at the top of page 2 and the page ending looks like this:

```
        2 February 1814  -  Last mention of sketches
.PA
------------------------------------------------------------------------P
          3 March 1814  -  Beethoven complains to Grump of
                           gastric problems
         26 April 1814  -  Beethoven performs the premiere of
                           the ^SSachertorte Sonata^S
```

Now that you've changed the normal page break between pages 1 and 2, WordStar will adjust the page endings for the rest of the file (if the file contains more than two pages!). You would continue to scroll through the file and check the other page breaks, inserting **.PA** commands where necessary.

Tip: To scroll slowly through a file from the beginning to check the page breaks, issue the command ^QQC. Then type a number to slow up the scrolling. When you reach a page break that you want to adjust, press any key to stop the scrolling. You may want to set up a macro to issue the continuous scrolling command, **^QQC.**

Note: Because WordStar saves the **.PA** commands with the file, they stay in effect. If you later edit the file, WordStar may change the page breaks, but *your* page break commands will also work! If you see any "short" pages, that's a good sign that you have a stray **.PA** command at that spot in the file. Yet another good reason *not* to break pages manually until the document has reached the final stage!

Tip: Insert a blank line with ^N *before* inserting a **.PA** command. You can later use **^QA** (**^F2**) to find and delete all **.PA** lines quickly by replacing them with nothing. When you remove all the **.PA** commands, you then don't accidentally delete a necessary blank line between text lines. This is especially important if the file is double spaced.

Press   **^KS** or **F9**

to save the file and resume where you left off.

The Conditional Page Break Command

WordStar always honors an unconditional page break command. There's another way to break pages: give WordStar a *condition* to look for. The condition is whether a certain stated number of lines remain on the page. If so, WordStar does nothing. If not, WordStar breaks the page at the point where the *conditional page break* command appears.

The conditional page break command, **.CP**, *must* include an integer representing the number of lines to look for as a test of the condition. The most frequent use of the command is to *keep* blocks of text on the same page. For example, if you wanted to ensure that WordStar didn't break the table of dates in the CH.27 file between two pages, you could use a conditional page break command.

Another good use of the **.CP** command is with headings or subheadings and the lines that follow them. As a matter of form, you shouldn't separate a heading from at least *the first two text lines* in the paragraph that follows it. For example, the page break in the following illustration is ugly and threatens to give your editor a heart attack!

```
^SThe Extant Material^S



    Aside from the completed sonata, there are several other

-----------------------------------------------------------------------------P
sketches in Beethoven's notebooks for the years 1813-1814 that

point to a tenth symphony.  For example, page 28 of Notebook 7
```

In this example, only one line in the paragraph connects to its heading at the bottom of the page. To rectify this problem, include the correct conditional page break command. Then, *any* time this section appears near the end of the page, WordStar will check if there are enough lines left on the page to include at least two lines with the heading. If not, WordStar begins a new page. Here are the steps for inserting a conditional page break command (you don't have to do them right now—just learn them!):

1. Count the number of lines that you want to keep together. In the example, the number is *seven,* because it includes the heading line, the blank lines between the heading and the paragraph, the two first lines of the paragraph, and the blank line between them.

2. Use ^N to insert a blank line *above* the heading line and add the dot command.

The result will be this:

```
-------------------------------------------------------------------------P
.CP 7
^SExtant Material^S



        Aside from the completed sonata, there are several other

        sketches in Beethoven's notebooks for the years 1813-1814 that

        point to a tenth symphony.  For example, page 28 of Notebook 7
```

If this section were at the bottom of a page and there were fewer than seven text lines left on the page, WordStar would begin a new page at the **.CP** command, as in the illustration. You're happy, and your editor stays healthy!

One advantage to the **.CP** command is that it remains in effect. If you edit the file, WordStar continues to check the condition to make sure that the text stays together. One disadvantage to the **.CP** command is that you have to insert it everywhere you want it. That is, if this file contained twenty headings and subheadings, you'd have to set up a **.CP** command for each. (Why not use a shorthand macro?) Still, once you've done it, it's finished!

A Brief, Working Interlude

Dear Reader: I've been rather lax with you in the last few chapters. Why, you haven't done any new typing at all! Before continuing, and as part of the next example, I'd like you to take a few moments to add a little bit of new text to this file.

Press   **^QC** or **^END**

to position the cursor at the end of the file, on line 46 of page 2. (The cursor should be at column 1.)

In a previous chapter you set up the formatting instructions, including a ruler line, to revert to the primary format of the file after the indented section. When you type the next paragraph, it should look exactly as shown:

Unfortunately, Beethoven never discusses the "current project" again. In fact, all other biographical material from the time points to a breakdown in his friendship with Grump. For instance, Grump's wife, Waltraute, mentions in her diary a "difference of opinion" between the composer and her husband about a certain kind of "fish sauce." According to her, Grump is "depressed about Ludwig again," but she fails to elaborate.

When you're finished:

Press   ^KS or F9

to save the file and resume where you left off.

The Good, the Bad, and the Ugly

Take a look at the very end of the file. What's "wrong" with it? The last line of the paragraph is an orphan! And what, in the name of all getout, is *that?* Why, the opposite of a widow, of course! Both are unfortunate entities that require a modicum of "eleemosynary" spirit on your part.

A *widow* is the beginning line of a paragraph stranded at the bottom of a page, while an *orphan* is the ending line of a paragraph left by itself at the top of a page. Because they are both short lines, widows and orphans look terrible if they're not "related" to at least one other line in the paragraph.

(An aside: Some people may tell you that a widow is the short line at the top of a page, while an orphan is at the bottom of the page. There's no complete agreement about which is which, but the semantical difference doesn't affect how you deal with widows and orphans. Read on!)

Right now WordStar has no compassion for widows and orphans. It will merely break each page according to the page formatting settings in effect. Perhaps by the time you read this there will be automatic widow and orphan control in WordStar, which means I'll have to change this section!

The way to correct the widow or orphan problem is to make sure that these short lines print with either the next line in the paragraph for a widow,

Before you check for widow or orphan protection: WordStar breaks pages using the default page format.

```
Widow line at bottom              Orphan line at top
of page                           of page


xxxxxxxxxxxxxxxxxxxxxxxxxxxxx     xxxxxxxxxxxxxxxxxxxxxxxxxxxxxx
xxxxxxx                           xxxxxxxxxxxxxxxxxxxxxxxxxxxxxx
    xxxxxxxxxxxxxxxxxxxxxxxxx     xxxxxxxxxxxxxxxxxxxxxxxxxxxxxx
------------------------------------------------------------------------P
xxxxxxxxxxxxxxxxxxxxxxxxxxxxx     xxxxxxxxx
xxxxxxxxxxxxxxxxxxxxxxxxxxxxx         xxxxxxxxxxxxxxxxxxxxxxxxx
xxxxxxxxxxxxxxxxxxxxxxxxxxxxx     xxxxxxxxxxxxxxxxxxxxxxxxxxxxxx
```

You insert unconditional page break instructions to "force" the pages early and thus prevent widows and orphans. The erstwhile widow prints with the next line in the paragraph, and the former orphan prints with the previous line in the paragraph.

```
Widow starts at top of            Orphan connected to             PAGE BREAK
next page                         previous line                    DISPLAY


xxxxxxxxxxxxxxxxxxxxxxxxxxxxxx    xxxxxxxxxxxxxxxxxxxxxxxxxxxxxx
xxxxxxx                           xxxxxxxxxxxxxxxxxxxxxxxxxxxxxx
.PA                               .PA
------------------------------------------------------------------------P
    xxxxxxxxxxxxxxxxxxxxxxxxx     xxxxxxxxxxxxxxxxxxxxxxxxxxxxxx
xxxxxxxxxxxxxxxxxxxxxxxxxxxxx     xxxxxxxxx
xxxxxxxxxxxxxxxxxxxxxxxxxxxxx         xxxxxxxxxxxxxxxxxxxxxxxxx
xxxxxxxxxxxxxxxxxxxxxxxxxxxxx     xxxxxxxxxxxxxxxxxxxxxxxxxxxxxx
```

Figure 15–1   Before and After Widow and Orphan Control

by breaking the pages early with unconditional page break commands, as or the previous line for an orphan. That means changing the page endings Figure 15–1 illustrates.

At present the last few lines of the file look like this:

```
"difference  of  opinion" between the composer  and  her  husband

about a certain kind of "fish sauce."  According to her, Grump is
------------------------------------------------------------------------P

"depressed about Ludwig again," but she fails to elaborate.
```

To correct an orphan, position the cursor at the left margin of the blank line between the first and second lines above. That should be line 55 of page 2. Then:

Type   .PA or .pa

Here's the result: the orphan is now related to the second-to-last line in the paragraph at the top of page 3.

```
"difference  of  opinion" between the composer  and  her  husband
.PA
-------------------------------------------------------------------P
about a certain kind of "fish sauce."  According to her, Grump is

"depressed about Ludwig again," but she fails to elaborate.
```

Similarly, suppose you discover a widow in a file that looks like this example:

```
In 1812, Beethoven moved from the west side of Vienna to the

-------------------------------------------------------------------P
east  side, but apparently the move was not without  frustration.

Although little extant material remains to help scholars  unravel
```

Position the cursor on the line *above* the beginning of the paragraph (the widow line) and insert an unconditional page break command. The result is:

```
.PA
-------------------------------------------------------------------P
In 1812, Beethoven moved from the west side of Vienna to the

east  side, but apparently the move was not without  frustration.

Although little extant material remains to help scholars  unravel
```

The widow is now related to the rest of the paragraph at the top of the next page.

Press   ^KD or F10

to save the file and return to the Opening menu.

Problems with Dot Commands in Paragraphs

In Chapter 4, I mentioned that you shouldn't insert dot commands lines in the middle of a paragraph, but in this chapter that seems to be exactly what you have to do! Heed my recommendation about differentiating between the "draft" and "final" stages of a document. Don't insert any dot commands in the middle of a paragraph until the document reaches its final stage and you want to get the best possible printout.

What's more, if you have to edit a paragraph that contains a dot command, delete the dot command first. WordStar will realign dot command lines and include them as part of the paragraph text when you press ^B or ^QU. Also, WordStar may "see" the end of the paragraph if there's a hard return at the end of the dot command line.

Because the dot commands that you'll probably insert most often in the middle of paragraphs are the .PA or .. commands (the latter to "blank out" a line at the top of the page—see the end of the chapter), use the find command to find these dot command lines and delete them *before* you edit the file. Additionally, if you change formats at the top of a page and the dot commands break the continuity of a paragraph that begins on the previous page, delete the dot command lines before you edit and realign the paragraph.

Leaving Space for Illustrations

There are many ways to make blank space on a page for illustrations or charts that you'll later "paste" onto the printout:

- Insert enough blank lines with ^N to make room for the illustration if you want it in the middle of a page.

- Make a "hole" in the text for the illustration if you want the text to "flow" around the illustration.

- Leave *part* of the page blank.

- Leave an entire page blank, but printed with any header or footer setup, including a page number.

- Skip a page number to leave an entire page blank, but with no header or footer.

Using ^N to insert blank lines for an illustration in the middle of a page is self-explanatory. However, you may want to include a .CP instruction to ensure that the blank lines stay together on one page and that WordStar doesn't break the page in the middle of the space you need for the illustration. For example, suppose you need 20 lines for an illustration. First press ^N once and insert this line at column 1:

```
.CP 20
```

Then press ^N 20 times for the blank lines.

Making a "hole" in the text means reformatting the text around the hole (called by publishers a "run-around"). In the example below, an illustration of the painting will appear within the paragraph. I changed the right margin setting on the second line to column 35, aligned the rest of the paragraph with ^B, then changed the right margin *back* to its original setting of column 65 further on in the paragraph. Finally, I used ^B again to align the last couple lines.

```
A  certain  famous painting has attracted a  great  deal  of

publicity   lately (Figure   7-2).

It's  one  of  Vincent  Van  Gogh's

"Sunflower" series, which  recently

carried  with  it a  price  tag  of

almost  forty million dollars at  a

London  sale.  What  induced   the

anonymous  collector to pay such a sum, the highest  in  history,

for this work?
```

In the previous chapter, you saw how to change the page number in the file to skip numbering, which covers the last option above. Here's how to accomplish options three and four.

To leave part of a page blank, merely insert an unconditional page break command, **.PA,** where you want the page to end. WordStar will still print any footer on the bottom of the page.

To leave an entire page blank but have headers or footers print on the page, insert a **.PA** command *between* the pages where you want the illustration to go. However, you must insert at least one blank line on the page, because WordStar won't let you put a **.PA** command on the *first* line of the page.

In the following illustration, WordStar has set up a normal page break between pages 3 and 4:

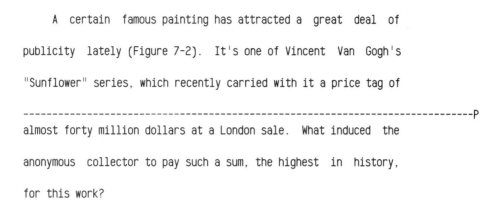

```
    A  certain  famous painting has attracted a  great  deal  of

publicity  lately (Figure 7-2).  It's one of Vincent  Van  Gogh's

"Sunflower" series, which recently carried with it a price tag of

---------------------------------------------------------------------------P
almost forty million dollars at a London sale.  What induced  the

anonymous  collector to pay such a sum, the highest  in  history,

for this work?
```

To include a blank, paginated page between these two pages, position the cursor at the top of page 4 under the *a* of *almost*. Then, press ^N to add a blank line. Move the cursor down to the next line, type **.PA**, and press **RETURN.** Here's the result:

```
    A  certain  famous painting has attracted a  great  deal  of

publicity  lately (Figure 7-2).  It's one of Vincent  Van  Gogh's

"Sunflower" series, which recently carried with it a price tag of

---------------------------------------------------------------------------P
.PA
---------------------------------------------------------------------------P
almost forty million dollars at a London sale.  What induced  the

anonymous  collector to pay such a sum, the highest  in  history,

for this work?
```

The status line will display the correct page numbers—3, 4, and 5—when you cursor through these pages.

Creating a Title Page

Now that you know about the unconditional page break command and how to set up top and bottom page margins, you should be able to figure out how to print a title page. Because I'm a nice guy, I'm providing a sample format for a fictitious file called CH.1 that begins with a separate title page. CH.1 is the first chapter file for a book on Ludwig van Beethoven.

```
.. This is the title page
.MT 20
.OP
                    THE BEST BOOK OF: BEETHOVEN


                                By

                        Vincent Alfieri, Ph.D.
.PA
-----------------------------------------------------------------------------P
.. This is real page 1
.MT 6
.MB 6
.PN 1
.PG
```

On the title page, you don't want page numbers (**.OP**), but you do want
the title to start further down on the page (**.MT 20**). You break the page early
to go on to real page 1 of the file, where you'll set the correct top and bottom
margins (**.MT 6** and **.MB 6**), reinstate page 1 (**.PN 1**), and start normal page
numbering (**.PG**).

Changing the Page Length

In the United States, we use paper with the standard length of eleven inches,
but WordStar lets you set up any page length you want. As you may know,
the legal profession takes perverse pleasure in using nonstandard (one might
say, anachronistic) page lengths. For example, in the law firm where I worked
we printed certain contracts on 14-inch paper and others on 12-inch paper.

The **.PL** dot command controls page length. If you plan to change the
page length, keep these things in mind:

- The page length is the *total* number of lines on the page, including the
  top and bottom margins.

- Normally, WordStar prints six lines per vertical inch.

- To determine the page length, multiply the length of the paper *in
  inches* times the number of lines per vertical inch. (See below for information on how to change the number of lines per vertical inch.)

Because page length governs the top and bottom margins and hence page
breaks, it's a good idea to put this setting before the **.MT** and **.MB** commands

at the very top of the file. WordStar then adjusts the page breaks correctly. To change the page length to 14 inches, then, multiply 14 times 6 to get 84 total lines. Insert this command at the top of the file:

.PL 84

Note: The page length must be an integer number. Some laser printers can't print on the first few lines at the top of the page and the last few lines at the bottom of the page, so you may have to set the page length of an 11-inch page to less than 66 total lines and adjust the top and bottom margin settings, too (Chapter 26). If you're working with a sheet feeder, you'd more than likely have to adjust the page length to accommodate the "push" that the feeder gives the paper. That's one of the topics of Chapter 17.

Tip: Experienced WordStar users who want to approximate the *old* ^**OP** command to get a *line count* can insert a **.PL 0** dot command at the beginning of the file. The status line then shows the line count. Continue to use ^**Q?** for a character count.

Using Paper Horizontally

In Chapter 11 you learned how to use the **.CW** dot command to print more characters per horizontal inch when you're printing with a different typesize and longer text lines. Now that you know about page formatting, especially how to change the paper length, learn a little about positioning the paper *horizontally* in the printer.

A standard, 8½ by 11 inch page used horizontally requires a new page format. The page length will be 8.5 × 6, or 51 total lines with six lines printed per vertical inch. You'll have to adjust the left and right margins, depending on how much blank space you want. An 11-inch page has 11 × 10 = 110 columns for 10 characters per horizontal inch, and 11 × 12 = 132 columns for 12 characters per horizontal inch. What's more, you may want to adjust the pagination defaults, or set up your own headers or footers.

The following dot commands represent the page formatting of a typical page inserted horizontally in the printer. There is a ten-column blank left margin and a ten-column blank right margin on the page.

.PL 51
.MT 4
.MB 6
.PO 10 [or whatever page offset you need]
.RM 90
.PC 45 [to center the default page numbers]

If you use a different **.CW** setting, adjust the **.RM** and **.PC** settings accordingly. **Note:** If you have a laser printer, you'll need to change the *paper orientation* to print pages horizontally (Chapter 26).

More About Envelopes

In Chapter 4 I discussed briefly how to set up the top and bottom margins to print envelopes. Now that you've learned about page formatting, here are a few more points to know about envelopes.

No matter what the actual paper is, think of it as a "page." For instance, legal-size envelopes contain 24 total lines, so the "page" format for an envelope might be something like this:

```
.PL 24
.MT 1
.PO 4
```

Here, I'm not concerned about the bottom margin setting (**.MB**), because most of the time you don't print on the entire envelope anyway. Notice that the top margin setting prints the return address closer to the top of the envelope "page," and the page offset command prints the left margin closer to the left side of the envelope. If you use letters with preprinted return addresses, adjust the top margin and page offset settings to start at the first *address line* of the envelope.

You can print an envelope with a letter by setting up the envelope as the second page of the file. Make sure you break the first page, containing the letter, with the **.PA** command. Then insert the above dot commands at the top of page 2.

Tip: You don't need to use the TAB key to position the cursor where the address lines are to print on the envelope. Just change the page offset setting. For example,

```
.PL 25
.MT 15
.PO 40
```

These commands work with standard business-size envelopes that have preprinted return addresses. The first address line prints on line 16 and at column 40. The advantage to this approach is that you can *block out* the return address in the letter and *copy* the block below these commands for the envelope. Even though the screen shows the block starting at column 1 (the left margin), the address will print at column 40 of the envelope.

Note: If you have a laser printer, you may have to change the *paper orientation* to print envelopes (Chapter 26). If you have paper and envelopes in different *sheet feeder bins,* you must indicate the bin number with a special dot command (Chapter 17). Other chapters show you how to set up the page formatting for mailing labels.

The PRVIEW Printer Driver Revisited

When you print to a disk file using the PRVIEW printer driver, discussed in Chapter 3, you'll note that WordStar inserts a **.PL** command at the top of the "printed" disk file. This command, used without an integer number, instructs WordStar not to show page breaks unless you specifically include a **.PA** command in the "previewed" file. (You can also insert a form feed command, ^PL, discussed in Chapter 17.)

You can scroll through the disk file version and see how the printed file will look, with top and bottom margins, headers and footers, page numbering, and so on. WordStar shows each page break as a *form feed,* that is, an instruction to the printer to start a new sheet of paper:

^L---

You can still use the **^QI (^F4)** command to go to specific pages in a "previewed" document.

Changing Lines per Vertical Inch

You may remember that WordStar measures horizontal character width in increments of 120ths of a inch—hence the strange rigmarole you have to accept to get the right setting. A similar case holds true for the number of lines per vertical inch, often known as *vertical pitch,* or in WordStar's parlance, *line height.* The dot command to change line height is **.LH.**

Many daisy wheel and laser prints can print line height in increments of 48ths of an inch, so the setting you use to determine the number of lines per vertical inch is a divisor of 48. That is, the default setting—six lines per vertical inch— is thus a setting of 48/8 = 6. This ends up being **.LH 8.**

As with horizontal character width, when you want *fewer* lines per vertical inch, you use a *greater* number as the divisor of 48. When you'd prefer *more* lines per vertical inch, and thus more tightly printed lines, use a *smaller* number as the divisor of 48.

You may opt to use WordStar's math feature (Chapter 18) to help you figure out the correct line height! If you have the WordStar manual handy, you'll see a useful chart that shows how various popular **.LH** settings affect the printout. It's listed under "Line Height."

Note: Some dot-matrix printers require an *even-numbered* integer for the .LH setting. Check the README file for more information about specific printers.

Squeezing More Lines on the Page

You can insert .LH commands anywhere you want to change the line height setting for individual sections of a file. For example, you may want an indented section to print more closely together on a page. Make sure you return the line height to its default setting where necessary.

Here's another example.

Press   **D** [open a document]

Type   form

Press   **RETURN**

Type   y

because this is a new file.

You have a very cheap, or very poor, school district that wants to run the following form off on mimeo paper but needs as many forms per page as possible.

CONSENT FORM

I hereby give my consent to my child's participation on the

outing to _____

on _____, 1988.

Child's Name _____

Parent's Name _____

Parent's Signature _____

At the beginning of the file, type the following dot commands, each at column 1:

```
.LH 5
.MT 3
.MB 3
.OP
.LS 2
```

Now type the form. Make sure you center the title and that the underlines extend to column *66* of each line. Press **RETURN** twice between the title and the body of the form. After typing the last line:

Press   **RETURN** twice

for spacing.

Now, block out the form and copy it as many times as you can fit it on the page (five times). When you're finished:

Press   **^PRT SC**

Press   **ESC**

to save and print the file.

Notice that even with more lines per vertical inch, the **.LH 5** command, the effect of the double spacing still appears in the printout.

When Double Spacing Really Isn't

One nifty way to use the line height setting is to print a single-spaced file in double spacing *without* changing the line spacing and reformatting the file! Just insert a **.LH 16** command at the top of the file. This setting results in 48/16 = 3 lines per inch. Use it, for example, to get a "draft" printout of a file. WordStar will still show the correct page breaks, by the way. You can delete the command later when you want to print the file in single spacing.

Line Height Need No Longer Be First

It used to be that the line height setting was, with due respects to Tennessee Williams, the "Big Daddy" of all page formatting commands. That is, previous versions of WordStar insisted that any specific **.LH** command occur before any other page formatting commands, such as **.PL,** because it governed these commands. That is no longer true. As long as the **.LH** command is at the top of the page, WordStar will honor it.

Other Page Formatting Tips

Now for other problem situations that you might encounter. What happens if you've printed a 20-page file only to find that you have to change page 12? If you delete or insert an extra line, this will throw off all the following page breaks. What a mess!

Here's how you save yourself unnecessary frustration. If you have to delete text on page 12, use the **.PA** command to break page 12 early, making sure that page 13 still starts at the right line according to your previous print-out.

If you have to *insert* a line, the problem is more complicated. Instead of having to reprint pages 12 through 20, change the bottom margin setting on page 12 only to reduce the bottom margin by one line. Insert the correct **.MB** command at the *top* of the page. Then at the top of page 13 reset the bottom margin. You can thus change individual page layouts by inserting the correct dot commands where necessary.

Another problem situation involves files in double spacing. You will notice that WordStar will not print the first line of each new page on line 1 if the previous page ends on an *even* number. For instance, if the last typing line of one page is line 54 and the file is double-spaced, WordStar will print the first line of the next page on line 2.

This is a drag, but here's one way to get around it: set the page format to have a possible *even* number of lines per page (for example, a top margin of 8 and a bottom margin of 6 would mean 66 − 14 = 52 possible typing lines per page). Then, make sure that you begin work on an *odd*-numbered line, such as 1. WordStar will then, in double spacing, automatically begin each new page on line 1.

Another nifty trick is to use the nonprinting comment dot command, .. or **.IG,** in blank lines at the tops of pages. WordStar will not include these blank lines in the total printed line count for the page, and the *next* line will print as line 1 of the page. This illustration shows what I mean:

```
"Sunflower" series, which recently carried with it a price tag of
-------------------------------------------------------------------------P

..
almost forty million dollars at a London sale.  What induced  the

anonymous  collector to pay such a sum, the highest  in  history,

for this work?
```

Here, WordStar would "print" the blank line between text lines at the top of the next page. I've inserted a .. dot command to "blank out" the blank line *without deleting it.* I often check my files at the last minute and insert .. commands in this fashion. Later, I can remove the dot commands quickly with find and replace to restore the blank lines. That is, I find the two dots (..) and replace them with two *spaces*.

Professional word processors are very picky people. They take the extra time to check page breaks during the final stage of a document and make any last-minute changes. That's because they want the best-looking printed results for their money. How about you?

Boilerplates, Format Files, and Document Assembly

In this chapter you will learn the following new commands:

File Command

.CS	Clear the screen of messages during printing
.DM	Display a message during printing
.FI	Insert a file during printing
.PF ON/OFF/DIS	Turn the print time reformatting on, off, or discretionary
.RP	Repeat printing

Other Feature

CHANGE (C)	Change the disk during printing

Dear Reader, you've probably already begun to think about how you can use boilerplate text and format files to help save time and work. Now that you know the ins and outs of page formatting, it's time to take another look at boilerplates and format files, to get the "big picture," as it were, of formatting. In this chapter, you'll discover ways to reduce the work load by reusing text and files. You'll also learn what document assembly is and the many ways to create documents during printing.

DO WARM-UP

An Historical Note

One of the major differences between older versions of WordStar and WordStar Professional Release 4 is the way WordStar now handles certain dot commands. In previous versions, many dot commands were only available during *merge printing,* and you needed a separate program, MailMerge, to access these commands.

Now, many original merge printing commands are available during regular printing operations, so you don't have to merge print a file to use these commands. Commands such as **.OJ ON** and **.LS** were once merge printing commands. You'll encounter several other changed commands, including **.FI** and **.PF**, in this chapter.

Another change from the original WordStar/MailMerge setup is the ability to print multiple copies of a file. That was originally part of MailMerge, but, as you know, it's now one of the print options. There's even a dot command that can determine how many copies of a file should print.

Inserting Boilerplates During Printing

Suppose you have to insert the same text repeatedly in a file. As you know, you can just block it out and copy the block wherever you need it. You can also set up the block as a file and use the file insert command, **^KR**, to read in the file. There's another way to go: have WordStar *insert* the boilerplate file during printing.

Press	**D** [open a document]
Type	`smith.ans`
Press	**RETURN**
Type	`y`

because this is a new file.

In a moment you'll create a file containing a deposition by a Mr. Smith in a certain law suit. Mr. Smith is not being terribly cooperative. His answer to each question is always the same; in legal jargon, he's "taking the Fifth":

```
Smith:  I refuse to say anything on the grounds that it may   tend
to incriminate me.
```

Deposition questions could go on for pages! You wouldn't want to type Mr. Smith's answer each time. Nor do you particularly want to copy in the answer. Instead, you'll use the file insert dot command, **.FI**.

Type Mr. Smith's answer, but make sure you press **RETURN** *twice* at the end of the sentence for spacing. You'll see why in a moment. When you're finished,

Press   **^KD** or **F10**

to save the file and return to the Opening menu.

The File Insert Command

Now, create the deposition file, which will include file insert commands. Wherever you need Mr. Smith's answer in the file, you type a command instructing WordStar to insert the SMITH.ANS file during printing. The **.FI** command must contain a correct file name.

Press   **D** [open a document]

Type   smith.dep

Press   **RETURN**

Type   y

because this is a new file.

Again, the deposition is not in the correct legal form; it's merely an example. Type the file exactly as you see it.

Smudge: Did you, or did you not, repeatedly threaten the Plaintiff with bodily harm if she did not keep her cat off your property?

.fi smith.ans
Smudge: Did you, or did you not, call the City Pound on numerous occasions and insist that they pick up a "stray cat" in your backyard, which you knew to be the Plaintiff's cat?

.FI SMITH.ANS
Smudge: Were you or were you not aware that Plaintiff's cat had a habit of chasing birds and, er, digging in your backyard?

.FI Smith.ans
Smudge: On November 11, 1987, the day prior to the alleged events, did you or did you not buy two boxes of Moist Munchies

```
cat  food  from the grocery store, even though you do not  own  a
cat?
```

```
.FI SMITH.ans
```

When you're finished:

Press   ^KS or F9

to save the file and resume where you left off.

You'll note that I've typed the **.FI** command lines in a variety of uppercase, lowercase, or mixed case. The case doesn't matter. Issues that do matter are that you include a file name and that you insert a space between the **.FI** command and the file name. **Tip:** When you have to insert the same **.FI** dot command many times, why not create a macro to do it for you? Then you'll save even *more* keystrokes.

Caution: The **.FI** command line *must* end with a hard return. Otherwise, WordStar will disregard the command entirely. If you insert an **.FI** command at the very end of a file, as in the last line of SMITH.DEP, make sure you press **RETURN** to finish the command. See also the section "Chaining Files."

Printing the File

When you print this file, every time WordStar comes upon a **.FI** command it *inserts*, that is, prints, the SMITH.ANS file. **Note:** The file must exist and be on the default drive or in the default directory. If the file is on another drive or in another directory, include the drive letter or directory path in the file name. For example:

```
.FI b:smith.ans
```

or

```
.FI \WS4\LEGAL\SMITH.ANS
```

When you print a file containing **.FI** commands, if WordStar can't find a file that you list on a **.FI** line, WordStar flashes the Print Wait message in the top right corner of the screen. Press **P** to see the problem **.FI** command line and this message underneath the Printing menu:

```
Can't find that file. Press C to continue anyway or ^U to stop.
```

It probably makes no sense to press **C**, because WordStar will print only what it can. Press ^U (**F2**) to cancel and make your corrections. You'll get the same message if you insert a blank **.FI** command line without a file name.

If you wish, prepare your printer and paper, then save and print the SMITH.DEP file with **^PRT SC ESC** to see the results.

Changing Disks During Printing

You can also instruct WordStar to *change disks* before it inserts a file during printing. Include the **CHANGE** option directly after the file name on the **.FI** line. You don't even have to type the entire word **CHANGE**; just type a **C**, but make sure there's a space between it and the file name:

```
.FI smith.ans c
```

> *or*

```
.FI smith.ans change
```

If you've instructed WordStar that you want to change disks for a file insert, when it encounters the **.FI** command WordStar will again flash the Print Wait message. Press **P** to see the file insert command line in question and this message:

```
Change disk. Press C when ready to continue.
```

 Caution: Make sure that the disk you're changing does *not* contain the WordStar program files. If you've set the help level to 0, WordStar doesn't flash a Print Wait message. I guess you just have to intuit when to press **P** to access the Printing menu!

Spacing Considerations with Boilerplates

You're probably wondering why there's no blank line between each **.FI** command line and the paragraph following it. Remember that you included the extra blank line in the SMITH.ANS file? When you set up boilerplates, always be careful about the spacing.

For instance, you could have added a blank line *above* Mr. Smith's answer in the SMITH.ANS file. Then, you wouldn't want a superfluous blank line in the SMITH.DEP file. The first part of the file would then look like this:

```
Smudge: Did you, or did you not, repeatedly threaten the
Plaintiff with bodily harm if she did not keep her cat off your
property?
.fi smith.ans

Smudge: Did you, or did you not, call the City Pound on numerous
occasions and insist that they pick up a "stray cat" in your
backyard, which you knew to be the Plaintiff's cat?
```

How you set up your boilerplates is your decision, but be consistent with spacing. Examples in this and other chapters illustrate different spacing setups.

Limitations of the .FI Command

A substantial limitation to the **.FI** command is that WordStar won't show on the screen the correct page breaks of the *final* printout. That's because it doesn't "go out" to the inserted files and count their lines during *editing*. If you wish, you could use the PRVIEW printer driver to print a file containing **.FI** dot commands to a disk file to check the page breaks.

Another potential limitation, but one that you'll learn how to overcome in a moment, is that files you insert at print time with the **.FI** command should be in the same format as the main file. In the deposition example, Smith's answer file has the same format as the deposition file.

A third, and related, limitation is that WordStar won't honor any formatting commands in the inserted file while you're editing. With this limitation in mind, don't use the file insert dot command to insert a format file at the beginning of a new file. You *can* do it, but WordStar won't follow the formatting instructions until it prints the file. It's a better idea just to use **^KR** to read in a format file so that the formatting commands take immediate effect and you can see the formatting on the screen as you edit.

Document Assembly

If you create documents that contain the same sections, such as contracts or other legal forms, you can take advantage of simple *document assembly* techniques. Set up each oft-used section of text in a separate boilerplate. Then, *assemble* the final document at print time with **.FI** commands, as examples in this chapter illustrate. Figure 16–1 presents a graphic description of document assembly techniques.

(An aside: There are much more powerful ways to assemble documents. You'll learn about them when you investigate WordStar's merge printing features in later chapters. This section is just a taste of great things to come.)

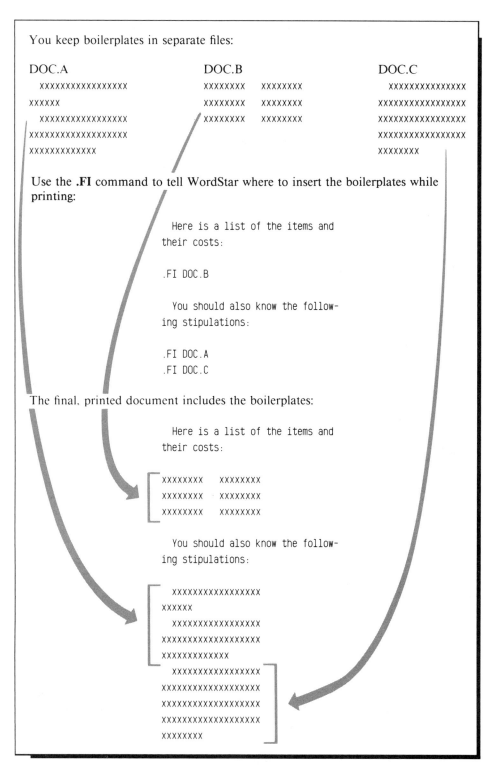

Figure 16–1 How Document Assembly Works

Aligning Text During Printing: The .PF Command

The key to document assembly is WordStar's ability to *reformat* a file at print time. That is, your boilerplates may be in a different format from the file into which you're planning to insert them. If you instruct WordStar to reformat while it is printing, the so-called *print time reformatter* will ensure that all inserted files print with the format of the main file.

The command to reformat while printing is **.PF ON**. This command works with and is governed by other line formatting dot commands, so you must include the other commands you need if the format settings in question are *not* the defaults. You can insert the dot commands in any order, but make sure the **.PF ON** command appears *before* any text in the file.

The word *reformat* clues you in to what format changes the **.PF ON** command affects—those commands that determine paragraph alignment and line spacing. That means any command that ^B or ^QU work with: **.OJ, .LM, .RM, .PM**, and **.LS**. No matter what the original format of the file was, the **.PF ON** command adjusts the format to one you specify. If you omit one of these dot commands, WordStar reformats according to the defaults.

Think of the **.PF ON** command as the print time equivalent of ^B or ^QU. However, **.PF ON** only works with dot commands, not onscreen formatting commands, such as ^OL, because you can't save onscreen commands in a file.

If there are sections of text that you *don't* want WordStar to reformat at print time, insert a **.PF OFF** command where necessary. For example, you may want to insert a boilerplate table that you don't want changed. Remember to turn print time reformatting back on where applicable with another **.PF ON** command. You can also use the **.AW OFF** and **.AW ON** commands to prevent reformatting.

Caution: Take care with *soft returns* at the ends of line. With **.PF ON**, WordStar may run two lines together during print time reformatting.

When you learn about merge printing, you'll see that by default the print time reformatter is in *discretionary* mode. That is, WordStar uses what little "discretion" it has to realign paragraphs that contain changing information. To return the print time reformatter to discretionary mode after you've turned it on or off, insert a **.PF DIS** command. This command only works with merge printing operations.

Smith Again!

You'll edit the SMITH.DEP file to learn how the **.PF ON** command works. You created the file using the defaults: single spacing, right margin justification on, and a 65-character line. Suppose you're assembling this document, with its related file, SMITH.ANS, but you want the file to print in a different format.

Press   **D** [open a document]

Type   `smith.dep`

Press   **RETURN**

Press   **^N**

to insert a line but leave the cursor where it is.

Type the following dot commands at the beginning of the file, pressing **RETURN** after each one except the last. Remember to begin the commands at column 1.

```
.PF ON
.RM 70
.LS 2
.OJ OFF
```

Prepare your printer and paper, then:

Press   **^PRT SC ESC**

to print the file in its new format.

The SMITH.ANS prints in the new format each time, too. The advantage of reformatting while WordStar is printing is that the *original* format doesn't change. You can still revert to it by deleting the dot commands from the SMITH.DEP file or changing the format for the next printout. Neat!

Thus, any time you insert a boilerplate into a file containing the **.PF ON** command, the boilerplate will print in the main file's format. Think of all the ways you can use, and reuse, boilerplates to assemble many different documents! To see just a couple possibilities, suppose you *don't* want Smith's answer to print in the new format. Instead, you'll keep it in the original format for emphasis.

Press   **D** [open a document]

Type   `smith.ans`

Press   **RETURN**

Add the **.PF OFF** and **.PF ON** commands to the file, but make sure there are two blank lines between the text and the **.PF ON** command, and that this command ends with a hard return. The file looks like this when you're finished:

```
.PF OFF
Smith:  I refuse to say anything on the grounds that it may  tend
to incriminate me.


.PF ON
```

Now, save the file with ^KD (F10) and print the *SMITH.DEP* file again to see what happens. With just a few changes to your files, you can get very different results!

Note: Keep in mind that WordStar always honors the *most current* formatting commands. Suppose you want to indent just Mr. Smith's answers. Set up the format changes in the SMITH.ANS file, but make sure you change the format *back* to that of the main file. Here's what I mean:

```
.LM 5
.RM 65
Smith:   I refuse to say anything on the grounds that it may   tend
to incriminate me.
.LM 1
.RM 70
```

In this example, the answer file will print with different left and right margins, but then WordStar reverts to the main file's format. Line spacing and justification have not changed from the main file. By setting up the format changes in SMITH.ANS, you only need determine them once. You *could* have put the changes directly before and after each **.FI** command line in the SMITH.DEP file, but that's a lot more work!

Note: Another problem you may encounter is with centered text when you reformat the file while it is printing. Until WordStar gets a specific "center" dot command, you'll have to recenter text manually before you print. The **.PF ON** won't help you. There *is* a way to have WordStar center text while it's merge printing a file—see Chapter 23.

Command Files

In document assembly, there's normally one file that "controls the show." That is, it contains the main formatting requirements, including a **.PF ON** command where necessary. All files that WordStar inserts during print time conform to the main format. The SMITH.DEP file is a controlling file.

Think of the main file as a *command file*. It contains all the formatting commands to govern the printing. However, if a boilerplate should print in a different format, you can control this from the boilerplate, as you did in the previous example. Notice that the **.PF ON** command in the SMITH.ANS file reverted to the format of the *main* file, SMITH.DEP.

Note: The WordStar documentation refers to command files as *master files*. Same difference.

Command, or master, files need not contain any text, just formatting commands. For example, say you're assembling a contract out of various boilerplate parts. You can construct a command file that sets the format and inserts the correct boilerplates. Here's an example:

```
.. CONTRACT.7 - Prints standard contract #7
.MT 7
.MB 5
.PF ON
.OJ ON
.LS 1
.LM 1
.RM 60
.FI opening
.FI section.2
.FI section.4
.FI section.7
.FI closing
.FI siglines
```

In this example, the various "section" files are different standard contract provisions, while OPENING is a standard contract opening, CLOSING is a standard closing section, and SIGLINES contains witnesses' signatures. **Tip:** You may want to maintain a "crib sheet" that tells you what text is in each boilerplate file.

Caution: I've discovered that if a file name doesn't end in at least one hard or soft return, the **.FI** command won't work properly, and WordStar will *skip* the next **.FI** line in the command file. For example, suppose the last character of the file SECTION.7 is at the end of a paragraph, but there is no hard return there. WordStar would not honor the **.FI closing** command!

To make sure that the last "inserted" file will print correctly, open the command file and position the cursor at the end of the file. If the column indicator in the status line doesn't show a 01, or the flag character display doesn't show a :, press RETURN to insert a hard return at the end of the line.

Remember to be careful about the *spacing* between boilerplate sections. In the above example, there are extra blank lines in each of the boilerplate files to separate each file from the next in the printout. Another way to go would be to have no extra blank lines in the boilerplate files, but to include them instead in the command file. For example:

```
.. CONTRACT.7 - Prints standard contract #7
.MT 7
.MB 5
.PF ON
.OJ ON
.LS 1
.LM 1
```

```
.RM 60
.FI opening


.FI section.2


.FI section.4


.FI section.7


.FI closing


.FI siglines
```

Here, there are two blank lines between each boilerplate insertion. It may take you a bit of time to get the spacing of your boilerplates—and how they work with each other—correct, but then think of the time you'll save later!

A command file can thus contain text and formatting commands. As another example, suppose you have a basic letter opening file that includes your return address and space for the recipient's name and address. Other paragraphs change depending on the letter you send. Here's a typical letter command file:

```
.MT 8
.MB 4
.OP
.PF ON
.OJ OFF
.LM 10
.RM 60
.LS 1
```

```
                              4118 Hollywood Boulevard
                              Hollywood, CA  90028
                              <today's date>



        Ms. Penelope Jones
        101 Pomander Walk
        Los Gatos, CA  94205
        Dear Ms. Jones:

        Thank you for your kind letter and for the numerous
```

```
photographs of your impressive cat, "Cozy Toes."
We are returning the photos herewith.
```

```
.FI accept
```

```
.FI ending
```

Here, the ACCEPT file contains a paragraph noting the acceptance of Ms. Jones's cat to the contest, while the ENDING file is a standard letter closing. In Chapter 21, you'll see an even better way to create letters for different recipients without having to edit the opening section to change the recipient's name and address or the current date.

Nesting Files

When you insert **.FI** dot commands in a file, you're *nesting* the commands. Each time WordStar comes to a **.FI** command, it stops printing the current file and prints the file listed on the **.FI** command line. A nested file can itself contain **.FI** commands. WordStar would print each file in its turn according to where the **.FI** commands appear. After it prints an inserted file, WordStar backtracks to the previous file, that is, the file containing the **.FI** line. This is the *calling* file. So, one file can "call" another, which in turn can "call" another.

Although it's possible to nest file *eight* levels deep, for the sake of your own sanity I don't recommend this approach. Try to nest files at only one level so you can keep track of what you want. If necessary, try *chaining* files, described next, instead of creating too many nesting levels.

Chaining Files

Suppose you're writing a book on WordStar, as I am doing this very moment. You maintain each chapter in a separate file: CH.1, CH.2, and so on. You can *chain print* the files when you want to print the entire book. There are *two* ways to chain print files:

1. Add a **.FI** command at the end of each file to instruct WordStar to insert the next file. You may also want to include a **.PA** command to start the next file at the top of a new page. That is, at the end of CH.1, insert these commands:

```
.PA
----------------------------------------------------------------------P
.FI ch.2
```

Notice that I show the page break display, but don't type it! Continue inserting the correct **.FI** commands at the end of each chapter file. Then print the *first* chapter file, and WordStar will continue chain printing the others in their turn, each with the correct pagination.

2. Set up a command file that includes just the **.FI** commands, with a **.PA** command between each. Then just print the command file. For example, to print the first four chapters of your book, determine whatever page formatting commands you want in a command file called, say, BOOK. After the page formatting commands, insert the file insert and page break commands. (Again, don't type the page break displays.) A representative BOOK command file might look like this:

```
.MT 6
.MB 6
.HE WordStar Book - Draft No. 5
.FO                              - # -
.FI CH.1
.PA
----------------------------------------------------------------------------P
.FI CH.2
.PA
----------------------------------------------------------------------------P
.FI CH.3
.PA
----------------------------------------------------------------------------P
.FI CH.4
```

Because there are page formatting commands in the command file, WordStar will print all files in the "chain" with the same page format. Now suppose you want page numbering for each chapter to begin with page 1. Insert **.PN** dot commands, like so:

```
.MT 6
.MB 6
.HE WordStar Book - Draft No. 5
.FO                              - # -
.FI CH.1
.PA
----------------------------------------------------------------------------P
.PN 1
.FI CH.2
.PA
----------------------------------------------------------------------------P
```

```
.PN 1
.FI CH.3
.PA
----------------------------------------------------------------------P
.PN 1
.FI CH.4
```

In this example, the pagination for each chapter starts with page number 1.

Keeping Track of What's Happening

When you work with command files that set up a large print job, you may want to know how the printing is progressing. You can insert a special dot command, **.DM**, to display a message during printing. In addition, you can clear the screen of previous messages with the **.CS** dot command.

Take a look at this changed version of the previous command file:

```
.MT 6
.MB 6
.HE WordStar Book - Draft No. 5
.FO                              - # -
.DM Printing chapter 1
.FI CH.1
.PA
----------------------------------------------------------------------P
.DM Printing chapter 2
.PN 1
.FI CH.2
.PA
----------------------------------------------------------------------P
.CS
.DM Printing chapter 3
.PN 1
.FI CH.3
.PA
----------------------------------------------------------------------P
.CS Printing chapter 4
.PN 1
.FI CH.4
```

As it prepares to insert the correct chapter file, WordStar displays a message about which chapter it's printing. Notice that after it prints the CH.2 file, WordStar clears the screen of the first two messages before displaying the next message, Printing chapter 3.

Wait, there's more! Look at the second **.CS** command in the example. Not only does it clear the screen, but it also displays a new message, Printing chapter 4. Thus, the **.CS** command can work like the **.DM** command, with the bonus that it clears the screen *before* displaying a message. You don't have to enclose the message in quotation marks. Just make sure there's a space between the message and the **.DM** or **.CS** command.

When it prints the command file, WordStar won't flash a Print Wait message on the status line. To see your messages, press **P** [print a file] from the Opening menu, or **^KP** from within a file to access the Printing menu. To resume printing in the background after viewing your messages, press **B**.

Printing an "Endless" File!

Just as it's possible to create a recursive macro, you can have a recursive **.FI** instruction that inserts the *same* file as the one you're printing. But then what happens is known in the computer world as an "endless loop." WordStar would print the file continuously until you press **^U** (**F2**) to cancel the printing.

As an example, use the **O** [copy a file] command from the Opening menu to copy the FORM file to a new file called FORM.2. You'll recall that FORM contains several copies of the same form on a page. FORM.2 will contain just one copy that prints repeatedly.

Use the **D** [open a document] command to open the FORM.2 file. Leave the *first* copy of the form, but block out and delete all other copies. That is, position the cursor on line 19 and block delete the rest of the file. Then, insert this command on line 19, the last line of the file:

```
.FI form.2
```

Make sure you press **RETURN** to end the dot command line. Otherwise, WordStar will ignore the command. Save and print the file. WordStar will print the form continuously until you press **^U** (**F2**) to cancel printing. Perpetuum mobile . . . wow!

Repeat Printing

Well, that was just an example of a funky way to print many copies of a file! Of course, you could just tell WordStar how many copies you want by answering the Number of copies? print option. In that case, make sure you remove the **.FI** command line from the FORM.2 file so that WordStar doesn't loop endlessly through the file during printing of the *first* copy.

There's another command that can govern how many copies of a file are to print. It's the repeat printing command, **.RP**. You insert this command at the top of the file, followed by the number of repetitions. (WordStar always "assumes" one copy unless you tell it otherwise.) So, in the FORM.2 file you could delete the **.FI** command line and insert an **.RP** line at the top of the file. For example, if you want to repeat printing 15 times, the command would be **.RP 15**.

Tip: If you have to print many copies of the same one-page form, set it up in file using the FORM.2 example, but include a **.PA** command at the end of the file so that each copy starts on a new page.

Hyphenating Your File as It Prints

Until WordStar has an automatic hyphenation feature, it technically can't hyphenate words during printing. However, you can help it along by inserting *soft hyphens* at correct syllable breaks. If the **.PF ON** command is in the file, or if the print time reformatter is in discretionary mode for merge printing (Chapters 19 through 24), the print time reformatter will honor soft hyphens where it can. Take a look at the following short example (you don't have to type it).

```
    The two parties to this Agreement, Software Supply House and
Compucat, do hereby warrant and state that they have not  entered
into   any  such  similar  agreement  with  any  other   company,
corporation  or  entity  for the same  purposes  as  agreed  upon
herein, which other agreement or agreements could be construed to
preclude  the terms, conditions and warranties herein.   Further,
Software  Supply  House  warrants that  it  shall  hold  Compucat
harmless  from  any  liability incurred should any  part  of  this
Section  be  disputed  by  Compucat in  a  court  of  law  having
jurisdiction over the terms of this Agreement.
```

If I wanted to take more control over hyphenation during printing, I could enter soft hyphens at correct syllable breaks in certain words. The command to insert a soft hyphen is ^OE. Remember that the ^OE command has changed from previous WordStar releases. Each time you press ^OE, you insert a soft hyphen at the cursor location. It's a good idea to turn the print code displays on with ^OD (SHIFT F1) so you can see the = where the soft hyphens are, just in case you insert one in the wrong place. Here are the words I've chosen to hyphenate and how they look on the screen:

```
        Agree=ment
        Soft=ware
        Compu=cat
        en=tered
        agree=ment
        com=pany
        corpo=ra=tion
        en=tity
```

```
pur=poses
here=in
agree=ments
con=strued
pre=clude
condi=tions
harm=less
Sec=tion
dis=puted
juris=dic=tion
```

I've gone overboard a little just to illustrate the point: *you* don't have to insert so many soft hyphens. Now, if I printed the same example with a **.PF ON** command in the file, single spacing, and right justification on, it would look like this:

```
The two parties to this Agreement, Software Supply House and
Compucat, do hereby warrant and state that they have not  entered
into any such similar agreement with any other company,  corpora-
tion or entity for the same purposes as agreed upon herein, which
other agreement or agreements could be construed to preclude  the
terms,  conditions  and  warranties  herein.   Further,  Software
Supply  House warrants that it shall hold Compucat harmless  from
any  liability incurred should any part of this Section  be  dis-
puted by Compucat in a court of law having jurisdiction over  the
terms of this Agreement.
```

If I changed the line length, the print time reformatter would again honor any syllable breaks it could when it realigns the paragraph.

More Practice with Format Files

You've already learned how to set up formatting dot commands in separate boilerplate files known as format files, and then how to use the ^KR command to read in the format whenever you start a new file. This section presents other ways to work with format files.

Creating a Format Library

A *format library* is merely a collection of format files that you set up once and then reuse whenever you need a specific format. Normally, format files contain only dot commands to govern page and line formatting, but they can contain text, too.

Everyone has different document format requirements, so I can only give some general examples. Remember that you should set WordStar's *default* formats to those you use most often. If the defaults that come with the program aren't to your liking, change the defaults with the WSCHANGE program (Chapter 27).

Then, set up the other format files you want to include in your format library. Use a *common file name* so you can copy all formats in the library when you start a new disk, or keep the format files on the WordStar *program* disk. Use short file names to save typing. For example, I have a format library that contains various files: F.1, F.2, F.3, and so on. I can copy these files from DOS with one command.

Tip: Create and print out a crib sheet that lists what each format file contains, and keep this sheet near your computer. After a while, you'll learn the format file contents anyway. A typical crib sheet might look like this:

```
F.1 - Standard contract
F.2 - Contract long form
F.3 - Letter
F.4 - Memo
F.5 - Weekly report
F.6 - Monthly report
```

The F.4 memo format file includes not only formatting dot commands, but also text that appears in all memos. It might look something like this:

```
.. Memo format
.MT 8
.MB 6
.LS 1
.OP
                    M E M O R A N D U M


To:

From:

Re:

Date:


-----------------------------------------------------------------
```

This type of setup is a *template*. When you start a new memo, you merely fill in the blanks. There are tabs after the *To:, From:, Re:,* and *Date:* lines so that each entry on these lines starts at column 11. To fill in the standard memo, position the cursor on the *To:* line and press ^**QD** (^**F10**) to move the cursor to the end of the line. Type the entry and continue with the other three lines. There are three hard returns in the file after the line of hyphens, so you need only press ^**QC** (^**END**) to enter the text of the memo. (Chapter 26 shows you how to jazz this memo up on a laser printer!)

Similarly, the F.5 format file might contain the following commands:

```
.. Weekly report format
.. Update header before printing!
.MT 10
.MB 8
.OP
.HE Weekly Report - Week of
.FO                              Page #
.LS 1
.OJ OFF
.CW 10
.LM 1
.PM 5
.RM 79
```

Whenever you start a new file in a nondefault format, such as the weekly report, either use the **O** [copy a file] command from the Opening menu to copy the format file to the new file name, or open the new file with the **D** [open a document] command and then read in the format file with ^**KR**. In this example, you would also cursor down to enter the week in the header, as the comment line reminds you.

The best thing about format files is that, once you've taken the time to set them up and test them to make sure that they are what *you* want, you can use them over and over again. No experienced word processor would be caught dead without a complete format library. *It makes work so much easier.*

Formatting Flexibility: A Script

This section presents a pseudo-real-life word processing situation that illustrates the use of various format files. You'll create part of a fictitious script to learn the patterns to follow when you're working with multiple formats.

Press   **D** [open a document]

Type   script

Press   **RETURN**

Type   y

because this is a new file.

Motion picture and television screenplays present a challenge to any word processing program. The basic problem with scripts is that they contain several distinctly different formats that change repeatedly. The harried word processor must continually change the text from one format to the other.

For the sake of simplicity, you'll limit your script to two basic formats: the outer format containing the stage directions, and the inner format for the dialogue. (Scripts also generally have the word *CONTINUED* as a header or footer on each page when the scene extends from one page to the next. I have left this out in the example.)

Before typing anything, take a look at how the script section will print. *INT.* and *EXT.* are standard abbreviations for "interior shot" and "exterior shot," respectively.

```
INT. - Hotel room, dusk

A lonely room in a fleabag hotel.  There are no lights on in the
room, but the light from a neon sign somewhere outside the one
window is flashing on and off at regular intervals.  The light
from this sign does not reach the bed, however, which is cast in
semi-darkness.  No one is immediately discernible, but soon two
figures can be seen slouched on the bed.  They are lying on top
of the bed, fully clothed.  They look -- and are -- exhausted.



                        MARY
              (Raises her head wearily
                 as she speaks)

        Oh, John!



                        JOHN

        Yes, Mary?



                        MARY

        John, why did it have to end this
        way?  Oh, John, why, oh why?  Why
        couldn't it have ended differently?
```

JOHN

I don't know, Mary: I guess things
just don't work out the way we hope
and plan them to sometimes. I'm
sure sorry about this, Mary ... I
sure am.

Suddenly the door is thrown open and the light is turned on in
the room, causing the two people on the bed to blink in order to
adjust their eyes to it. It is STANLEY, who stands formidably at
the doorway. We see his powerful frame silhouetted by the strong
light from the corridor. He stands there with a towering pose,
arms folded imperiously across his chest.

MARY
(Hastily collecting herself)

Who's there? Oh, who's there?

STANLEY

I thought I'd find you two here!
You see, you couldn't fool me! In
fact, you can't fool anybody! We're
all onto your little game. Well,
the party's over ... this time for
good!

JOHN
(Stands up)

You have no right coming in here
like that. How dare you! Get out,
get out, or I'll make you get out.

STANLEY

You'll make me! What a joke. Who
do you think you are ... her
husband?

```
JOHN looks dejectedly around him.  He knows he is defeated.  He
walks slowly toward the window, away from MARY, who holds out her
hands imploring him, but says nothing.  She starts to weep.
STANLEY keeps his majestic pose at the door as the scene FADES
INTO

EXT. - Hotel Parking Lot, Night (and so on)
```

There are several format files that you'll need for this script. First, there's the format for the script as a whole. This format includes the page formatting, the line spacing, and the justification setting, because the latter two settings don't change. Second, there's the dialogue format for each of three characters, which is the same except for the character's name. Finally, there's the change to return to the outer format for the stage directions.

The first format, in a file called F.S, is simple enough:

```
.. Script format
.MT 10
.MB 10
.LS 1
.OJ OFF
```

The second, third, and fourth formats are all similar. You can create one and then copy it to create the other two. The second format, M for Mary, looks like this:

```
.LM 15
.RM 50
                        MARY
```

Each time you insert a dialogue format, it changes the left and right margin for the shortened dialogue lines and inserts the character's name. The file ends with a hard return after the centered *Mary* line so you're ready to type her stage directions and dialogue. This is another example of a template. You can copy this format file to new files called J for John and S for Stanley, and merely change the names. Don't forget to center each name line before saving the files.

The final format just returns the left and right margins to the original settings:

```
.LM 1
.RM 65
```

You're now ready to construct the script using the ^**KR** command to insert the correct format file at each point in the text. Start by inserting the F.S file, then type the stage direction. Press **RETURN** enough times for proper spacing. Then use ^**KR** to read in the M file for Mary's first lines, and so on. The result looks like this on the screen:

```
.. Script format
.MT 10
.MB 10
.LS 1
.OJ OFF
INT. - Hotel room, dusk

A lonely room in a fleabag hotel.  There are no lights on in the
room, but the light from a neon sign somewhere outside the one
window is flashing on and off at regular intervals.  The light
from this sign does not reach the bed, however, which is cast in
semi-darkness.  No one is immediately discernible, but soon two
figures can be seen slouched on the bed.  They are lying on top
of the bed, fully clothed.  They look -- and are -- exhausted.


.LM 15
.RM 50
                        MARY
                (Raises her head wearily
                    as she speaks)


            Oh, John!



.LM 15
.RM 50


                        JOHN


            Yes, Mary?



.LM 15
.RM 50


                        MARY


            John, why did it have to end this
            way?  Oh, John, why, oh why?  Why
            couldn't it have ended differently?
```

```
.LM 15
.RM 50
```

                    JOHN

          I don't know, Mary: I guess things
          just don't work out the way we hope
          and plan them to sometimes. I'm
          sure sorry about this, Mary ... I
          sure am.


```
.LM 1
.RM 65
```
Suddenly the door is thrown open and the light is turned on in
the room, causing the two people on the bed to blink in order to
adjust their eyes to it. It is STANLEY, who stands formidably at
the doorway. We see his powerful frame silhouetted by the strong
light from the corridor. He stands there with a towering pose,
arms folded imperiously across his chest.


```
.LM 15
.RM 50
```

                    MARY
          (Hastily collecting herself)

          Who's there? Oh, who's there?


```
.LM 15
.RM 50
```

                    STANLEY

          I thought I'd find you two here!
          You see, you couldn't fool me! In
          fact, you can't fool anybody! We're
          all onto your little game. Well,
          the party's over ... this time for
          good!


```
.LM 15
.RM 50
```

                    JOHN
          (Stands up)

          You have no right coming in here

```
                          like that.  How dare you!  Get out,
                          get out, or I'll make you get out.


        .LM 15
        .RM 50

                               STANLEY

                          You'll make me!  What a joke.  Who
                          do you think you are ... her
                          husband?


        .LM 1
        .RM 65
        JOHN looks dejectedly around him.  He knows he is defeated.  He
        walks slowly toward the window, away from MARY, who holds out her
        hands imploring him, but says nothing.  She starts to weep.
        STANLEY keeps his majestic pose at the door as the scene FADES
        INTO

        EXT. - Hotel Parking Lot, Night (and so on)
```

When you're finished:

Press   ^KS or F9

to save the file and resume where you left off.

What's wrong with this setup? Nothing really, but there is a bit of duplication of formatting commands because each character's dialogue format file inserts left and right margin changes into the file. This looks a bit messy on the screen, but it's acceptable. You can turn off the dot commands with ^OP to see just the text, if you wish.

Another way to go would be *not* to set up the left and right margin changes in each character's dialogue format file. Have a format file for this change only, and then just have the centered character name in the M, J, and S files. Then you'd only need the format change for the first character in a series of dialogues. The first part of the example would look like this:

```
        .. Script format
        .MT 10
        .MB 10
        .LS 1
        .OJ OFF
        INT. - Hotel room, dusk
```

A lonely room in a fleabag hotel. There are no lights on in the
room, but the light from a neon sign somewhere outside the one
window is flashing on and off at regular intervals. The light
from this sign does not reach the bed, however, which is cast in
semi-darkness. No one is immediately discernible, but soon two
figures can be seen slouched on the bed. They are lying on top
of the bed, fully clothed. They look -- and are -- exhausted.

.LM 15
.RM 50
                        MARY
                (Raises her head wearily
                    as she speaks)

        Oh, John!

                        JOHN

        Yes, Mary?

                        MARY

        John, why did it have to end this
        way? Oh, John, why, oh why? Why
        couldn't it have ended differently?

                        JOHN

        I don't know, Mary: I guess things
        just don't work out the way we hope
        and plan them to sometimes. I'm
        sure sorry about this, Mary ... I
        sure am.

.LM 1
.RM 65
Suddenly the door is thrown open and the light is turned on in
the room, causing the two people on the bed to blink in order to
(and so on)

Some bright soul out there in Readerland may have intuited that you can insert ruler lines instead of left and right margin dot commands. That is, use ^OL and ^OR to change the margins, then press ^OO (F8) to insert the ruler line once. Copy the ruler line whenever you need it. Here's how a section of dialogue would look with its ruler line:

```
.RR                L!----!----!----!----!----!----!---R
                             MARY

                   John, why did it have to end this
                   way?  Oh, John, why, oh why?  Why
                   couldn't it have ended differently?


                             JOHN

                   I don't know, Mary: I guess things
                   just don't work out the way we hope
                   and plan them to sometimes.  I'm
                   sure sorry about this, Mary ... I
                   sure am.
```

Save the file with ^KD (F10) when you're finished.

Of course, I'm discussing format files here, but don't forget WordStar powerful shorthand macros. You could set up macros to accomplish the same type of format changes *and* type and center each character name. Or use a combination of macros and format files.

How you reach your goal is up to you; WordStar has the flexibility to work with you. Unfortunately, no program has the means to help you *sell* your script ... find yourself a hot-shot agent. Good luck!

Chapter 17

More Special Printing Effects

In this chapter you will learn the following new commands:

File Commands

.BN	Select a sheet feeder bin
.BP ON/OFF	Turn bidirectional printing on/off
.LQ ON/OFF	Turn letter quality printing on/off
^P@	Print the following text at a fixed column
^PA	Turn the alternate character width on
^PE	User-defined print code
^PF	Phantom space
^PG	Phantom rubout
^PH	Backspace and overprint a character with the next character
^PI	Insert a nondocument fixed tab in a document file
^PJ	Insert a line feed
^PL	Insert a form feed
^PN	Turn the normal character width on
^PQ	User-defined print code
^PR	User-defined print code
.PS ON/OFF	Turn proportional spacing on/off

more . . .

	^PT	Turn superscript on/off
	^PV	Turn subscript on/off
	^PW	User-defined print code
	.SR	Set sub/superscript roll
.UJ ON/OFF/DIS		Turn microjustification on, off, or discretionary
	.XE	Define the ^PE command string
	.XL	Define the form feed string
	.XQ	Define the ^PQ command string
	.XR	Define the ^PR command string
	.XW	Define the ^PW command string

Other Features

ALT F1 through	Line and box drawing characters
ALT F10	

It's time to pick up the discussion of special printing effects that I began 'way back in Chapter 3, so make sure you study that chapter first. There are a lot of new commands, but you won't ever need to use them all! For the sake of completeness, however, this chapter lists all the ^P commands you didn't learn in Chapter 3, and a variety of dot commands that control specific printing situations.

In this chapter you'll learn how to print subscripts and superscripts, how to do complex equations, how to print special legal and foreign language characters, how to set up printer escape codes, how to draw lines and boxes, and a variety of other nifty printing effects. At the end of the chapter I'll discuss how to select printer sheet feeder bins from within a file.

> **DO WARM-UP**

Before You Begin

Even though WordStar theoretically supports many special printing features, that doesn't necessarily mean that your printer can. It's possible that your printer can't handle a particular special print effect. Check MicroPro's

"Printer Information" pamphlet to determine what features WordStar supports on your printer.

You may also find important information about your printer in the README file (see the Introduction). **Note:** Laser printer owners should read this chapter for an understanding of the generalities, but should also peruse Chapter 26 for specific examples.

If you're still having problems, I urge you to consult a printer expert. Printers are very funny beasts, and getting *any* printer to work correctly is one of the biggest hassles in computerdom. I wish I had a dollar for every time someone asked me a question about printers. Why, I'd be a rich man and wouldn't have to write books!

So much for "Alfieri's lament." Getting back to the business at hand, you'll open a test file to experiment with the various print features:

Press   **D** [open a document]

Type   **effects**

Press   **RETURN**

Type   **y**

because this is a new file.

You don't have to try out the examples in this chapter in any order. Just remember to open this file before you study a section if you want to type in the examples.

Subscripts and Superscripts

Subscripts and superscripts print slightly below or above the current line, respectively. The command for subscripts is **^PV** and for superscripts, **^PT**. Both are toggle switches, so make sure to turn the command off at the correct spot in the file.

The **^PT** and **^PV** commands are "toggles with a twist." When you issue the command, WordStar adjusts the print head either up or down. When you turn off the command, WordStar readjusts the print head to the normal position. Thus, the first **^PT** tells WordStar to shift the print head up a bit, and the second **^PT** instructs WordStar to shift it back down.

Tip: Many dot-matrix printers can only print subscripts and superscripts one whole line below or above the current line. To avoid overlapping, you may want to change line spacing from single to double. See "The Sub/Superscript Roll" for more information about adjusting the printing of subscripts and superscripts.

Subscripts

As with all print toggles, the subscript command remains in effect until you turn it off. This example sets up the correct printing of the following sentence: Be careful with the CO_2 cartridges.

Type   `Be careful with the CO`

Press   **^PV**

to start subscripting.
     The symbol ^V appears on the screen, and WordStar shows the subscript in highlighting or a different color, depending on your monitor.

Type   `2`

Press   **^PV**

to end subscripting.
     Another ^V appears.

Press   **SPACEBAR**

for correct spacing.

Type   `cartridges.`

The entire sentence looks like this on the screen:

`Be careful with the CO^V2^V cartridges.`

Press   **RETURN**

for spacing here and between *each* example you try in this chapter.

Superscripts

As an example of a superscript, you'll include a footnote reference at the end of a sentence. Chapter 25 discusses footnotes at more length.

Type   `See Figure 1, page 6.`

Directly after the period,

Press   **^PT**

to start superscripting.
The symbol ^T appears on the screen.

Type   17

Press   **^PT**

to end superscripting.
This is the result:

See Figure 1, page 6.^T17^T

It will print:

See Figure 1, page 6.^{17}

Both the **^PT** and **^PV** commands throw off the appearance of the right margin on the screen, but you can use the **^OD (SHIFT F1)** command to see how the lines will print. Still, there may be times when things get a little complex. For example, consider the following chemical symbol of a common substance found in many households during the 1960s:

$C_{15}H_{15}N_2CON(C_2H_5)_2$

It will appear as *this* on the screen:

C^V15^VH^V15^VN^V2^VCON(C^V2^VH^V5^V)^V2^V

And that is *no* hallucination! Later in the chapter you'll learn more about doing complex equations in WordStar.

Note: Some laser printers offer a smaller character set for subscripts and superscripts. You may have to insert *font change* codes instead of the ^PT or ^PV commands (see Chapter 26 for an example). You can search and replace codes if necessary.

The Sub/Superscript Roll

In Chapter 15 you learned that WordStar can accommodate vertical pitch in increments of 48ths of an inch. The default setting is **.LH 8**, which means that there are $48/8 = 6$ lines per vertical inch. Similarly, there are $48/6 = 8$ "ticks" per line. WordStar normally prints subscripts and superscripts *three* ticks—3/48ths of an inch—below or above the line by "rolling" the printer up or down.

You can change the amount of printer roll with the sub/superscript roll dot command, **.SR**. Use an integer number representing the number of ticks you want. The default setting is **.SR 3**. To roll up an entire line whenever you insert a **^PT** command, for example, insert an **.SR 8** line in the file *before* you issue any **^PT** or **^PV** commands.

Note: On certain laser printers you can get the smaller character set for subscripts and superscripts by setting the roll to 0: **.SR 0**. Some dot-matrix printers can print subscripts and superscripts half-way between lines if you insert an **.SR 0** setting in your files. You may want to change WordStar's defaults accordingly (Chapter 27).

This seemingly innocuous and rather esoteric command can help you do some *very nifty* things, as later sections in this and other chapters illustrate. Stay tuned!

Printing Double Underlines

Now that you know about subscripts, and using your knowledge of the line overprint command, you can learn how to print double underlines. (Dear Reader: You *do* remember the line overprint command, **^P RETURN**, don't you? I introduced it in Chapter 11.)

There are at least two, if not more, ways to print double underlines. If you know the correct *printer escape code,* you can issue it directly (see "Sending Special Printer Codes"). However, as an illustration of WordStar's flexibility, you'll print double underlines in a more creative fashion.

Suppose this is the line you want to print with double underlines:

<u>SPECIAL!   FOR A LIMITED TIME ONLY!!</u>

First, insert a **.UL ON** dot command in the file. Then, press **^PS** for the regular underline. Then type the line and press **^PS** again to turn off regular underlining. Press **^OC** (or **SHIFT F2** or **ESC C**) to center the entire line. Then, press **^P RETURN** to print the next line over this one. (A - appears in the flag character display.)

Here's the tricky part. You want to make sure that the second line of underlines is correctly positioned under the text, so you want to turn the print codes *off* with **^OD** (**SHIFT F1**). Then space over to underneath the *S* of *SPECIAL*. Now, because the second line of underlines has to print slightly *below* the first line, issue the subscript command: **^PV**. Then *type* a string of underlines as far as the last exclamation point on the line. Turn off subscripting with another **^PV** command and press **RETURN** enough times for spacing.

When you turn the print code display back on with **^OD** (**SHIFT F1**), here's what the screen shows (notice the hyphen in the flag character display):

```
^SSPECIAL!  FOR A LIMITED TIME ONLY!!^S
^V_____^V
```

Another way to do double underlines is to have *two* overprinted lines, but to change the subscript roll before the second line. I'll let you try that one yourself!

Alternate and Normal Character Width

In Chapter 10 you learned how to adjust the number of characters that WordStar prints per horizontal inch—with the **.CW** command. The examples in that chapter used a different character width for entire lines. The default character width setting is **.CW 12** for 10 characters per horizontal inch.

Suppose, however, that you want to switch character widths *in the middle* of a line and then switch back to the standard width on the same line. There is a command, **^PA**, that turns on what WordStar calls the *alternate character width.* By default, the alternate character width prints 12 characters per horizontal inch, so it's a **.CW 10** setting. **Note:** If you have a laser printer, the **^PA** command switches *fonts,* and it's the only way to change fonts in the middle of a line (Chapter 26).

The **^PA** command is *not* a toggle switch. To return to *normal* printing—that is, to whatever was the character width setting *before* you issued the **^PA** command—insert a **^PN** command in the file. So it's *A* for *alternate,* and *N* for *normal.* To see how the **^PA** and **^PN** commands work, follow this example after pressing **RETURN** once or twice to space down from the last example:

Type   This is the normal character width

Press   **SPACEBAR**

for correct spacing.

Press   **^PA**

to turn on the alternate character width.
    A ^A appears on the screen.

Type   and this is the alternate width.

Press   **^PN**

to return to the normal character width.
    A ^N appears on the screen.

Press   **SPACEBAR** twice

for correct spacing at the end of the sentence.

Type   `Now you're back to the normal width.`

Always insert the ^PN command as soon as possible to return to normal printing. That is, if the text is at the end of a line, insert the ^PN command on that line instead of the next line.

You can override whatever is the default alternate character width with a **.CW** dot command. Then, whenever you insert a **^PA** command, WordStar switches to the character width setting in the **.CW** command. However, you have to tell WordStar what the normal character width is, too, if it's not the default **.CW 12** setting. For example, you want to print 15 characters per horizontal inch whenever you issue the **^PA** command, and 12 characters per inch for the normal width. After checking the table in the WordStar manual about what **.CW** settings to use, this is how you set up the commands:

```
.CW 10
^A
.CW 8
^N
```

The first line sets up the normal character width to be 12 characters per inch (120/10). The second line is a blank line with just the **^PA** command on it. Recall that you only see the ^A part of the command in your file. The third line tells WordStar what setting to use for the alternate width. Notice that there's a superfluous blank line in the file.

Because you just turned on the alternate character width, you must return to normal width on the line directly below the dot commands. As shown, issue a **^PN** command at the left margin of that line. You can't include it at the end of the .CW 8 line—that won't work.

If you insert these settings at the beginning of the file, adjust the page formatting for this first page to accommodate that extra blank line. (A later version of WordStar may solve the problem of the blank line, so check your WordStar documentation.) **Tip:** If you want to change typewheels or thimbles for the alternate section, insert stop printer commands (^PC) where appropriate.

You may have to adjust the right margin setting and realign the paragraph when you switch character widths in the middle of lines. That is, extend the right margin a bit on the lines containing ^PA/^PN commands, then return to the regular right margin where necessary. **Caution:** Even with a bit of experimenting, you probably won't be able to use these commands with justified right margins, so don't tell me I didn't warn you!

Tip: In Chapter 10 you learned that using a large **.CW** setting is one way to get *expanded* print. For instance, **.CW 24** prints five characters per inch instead of 10. See "Sending Special Printer Codes" to learn another way.

Backspace Overprint a Character

In WordStar the BACKSPACE key has nothing to do with moving the print head while a file is printing. However, there is a special print command, ^PH, that moves the print head back one position and prints something else over the previous character.

The ^PH command is *not* a toggle switch. It moves the print head back one column for every occurrence of the command. The character that follows the ^PH command in the file will print over the character that precedes the command. Please note that some printers can't backspace, so you might not get the correct results in the next example.

Probably the most common use of the ^PH command is for accent marks or special symbols. In a moment, you'll learn about the computer's *extended character set,* which provides many special symbols already. For the time being, use the standard keyboard keys to study the ^PH command. You'll type the word *vis-à-vis,* which uses a grave accent. (The grave accent key is directly to the right of the single quotation key on the IBM PC computer.) Here's how:

Type   **vis-a**

Press   **^PH**

The symbol ^H appears on the screen.

Type   `

(the grave accent).

Type   **-vis**

The screen looks like this—

vis-a^H`-vis

—but the word will print correctly. Another useful way to apply the ^PH command occurs when you want to underline just one or two characters without using ^PS:

Press   **RETURN** twice

for spacing.

Type   `It's his un`

Press   **^PH** twice

    Two ^H symbols appear on the screen.

Type   __

(two underlines, SHIFT HYPHEN).

Type   `official attitude that I don't like!`

    The screen will look like this:

`It's his un^H^H__official attitude that I don't like!`

    I promised you some nifty uses of the **.SR** command, and now that you know how to backspace the print head here's one to try out. My daisy wheel printer doesn't have an acute accent mark (´), but the comma looks so similar that I use it instead. However, as you know the comma prints far too low on the line to be an accent mark. Even the normal superscript roll doesn't print the comma high enough above the letter. So, whenever I have to print my friend's name, *Ramón,* I set the superscript roll to five with the **.SR 5** command. Then I type his name like this:

`Ramo^H^T,^Tn`

    The ^H tells WordStar to print the next character, the comma, over the *o*. The ^T command is the normal superscript to print the comma higher on the line. Because the superscript roll is 5, the comma prints over the *o* exactly as if it were an acute accent!

Legal, Foreign Language, and Scientific Characters

    All well and good, but there are only a limited number of characters you can form with the standard keyboard keys and the **^PH** command. Not to worry; there are many more characters lurking in the background on the IBM PC and compatibles. They are part of the *extended character set.*

I don't want to go into the history of computer keyboards here. All you need know is that the extended character set supplies many legal, foreign language, scientific, and graphics characters. For some bizarre reason, it even includes *two* versions of the Happy Face! The ASCII code numbers for extended characters are between 1 and 31 and between 128 and 255. The WordStar manual contains a listing of the ASCII codes.

You may recall that I introduced the ASCII coding scheme in Chapter 3 when I discussed the special ASCII printer driver. At that time I mentioned that WordStar uses the extended ASCII codes for its own purposes. So how can you now use these codes for extended characters? Simple! WordStar keeps track of when *you* issue an ASCII code and when *it* uses the same code for formatting. You never have to worry about the difference.

Note: You may have to change typestyles or thimbles to print extended characters. Include the necessary ^PC codes. Many dot-matrix and laser printers can now print the extended character set with no extra fuss, but on some laser printers you may have to change the *default internal font* (Chapter 26).

To insert any extended character between 128 and 255, press and hold down the ALT key while you type the character's code number on the *numeric keypad only*. Don't use the regular number keys on the top line of the keyboard. For instance, ALT 227 gives the lowercase Greek p (π) that represents *pi*. **Caution:** If you're using a memory-resident *keyboard enhancer* program, such as SuperKey, you might have to press both the ALT and the SHIFT keys together to get the extended characters. You'll see the extended character on the screen.

Try typing this example. For the German double s, use ALT 225, and for the umlauted *o*, ALT 148:

Neulich sagte mir Beethoven: "Ach, die Kram wird mir endlose Schwierigkeiten machen! Wissen Sie, daß sie noch mal die Miete erhöhen will?"

Unfortunately, WordStar Professional Release 4 can't access code numbers 1 through 31, but by the time you read this that defect may be a thing of the past. You would use the same ALT key method to insert these codes, which include the very useful paragraph and section symbols: ¶ (ASCII 20) and § (ASCII 21).

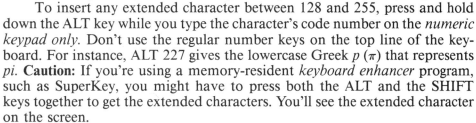

Tip: If you need certain extended characters regularly, why not assign them to macros? That way, you won't have to remember what their ASCII codes are. Just press **ESC** to see what shorthand key inserts the extended character you want.

Entering Complicated Equations

Multiline equations require a little thought and planning on your part, as well as several extra formatting steps. Here's a sample equation with many superscripts and subscripts, but please don't ask me what it does!

$$x^2 \frac{\frac{dy^2}{}}{dx^2} \quad + \quad x \frac{dy}{dx} \quad + \quad (x^2 - a^2)y = 0$$

There are some general steps to follow when you do a complicated equation in WordStar:

1. Determine the total number of *half*-lines in the equation, including the superscript or subscript lines, too. The example here has six half-lines. Then determine the *middle* line of the equation (the fourth line in this example), which will be your starting point when you type the equation.

2. Position the cursor at the location in the document where you want the equation to appear. You may wish to add blank lines for spacing from the preceding text.

3. Insert dot commands to set the line spacing to single spacing and turn paragraph alignment off. You may also want to include a different **.LH** setting to "squeeze" the equation together when it prints.

4. Use ^N to add enough blank lines to fit the entire equation. Remember that each half-line of the *printed* equation will be a separate *full* line on the screen.

5. With the **TAB** key, tab over several times on *each* blank line to insert spaces in the line. You'll then write over these spaces with the actual equation.

6. Turn insert mode *off.* Position the cursor at the correct line and type the equation. Start with the middle line and work up and down as necessary. Type from the left margin, unless you know exactly how far over you have to move the cursor to center the equation on the page. Later, you can use the **.PO** command to print the entire formula farther over on the page.

7. On the correct line below the equation area, change the format back to the original settings and turn insert mode on again.

8. Save your work!

Whew! Actually, it's a lot less complicated than it seems. Now, do the sample equation, step by step (slowly I turned . . . Niagara Falls!—oops, wrong movie). Just space down in the EFFECTS file by pressing **RETURN** once or twice. Then type these dot commands at column 1, ending each with a hard return (the file is already in single spacing):

```
.LH 6
.AW OFF
```

You can use a different line height setting if this squeezes the lines in the equation too closely together. If the equation is longer than 65 characters, change the **.RM** setting, too. Now, add enough blank lines for the equation and add spaces to each line:

Press   ^N six times

Press   **TAB** nine times

to insert spaces.

(How many spaces you need to insert depends on how wide the equation is. To be on the safe side, you could tab over to the furthest tab stop on each line.)

Press ^X (**DOWN ARROW**) and repeat the tabbing procedure to add spaces to the other five lines. When you're finished, move up to the fourth blank line, the middle line of the equation. Then:

Press   ^V or **INS**

to turn insert mode off.

Start typing the equation at the left margin:

Type   x

Press   **UP ARROW**

Type   2

Notice that you *aren't* using the superscript command here.

Press   **SPACEBAR**

Press   **SHIFT HYPHEN** eight times

for the line.

Using this section of the equation as your guide, complete the entire equation. When you're finished:

Press   ^V or **INS**

to turn insert mode on.

Press   ^QC or ^**END**

to position the cursor at the end of the file.

Reset the formatting of the file by inserting the correct dot commands. For example:

```
.AW ON
.LH 8
```

Now, save your work! If you wanted this equation to print over on the page, insert the correct **.PO** command before the equation. Reset the page offset below the equation. You could also *move* the entire equation over as a block, but make sure you turn column mode on with **^KN** first to set up the block as a rectangle. You may also have to turn column insert mode on with **^KI**.

Tip: If you do equations like this a lot (heaven help you!), set up a format file with the correct dot commands, blank lines, and filled in spaces on each line. Then just use **^KR** to read in the format file when you want to type a new equation.

Drawing Lines and Boxes

Many of the extended characters let you draw lines and boxes in your files. Of course, you'll still have to determine whether your printer can print these special characters, but for the time being assume that it can. WordStar will substitute other characters that are most similar to the special characters on some printers. For example, it may use a \ for a bottom left box corner if your printer can't print the actual corner character.

To help you with your drawing requirements, the folks at MicroPro set up the ALT function keys to access 10 popular line and box drawing characters. At the risk of being considered a party pooper or curmudgeon, or both, I don't particularly consider this setup very useful. I use the ALT function keys for other commands, because it's a lot easier to press ALT F1 than, say, SHIFT F1.

In any case, the WordStar manual under "Drawing" shows you what character each ALT function key provides. You can still access these codes by pressing the ALT key and typing the ASCII code number on the numeric keypad, if you decide as I did to change the function key assignments. Figure 17–1 shows you the box drawing possibilities, including those characters that don't have ALT function key equivalents.

The chart in the WordStar manual mentions that the four corners of a single-line box are on the "square" represented visually on many keyboards by the placement of the F3 through F6 keys:

ALT F3	⌐	¬	ALT F4
ALT F5	L	⌐	ALT F6

ALT F1 (ASCII code 179) draws vertical connecting lines, and ALT F2 (ASCII code 196) draws horizontal connecting lines between box corners.

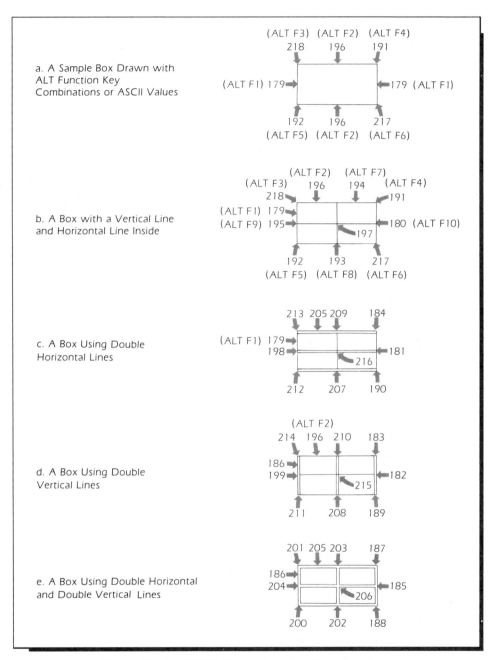

Figure 17–1   ASCII Characters for Drawing Boxes

ASCII 186 (vertical) and 205 (horizontal) are the double equivalents. Use these keys alone to create lines instead of boxes.

There are two basic ways to draw boxes: (1) start from scratch using the ASCII characters listed in the figure or, whenever possible, the ALT function key equivalents; (2) modify a box setup supplied with WordStar in the file appropriately named BOX.

If you choose the former route, you'll need to fill in a box with spaces just as you did when setting up a complex equation. So you may want to use the TAB key to insert spaces on each line *before* you enter the box characters. Follow the procedure for setting up the number of blank lines you need and then inserting spaces with the TAB key. Then, with insert mode off, type in the box characters. Use the cursor keys to move around on the lines.

If you choose the latter option, just read in the BOX file with **^KR**, then edit it to your liking. You may, for instance, want to expand the box horizontally or vertically. You may also wish to insert text within the box. Make sure insert mode is off before you do this, else you'll destroy the box boundaries.

Caution: Whichever route you take, make sure you insert an **.AW OFF** command above the box and an **.AW ON** command below the box so that you don't inadvertently realign the box with a **^B** or **^QU** command.

Using the BOX file as your guide, set up other box sizes by editing this file in a new file for each different size. Here's an example to try in the EFFECTS file.

Press   **RETURN** two or three times

for spacing.

Press   **^KR**

I'm assuming that the BOX file is on the WordStar program disk in the A drive:

Type   a:box

Press   **RETURN**

You want to enlarge the box so that it extends to the right margin, column 65. But instead of pressing **ALT F2** repeatedly to add more horizontal lines, just block out the entire horizontal line (minus the corners) and copy the block.

Press   **^D or RIGHT ARROW**

to position the cursor on the first horizontal line character at the top of the box.

Press   **^KB or SHIFT F9**

to begin the block.

Press   **^QD** or **^F10**

to position the cursor at the end of the line.

Press   **^S** or **LEFT ARROW** twice

to position the cursor on the last horizontal line character.

Press   **^KK** or **SHIFT F10**

to end the block here.

Press   **^KC** or **SHIFT F8** twice

to copy the block twice.
    Well, the box still doesn't extend to the right margin:

Press   **ALT F2** twice

    Now, fill in the next lines with spaces:

Press   **^X** or **DOWN ARROW**

Press   **^S** or **LEFT ARROW**

to position the cursor on the vertical bar character.

Press   **TAB** or **^I** seven times

to position the cursor at the last default tab stop.

Press   **SPACEBAR** nine times

to extend the box to the right margin.
    Repeat these steps for the other lines except the bottom line of the box. When you get to that line:

Press   **^KC** or **SHIFT F8** twice

to copy the horizontal lines twice again.

Press   **ALT F2** twice

to extend the box to the right margin.
    Sheesh! Now that you've enlarged your box, you can block it out and write it to another file with the **^KW** command so you don't have to go through all that work again!

Tip: To draw a single horizontal line with a minimum of keystrokes, press **^QQ**, then press and hold down the **ALT** key and type **196** from the numeric keypad. Release the **ALT** key. Press the **SPACEBAR** or any other key to stop the repeating command when you have the line length you want.

Sending Special Printer Codes

Many printers use special codes that begin with the ASCII value for the ESC key to provide such features as compressed or expanded printing. These printer codes are, understandably, called *escape codes.* For example, a code might be ESC A to turn on double underlining and ESC B to turn it off. As you know, WordStar has other uses for ESC, but you can still insert a printer escape code, or any printer code, in a file.

WordStar provides four *user-defined print controls* that are purposely left "blank" so you can set them up as you wish to get those special printing effects not available through the regular print codes. The four user-defined print controls are **^PE**, **^PQ**, **^PR**, and **^PW**.

If you only want one or two special effects, you can use the WSCHANGE program to set up the user-defined print controls (Chapter 27). However, there's another way that lets you *change* the definitions for these commands "on the fly." For each user-defined command there's a corresponding dot command beginning with **.X** that defines what the command does. That is, **.XE** defines the **^PE** print code, **.XQ** defines **^PQ**, **.XR** defines **^PR**, and **.XW** defines **^PW**. **Tip:** You can thus change, say, what **^PE** does as many times as you like in a file just by inserting a correct **.XE** dot command with the new setting.

You can also use the four dot commands to set up the same codes for different printers in different format files. You can insert the format file for one printer. Then if you use another printer, you can delete the **.X** commands and insert another format file for the new printer without having to change the print codes throughout the file.

That was the good news; now for the bad news. You must insert the escape code sequence in *hexadecimal* format. What the dickens is that? Hexadecimal is merely another numbering scheme, with a base of 16 instead of 10, that works well with computers, although not so well with humans. (If human beings had 16 fingers, then hexadecimal would seem normal and decimal would seem bizarre.)

Be that as it may, Dear Reader, take heart: you *don't* have to learn hexadecimal. After you determine what the printer escape codes are, just look up the correct hexadecimal numbers in the chart in the WordStar manual. Your printer manual may also show the hex codes. Do notice, however, that some hexadecimal numbers have A, B, C, D, E, or F as part of the number. That's normal for hexadecimal!

Note: Each **.X** command requires a string containing the printer codes in the correct order. Separate each hexadecimal code from the next with a space. The longest string for any **.X** command is 24 bytes. Each hexadecimal number counts as one byte. If you insert a *blank* **.X** code in a file, such as **.XE**, that disables the corresponding command (**^PE**).

So you first have to refer to your printer's manual for the correct escape codes. Remember there are most likely *two* codes: one for "on" and one for "off." Also, some printers may distinguish between upper- and lowercase letters, so be careful how you type the hexadecimal codes. **Tip:** Use **^PE** to turn a feature on and **^PR** to turn it off as one "set." Notice where these keys are on the keyboard. Use **^PQ** and **^PW** as the other set for another feature.

As an example, suppose your printer switches to expanded printing when it sees the code **ESC F** and returns to normal printing when it encounters the code **ESC G.** You decide to issue these codes with the **^PE** and **^PR** commands, respectively. Checking the WordStar manual, you note that the hexadecimal value for the ESC key is 1B; for the *uppercase F,* 46; and for the uppercase *G,* 47. You would insert these commands in the file to govern the **^PE** and **^PR** commands:

```
.XE 1B 46
.XR 1B 47
```

Then, whenever you issue a **^PE** command, you'll get expanded printing until you insert a **^PR** command in the file. Remember to adjust the margins to accommodate the change in printing. **Note:** WordStar automatically clears any printer escape codes when you finish printing one file and open another file. Thus, each file should include the necessary codes for special printing if these codes aren't part of the defaults.

Don't defeat the purpose of WordStar's printer drivers by trying to set up user-defined codes for printing effects that are *already* available. For example, it makes more sense to use the standard **^PB** for boldface—because WordStar already "knows" how to handle boldface print on your printer—than to set up a code to do this. It's best to enter the user-defined print codes for nonstandard printing effects, such as condensed or expanded print. Also, you may notice interferences between the various user-defined print controls and the built-in controls in the printer driver. If that's the case, try using the generic printer driver, DRAFT.

Proportional Spacing

Normally WordStar "assumes" that each character occupies the same amount of space on the printed page. This is *fixed width printing.* As you edit a file, the letters you see on the screen each take up one screen column. So an *i* requires just as much space as a *W*, and characters line up vertically. With *proportionally spaced* printing, however, each character has a different width that represents its true size, so one line of characters won't align directly under the previous line.

To print in proportional spacing, WordStar has to maintain a *table of spacing values* for all characters. Because each printer has different proportionally spaced typestyles, WordStar keeps the table of spacing values in the printer driver files. To justify proportionally spaced text during printing, WordStar uses its own special formula to determine how many extra spaces it needs on each line. The formula includes the character width setting and an average mix of lowercase and uppercase letters.

You have to tell WordStar when to use the proportionally spaced table by including a **.PS ON** dot command in the file. To turn proportional spacing off, insert a **.PS OFF** command. (Remember that you can use **1** for **ON** and **0** for **OFF**.) **Caution:** If the right margin is to be right-justified, always include an explicit **.OJ ON** command in the file. Otherwise, the file may not print correctly justified with a proportionally spaced typestyle. See also "Microjustification Again," below.

On some printers, you have to flip a *switch* to instruct the printer that you're using a proportionally spaced typestyle. The **.PS ON** command in WordStar can't set the switch for you because the latter is a hardware item. Make sure you insert the correct proportionally spaced typewheel or thimble into the printer, too. On laser printers, the settings of the **.PS** and **.CW** commands determine which *font* you are using (Chapter 26).

It's *very* important to keep in mind that WordStar doesn't show proportional spacing on the screen. Nor will it change the lines when it prints the file, unless you insert a **.PF ON** command in the file. You may find, depending on the proportionally spaced typestyle that you use, that the words appear either too "spaced out" or too "squeezed together." You can rectify this problem by choosing a different horizontal character width setting, the **.CW** command, and trying again. See the README file for suggested **.CW** settings on your printer.

Tip: When you print standard text lines in a proportionally spaced typestyle, normally you can get more characters on a line than with a fixed width typestyle. You may have to increase the line length accordingly to fill in the page.

Alas, only experimentation or luck, or both, will help you get the results you want. As a general rule, use a *higher* **.CW** setting to expand the line if it's too tight, or a *lower* **.CW** setting to tighten up the line if it's too spaced out. **Another Tip:** To close lines up as much as possible, turn hyphen help on and realign the file to hyphenate any long words *before* you print the file with a proportionally spaced typestyle. Then adjust the **.CW** setting as necessary.

One final note: I have not found an easy way to mix a nonproportionally spaced font with a proportionally spaced one on the *same line.* You could use the overprint line command, **^P RETURN**, but that gets messy and frustrating. Any suggestions from the Readers' Gallery?

Fixed Column Printing

Even though it may look correctly aligned on the screen, columnar text—any text arranged along tab stops—may not print correctly aligned with a proportionally spaced typestyle. That's because of the different spacing value for each character. However, you can make sure that columns begin at a *fixed* column position when you indicate these positions with the ^P@ command. This command prints the text starting at the exact column position at which the command appears in the file.

You can use the ^P@ command any time you want to line up columnar text. You don't necessarily have to use it with a proportionally spaced typestyle. As one of the merge printing chapters will show you, this command comes in very handy when you want to set up fill-in forms. You can also use ^P@ to your advantage when you have columnar text in the alternate character width and WordStar doesn't align the columns correctly. **Tip:** Set up a shorthand macro to issue this command so that you don't have to fiddle with the CTRL and SHIFT keys.

Here's an example of how to apply the ^P@ command.

Press   **^KD** or **F10**

to save the EFFECTS file and return to the Opening menu if you haven't done so already.

Press   **D** [open a document]

Type   `meeting.apr`

Press   **RETURN**

You may recall that this file illustrated ways to do an outline in WordStar. Suppose you're having problems getting the indented outline sections to line up correctly in the printout. To rectify the problem, insert a ^P@ command on the *first* line of each paragraph where the indent should start. For example, to change the first paragraph:

Press   **^X** or **DOWN ARROW** eleven times

Press   **^F** or **^RIGHT ARROW**

to position the cursor under the *C* of *Call.*

Press   **^P@**

(remember that @ is **SHIFT 2**).

If the print code display is on, this is how the first section of the outline now looks:

I.   ^@Call the meeting to order at 8:00 p.m. sharp (even if Joe
      and Laura aren't there yet)

As with all print codes, the ^@ seems to throw off the rest of the line, but WordStar will now print the indented sections correctly at the column location of the **^P@** command (column 6). Continue inserting **^P@** commands in each section. When you're finished:

Press   **^KD** or **F10**

to save the file and return to the Opening menu.

Print the file if you wish.

Note: You can find or find and replace this command, but if you're using a keyboard enhancer program such as SuperKey (Chapter 28) it's a little tricky. After pressing **^QF** (**^F1**) or **^QA** (**^F2**), press **^P**. Then *hold down* the CTRL key as you press **SHIFT 2** for the @ symbol. What you'll see is ^@ and one of the extended characters, most likely an umlauted *A*. Press **BACKSPACE** to delete the extra character so that only ^@ remains. Then continue the find or find and replace as normal.

(An aside: If you want to see what this command can do when it works with proportionally spaced typestyles, open the file LASER1.DOC. Even if you don't have a laser printer, I think you'll realize just how necessary **^P@** is, especially when you're attempting fancy printing!)

Making Your Printer Run More Efficiently

Here are three other dot commands that can make your printer run more efficiently in certain situations. Most of the time you won't need to use these commands, but browse through this section at least once anyway.

Bidirectional Printing

Many printers print *bidirectionally*. That is, one line prints from left to right, while the next prints from right to left, and so on. By default, WordStar sets bidirectional printing *on* for printers that have this feature. However, you may get slightly better print quality when bidirectional printing is off, although the printer will operate more slowly. Just insert a **.BP OFF** command in your file. To return to bidirectional printing, insert a **.BP ON** command.

Near Letter Quality Printing

 Some dot-matrix printers let you print in *near letter quality* mode. This, too, is WordStar's default, but it can also slow down your printer. To print a file quickly in *draft mode,* turn letter quality mode off with a **.LQ OFF** command. Turn it back on with a **.LQ ON** command. **Note:** On some laser printers, where near letter quality printing is not an issue, the **.LQ** command selects a font.

Microjustification Again

When right margin justification is on, WordStar inserts microspaces between letters and words to fill in each line. It will attempt to allocate extra microspaces on the line as evenly as possible. As you know, this is *microjustification.* By default, WordStar relies on what little "discretion" it has to microjustify according to the printer driver you're using.

Especially on dot-matrix printers, microjustification may slow things down quite a bit. You can insert a command, **.UJ OFF**, to turn microjustification off, and **.UJ ON** to turn it on again. The default setting is **.UJ DIS**, that is, WordStar uses its discretion again to determine microjustification depending on the printer driver you select. When you're printing with a proportionally spaced typestyle on dot-matrix printers, you may need to include an explicit **.UJ ON** command in your file.

With earlier versions of WordStar people used the **.UJ OFF** command to avoid problems with inadvertent alignment of text in tables and charts. Now it's a much safer bet to insert the **.AW OFF** command before text that you don't want WordStar to align or realign during editing or printing.

More Esoteric Print Commands

There are a few other print control commands worth including here for the sake of completeness, although you'll probably use them seldom, if at all.

Phantoms

On some printers there are special characters lurking behind the **DEL** ("rubout") key and the **SPACEBAR**. The computer industry calls them *phantoms.* If your printer has phantom characters, you can print them with **^PG** for the phantom rubout character and **^PF** for the phantom space character. Neither is a toggle switch.

Nondocument Fixed Tabs

When you press **TAB** (**^I**) in a document file, WordStar normally inserts enough spaces to move the cursor from its current position to the next tab stop. That's why when you delete a tab with **BACKSPACE** (**^H**) you generally have to delete several spaces. In nondocument mode, WordStar inserts a special *nondocument tab character* (ASCII code 9) or *variable tab* instead of spaces when you press **TAB** (Chapter 11).

Although you may never have to insert a nondocument tab character in a document file, you can do it with the **^PI** command. The **^PI** command doesn't honor whatever tab stops are in the file: the special tab character just moves the cursor over eight columns. You may need to insert nondocument tabs instead of the spaces when you want to convert a WordStar document file to another word processing format (Chapter 28).

Form Feeds and Line Feeds

Finally, there are commands that can insert two special printer codes into a file, but most users won't ever need these commands. When you're in doubt, *don't* use them! The **^PL** command issues a *form feed,* while the **^PJ** sends a *line feed* to the printer. If you press **^PL**, you'll see a page break display with an **^L** in the first column. If you press **^PJ**, you'll see a J in the flag character display, and WordStar positions the cursor at the beginning of the next line.

WordStar generally "knows" what form feed string to send to your printer to start a new page, that is, to feed it a blank piece of paper. However, if you have to change this string, there's a dot command, **.XL**, to do it. You set up the string exactly as you would for a user-defined print control, using hexadecimal numbering.

Note: One of the only times you may need to change the form feed string with an **.XL** dot command occurs when you have a sheet feeder that requires a special code to feed each page into your printer. Check your printer or sheet feeder documentation. This brings me to, last but not least . . .

Changing Sheet Feeder Bins

If you have one or more sheet feeder bins attached to your printer, you can instruct WordStar which bin to use with the correct *bin number.* You can access as many as four different sheet feeder bins. Insert a **.BN** command followed by the number of the sheet feeder bin. Until you tell it otherwise, WordStar uses that sheet feeder number to feed paper into the printer.

Make sure you insert the **.BN** command at the *top* of a page in your file. For example, if you print multipage letters from two feeders—one containing the first (letterhead) page and one containing other pages—at the top of page

2 of the file insert the correct bin number, such as **.BN 2**. You may also have a separate sheet feeder bin containing envelopes, as the example in the WordStar documentation notes. At the top of the "envelope page" in your file, insert the correct **.BN** command to insert an envelope from that sheet feeder into your printer.

When you use the command **.BN 0** (that's a zero), WordStar disables the sheet feeder and you can supply paper from another source. If necessary, you can include a **.BN 0** command as the last thing in a file to eject the last page from the printer without inserting a new page from the sheet feeder.

Most sheet feeder setups require you to change the page formatting defaults so that WordStar "thinks" the page is longer or shorter than it really is. That way, the program can force a form feed at the correct spot. Check your documentation and the README file for the correct page length, top margin, and bottom margin settings. You'll also have to answer "yes" to the Use form feeds (Y/N)? print option.

That was a lot to learn! But now you've taken a look at virtually all the print enhancements supported by WordStar. You can use these print features in any number of ways to create special effects for your finished product. By now, you should have realized that you are worlds away from that old typewriter!

Chapter
18

Math Maneuvers

In this chapter you will learn the following new commands:

File Commands

^KM   Total the numbers in a marked block

^QM   Turn on the calculator

Other Features

ESC =   Insert the result of the last ^KM or ^QM calculation into the file

ESC $ Insert the dollar formatted result of the last ^KM or ^QM calculation into the file

ESC#   Insert the last ^QM equation into the file

^R   Restore the last equation in the calculator

Dear Reader: I bet you thought WordStar was just a word processing program. Wrong! WordStar can also help you with your math, because it contains a built-in calculator. You can do calculations on the fly, insert the results of any number of different types of calculations into a file, or tally totals of marked blocks. You'll learn how in this chapter.

DO WARM-UP

WordStar's Calculator: The Math Menu

You can access WordStar's calculator at any time while you're editing a file, but not from the Opening menu. Open a test file to experiment with the calculator:

Press   **D** [open a document]

Type   math.ex

Press   **RETURN**

Type   y

because this is a new file.

First, do a couple math equations before learning how to insert the results into a file.

Press   ^QM

The Math menu appears. You can't edit your file until you leave the Math menu by pressing ^U (**F2**). If there's no equation showing, you can also press **RETURN** to leave the Math menu. While the menu displays, anything you type becomes part of an equation that you're asking WordStar to evaluate for an answer.

Simple Operations

At the bottom of the Math menu is a listing of *math operators.* WordStar follows the standard convention in the computer world of representing multiplication by an asterisk (*), *not* an ×, division by a slash (/), and exponentiation by a caret (^). **Tip:** Press the unshifted PRT SC key for an asterisk.

So, to multiply 5 times 2:

Type   5 * 2 or 5*2

Press   **RETURN**

The result, 10, appears next to Last result: at the top right corner of the Math menu.

Editing an Equation

WordStar "remembers" the last equation you typed, so you can call it back to the edit line and change it:

Press   **^R**

to restore the last equation.

Press   **DEL** or **^G**

to delete the *5*.

Type   **225.8**

Press   **RETURN**

The result, 451.6, appears. You can use the following keys to move the cursor or edit the equation: **DEL (^G)**, **BACKSPACE (^H)**, **^T (F6)**, **^Y (F5)**, **^F (^RIGHT ARROW)**, **^A (^LEFT ARROW)**, and the standard arrow or cursor diamond keys. Insert mode is always on in the Math menu.

Scientific Stuff

For the operators listed as strings next to the standard math operators, enclose the figure in parentheses. For example, to find the cosine of 15 degrees,

Type   **cos(15)**

Press   **RETURN**

If you don't *balance* the parentheses—that is, if you leave the ending one out—WordStar displays the following error message when you press RETURN:

Mismatched parentheses.

Press Esc to continue.

After you press **ESC**, press **^R** to restore the equation, then edit the line where necessary.

To find the square root of 10:

Type   **sqr(10)**

Press   **RETURN**

You can express numbers in *scientific notation*. For example, try this:

Type   **1e65 * 4.32**

Press   **RETURN**

Oops! Something went wrong, because WordStar prompts:

Can't do that equation. Check for correctness.

Press Esc to continue.

It turns out that *1e65* is too large a number for WordStar to handle. The largest number you can work with is 1e63 (that's 1 times 10 raised to the 63rd power).

Press   **ESC**

Type   1e55 * 3.3

Press   **RETURN**

 WordStar shows the result in scientific notation, too. *Question:* Does WordStar recognize *pi? Answer:* Unfortunately, no. I suppose you'll have to use an equivalent, like 3.14, or whatever *pi* is.

Order of Precedence

WordStar evaluates the numbers and operators in an equation from left to right, but certain operations take precedence over others. For example, division has a higher *order of precedence* than subtraction, so WordStar divides before it subtracts. This can cause problems if you're not careful. For example, suppose you want to multiply 5 times the result of 30 plus 5. Try it!

Type   5 * 30 + 5

Press   **RETURN**

Wait! The answer, 155, isn't correct. Even *you* know that 5 times 35 = 175! What happened? WordStar multiplied 5 times 30 *first*, because multiplication takes precedence over addition, and then it added 5 to the result.

How *do* you get the correct results when order of precedence could throw you off? Use parentheses to *override* the natural order of precedence. Here's how to type the equation:

Type   5 * (30 + 5)

Press   **RETURN**

You can *nest* parentheses up to 32 levels deep. WordStar always evaluates the operations in the innermost parentheses first and then continues outward. **Caution:** Make sure you balance the parentheses.

Press   ^U or **F2**

to leave the Math menu.

Inserting Math Results into a File

There are three predefined shorthand keys that insert either an equation or the result of an equation at the cursor location in a file. You can insert the result as it appears in the Math menu, or *formatted* as a dollar amount. The shorthand keys are **ESC #** to insert the last equation, **ESC =** to insert the last result, and **ESC $** to insert the last result as a dollar amount.

Type   Here is the equation and its result:

Press   **RETURN** twice

for spacing.

Press   **TAB** or **^I**

Press   **^QM**

to bring up the Math menu.

Type   (4,987 / 5) + (22.7 * 401.26)

Press   **RETURN**

to calculate the equation.

Press   ^U or **F2**

to leave the Math menu.

Press   **ESC #**

to insert the last equation at the cursor location.

Press   **TAB** or **^I** twice

Press   **ESC =**

to insert the result of the last equation at the cursor location.

Notice that you'd have to add the comma to the result if you wanted to so that it looks like this: 10,106.002.

Now try an example with a dollar amount. You may think that the amount will include the dollar sign, but you'd be wrong. The shorthand command **ESC $** merely inserts an amount that WordStar rounds to two decimal points. WordStar will, however, include a comma in the figure if it's more than 999.99. You can change the default format for this shorthand key (Chapter 27).

Press   **RETURN** twice

for spacing.

Press   **^OJ**

to turn right margin justification off.

Type the example below as you see it. Stop directly after typing the dollar sign (**SHIFT 4**):

Dear Ms. Kumquat:

    Our records indicate that there is an overdue balance on your account of $

Now, get the figure:

Press   **^QM**

Type   505.05 * 1.125

(That is, you're multiplying the balance, $505.05, times itself and 12½ percent interest: 1.125.)

Press   **RETURN**

Press   **^U** or **F2**

to leave the Math menu.

Press   **ESC $**

to insert the amount, *568.18,* at the cursor location.

Type   .

(that's a period) to finish the sentence.

Press   **^KD** or **F10**

to save the file and return to the Opening menu.

Block Math

You can total the numbers in a marked block without calling up the Math menu. Use the block math command, **^KM**. As usual, delimit the beginning and end of the block. WordStar only totals numbers; it disregards all other characters in the block. However, it makes several important assumptions about the block:

- WordStar "assumes" it's supposed to total all numbers in the block. This can cause problems if you include, say, street numbers in a block. Be careful!

- If WordStar sees a hyphen directly in front of a digit, it assumes the number is negative. It also assumes a negative number if it finds digits enclosed in parentheses, such as (509.80).

- If WordStar sees a period followed immediately by a number, it assumes that the period is a decimal point; otherwise, it assumes the period is a period.

- If WordStar sees an **e** or **E** surrounded by digits, it assumes that this is a number in scientific notation.

- The largest possible number that WordStar can work with has 30 digits.

So, the basic rule of thumb to follow when you work with block math is simple: block out only those figures that you *really* want to total!

 Caution: Despite the term *block math,* the **^KM** command only *totals* numbers in a block. Keep in mind that subtraction is just negative addition. Even if there are other math operators such as * or / in a block, the block math command won't give you a correct mathematical result. If you need the results of other operators like multiplication, use the **^QM** command.

Totaling Regular Blocks

In an earlier chapter you created an file listing monthly expenditures. Use this file to learn about block math.

Press   **D** [open a document]

Type   `expenses.jan`

Press   **RETURN**

Press   **^X or DOWN ARROW** twelve times

to position the cursor on the first expenditure line.

In another example, you'll learn how to total individual columns. Here, because the first column of labels doesn't contain numbers anyway, you can use a standard—that is, horizontal—block setup.

Press   **^KB or SHIFT F9**

to begin the block.

Press   **^QC or ^END**

to position the cursor at the end of the file.

The cursor should be directly after the word *Total*. If it isn't, use the BACKSPACE key to move the cursor back. Then:

Press   **^KK or SHIFT F10**

to end the block.

Press   **^KM**

to total the block.

WordStar tells you at the top of the screen:

`Result: 1268.99`

`Press Esc to continue.`

Press   **ESC**

to remove the total from the screen.

Now you want to insert the total at the correct location.

Press   **TAB or ^I**

to move to the cursor to the decimal tab stop.

Type $

for the dollar sign.

Press   **ESC $**

to insert the total as a dollar amount.

Notice that WordStar includes the *comma* in the figure, and that it aligns the inserted total around the decimal tab stop.

Note: The two shorthand commands, **ESC =** and **ESC $**, always insert the *last* math result, whether it be after you've used the ^QM or ^KM command. The shorthand command **ESC #** only works with the equation you entered during the last ^QM command.

Press   **^KD** or **F10**

to save the file and return to the Opening menu.

Totaling Column Blocks

In this last example you'll create a report listing first quarter sales for certain bakery products. You'll use a column format, then you'll total each column. As a bonus, you'll also total the rows horizontally.

Press   **D** [open a document]

Type   sales.1q

(for "1st quarter sales").

Press   **RETURN**

Type   y

because this is a new file.

The completed sales report is below. Take a look at it, but don't start typing yet.

```
.RM 85
.OJ OFF
.RR------------------------#------------#------------#----------------#---------R
    Product              January     February     March     Total for Product

Apple Pie              5,344.25    5,487.65    6,001.50       16,833.40
Bear Claw              2,567.80    2,010.36    1,998.66        6,576.82
Chocolate Eclair       3,558.22    (500.01)    2,775.12        5,833.33
```

Linzertorte	1,783.15	776.75	-765.43	1,794.47
Strawberry Shortcake	981.00	865.40	1,115.50	2,961.90
Truffled Delight	3,299.25	3,005.22	4,004.04	10,308.51
	———	———	———	———
TOTAL	17,533.67	11,645.37	15,129.39	44,308.43

After you type in the columns of figure for January, February, and March, you'll add each row to get a total for the fourth column. Then you'll total each column at the bottom. Notice that there are two negative amounts, one shown in parentheses and one shown with a minus sign.

Because this example is good practice for a variety of tasks (including setting up decimal tabs), I'm going to step you through it. First, type the **.RM 85** and **.OJ OFF** dot commands in the file. Then set up the tab stops:

Press   **^ON**

Type   a

Press   **RETURN**

to clear all tabs.

Press   **^OI**

Type   #31

Press   **RETURN**

to set a decimal tab at column 31.

Repeat these steps to set decimal tabs at columns 44, 57, and 74. When you're finished:

Press   **^OO** or **F8**

to insert the ruler line into the file.

Because there are decimal tab stops in the file, you can't tab across and easily type the titles over the columns. Instead, just use the SPACEBAR to move the cursor before you type each title starting at the column listed below. As you can see, I'm doing a lot of your work for you, because I want to move along and get to the math part!

Product	Starts at column 3
January	26
February	39
March	54
Total for Product	65

When you've entered the titles,

Press   **RETURN** twice

for spacing.

Now you'll enter the name and three months' figures for each product. In the process, why not block out the figures in the row so you can quickly add them for the *Total for Product* column? Here's how to do the first line:

Press   **^KB or SHIFT F9**

to begin the block.

Type   `Apple Pie`

Press   **TAB or ^I**

Type   `5,344.25`

Don't worry that the figure appears a bit too far over to the right. Recall that the beginning block marker throws off the look of the line.

Press   **TAB or ^I**

Type   `5,487.65`

Press   **TAB or ^I**

Type   `6,001.50`

Stop! Now you want to end the block and total the row.

Press   **^KK or SHIFT F10**

to end the block.

Press   **^KM**

to total the block.

Press   **ESC**

to remove the total from the screen.

Press   **TAB or ^I**

to position the cursor at the last decimal tab stop.

Press   **ESC $**

to enter the total as a dollar amount.

Press   **RETURN**

to end the line.

Repeat the same steps for the other products. Enter the figures exactly as you see them so that the totals come out correctly. When you're finished with "Truffled Delight," press **RETURN** once. Then use the **SPACEBAR** to eye-ball where the underlines should go. Enter them from the keyboard, SHIFT-HYPHEN. Space down and type the word *TOTAL* at column 6 of line 11. Then stop!

To total each column, you must first turn column mode on:

Press   **^KN**

to turn column mode on.

Then you block out each column and total the columns individually. First, position the cursor under the Apple Pie figure in the *January* column. It should be under the beginning *5* (column 26 of line 3). Then:

Press   **^KB or SHIFT F9**

to begin the block.

Press   **^X or DOWN ARROW** five times

Press   **^D or RIGHT ARROW** five times

to position the cursor after the last figure on the last column.

Press   **^KK or SHIFT F10**

to end the block.

Press   **^KM**

to total the block.

Press   **ESC**

to remove the total from the screen.

Press   **^QC or ^END**

to position the cursor at the end of the file.

Press   **TAB** or **^I**

to position the cursor at the first decimal tab stop.

Press   **ESC $**

to insert the total as a dollar amount.

Now, here's a quick way to start the next column:

Press   **^QB**

to position the cursor at the beginning of the marked block.

Press   **^F** or **^RIGHT ARROW** three times

to position the cursor at the beginning of the next column.

Repeat the procedure for each column, but for the *second* column make sure you extend the block one column position more to the right so that the *ending* parenthesis on the third line is part of the column block. Continue blocking and totaling each column and inserting the total in the correct spot. When you're finished:

Press   **^KN**

to turn column mode off.

Press   **^KS** or **F9**

to save the file and resume where you left off.

Tip: As a way of checking your work, after you total the fourth and last column, block out the *row* of totals for the first three columns only. Make sure column mode is off. Then press **^KM** to get the total for the row. It should be the same as the total for the fourth column.

Recalculating

If you change any figures, WordStar won't automatically recalculate the columns. So sorry; you'll have to repeat all the steps: turn column mode on, block out the column, press **^KM** to total the column, press **ESC** to remove the total, delete the previous total and insert the new total. Consider using a shorthand macro to do these steps.

Press   **^KD** or **F10**

to save the file and return to the Opening menu.

Dear Reader: There you have a quick perusal of WordStar's math features. Go ahead, practice them some more if you wish. When you're ready to continue, you'll explore an entirely different world: merge printing. Later, in Chapter 24 to be exact, you'll learn how to combine merge and math using one of the same examples from this chapter.

Chapter 19

A Form Letter Course, Part 1

In this chapter you will learn the following new commands:

Opening Menu Command
- **M**   Merge print a file

File Commands
- **.DF**   Define the data file
- **.RV**   Read the name and order of variables in the data file

Other Points
- **,**   Field delimiter in the data file
- **&**   Variable field identifier
- **&@&**   Insert today's date during merge printing
- **/O**   Omit a variable entry without leaving a blank line

The next few chapters devote themselves to WordStar's extensive *merge printing* capabilities. Although the most common duty of merge printing is to generate form letter mailings, there are countless other practical applications that can save you a lot of time and effort. I can only touch on the "tip of the merge printing iceberg," as it were. With the examples as starting points, you'll no doubt develop your own uses for this hard-working friend. Prepare to be amazed at what merge printing can do for you!

But first some words of advice: merge printing is in some respects different from normal word processing, and it may take *a bit of getting used to.* Don't despair if things don't work out right the first time. Keep trying! Look at it this way: when you have to drive on the freeway, you *merge with caution.*

Follow the same wisdom when you merge print, and you'll have some impressive results to show for it. I promise!

I've designed the lessons to show you how to eliminate many minor technicalities that can throw you off, so study the examples thoroughly. And, please, go through the merge printing chapters *in order!* Each one builds upon the previous ones.

> **DO WARM-UP**

Merge Printing in a Nutshell

As its name implies, *merge printing* refers to the process of combining information from one or more separate files during printing. The printed result is a composite of these different files—for example, a set of form letters. That is, the text of the letter is the same for each recipient, but the names and addresses are different. Instead of typing the letter many times, you type it *once* and instruct WordStar where to "plug in" the information for each different recipient. You maintain the list of recipients in a separate file.

But merge printing goes far beyond form letters. You can merge print a file with information that you've typed in at the keyboard to create what I call *fill-in documents,* such as a stock reply letter or generic envelope. You can use merge printing to automate document assembly procedures, create fancy reports with totals that WordStar calculates automatically, and do any number of other nifty feats.

One of the main advantages of merge printing—besides saving you the drudgery of having to type the same file many times—is that you don't change the original files. You can use them again and again. For example, in the next chapter you'll see how to print envelopes for a form letter mailing with the same names and addresses that you typed for the letter itself.

If a computer can't read, how can it know where to put text from one file or from the keyboard into another? It can only follow your *explicit instructions,* which you insert in the file as a series of dot commands and other special operators. The merge printing commands and operators are the signals that WordStar follows to create the merged printout.

Because these commands must be exactly as WordStar expects them, the secret to successful merge printing operations is to be patient, precise, and very, very careful. Don't despair: there are easy ways to *test* your merge printing task before you actually print, so you won't waste paper!

There is always at least one file that controls the merge. It could be the letter file for form letter mailings, or a command ("master") file similar to the ones you saw in Chapter 16. The controlling file generally contains the special dot commands and operators that govern the merging of other files during printing.

Also in Chapter 16 you met the print time reformatter, in the guise of the **.PF ON** command. When you use this command with normal printing, you have to turn it on explicitly. During merge printing, the print time reformatter is in *discretionary* mode by default. That's because the lines may change depending on the variable information, so WordStar has to realign the lines where necessary. You'll see all this in action shortly.

Although many former merge printing commands from earlier versions of WordStar are now available during regular printing, the new dot commands and operators you'll meet in the next few chapters generally work *only* with merge printing. As time goes by and newer versions of WordStar appear, however, the distinction between regular printing and merge printing is becoming less and less obvious.

As I've mentioned a couple of times, there is no longer a separate merge printing program called MailMerge. All merge printing operations are part of WordStar now. The only difference you'll have to keep in mind is to use the **M** [merge print a file] command from the Opening menu instead of the **P** [print a file] command, or to answer **y** when you press **^KP** to merge print a file while you're editing another.

Note: WordStar shows a colon (:) in the flag character display for all dot commands that govern formatting when you print or merge print a file. WordStar no longer identifies merge printing dot commands with an M in the flag character display.

Even with the new commands and operators, though, a merge printing application is *not* an editing application. You first work with WordStar as normal to create and edit the files that you will eventually merge print. For instance, up to a certain point a form letter file is just like any other letter file: you have to establish its formatting and type in the text. I think all this will become clear to you when you dive into the world of merge printing. Ready? Not quite! Now learn a little about how WordStar handles form letters.

Form Letters: An Overview

If you've ever had to type the *same* form letter 100 times, you know what boring and back-breaking work it can be. Never again! By setting up the form letter application as a merge printing task, you need type the letter only once. WordStar then plugs in a different name and address, stored in a separate file, for each letter during merge printing.

Constant and Variable Information

A form letter contains two kinds of information: (1) information that remains *constant* in each letter—that is, the body of the letter itself; and (2) information that changes for each recipient—what WordStar calls *variables.* For example, if you're preparing a form letter mailing to 100 recipients, there are 100 sets of different names and addresses.

Shell Files and Data Files

The letter file that contains the constant text and the commands to govern merge printing is the *shell* file. Think of the shell as a framework into which WordStar will insert the variable names and addresses. Because it's a letter like any other, the shell file contains the necessary formatting commands, too. But it also contains dot commands and other operators to control the merge printing.

You set up the variables in a separate file called a *data file.* As you'll see, the data file is a nondocument with no formatting. It just contains the "raw data" that you'll use for the form letter, envelopes, mailing labels, even a mailing list! The data file is actually a simple *data base.* There can be many different variables, but you don't have to use all the variables all the time. You can select which variables to print in a particular form letter.

Tip: You can use many data base programs, such as dBASE III PLUS, to keep track of your data. When you set up a merge printing application, have these programs generate "delimited ASCII" files that WordStar can read as data files. See Chapter 28.

Fields and Records

In the data file you break down the variable information into *fields,* each field generally containing one piece of information. For example, you may have different variable fields for a recipient's name, street address, city, state, and zip code. You give each field an easy-to-remember *name,* such as *street* for the street address field. The field name should identify the field's contents.

WordStar finds the field's contents by its name and its position in the data file. It then *substitutes* the contents of the field for the variable name in the shell file. Voilà: a form letter!

The *combined* fields for each person compose a *record.* Every record must contain the *same* number of fields, and the type of information in each field must be in the same *order* in each record. That is, if the first field contains a person's street address, then all first fields in all records must contain street addresses or else be blank. The field names don't change, but their contents do, for each record.

The Setup

There are specific rules governing how you set up the shell file and data file so that WordStar "knows" where the information is and how to use it. In brief, you must supply WordStar with the following information:

- The name of the data file and its location
- The names of the variable fields in the data file
- The order in which you've typed the variable fields in the data file
- Where the information in each variable field for each record is to print on the form letter
- Where one variable field ends and another begins in the data file so that WordStar doesn't mix up the variable information
- Where one record ends and another begins in the data file so that WordStar doesn't mix up the different records

What you must *not* include are superfluous characters, such as spaces, at the end of the data file. They throw WordStar off to no end! When it's merge printing, WordStar is very finicky about superfluous characters—much more finicky than normal.

The Result

When you merge print the shell file, dot commands and other operators instruct WordStar to put the information from the data file into the correct location in the letter for each record. It's important to understand that WordStar *can't read* the information in the fields. It only looks for the *field names* and the *order* they appear in the data file. Then it makes a match according to where the field names appear in the shell file. Figure 19-1 illustrates the process.

After it finishes one letter, WordStar goes on to merge print the same shell letter with the variable information for the next record in the data file, and continues to do so until there are no more records in the data file. With a minimum of effort, you can then reuse both the shell letter for another form mailing with a different set of names and addresses, or the original names and addresses with any number of other shell files.

Dear Reader: *now* you're ready to begin!

Creating the Shell File

You first create the shell letter as you would any other letter, with the addition of special merge printing dot commands and operators. Don't worry: I'll step you through the entire process. That's what I'm here for!

Press   **D** [open a document]

Type   burbank.1

(that's the number one).

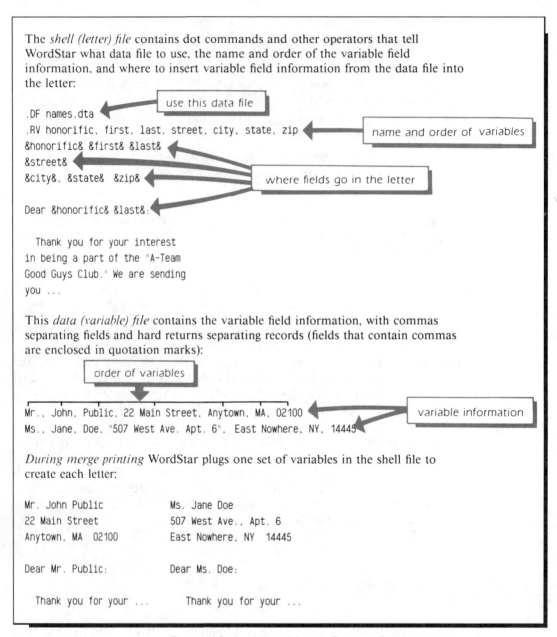

The *shell (letter) file* contains dot commands and other operators that tell WordStar what data file to use, the name and order of the variable field information, and where to insert variable field information from the data file into the letter:

.DF names.dta ◄─── use this data file

.RV honorific, first, last, street, city, state, zip ◄─── name and order of variables

&honorific& &first& &last&

&street&

&city&, &state& &zip& ◄─── where fields go in the letter

Dear &honorific& &last&:

Thank you for your interest
in being a part of the "A-Team
Good Guys Club." We are sending
you ...

This *data (variable) file* contains the variable field information, with commas separating fields and hard returns separating records (fields that contain commas are enclosed in quotation marks):

order of variables

Mr., John, Public, 22 Main Street, Anytown, MA, 02100 ◄─── variable information
Ms., Jane, Doe, "507 West Ave. Apt. 6", East Nowhere, NY, 14445

During merge printing WordStar plugs one set of variables in the shell file to create each letter:

```
Mr. John Public          Ms. Jane Doe
22 Main Street           507 West Ave., Apt. 6
Anytown, MA  02100       East Nowhere, NY  14445


Dear Mr. Public:         Dear Ms. Doe:

  Thank you for your ...     Thank you for your ...
```

Figure 19–1   How Merge Creates Form Letters

Press   **RETURN**

Type   **y**

because this is a new file.

This form letter mailing is a promotional offer. Take a look at the letter, but don't type it yet. There are some weird things in it, aren't there?

```
.. promotional letter no. 1
.MT 13
.MB 10
.OP
.PO 14 [or whatever setting your printer requires, if any]
.RM 60
.LS 1
.OJ OFF
.RR--!------------------------!--------------------------R
.DF burbank.dta
.RV title, first, last, street, city, state, zip, sponsor
                          66 Golden Mall
                          Burbank, CA  91300
                          &@&
```

```
&title& &first& &last&
&street&
&city&, &state&  &zip&

Dear &first&:

     You have been chosen as one of the lucky recipients of
a trip to Beautiful Downtown Burbank, as part of this
station's anniversary celebration, commemorating 25 glorious
years of service to the San Fernando Valley!

     Each prize winner receives an all expenses paid day for
two in Burbank.  You are whisked to Burbank in comfort and
luxury from anywhere in Southern California by Speedy-O
Limousine Service.  Speedy-O will call for you and your
companion in &city& and return you home after your exciting
day in Burbank.

     We are sure, &first&, that you will be thrilled to take
part in sharing our anniversary with us, and we look forward
to hearing from you and making final plans for your day in
Burbank.  Please call us at your earliest convenience.

     Congratulations again!
```

```
                    Yours truly,



                    Seymour F. Fayke
                    President, XKBBK
     .PA
```

The first nine dot commands are straightforward. You've seen similar formatting setups in previous examples. The shell letter is like any other letter: it must still have formatting! On the tenth dot command line things start to look a little strange, and become even stranger in the body of the letter. Here's what all the strangeness means.

Defining the Data File

You must tell WordStar the name of the separate data file that contains the variable names and addresses. Supply the name on the merge printing dot command line beginning with **.DF** for "data file." Here, the names and addresses are—or will be—in a file called BURBANK.DTA.

Tip: You can name data files as any others, but supplying the extension .DTA is a good way to identify them as data files. Or use any file-naming convention that makes sense to you!

If the data file is on another disk or in another directory, supply the correct drive designator or path. For example,

```
.DF B:BURBANK.DTA
```

or

```
.DF \WS4\LETTERS\BURBANK.DTA
```

If you want WordStar to wait while you *change* disks during merge printing, insert a CHANGE or C directive after the file name, as you saw in Chapter 16. For instance,

```
.DF BURBANK.DTA C
```

For the sake of your sanity, though, try to keep the shell letter file and the data file on the same disk or in the same directory until you get to be a WordStar pro!

Setting the Names and Order of Variables

The next merge printing dot command, **.RV**, instructs WordStar about how to "read the variables." That is, it tells WordStar two things: (1) the *order* in which the variables appear in the data file, and (2) the *field name* you've assigned to each variable. You list each field name separated by commas from the next. Don't end the line with a comma, though.

Caution: The **.DF** command must appear *before* the **.RV** command in the file, and the **.RV** command must appear *before* any of the field names in the letter itself. So, get into the habit of inserting the **.DF** and **.RV** commands together at the top of the file.

A field name can be up to 39 characters long, but it makes most sense to use short names, thus saving keystrokes. Do, however, use names that remind you what the field's contents are. I bet you already understand what each field name in this letter represents!

You can insert as many **.RV** lines as you need, provided that the variable field names are in the correct order. So you could have typed the **.RV** lines in the BURBANK.1 letter like this:

```
.RV title, first, last
.RV street, city, state
.RV zip, sponsor
```

I've used lowercase letters in the field names for convenience so you don't have to press the SHIFT key. I suggest that you *be consistent* in how to set up variable names. By the way, WordStar ignores the spaces between the comma and the next name. **Note:** The variable name must be one "word" and can't contain a space, although you can use underlines or hyphens. For example, *mr-ms* or *last_name* are acceptable variable names, but *mr ms* is not.

Entering the Variables in the Letter

Every time you want WordStar to *substitute* the contents of the variable field from the data file into the shell letter, you insert the variable name in the shell file. However, you must enclose the variable name in ampersand signs (**&**). The ampersands tell WordStar that this is a variable, not constant text.

Think about it: normally an ampersand isn't directly connected to another word. That's the signal to WordStar to consider the text as a variable. You can still use ampersands in normal text, for instance, *Smudge & Smudge*. **Note:** In the **.RV** line you don't enclose the variable names in ampersands.

WordStar is no longer picayune about leading spaces or the case in variable names. For example, the following variables are all the same: **& first&** (notice the space), **&FIRST&**, **&FirST&**, and **&first&**. *However . . .*

Tip: Take extra care when you type the variable names because incorrect typing is the major source of merge printing headaches. WordStar can't read, so it won't be able to make a match if it sees a variable name that it can't identify. For example, if you typed &firstt& instead of &first&, WordStar would not be able to locate the correct variable name on the **.RV** line. Your form letter would be a mess! See "Testing the Merge Printing," below.

Take Care with Spacing and Punctuation

It also bears noting that you should include all necessary spacing and punctuation as part of the constant portion of the file. Take a look at the salutation line. Mr. Fayke is being quite informal in addressing the recipient by his or her first name! Be that as it may, notice that there is a space between the title and the first name, and that there is a colon at the end of the salutation. These are part of the letter itself, *not* of the variable information.

In the interior address section, the city line is worth investigating. There are a comma and space between the city and the state, and two spaces between the state and the zip code. This would be wrong: &city, &&state &&zip& . The spaces or punctuation marks shouldn't be within the ampersand signs!

Reusing Variables

Notice that in the second and third paragraphs and in the salutation you've *reused* certain variable names. That's completely possible. Because WordStar already "knows" the order of the names from the **.RV** line, it can always make the correct substitutions. You can use variable names as many times as you want in the shell letter, provided the names match those in the **.RV** line.

A "Missing" Variable!

Dear Reader: Take a close look at the letter. Nowhere does the last variable on the **.RV** line, by name *sponsor,* appear in the letter! I stuck it in to illustrate two important points:

1. You must include the names of *all* variables in the data file and their correct order.

2. However, you don't have to use all variables in the shell letter file.

You'll work with this variable only when you learn about conditional printing in Chapter 22. You can thus have *many* types of variable information in a data file, but you can pick and choose which information to include in a form letter mailing or other merge printing task. Just keep in mind that you have to list all variable names so that WordStar maintains the correct order of the variables during merge printing.

Inserting the Current Date During a Merge

There's a special variable directly below the station's address: **&@&**. This is a predefined variable that inserts the current date *when you merge print the letter.* Thus, you can merge print the same letter again at any time without having to worry about changing the date in the letter file. (You *did* enter the correct date when you started your computer today, didn't you?)

Note: Unlike the predefined shorthand key, **ESC @**, this predefined variable doesn't show the date on the screen. However, it does use the same date format as **ESC @**. See Chapter 20 to learn about the other predefined merge printing variables.

The Unconditional Page Break Command

Note: At the end of the letter is an unconditional page break command, **.PA**. In form letter mailings, you *must* include this command to tell WordStar to start the next letter at the top of a new page. If you didn't add this command, WordStar would begin printing the next letter on the same page.

Because WordStar starts a new page for each new record in the data file, you can print only certain records by choosing the correct starting and ending page. Another section shows you how.

Get to Work!

Okay, I've done enough explaining for a few minutes. It's time for you to type the letter exactly as you see it. Notice that I've included a ruler line with tab stops at columns 6 and 31 only so you don't have to press the TAB key too often. When you're finished:

Press   **^KS or F9**

to save the file and resume where you left off.

A Very Important Tip

Because this letter is going out to several—perhaps hundreds—of people, make sure it's *completely correct* before you merge print it. Think of your frustration if you printed 100 letters, each with the same typo! At this point, position the cursor at the beginning of the file and press **^QL (SHIFT F3)** to do a spelling check of the entire letter. Or just eye-ball it to make sure that there are no mistakes. When you're finished:

Press   ^KD or F10

to save the file and return to the Opening menu.

See "Testing the Merge Printing" for more ways to check the accuracy of your letter before you print the form mailing.

Creating the Data File

A long time ago I mentioned that perhaps the only uses you may have for nondocuments, if you're not a programmer, are to edit your personal dictionary file now and again and to work with merge printing. Here's where you learn about using nondocuments with merge printing. The advantage to setting up data files as nondocuments is that there is no extraneous formatting (margins, word wrap, and so on) to get in the way of the data itself.

Press   N [open a nondocument]

Type   burbank.dta

Press   RETURN

Type   y

because this is a new file.

Caution: If you open a data file as a document by mistake, press ^KQ to abandon the new file *now* and start over!

Again, I'm going to ask you to take a look at the records in the data file before you type them, so I can explain everything first.

```
Dr., Jorge, Rivera, 1155 Soto Street, Los Angeles, CA, 90033, yes
Mr., J. Jacob, Grump, P.O. Box 88, Victorville, CA, 92433, yes
Ms., Fernanda, Hopkins, , Mountain Hole, CA, 93777, no
Mr., Jamie, Sutter, "909 Grant Avenue, Suite 10", San Francisco, CA, 94111, yes
Rev., Manny, Kant, '510 "R" Street, N.W.', La Mirada, CA, 91444, no
```

Remember the Order and Number of the Variables!

Before you type entries into a data file, make sure you remember the order in which you listed the variable field names in the shell file and what the total number of variables is. You could have printed the BURBANK.1 file to produce a hard copy version to which you could then refer. To refresh your memory, here is the order as listed in the **.RV** line:

```
.RV title, first, last, street, city, state, zip, sponsor
```

Always keep in mind that the information must be in the same order for each record, and that there must be the same number of fields for each record. A field can be blank, as you'll see in a moment. In this example, there are eight variable fields.

Separating the Field Information

WordStar expects to see a *comma* or a *hard return* as the field separator. That's how it determines where the information for one field ends and the information for the next field begins. When you use the comma as field separator, insert a hard return at the end of each record. Take a look at the first record to see what I mean. In the next chapter, I'll show you how to use another character, such as a hard return, a backslash (\), or a vertical bar (¦), as the field separator.

Note: The last field in each record does not end with a comma. That's the *sponsor* field, by the way. In Chapter 22, you'll see why I'm using yes and no in this field.

Separating Records

I'll first follow the traditional WordStar approach of using the comma as the field separator and the hard return to tell WordStar where one record ends and another begins. So, each record is on a separate line in the data file. Don't worry that the information scrolls right on the screen, as long as all fields for a particular record are on the same line that ends with a hard return.

Tip: Count the number of comma field separators for each record. It should always be one number fewer than the number of fields. Getting into the habit of relying on the comma as field separator, instead of the hard return, will benefit you if you use other data base programs with WordStar.

How WordStar Handles Spaces

You can enter spaces after a comma and before the information in the next field to make each entry stand out visually from the next. You can also type spaces at the ends of fields. WordStar *disregards* these leading and trailing spaces at the beginnings and ends of the field, but honors any spaces within the field. Notice, for instance, in the second line that Mr. Grump's first name will print correctly as *J. Jacob.*

Commas as Part of the Field Information

Because WordStar uses the comma as the field separator, it "assumes" each time it sees a comma that another field is to begin. In the fourth record, there's a comma that's part of the street address information. To *override* the use of this comma as a field separator and tell WordStar instead that it's part of the actual information in the field, enclose the *entire* field in double quotation marks.

Caution: Make sure you still have a comma at the end of the field, and that it's not within the quotation marks. For example, this is wrong:

```
Mr., Jamie, Sutter, "909 Grant Avenue, Suite 10," San Francisco, CA, 94111, yes
```

You've misplaced the comma separating the street address field from the city field *within* the quotation marks. WordStar would mess up the order of the fields because there are now fewer fields than expected in the record. Be careful!

Note: You could enclose *all* fields in quotation marks! When you transfer information from some data base programs, such as dBASE III PLUS, to a WordStar merge printing format, this is exactly what happens. For example, the following data file format is acceptable (sorry about the teeny tiny type):

```
"Mr.", "Jamie", "Sutter", "909 Grant Avenue, Suite 10", "San Francisco", "CA", "94111", "yes"
```

Don't worry! As long as there are commas correctly separating the fields, and as long as the commas are outside the quotation marks, the merge will work. See Chapter 28 for more about transferring information from other programs to WordStar.

Quotation Marks as Part of the Field Information

The last record illustrates how to have quotation marks print as part of the actual field contents when you need quotation marks to enclose a field that also contains a comma. Enclose the entire field in single quotes. If you need single quotes within the field's contents and the field also contains a comma, enclose the entire field in double quotes.

Leading Spaces as Part of the Field Information

If on the odd chance you need to include a space at the beginning of a field as part of the field's contents, enclose the entire field in quotation marks. For example: " Sunnyvale" will print with the leading space.

Tip: Any time you want WordStar to treat a field's contents literally, enclose the entire field in quotation marks.

Empty Fields

Take a close look at the third record. There is no street address, so the field is empty. *However, you must still separate an empty field from the next with a comma.* Otherwise, WordStar wouldn't be able to substitute the correct field information in each record with the field name in the letter file. Think of each comma as a "place marker" for the location of the end of one field and the beginning of the other. What's *in* the field is another matter altogether.

This empty field will cause a slight problem when you print the form letters: there will be an ugly blank line in the interior address where the street should be. In a moment, I'll show you how to correct this problem.

Back to Work!

Type the five records as you see them. Make sure you position commas correctly as field separators, and that each record (line) ends with a hard return.

Caution: The *last* record in a data file must end with a hard return, too. Otherwise, WordStar might not print a letter for this record. In addition, don't type any superfluous *spaces or blank lines* at the end of the file. WordStar will merge print a "blank" letter! Make sure that the cursor is at the *beginning* of the line directly below the last record.

When you're finished, check your typing before you

Press   **^KD or F10**

to save the file and return to the Opening menu.

Editing the Data File

You can, of course, open the nondocument data file and edit its contents at any time. For instance, suppose one of the addresses is wrong. Just make your changes, but remember to retain the commas as field separators.

Dealing with Empty Fields

Before testing the form letter setup, learn how to instruct WordStar *not* to insert a blank line when a field is empty. First, open the shell file again:

Press   **D** [open a document]

Type   burbank.1

Press   **RETURN**

Position the cursor on the line with the &street& field name in the interior address (it's line 8). Move the cursor to the second & and type this: /o. You could also have typed /O with an uppercase *O*, but don't use a zero and don't add any superfluous spaces! The line should now look exactly like this:

&street/o&

The **/O** is a special operator that tells WordStar: "if the field is empty, *omit* it and don't put in a blank line here." In the next chapter I'll show you how to avoid blank spaces when there are several fields on a line. **Note:** You include the **/O** operator in the field identifier in the text part of the letter, *not* on the **.RV** line. It must always be at the end of the field name but before the closing **&**.

Press   **^KD** or **F10**

to save the file and return to the Opening menu.

Merge Printing the Form Letter

At the end of the chapter are some tips for testing the form letter setup. Assuming, however, that everything is correct, here's how to merge print the letters. First, prepare your printer and paper. You always print the "controlling" file, that is, the one containing the merge printing commands.

Press   **M** [merge print a file]

WordStar responds:

Specify the name of the document to be merge printed. If you respond with the Esc key to any question after naming the document, further questions will not be asked and defaults will be used for them. If you don't enter anything after a question, a default will be used.

Document to merge print?

Type   burbank.1

At this point, if you can bypass the print options, press **ESC**. Otherwise, press **RETURN** and answer the print options as usual.

From within a file, press **^KP**, then type **y** for "yes" in response to WordStar's message:

```
You can print your file using either standard printing or merge printing.

Merge print (Y/N)?
```

Then supply the file name and continue as usual.

Viewing or Canceling the Merge Printing Job

Even though you press **M** to merge print a file, while WordStar is merge printing you can press either **M** or **P** from the Opening menu, or **^KP** from within a file, to bring up the Printing menu. For example, you may want to see how many letters WordStar has printed up to a certain point. WordStar displays the current page it's printing at the top of the Printing menu. Or you may want to press **^U (F2)** to cancel the merge printing job altogether.

If you've included a **CHANGE** instruction in the shell letter file, after you begin a merge printing WordStar will flash the Print Wait message. Press **M** or **P** from the Opening menu, or **^KP** from within a file, to see the Printing menu and the message to change disks. Press **C** to continue after you've made the change.

Merge Printing Selected Records

Suppose you made a mistake in one record and you want to reprint a letter for that record. You don't have to reprint letters for all records in the data file. Here's where you use the starting and ending page print options.

Take the example of a one-page letter first, because that's the easiest to understand. Because each record of the data file starts a new letter "page," all you need do is find the *line number* of that record. The line number corresponds to the page number of the merged printout. For instance, in the BURBANK.DTA file the record for Ms. Fernanda Hopkins in on line 3, so you would supply **3** as the starting and ending pages to reprint a letter for this record only.

Tip: To position the cursor on a specific line number in a large non-document file, press **^QI**, then type the line number and press **RETURN**.

You can also print one-page letters for a range of "pages" in the data file by supplying the correct starting and ending page (line) numbers or the individual page numbers. See Chapter 3 if you've forgotten how to do this.

For *multiple page* letters, multiply the starting and ending "pages" in the data file by the number of actual pages in the letter, then subtract 1 from the resulting starting page figure. That's because, for a two-page letter, for example, the letter for the *first* record in the data file starts on page 1 and continues to page 2. The second letter would then start on page 3, and so on. So, to print "pages" 3 and 4 in the data file on a two-page merge letter, supply the starting page of 5 ($3 \times 2 = 6 - 1$) and the ending page of 8.

Another way to print selected records is to use *conditional merge printing* commands, but you haven't learned about them yet! Just be patient: they're the topic of Chapter 22.

Print Time Reformatting During a Merge

Whenever you merge print a file, the print time reformatter feature is in discretionary mode by default. You don't have to insert an explicit **.PF** command (although you can if you want to). Wherever WordStar encounters variable information, it reformats the file when necessary. In the example form letter, WordStar would reformat the second and third paragraphs depending on the length of the city and first name fields for each record.

Because the print time reformatter is always lurking in the background, be careful when you're using format settings that aren't the default format. For example, if you've set the default line spacing to double, make sure you insert an **.LS 1** command in your form letter file to print it in single spacing. That way, you'll always get the correct format. Include the correct **.LM** and **.RM** commands, too. If you're printing with a proportionally spaced typestyle, include the correct **.OJ** command—either **.OJ ON** or **.OJ OFF**—to achieve proper justification.

Testing the Merge Printing

Because you have to be so precise in how you set up a merge printing application, and because you're still a novice, it's a good idea to test the merge printing *before* you actually do it. That way, you don't waste your expensive stationery! Remember to run the letter file through a spelling check first, too.

Print Hard Copies of the Letter and Data Files

Often it's easier to correct mistakes from a hard copy instead of from the screen. You can use the regular print command, **P** from the Opening menu or **^KP** from within a file, to print both the shell letter and data files. Answer n for "no" when WordStar asks if this is a merge printing job.

However, do answer "yes" to the question, Nondocument (Y/N)? so that WordStar prints the dot commands as text instead of as commands in the letter file. That way, you can check the accuracy of the commands. Use the same approach with the data file to print this file with a document-style page layout.

Merge Print to Disk

If everything seems to be okay, you can then merge print the shell letter to a disk file using the preview printer driver (PRVIEW). That way, you'll see every letter with—if you're lucky—all the field information in the correct spots.

Note: Remember that if you don't supply a file name after selecting the PRVIEW printer driver, WordStar "prints" to a disk file called PRVIEW.WS. Use **D** [open a document] to view this file.

Scroll through the file and check each letter. If something is wrong, more than likely there's a misplaced comma, or no comma where WordStar expects one, in the data file and that problem has thrown off the order of the fields. Make sure you also see a page break between each letter. If you don't that means you forgot to include the **.PA** command at the end of the shell letter file.

But maybe your data file is a large one and you don't have enough disk space to print the entire form mailing to a disk file. Do a *selective* printing: perhaps the first 20 pages or so. If nothing is amiss, chances are the rest of the data file is okay, too. Or, better yet, break the data file down into smaller files and merge print the letter with each data file. Remember to change the file name on the **.DF** line.

Dear Reader, you now have a form letter ready to go, but it still needs envelopes or mailing labels. You're probably tired of merge printing by now—what with all the do's and don'ts—so why not take a break? Get a good night's sleep before continuing. When you do, you'll be happy to know that the worst is over and you can start *really* learning about the nitty-gritty of merge printing!

Chapter

20

A Form Letter Course, Part 2

In this chapter you will learn the following new features:

Other Features

        XTRACT printer driver

  &!&   Insert the current time during merge printing

  &#&   Insert the current page number during merge printing

  &_&   Insert the current line number during merge printing

Well, you've successfully printed your form letters, but they aren't much good if you don't send them out! This chapter shows you how to create envelopes or mailing labels for your letters, how to set up a mailing list, and other ways to fine tune your merge printing tasks. You'll also learn about the special XTRACT printer driver.

> **DO WARM-UP**

Envelopes for the Form Letters

A merge printing shell file need not be a letter. It can be any type of document that uses information from a separate data file. Because you already have the names and addresses ready to go, all you need do now is create a new shell file for envelopes. The trick here is that you use *only* the variables that you need from the data file and skip the rest.

Press   **D** [open a document]

Type   burbank.1e

Press   **RETURN**

Type   y

because this is a new file.

The envelope setup below is for standard business envelopes. Apparently Mr. Fayke has run out of preprinted stationery, so you're including his return address. Type the text as you see it. Make sure you type the dot commands correctly. Press **RETURN** ten or twelve times where I instruct you to space the recipient's address from the return address. Notice the **.PO** commands—I'll explain them in a moment.

```
.. envelopes for promotional letter no. 1
.PL 25
.MT 1
.PO 7
.PF OFF
.LS 1
.OP
.DF burbank.dta
.RV title, first, last, street, city, state, zip, sponsor
XKBBK
66 Golden Mall
Burbank, CA  91300
```

Ten or twelve blank lines here

```
.PO 42
&title& &first& &last&
&street/o&
&city&, &state&  &zip&
.PA
```

When you're finished:

Press ^KS or F9

to save the file and resume where you left off.

As in the shell letter file, even though you aren't using all the variable fields in the BURBANK.DTA file, you *must* include their names and correct order on the .RV line. Notice also the /O in the &street/o& variable to suppress the printing of a blank line if the field is empty. **Tip:** You could have copied the letter file and then made the necessary changes for the envelope file.

I've used a little trick to position the recipient's name and address on the envelope. Instead of pressing the TAB key several times, I've changed the *page offset* setting. You'll have to experiment with the correct .PO setting for printing the interior address on your printer. Here, it's .PO 7, but your setting depends on where you position the envelopes in your printer. The return address should print almost at the left edge of the envelope. Then, increase the .PO setting by *35 or 40* columns to print the names and addresses in the middle of the envelope.

You'll also have to test the correct top margin setting. I've used a page length of 25, which is about right for business envelopes. **Note:** If you own a laser printer, you may have to change the *paper orientation* to print envelopes (Chapter 26).

Question: Why is the print time reformatter off? *Answer:* If one of the name and address lines is long, the print time reformatter won't wrap the lines to the default right margin at column 65. It just ignores any print time reformatting and prints each line as is.

Once again, there's a .PA command at the end of the file to force a page break so that each envelope prints correctly at the top of the next "page." **Tip:** If you want to have your printer stop after printing each envelope, insert a ^PC command, followed by a hard return, directly after the page break. Better yet, answer "yes" to the Pause between pages (Y/N)? print option.

Press ^KD or F10

to save the file and return to the Opening menu.

Follow the same testing procedures as outlined in the previous chapter before printing your envelopes. To merge print the envelopes, remember to press **M** [merge print a file] from the Opening menu and type the correct file name, BURBANK.1E.

Mailing Labels

You may wish to print on *mailing labels* instead of envelopes, because labels are cheaper and printing them takes less time. Sure, you can use your data file again! The format for mailing labels depends on whether you have rolls of single labels or pages of labels that are two, three, or more across.

Rolled Single Labels

The problem many people often have with mailing labels is a conceptual one, not a technical one. Labels are just a series of small "pages," one strung after the other on a continuous roll, just like a continuous roll of printing paper. So, half the battle is merely one of setting the correct page length and top and bottom margins.

Press   **D** [open a document]

Type   burbank.1l

[that's a lowercase *L*].

Press   **RETURN**

Type   y

because this is a new file.

Here's a standard format for rolled labels that are two inches high. Use it as a guide for your needs.

```
.. rolled labels for promotional letter no. 1
.PL 12
.MT 3
.MB 0
.PO 7
.RM 80
.LS 1
.OP
.DF burbank.dta
.RV title, first, last, street, city, state, zip, sponsor
&title& &first& &last&
&street/o&
&city&, &state&  &zip&
.PA
```

In this example the page length is 12 lines: six lines per inch times two inches. I've included a **.MB 0** setting because the normal bottom margin is eight lines. Add this to the top margin of three, plus the three text lines, and you get a figure that's greater than the page length. So I've changed the bottom margin to provide more room on the page. If you're using three-inch high labels, the page length setting would be **.PL 18** for six lines per inch.

You still might have to adjust the margin and page offset settings; again, it depends on where you position the mailing labels to print in the printer. Trial print the label file on scrap paper to determine the necessary adjustments. **Caution:** If your printer normally pauses after each page, remember to answer "no" to this question when you merge print rolled labels.

Two- and Three-Across Labels

To set up the merge printing of two- or three-across labels—or four-across, or five-across, or whatever—is not particularly easy. In fact, it's a royal pain, even though there are *two* ways to set up multiple label printings. I'll show you one—somewhat unsatisfactory—way here, and the other one in a later chapter.

A problem with multiple-across labels involves the differing lengths of variables. Take two-across labels as an example. There are two "name" lines on the same printed line, one for each label. The variable information in each line changes with each record, so the first name line might push the second one over too far. But you still want WordStar to print the second label starting at the same column position each time. To accomplish this tricky task, you'll use the overprint line command, **^P RETURN**. You'll also work with this command in the next chapter when you learn how to fill in preprinted forms.

Another problem revolves around the page formatting for the label "pages." How you set that up depends on the size of the labels you're using. With a thorough understanding of the technical difficulties, you're ready to see one method of merge printing labels. You'll prepare two-across labels now, and three-across labels later in your WordStar apprenticeship.

Press   **D** [open a document]

Type   burbank.112

(that's a lowercase *L* in the middle of the file extension).

Press   **RETURN**

Type   y

because this is a new file.

Below is a setup for two-across labels using the BURBANK.DTA data file. Each label is one inch high, and there are *two blank* lines between rows of labels. You'll adjust the page offset to print the default left margin for the first label, and column 45 as the starting point for the second label. Your settings, of course, may be slightly different. Take a look at the file, then read the explanations.

```
.. two-across labels for promotional letter no. 1
.PL 8
.MT 1
.MB 0
.PO 7
.PF OFF
.LS 1
.OP
.DF burbank.dta
.RV title1, first1, last1, street1, city1, state1, zip1, sponsor1
.RV title2, first2, last2, street2, city2, state2, zip2, sponsor2
&title1& &first1& &last1&
                                    &title2& &first2& &last2&

&street1&
                                    &street2&

&city1&, &state1&  &zip1&
                                    &city2&, &state2&  &zip2&
.PA
```

Why a page length of eight? The actual page length is six lines, but I've included the two lines *between* labels so that WordStar ejects each "page" correctly. Remember that these labels are presumably on sheets.

I've changed the variable names slightly from previous examples, but that's okay as long as the *order* and *number* of variables is still the same in the data file. The reason I changed them was to emphasize the *two* **.RV** lines. Because this file prints two-across labels, you have to instruct WordStar to read *two* sets of variables at a time. For three-across labels, you would have *three* sets of variables and three **.RV** lines, and so on.

So, the first set of variables prints the first label, while the second set prints the second label on the same line. To accomplish this, the instructions for all *second label* lines must be on separate screen lines that overprint the previous line. That is, after you type the first variable line—

```
&title1& &first1& &last1&
```

—you then press **^P RETURN** to insert an overprint line command. The flag character display will show a hyphen (-). Use the **SPACEBAR** to position the cursor at column 45, where the second label is to start printing. Then you type the first line for the second label:

```
&title2& &first2& &last2&
```

After typing this line, you press **RETURN** because you now *do* want to begin a new printed line for the street address. Repeat the procedure of using the overprint line command for the other two lines. Only the second, fourth, and sixth lines should end in hard returns. The first, third, and fifth lines should show that - in the flag character display.

Tip: If you're using a proportionally spaced typestyle, at the column positions where the second label's variable entries go include a ^P@ command directly in front of the variable. This guarantees that WordStar will always print the variable exactly at column 45.

When you're finished,

Press   **^KD or F10**

to save the file and return to the Opening menu.

Using scrap paper, merge print this file to see the results. **Caution:** If you have a laser printer, don't use the form feed as you would normally. Answer "no" to the Use form feeds (Y/N)? print option so that WordStar doesn't issue a form feed at the end of each label "page."

Unfortunately, the results are not *exactly* perfect! That's because if there's an empty field in the data file, such as Ms. Hopkins' nonexistent street address, you have to use a *conditional merge printing* command and establish variables on the fly, as it were, to handle this problem. The /O operator won't work to suppress the blank line. That's why I didn't include it in the setup. But you don't *know* how to do these things yet, so you'll have to wait a while. There are plenty of other features to learn in the meantime. Thanks for bearing with me!

Creating a Mailing List

So now you have a huge form letter mailing and either the envelopes or labels to boot. Why not create a mailing list of the recipients for future reference? Once again, because you already have the data file, it's easy to use it *a third time*. But there are a couple of changes from the previous setups.

Press   **D** [open a document]

Type   burbank.1m

Press   **RETURN**

Type   y

because this is a new file.

Here's how a typical mailing list setup might look. After checking it out, type it!

```
.. mailing list for promotional letter no. 1
.MT 6
.MB 6
.HE "Burbank Promotion" \#1 - &@&
.LS 1
.DF burbank.dta
.RV title, first, last, street, city, state, zip, sponsor
.CP 3
&last&, &title& &first&
&street/o&
&city&, &state&  &zip&
```

Three blank lines here

When you're finished:

Press   **^KS** or **F9**

to save the file and resume where you left off.

Here, you've listed each recipient's last name first. Remember that you don't have to use the variables in any specific order, as long as you show the correct order on the **.RV** line.

When you print a mailing list, you wouldn't want to start a new page after each new name and address. Instead, you'd want to squeeze as many names and addresses on a page as possible. So, there's no **.PA** command at the end of the file. That's one change from previous shell files.

However, you *would* want to separate each name and address from the next, so you've inserted three blank lines below the city line to space down before WordStar inserts the next name and address.

You'd also be printing on normal paper, so the page defaults will be standard. Notice this time that you're not omitting pagination, so that standard page numbers will print on each page of the mailing list. You've also included a *header* as an added touch. Take a look at what the header also contains.

Finally, so as not to break up a name and address listing over two pages, you've inserted a conditional page break command, **.CP 3**. Neat!

Press   **^KD** or **F10**

to save the file and return to the Opening menu.

(Because the BURBANK.DTA file only contains five records, you could add a few records using your friends' names and addresses, or merely copy the existing records a couple of times to see how WordStar handles more records than can fit on one page of the mailing list. Make sure you open the file with the **N** [open a nondocument] command from the Opening menu.)

If you wish, try merge printing the BURBANK.1M file to a disk file with the PRVIEW driver to see how the list looks.

A Merge Miscellany

This last section provides a variety of ways to enhance your form letter mailings and other points about merge printing that can come in handy at times. You'll see many of these features in action in other chapters.

Variables in Headers and Footers: A Multipage Letter!

In my own sneaky fashion I just introduced something that can be beneficial in your form letter mailings. In the previous example you used the predefined variable **&@&** to insert the current date in the header of your mailing list. By the process of deduction—or is it induction?—you've probably already figured out that you can include any variable in a header or footer, provided the setup appears *after* the **.RV** line in the file.

For example, suppose your form letter contains several pages of text and you want a header to print on the top of each page starting on page 2. The header will show the recipient's name and the page number. If the header dot command lines appear after the **.RV** line in the file, here's an example using the same variable names from the BURBANK.1 letter file that you'd insert at the top of page 2. As an added bonus, the first header line prints in boldface.

```
.H1 ^B&title& &first& &last&^B
.H2 Page #
```

If you wish, open the BURBANK.1 file and insert a *footer* instruction that includes the same variables. *Question:* Where would the instruction go? *Answer:* Directly *below* the **.RV** line. If you insert the footer instruction above the **.RV** line, you'll get unwelcome results. Try it if you don't believe me!

Caution: Using headers or footers in form letters can be tricky. In the example above, the header or footer would print starting on page 2 of the *first* letter, but would print on *each* page of letters for other records! That's because you didn't turn the header or footer instructions back off for the first page of the letter. So, at the top of page 1 of the shell letter file, insert blank header or footer lines, like so:

```
.H1
.H2
```

Now for another problem: because you've included the page numbering symbol (#) in the header, WordStar continues to increment the page numbers for each printed page. It's not smart enough to realize that this is a form letter mailing! Thus, for a two-page letter, the first record in the data file would print on pages 1 and 2 of the letter, while the second record would print as pages 3 and 4, and so on—definitely not what you want! To get around this problem, insert a **.PN 1** command at the top of the letter file to reset the page numbering at the beginning of each new letter.

Displaying Messages While You Merge Print

Using the **.CS** and **.DM** commands that you learned in Chapter 16, you can display helpful messages during the merge printing of a form letter mailing. For example, take a look at these commands:

```
.CS
.DM Now printing letter to &first& &last& of &city&, &state&
```

If you insert these two lines directly *below* the **.RV** line in the BUR-BANK.1 file, WordStar displays a message telling you whose letter is printing. After you begin merge printing, WordStar flashes the Print Wait message. Press **M** or **P** from the Opening menu, or **^KP** from within a file, to see the Printing menu and your message. Try it! Include the two lines in the BURBANK.1 and then merge print the file using the PRVIEW printer driver.

Breaking Down Fields

In the example you've been working with, I deliberately broke down information into small units to illustrate what fields are and how to set them up in the data file. For example, there are separate fields for each person's *honorific* (title), first, and last names. How you set up your fields is up to you and depends on the way you plan to use the fields in your form letters.

As a general rule, having each field contain one specific piece of information is beneficial. When you learn about conditional printing, you'll see just how useful this approach can be. For example, if you had the city, state, and zip code information all in one field, you wouldn't be able to *select* certain records based on, say, state or zip code. That's because WordStar can't *extract* information from a field's contents. It can only check the contents of a field starting from its first character. When each piece of information is in a different field, your options for manipulating the information are greater.

Using a Different Field Separator

WordStar's default field separator, the comma, may cause you excessive grief and give you a headache *this big* when you have a lot of fields containing commas. If you forget to enclose these field in quotation marks, you'll throw off the ordering of the fields during merge printing. The result: a mess!

A simple solution to the problem is to use another character as the field separator. For example, it's not likely that you'll need to print a backslash (\) or vertical bar (¦) in name and address information, so you can use one of these characters as a separator. That way, you don't have to enclose any fields in quotation marks (unless, of course, the field contained the separator character).

You can also list fields on individual lines, with *no* separator except a hard return, but that's the topic of another section. It's also not a totally satisfactory solution, as you'll see.

There are two ways to tell WordStar that you're using another character as the field separator. Either change the merge printing defaults (Chapter 27), or tell WordStar what the separator is on the **.DF** line. The latter approach is useful if you employ different separators in different data files, or if you're just too lazy to change the defaults.

For example, suppose you decide that you want the backslash as the field separator in the BURBANK.DTA file. In each shell file that uses this data file, change the **.DF** line so that it reads:

```
.DF burbank.dta, \
```

You must separate the file name from the separator character with a comma. Here's how the edited BURBANK.DTA file would look with the new separator:

```
Dr.\ Jorge\ Rivera\ 1155 Soto Street\ Los Angeles\ CA\ 90033\ yes
Mr.\ J. Jacob\ Grump\ P.O. Box 88\ Victorville\ CA\ 92433\ yes
Ms.\ Fernanda\ Hopkins\ \ Mountain Hole\ CA\ 93777\ no
Mr.\ Jamie\ Sutter\ 909 Grant Avenue, Suite 10\ San Francisco\ CA\ 94111\ yes
Rev.\ Manny\ Kant\ 510 "R" Street, N.W.\ La Mirada\ CA\ 91444\ no
```

You no longer need double quotation marks around the fifth address, even though it contains a comma, so the street will print correctly as *"R" Street*.

 Note: If you want to instruct WordStar to wait while you change disks for the data file, *and* you want to use a different field separator, include the **CHANGE** or **C** command before the separator:

```
.DF burbank.dta c, \
```

Putting Fields on Separate Lines

You can set up your data files so that each field is on its own line ending in a hard return. That way, you don't have to have any field separator at all. There are potential problems with this approach, however.

For example, here's how the BURBANK.DTA file would look if each field were on a separate line:

```
Dr.
Jorge
Rivera
1155 Soto Street
Los Angeles
CA
90033
yes
Mr.
J. Jacob
Grump
P.O. Box 88
Victorville
CA
92433
yes
Ms.
Fernanda
Hopkins

Mountain Hole
CA
93777
no
Mr.
Jamie
Sutter
909 Grant Avenue, Suite 10
San Francisco
CA
94111
yes
Rev.
Manny
Kant
510 "R" Street, N.W.
La Mirada
CA 91444
no
```

The problems with this method are:

- It's difficult to tell where one record ends and another begins. The normal approach—separating fields by a comma or other separator and listing the entire record on one line—is visually easier to handle.
- You still have to include blank fields where necessary (as in the third example).
- It's more difficult to merge print only certain records by "pages," because each line doesn't correspond to a different record and, hence, to a different page.
- You still have to use a noncomma field separator so that regular commas don't give you trouble.

If your data files contain only a few fields, and if they don't have too many empty fields, you may find this approach to setting up fields satisfactory. One way to get around the problem of not knowing where one record ends and another begins is to use spaces or tabs as indentations. Remember that WordStar disregards leading spaces. So, the first two records could appear like this:

```
Dr.
  Jorge
  Rivera
  1155 Soto Street
  Los Angeles
  CA
  90033
  yes
Mr.
  J. Jacob
  Grump
  P.O. Box 88
  Victorville
  CA
  92433
  yes
```

Spaces indent each field except the first to demarcate the records visually. If you use tabs, remember that you can change the tab interval in nondocuments with the ^O command. If you're doing a *bibliography,* this might be one way to go. In any case, the decision is ultimately yours!

Caution: Make sure there are *no* superfluous tabs or spaces at the end of the data file. If there are, WordStar will merge print a "blank" letter. The cursor should be at the beginning of the line directly below the last field of the last record in the data file.

More on Dealing with Empty Fields

The /O (omit) operator is useful to avoid unsightly blank lines when a field is empty. However, how do you avoid blank *spaces* on a line when there are several fields on the line and one field in the data file is empty? For example, recall that the first line of the interior address in BURBANK.1 reads:

```
&title& &first& &last&
```

What if the *title* field for a record were empty? WordStar would still insert a space, because there's a constant space between **&title&** and **&first&** on the line. There are two ways to avoid this problem. One way requires conditional printing, so I'll defer discussion of that until Chapter 22.

The other method involves bypassing the /O operator. Instead, include the space *in the field information,* but not as a constant in the file. **Note:** Don't do this example, because you should keep the BURBANK.DTA file as it is for examples later. Just read!

The interior address line in BURBANK.1 would thus have to look like this:

```
&title&&first& &last&
```

You'd then also have to edit the BURBANK.DTA data file so that each title field contained a space. Remember that WordStar normally disregards trailing spaces, so enclose each field in quotation marks. Suppose you're using this method and there's no title for J. Jacob Grump. The amended BURBANK.DTA data file would look like this:

```
"Dr. ", Jorge, Rivera, 1155 Soto Street, Los Angeles, CA, 90033, yes
, J. Jacob, Grump, P.O. Box 88, Victorville, CA, 92433, yes
"Ms. ", Fernanda, Hopkins, , Mountain Hole, CA, 93777, no
"Mr. ", Jamie, Sutter, "909 Grant Avenue, Suite 10", San Francisco, CA, 94111, yes
"Rev. ", Manny, Kant, '510 "R" Street, N.W.', La Mirada, CA, 91444, no
```

There still has to be a comma separating the blank *title* field from the next field for J. Jacob, and all the other *title* entries must include a trailing space.

Extracting Information from a Data File

Suppose you have a large data file with a variety of fields and you want to set up *another* data file that will contain some of the same information. Don't retype! You can *extract* the fields you need by setting up a shell file and then "printing" the file to a new file with the special XTRACT printer driver. The XTRACT printer driver creates a file with no page formatting at all. Here's how it works.

Pretend you want to extract the name, city, state, and zip code information from the BURBANK.DTA file. You first create a shell file that governs the merge. The file would look like this:

```
.OP
.LS 1
.DF burbank.dta
.RV title, first, last, street, city, state, zip, sponsor
&first&, &last&, &city&, &state&, &zip&
```

You must still include the correct **.DF** and **.RV** lines so that WordStar can read the data file. When it extracts the information, WordStar supplies the comma as field separator in the new data file! You must include the **.OP** command so that WordStar doesn't set up pages—WordStar will end the new file directly below the last record, and there will be no extra blank lines.

Caution: The line containing the variable information that you want to extract *must* end in a hard return so that WordStar creates a new data file with a hard return at the end of each record. Don't add any superfluous spaces to the file: the cursor should be at the left margin of the line below the variables.

When you merge print this file, supply the name of the XTRACT printer driver after the Name of printer? question. If you don't supply a file name, WordStar creates a file called XTRACT.WS. Be careful! WordStar overwrites this file the next time you "print" with the same driver. A better bet would be to supply a file name like this: xtract>filename.

The new data file will contain only the fields you want. This is what you see when you open the file with **N** [open a nondocument] from the Opening menu.

```
Jorge, Rivera, Los Angeles, CA, 90033
J. Jacob, Grump, Victorville, CA, 92433
Fernanda, Hopkins, Mountain Hole, CA, 93777
Jamie, Sutter, San Francisco, CA, 94111
Manny, Kant, La Mirada, CA, 91444
```

Exactly what you want! You can then add new fields if necessary. In the next chapter you'll learn how to set up a *data entry form* using the special ASCII printer driver.

A Reminder About Hyphenation

In Chapter 16, I mentioned that you can insert *soft hyphens* in a file. The print time reformatter will honor a soft hyphen—that is, a syllable break—if it appears at the end of the line and if there's a **.PF ON** command in the file. (Perhaps by the time you read this WordStar will have an automatic hyphenation feature, which might eliminate the discussion entirely!)

For all merge printing applications the print time reformatter is automatically in discretionary mode—unless you explicitly turn it off or on with **.PF OFF** and **.PF ON** commands, respectively. So, you might want to insert soft hyphens in those paragraphs that contain variable information, and the print time reformatter will honor them as necessary.

You insert soft hyphens with the **^OE** command, but make sure the print code display is on (press **^OD** or **SHIFT F1**) so you see exactly where the hyphens appear. WordStar shows them as equals signs (=) on the screen. I suggest that you take a good look at your test form letter file to see if the line endings are okay. If the text lines appear too ragged, insert soft hyphens in those longs words that you'd want to hyphenate if they fall at the end of the line but don't entirely fit.

When Merge Printing Is Really Just Printing

Now for a little secret: A merge printing task need not be a form letter or involve a true merging of files at all. The only thing that determines whether you *print* or *merge print* a file is if the file contains merge printing dot commands or operators.

Suppose, for example, that you just *love* the predefined date variable, **&@&**, and you want to use it to print the current date in a header or footer every time you print a copy of a file. That way, you don't have to edit the file to include the correct date. Why, insert the variable in the header or footer instruction and then just merge print the file instead of printing it. No problem!

Well, there *are* just a couple tiny problems: the print time reformatter and the length of the variables themselves. The print time reformatter may unexpectedly realign paragraphs when you merge print a file that you normally would print. So, to be on the safe side, include a **.PF OFF** command at the top of the file. And remember that WordStar substitutes a longer string, such as the date, when it sees the **&@&** variable. If this variable is in the middle of a paragraph, you might *want* **.PF ON** to realign the paragraph. Keep these two points in mind.

Other Predefined Variables

Apropos predefined merge printing variables, you might as well learn the other ones available to you:

- **&!&** inserts the current time during merge printing, using the same format as that provided by **ESC !**.
- **&#&** inserts the current page number during merge printing.

- **&_&** (that's an underline, SHIFT HYPHEN) inserts the current line number during merge printing, something programmers might appreciate.

You can insert these predefined merge variables in any file, as long as you plan to merge print the file.

Well, Dear Reader, for once a short chapter! Now that you have form letter mailings down pat, it's time to try your hand at another type of merge correspondence: stock reply letters and other types of fill-in documents.

Fabulous Fill-Ins

In this chapter you will learn the following new command:

File Command

.AV   Ask for a variable from the keyboard

Now that you know the basics of merge printing, you're ready to explore other powerful applications. Merge printing is not for form letters alone! For example, it would be a colossal pain to have to do an entire form mailing for, say, just one or two letters. And it would be a waste of time to create a new file every time you wanted to send out the same form or print a standard envelope.

With WordStar you can create *stock* documents with *fill-in variable* locations. Unlike form letters, fill-in documents don't use a data file. Instead, you supply the variable information from the keyboard during merge printing. WordStar even prompts you to type each variable! What's more, you can expand your original form letter setup to include a *data entry form* to make adding information to a data file much easier.

DO WARM-UP

How Fill-In Documents Work

A fill-in document, such as a stock reply letter, requires a certain amount of variable information that changes for each printout, although *most* of the file remains the same. You could, if you wanted to, type the letter as normal and then type over the old information with the new information. You have done this already, but that's kid's stuff! In a complicated or lengthy document you might risk the chance of missing something.

WordStar has a much better way to avoid these problems. For each variable you insert a special dot command, **.AV**, that tells WordStar to "ask for the variable" from the keyboard. Then you set up the variable in the document where you want it to print, much like a form letter shell file. Remember to supply the correct constant spacing and punctuation around the variable information in the fill-in file.

When you merge print the file, however, WordStar requests the information for each variable *from the keyboard* before it prints. Then it substitutes the information you've typed for the variable names in the file. Because the variables may change the line length, the print time reformatter is in discretionary mode to realign any affected paragraphs. You don't have to edit the file at all!

Substitution Is the Key!

Dear Reader: By now you've probably realized that the process of *substitution* is the driving force of merge printing. For every variable name in a file, WordStar substitutes something else. I'll keep reinforcing this idea throughout the remaining merge printing chapters, because it's *that* important!

A Stock Reply Letter

A stock reply letter is correspondence that you send out at regular intervals—once a day, once a week, or even less frequently. It turns out that Mr. Fayke has asked his secretary to set up a stock reply letter to handle a certain unfortunate problem that cropped up as a result of his promotional offer.

Press	**D** [open a document]
Type	`burbank.stk`
Press	**RETURN**

Type   y

because this is a new file.

Below is the entire letter. Take a look at it, then type it as you see it.
Make sure each dot command starts at column 1.

```
.MT 15
.MB 6
.OP
.PO 14   [or whatever setting your printer uses]
.RM 60
.OJ OFF
.LS 1
.AV name
.AV street1
.AV street2
.AV city
.AV salutation
.AV othercity
```

```
                              66 Golden Mall
                              Burbank, CA 91300
                              &@&



&name&
&street1/o&
&street2/o&
&city&

Dear &salutation&:

We are sorry that you cannot attend our anniversary
celebration and that your plans don't call for visiting
Beautiful Downtown Burbank soon.

In response to your inquiry, please be advised that you may
not take a free trip to &othercity& instead of to Burbank.

Thank you.

                    Yours,



                    Prudence Malloy
                    Assistant to Mr. Fayke
```

When you're finished,

Press   ^KS or F9

to save the file and resume where you left off.

The Ask for Variable Feature

Instead of instructing WordStar to read the variables from a separate data file, you insert **.AV** dot commands that tell WordStar to request the information from the keyboard. Unlike the **.RV** command, which can—and usually does—contain all the variable names on one line, each **.AV** line handles *one* variable only. So, you must set up a different **.AV** line for each variable.

Like the **.RV** line, the **.AV** lines must precede the actual text of the file. WordStar has to know the variable names first before it can substitute the contents of the variables. As in form letter mailings, variable names can be up to 39 characters in length but cannot contain spaces.

When you merge print the file, WordStar asks for each variable by name, so it's a good idea to use names that call to mind the variable information you want. You can also have WordStar display a helpful prompt or message on the screen when it asks for the variable. I'll discuss that in another section.

You insert the location of the variable information in the file just as in a form letter mailing. That is, you must enclose each variable with ampersands. Notice that the two street variables also contain the **/O** (omit) operator to handle blank street information. The variable names in the file must match the names on the **.AV** lines *exactly*. Be careful to check for possible spelling mistakes!

You don't have to enter the variables on the **.AV** lines in any particular order. For example, I could have listed the **.AV othercity** line first. However, WordStar requests the variables in the order in which the **.AV** lines appear in the file. You can use the variables as many times as you wish in the actual text of the letter.

Tip: Merge print the file to a disk file with the PRVIEW printer driver to test the accuracy of the dot commands and variable operators.

Supplying Variables from the Keyboard

Because the **.AV** dot command only works with merge printing, remember to merge print the file. First, prepare your printer and paper. Then,

Press   **M** [merge print a file]

from the Opening menu or **^KP** from within a file (then type **y** because this is a merge printing)

Type   burbank.stk

If you've set up the print defaults, you can now press **ESC** to begin merge printing. Otherwise, press **RETURN** and answer the print options. As soon as it sees the first **.AV** line (and if the help level is not set at 0), WordStar flashes the Print Wait message on the screen.

Press   **M** or **P**

from the Opening menu, or **^KP** from within a file to see the Printing menu.

WordStar displays the first variable name, followed by a question mark and a space. It always displays the variable in uppercase, no matter how it appears in the .AV line. Type the information for this variable and press **RETURN**. WordStar then displays the next variable. To *skip* a variable—for instance, if there is no "second street" information—press **RETURN** alone.

If you make a mistake while typing, press **BACKSPACE** (**^H**) to correct it *before* you press RETURN to go to the next variable. **Caution:** Once you've pressed RETURN to complete one variable, you can't backtrack. Suppose you made a mistake in the name variable and you've already pressed RE-TURN at the end of the line. You'd have to press **^U** (**F2**) to cancel the entire operation and start again.

Below is an example of the screen display after you've filled in all variable entries. When you press **RETURN** after the last entry, WordStar plugs the variable information into the printout.

```
NAME? Vincent Alfieri, Ph.D.
STREET1? 4118 Loony Tunes Blvd.
STREET2? Apartment 2
CITY? Los Angeles, CA  90027
SALUTATION? Dr. Alfieri
OTHERCITY? Pasadena
```

(An aside: the street2 variable actually handles any second street address line, such as a suite number, apartment number, or what have you. Notice that there is a constant colon at the end of the salutation in the file, so you *don't* type the colon when prompted for the variable.)

Question: What do you do if you have to send this letter to five different recipients today? *Answer:* Just type **5** after the Number of copies? print option. After requesting the first set of variables and merge printing the file, WordStar clears the screen below the Printing menu and requests the next set, and so on.

Displaying Prompts and Messages

In this particular fill-in document, the name variable is supposed to contain the recipient's full name, including honorific if desired. The city variable includes the city, state, and zip code. You might forget what information to supply for each variable, and the variable name doesn't give you enough of a clue.

To get around this problem, you can instruct WordStar to display a helpful prompt or other message *instead of* the variable name. If you're at the Opening menu:

Press   **D** [open a document]

Press   **ESC**

to open the same file, BURBANK.STK.

To display a custom message, supply the message you want enclosed in quotation marks directly after the **.AV** command. Then type a comma and the variable name. Use correct case in the message. Change the **.AV** lines in the file so that they look like this:

```
.AV "Recipient's full name: ", name
.AV "First street line (RETURN if none): ", street1
.AV "Second street line (RETURN if none): ", street2
.AV "City, state, and zip code: ", city
.AV "Salutation (without a colon): ", salutation
.AV "Other city: ", othercity
```

Notice there is a space at the end of each message to separate the message from the variable entry. The space is part of the message string, so it's within the quotation marks. WordStar doesn't supply a default space after a message unless you tell it to. If you want to include a double quote in the message, enclose the entire message in single quotes.

Caution: The comma separating the message from the variable name must *follow* the ending quotation mark. Take a look at the extra help that I've provided for the two street variables!

Press   **^KD or F10**

to save the file and return to the Opening menu.

When you merge print the file, you'll see the messages instead of the variable names. Here's one example of a completed screen. Notice that I pressed RETURN for the second address line because that line is blank.

```
Recipient's full name: Mrs. Jean Hill
First street line (RETURN if none): 222 Del Gato Drive
```

```
Second street line (RETURN if none):
City, state, and zip code: San Ramon, CA  94099
Salutation (without a colon): Mrs. Hill
Other city: Santa Monica
```

just a RETURN here

Caution: Both the message line *and* the information you type for the variable must all fit on one line of the screen. That is, the total number of characters can't be more than 80. I've deliberately kept the messages short for that very reason, especially because the street information might be lengthy. There's a way to get around this problem: Use a **.DM** or **.CS** command to display the first line of the message, then the **.AV** command with a shorter message line. For example:

```
.DM Enter the first street address line
.AV "(RETURN if none): ", street1
```

Whereas the **.CS** and **.DM** lines don't require quotation marks around the message text, the **.AV** command does. Be careful!

A note to old timers: You used to be able to *restrict* the length of a variable entry in the **.AV** line. For example, you could ensure that a zip code variable be no longer than five characters. That feature apparently has disappeared. To get around it, supply a message informing the user the limit of the entry or rely on conditional merge printing (discussed in the next chapter) to test the validity of an entry.

Envelope Madness!

There are many other ways to apply the **.AV** command. This section shows you how it can help you deal with a common annoyance: addressing envelopes.

The First Best Way to Address Individual Envelopes

By far the most frequent use of the **.AV** command in the Alfieri household is to print individual envelopes without a lot of hullabaloo. Here's what I mean.

Press   **D** [open a document]

Type   **e**

Press   **RETURN**

Type   y

because this is a new file.

Here is a setup for standard business envelopes. It is similar in format to the BURBANK.1E file from the previous chapter, but it uses **.AV** lines instead of a data file. You may have to adjust the page formats for your setup. If you have a laser printer, you may also have to change the *paper orientation* to print envelopes (Chapter 26).

```
.. "stock" envelope setup
.PL 25
.MT 1
.PO 7 [or whatever setting you need]
.PF OFF
.LS 1
.OP
.AV line1
.AV line2
.AV line3
.AV line4
.AV line5
.AV line6
4118 Loony Tunes Boulevard
Los Angeles, CA 90027
```

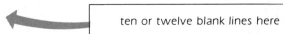
ten or twelve blank lines here

```
.PO 42
&line1&
&line2&
&line3/o&
&line4/o&
&line5/o&
&line6/o&
```

This file handles addresses of up to six lines, which is usually more than adequate for my needs. I don't bother adding messages, because I know that each "line" just contains standard name and address information. If I don't supply information for a couple of lines, nothing prints anyway, although I've included /o operators just for fun. I named the file E to save keystroking! When you've typed the file and checked it for accuracy:

Press   ^KD or F10

to save the file and return to the Opening menu.

The Second Best Way to Address Individual Envelopes

As a variation on this theme, I have another envelope setup that prints the envelope from information in a file. Suppose I've just composed a letter to someone, and now I want to address the envelope. I use a shorthand macro to *block out* the interior address in the letter file and write the block to a file with the ^KW command. After printing the letter, I merge print the envelope file.

This envelope file, which I call EX, first asks me the name of the file containing the recipient's information. It then plugs this information into the envelope. Notice how I've used the .AV command to supply information to *another* dot command, .FI!

```
.. envelope setup using a file
.PL 25
.MT 1
.PO 7 [or whatever setting you need]
.PF OFF
.LS 1
.OP
.AV "What is the file name? ", file
4118 Loony Tunes Boulevard
Los Angeles, CA  90027
```

ten or twelve blank lines here

```
.PO 42
.FI &file&
```

In other examples, you'll see many uses of the .AV command with other dot commands.

A "Dummy" Variable

A *dummy* variable is one that doesn't ever print. It's there mainly to act as a pause, usually with a prompt or message. For example, in the form letter envelope that you set up (BURBANK.1E) you want to prompt your users to insert an envelope in the printer. Add these lines to the top of the file:

```
.AV "Insert a blank envelope and press RETURN to continue", x
.CS
```

After the user inserts a new envelope and presses RETURN, Wordstar clears the message and prints the envelope. It pauses for each envelope in the form letter mailing.

Letter and Envelope in One File

The next example brings it all together, as it were. It sets up a stock reply letter *and* its envelope in the same file. When you merge print this file, you'll also see how the print time reformatter handles variable information in paragraphs.

Press   **D** [open a document]

Type   ordered

Press   **RETURN**

Type   y

because this is a new file.

As you type the file, try to figure out why I included the dot commands as I did and what each one does. *Don't* type the page break displays! Notice that there are underline print codes (^S) enclosing the **&book&** variable in the letter, so WordStar will underline the book title when it merge prints the letter!

```
.. stock reply for out of stock book order
.PL 66   [or whatever setting you use]
.PF DIS
.MT 14
.MB 10
.OP
.PO 15   [or whatever setting you use]
.RM 60
.LS 1
.OJ off
.UL ON
.RR--!------------------------!--------------------------------R
.AV "Insert letterhead stationery and press RETURN to continue", x
```

```
.AV "Title (Mr., Ms., etc.): ", title
.AV "First name: ", fname
.AV "Last name: ", lname
.AV "Address line 1 (RETURN if none): ", street1
.AV "Address line 2 (RETURN if none): ",  street2
.AV "City, state, zip code: ", city-state-zip
.AV "Order date: ", orderdate
.AV "Book on order: ", book
.AV "Weeks until delivery (spell out): ", weeks
```

```
                              Everyman's Computer Book Store
                              555 West Alameda Avenue
                              Orange, California  93301
```


```
&title& &fname& &lname&
&street1/o& &street2/o&
&city-state-zip&
```

Dear &title& &lname&:

     We are in receipt of your order of &orderdate& for one
copy of ^S&book&^S. Unfortunately, that book is presently out
of stock, but we do expect a shipment of it to arrive within
&weeks& weeks. We will, of course, forward you a copy at
the earliest possible moment.

     We are sorry for any inconvenience caused you by this
delay. Because ^S&book&^S is a very popular book, we are sure
that you will be pleased with it.

     Once again, thank you for your order.

                    Yours truly,

                    J.R. Dalrymple
                    Director, Mail Order Sales

```
JRD/wpc
&@&
.PA
```
--P
```
.PL 25
.MT 1
.PO 7  [or whatever setting you need]
```

```
.PF OFF
.CS
.AV "Insert envelope and press RETURN to continue", y
Everyman's Computer Book Store
555 West Alameda Avenue
Orange, California 93301
```

ten or twelve blank lines here

```
.PO 42
&title& &fname& &lname&
&street1/o&
&street2/o&
&city-state-zip&
.PA
------------------------------------------------------------------------------P
```

You may want to merge print several copies of this file at one time. Because you've changed the paper length for the shorter envelope page, you must include a **.PL** command at the top of the letter page, too. Additionally, notice that the print time reformatter is off for the envelope so that WordStar doesn't realign long address lines. You set it back to discretionary mode on the first page. You're also using helpful messages, including dummy variables with prompts to tell the user when to insert the paper and the envelope.

Press   ^KD or F10

to save the file and return to the Opening menu.

Fun with Forms

Okay, so perhaps forms aren't much fun, but there are any number of ways the **.AV** command can help you prepare forms. In this section I'll show you how to create a data entry form for a form letter mailing and how to have WordStar fill in preprinted forms.

A Data Entry Form

As you know, you have to be *very* careful when setting up the fields in a data file for a form letter mailing. Not only do you have to remember to put a comma between fields, but you also have to enclose a field in quotation marks if the field information contains a comma. Additionally, you must end each line with a hard return.

Using the ask for variables feature and the ASCII printer driver, you can set up a data entry form that requests the information and then creates the new data file for you! The data entry form file contains all the extra stuff, like commas and hard returns. You don't have to worry about them!

Press   **D** [open a document]

Type   burbank.frm

Press   **RETURN**

Type   y

because this is a new file.

This file creates a new data file with the same field information as BURBANK.DTA. Here's the setup:

```
.OP
.LS 1
.PF OFF
.CS
.AV "Enter the title (Mr., Ms., Dr., etc.) -> ", title
.AV "Enter the first name -> ", first
.AV "Enter the last name -> ", last
.DM Enter the first street address line
.AV "(RETURN if none) -> ", street1
.DM Enter the second street address line
.AV "(RETURN if none) -> ", street2
.AV "Enter the city -> ", city
.AV "Enter the state code (two letters) -> ", state
.AV "Enter the zip code (five numbers) -> ", zip
.DM If the person is a sponsor, type yes;
.AV "otherwise, type no -> ", sponsor
&title/o&,&first&,&last&,&street1/o&,&street2/o&,&city&,&state&,&zip/o&,&sponsor&
.FI burbank.frm
```

Notice that I've supplied a lot of help! The **.PF OFF** instruction just ensures that WordStar doesn't wrap variable entries across lines. Because you want this file to repeat itself for each new record, the **.FI** command reads in and repeats the same file. The **.CS** command clears the screen of the previous form. Notice the use of the **/O** operator for certain fields: if you don't supply an entry, WordStar still supplies the field separator so that the number of the fields for each record is always the same.

There are a few tricks to using this form. First, when you merge print the file, supply ASCII as the printer driver after the Name of printer? question. Second, because WordStar creates a file called ASCII.WS and will overwrite this file the next time you use the same driver, supply a different file name, for example, ascii>newfile. Finally, the file will repeat itself endlessly, but when you're finished entering new records, press ^U (F2) to cancel printing at the top of the next *blank* data entry form.

Caution: If you use this setup at different times, supply *different* file names for the new data file each time. Later, you can combine files by opening one (as a nondocument) and then inserting the others with the ^KR command. Also, if you plan to use commas as part of field information, substitute a noncomma field separator in the setup above. You could also enclose each field variable in quotation marks, like so:

"&title/o&","&first&","&last&","&street1/o&", and so on

That way, any entries containing commas don't throw off the commas as field separators.

Filling In Preprinted Forms

WordStar is not adept at helping you fill in forms on the fly, so for the occasional form you might as well just get out the old ballpoint. But if you work with the same form a great deal it might behoove you to set up a file with ask for variable commands. It takes a bit of time and effort, but in the long run you'll come out ahead.

The most difficult parts of the setup are figuring out where the information is to print on the form and establishing the correct page defaults. Here's a trick: use a *grid* to mark where each entry is to go. The grid prints characters on the *entire page.* You mark the line numbers and column positions of all entries and then create the form file.

To learn the entire procedure, assume you have a form that's on standard, 8½ by 11 inch paper. First create the grid file.

Press   **D** [open a document]

Type   grid

Press   **RETURN**

Type   y

because this is a new file.

Set up the page format for the grid like this:

```
.LH 8
.PL 66
.OP
.MT 0
.MB 0
.PO 0
.RM 85
```

The top and bottom margins are zero, so WordStar prints on each line of the page. The page offset is zero to ensure that WordStar prints starting at the *left edge* of the paper. Because the page is 8½ inches wide, a **.RM 85** setting works for the standard 10 characters per horizontal inch. You don't need the **.LH 8** or **.PL 66** commands if you haven't changed the page defaults, but I threw them in anyway. Adjust the page length and right margin settings if the form is a different size.

Next, type *one* line of characters all the way to column 85, as in the example below (it's been reduced to fit on the page). Press **RETURN** at the end of the line.

1234567890123456789012345678901234567890123456789012345678901234567890123456789012345

Now for the trick: after typing the line, position the cursor back on it and press **^Y (F5)** to delete it. Now you want to copy the *same* line 66 times for the entire page. Press **^QQU** to repeat the unerase! WordStar leaves the cursor on line 1, but repeatedly unerases the same line. Wait about two minutes, then press any key to stop the repetition. Press **^QC (^END)** to position the cursor at the end of the file. Delete any lines on page 2. Make sure that there is no page break and that the file ends at the bottom of page one. You now have a grid that fills in the entire page.

Print the GRID file on a blank form. Then mark the column positions of each entry and note the *exact* line and column numbers. You're now ready to create the form file with ask for variable commands. (You can use the GRID file again to help you set up other forms.) So that the grid lines match the form lines and the entry positions match those on the grid, use the same zero settings for the top and bottom margins and page offset.

Set up each variable entry on its own **.AV** line, supplying any prompts or messages to help you when you enter information. To insert the variables at their correct locations in the file, you have a little work ahead of you! If there are two or more variables on the same line, you must use the overprint line command, **^P RETURN**, to print the variables at the correct spot on the form. Take a look at this example:

```
&company&                    &invoice_no&
&street1&                    &invoice_date&
&street2&
```

The **&invoice_no&** and **&invoice_date&** variables have to print at column 50, no matter what! The **&company&** and **&street1&** variables change in length, so WordStar wouldn't normally be able to print the **&invoice_no&** and **&invoice_date&** variables at a fixed column on the form. It always prints however many spaces are *between* the variables. You saw the same basic problem when you learned about two-across mailing labels in the previous chapter.

To correct the problem, use the overprint line command again. Type the **&company&** variable, then press **^P RETURN**. A - appears in the flag character display. Press **TAB (^I)** or the **SPACEBAR** to position the cursor at the correct column for the **&invoice_no&** variable. Type it and press **RETURN** to end the line. Repeat this procedure for all lines. The example above (including the flag character display) would now look like this:

```
&company&                                                    -
                              &invoice_no&                    <
&street1&                                                     -
                              &invoice_date&                  <
&street2&                                                     <
```

Only the second *screen* line ends in a hard return to indicate the end of the first *printed* line. If you have three variables on the same line, you'd end the first two lines with overprint commands. The screen line containing the *last* variable is the one that ends in a hard return. I *told* you setting up forms takes time!

Tip: If you're using a proportionally spaced typestyle, at the column positions where the variable entries go include a **^P@** command directly in front of the variable. This guarantees that WordStar will always print the variable exactly in the blank on the form.

Dealing with Long Variable Entries

WordStar only lets you type a entry that fits on the screen. Remember that the message or variable name takes up part of the line. If you have to type in long variable entries, break them up into two or more separate variables in the file. Then let the print time reformatter help you.

Press	**D** [open a document]
Type	**bib**
Press	**RETURN**

Type   y

because this is a new file.

Below is a setup that requests information from the keyboard and then prints a *bibliography* on 4 by 6 inch index cards. The exact page formatting would depend on your printer and where you insert the card.

```
.PL 24
.MT 1
.MB 0
.PO 7  [or whatever setting you use]
.LS 1
.OP
.OJ OFF
.PM 1
.LM 6
.RM 55
.AV "Author's first name: ", first
.AV "Author's middle name: ", middle
.AV "Author's last name: ", last
.DM Enter as much of the title as will fit on the screen,
.DM  next to the -> below
.AV "-> ", title1
.DM Enter the rest of the title on the screen,
.DM  next to the -> below
.AV "-> ", title2
.AV "Publication date: ", pdate
.AV "Publisher: ", pub
.AV "Publisher's city: ", pcity

&last&, &first& &middle&

&title1& &title2/o&

&pdate&, &pub&, &pcity&
```

I've kept the example short, but you can customize it for your own particular needs. Notice that the **.LM** and **.PM** commands set up a hanging indent for the first line, so that long title and publishing information lines indent nicely on the card. Because you want two of the message lines to indent, you include extra spaces. WordStar disregards the *first* space following the **.DM** command, but displays the others.

If the title is longer than one screen, you can enter the rest of the title for the **&title2&** variable. For this to work properly, the **&title1&** variable shouldn't end in a space, because WordStar supplies the spaces between it and the **&title2&** variable. An example of a filled-in screen form follows.

```
Author's first name: Janice
Author's middle name: Q.
Author's last name: Johnson
Enter as much of the title as will fit on the screen,
  next to the -> below
-> The Howdy Doody Show, or How I Learned to Love Television in Spite
Enter the rest of the title on the screen,
  next to the -> below
-> of Myself
Publication date: 1986
Publisher: Fancy Free Press
Publisher's city: San Francisco, CA
```

The printed card looks like the one in Figure 21–1.

Figure 21–1
A Merge Printed
Index Card

```
Johnson, Janice Q.

The Howdy Doody Show, or How I Learned to Love
        Television in Spite of Myself

1987, Fancy Free Press, San Francisco, CA
```

A "Generic" Form Letter Setup

Suppose you send the same form letter to many different recipients, but your recipients' records aren't all in the same data file. Perhaps you've divided the names alphabetically so that names starting with *A* to *L* are in one file, and *M* to *Z* in another. The structure of the data files is the same, of course.

You could merely edit the **.DF** line in the form letter file when you want to change the file name and print more form letters, but here's another way to go. Use the ask for variable command in a separate *command file* to request the name of the particular data file. Then use the file insert command to insert the letter file.

Don't type these examples, because I want you to keep the "Burbank" files the way they are. Just look! A command file might contain the following commands:

```
.AV "Enter the name of the data file: ", file
.FI burbank.1
```

To use this command file, you'd have to edit the **.DF** line in the BUR-BANK.1 file so that it reads:

```
.DF &file&
```

When you merge print the command file, WordStar requests the name of the data file. It then runs the BURBANK.1 file and *passes* the name you supply for **&file&** to the **.DF** line in BURBANK.1. When it finishes printing all letters, it returns to the command file. Because there are no more commands in the command file, the merge printing is done.

If all your data files have the same extension, such as .DTA, you can avoid having to type even that. Here's how to set up the command file:

```
.AV "Enter the name of the data file without extension: ", file
.FI burbank.1
```

Then edit the BURBANK.1 file so that the **.DF** line reads:

```
.DF &file&.dta
```

WordStar joins, or *concatenates,* the file name you supply with the extension .DTA and uses the result as the data file!

Question: Why can't you just put the **.AV** line in the letter file itself? *Answer:* You could, but WordStar would stop and request the data file name for *each* pass of the letter—not what you want!

What you just did was create a simple type of document assembly application using merge printing techniques. There are more examples in other chapters. Before you can investigate them, however, you should learn yet another useful feature: conditional merge printing.

Conditional Merge Printing

In this chapter you will learn the following new commands:

File Commands

.EI	End a condition
.EL	Begin a conditional alternative
.GO TOP/BOTTOM	Go to the top or the bottom of the file and continue
.IF	Begin a condition

Other Features

Alphabetical Operators

=	Is the same as
<	Comes before
>	Comes after
<=	Comes before or is the same as
>=	Comes after or is the same as
<>	Is not the same as

Numerical Operators

#=	Is equal to
#>	Is greater than
#<	Is less than

more . . .

#>=	Is greater than or equal to
#<=	Is less than or equal to
#<>	Is not equal to

Dear Reader: You are about to enter another dimension in the fascinating world of merge printing, a dimension that goes far beyond simple form letters and fill-in documents. This new and unfamiliar realm is conditional merge printing. At first, you may think you really *are* in the "twilight zone," but I'm here to help guide you over the rough spots. Be patient! Be alert! Be brave!

> ### DO WARM-UP

Some Preliminary Notes

Conditional merge printing—which I'll just call conditional printing—depends on whether a stated condition occurs or doesn't occur. In other words, you'll ask WordStar to act in a certain fashion if the condition is *true* and in another fashion if the condition is *false*.

An Iffy Situation

Suppose you want to send form letters only to people who live in Massachusetts, but there are many other states represented in a particular data file. You've typed the two-letter postal abbreviation for each state. You can instruct WordStar to *select* only those records that contain *MA* in the state field, and bypass the others. The condition here is "*if* the state is MA, *then* send a letter; *else*, skip the record." I deliberately used awkward English because the words *if*, *then*, and *else* are important to your understanding of conditional printing.

You can also state a condition in negative terms. For instance, assume you want to send form letters to everyone who *doesn't* live in Massachusetts. The condition would be "*if* the state is *not* MA, *then* send a letter." How you set up conditions depends in large part on what you want to do and the structure of your files. You can use conditional commands in many different ways, not just in form letter mailings.

Conditional Commands and Operators

Unfortunately, WordStar can't read English, so you have to state a condition in a way that WordStar can "understand." To do this you use *conditional commands and operators,* a list of which is at the beginning of the chapter. All conditional commands are dot commands, such as **.IF** to begin a condition. You've probably noted that the conditional operators are similar to mathematical ones. I think the examples in this and later chapters will help you learn how to use them.

Suffice it to say at this point that a condition always requires a comparison of two items to see if the items are the same or different. The operators let you determine whether one item is greater than, less than, equal to, or not equal to the other item. However, the *order* in which you state the condition is fixed. You always compare the *first* item to the *second.*

In my original example, suppose you're using the variable name **&state&** to designate the state field in your data file. To have WordStar determine if the state is Massachusetts, the command would be:

```
.IF &state& = MA
```

To ascertain if the state *isn't* Massachusetts, the command would be:

```
.IF &state& <> MA
```

WordStar will always do one of two things depending on the "truth" or "falseness" of the condition. Sometimes you'll also want to give it an *alternative* condition or other options. As you'll see, you can provide an "else" statement for the alternative, or you can *nest* several conditions. An example of nesting conditions would be sending letters to those people who live in Massachusetts *and* whose zip code is greater than 02100. You would need two conditions for this one.

How WordStar Makes Comparisons

Recall from Chapter 7 that a *string* is a series of characters "strung together." Strings can contain letters, numbers, print codes, and punctuation marks. WordStar compares strings differently from numbers alone. As the chart of operators suggests, WordStar "assumes" it's comparing two strings unless you append a number sign (#) to the operator.

When it compares two strings, WordStar compares only the letters in the string. For one string to be "equal to" another, both strings must contain the same characters in the same order. WordStar disregards leading spaces and case differences, so this command line—

```
.IF &state& <>      ma
```

—is the same as the previous one. You can, however, enclose a string in quotation marks when the spaces are necessary to the comparison. In that case, you must enclose *both* items in quotes:

```
.IF "&state&" <> " MA"
```

How can one string be "greater than" or "less than" another? No, it has nothing to do with the length of the string, because strings of different lengths are by their very nature not the same. WordStar determines the *alphabetical* position of the *first* character in the first item to the first character in the second item. Suppose a state field contained the entry *CA* for California. This command—

```
.IF &state& < MA
```

—would evaluate to true, because *C* comes before *M* in the alphabet. That is, *C* is "less than" *M*. WordStar doesn't even have to look at the second letter! If the state in question were *RI*, then the condition would evaluate as false, because *R* is "greater than" *M*.

If the first letter of both items is the same, WordStar compares the second letter. If that's the same, it compares the third, and so on. So, *Maine* is less than *Massachusetts*, as you would expect, but *MA* comes before *ME*. That's the post office for you!

When you tell it to compare numbers, WordStar disregards non-numeric characters altogether. The only exceptions are the minus sign (−) and the decimal point (.). So $27.95 is equal to 27.95, because the dollar sign doesn't matter. Comparisons of numbers are easier to understand than comparisons of strings, because it's more obvious to you whether the numbers are equal or not, or whether one is larger than the other.

Caution: If you don't tell WordStar that you want to compare numbers, it treats any numeric characters as just text. Thus, $27.95 is *not* equal to 27.95! Always use the # symbol to compare numbers, such as dollar amounts.

By the way, when WordStar treats numbers as text, they come "alphabetically" before letters. So the string *23-Skiddoo* comes before *Hello 'dere!* The reason for this is simple: in the ASCII coding scheme, numbers come before uppercase or lowercase letters. For example, the ASCII code for *1* is 49, while the code for *A* is 65.

Location Means a Lot

Most of the time you'll want to compare a *merge variable* to a *constant,* such as whether the contents of a **&state&** variable are the same as the string *MA.*

That means you must have first *declared* the variables by name, either in **.RV** or **.AV** lines. So it's important to insert any conditional commands *after* the **.RV** or **.AV** lines in the file.

A Cardinal Rule

You're almost ready to try your hand at conditional printing and learn the fine points as you go. Before you do, there's just one simple rule to appreciate and follow: *Every if must have an end.* That is, after you begin a condition you have to tell WordStar where in the file the condition ends. The command to do this is **.EI** for "end if." To put this in conditional terms: *If* you don't include an "end if," *then* you'll be sorry!

Start with a Single Condition

For the first example, pretend that the BURBANK.DTA data file contains hundreds of records. Mr. Fayke is a cheapskate at heart, although even Ms. Malloy doesn't know that, so he's convinced himself that he has to limit his free promotional offer. He's decided to send letters only to people who live in Los Angeles. That means he has to change the original form letter shell by including a conditional setup.

Press   **D** [open a document]

Type   burbank.1

Press   **RETURN**

Press   **^X** or **DOWN ARROW** eleven times

to position the cursor on the first *real* text line of the file.

There are two ways to establish the condition: either in "positive" or "negative" terms. That is, you could ask WordStar to test whether the **&city&** variable is the same as *Los Angeles,* or whether it isn't the same. I'm belaboring the point because you'll see later that it's often easier to state the condition in negative terms. For the sake of this example, though, you'll look at both ways.

Press   **^N**

to insert a line but leave the cursor where it is.

A Positive Approach

Being a cock-eyed optimist, you always look at the positive side of things. Type this line at column 1:

```
.IF &city& = Los Angeles
```

You must enclose the variable name in ampersands, just as you've done all along in the other merge printing examples. At this point, the conditional statement is telling WordStar to evaluate the contents of the **&city&** variable in the data file. If it's *Los Angeles,* then you want to print a letter for that record.

However, what if it's *not* Los Angeles? What does WordStar do? Presumably it doesn't print the letter, but instead skips the record and goes to the next. How? You must tell it where to *end* the current condition. Because you want WordStar to print the entire letter if the **&city&** variable is *Los Angeles,* the location of the **.EI** line must be at the end of the file.

Press   **^QC or ^END**

to position the cursor at the end of the file.

If you didn't enter a hard return after the **.PA** line, do so now. The **.EI** dot command line must be below it. Type this dot command and press **RETURN** to end the line so that the command looks like this:

```
.EI
```

You now have one command on "page 2," but it won't print anyway. You've told WordStar to print the contents of the file, all the text following the **.IF** line, if the condition is true. Otherwise, you've told WordStar to go to the end of the condition, the **.EI** line. Because there's nothing past the **.EI** line, WordStar skips the record in the data file and tries the next one. If the city *is* Los Angeles, WordStar prints the letter, ejects the page, and then comes to the **.EI** line. Again, it goes to the next record in the data file and continues its evaluation of the **&city&** variable.

If you wish, save the file and merge print it to a disk file with the PRVIEW driver. Sure enough, WordStar generates only one form letter, and Mr. Fayke has saved himself a bundle!

Note: You'd probably give Mr. Fayke a heart attack if you now printed all the envelopes or mailing labels for your form mailing. Insert the *same* conditional commands in the envelope or label file so that you only print the ones you need.

A Negative Approach

The other way to go would be to instruct WordStar to determine if the **&city&** variable doesn't contain *Los Angeles*. Open the BURBANK.1 file and delete the **.EI** line at the end of the file. Then position the cursor on the **.IF** line. Change it to this:

```
.IF &city& <> Los Angeles
```

You now have to tell WordStar what to do if the city isn't Los Angeles. That is, WordStar should *skip* the letter and try the next record. That is, you tell WordStar to *go to the bottom* of the file with the **.GO BOTTOM** command. Below this command you insert the end if command, because if the city *is* Los Angeles, the condition has been met and WordStar should print the letter. Add these two lines directly *below* the **.IF** line so that the entire conditional setup is this:

```
.IF &city& <> Los Angeles
.GO BOTTOM
.EI
```

Note: You can type .GO B , but I'll show the entire word BOTTOM to keep things clear. Later you'll learn how to use the alternate to this command, **.GO TOP**.

One nice thing about the negative approach here is that you can keep all the conditional commands together. The results in this case are the same, but if BURBANK.1 were a long file the negative approach would be faster. Why? Because if the condition is false, WordStar goes *immediately* to the end of the file. It doesn't have to read the entire file looking for the **.EI** line, as it would have to do in the first example.

Save the file and merge print it using the PRVIEW printer driver. You should get the same results.

Multiple Conditions

When you want to supply two or more conditions, you might have to *nest* one within the other. *Nesting* means setting up one conditional structure within another. There are a few pratfalls along the way, so take care.

The first potential problem is with the **.EI** lines. When you nest conditions, each **.IF** line must have a corresponding **.EI** line, but you must reverse the *order* of the **.EI** lines! Nested conditions are like those Russian folk art dolls. You open one doll only to find a smaller one inside, and so on. Each *level* of the nest must therefore be complete in itself. That is, there must be an **.EI** line for each **.IF** line and the order of the **.EI** line is reversed, as Figure 22–1 illustrates.

The second problem is getting the *logic* of the conditional statements correct. That is, do you want WordStar to act if *either* one condition *or* the other is true, or do you want WordStar to act if *both* the first condition *and* the second are true? They're entirely different situations! **Note:** Often you have to state the logic of a condition in a negative manner, as the examples will illustrate.

You've probably realized that a computer's logic is often not the same as a person's. With all due respect to the human race, I must say that people are a little more "muddle-headed" at times than computers. Therefore, it's always a good idea to *test* conditional merge printing before you merge print. Use the good old print to disk routine.

Finally, there's the *order* in which you state the conditions, depending on what you want to accomplish. **Tip:** Because you're attempting to rule out the possibilities that *don't* apply and leave in the ones that *do,* try to set up the order so that the first condition eliminates as many nonapplicable situations as possible. Then *narrow down* the possibilities with other conditional statements.

An "Either or" Situation

Assume that Mr. Fayke has had a change of heart. He's decided to offer free trips to Burbank *either* to those people who live in Los Angeles *or* to people who are sponsors of the station, no matter where they live. Recall that you entered "yes" or "no" in the sponsor field when you set up the name and address file, BURBANK.DTA.

Press   **D** [open a document]

When you nest conditional commands, there must be one **.EI** line for each **.IF** line. The order of the **.EI** lines is reversed. That is, WordStar "backtracks" to match an **.EI** with the most previous **.IF** line.

```
.IF   <condition>  ←──────────────┐
        Some text here . . .       │
.IF   <another condition>  ←────┐  │
        Some more text here . . . │  │
.EI   <goes with last .IF condition>  ←──┘  │
.EI   <goes with first .IF condition>  ←────┘
```

Figure 22–1 Nesting Conditional Commands

Press   **ESC**

to open the same file, BURBANK.1.

You'll add the second condition *below* the first. That is, if the city isn't Los Angeles, WordStar then has to evaluate whether the sponsor field contains "yes." Using the negative approach, you'll ask WordStar if the sponsor field doesn't contain "yes." If it doesn't, *then* WordStar should go to the end of the file. Otherwise, one or the other condition is true, and WordStar prints the letter. Remember to include an "end if " line for the second "if." The new setup would look like this:

```
.IF &city& <> Los Angeles
.IF &sponsor& <> yes
.GO BOTTOM
.EI
.EI
```

Tip: WordStar disregards any text *after* the **.EI** command, so you can put in a helpful message *to yourself* that reminds you which **.IF** line goes with each **.EI** line. This can save you a lot of frustration! For example, you could set up the condition like this:

```
.IF &city& <> Los Angeles
.IF &sponsor& <> yes
.GO BOTTOM
.EI end of sponsor condition
.EI end of city condition
```

Save and merge print the file using the PRVIEW printer driver. How many letters does WordStar generate?

A "Both and" Situation

Mr. Fayke realizes that one of his sponsors lives in San Francisco. It would be a burdensome expense to provide free transportation for this individual! So Mr. Fayke has decided to have another change of heart and of condition. He wants to offer free trips only to people who meet *both* the following conditions: they must be sponsors *and* their zip code must be less than 92000.

Press   **D** [open a document]

Press   **ESC**

to open the same file, BURBANK.1.

First, position the cursor on the first **.IF** line and press **^Y (F5)** five times to delete *all* the conditional command lines to start with a fresh slate. With the cursor on the same line, press **^N** to add a blank line. Then enter the following commands, pressing **RETURN** after each one except the last:

```
.IF &sponsor& <> yes
.GO BOTTOM
.EI sponsor condition
.IF &zip& #>= 92000
.GO BOTTOM
.EI zip code condition
```

This time you *aren't* nesting conditions. Each conditional structure is a separate unit. WordStar first checks whether the **&sponsor&** field doesn't contain *yes.* If that's the case, it goes to the bottom of the file and continues with the next record in the data file. Notice the position of the **.EI** line.

WordStar then checks whether the zip code is *greater than or equal to* 92000. Because this is a number, you've added the **#** symbol. You use the **>=** operator to rule out zip code 92000, too. So, if the individual's zip code is less than 92000, then WordStar prints the letter. Otherwise, it goes to the end of the file and continues with the next record in the data file.

You could have set up the second condition like this:

```
.IF &zip& #< 91999
```

Caution: Always be careful about the *limits* of the actual amounts you want to test. For example, if you want to evaluate amounts *greater than* $100.00, use **#> 100.00.** I'm not going to take the time to illustrate each operator in an example, but you'll see them again in the chapter on math reports, Chapter 24.

Save the file and merge print it with the PRVIEW driver. As it turns out, Mr. Fayke can breath easy again, because now he just has to pay for one free trip to Burbank!

One of Two Possibilities: A Range

Sometimes a condition can contain an alternate: *"if* such and such is true, do this; *else,* do that." There's a command for the "else" part. Wouldn't you know it would be **.EL?** The else command always sets up *one and only one* alternate to the original if. That is, you can have only one **.EL** line for every **.IF** condition.

For example, you want to print letters to all people whose last names, the **&last&** variable, begin with *M* through *P.* You'll exclude the rest. Unfortunately, ranges can be tricky! Here's the setup you *think* will work . . . does it?

```
.IF &last& < M
.GO BOTTOM
.EL
.IF &last& > P
.GO BOTTOM
.EI last name starts with Q or above
.EI last name starts with L or below
```

It turns out that this setup won't work the way you want it to. Why not? The first part is okay. WordStar evaluates whether the last name starts with a letter less than *M,* in other words, *A* through *L.* If such is the case, it goes to the bottom of the file and starts a new record. Then there's the **.EL** line, which brings up the second **.IF** condition.

It's this second if condition that's wrong. If the last name is greater than *L,* WordStar checks if the last name is greater than *P.* However, this statement doesn't mean that the last name is in the range of *Q* through *Z. Au contraire!* WordStar evaluates any last name that begins with *P* and *continues to evaluate the rest of the name.* As it turns out, *any* last name that is longer than just *P* but includes *P* as the first letter will evaluate as "false." For instance, *Park* is greater than just *P,* because it has more letters. So, the correct setup has to evaluate if the name is greater than *Q. This* will work:

```
.IF &last& < M
.GO BOTTOM
.EL
.IF &last& > Q
.GO BOTTOM
.EI last name starts with Q or above
.EI last name starts with L or below
```

The moral? Keep in mind the length of constants when you're comparing them to variables, and the order of the letters in the constants. *Lane* is definitely less than *Morris* because the *L* is less than the *M.* However, *Morris* is greater than *M* because it has more letters. Sheesh!

Other Possibilities

Dear Reader: You haven't done any real work in a while! To illustrate other conditional printing commands and possibilities, you'll create another form letter mailing and data file. (If you're tired or bored, stop here and continue later.)

This time, create the data file first:

Press   **N** [open a nondocument]

Type	publish.dta
Press	**RETURN**
Type	y

because this is a new file.

This is a list of fictitious book publishers. Type the following entries *exactly* as you see them. Make sure you use correct upper and lowercase and that you include the comma field separators and quotation marks. In a moment you'll understand what role the first field plays.

```
Computer, MicroMicro Press, 1000 Westway, Bellevue, WA, 98005
Cook, "Blue, Brown & Co.", 32 Beacon Street, Boston, MA, 02107
Cook, Ballyhoo Books, 201 E. 51st Street, New York, NY, 10022
Computer, The Merit-Bobby Co., 625 Third Avenue, New York, NY, 10017
```

When you're finished,

Press	^KD or **F10**

to save the file and return to the Opening menu.

Now for the form letter file:

Press	**D** [open a document]
Type	proposal
Press	**RETURN**
Type	y

because this is a new file.

The correspondent is a writer with two basic interests: food and word processing. (Sound familiar?) He has proposals for two new books, and he wants to find publishers for them. To save time, he'll use conditional commands to print different letters depending on whether he's writing to a computer book company or a cookbook company. He can set up everything in *one* file! Take a look at the letter before you type it.

```
.MT 10
.MB 6
.OP
.PO 12
.RM 60
.LS 1
.OJ OFF
```

```
.DF publish.dta
.RV department, publisher, street, city, state, zip
.RR--!-----------------------------!---------------------R
                              100 Cheyenne Highway
                              Dead Pine, WY  82910
                              &@&



Acquisitions Editor
&department& Books
&publisher&
&street&
&city&, &state&  &zip/o&


To the Editor:

.IF &department& = Cook
     I am planning a trip to &city& soon and would like to
discuss with you my latest book idea: "Pasta Without Pain."
Enclosed please find a written proposal for this project.
.EL
     I am planning a trip to &city& soon and would like to
discuss with you my latest book idea: "What to Do About
WordStar."  Enclosed please find a written proposal for this
project.
.EI

     I shall call you after I arrive in &city&, but please
don't hesitate to contact me in the interim regarding this
project.  Thank you.

                              Yours truly,



                              Salvatore P. Tettrazzini

encl.
.PA
```

Here, Mr. Tettrazzini has created two different paragraphs, one for computer books and one for cookbooks. Depending on the contents of the **&department&** field, which also prints in the interior address, WordStar inserts the correct paragraph.

Notice the placement of the conditional commands and the *blank line* separating the first paragraph from the second. Always make sure the constant text, including spaces and blank lines, is correct in your files.

Type the letter and run a spelling check. When you're finished,

Press   **^KD** or **F10**

to save the file and return to the Opening menu.

Try merge printing PROPOSAL using the PRVIEW printer driver to see how the different letters come out.

Conditional Customizing

There's virtually no limit to the ways you can *customize* your merge printing tasks with conditional commands. In later chapters you'll see how to set up rather complicated document assembly procedures. To whet your appetite, take a look at what else Mr. Tettrazzini has done.

Because he used to live in New York, Mr. Tettrazzini has succumbed to a moment of temporary nostalgia. He's inserted the following passage directly above the last paragraph, but below the blank line.

```
.IF &city& = New York
    It's been a long time since I visited my old stomping
grounds in the Big Apple.  I look forward to "giving my
regards to Broadway" again.

.EI
```

Because this paragraph doesn't print for each letter, Mr. Tettrazzini has included the blank line between it and the last paragraph *within* the conditional structure. There's no blank line after the **.EI** command. You've probably realized that this section is a boilerplate, and as with all boilerplates you have to be careful about the formatting.

Go ahead, insert this section in the PROPOSAL file, then merge print the file, again using the PRVIEW printer driver.

Dear Reader: Mr. Tettrazzini and I can't resist just *one* more example! Take a look at it first:

```
.IF &city& = New York
    It's been a long time since I visited my old stomping
grounds in the Big Apple.  I look forward to "giving my
regards to Broadway" again.
```

This is a blank line

```
.EL
.IF &city& = Boston
     Ah, Boston!  Durgin Park, Filene's Basement, the MTA!
I hope my favorite city hasn't changed too much over the
years.  I look forward to my visit.


.EI city is Boston
.EI city is New York
```

This time, there's an **.EL** line that contains *its own* nested **.IF** condition. Notice the placement of the two **.EI** commands and the blank lines. WordStar first checks if the **&city&** variable contains *New York* and adds a paragraph. If not ("else"), it checks if the variable contains *Boston* and prints a different paragraph. If neither condition is true, it just finishes the letter.

Type the extra section, check it for accuracy, then save the file with ^KD (**F10**). Merge print it to see the results, if you wish.

Dealing with Potential Input Errors

Using conditional commands, you can reduce the possibility of input errors by setting up *error traps* in certain situations. Unlike sand traps, the bugbears of all golfers, error traps are good for you! At least they avoid a potential waste of paper.

Empty Variables, Part 1

As an example, consider the second envelope setup, EX, that I showed you in the previous chapter. WordStar requests a file containing the recipient's name and address, then uses the **.FI** command to insert this file during merge printing. Suppose you press RETURN without entering a file name? WordStar would still print the envelope, but without any name and address!

You can provide an error-trapping routine to prevent this. You would insert these commands directly *below* the .AV "What is the file name? ", file line:

```
.IF &file& =
.CS You didn't supply a file name!
.AV "Press RETURN to try again", x
.CS
.GO TOP
.EI
```

The **.IF** line tests for an *empty* variable. If you press RETURN without supplying a file name, the variable **&file&** is empty and the condition evaluates as true. WordStar clears the screen, displays an error message, and waits for you to read the message and press RETURN. It then clears the message again. The **.GO TOP** command returns to the beginning of the file to let you try again.

Now for another nifty error trap. Remember the *first* envelope file, E? It just requests the name and address information from the keyboard. Suppose if you don't type a file name when you merge print EX, you want WordStar to request the information from the keyboard instead. Here's a way to set this up in the EX file, again directly below the **.AV** line. Delete the previous example and insert these lines instead:

```
.IF &file& =
.CS You didn't supply a file name, so enter
.DM the information from the keyboard ...
.DM
.FI E
.GO BOTTOM
.EI
```

This time, if the **&file&** variable is empty, WordStar presents a different message. The second **.DM** line just displays a blank line on the screen. WordStar inserts the E file, and all the **.AV** commands in that file start working to request the name and address information. After the E file prints the envelope, WordStar *returns* to the "calling" file, EX. You now *don't* want to continue—because if you did WordStar would print a second, blank envelope with a return address—so you've included a **.GO BOTTOM** command that instructs WordStar to stop. Try it!

As Chapter 16 pointed out, a file containing **.FI** lines is a command or master file. After performing each **.FI** command, WordStar returns to the next line in the command file and generally evaluates the dot commands in their turn until it reaches the end of the file. With the **.GO TOP** or **.GO BOTTOM** command, you can change this order of evaluation.

Empty Variables, Part 2

You now know one way to deal with empty variables, but there's another. Remember that in Chapter 20 I taught you how to ensure that WordStar doesn't print a blank space if there's no title variable in the BURBANK.1 file? Using conditional commands is easier than including the spaces in the data file.

Press   **D** [open a document]

Type   **burbank.1**

Press   **RETURN**

You could set up the interior address like this:

```
.IF &title&
&title& &first& &last&
.EL
&first& &last&
.EI
&street/o&
&city&, &state&  &zip&
```

The **.IF &title&** line tests for the *existence of something* in the variable **&title&**. That is, it evaluates whether the variable is not zero and not blank. If so, then the **.IF** statement evaluates as true.

Unfortunately, WordStar can't do much more testing than just if the field contains some text, so assume that you've typed the entries correctly. If there *is* a title entry, then WordStar prints it. If not, it prints just the first and last names. The above setup is the same as this one:

```
.IF &title& =
&first& &last&
.EL
&title& &first& &last&
.EI
&street/o&
&city&, &state&  &zip&
```

Here, you're performing the conditional test the other way around. WordStar evaluates whether the **&title&** field is empty, in which case it prints just the name. Otherwise (else), it prints all three fields. Examples in later chapters illustrate other error-trapping procedures.

Drafts and Finals Again

Suppose you own a dot-matrix printer that can print in both draft mode and near letter quality mode. You're constantly switching between the two by inserting **.LQ OFF** and **.LQ ON** commands in your files. Why not have WordStar do this for you? By the way, even if you don't own a dot-matrix printer, try this example anyway—it's good practice!

Press   **D** [open a document]

Type   draft

Press   **RETURN**

Type   y

because this is a new file.

The following file requests whether you want to print in draft mode or near letter quality mode. Using conditional statements, it then determines what command to issue *before* it "inserts"—that is, prints—the file. It even determines whether you're printing or merge printing! **Note:** For this file to work correctly, remove any **.LQ** commands in your other files. I've included nonprinting comment lines to break up the commands visually so you can understand them more easily.

```
.AV "What file do you want to print? ", filename
.AV "Is this a merge printing file (type a lowercase y or n)? ", merge
.AV "Type a lowercase d for draft, or f for final -> ", draft
..
.IF &draft& =
.CS
.GO TOP
.EL
.IF &draft& = d
.LQ OFF
.EL
.LQ ON
.EI you typed d
.EI you pressed RETURN

..
.IF &merge& =
.CS
.GO TOP
.EL
.IF &merge& = y
.PF DIS
.EL
.PF OFF
.EI if you typed y
.EI you press RETURN

..
.IF &merge& = y
.DM You're merge printing &filename&
.EL
.DM You're printing &filename&
.EI
.IF &draft& = d
```

```
.DM in draft mode.
.EL
.DM in near letter quality mode.
.EI
..
.FI &filename&
```

After you answer the three questions, the file first checks if you just pressed RETURN in response to the third question. If you did, WordStar clears the screen and starts over. Otherwise, the **.EL** line checks if you typed **d** and sets the **.LQ** command accordingly.

Because the file you're printing may be a standard file or a merge printing setup, the next conditional commands check whether you typed **y** or **n** in response to the second question. The commands also check if you pressed RETURN. If the file is a merge file, WordStar sets **.PF DIS**; otherwise, it sets **.PF OFF**. I put the conditional statements in this way to remind you that you can check the variables in any order.

The third set of conditional commands merely displays the appropriate message on the screen depending on whether you're printing or merge printing in either draft or near letter quality mode. The last command inserts the file you want to print or merge print.

After typing the file and saving it with ^**KD** (**F10**), merge print it with any short file to see how it works.

Asking for the Number of Repetitions

Suppose you want to send a stock reply letter, such as BURBANK.STK, to several people. Of course, you could supply a amount after the Number of copies? print option. Here's another way to go. Set up a generic command file that requests both the number of copies *and* the particular stock letter you want to send. Then learn why your file doesn't work!

Press   **D** [open a document]

Type   stock.1

Press   **RETURN**

Type   y

because this is a new file.

Just look at the example below, but don't type it. Everything looks straightforward, doesn't it?

```
.AV "What stock reply letter do you want to send?: ", file
.AV "How many copies do you want to print?: ", number
.CS
.RP &number&
.FI &file&
```

It turns out, however, that this setup doesn't work. The repeat printing command, **.RP**, repeats *all* the commands in the *current* file. That means that after WordStar prints one stock letter, it again requests a file name and number of repetitions. A mess indeed. If you don't believe me, try it!

If you *do* believe me—and I hope you do—this is how you would set up a generic request file. You need *two* files. The first, STOCK.1, contains these lines:

```
.AV "What stock reply letter do you want to send?: ", file
.AV "How many copies do you want to print?: ", number
.FI stock.2
```

This file just requests the information from the keyboard. It then calls the second file, STOCK.2. Make sure there's a hard return after the third line!

Type the commands and save the file with ^**KD** (**F10**). Then:

Press   **D** [open a document]

Type   stock.2

Press   **RETURN**

Type   y

because this is a new file.

The second part of the generic setup contains these commands:

```
.IF &number& #> 0
.RP &number&
.CS
.FI &file&
.EI
```

I've stuck in an error trap just for good measure. If you don't type a number greater than zero—that is, if you press RETURN in answer to the "How many copies do you want to print?" prompt—nothing happens. WordStar returns to the calling file, STOCK.1. Because there are no more commands in STOCK.1, WordStar ends the operation altogether.

If you *did* type a valid number, then WordStar sets up the repeat printing, clears the screen before each copy, and inserts the stock reply letter file. Because the letter file contains ask for variables, WordStar requests the variables for each copy.

To see how far you've come, merge print the DRAFT file. Supply STOCK.1 as the file you want to print, and answer y to the merge printing question. You've just have one file call another, which in turn calls a third file!

Other examples will show you that you may have to set up a "double command file" like this one to handle certain merge printing tasks. These last two examples were a tie-in to *automated* document assembly projects, the topic of the next chapter.

Automated Document Assembly

In this chapter you will learn the following new commands:

File Command

   .SV   Define the data or format for a variable ("set variable")

Other Points

   /   Assign a format to a variable

Variable String
Formatting Symbols
        C   Centered format
        L   Left-justified format
        R   Right-justified format

If you've been studying the merge printing chapters in their turn—and I hope you have—you now know all the basic concepts and features. You've learned what variables are, how to create shell files and data files, how to ask for information from the keyboard, and the conditional printing commands. With these features under your belt, you can investigate ways to automate your document assembly applications.

Recall that Chapter 16 introduced you to manual document assembly techniques. They're useful for many tasks, but you'll discover that merge printing commands can often save you even more time and effort. Once you get the setup right, WordStar does most of the work for you! This chapter shows you just a few illustrations of automated document assembly. Of special importance is the discussion of *variable formatting* later in the chapter, because the examples at the end of the chapter and in the next rely heavily on this powerful feature.

DO WARM-UP

Menu Madness

As editor-in-chief of *Recipes "R" Us* magazine, Simone Fourchette receives countless contributions from her readers. Some of them are good; some not so good! Often a recipe is incomplete or illegible. Using merge printing commands, Ms. Fourchette has created a stock reply letter that handles *all* these situations and more.

When she was thinking over how to deal with all the many possibilities, Ms. Fourchette realized that each letter is the same except for one paragraph. There's always a standard opening section containing the magazine's address, the interior address, salutation, and a general "thank you for the submission" paragraph. Similarly, there's the standard closing section. It is the *middle section* that changes depending on the type of response she wants to send.

So, Ms. Fourchette used conditional printing commands to determine what text to print for that middle section. All she does is select the type of letter she wants to send from a *menu* of possibilities. Whenever she needs a letter, she merge prints the file, supplies the necessary information from the keyboard, and takes a short coffee break while WordStar does the rest.

Press	**D** [open a document]
Type	`reply`
Press	**RETURN**
Type	`y`

because this is a new file.

The entire setup is in this one file. Later I'll show you another way to accomplish the same thing. Do you understand what all the dot commands do?

```
.. REPLY - stock reply letter for recipe submission
.CS What type of letter do you want to send?
.DM
.DM
.DM             1 - Acceptance of recipe as is
.DM             2 - Acceptance of recipe with revisions
.DM             3 - Rejection of recipe
.DM             4 - Incomplete recipe
.DM             5 - Illegible recipe
```

```
.DM
.DM Type your choice and press RETURN
.DM or press ^U to cancel
.DM
.AV "Your choice please: ", choice
..
.IF &choice& #=
.GO TOP
.EI no choice
..
.IF &choice& #> 5
.GO TOP
.EI choice is too high
..
.CS
.AV "Title (Mr., Ms., etc.):    ", honorific
.AV "First name (and initial): ", first_name
.AV "Last name:                ", last_name
.AV "Street 1 (RETURN if none): ", street1
.AV "Street 2 (RETURN if none): ", street2
.AV "City:                     ", city
.AV "State:                    ", state
.AV "Zip code:                 ", zipcode
.AV "Date of submission:       ", letter_date
.AV "Name of recipe:           ", recipe
..
.IF &choice& #< 3
.AV "Issue date (month & year): ", issue_date
.EI choice is 1 or 2
..
.MT 15
.MB 6
.OP
.PO 12 [or whatever setting you need]
.RM 60
.OJ OFF
.LS 1
.UL ON
.RR--!--------------------------!----------------------R
                          Recipes "R" Us
                          1776 Cahuenga Boulevard
                          Hollywood, CA  90028
                          &@&


&honorific& &first_name& &last_name&
&street1/o&
```

503

```
&street2/o&
&city&, &state&  &zipcode&

Dear &honorific& &last_name&:

     We have received your letter dated &letter_date&.
Thank you very much for submitting the following recipe for
our consideration: &recipe&.

.IF &choice& #= 1
     We are pleased to inform you that your recipe will
appear in our &issue_date& issue.  A copy of that issue will
be sent to you as soon as possible after printing.
..
.EI
.IF &choice& #= 2
.AV "Enter the cut-off date:    ", cutoff
     We are accepting your recipe for publication in our
&issue_date& issue.  However, we have made a few editorial
changes.  Please review the attached page and notify us by
&cutoff&, whether the changes are acceptable.
.EI
..
.IF &choice& #= 3
     After careful review of your entry by our Reviewing
Committee, we are sorry to inform you that your recipe does
not meet our present needs.  Please feel free to submit
other recipes at any time.
.EI
..
.IF &choice& #= 4
     Unfortunately, our Reviewing Committee cannot read your
instructions, because they were not presented clearly.  Would you
please resubmit your recipe in either a printed or a typewritten
form?  By the way, each instruction should begin on a new line.
.EI
..
.IF &choice& #= 5
     Our Reviewing Committee has attempted on several
occasions to create this recipe, but has found it inedible
each time.  Perhaps you have left out some of the steps or
ingredients?  Please check your original recipe and submit a
corrected version as soon as possible.
.EI

     Thank you for your interest in our magazine.  Best
wishes, and happy cooking!
```

```
                        Sincerely,



                        Simone Fourchette
                        Editor-in-Chief

.IF &choice& #= 2
encl.
.EI
```

Follow along with me as I explain the commands, step-by-step. Note that I've included a lot of nonprinting dot commands (..) to separate the sections visually and thus make them easier to read and understand.

The **.CS** and **.DM** lines at the beginning of the file clear the screen and display a message and the menu items. Notice the other help that I've provided. After the user types a number, WordStar evaluates whether the choice is nothing (**.IF &choice& #**=), or whether it's greater than 5 (**.IF &choice& #**> **5**). In either of these cases, WordStar "loops back" (**.GO TOP**) and presents the menu again. Because the choice is a number, I've included the # symbol in the condition.

If the choice is between 1 and 5, WordStar then clears the screen and requests the recipient's information from the keyboard. The line **.IF &choice& #**< **3** only applies to choices 1 or 2, because only those choices require an issue date. Then standard dot commands set up the page formatting.

The opening of the letter is the same for each recipient. Depending on the type of letter, however, the second paragraph differs. Notice the blank line between the first paragraph of the letter and whatever is the second paragraph. A series of **.IF** lines handle the second paragraph.

If the choice is 2, WordStar has to request one more variable from the keyboard, a cutoff date. In addition, because there's an enclosed revised recipe, at the end of a letter WordStar prints the standard **encl.** for this choice only. Once again, there's a blank line between the second paragraph and the closing.

The menu is *modular*. That is, you could easily add several more menu choices with very little adjustment to the rest of the file. You may also want to press ^**OH** to turn hyphenation on and realign the file to see if you can split any long words between two lines. When you're finished typing the example,

Press   ^**KD** or **F10**

to save the file and return to the Opening menu.

When you merge print the file, WordStar flashes the Print Wait message, because printing is in the background. Press **M** or **P** to display the Printing menu. This is what you see:

```
What type of letter do you want to send?

        1 - Acceptance of recipe as is
        2 - Acceptance of recipe with revisions
        3 - Rejection of recipe
        4 - Incomplete recipe
        5 - Illegible recipe

Type your choice and press RETURN
or press ^U to cancel

Your choice please:
```

Suppose you type 2. Below is an example of what WordStar requests and what you might enter:

```
Title (Mr., Ms., etc.):     Mrs.
First name (and initial):   Josepha
Last name:                  Ramos
Street 1 (RETURN if none):  105 Albany Road
Street 2 (RETURN if none):  Apartment 2B
City:                       Staten Island
State:                      NY
Zip code:                   10299
Date of submission:         May 8, 1987
Name of recipe:             Puerto Rican Pasteles
Issue date (month & year):  November 1987
Enter the cut-off date:     August 31, 1987
```

Try merge printing the file, using the PRVIEW printer driver. Experiment with each of the possible choices.

An Alternative Approach Using Boilerplates

You could have set up the REPLY letter using separate boilerplate files. For example, each "second" paragraph is in a different boilerplate. Then you'd just include a **.FI** line with the name of the file for each different choice. For example, if the text for choice 1 were in a file called ACCEPT, the commands would read:

```
.IF &choice& #= 1
.FI accept
.EI
```

I like my way better, because I can see at a glance exactly what paragraph each choice will print.

A Generic Print Formatter

The next example is an all-purpose file that requests many different format settings at the time of merge printing. You supply the name of the file you want to print and each format setting. WordStar sets up the format and prints the file at the same time.

Note: For this file to work properly, there should be *no* format settings in the file you want to print, because they would override the settings you're supplying from the keyboard. You can enhance or customize this file for your particular needs. For instance, perhaps all you want to do is determine the line spacing from the keyboard, or you want to include a question about draft or near letter quality mode à la the example in the last chapter. Just use the commands you need.

```
.AV "  Name of file to print? ", filename
.DM
.DM Type a valid integer and press RETURN --
.DM
.AV "Lines per vertical inch? ", height
.AV "            Page Length? ", page
.AV "             Top margin? ", top
.AV "          Bottom margin? ", bottom
.AV "            Page Offset? ", offset
.AV "            Left margin? ", left
.AV "           Right margin? ", right
.AV "           Line spacing? ", spacing
.DM
.DM Type a lowercase y or n and press RETURN --
.DM
.AV "     Page numbers (y/n)? ", pages
.AV " Justification on (y/n)? ", just
.AV " Underline spaces (y/n)? ", under

..
.IF &filename& =
.GO TOP
.EI

..
.CS Printing &filename&
.PF ON

..
.IF &height&
.LH &height&
```

```
.EI
..
.IF &page&
.PL &page&
.EI
..
.IF &top&
.MT &top&
.EI
..
.IF &bottom&
.MB &bottom&
.EI
..
.IF &offset&
.PO &offset&
.EI
..
.IF &left&
.LM &left&
.EI
..
.IF &right&
.RM &right&
.EI
..
.IF &spacing&
.LS &spacing&
.EI
..
.IF &pages& = n
.OP
.EI
..
.IF &just& = n
.OJ OFF
.EL
.OJ ON
.EI
..
.IF &under& = y
.UL ON
.EL
.UL OFF
.EI
..
.FI &filename&
```

If you don't supply a setting, that is, if you press RETURN alone in answer to a prompt, WordStar uses whatever is your particular default setting. The only exceptions are the three "yes/no" answers: WordStar uses an **.EL** line to set them one way or the other. The conditional commands handle this by checking whether there's an entry in each variable. Notice that you must include the **.PF ON** command for this file to work properly.

Tip: You could use **.EL** lines to determine the default format setting if the variable is blank. For example:

```
.IF &left&
.LM &left&
.EL
.LM 1
.EI
```

Here, WordStar sets the left margin at column 1 if you don't enter a new value.

Introducing the Set Variable Command

The set variable command, **.SV**, has a dual personality. (Old timers should read the next section to learn about the new features of this command.) With the **.SV** command you can insert the values of variables once in a file—usually at the beginning. Whenever WordStar comes to the variable name, it substitutes the value defined by the **.SV** line. You'll see how in a moment.

The **.SV** command can also define the *format* of a variable within the file. Because this is a very powerful—and very complicated—feature, I plan to spend a lot of time on it in the rest of this chapter and in the next. For example, you'd use the **.SV** command to set up those multiple mailing labels that I told you about in Chapter 20. First things first, however: learn the basic use of **.SV**.

Saving the Values of Variables in a File

A typical application of the **.SV** command is to define and save the values of variables in contracts or other documents where the variables appear many times. For your example you'll work with a school report.

Press   **D** [open a document]

Type   `report.1`

Press   **RETURN**

Type   y

because this is a new file.

Take a look at the entire report before you type it.

```
.MT 8
.MB 8
.OP
.LS 1
.LM 1
.RM 65
.OJ ON
.SV child, Stuart
.SV pronoun, he
.SV teacher, Ms. Jenkins
.SV year, 1988
              Hidden Hills Consolidated School District
                    STUDENT'S SEMIANNUAL REPORT
                        December &year&


        We  are  happy to inform you that the  performance  of  your
    child, &child&, during the first half of the current school  year
    has been exemplary.   The  child's  teacher, &teacher&,  finds
    &child& to be an excellent student.

        &child&  is  well-liked  by the rest of the  class  and  has
    proven  remarkably attentive to the scholarly pursuits which  are
    the  most  important part of school life.  &teacher& assures  us
    that &child& has remarkable ability and will probably be rich and
    famous by the time &pronoun& is thirty.

        You should be proud of &child& -- we are!  Best wishes.
```

By setting the variables at the top of the file, you can quickly see exactly
what variables the file contains and what their current values are. Every time
WordStar sees a variable, it substitutes its assigned value and realigns the
paragraph.

When you set variables, don't enclose them in ampersands on the **.SV**
lines. You can separate the variable name—the first item—with its value—the
second item—either with a comma or an equals sign. So the **.SV** lines above
could read:

```
.SV child = Stuart
.SV pronoun = he
```

```
.SV teacher = Ms. Jenkins
.SV year, 1988
```

WordStar disregards leading or trailing spaces unless you enclose the entire value in quotation marks. If you had typed .SV child = " Stuart" WordStar would include the leading space in the value.

Tip: When you type the file, use a *binding space* (^PO) between *Ms.* and *Jenkins* so that the print time reformatter doesn't break up her name over two lines. It would look like this on the screen: Ms.^OJenkins.

Later, to merge print this file for another student, merely substitute the correct values, such as:

```
.SV child, Tiffany
.SV pronoun, she
.SV teacher, Mr.^OChipps
```

When you're finished typing the example,

Press   **^KD or F10**

to save the file and return to the Opening menu.

Merge print the file to see the results. Because there are variables in the text, the print time reformatter is in discretionary mode and will realign the text as necessary.

As an astute reader you've probably realized that you could just as easily use **.AV** commands to request the variables from the keyboard. The only difference is that then you aren't saving the values with the file. Not a big deal, to be sure, but when you're editing and merge printing the file several times, it makes more sense to save the variables than to enter them each time you want another printout.

Recursion in Merge Printing

You can also use the set variable command in a *recursive* merge printing application. Wha? It's not as complicated as it sounds. Take a look at this small data file called NAMES.DTA (you don't have to type it!):

```
John Q. Public, 55 Main Street, "West City, PA  19000", &bad&
Jane Doe, 111 Commercial Avenue, "Omaha, NE 43211", &good&
Frank R. Smith, Route 10, "Joplin, MS  40201", &good&
Mary Jane Jones, 3 Maple Lane, "Portland, ME  01817", &bad&
```

As strange as it may seem, you can include variables in a data file! That's what **&good&** and **&bad&** are. Remember to enclose the variable names in ampersands. Now look at a very short controlling file that works with NAMES.DTA:

```
.SV good, One Week
.SV bad, Two Weeks
.DF names.dta
.RV name, street, cityline, prize
.OP
&name&
&street&
&cityline&

Dear Friend:

    I am pleased to inform you that you are a winner in our
recent "Go for Burbank" contest.  Your prize is &prize& in
Beautiful Downtown Burbank.

                    Best wishes, etc.
    .PA
```

Recursion in merge printing means that WordStar has to substitute variables at least *twice* before doing anything else. In the controlling file the **.SV** commands define what the **good** and **bad** variables contain. Then the **.DF** and **.RV** lines set up the data file and the order and names of the variables as usual.

During merge printing, when WordStar reads the variables from the NAMES.DTA, it "realizes" that the fourth variable—called **prize**—could be one of two other variables, **&good&** or **&bad&**! So, it substitutes either **&good&** or **&bad&** for **&prize&** in the text. That's round one.

Because it's substituted one set of variables for another, WordStar now has to determine what the actual values of **&good&** and **&bad&** are. So, it checks the controlling file's **.SV** lines and makes another substitution, this time with the correct values. After this recursive double-take, as it were, it can finish printing the text (the idea for which, as you may know, came from W. C. Fields).

Defining Variable Formats

You've strayed a little from the main topic of this chapter: automated document assembly. Now learn how the **.SV** command fits into the discussion. Where the **.SV** command really shines is in its ability to *define and save a format* for a variable so that you can control exactly how your merged printout will appear. You can also use the command to *assign the value of one variable to another,* a very powerful tool.

Because the print time reformatter may change the lines, and because of the different lengths of variable values, being able to govern the variable formatting is essential to your work with automated document assembly. For example, WordStar can't normally recenter a variable depending on its length, but you can get WordStar to do this with the **.SV** command.

Note: Take your time studying this section, because it's complicated! What's more, it forms the foundation for all the examples in this and the next chapter.

The Basics of Variable Formatting

Before getting into the nitty-gritty of variable formatting, learn how to define a variable's formatting requirements with the **.SV** command. In brief, there are three steps to the process:

1. Decide the *name or number* of the format.
2. Set up the format as a *template.*
3. Assign the format to a defined variable.

I'll explain each step in detail. Then I'll discuss exactly what's going on during variable formatting. Finally, you'll work with some practical examples.

The Format Name. You can use any *one digit or letter* as the format name, but *don't* use the letter *O.* You'll see why in a moment. Notice that unlike standard variable names, which can be up to 39 characters long, variable format names must be one character in length only. Both *A* and *2* are "legal," but *F2* is not. **Caution:** WordStar disregards case, so *A* and *a* are the same. Don't assign two different formats to *A* and *a.*

The Format Template. The format template tells WordStar (1) the total length of the variable, and (2) its format. In this chapter I'll concentrate on *string* formats. In the next chapter you'll take a look at *number* formats, which are a bit more complicated.

String formats can be left-justified, centered, or right-justified. You use the symbols **L**, **C**, and **R**, respectively, for these formats. (You can also type **l**, **c**, and **r**, but for the purposes of clarity I'll stick to uppercase.) Designate the length of the variable by filling the template with the formatting symbol. That is, for *each* character position in the variable you supply an **L, C,** or **R.** However, only the *first* letter in the template tells WordStar the formatting: left-justified, centered, or right-justified.

Caution: For the sake of your sanity at this point, always use the *same* formatting symbol in the entire format. In a moment you'll see why.

Some Examples. Putting all you've learned so far together, you assign a variable name and template on the same **.SV** line. For example,

```
.SV C = CCCCCCCCCCCCCCCCCCCC
```

This line assigns the format name **C** to the format, determines that the format is a centered string, and sets its maximum length to 20 characters. You can also separate the format name from the template with a comma:

```
.SV C, CCCCCCCCCCCCCCCCCCCC
```

Suppose you want to set up a left-justified format called **1** that is 10 characters long. Here it is:

```
.SV 1 = LLLLLLLLLL
```

You can include leading or trailing spaces in a left-justified or right-justified format, a process known as *masking,* but I don't recommend it until you're completely comfortable with variable formatting. Stick to simple things for a while! To include spaces, you enclose the entire format in quotation marks:

```
.SV X, "  LLLLL"
```

Here, **X** will always print with two leading spaces. Because WordStar determines the format from the *first* L, C, or R that it sees, if you type one of these letters—on any other character—in the *middle* of a left-justified or right-justified format, WordStar prints it literally. Take this format as an example:

```
.SV X = LLCL
```

If the variable assigned to this format contained the word *TYPE,* then WordStar would print *TYCE.* Don't use masking unless you know what you're doing!

Assigning the Format to a Variable. Once you've defined a format, you assign it to a defined variable by appending a slash (/) and the format name to the end of the variable *within the ampersands.* Take a look at these lines:

```
.RM 40
.DF test.dta
```

```
.RV name, street, city-state-zip
.SV A = CCCCCCCCCCCCCCCCCCCCCCCCCCCCCCCCCCCCCCCC
&name/a&
&street/a&
&city-state-zip/a&

To &name&:
```

The format **A** is a centered string that's 40 characters long, the same length as the line (**.RM 40**). You must define the format *before* you assign it to a variable, just as you must define variables before you can use them. WordStar will center the first three lines when it merge prints this example, but it *won't* center the **&name&** variable on the last line. That way, you can use a format only when you want to.

So, append the / and variable name *whenever you want the variable to print with the format* in the file. If you don't add the format to the variable, WordStar doesn't use the format, even if you've already assigned the format to the variable before.

What's Going On Here?

As you know, in all merge operations WordStar uses a process of *substitution* to replace a defined variable with a value. The definition of a variable can be in one of three places, and WordStar looks for the contents of the variable accordingly:

- If you've defined a variable in an **.RV** command, WordStar looks for the variable in the data file that you list after the **.DF** line.
- If you've defined the variable in an **.AV** line, WordStar requests the variable from the keyboard.
- If you've defined the variable in an **.SV** line, WordStar checks that line.

Normally, WordStar then substitutes the value of the variable wherever it sees the variable name enclosed in ampersands throughout the file. If, however, you assign a format to a variable, WordStar substitutes the format template *before* the value. This has important and far-reaching implications for how your printouts will appear, so listen up!

When it sees a variable in the file and the variable has an assigned format, WordStar substitutes the format template starting at the column position of the *left* ampersand sign. *Then* it substitutes the contents of the variable within the format template.

If the template format is left-justified, WordStar inserts the contents of the variable at the left side of the template. Then it pads the rest of the template with spaces if the contents of the variable don't entirely fill in the template. If the format calls for centering, WordStar inserts the contents of the variable into the center of the template, with extra spaces on each side. If the format is right-justified, WordStar inserts the contents of the variable at the right end of the template and pads the left side with spaces.

Of course, the number of spaces that WordStar uses to pad the template depends on the length of the template and the length of the actual contents. For example, Figure 23–1 shows a template that's 30 characters long and a variable that's 22 characters long. There are eight spaces that WordStar has to insert into the template depending on the format.

What does this mean in realistic terms? Take a look at the following example:

```
.RM 65
.DF test.dta
.RV name, street, city-state-zip
.SV A = CCCCCCCCCCCCCCCCCCCCCCCCCCCCCCCCCCCCCCCC
        &name/a&
        &street/a&
        &city-state-zip/a&

        To &name&:
```

Here, the **A** format is a centered string that's 40 characters long, as in the previous example, but this time the line length is 65 characters. When WordStar "sees" the **&name/a&** variable, which begins at column 6, it inserts the format template starting at this column. So the format template extends from column 6 to column 46, and WordStar centers the contents of the variable *within that space*. The result: WordStar doesn't center the variables to the entire line length!

Now look at this one:

```
.RM 65
.AV name
.AV street
.AV cityline
.SV X, RRRRRRRRRRRRRRRRRRRRRRRRRRRRRR
                &name/x&
                &street/x&
                &cityline/x&
```

In this example, the right-justified **X** format is 30 characters in length. When WordStar sees the **&name/x&** variable at column 26, it inserts the format. Because 26 + 30 = 56, WordStar will right-justify the variables at column 56.

WordStar substitutes the variable format template before it inserts the actual contents of the variable. The variable **&example&** contains a string of 22 characters: THIS IS ONLY A TEST!!! The format template is 30 characters long.

If the format is left-justified:

```
.SV X = LLLLLLLLLLLLLLLLLLLLLLLLLLLLLL
&example/X&
```

WordStar inserts the format template at the position of the left ampersand and then inserts the contents of the variable at the left side of the template. WordStar "pads" the rest of the template with spaces:

```
THIS IS ONLY A TEST!!!
------------------------------
```

Contents with spaces at right end
Length of template

If the format is centered:

```
.SV X = CCCCCCCCCCCCCCCCCCCCCCCCCCCCCC
&example/X&
```

WordStar inserts the format template at the position of the left ampersand and then inserts the contents of the variable centered within the template. WordStar "pads" both sides of the template with spaces:

```
    THIS IS ONLY A TEST!!!
------------------------------
```

Contents with spaces at either end
Length of template

If the format is right-justified:

```
.SV X = RRRRRRRRRRRRRRRRRRRRRRRRRRRRRR
&example/X&
```

WordStar inserts the format template at the position of the left ampersand then inserts the contents of the variable flush right within the template. WordStar "pads" the left side of the template with spaces:

```
        THIS IS ONLY A TEST!!!
------------------------------
```

Contents with spaces at left end
Length of template

Figure 23–1   How Variable Formatting Works

This may all seem like a royal pain to you, because there are so many things to think about, but it has certain advantages. For instance, consider the setting up of columnar material. Because the format's length remains the same—no matter what the contents of the variable—WordStar will *line up* information nicely into columns. You'll soon see several examples of what I mean!

Some Simple Rules to Follow

There are just a few easy rules of thumb to follow when you set up variable formatting. The first rule of thumb is: *for left-justified formats, set up the length of the format to accommodate the largest possible value in the variable.* Otherwise, WordStar will cut off (truncate) the characters that don't fit. For example, if you define a left-justified format that's 30 characters long and one of the variables contains 40 characters, WordStar result print the first 30 characters only and drop the last 10.

The second rule of thumb is: *for centered or right-justified formats, when you're in doubt use a format length that's the same as the line length.* That way, you can keep the variable names at the left margin and WordStar will still center or right justify the contents according to the line length.

The third rule of thumb is: *if the variables are on separate lines, keep them at the left margin whenever possible.* This one works with rule number two! Of course, if the variables are within a paragraph, this rule doesn't apply.

The fourth and final rule is one that you should have ingrained on your soul a long time ago: *test and test again until you get it right!* Then sit back and relax.

A Conflict!

Don't be confused by the way WordStar uses the slash for both formatting and omitting empty fields—the **/O** operator. Technically, the **/O** is not a format: it always omits blank lines. What happens, then, when you're using a format and you want to suppress empty fields, too? Use conditional statements! Take a look at a revised version of the first example:

```
.RM 40
.DF test.dta
.RV name, street, city-state-zip
.SV A = CCCCCCCCCCCCCCCCCCCCCCCCCCCCCCCCCCCCCCCC
&name/a&
.IF &street&
&street/a&
.EI
&city-state-zip/a&

To &name&:
```

The **.IF &street&** command determines whether there's a value in the **&street&** field. If so, WordStar prints the street using the designated format. If not, it just goes on to the city line. Using conditional commands is the *only* way to rule out empty variables when you're working with variable formatting.

Some Practical Examples of Variable Formatting

You may not have a "handle" on variable formatting yet, so perhaps a few examples might help clarify how to work with this powerful WordStar feature. Guess what, Dear Reader: At the end of this section you're *finally* going to learn the right way to print multiple columns of mailing labels! But first . . .

A "Generic" Contract

You'll begin with the setup for a generic contract between two parties.

Press	**D** [open a document]
Type	contract.7
Press	**RETURN**
Type	y

because this is a new file.

The file illustrates a couple of interesting ways to use variable formatting. Take a look at it before you start typing.

```
.AV "Who is the party of the first part? ", party1
.AV "Who is the party of the second part? ", party2
.AV "What is the day of the month (e.g., 1st, 2nd)? ", day
.AV "What is the month spelled in full? ", month
.AV "What is the year? ", year
..
.. The following format contains 65 characters
.SV C, CCCCCCCCCCCCCCCCCCCCCCCCCCCCCCCCCCCCCCCCCCCCCCCCCCCCCCCCCCCCCCCCCCCCC
.SV firstpart = The Party of the First Part - &party1&
.SV secondpart = The Party of the Second Part - &party2&
.SV footer = &party1& and &party2&
..
.MT 10
.MB 10
.FM 4
.F1                       Agreement between:
.F2 &footer/C&
.F3                              Page #
.LM 1
.RM 65
.OJ OFF
.LS 2
```

```
                    A G R E E M E N T

                        between

&firstpart/C&

                          and

&secondpart/C&



     BE IT HEREBY KNOWN THAT the party of the first part,

&party1&, and the party of the second part, &party2&, in

consideration of the mutual interests outlined below, have duly

signed their names to this Agreement, dated the &day& day of

&month&, &year&.

     WHEREAS, &party1&, being presently a tenant of &party2&,

agrees to be retained in the employ of &party2& as Apartment

Manager for the property listed below.

     WHEREAS, &party2& agrees to provide &party1& a remuneration

for services rendered as Apartment Manager.  Such remuneration

shall include, but not be limited to, rent for a one-bedroom

apartment at the said property and a monthly stipend as outlined

below.
```

I don't think I have to explain the **.AV** lines: they just request the variable information from the keyboard. The first **.SV** line defines a string format, **C**, that's centered and 65 characters long. I've included a nonprinting comment line to remind you about the length.

The next three **.SV** lines are the real stars of this example. These lines define three new variables, **firstparty**, **secondparty**, and **footer**, that include *regular text* and the contents of previously defined variables! The point I'm getting to here is that you can define a variable that is a mixture of text and other variables. But why do you want to do this in the first place?

You're defining new variables like this because you want to center the entire string on the page. To center *both* the constant text and the variable "party" names, you must include both in a new variable.

The **footer** variable points out that you can include variable formatting in a header or footer line. Neat! Further down you'll see the setup for the three footer lines. For **.F1** and **.F3**, I centered the text *first* before inserting the command (don't forget the space after the command).

Notice that the length of the **C** format takes care of centering each variable on the page, so I've typed the variables at the left margin. However, you must center the constant text with the standard **^OC** (**SHIFT F2** or **ESC C**) command.

After typing the file, running a spelling check, and saving the file with **^KD** (**F10**), merge print the file using the PRVIEW driver. Here's a sample of the information you'd supply from the keyboard.

```
Who is the party of the first part? Gertrude Stein
Who is the party of the second part? Alice^OB. Toklas
What is the day of the month (e.g., 1st, 2nd)? 26th
What is the month spelled in full? April
What is the year? 1909
```

Again, I've used a binding space between *Alice* and *B.* so the print time reformatter doesn't break the lines incorrectly.

A "Simple" Columnar Report

The next example takes you back to Beautiful Downtown Burbank, or at least to the BURBANK.DTA data file. It illustrates a simple columnar report that turns out to be more complicated than you think. This is how you want your report to look when you merge print it (only the date will be different):

```
                                                    8 May 1987


                       Promotional Mailing #1

                          List of Recipients


Name                Street                  City

Dr. Jorge Rivera    1155 Soto Street        Los Angeles, CA  90033
Mr. J. Jacob Grump  P.O. Box 88             Victorville, CA  92433
Ms. Fernanda Hopkins                        Mountain Hole, CA  93777
```

```
Mr. Jamie Sutter        909 Grant Avenue, Suite 10    San Francisco, CA  94111
Rev. Manny Kant         510 "R" Street, N.W.          La Mirada, CA  91444
```

It looks easy enough, but beware. Here's the problem: If you attempt to set this up in one file, WordStar will print the title and heading lines above *each* record in the data file. Here's the solution: Set up a command file that establishes the page formatting, then use the **.FI** command to insert the file that merges in the records.

Press	**D** [open a document]
Type	burbank.r1
Press	**RETURN**
Type	y

because this is a new file.

The report employs a left-justified and a right-justified format, but you can't set up the left-justified format until you define the variables from the BURBANK.DTA file. Here's the command file in its entirety:

```
.. This time, 20 characters for the following format
.SV X = RRRRRRRRRRRRRRRRRRRR
.HE                                                                    &@/X&
.LS 1
.OJ OFF
.RM 85
                              Promotional Mailing #1

                                List of Recipients


Name                    Street                          City

.FI burbank.rr
```

The **X** format will right justify text, but because the right margin is at column 85, it would look bizarre to have the format contain 85 *R's*. So, I've used a trick: I've set the length of the format to 20, and when I use this format with a variable I'll put the variable at column 65. That is, 85 − 20 = 65!

So, where do I use the format? That's right: to print today's date in a header. Yes, you can use variable formatting with the predefined variables! Because the **.HE** command and space take up four columns, the **&@/X&** is at column 69 of the screen.

The titles are centered, and the headings above the variables start at columns 1, 26, and 56 to line up with the columns below them. The column containing the name will be 25 characters wide, while the other two columns will be 30 characters wide.

Note the blank line between the headings and the **.FI** line—that's for spacing. The **.FI** line inserts the file that governs the merge of the records in the data file. This line must end in a hard return!

Type the file as you see it. When you're finished:

Press   **^KD** or **F10**

to save the file and return to the Opening menu.

Now you'll do the BURBANK.RR file.

Press   **D** [open a document]

Type   burbank.rr

Press   **RETURN**

Type   y

because this is a new file.

The other file governs the page formatting, so all you need do is define your variables and variable formats, then determine where you want the variables to print. The entire setup is:

```
.DF burbank.dta
.RV title, first, last, street, city, state, zip, sponsor
.. This format has 25 characters
.SV A = LLLLLLLLLLLLLLLLLLLLLLLLL
.. This one has 30 characters
.SV B = LLLLLLLLLLLLLLLLLLLLLLLLLLLLLL
.SV fullname, &title& &first& &last&
.SV fullcity, &city&, &state& &zip&
&fullname/A&&street/B&&fullcity/B&
```

The **A** format is 25 characters long and left-justified, while the **B** format is 30 characters long. The **.SV** lines below these lines define two new variables, **fullname** and **fullcity**, to hold the recipient's name and city/state/zip code. This time, there's no constant text in the new variables.

Take a look at the only printed line in the file. Why are the three variables next to each other? Because WordStar will still print the first with 25 characters and the second two with 30 characters. That is, it *pads* the right side of each variable with spaces to fill in the entire format template. Even Ms. Hopkins' nonexistent street address will "print" correctly aligned!

Caution: Even though the variables are strung together, make sure there are ampersands around each one. If you forget just one ampersand, you're in trouble!

By the way, the last text line must end with a hard return so that WordStar prints a new line for each record in the data file. Type the file. When you're finished:

Press   **^KD** or **F10**

to save the file and return to the Opening menu.

Question: Which file do you now merge print? *Answer:* Always the controlling file, in this case BURBANK.R1. Go ahead, try it!

The Truth About Multiple Mailing Labels

Dear Reader: I set you up quite nicely for the next and last example in this chapter. If you look closely at the report you just created, you'll realize that it won't take much to change the format around slightly for two- or three-across mailing labels. After all, multiple labels are just columns across the page, too. But what about that empty street address? All in due time . . .

Press   **D** [open a document]

Type   burbank.113

(that's a lowercase *L* after the *1*).

Press   **RETURN**

Type   y

because this is a new file.

You'll experiment with three-across labels. Each label is one inch high and four inches wide. There are three blank lines between rows of labels and five blank spaces between each column of labels. You'll print the first column of labels at the left margin of the file and adjust the page offset accordingly.

Because each label is three inches wide, you'll set up a left-justified variable format that's $4 \times 10 = 40$ characters long (four inches times ten characters per inch). You also have to create new variables for the full name and full city lines.

```
.. three-across labels for promotional letter no. 1
.PL 9
.MT 1
.MB 0
.PO 7 [or whatever setting you need]
```

```
.PF OFF
.RM 130
.LS 1
.OP
.. Set up data file and order of variables
.DF burbank.dta
.RV title1, first1, last1, street1, city1, state1, zip1, sponsor1
.RV title2, first2, last2, street2, city2, state2, zip2, sponsor2
.RV title3, first3, last3, street3, city3, state3, zip3, sponsor3
..
.. This variable format has 40 characters
.SV L = LLLLLLLLLLLLLLLLLLLLLLLLLLLLLLLLLLLLLLLL
..
.. New variables
.SV fullname1 = &title1& &first1& &last1&
.SV fullname2 = &title2& &first2& &last2&
.SV fullname3 = &title3& &first3& &last3&
.SV fullcity1 = &city1&, &state1&  &zip1&
.SV fullcity2 = &city2&, &state2&  &zip2&
.SV fullcity3 = &city3&, &state3&  &zip3&
..
&fullname1/L&    &fullname2/L&    &fullname3/L&
&street1/L&      &street2/L&      &street3/L&
&fullcity1/L&    &fullcity2/L&    &fullcity3/L&
.PA
```

You must have *three* .RV lines and three sets of variables so that WordStar reads in the information for three labels at a time. (You'd need four lines for four-across labels, and so on.) Because the L format is 40 characters long, you insert five spaces between each variable to align the columns correctly when they print. The positioning of the variables looks wrong here, but they'll print correctly. The print time reformatter is off because you don't want WordStar to realign the lines on the odd change that one line in the third column extends past the right margin.

If you don't mind that blank line caused by Ms. Hopkins' nonexistent street address, then you're finished. However, if you're as much of a nitpicker as I am, you still have some work to do. You must "close in" the lines by *bringing up* the full city line so that it prints on the street line. Then you *blank out* the full city line. For example, to set up the empty record condition for the first set of names and addresses, you would insert these lines directly *above* the actual printed part of the file:

```
.IF &street1& =
.SV street1 = &fullcity1&
.SV fullcity1 =
.EI
```

What this does is check if the **&street1&** variable is empty. If so, WordStar assigns the contents of **&fullcity1&** to **street1** so that the city line will print where the street line is. You then blank out the original **&fullcity1&** variable so that nothing prints on the third line.

You set up the same basic conditional statements for each street line. The entire file, when you're finished, is this:

```
.. three-across labels for promotional letter no. 1
.PL 9
.MT 1
.MB 0
.PO 7 [or whatever setting you need]
.PF OFF
.RM 130
.LS 1
.OP
.. Set up data file and order of variables
.DF burbank.dta
.RV title1, first1, last1, street1, city1, state1, zip1, sponsor1
.RV title2, first2, last2, street2, city2, state2, zip2, sponsor2
.RV title3, first3, last3, street3, city3, state3, zip3, sponsor3
..
.. This variable format has 40 characters
.SV L = LLLLLLLLLLLLLLLLLLLLLLLLLLLLLLLLLLLLLLLL
..
.. New variables
.SV fullname1 = &title1& &first1& &last1&
.SV fullname2 = &title2& &first2& &last2&
.SV fullname3 = &title3& &first3& &last3&
.SV fullcity1 = &city1&, &state1&  &zip1&
.SV fullcity2 = &city2&, &state2&  &zip2&
.SV fullcity3 = &city3&, &state3&  &zip3&
..
.. Are any street lines empty?
.IF &street1& =
.SV street1 = &fullcity1&
.SV fullcity1 =
.EI empty street1
..
.IF &street2& =
.SV street2 = &fullcity2&
.SV fullcity2 =
.EI empty street2
..
.IF &street3& =
.SV street3 = &fullcity3&
```

```
.SV fullcity3 =
.EI empty street3

..
&fullname1/L&      &fullname2/L&      &fullname3/L&
&street1/L&      &street2/L&      &street3/L&
&fullcity1/L&      &fullcity2/L&      &fullcity3/L&
.PA
```

You can now type, save, and merge print this file to see the results. **Note:** Make sure you answer "no" to the Pause between pages (Y/N)? and Use form feeds (Y/N)? printer questions. You'll probably notice that if the number of records in the data file isn't evenly divisible by three, WordStar prints a label with the only real text in the file: that comma between the city and state. Well, so you wasted one or two labels!

Tip: Some word processing professionals recommend that you don't print directly on sheets of labels at all. Instead, print on regular paper, then *photocopy* the printed pages onto the label sheets. That way, you avoid the possibility of the labels ungluing in the printer!

Dear Reader: This has been quite a chapter, but you'll perhaps be happy to know that you're almost finished with merge printing. The next, and last, merge printing chapter covers merge and math features, and in the process shows even more examples of automated document assembly. Carry on!

Merge Plus Math

In this chapter you'll learn the following new command:

File Command
   .MA   Define a math equation variable

Other Points

Variable Number
Formatting Symbols

*	Format a number with leading asterisks
$	Format a number with a leading question mark
–	Format a negative number with a minus sign
.	Insert a decimal point
,	Insert a comma
()	Enclose a negative number in parentheses
9	Substitute a digit or zero
Z	Substitute a digit or a space

In the still of the night, when smart people are already fast asleep, I sit in front of my computer and dream up ever more complicated merge printing applications. Am I crazy or just a WordStar fanatic—or both? Unfortunately, I can only show you a few more ways to work with merge printing, then it'll be time to move on to other topics.

This chapter introduces variable number formatting and math features for merge printing. In the process, you'll see some other nifty examples of automated document assembly. I hope that they inspire you to develop some applications on your own. If you feel you have a particularly good one that you'd like to pass on, please send it to me in care of the publisher. Thanks!

DO WARM-UP

Variable Number Formatting

Just as the symbols **L**, **C**, and **R** indicate to WordStar a type of string format, so, too, other symbols tell WordStar that the format is for numeric variables. Numbers have different formatting requirements than strings. Sometimes the format even determines how *you* interpret the number.

For example, the number *1234.5678* is harmless enough, but if you format it like this—**$1,234.56**—it takes on quite a different meaning than this—**1234.5**—or this—**001234.5678**. Most of the time, of course, it's obvious exactly what the number is anyway, but WordStar still gives you great flexibility in formatting it.

Another advantage to variable number formatting is that you don't have to worry about the format when you enter the variable information. Suppose you have a data file filled with numbers. As long as the shell file contains the correct formatting instructions, you don't have to include the formats in the data file. Again, WordStar is saving you work!

Some Guidelines

Before taking a look at the special variable number formatting characters, study and learn these general guidelines:

- You still use the .SV command to assign the variable's name and format. You can separate the name from the format template with either a comma or an equals sign.

- If WordStar doesn't "see" an **L**, **C**, or **R** as the *first* character in a format template, it "assumes" that the format is for a numeric variable. However, if you use a character that's *not* in the list of special numeric symbols, the results are—as the manual states, "unreliable." Translated: don't do it!

- As with string formats, you must tell WordStar the *length* of the format template by filling the template with symbols, one for each column position.

- If you don't supply a template long enough to handle every numeric variable that is to print with the format, WordStar will substitute a series of question marks when you merge print the file!

■ WordStar automatically right justifies all numbers by filling in the left side with spaces or other characters, depending on (1) the symbols you've used, (2) the length of the format template, and (3) the length of the variable's contents. There's a way to left justify numeric variables, as you'll see later in the chapter.

■ You can mix and match symbols wherever necessary. That's the most common way to use the symbols.

■ Some symbols substitute one of two values, depending on whether the content of the variable *in that column position* contains a digit or nothing.

■ WordStar cuts off, or *truncates,* numbers according to the number of decimal positions in the format template. That is, if the variable is *506.789* and the template allows two decimal points, the result will be **506.78**. WordStar does *not* round out numbers.

■ If you don't use a numeric format at all, WordStar treats the number as a string. That is, it removes leading blanks and prints the number exactly as it appears.

Sheesh! If you're thoroughly confused and ready to take a break or give up, bear with me a little while longer. As usual, a few examples will help you realize that none of this is too difficult after all. Now for the symbols themselves . . .

Number Formatting Symbols

There are just nine number formatting symbols—eight if you count the left and right parentheses as one symbol, because you must use these two together anyway. You can break down the way the symbols work into certain groups:

General Number Formatting. The **9** and **Z** symbols substitute digits where digits appear in the variable. For positions in the template that contain no digits, the **9** symbol substitutes zeros (**0**), while the **Z** symbol substitutes leading spaces.

Negative Numbers. There are two ways to format negative numbers. The **(** (left parenthesis) and **)** (right parenthesis) enclose a negative number in parentheses. You must surround the *entire* format template in **()** for these symbols to work properly. The **–** (minus sign or hyphen) inserts a minus sign in front of a negative number. You insert it as the *first* character in the format. Use one or the other symbol, but not both. By the way, whichever you use, if the number is *positive* the parentheses or minus sign don't print.

Caution: If you *don't* include either the **()** or **–** symbol to handle negative numbers, WordStar displays them as *positive* numbers! Remember to make provision for negative number formatting for those variables whose contents may at times be negative.

Decimal Point and Thousands Separator. Perhaps the easiest symbols to remember are the . (decimal point) and , (comma). You insert these symbols wherever you want a decimal point or comma as a thousands separator to appear in the number.

Dollar Sign and Asterisk. The $ (dollar sign) symbol prints *one* leading $ before a number and fills any nondigit spaces with leading blanks. Use this symbol on the *left* side of a decimal point only.

The * (asterisk) symbol, in contrast, prints as many stars as necessary to fill in the left side of the number. Many banks use this symbol for check amounts. If you include this symbol on the right side of a decimal point in the template, WordStar prints zeros where no digits occur. You can use both $ or * in a format, if you wish.

A Few Examples

By far the most common variable number format is for *dollar amounts,* so that's a good place to start. Here's your first example:

```
.SV 1, $$$.99
```

This format template, **1,** is six characters long. It inserts a decimal point and prints a dollar sign in front of the number. Notice that you use the **9** symbol for the cents part of the amount—why? Because you always want to print either the digit or a zero in an amount. If you had used the **Z** symbol and if the variable were 50, then WordStar would print **$50.** and two spaces!

Unfortunately, this format only handles amounts up to $99.99! Why? Because you need at least one character position for the dollar sign itself. Recall also that the $ symbol fills in the left side of the template with leading spaces. If the variable were *5.01,* the format prints one space, followed by **$5.01**.

Well, that one wasn't very useful for large amounts. Try this one instead:

```
.SV 1 = $$$$,$$$,$$$.99
```

This format handles amounts up to *$999,999,999.99* and even inserts the commas where necessary. If the amount doesn't require commas, then WordStar doesn't print them, but keep in mind that WordStar still fills in the template length with spaces.

Underline characters represent spaces in the following examples. If the variable contained *505.10,* WordStar would print _____$505.10 —that's eight spaces. If the amount were *770823.00,* WordStar would print ___$770,823.00. Later you'll see how to deal with the leading spaces.

Tip: Use a template that can accommodate the largest amount you need to format.

To change the format template so that it can designate negative numbers, use either method you know. Thus:

```
.SV 1 = -$$$$,$$$,$$$.99
```

or

```
.SV 1 = ($$$$,$$$,$$$.99)
```

Here's a format that just prints dollar amounts *without* the cents.

```
.SV 2, $$$,$$$
```

The next format prints asterisks to fill in the left side of the template, but zeros on the right side. How large an amount does it handle?

```
.SV X, ***,***.**
```

The answer is *999,999.99.* If the amount were *505.10,* WordStar would print ******505.10,** including one asterisk for the unused comma. If the amount were *5000,* WordStar would print ****5,000.00.** Notice that WordStar will still print the decimal point and zeros in this format, because they're part of the template. If you didn't want the decimal point, the template would look like this:

```
.SV X, ***,***
```

The most general number format just contains either **9** or **Z** symbols. For example:

```
.SV T = 999999
```

If the number were 1234.56, WordStar would print it as **001234.** Note the two leading zeros and the truncated decimal positions. To include the decimal positions, use a template like this one:

```
.SV T = 999999.99
```

Use the **Z** symbol if you want WordStar to pad the number with leading spaces instead of zeros.

```
.SV Y, ZZZZZZ.99
```

If the number were 1234.56, WordStar would print two leading spaces, then **1234.56**.

Testing the Formatting

Before you experiment with math and merge examples, here's a test file that you might want to try.

Press   **D** [open a document]

Type   numbers.tst

Press   **RETURN**

Type   y

because this is a new file.
Type the file as you see it.

```
.. Various sample number formats
.SV A, $$$$
.SV B, ($$$$,$$$.99)
.SV C, 99999
.SV D, -999999.99
.SV E, ******
.SV F, ***,***.**
.SV G, ZZZZZZZ.Z
..
.. Various sample numbers
.SV n1 = 234
.SV n2 = 1234.567
.SV n3 = -09877
.SV n4 = 5000
.SV n5 = 6.22
..
.RM 80
.LS 1
&n1/A&    &n1/B&    &n1/C&    &n1/D&    &n1/E&    &n1/F&    &n1/G&

&n2/A&    &n2/B&    &n2/C&    &n2/D&    &n2/E&    &n2/F&    &n2/G&
```

```
&n3/A&    &n3/B&    &n3/C&    &n3/D&    &n3/E&    &n3/F&    &n3/G&

&n4/A&    &n4/B&    &n4/C&    &n4/D&    &n4/E&    &n4/F&    &n4/G&

&n5/A&    &n5/B&    &n5/C&    &n5/D&    &n5/E&    &n5/F&    &n5/G&
```

When you're finished, save the file with **^KD (F10)** and merge print it to see how WordStar formats the various examples. Do you understand how WordStar arrived at each result? If you wish, change the sample numbers and merge print the file again.

Math Equations in Merge Printing

To be sure, being able to format numeric variables in different ways is useful. Of equal utility is WordStar's **.MA** dot command, which lets you set up *math equations* in a merge printing application. Together, the two features provide an unbeatable combination, because you can do calculations and format results during merge printing!

The **.MA** command works exactly like the **.SV** command to "set" or define a variable, except that the variable you're defining is an equation. The format of the definition is the same as in **.SV** lines—that is, you can separate the new variable from its definition with either a comma or an equals sign.

You use the same standard math operators as on the Math menu, so if you've forgotten them, press **^QM** to refresh your memory. Press **^U (F2)** when you're finished to return to the text area. You can include any *defined* variables in the **.MA** equation. That is, there must be **.RV**, **.AV**, or **.SV** lines that set up the variables you include in an equation. Make sure you enclose the variables on the right side of the assignment in ampersands. The new variable you're defining in a **.MA** line is *not* enclosed in ampersands.

Take a look at this example, but don't type it:

```
.DF monthly.dta
.RV jan, feb, mar, apr, may, jun, jul, aug, sep, oct, nov, dec
.MA average6 = &jan& + &feb& + &mar& + &apr& + &may& + &jun& / 6
.SV A = $$$$.99
Your average bill for the first six months is: &average6/A&
```

In this example WordStar computes the six-month average bill, **average6**, as the sum of the amounts for the first six months of the year divided by six. Notice the ampersands on the right side of the assignment only. When it prints the average, WordStar uses a numeric format, **A**.

WordStar employs the same *order of precedence*—left to right—when calculating merged math equations as it does on the Math menu, so you may have to use parentheses to change the "natural" order of calculation or to clarify the equation for yourself. In this example—

```
.AV first_num
.AV second_num
.AV third_num
.MA result = &first_num& * (&second_num& - &third_num&)
```

—WordStar would normally first multiply **&first_num&** times **&second_num&**, but the parentheses change the order of calculation.

Note: Because a math equation is by its very nature a number, you'll more than likely want to include a numeric format to print the equation exactly as you want it. If you don't use a format, WordStar may print the equation with too many decimal places.

During merge printing, if WordStar can't "understand" a **.MA** equation, it flashes the Print Wait message while printing is in background mode. Press **M** or **P** to display the Printing menu, the recalcitrant equation, and this message:

```
Can't do that equation. Check for correctness.
```

Press **^U (F2)** to cancel the merge printing and check your file before trying again. So much for the lengthy preliminaries. The rest of the chapter shows practical examples using variable number formatting, merged math equations, and automated document assembly techniques.

Another Promotional Letter

The first example is a stock letter that offers a different promotional price for a product depending on whether the customer is "preferred" or not. WordStar also computes the necessary sales tax and total sale.

Press   **D** [open a document]

Type   `flea.ltr`

Press   **RETURN**

Type   `y`

because this is a new file.

There are several interesting things in this letter. Take a look at it and try to understand what all the commands do. I'll explain them in a moment.

```
.AV "Customer number (five digits or less): ", customer
.AV "Customer's first name: ", firstname
.AV "Customer's last name: ", lastname
.AV "First street line (RETURN if none): ", streetline1
.AV "Second street line (RETURN if none): ", streetline2
.AV "City, state, zip code: ", citystatezip
.AV "Pet's name: ", petname
.AV "Type of animal (lowercase d for dog or c for cat): ", dogcat
.AV "Preferred customer? (type lowercase y or n): ", preferred
..
.IF &dogcat& = d
.SV dogcat = dog
.EL
.SV dogcat = cat
.EI
..
.. Variable number formats:
.SV 1 = 99999
.SV 2 = $$$.99
.SV 3 = ZZZ.99
..
.. New variable
.SV price, 22.50
..
.MT 12
.MB 6
.OP
.OJ OFF
.LS 1
.RM 60
.PO 12  [or whatever setting you need]
.. Tabs at columns 6 and 31:
.RR--!-----------------------!---------------------------R
                             Frisky Farms, Inc.
                             A Division of Exxo Worldwide
                             22 Pomander Walk
                             Los Perros, NM 87777
                             &@&


&firstname& &lastname&
&streetline1/o&
&streetline2/o&
&citystatezip&


     Re: Customer Number &customer/1&
```

```
Dear &firstname&:

    It's that season again when &petname& suffers so much
from the pain and irritation of flea bites.  This year, why
don't you do something about them?

    We have a special offer just for you and &petname&, and
we don't think you can refuse!  For a limited time only, you
can purchase not one can, not two cans, but an entire case
(twelve cans!) of Frisky Flea-Away for your &dogcat& at the
incredible low price listed below.

.IF &preferred& = y
    For our preferred customers, we'll even throw in a
discount of five percent if you act now.  That's our way of
saying "Thank You!" for your past patronage.  The price you
see reflects your five percent discount.

.EL
.MA price, &price& * 1.05
.EI

    One case of Frisky        &price/2&
    Flea-Away
.MA tax, &price& * 0.065
.MA total, &price& + &tax&
    State sales tax           &tax/3&

                          _____

    Total                     &total/2&


    We urge you to place your order as soon as possible.
At these prices, our special offer won't last long!

                    Best wishes,




              The Folks at Frisky Farms
```

I won't comment on the standard page formatting dot commands, or
on the **.AV** lines. Below the **.AV** lines there's an interesting use of conditional
commands—to substitute one value for another in the same variable. If you
type **d**, WordStar substitutes the word *dog* for the **&dogcat&** variable; otherwise, it substitutes the word *cat*.

Below the conditional commands are three variable number formats. The first format, **1**, prints a number with leading zeros. The number that uses this format is on the *Re:* line. No matter what number of five digits or less you type, WordStar fills it in to make it five digits long. You can use the same technique for invoice or billing numbers.

The **2** format prints an amount with a leading dollar sign. It can handle amounts up to $99.99, more than adequate for the needs of this letter. Both the **&price&** and **&total&** variables print in this format.

The third format, **3**, contains the same *length* as format **2** so that the amounts line up correctly. This format, however, doesn't print a leading dollar sign. Instead, it prints leading spaces. Many accountants only want the top and bottom figures in a column to print with dollar signs, so this format handles the other figures. In the letter, the **&tax&** variable uses this format.

The next .SV line defines a new variable called **price** to be 22.50. Notice that you *don't* use the .MA command, because this is just a number. The .MA command only defines equations.

In the body of the letter is another conditional structure that checks if you typed **y** to note if the customer is a "preferred" one. If so, WordStar prints an extra paragraph. If not, it changes the original **price** variable by increasing it five percent! (The Folks at Frisky Farms are not averse to a little bit of tomfoolery, I'm afraid.)

In other words, you're *redefining* the variable using the same variable name on both sides of the assignment. This time, you *do* have to use a .MA command to create the new price, which is 105 percent greater than the original price.

After you've determined which price to use, you can include the equations to compute the **tax** and **total** variables. Notice that you must insert these equations *below* all different values of the **price** variable. If you had inserted either equation at the top of the file below the .SV price, 22.50 line, WordStar would have computed the tax and total for the original amount only! The tax for the higher amount would then be wrong, and the Folks at Frisky Farms would be losing money.

Remember that WordStar inserts the format template at the location of the left ampersand. The dividing line above the total appears to be too short, but when you merge print the file you'll see that it is exactly right for the resulting figures. By the way, it's eight characters wide.

Type the letter, press ^KD (**F10**) to save it, and merge print it.

Problems with Characters That Aren't Numbers

If you type a non-numeric character into a variable and then format the variable with a template, WordStar prints zeros in the entire format! Suppose you typed R22 for a customer number. WordStar would format the five-digit "number" as 00000.

So, you may want to include an error trap to deal with incorrect input. For example, *below* the **.SV** line that declares the **1** format, you could insert this conditional structure:

```
.IF &customer/1& = 00000
.CS You typed an incorrect customer number!
.DM Please re-enter it using numbers only
.AV "(five digits or less): ", customer
.EI
```

This condition checks for the *formatted* value of the **&customer&** variable, not its *real* value. For example, if you typed R22 into the variable, its real value would be *R22,* but its formatted value using the **1** format would be *00000.*

Dealing with Leading Blanks

In the previous example all the variable number formats appear on short lines or at tab stops, so there's no problem getting the numbers to align correctly. Remember that WordStar always fills in the *left* side of a numeric template to right justify the number. With most symbols, WordStar uses leading spaces to fill in the template, and these spaces will present a problem when the number appears *within* a paragraph. That is, there may be extra and unsightly spaces in front of the number.

There's a way to trim off the leading spaces from a variable number format when the variable appears in the middle of a paragraph. The next example shows you how.

Press   **D** [open a document]

Type   `arrears.let`

Press   **RETURN**

Type   **y**

because this is a new file.

As you type the letter, try to understand what each command does.

```
.SV yearly.interest = 19.5
.DF arrears.dta, \
.RV account, title, first, last, address
.RV cityline, amount.due
..
```

```
.. Variable number formats
.SV W = 9.9999
.SV X = ZZ.9
.SV Y = $$,$$$.99
..
.. New variables
.MA monthly.interest = &yearly.interest& / 1200
.MA charges = &amount.due& * &monthly.interest&
.MA total = &charges& + &amount.due&
..
.. Redefinitions
.SV amount.due = &amount.due/Y&
.SV monthly.interest = &monthly.interest/W&
.SV charges = &charges/Y&
.SV total = &total/Y&
..
.MT 12
.OP
.PO 10   [or whatever setting you need]
.LS 1
.RM 60
.OJ OFF
.. Tabs at columns 6 and 31
.RR--!----------------------!-------------------------R
.IF &title&
&title& &first& &last&
.EL
&first& &last&
.EI
&address/o&
&cityline&


        Re: Account Number &account&

.IF &title&
Dear &title& &last&:
.EL
Dear &first&:
.EI


        Our records indicate that the amount of &amount.due& is
overdue on the above-captioned account.

        If we do not receive payment within ten (10) days from
the date of this letter, we shall be forced to charge you
interest at the rate of &yearly.interest&% per year
```

```
(&monthly.interest&% per month).   That means the new payment
due us would be &amount.due& plus interest charges of
&charges&, for a total of &total&.

     Should you fail to make payment within thirty (30) days
from the date of this letter, we have no other recourse but
to break both your legs.

     To avoid any problems, please remit your payment
immediately.  Thank you.

                    Yours sincerely,



                    Benji's Buy-By-Mail, Inc.
&@&
.PA
```

Because interest rates change, the first **.SV** line is at the top of the file so you can edit it quickly whenever necessary. The letter gets most of its information from a data file called ARREARS.DTA. The field separator in the data file is a backslash. Notice that this time I've used a period in many variable names—entirely possible!

There are three variable number formats. The format **W** displays the monthly interest rate with a leading zero and four decimal places, while **X** displays the yearly interest rate with only one decimal place. The third format, **Y**, prints dollar amounts up to $9,999.99, adequate for the needs of this letter.

The **.MA** lines set up three equations. The first new variable, **monthly.interest**, is worth noting for the formula itself. To arrive at the monthly interest, you first have to divide the yearly interest by 12. However, to put the rate in the correct decimal format before you can use it, you must divide it by 100, too. For example, 19.5 percent interest is .195. The **.MA** line combines both operations: it divides the yearly interest by 1200. The other two **.MA** lines set up the **charges** and **total** variables.

Below the line with *Redefinitions* on it is where you deal with leading spaces for variables that appear in paragraphs. Each **.SV** line *redefines* the variable as *itself plus a format template*. For example, you've assigned to the **amount.due** variable from the ARREARS.DTA file its contents (**&amount.due&**) plus the format template, **Y**. When WordStar prints the variable, it trims off any superfluous leading spaces.

Notice that you *do not* append a format name to the variable in the paragraph, because the variable itself now contains the format, too. For example, take a look at the **&amount.due&** variable in the first paragraph. Use this technique of redefinition whenever you want to use a variable number format in a paragraph.

Caution: If you change the actual *contents* of a variable, then you must redefine it again to include the format template and trim leading spaces. For example, suppose later in this letter you set up another **.MA** line to compute the **total** variable with a discount. You'd then add a **.SV** line to redefine total as **&total/Y&** to include the format.

The rest of this file is straightforward. What do the conditional lines do? When you type the file, make sure the percent sign (**%**) is directly after the **&yearly.interest&** and **&monthly.interest&** variables in the second paragraph. Don't forget the **.PA** line at the end of the file.

By the way, the second paragraph might benefit from a few strategically placed soft hyphens at syllable breaks. You may also want to turn hyphen help on (**^OH**) and check the other paragraphs for possible hyphenation spots.

When you're finished, save the file with **^KD (F10)**. Now you need the data file.

Press	N [open a nondocument]
Type	arrears.dta
Press	**RETURN**
Type	**y**

because this is a new file.

Here are sample records for the file. You can use ones of your own, or add others to those below.

```
WT201\ Mr.\ Walter\ Theurer\ 200 Cathedral Parkway\ New York, NY  10027\ 5199.22
OH727\ \ Orlando\ Higgins\ 12001 Ventura Boulevard\ North Hollywood, CA  91308\ 705.90
LA444\ Ms.\ Leslie\ Adams\ 327 Main Street\ Calumet City, IL  66321\ 395.25
```

Keep in mind that the variable number formats print the amounts with dollar signs, commas, and decimal points. So, you don't have to include the formatting—except the decimal places—in the variables here.

When you're finished, save the file with **^KD (F10)** and merge print ARREARS.LET using the PRVIEW printer driver.

Using String Formats with Numbers

Once you've reassigned a variable to include a variable number format and the variable's contents, you can then format the variable as a string. Take a look at this short file:

```
.AV "First number?  ", first#
.AV "Second number?  ", second#
```

```
.AV "Third number?  ", third#
.MA total, &first#& + &second#& + &third#&
.SV 1, ZZZ,ZZZ,ZZZ.99
.SV C, CCCCCCCCCCCCCCCCCCCCCCCCCCCCCCCCCCCCCCCCCCCCCCCCCCCCCCCCCCCCCC
.SV first#, &first#/1&
.SV second#, &second#/1&
.SV third#, &third#/1&
.SV total, &total/1&
&first#/C&
&second#/C&
&third#/C&
&total/C&
```

The file requests three numbers, then computes their total. To trim leading spaces, the file reassigns each variable to be its contents plus the format template **1**. Finally, the file centers and prints each variable, using string format template **C**.

A Columnar Math Report

Because WordStar keeps the length of each variable format the same, you've already learned how to use this fact to your advantage for printing multiple-column mailing labels. The next example is similar, except you're printing a columnar math report instead of names and addresses.

The report you'll prepare is the very same one called SALES.1Q from Chapter 18. You may wish to have a printout of that file handy to check the accuracy of your typing. This time, however, WordStar will generate the entire report—including totals—from "raw" data in a nondocument file. You don't have to do a thing once you've set up the report.

This time you'll create the data file first to set up the information that WordStar will use.

Press   **N** [open a nondocument]

Type   **sales.dta**

Press   **RETURN**

Type   **y**

because this is a new file.

Type the data as you see it below. Notice that a couple amounts are negative, but *none* contains commas.

```
Apple Pie, 5344.25, 5487.65, 6001.50
Bear Claw, 2567.80, 2010.36, 1998.66
Chocolate Eclair, 3558.22, -500.01, 2775.12
Linzertorte, 1783.15, 776.75, -765.43
Strawberry Shortcake, 981.00, 865.40, 1115.50
Truffled Delight, 3299.25, 3005.22, 4004.04
```

When you're finished, press ^KD (F10) to save the file. Now for the report itself.

Press	**D** [open a document]
Type	sales.1m
Press	**RETURN**
Type	y

because this is a new file.

As you type the report, try to figure out what the commands do. For example, why *six* **.RV** lines? And how do the variable number formats **E** and **F** work? Don't worry—I'll explain them later!

For the column positions of the titles, here they are: *Product* starts at column 3; *January* at column 26; *February* at column 39; *March* at column 54; and *Total for Product* at column 65. There are three spaces between the variable names in column 1 and column 2, and between those in column 2 and column 3. There are six spaces between columns 3 and 4. Use the relative position of the text above them to eye-ball the location of the dividing lines.

```
.MT 8
.PO 6 [or whatever setting you need]
.RM 90
.OP
.LS 1
.OJ OFF
..
.DF sales.dta
.RV item1, jan1, feb1, mar1
.RV item2, jan2, feb2, mar2
.RV item3, jan3, feb3, mar3
.RV item4, jan4, feb4, mar4
.RV item5, jan5, feb5, mar5
.RV item6, jan6, feb6, mar6
..
.. The first one is 24 characters long
.SV D = LLLLLLLLLLLLLLLLLLLLLLLL
.SV E = (Z,ZZZ.99)
```

```
.SV F = (ZZ,ZZZ.99)

..
.MA tline1 = &jan1& + &feb1& + &mar1&
.MA tline2 = &jan2& + &feb2& + &mar2&
.MA tline3 = &jan3& + &feb3& + &mar3&
.MA tline4 = &jan4& + &feb4& + &mar4&
.MA tline5 = &jan5& + &feb5& + &mar5&
.MA tline6 = &jan6& + &feb6& + &mar6&
.MA tcol1 = &jan1& + &jan2& + &jan3& + &jan4& + &jan5& + &jan6&
.MA tcol2 = &feb1& + &feb2& + &feb3& + &feb4& + &feb5& + &feb6&
.MA tcol3 = &mar1& + &mar2& + &mar3& + &mar4& + &mar5& + &mar6&
.MA tcol4 = &tline1& + &tline2& + &tline3& + &tline4& + &tline5& + &tline6&

..
  Product                 January    February     March     Total for Product

&item1/D&&    jan1/E&    &feb1/E&    &mar1/E&    &tline1/F&
&item2/D&&    jan2/E&    &feb2/E&    &mar2/E&    &tline2/F&
&item3/D&&    jan3/E&    &feb3/E&    &mar3/E&    &tline3/F&
&item4/D&&    jan4/E&    &feb4/E&    &mar4/E&    &tline4/F&
&item5/D&&    jan5/E&    &feb5/E&    &mar5/E&    &tline5/F&
&item6/D&&    jan6/E&    &feb6/E&    &mar6/E&    &tline6/F&

              _____   _____   _____   _____

TOTAL         &tcol1/F&  &tcol2/F&  &tcol3/F&      &tcol4/F&
```

Press   ^KS or F9

to save the file and resume where you left off.

Of course, there are six **.RV** lines because presumably there are six and only six entries in the SALES.DTA data file—one entry for each product. You want WordStar to read them all in at once so that one set prints on each line next to its product name.

The **D** format is for the left-justified product names. Because it's 24 characters long, there's no space between each item and its January sales figure. The **E** and **F** formats display the amounts with leading blanks and dollar signs. The **F** format is one character longer than the **E** format. If any amount is negative, WordStar encloses it in parentheses.

I think the **.MA** equations are obvious. Each tline represents the sum *across* a line, while each tcol is the sum *down* a column.

The most difficult part about creating this automatic reporting file is to line up the figures correctly. You aren't using decimal tabs at all here! The starting position of the variables in each of the monthly columns has to take into account the entire length of the format, *including* the beginning and ending parentheses symbols. Because the TOTAL line uses the F format, it doesn't align with the columns above it. With a little luck, this file will print correctly, however. Try it!

Tip: I found the best way to set up column alignments is just to merge print the file to disk with the PRVIEW driver and note any necessary changes. It will require a few trial runs, but this way is easier than trying to keep track of the format lengths.

Press ^KD (F10) to save the file, then merge print it to see the results. The totals should be *exactly* the same as on your printout of the SALES.1Q file!

Note: If it's a rainy day and you don't have much to do, why not try to create a completely automated data entry and reporting application? Using the techniques you've learned in the last few chapters, create a command file that runs the show. The command file would first call a data entry form file to request from the keyboard and set up the sales figures for the products in a nondocument data file. Then the command file would call this report to merge print the results. Good luck!

Going for Broke: An Invoice

Dear Reader: Here's just one more automated document assembly example for you to try—if you feel like it—and then you're finished with merge printing! I *told* you I spend my nights thinking up complicated merge printing applications; well, this one takes the cake. It's a file to print an invoice of up to five items, and it illustrates a variety of features and techniques.

Press	**D** [open a document]
Type	invoice
Press	**RETURN**
Type	y

because this is a new file.

This time, I'm not going to explain *anything!* Try to figure out what all the commands do as you type the file. If you don't understand the entire setup, then you'll have to merge print the file. Notice that I've included a message line to remind you about the beginning column numbers for the titles.

```
.CS
.AV "How many items are on the invoice (1-5)? ", items
..
.IF &items& =
.GO TOP
.EL
.IF &items& #> 5
```

```
.GO TOP
.EI
.EI
..
.AV "Invoice number (up to 6 digits only)? ", invoice
.AV "Invoice date? ", date
.DM Send to --
.AV "  Name: ", name
.AV "  Address 1: ", address1
.AV "  Address 2: ", address2
.AV "  City/State/Zip: ", city
.AV "  Attention: ", attention
.DM Terms (choose one) --
.DM   1 - Net 10 days
.DM   2 - Net 15 days
.DM   3 - Net 20 days
.DM   4 - Net 30 days
.AV "  Your choice? ", terms
..
.IF &terms& =
.GO TOP
.EL
.IF &terms& #> 4
.GO TOP
.EI
.EI
..
.IF &terms& = 1
.SV terms = Net 10 days
.EL
.IF &terms& = 2
.SV terms = Net 15 days
.EL
.IF &terms& = 3
.SV terms = Net 20 days
.EL
.SV terms = Net 30 days
.EI
.EI
.EI
..
.CS First item --
.AV "  Name of item: ", item1
.AV "  Amount sold: ", sold1
.AV "  Unit price: ", price1
.MA tot1 = &sold1& * &price1&
.MA grand = &tot1&
```

```
..
.IF &items& #> 1
.CS Second item --
.AV "  Name of item: ", item2
.AV "  Amount sold: ", sold2
.AV "  Unit price: ", price2
.MA tot2 = &sold2& * &price2&
.MA grand = &grand& + &tot2&
.EI
..
.IF &items& #> 2
.CS Third item --
.AV "  Name of item: ", item3
.AV "  Amount sold: ", sold3
.AV "  Unit price: ", price3
.MA tot3 = &sold3& * &price3&
.MA grand = &grand& + &tot3&
.EI
..
.IF &items& #> 3
.CS Fourth item --
.AV "  Name of item: ", item4
.AV "  Amount sold: ", sold4
.AV "  Unit price: ", price4
.MA tot4 = &sold4& * &price4&
.MA grand = &grand& + &tot4&
.EI
..
.IF &items& #> 4
.CS Fifth item --
.AV "  Name of item: ", item5
.AV "  Amount sold: ", sold5
.AV "  Unit price: ", price5
.MA tot5 = &sold5& * &price5&
.MA grand = &grand& + &tot5&
.EI
..
.. Variable formats
.SV R = RRRRRRRRRRRRRRRRRRRR
.SV L = LLLLLLLLLLLLLLLLLLLL
.SV 1 = ZZZZZZ,ZZZ,ZZZ
.SV 2 = $$$9.99
.SV 3 = $$$,$$$.99
.SV 4 = ZZ,ZZZ.99
.SV 5 = 999999
..
.MT 8
```

```
.OP
.PO 10  [or whatever setting you need]
.OJ OFF
.LS 1
.LM 1
.RM 70
.. The &date/R& variable is at column 45
                                              &date/R&


Invoice Number: &invoice/5&


Send to:

        &name&
        &address1/o&
        &address2/o&
        &city&
.IF &attention&
        Attention: &attention/o&
.EI

Terms: &terms&


.. Column numbers      26            43           60
Item                   Amount Sold   Unit Price   Total
```

```
&item1/L&&sold1/1&      &price1/2&    &tot1/3&
.IF &items& #> 1
&item2/L&&sold2/1&      &price2/2&    &tot2/3&
.EI
.IF &items& #> 2
&item3/L&&sold3/1&      &price3/2&    &tot3/3&
.EI
.IF &items& #> 3
&item4/L&&sold4/1&      &price4/2&    &tot4/3&
.EI
.IF &items& #> 4
&item5/L&&sold5/1&      &price5/2&    &tot5/3&
.EI

        Subtotal                                  &grand/3&
```

```
.MA tax = &grand& * .065                          &tax/4&
     State sales tax


                                                  _____

.MA grand = &grand& + &tax&
     Grand total                                  &grand/3&



.IF &grand& #> 1000.00
Thank you for your patronage!
.EI
```

Okay, I've decided to call your attention to one point about this file. How many times do I *redefine* the **grand** variable, and why?

After you're finished typing, press ^KD (F10) to save the file. Prepare your printer and paper, and merge print the file using the following responses to the prompts:

```
How many items are on the invoice (1-5)? 5
Invoice number (up to 6 digits only)? 1099
Invoice date? April 26, 1988
Send to --
  Name: Dos Gatos Support Group
  Address 1: 4118 Loony Tunes Blvd.
  Address 2: Suite 77
  City/State/Zip: Los Angeles, CA  90027
  Attention: Ms. Lennie Gladstone
Terms (choose one) --
  1 - Net 10 days
  2 - Net 15 days
  3 - Net 20 days
  4 - Net 30 days
Your choice? 4

First item --
  Name of item: Floppy disks
  Amount sold: 100
  Unit price: 1.99

Second item --
  Name of item: Drafting pencils
  Amount sold: 1000
  Unit price: .25

Third item --
  Name of item: Printer ribbons
```

Amount sold: **50**
Unit price: **11.99**

Fourth item --
  Name of item: **Binders**
  Amount sold: **100**
  Unit price: **2.50**

Fifth item --
  Name of item: **Computer paper**
  Amount sold: **75**
  Unit price: **4.72**

You should see the same printout as in Figure 24–1.

Dear Reader: I've given you a head start in the wonderful world of merge printing, but it will still take you a while to set up the merge applications that fit your needs. Just a few more chapters to go before your WordStar apprenticeship is over!

```
                                        April 26, 1988

Invoice Number: 001099

Send to:

        Dos Gatos Support Group
        4118 Loony Tunes Blvd.
        Suite 77
        Los Angeles, CA  90027
        Attention: Ms. Lennie Gladstone

Terms: Net 30 days


Item                    Amount Sold      Unit Price        Total
_____

Floppy disks                    100          $1.99       $199.00
Drafting pencils              1,000          $0.25       $250.00
Printer ribbons                  50         $11.99       $599.50
Binders                         100          $2.50       $250.00
Computer paper                   75          $4.72       $354.00

    Subtotal                                            $1,652.50
                                                     _____

    State sales tax                                       107.41
                                                     _____

    Grand total                                        $1,759.91

    Thank you for your patronage!
```

Figure 24–1   A Completed Invoice

For Bibliophiles Only

In this chapter you'll learn the following new commands:

Opening Menu Commands

I	Generate an index
T	Generate a table of contents

File Commands

.IX	Insert an index reference
^PK	Enclose file text as an index reference
.TC	Insert a table of contents reference
.TC1–9	Insert an alternate (list) reference

Other Points

,	Separate an index subreference from its reference
-	Indicate an index cross-reference
+	Indicate an index primary reference
\	Print the next character literally in the table of contents or index

Even if you're not strictly speaking a bibliophile, a "lover of books," you'll appreciate WordStar's table of contents and index generation features. They are the topic of this chapter, along with that other bugbear of scholars and nonscholars alike: footnotes.

DO WARM-UP

Some Preliminary Notes

One of the world's most boring and tedious jobs is creating a table of contents, a list of figures or illustrations, or an index. You must locate all the references you need, jot down the page numbers, and consolidate them into a separate table or index. Doing an index is especially difficult, because you might have many pages for just one topic, along with cross-references and other nasty things.

WordStar can help you with these most thankless tasks. You include special dot commands in your files for table, list, or index entries. You can even *mark* existing text as an index reference without retyping simply by enclosing the text with a special print command. Later, WordStar will generate the table, list, or index for you and save them in separate files. You can then insert the table, list, or index files into another file, or you can print them separately.

Note: Earlier versions of WordStar included a separate program called *StarIndex* that generated a table of contents and index. The StarIndex commands are totally different from the WordStar Release 4 commands and, boy, are they a *bear* to learn! This chapter discusses only the WordStar commands, although you can still insert StarIndex commands in WordStar files and use StarIndex to generate tables and indices. There's one problem, though: StarIndex can't read the extended ASCII character set.

Inserting table of contents and list entries in a file is easy. You'll probably use existing headings, subheadings, and figures in the table or list. But a caveat is in order about constructing an index. WordStar can only *help* you; its power is necessarily limited in this area. Why? Because even the most experienced bibliophile knows that generating an index is an art in itself. As you'll see, it's one thing to mark index references, but quite another to be organized enough to get them right the first time.

Tip: Because generating tables of contents, lists, and indexes requires a slew of added dot command lines in a file, wait until the file is in its final stages. That way, the presence of so many extra dot command lines won't distract you from your editing work. Also, remember that you can temporarily turn off the dot command lines with ^OP.

Caution: For heaven's sake, make sure your page breaks are correct before you begin generating a table of contents or index. WordStar can only use the current page numbering—it can't read your mind! Use unconditional page breaks (.PA) where necessary. If you edit the file after you create your index or table and the page breaks change, you'll have to regenerate everything or edit the table and index files that WordStar created for you.

By the way, WordStar can only read the page number, not anything else in a header or footer that may compose the printed number. That is, if you've set up the page numbers for Chapter 7 to be 7-1, 7-2, and so on, WordStar won't include the *7-* part of the setup in the table or index files. So sorry!

Tables of Contents and Lists

A table of contents is just a *list,* isn't it? Usually, tables of contents include chapter numbers and titles, and all headings and subheadings in each chapter. Similar to a table of contents is a list of figures or illustrations. You can do both in WordStar.

Inserting Table Entries

The **.TC** dot command sets up a table of contents or list reference. When you insert these references, you include three facts in the **.TC** command line:

1. The *text* of the reference. Often you can just copy existing text for the reference, but you can make cosmetic changes to it. For example, you may want to print in uppercase, or use boldface and underlining in your table.

2. The table of contents *level,* which I'll discuss in a moment.

3. The way you want the reference to look, that is, its *format.* The format includes page numbers and perhaps leaders of one kind or another. The format usually depends on the level of the reference.

Caution: As with other dot commands, each **.TC** command should be on its own blank line so that it doesn't throw off the actual text lines of the file. Use ^N to insert the blank line before you enter the table of contents reference.

Normally, the *highest* level of a table of contents is the chapter title itself. Below that, at other levels, are major headings, then possibly subheadings, sub-subheadings, and so on. You must determine how to format the table so that it clearly shows the levels in the file, and include this formatting in the **.TC** line.

For example, suppose you've numbered your headings and subheadings like this:

```
I.   My Life with Animals
     A.  Cats
         1.  Stray Cats
         2.  Domestic Cats
```

```
          B.  Dogs
      II.  My Life With Insects
          A.  Flies
          B.  Mosquitoes
```

You may want to include the numbering and indentation scheme in your table of contents, too. Or you may want to indent subheadings with fewer spaces. It's up to you, but be consistent in the way you determine each level. (Emerson said only *foolish* consistency was the "hobgoblin of little minds"; Alfieri says that *useful* consistency is another thing altogether.)

You also determine where the page numbers are to print, and whether you want leaders between references and page numbers. A standard table of contents is one that has dot leaders. Notice in this example that I've changed the indentation of the subheadings:

```
I.    My Life with Animals.....................................1
      A.  Cats..................................................2
          1.  Stray Cats.......................................2
          2.  Domestic Cats....................................3
      B.  Dogs..................................................5
II.   My Life With Insects...................................10
      A.  Flies................................................11
      B.  Mosquitoes...........................................13
```

For *each* table of contents reference, that is, each **.TC** line, you must include the leaders and page number reference. As with page numbers in headers and footers, you use the number sign (#). WordStar later replaces it with the correct page number when it generates the table. For example, the first entry looks like this in the file:

```
.TC I.    My Life with Animals.....................................#
```

There's a *space* between the **.TC** command and the actual text of the entry. Although the page number symbol will print at column 65, the four positions required by the **.TC** and space push the entry over a bit on the screen.

The format is up to you. For example, you may want hyphen leaders only for headings, and left-justified page numbers positioned at a different column:

```
I.    My Life with Animals ------------------------- 1
      A.  Cats                                        2
          1.  Stray Cats                              2
          2.  Domestic Cats                           3
```

The first reference would then look like this in the file:

```
.TC I.   My Life with Animals ------------------------ #
```

But the second entry would be this:

```
.TC   A.  Cats                                    #
```

Note: Well, the format is not *entirely* up to you. Your printer has a say in the matter, too. That is, there is a problem with any kind of leader—such as a dot or hyphen. Leaders have *very small* characters widths. Fixed-width typestyles are okay, but if you try to print a table of contents with leaders in a proportionally spaced typestyle, you'll get the shock of your life. If you *must* use a proportionally spaced typestyle, omit the leaders and insert the fixed column command, **^P@**, directly in front of each page number symbol in the **.TC** dot command lines. That way, at least you'll be able to line up the page numbers correctly!

If you want the number sign to print literally in a table of contents or index reference, insert a backslash (\) directly in front of it: \#. If you want a backslash character to print literally, use two backslashes: \\. To include print commands such as boldface or underlining, you must insert them in the **.TC** lines, too. Make sure you press **^OD (SHIFT F1)** to turn the print code display on and check that you've included an ending toggle. Then turn the display off to set up the page number position. Another way to go would be to edit the table of contents file later after WordStar has generated it. It's up to you.

Tip: By default WordStar left justifies page numbers. However, now that you know about merge printing, learn an easy way to get right-justified page numbers in a table of contents. Use a page number merge variable (**&#&**) with a number format *instead of* the normal number symbol. For example, suppose you set up a merge printing variable format like this in your file (make sure it's in front of any table of contents entries):

```
.SV 1 = ZZ9
```

If you use this format with the page number as a merge printing variable, then WordStar right justifies the page numbers when you generate the table of contents! How? It adds leading spaces (the **Z** symbol) to the left of the numbers that don't contain three digits. A sample table of contents entry with page number reference might thus be:

```
.TC My Life with Animals........................................&#/1&
```

When it generates the table of contents file, WordStar formats the page numbers right-justified correctly. Try it!

A Nifty Trick and General Pattern to Follow

The easiest way to mark table of contents entries is to follow these steps:

1. Position the cursor at the left side of the line containing an entry, such as a heading or subheading.
2. Press ^QY to delete from the cursor position to the right side of the line. Don't use ^Y (F5) for reasons explained below. This is part one of the trick!
3. Press ^U (F2) *immediately* to restore the deleted line. This is part two of the trick!
4. Press ^N to insert a blank line for the table of contents reference.
5. Press the **SPACEBAR** to indent the reference as much as you want.
6. Press ^U (F2) to restore the same line as your table of contents entry. This is part three of the trick! If you had used ^Y, WordStar would have inserted a return, too. Recall that ^QY doesn't delete a return.
7. Press ^QD (^F10) to position the cursor at the end of the line, then type the leaders and the page number symbol.
8. Press ^QS (^F9) to position the cursor at column 1.
9. Type .TC and a space to complete the reference.

Why not type the .TC and space *first?* You could, but I've found that WordStar slows up considerably when you're entering any repeating characters, such as dot leaders. On my machine, I can hold down the period key to repeat the character quickly, and this feature works faster on a normal text line. Also, I can line up the page number at the correct column position without having to worry about the offset of four characters caused by the .TC command itself.

Macros to Do It!

You can create a macro that does the first few steps for you and another to finish off the procedure. The next example sets up a macro, **ESC 1**, that deletes the entry, restores it, creates a blank line, indents two spaces for a level two heading, inserts the reference text, and positions the cursor at the end of the line.

Press   **ESC**

Type   ?

to define a new macro.

Type   1

Type   Table entry

for the description if you wish.

Press   **RETURN**

Careful! Remember to use ^P each time you want to insert a WordStar command in the macro:

Press   **^P^Q**

Type   Y

Press   **^P^U^P^N**

Press   **SPACEBAR** twice

Press   **^P^U^P^Q**

Type   D

Press   **RETURN**

to enter the definition.
The entire definition should look like this:

^QY^U^N ^U^QD

You can't set up a macro to type the dot leaders, because there will be a different number of them for each entry. However, you can set up a macro, **ESC 2**, that types the page number symbol, positions the cursor at column 1, and enters the **.TC** command and space. The Shorthand menu should still be on the screen.

Type   2

to define this key.

Type   `Finish table`

Press   **RETURN**

for the description if you wish.

Type   `#`

Press   **^P^Q**

Type   `S.TC`

Press   **SPACEBAR**

Press   **RETURN**

for the macro definition.

The entire definition looks like this:

`#^QS.TC`

To save the two new macros:

Press   **RETURN**

Type   `y`

In a moment, you'll use them!

Lists

The procedure for setting up a list is essentially the same as for a table of contents, with only one slight difference. You designate the *list number* directly after the **.TC** command. This number represents an *alternate* table of contents file that WordStar will create for you. For example, this command line inserts an entry in list number 1:

`.TC1 Figure 1-1 WordStar Deletion Commands ........................#`

There is still a space between the **.TC1** command and the actual text of the entry. Do *not* insert a space between **.TC** and **1**. You can have up to *nine* different alternate table files, for instance, one for figures (**.TC1**), one for illustrations (**.TC2**), and one for tables (**.TC3**). You don't have to use the numbers in any order, provided you mark each entry in a list with the correct number. WordStar keeps track of where the entries go when it generates the tables.

WordStar puts the table of contents listing in a file with the extension .TOC, and each alternate in a file with the extension .TO1, .TO2, and so on. More about file names later.

Tip: Even though you work with it as a table of contents, a list can be a compendium of practically anything. If you don't include leaders and page numbers, then you can just generate a simple list of entries in your **.TC** lines.

Back to Beethoven

Pretend that you want to generate a table of contents and a list of tables for the CH.27 file, although it's not terribly long. You'll use your macros for creating some of the entries.

Press	**D** [open a document]
Type	ch.27
Press	**RETURN**

It's back to Beethoven once again! You first want to enter level one references to the chapter number and title, but you don't want them centered in the table of contents. If you used the **ESC 1** macro, it would indent the entry two spaces. You don't want that here, because this will be a level one heading. So, first position the cursor on the real text line 1, the line with *27* on it.

Press	**^N**

to insert a line but leave the cursor where it is.

Type	.TC 27
Press	**RETURN**

to add a blank line.

Type	Beethoven's "Tenth" Symphony

but leave the cursor at the end of the line.

Now, type a period all the way to column *65*. Then:

Press   **ESC 2**

to add the page number symbol and finish the table of contents entry.

Don't press RETURN because then you'd have a superfluous blank line. The table of contents entries will look like this:

```
.TC 27
.TC Beethoven's "Tenth" Symphony...................................#
```

Notice that the first line won't print page numbers; it just prints the chapter number. Now you want level *two* entries for each heading in the file. Each level two entry will indent two spaces in the table of contents. So this time you *will* use your **ESC 1** macro.

Position the cursor at column 1 of the first heading, *Background.*

Press   **ESC 1**

Type   .

but hold down the key until you reach column 65.

Press   **ESC 2**

to finish the macro.

When you generate the table of contents, WordStar includes the underline codes. If you don't want them, you can quickly delete them from the table of contents file.

Now, repeat the above steps for the remaining level two headings in the file: *Chronology* and *The Extant Material.* When you're finished, you want to add an entry for a list of tables. Position the cursor directly on the .AW OFF command line above the table on page 1 (line 37).

Press   **^N**

to insert a line but leave the cursor where it is.

Type   `Table of Dates Pertaining to the "Tenth Symphony"`

Type   .

but hold down the key until you reach column 65.

Press   **ESC 2**

Press   ^S or **LEFT ARROW**

Type   1

to finish the entry.
    The list entry looks like this:


```
.TC1 Table of Dates Pertaining to the "Tenth Symphony"..............#
```


    Now you have all your entries and are ready to generate the two tables.
If you wish, insert **.PA** commands to break up this short file into several more
pages just for fun! Then:

Press   **^KD** or **F10**

to save the file and return to the Opening menu.

Generating Tables of Contents and Lists for One File

    When you generate a table of contents, WordStar also creates any tables of
lists, too. So, you'll have a .TOC file and a .TO1 file for CH.27:

Press   **T** [table of contents]

    WordStar responds:


```
Type the name of the document for which tables of contents are to be made.
If you press Esc at any question after naming the document, further
questions will not be asked and defaults will be used for them. If you
press ↵   after a question, a default will be used. The main table
of contents will be in a file with the same name, but file type TOC. Up to
nine more tables will be in files with types TO1 to TO9.

Table of contents for what document?
```

    Most of the time you'd want to generate a table of contents and any lists
for an entire file, so type the document name and press **ESC** to bypass any
further questions. **Tip:** If you were generating a table of contents for the same
file that you just saved, press **T** [table of contents] and then press **ESC**.
    If you type the file name and press **RETURN**, WordStar requests the
beginning and ending pages. You can therefore specify a page range for which
WordStar is to generate the table or tables.

Caution: Use page numbers that make sense according to the file's pagination scheme. That is, if you tell WordStar to start generating a table from page 7, but the first page of the file is page 42, WordStar unceremoniously drops you back to the Opening menu.

After that, WordStar displays this message:

```
Generating table of contents...

^U cancels in the middle
```

WordStar displays the page it's on at the top of the screen. Now all you can do is wait, unless you want to cancel the operation by pressing **^U (F2)**. WordStar will stop and save the table of contents entries that it's read so far. Otherwise, in a moment or two the new table files are ready!

You can't work with any other file or command while WordStar is generating a table of contents or an index (see below). Conversely, WordStar can't generate a table of contents or index while it's printing. If, for instance, you're printing a file and you press **T** [table of contents] from the Opening menu, WordStar retorts:

```
Cannot make an index or tables of contents while printing.

Press Esc to continue.
```

Patience, please, Dear Reader! Let WordStar finish printing first. If you get this message—

```
Can't use that printer. Incorrect name or not enough memory.

Press Esc to continue.
```

—either you don't have enough memory to run the table of contents program, or you don't have the correct *printer driver* for it. As strange as it may seem, WordStar uses a specific printer driver called $TOC to generate tables of contents. If you've reduced the size of the printer driver file, WSPRINT.OVR (Chapter 27), perhaps you didn't include this driver.

Caution with File Names!

WordStar always creates a table of contents file using the file name *without* the file extension. WordStar then appends the extension .TOC to the file containing the table of contents, and extensions .TO1, .TO2, .TO3, and so on, to files containing separate lists. WordStar saves these files on the default drive or in the default directory.

Take care if you're generating separate tables of contents for files with similar names. For example, you generate a table of contents for CH.1. The table's file name is CH.TOC. Then you generate a table of contents for CH.2. WordStar *again* uses CH.TOC for the table of contents file but—at least at present—doesn't warn you that it's about to overwrite the first file! (The folks at MicroPro may have corrected the problem by the time you read this.)

Tip: *As soon as* you generate a table of contents, use the **E** command from the Opening menu, or **^KE** from within a file, to rename the table of contents and list files.

Generating Tables of Contents and Lists for Many Files

Okay, everything is easy when you're just working with individual files. But now you have to create a table of contents for an entire book, which you've broken down into modules. Each file contains a different chapter.

As you probably have figured out, use a *command file* to "run the show" with file insert (**.FI**) commands. For example, suppose the book contains ten chapters. Here's a command file to generate a table of contents. There are a couple nifty tricks here—what are they?

```
.. command file to generate table of contents for my magnum opus
.TC                        Table of Contents
.TC
.TC
.FI CH.1
.TC
.FI CH.2
.TC
.FI CH.3
.TC
.FI CH.4
.TC
.FI CH.5
.TC
.FI CH.6
.TC
.FI CH.7
.TC
.FI CH.8
.TC
.FI CH.9
.TC
.FI CH.10
```

You've included the title *Table of Contents* in the command file; WordStar will insert it at the top of the table of contents file. That's trick number one. The other trick involves those blank .TC lines. Even if you insert blank lines between the .FI commands, WordStar won't separate the table of contents entries for one chapter from the next. You've accomplished this with the blank .TC lines.

Remember to type the file name of the command file when you use it to generate a table of contents for all the other files. **Caution:** I've discovered the hard way that if a file doesn't end in at least one hard or soft return, the .FI command won't work properly and WordStar will *skip* the next file in the list. For example, suppose the last character of CH.8 is at the end of a paragraph, but there is no hard return there. WordStar would skip CH.9 altogether and go on to CH.10! *Caveat scriptor . . .*

Editing a Table of Contents

Once you have generated the table of contents and lists, you can open the table files and edit them. In this example, WordStar has created two file: CH.TOC and CH.TO1. Use **D** [open a document] from the Opening menu to edit these files.

You might want to pretty them up a bit, or even insert them into the main file (probably at the beginning of the file, no?). Perhaps you'll decide to include page formatting commands, or what have you, then print the table of contents file separately or along with the other file. This brings me to the last topic before you proceed to indexing . . .

Pagination with Roman Numerals

Traditionally, the page numbering for tables of contents uses *lowercase Roman numerals.* WordStar can only correctly paginate with integer numbers (Arabic numerals), so how do you get Roman numerals instead? Right! Use a different footer setup for each page—a hassle, but what can *I* do about it? For instance, for a centered page ii, this is how the footer command might appear:

```
.F1                                    ii
```

Remember to change the footer for each page because WordStar would use the same footer if you didn't instruct it otherwise. This is the *only* way to do noninteger pagination in WordStar—at least for the present.

Creating an Index

WordStar can generate an index of a file—or of several files—in two different ways:

- It can read *only* entries that follow the index dot command, **.IX**, or those marked by the toggle switch **^PK** in the file, and then arrange the entries alphabetically in a separate index file.

- It can index *all* words in a file except those in an optional *exclusion list*. This is a separate file that contains an alphabetical listing of common words that you don't want to index. Many people call them "noise" words. *The, a,* and *in* are typical noise words. Once again, WordStar creates a separate index file.

Caution: If you instruct WordStar to index all words in a file, it will include separate index entries for any **.IX** lines or phrases enclosed in **^PK** commands. It's a good idea to use one approach or the other. That is, if you want to index all words, don't include any **.IX** lines or **^PK** commands.

Types of Index Entries

There are four kinds of index entries: (1) a single reference, (2) a reference with a subreference, (3) a cross-reference, and (4) a primary reference. You'll prepare all three in a moment.

There are two ways to insert a single reference into a file:

1. Directly *above or below* the paragraph in which the reference occurs, insert a blank line and a new **.IX** dot command line with the reference. Separate the **.IX** from the text of the reference with a space. (Whether you insert the **.IX** line above or below the paragraph is the topic of the next section.) Here are two examples:

   ```
   .IX cats
   .IX domestic animals
   ```

2. Enclose the word or phrase *in the text itself* with the indexing print command, **^PK**. This is a toggle switch, so there must be two commands for each reference. WordStar shows the command as **^K** on the screen:

   ```
   As you know, ^Kcats^K are one of the most popular kinds of
   ^Kdomestic animals^K.
   ```

In the example above, notice that the ending ^K after *animals* occurs *before* the period. You don't want to include the period in the index reference! You can use **^PK** only for single references.

Recall from Chapter 14 that the **^PK** command has a entirely different task in headers and footers: it sets up alternating pagination. Thus, you can't include an index reference in any dot command line.

In either case above, WordStar displays the references in the index file like this:

```
Cats, 2
Domestic animals, 2
```

Note: In all the examples I'm using page numbers arbitrarily just to show you how the final index entries appear.

The *only* way to insert a reference with a subreference is to use the **.IX** dot command. Separate the two parts with a comma:

```
.IX animals, domestic
.IX animals, cats
.IX animals, dogs
```

WordStar will consolidate all subreferences under the *same reference name* in the index file and list the page numbers for each *exact* reference:

```
Animals
  cats, 2
  dogs, 2
  domestic, 2
```

WordStar always capitalizes the first letter of the reference, even if you don't, but WordStar won't change the case of anything else. If you need uppercase elsewhere in a reference or subreference, type it correctly:

```
.IX dog breeds, Akita
.IX dog breeds, German Shepherd
```

This appears as:

```
Dog breeds
  Akita, 5
  German Shepherd, 5
```

If you want the reference to appear as Dog Breeds, make sure you type *each* reference with the correct case:

```
.IX Dog Breeds, Akita
.IX Dog Breeds, German Shepherd
```

 Tip: Once you've created your index, follow these easy steps if you want all references in lowercase: (1) press ^KN to turn column mode on, (2) block out the first letter of each line in the entire index as the column block, (3) press ^K' to turn the block into lowercase, (4) press ^KN again to turn column mode off.

When marking index entries, you can use the backslash to have WordStar print a comma literally and thus not interpret it as the reference/subreference separator:

```
.IX Beethoven\, Ludwig van
```

This will appear as:

```
Beethoven, Ludwig van, 5
```

You can still include a subreference:

```
.IX Beethoven\, Ludwig van, stomach problems
```

WordStar always treats the *first* and *only the first* comma that doesn't have a backslash in front of it as the separator between reference and subreference. WordStar prints any other commas past the first one as just literal commas. Look at these entries:

```
.IX Beethoven, childhood, in Bonn
.IX Beethoven, childhood, in Vienna
```

WordStar sees the first comma as the separator and includes the second in the subreference. Here is the result in the index file:

```
Beethoven
  childhood, in Bonn
  childhood, in Vienna
```

Notice that WordStar did *not* consolidate the subreferences!

To mark a cross-reference you also use the **.IX** command, but append a hyphen to the command. The hyphen must immediately follow the **.IX**. In addition, include any extra words in the cross-reference. For example:

```
.IX- dogs, see Domestic animals
```

Cross-references don't have page numbers, so WordStar shows this example as:

```
Dogs
  see Domestic animals
```

You can include any cross-referencing text that you want and in any case:

```
.IX- geniuses, see also: Alfieri\, Vincent
```

This appears in the index as:

```
Geniuses
  see also: Alfieri, Vincent
```

Finally, you can indicate a *primary* index reference, that is, where you discuss a topic most thoroughly. The plus sign (+) symbol notes a primary reference. WordStar prints a primary reference page number in boldface. (Only copies of WordStar Release 4 available after June 1987 include this feature.) For example, your text contains many references to Beethoven's *Ninth Symphony,* so you want to note where the primary reference is:

```
.IX+ Ninth Symphony
```

By the way, WordStar *ignores* print codes in the **.IX** lines or when they're enclosed in **^PK** commands. So the only way to add codes to an index—other than on primary reference lines—is to edit the index file after WordStar has generated it. Use find and replace to help you.

Above or Below?

Where an index entry goes depends on where the page breaks occur in relationship to the text that you're referencing. For example, take a look at this paragraph, which extends from one page to the next, and the index entries for it:

```
.IX Benson\, E.F., Miss Mapp
     After experiencing to the very fullest Lucia's whirlwind of
activity in Riesholme and London, the reader enters an altogether
different world in the third book of the series.  Indeed, Miss
Mapp isn't about Lucia at all!  To introduce his readers to
--------------------------------------------------------------------------P
picturesque Tilling (actually, Rye) and to Lucia's ultimate
"match," E.F. Benson goes on a delightful tangent.  The inevi-
table and hilarious confrontation doesn't happen until Mapp and
Lucia.
.IX Benson\, E.F., Mapp and Lucia
```

Here, the reference for Benson's book, *Miss Mapp,* goes above the paragraph, but the reference for his other book, *Mapp and Lucia,* must appear below the paragraph, because of the location of the page break. **Caution:** Don't ever insert dot command lines in the middle of a paragraph: WordStar may align the **.IX** into the paragraph at some point!

"Words to the Wise"

The most common index is one containing only those entries you mark in the text, but it's also the most tedious because *you* have to set up the entries yourself. Now that you know how to mark entries, a few preliminary words to the wise about creating an index are in order.

First, try to determine the specific index topics you want *before* you begin. Do you plan to have separate entries for *Apple Pie* and *Pie, Apple?* If you do, you must put in a dot command line for each. WordStar can't help you decide your index topics, but a good style book—such as the *The Chicago Manual of Style*—can.

Second, even though it takes more time, try to find the entries for each topic separately and mark them, one topic at a time. That way, you can concentrate on one topic without distraction from others, and you won't miss a reference location. What's more, you can then create a *temporary macro* to set up the index reference for the topic repeatedly throughout the file, or the ^Y/^U trick to delete the reference the first time you type it, then restore it immediately there and everywhere else in the file quickly. Use the find command to help you find the locations of the reference.

Third, and most important, *be consistent.* (It's the Emerson/Alfieri debate again!). If you mark one section of text as an entry called *Pies,* make sure you mark all other applicable text in the same fashion. For instance, if you marked a section with the topic *Apple Pies,* then WordStar will generate a separate entry in the index for this entry. It might be better if you used a heading and a subheading in the index. The heading, of course, would be *Pies,* while each subheading would be a type of pie: *apple, cherry,* and so on.

Be consistent in your use of case, too. If you type *pies, apple* in some places and *Pies, Apple* in other places, WordStar considers these separate entries for the index. It always capitalizes the first letter of the entry, but doesn't change the other letters. Again, an ounce of prevention is worth a pound of headaches later.

Finally, there's no getting around the harsh reality that *after* WordStar generates an index for you, you'll still have to do a bit of "housekeeping" to pretty it up. Even the best-planned index may not turn out exactly as you intended. For instance, you might decide to consolidate a few entries or add more cross-references. But it's an easy matter once you *have* the drafted index to make changes to it.

Try Your Hand!

Why not follow along with me and mark a few index entries for your Beethoven book?

Press	**D** [open a document]
Type	ch.27
Press	**RETURN**

First, position the cursor at the left margin of the first paragraph, line 11 of page 1. You'll insert two index entries here.

Press	^N

to insert a line but leave the cursor where it is.

Type	.IX Grump\, Johann Friedrich
Press	**RETURN**
Type	.IX symphonies, "tenth"

Next, position the cursor on the *S* of *Sachertorte* on the second to last line of the paragraph.

Press	^PK
Press	^F or ^**RIGHT ARROW** twice
Press	^S or **LEFT ARROW**

to position the cursor directly after the *a* of *Sonata*.

Press   **^PK**

Now, position the cursor on the line in the chart of dates that begins *15 October 1813*.

Press   **^N**

to insert a line but leave the cursor where it is.

Type   .IX Kram\, Gertrude

Press   **RETURN**

Type   .IX- landlady, see Kram\, Gertrude

In the listing for *5 January 1814* enclose the words *Sacher Hotel* in **^PK** codes.

Then, position the cursor at the left margin of the first line of the paragraph after *The Extant Material,* line 12 of page 2.

Press   **^N**

to insert a line but leave the cursor where it is.

Type   .IX notebooks

Finally, position the cursor at the left margin of the first line of the last paragraph.

Press   **^N**

to insert a line but leave the cursor where it is.

Type   .IX Grump\, Waltraute

There are many more possible index entries, but I think you get the picture!

Press   **^KD** or **F10**

to save the file and return to the Opening menu.

Generating an Index for One File

The same points that govern table of contents generation apply to generating an index, too. They are:

- You can't print or edit while WordStar is creating an index.
- You can specify page ranges or index an entire file.
- WordStar saves the index in a file using the file name, but with the extension .IDX for "index." You can then edit the file as you wish.
- If you press ^U (F2) to cancel the index generation, WordStar saves the index entries that it's read up to the moment you canceled.
- You must have a special indexing printer driver in the WSPRINT.OVR file. The driver is called $INDEX.

The only big difference between generating a table of contents and generating an index is that you have to tell WordStar when you'd like to index all the words in a file except for any possible noise words.

Press   **I** [index a document]

WordStar responds:

```
Type the name of the document to be indexed.  If you press Esc at any
question after naming the document, further questions will not be asked
and defaults will be used for them.  If you press ↵  after a question,
a default will be used. The resulting index will be in a file with the
same name, but file type IDX.

Document to index?
```

Type   ch.27

Press   **ESC**

to bypass the other index questions.
     WordStar tells you—

```
Indexing...

^U cancels in the middle of indexing
```

You can then edit the CH.IDX document to add, say, a heading ("Index") and make any other changes you'd like. Notice that WordStar separates entries for each letter—*A, B, C,* and so on—with a blank line. If you wish, insert the index into the main file with the *^KR* command. Remember to *rename* the index file if you plan to generate another index from another file with the same name but different extension.

Generating an Index for Many Files

You can use the same command file approach to set up an index for an entire book, or whenever you want a composite index for many files. You can use the very same command file, even if it has **.TC** commands! WordStar just honors the **.FI** commands and disregards the **.TC** commands when it generates the index.

Using an Exclusion List and Indexing All Other Words

If you plan to index all words in a file except those in an exclusion list of noise words, here's what you should know:

- You don't have to mark anything in the file, but keep in mind that WordStar just generates a list of words, *not* phrases.

- WordStar automatically excludes the standard noise words that are in a nondocument file called WSINDEX.XCL (the .XCL stands for "exclusion"). If it can't find this file on the default drive or in the default directory, WordStar won't exclude the noise words from the index.

- WordStar also looks for another exclusion file with the same name as the file you're indexing, but again with the extension .XCL. For example, before starting to index all words in CH.27, WordStar checks for the existence of a file called CH.XCL and excludes any words in that file, too. You can thus maintain the standard noise words in the WSINDEX.XCL file, and a separate list of other unwanted words for each different file.

However, you must be a little careful about creating the exclusion file. First, it has to be a nondocument. Second, it must have the same name as the file you want to index, and it must have the extension .XCL. Third, the words you want to exclude must be in *alphabetical order.* Finally, you can type the words in any mixture of case, but using lowercase requires fewer keystrokes.

If you wish, open the WSINDEX.XCL file with the **N** [open a nondocument] command from the Opening menu to see the noise words. You can add or delete words, but make sure you maintain the list in strictly alphabetical order.

Tip: You can have a special transient DOS command sort the entries in an exclusion file for you! See the discussion of the SORT command in Chapter 28.

To generate a list of all words except those on your two exclusion lists, press **I** [index a document], type the file name, and press **RETURN**. WordStar then asks:

```
Index every word (Y/N)?
```

Type   **y**

Answer the page range questions or press **ESC** to bypass them. Normally, WordStar "assumes" you *don't* want to index all words—that is, that you just want to extract the **.IX** and **^PK** entries. However, if you most often index all words, you can make that the indexing default (Chapter 27).

Tip: Generating an index using every word in a file can help you build your final index, because it can show you where every occurrence of a word appears. For instance, if the word *pies* appears on pages 1, 2, 3, 4, and 7, you can easily see that you'd want to combine the page numbers to list them instead as 1-4, 7.

Footnotes and Not So Fancy Free

Dear Reader: It's almost a certainty that sometime soon WordStar will be able to "do" footnotes, just as it more than likely will be able to "do" windows. That is, there will be some kind of *automatic footnote feature,* which means you don't have to worry about placing footnotes at the bottom of a page. WordStar will place them for you.

Until automatic footnoting comes along, however, rely on the old—that is, manual—ways to do footnotes. Who knows, maybe you'll like one of these methods better! Although there are any number of ways to handle footnotes, I'll concentrate on just two popular alternatives in this section.

I prefer to keep all footnotes in separate files, one note per file. Later, when a project is getting close to its final stages, I use **^KR** to insert the footnotes into the main text. Of course, whenever possible I make sure that I've made all editing changes to the file before adding the footnotes, but I can still edit the file later if necessary.

You may prefer to have footnotes in the text itself to get a rough idea of the page makeup in a file's draft stages. That is, directly *below* a paragraph that contains a footnote reference, include the note itself with its divider line and the correct spacing. Later, when you're ready to place the notes, just block each one and move the block to the bottom of the page.

No matter what route you take, your biggest problem with footnotes will be placing them correctly. You must first ascertain the size of the entire note in lines, including any blank lines between the text and the note and line divider line. Then you insert a **.PA** command to break the file page at the correct location that allows you to place the note at the bottom of the page. Finally, you position the note, either by reading it in from a separate file, or by moving it.

Tip: If a note isn't at the very bottom of the page, add a few blanks lines with ^N directly *above* the note to "push it down" the page.

If you prefer *endnotes* that appear at the end of a chapter or section, your life will be much simpler. At the end of the file, just change the format for the notes and type each note in its turn. *Question:* How could the table of contents feature help you generate endnotes? Think about it sometime!

A Footnote Format File

You might find it advantageous to create a format file for the footnote format that you use. Because footnotes are almost always in single spacing and may require other special formatting, make sure you include dot commands to *restore* the default format of the main file directly below the footnote.

Here's my example footnote format. It's in a file called simply FN.

Press	**D** [open a document]
Type	fn
Press	**RETURN**
Type	y

because this is a new file.

In the footnote the lines are single spaced and justification is on, as in the main file into which you'll place the footnotes (CH.27). A 25-character divider line separates the file text from the first note, and there is one blank line between the divider and the note, and then between notes. The footnote reference number is flush to column 1, but the note itself indents to the first tab stop. That means I can use the paragraph margin command for the first line of the note; the **.LM 6** command handles the other lines in the note.

```
.. footnote format
.LS 1
.PM 1
.LM 6
_____

.. restore file format
.LS 2
```

```
.LM 1
.PM
```

If your right margin justification setting is off, include an **.OJ ON** command in the format file so WordStar correctly formats the lines for each note. You may also decide to leave out the divider line, because if there are several notes on the same page the divider line only has to appear once. Either use a macro to type the divider line and blank line for you, or create another format file to read it in whenever you need it.

Type the file, then press **^KD (F10)** to save it.

Footnotes in Separate Files

One of the important advantages to maintaining notes in separate files is that they don't get in the way of your editing routine when you're working with the main file. I generally label footnote files by their number: F.1, F.2, and so on. If I have several current projects all requiring footnotes, I keep each in a different directory or on different floppy disks to avoid confusing the footnote files.

To create a new note file, say F.7 for "footnote number seven," follow these steps:

Press	**D** [open a document]
Type	f.7
Press	**RETURN**
Type	y

because this is a new file.

Press	**^KR**
Type	fn
Press	**RETURN**

to insert a copy of the format file.

Position the cursor on the blank line above the ..restore file format line, type the footnote number, press **TAB**, and type the text of the note. Here's a finished note:

```
.. footnote format
.LS 1
```

```
.PM 1
.LM 6
```

```
7.   Douglas  T.  Gladstone,  Ph.D.,  "Cuisine  and  Counterpoint:
     Beethoven"s  Letters  to Johann Friedrich Grump,"  Food and
     Music Review, Vol. X, No. 2 (June 1987), pp. 22-39; Claudia
     Trelawny,  "Beethoven's 'Sachertorte' Symphony,' Journal of
     the  Canadian  Beethoven Society, Vol. 31,  No.  7 (October
     1983), pp. 199-234.
..  restore file format
.LS 2
.LM 1
.PM
```

If you wish, press ^OH to turn hyphen help on and check possible hyphenation spots. When you're finished, press ^KD (F10) to save the file.

Once you have all your separate footnote files ready, make a *printout* of their contents so you can see at a glance how long each note is. **Tip:** Use a command file that contains **.FI** commands to print all the footnotes you need. For example:

```
.FI F.1
.FI F.2
.FI F.3
.FI F.4
.FI F.5
.FI F.6
.FI F.7
```

When you print this command file, WordStar prints each footnote file in its turn. Next you'll place the note at the correct spot on the page.

Press   **D** [open a document]

Type   ch.27

Press   **RETURN**

You first need a *footnote reference number* in the text itself. Position the cursor at the end of the first paragraph on line 23. The cursor should be directly after the closing quotation mark so that you attach the number to the end of the sentence. Although footnote references can have different styles, you'll stick to a "plain vanilla" superscripted number:

Press   **^PT**

Type   **7**

Press   **^PT**

You're ready to place the note at the bottom of page 1. It turns out that the note, including divider, contains 8 lines. Add to that 2 blank lines for spacing from the text itself, so you need a total of 10 blank lines at the bottom of the page.

Position the cursor at the bottom of the page. It turns out that there's a **.PA** command line there from an earlier lesson. Position the cursor on this line and *delete it* with **^Y (F5)** before continuing.

Now, count 10 lines starting on the *last line* of the page and counting up. That's where you have to break the page. The page break might be in the middle of a table entry (*15 January 1814*), so why not break the page instead on the line that starts the entry? Position the cursor on that line (it should be line 48).

Press   **^N**

to insert a line but leave the cursor where it is.

Type   **.PA** or **.pa**

to break the page here.

You could have just inserted the footnote here without adding an unconditional page break. You'll delete the **.PA** command after placing the note. I just wanted to show you different ways to go.

Press   **^QS** or **^F9**

to position the cursor at the beginning of the line.

Now, insert the footnote:

Press   **^KR**

Type   **f.7**

Press   **RETURN**

Because you broke the page with *more* than 10 lines left, you should add a couple of blank lines above the note to push it down to the bottom of the page. How many lines do you add? You don't know yet! To find out, delete the **.PA** line and the blank line directly above it:

Press   **^QF** or **^F1**

Type   .PA or .pa

(whichever way you originally entered the command).

Press   **ESC**

Press   **^Y or F5**

to delete the line.

Press   **BACKSPACE**

to delete the previous blank line.

There should now be at the bottom of page 1 *five* lines of the table that you want at the top of page 2. Position the cursor above the footnote and add five blank lines to push the note to the bottom of the page:

Press   **^E or UP ARROW** sixteen times

Press   **^N** five times

to insert five blank lines but leave the cursor where it is.

Here's how the bottom of page 1 and the top of page 2 will appear with the note in place:

```
15 October 1813   -   Composer shows sketches for "first
                      movement" of something to landlady,
                      Gertrude Kram, who is not impressed




.. footnote format
.LS 1
.PM 1
.LM 6
```

---

7.   Douglas T. Gladstone, Ph.D., "Cuisine and Counterpoint: Beethoven's Letters to Johann Friedrich Grump," Food and Music Review, Vol. X, No. 2 (June 1987), pp. 22-39; Claudia Trelawny, "Beethoven's 'Sachertorte' Symphony," Journal of the Canadian Beethoven Society, Vol. 31, No. 7 (October 1983), pp. 199-234.

```
--------------------------------------------------------------------------P
.. restore file format
.LS 2
.LM 1
.PM
              5 January 1814      -    Dispute with landlady forces
                                       composer to move, disrupting all
                                       work in progress; Beethoven spends a
                                       great deal of time at the Sacher
                                       Hotel, devouring pastries
```

Whew! That was a lot of work, but I think you see that there are many points to keep in mind when you place footnotes.

Press   ^KS or F9

to save the file and resume where you left off.

Inserting Footnotes as You Type

If you want to see the footnote text, add the note directly *below* the paragraph containing the reference number. **Caution:** Don't add the note to the middle of the paragraph because the two entities should be separate. For example, suppose you want to add a reference after the words *Notebook 7* on the third line of the next paragraph. Position the cursor directly past the *7*. Then add the next number:

Press   ^PT

Type   8

Press   ^PT

Now, align the paragraph because you've made changes to it.

Press   ^B

The cursor is directly past the paragraph, exactly where you want to be to insert the note:

Press   ^KR

Type   fn

Press   RETURN

to insert the footnote format.

Press   ^X or **DOWN ARROW** six times

to position the cursor on the blank line.

Type the text of the note, shown below with the dot commands from the FN format file:

```
.. footnote format
.LS 1
.PM 1
.LM 6
```

```
8.   All page references to Beethoven's notebooks are from the
     edition edited by Karl Heinz Kleinhirn, 1912-1914.
.. restore file format
.LS 2
.LM 1
.PM
```

When you're ready to place the note at the bottom of the page, block it out—including the dot commands—and move it with **^KV (SHIFT F7)**. You'll still have to finagle a bit with the page endings, because you're never completely sure how the page will look until you've positioned the note at the bottom of the page.

Editing a File with Footnotes Already in Place

Another advantage to keeping footnotes in separate files is that you can delete a note from the main file, edit the file, and restore the note quickly. That way, you won't have any trouble aligning paragraphs.

That is, if you break a page in the middle of a paragraph to make room for a footnote, you can't realign the paragraph correctly. The page break and footnote interrupt the "flow" of the paragraph. To edit the paragraph, delete the note—and all footnote related dot commands and extra blank lines—and bring the two halves of the paragraph together. Make your changes and press **^B** to realign the paragraph. Then reinsert the note.

Tip: Don't delete separate footnote files until you are totally finished with a project. You never know when you'll need them again!

Well, Dear Reader, after struggling through this long and complicated chapter you should definitely consider yourself a true bibliophile! And if you admire the printed page as much as your fellow bibliophiles do, there are many nice surprises awaiting you in the next chapter.

Laser Legerdemain

In this chapter you will learn the following new command:

File Command

.PR OR=P/L   Change the laser printer paper orientation

One of the biggest buzzwords these days in the ever-changing world of computers is *desktop publishing,* also known as *personal publishing.* What made personal publishing such an interesting idea, and a potentially revolutionary one, was the appearance of desktop size laser printers. Provided you have a couple of grand to buy a laser printer, you can create near typeset-quality documents for a fraction of the cost of typesetting.

New software products have emerged to tap the desktop publishing capabilities of laser printers. Most desktop publishing programs can read, and often write, WordStar files. If you don't want to learn another program, however, with a little practice—and a lot of patience—you can produce some rather stunning documents with WordStar alone. This chapter starts you on your way.

Note: I use the Hewlett-Packard LaserJet Series II as the representative laser printer in this chapter. The Series II is similar to its predecessor, the LaserJet Plus. Even if you own another brand, the general remarks in the chapter still apply, and you can extrapolate the information you need from the examples.

DO WARM-UP

Terminology Trouble

As much as I would like to avoid jargon, there are unfortunately a few terms and concepts indigenous to the world of laser printers that you must understand. Even more unfortunate is the perplexing way the meaning of a particular term changes depending on who's using the term. So the first order of business is to explain and clarify the terminology mess.

One reason for all the confusion is a matter of history. Word processing programs like WordStar trace their roots back to the milieu of the office and the typewriter, while the laser printer's antecedents are in the domain of typesetting and printing. Both worlds have different sets of terminology, to be sure. Now the two worlds are coming together, but no one yet has standardized the terminology. You'll find, however, that the jargon associated with desktop publishing and laser printers is generally more akin to the typesetting world than to the typewriter world.

Typestyles, Fonts, and Families

A dot-matrix or daisy wheel printer prints a particular typestyle that may either be built into the character set of the printer or on a daisy wheel or thimble. A *typestyle* is, as its name implies, one particular style of type such as Times Roman or Courier. You'll also see the word *typeface* to mean typestyle. (By the way, some typestyles are under copyright or trademark protection; for example, Times and Helvetica are registered trademarks of Allied Linotype Company.)

A *font* is one particular version of a typestyle in one particular size. Laser printers usually have several built-in, or *internal,* fonts. You can also purchase additional *font cartridges* that plug into a slot on the printer, or *soft fonts* to load into the printer's memory from disk files. The LaserJet Series II, for example, has several 12 point and 8 point, fixed-width, internal fonts. To print with proportional fonts, you'd need a cartridge or a soft font package.

When you're doing special printing effects, keep in mind the important distinction between typestyles and fonts. Conventional printers handle many effects by a purely mechanical printing action. For example, to print text in boldface, the printer normally overprints each letter two or three times, sometimes even moving the printhead slightly to make a filled in look.

A laser printer, like typesetting equipment, does not necessarily use the same mechanical techniques as conventional printers to accomplish special effects. For instance, it usually prints in boldface by switching to a separate *boldface font,* which is an emboldened version of a particular typestyle in a particular size. The same procedure applies for italics. This means that the printer uses several different versions of the same typestyle in the same size. Each version is a different font.

A *family,* or *font family,* is a collection of all fonts available in a particular typestyle on a particular laser printer. For instance, the Times Roman family may include regular, bold, and italic fonts in 10 point, 12 point, and 14 point sizes (I'll discuss *points* in a moment), but only bold fonts for 18 point and 24 point. This particular font family thus contains 11 different fonts.

How many of the fonts in a family you can use depends on whether they're (1) internal, (2) on a font cartridge, or (3) soft fonts. You can use any internal font at any time because internal fonts are always available. You can only use cartridge fonts after you've inserted the correct cartridge, but you *cannot* switch cartridges during printing. The number of soft fonts that you can access at any one time depends on how much memory your printer has. (Oh, yes, a laser printer has memory, just like a computer.) See the separate section on soft fonts, below.

Points, Picas, Pitch, and Proportionals

Okay, that wasn't too difficult to understand, but now the confusion begins in earnest. Typesetters and printers normally refer to font sizes in terms of *points* or *picas.* There are 72 points in an inch, 12 points in a pica, and thus 6 picas per inch. The font size is usually just a little bigger than the height of a font's tallest character, so think of font size as a vertical measurement. On laser printers font size is usually displayed in points. (To save your sanity, you'll bypass the metric system altogether!)

Pitch, as you know, refers to the number of printed characters per horizontal inch. The larger the font, the fewer characters will fit on an inch. Traditional pica type prints 10 characters per horizontal inch, while elite prints 12. You also know that 10 characters per inch is a **.CW 12** setting (because you divide 12 into 120 to get 10), and 12 characters per inch is **.CW 10**. The **.CW** setting is very important for WordStar's use of laser fonts because it approximates the point size.

It's easy to determine a character width setting when each character is a fixed width. Proportionally spaced fonts, however, present a problem because character widths change. That is, using the same font you may get 12 characters per inch or 10, depending on the actual characters.

Portraits and Landscapes

What is this, an art history lesson? Not really, but the laser printer terms *portrait* and *landscape* do come originally from the world of painting. This section is a short primer on paper handling. The paper on which a laser printer prints enters the printer from a paper tray and can only enter one way. You can't shift the paper around to print, say, horizontally on the page. What you must do instead is change the *paper orientation.*

Normally, you print across the width of the paper. This is *portrait orientation,* so named because most portrait paintings are vertical. When you want to print across the length of the page, that's called *landscape orientation,* because landscape paintings are generally horizontal. Laser printers work in portrait mode unless you instruct them to print in landscape mode. You'll see how in a moment.

It's very important to understand that, depending on what types of fonts you're using, there may be far fewer fonts available in landscape orientation than in portrait orientation. Similarly, some fonts only print in landscape orientation.

Symbol Sets

The last terminology issue to address concerns *symbol sets.* A symbol set is merely a list of the characters available in a font. The problem with symbol sets is that they may not use the same codes as the ASCII character set of your computer. The Hewlett-Packard LaserJet series, for instance, has Roman-8, USASCII, and LINEDRAW symbol sets, among others.

Virtually all text symbol sets contain the standard letters, numbers, and punctuation marks and, fortunately, use the same *7-bit* ASCII codes. That is, code numbers 32 through 127 are standard. However, many symbol sets can't print the "extended ASCII" characters—that is, ASCII codes 1–31 and 128–255—or use different codes for the characters. You may have to find out what code, if any, represents the extended character you want, or modify the printer driver to include this character. See also "Important Default Settings."

"Soft" Fonts

Soft fonts are *software-based* fonts. Because they are on disk, you must *load*— that is, copy—the fonts you want from the disk into the printer. This process is called *downloading.* Soft fonts remain in the printer's memory until you turn the printer off. In that respect they are like any other program.

Advantages. One big advantage to soft fonts over cartridge based fonts is that you can choose exactly which fonts you want to use. You can't alter the configuration of a cartridge. In addition, soft fonts last longer than cartridge fonts. For all intents and purposes, soft fonts last "forever," provided you always use a copy of the font disk. They're also cheaper than cartridges.

Disadvantages. Unfortunately, there are a few disadvantages to soft fonts. The first is that WordStar doesn't have proportional spacing tables for all proportionally spaced soft fonts, or even for all fonts in a particular package. For example, WordStar handles the Times Roman fonts in the AC soft font package well, but it doesn't "know" too much about the Helvetica fonts in the same package.

You may still be able to use other fonts, but that depends on their size. I've found that if I want to use one or two sizes of Times Roman (say, 12 and 14 point) and a *different* size Helvetica font (18 point), then there's no problem. However, if I want to have a 12 point Times Roman and a 12 point

Helvetica, WordStar won't let me use the Helvetica. That's because they both require the same point setting, which "confuses" WordStar to no end.

The *order* in which you load the fonts may be important, too. Generally, try to load fonts in families, smallest to largest. That is, load all Times Roman fonts first before loading any Helvetica fonts.

Finally, there's the other disadvantage to soft fonts: memory limitations. Cartridge fonts contains their own internal memory that's separate from the printer's memory. Soft fonts, however, take up the printer's memory, and quite a lot of it. Depending on the size of the font and how much memory your printer has, you may only be able to download a few different fonts.

For example, the LaserJet Series II without a memory expansion board can handle about five or six fonts at once that are 12 to 14 point sizes. If you use 18, 24, or 30 point sizes, you'll quickly run out of memory. Unfortunately, the printer doesn't tell you that until it's too late and you've already started to print! This brings me to . . .

Downloading the Fonts. After you determined which fonts you want to use, you must *download* them to the printer before you can print with them. Although you can download fonts individually, you'll soon find this a tedious—not to mention boring—process on a day-to-day basis.

You select soft fonts by file name, each font in a different file. Hewlett-Packard maintains a standard nomenclature that includes the abbreviated typestyle name, the point size, whether the font is "regular," "bold," or "italic," and whether it's in portrait or landscape orientation. For example, the file TR120RPN.USP contains the 12 point Times Roman regular font for portrait orientation. Its landscape counterpart is TR120RPN.USL.

To save your sanity, follow the instructions in the font manual to create a *setup file* with the Hewlett-Packard *PCLPak* program. The setup file contains all the fonts you've decided you need. The order in which you load the fonts in the setup file determines the order in which the printer receives them.

Caution: You must set up all soft fonts as what Hewlett-Packard terms "permanent" fonts for WordStar to use them correctly. The printer doesn't clear its memory of permanent fonts after each print job. Don't use "temporary" fonts.

Once you've set up the setup file, you merely copy it to the printer from DOS. For example, my font setup file is, wouldn't you know it, FONTS. My printer is connected to the parallel port, which DOS likes to call LPT1: (with a colon at the end). Before I print, I go out to DOS with **R** [run a DOS program] from the Opening menu, or **^KF** from within a file, and issue this command:

```
C> copy fonts lpt1:/b
```

This command copies the FONTS file to the parallel printer port and, hence, to the printer itself. (The printer must be on and on-line, by the way.) The **/B** switch informs DOS that the file is in *binary* format. DOS copies more quickly when you add this switch to the command. That's all you have to know about binary!

To check whether the printer's memory was able to accommodate all the fonts in the setup file, you'll have to run the standard font test. If all the fonts print on the test, then they loaded successfully. However, if the printer can't handle all the fonts in the file, it generally starts removing the first fonts loaded to accommodate a larger font. You may *think* you're loading five fonts only to discover after running the font test that you've only loaded one!

Tip: You can have as many different setup files as you like, each with its own set of fonts. I strongly suggest that you insert *nonprinting comment lines* at the beginnings of your files to remind you which fonts the document uses. That way, you never get confused about all those different fonts.

If you want to clear the fonts from the printer, turn off the machine briefly. Then turn it on again and load whatever new soft fonts you want.

Using WordStar with Laser Printers

So much for the generalities of laser printers. Now turn your attention to how WordStar fits into the discussion at hand. **Note:** Always refer to MicroPro's README file for the latest information about laser printers, including which fonts WordStar supports. If you continue to have problems getting WordStar to work correctly with your printer, call MicroPro's Technical Service Department.

Selecting the Printer Driver

For most laser printers that WordStar supports, you just choose the printer name from the list. Of course, if this is your only printer, set it up as the primary printer. An exception to the rule is the Hewlett-Packard LaserJet series. You choose the printer driver according to the cartridge or soft font package you're using.

For example, the HPLJ:B printer driver works with the B cartridge, while the HPLJ:Y driver works with the Y cartridge and the Times Roman soft fonts in the AC font package. If your cartridge doesn't have its own printer driver, choose the generic HPLJET driver. See the README file for more information. I used the HPLJ:Y printer driver and soft fonts to print all the figures in this chapter.

Form Feeds and Default Fonts

All laser printers have to receive a form feed instruction to eject the paper at the end of each page, so change the printing defaults to answer "yes" to the Use form feeds (Y/N)? question. You may also have to tell WordStar the *port* to which the printer is attached if it's a serial port or if it's not the first parallel port (LPT1).

On the LaserJet Series II, the *default internal font* is a 12 point Courier font. But it contains the Roman-8 symbol set, so the extended ASCII characters (those between 128 and 255) are different from what your computer displays. If you print the standard internal font test, you'll note that there are other, 12 point, internal Courier fonts with *some* ASCII extended characters. You can select the font you want as the default internal font from the control panel. See the "Fonts" chapter in the user's manual for instructions.

Tip: Create a file containing a chart with the code numbers 128 through 255 and each extended character next to its number. Then print the file with the different internal fonts to see what you get for each code.

If you work a lot with foreign languages and their accent marks, stick with the default internal font and just use the codes on your chart instead of the normal extended ASCII codes for the PC. If you print a lot of lines, boxes, and other graphics, choose one of the other internal fonts that contain these characters. Unfortunately, *none* of the internal fonts contains the entire extended ASCII code set. Only the Y cartridge has the complete IBM ASCII scheme.

Note: When it comes upon an extended ASCII code, WordStar *may or may not* revert temporarily to the default internal font to print the character associated with that code. It generally reverts to the default internal font if the code represents a letter with an accent mark, but not if the code represents a graphics character. For letters with accent marks, such as the umlauted *o* (ö), the result could look a bit strange because of the change in typestyles! To get around this, you *might* be able to use the standard *o* character and the *separate* umlaut character, with a backspace command (^PH) to print the latter over the former. An umlauted *o* would thus appear on the screen as o^H½. The ^PH command won't work well with proportional fonts, however, because WordStar doesn't maintain spacing values for the extended characters.

Page Formatting Issues

Laser printers can't print in the blank lines at the very top or bottom of the page. That means you should change the default page length from 66 to the settings recommended in the README file so that WordStar shows the correct page breaks on the screen. Generally, use a page length of 62 in portrait orientation and a page length of 47 in landscape orientation. You may also want to change the default top and bottom margins. Again, the README file has recommended settings.

Laser printers also can't print at the exact left or right edges of the paper. To print closer to the left edge of the paper, use a smaller page offset setting, **.PO**. To print closer to the right side, use a higher right margin setting, **.RM**. You'll have to experiment to see which settings work best for your printer.

Paper Orientation

A dot command changes the paper orientation from within a file. It's **.PR OR** followed either by =**L** for landscape or =**P** for portrait. Thus, to switch to landscape orientation, insert this command at the top of the correct page:

```
.PR OR=L
```

Note: Switching from portrait to landscape orientation does nothing to the actual page formatting. You must still insert the necessary dot commands to change the top and bottom margins and page offset, for instance.

To return to portrait orientation, use **.PR OR=P**, or just **.PR OR**.

Caution: If you insert a **.PR** command anywhere else than at the top of the page, WordStar doesn't change the paper orientation until it reaches the *next* page.

Guidelines for Selecting Different Fonts

What font you need depends on what you're doing. For example, if the font represents a special printing effect such as boldface or italics, WordStar selects the font for you automatically when it comes upon the corresponding print code—that is, **^PB** or **^PY**. If you're just switching to a different sized font, you have more work to do. Here then are some general guidelines to help you select fonts:

1. WordStar can only access those fonts that are *already* in the printer—that is, internal fonts, a cartridge that's plugged in before you begin printing, or soft fonts that you've downloaded before you begin printing. All soft fonts must be "permanent."

2. For certain standard print effects, such as boldface or italics, WordStar automatically chooses the right font—provided the font is already in the printer. That is, when it sees a **^PB** command it switches to the bold font in the current point size and then switches back to the previous font when it encounters the ending **^PB**. When it comes to a **^PY** command, it switches to the italic font.

3. WordStar handles most other print effects as on other printers. For example, underlining (**^PS**) is just underlining, *not* italics. (To print in true italics, use the find and replace command to replace all **^PS** commands with **^PY** commands.) Superscripts and subscripts appear three ticks above or below the line with the default "roll." See below for more information about the **^PA** and **^PN** commands.

4. If there's no font available for a special effect, WordStar keeps using the current font. An exception on most, but not all, laser printers is

the doublestrike command, ^PD. When it sees this command, Word-Star prints the character and then shifts the print head over 1/120ths of an inch to print the character again, thus producing a "simulated bold" effect. **Tip:** If no bold font is available, use ^PD instead of ^PB.

5. To use proportionally spaced fonts, you must include a **.PS ON** command in the file before you can access the fonts.

6. To switch to a different sized font at the beginning of a new line, you insert a **.CW** command line at that point in the file where WordStar is to use the new font. The actual **.CW** setting depends on the size of the font and whether it's proportionally spaced or fixed-width. (On one or two laser printers you must also use the correct **.LQ** setting, **.LQ ON** or **.LQ OFF**.)

7. To switch fonts in the *middle* of a line, you must have already defined the alternate character width (the ^PA setting).

8. You will more than likely have to adjust the line length—the left and right margins—and perhaps the page offset and vertical pitch when you switch between fonts of different sizes.

Because items 6, 7, and 8 in this list are the most complicated, I'll discuss them at length next.

What Fonts Can You Use?

Theoretically, you can use any font now in the printer. In actuality WordStar only works well with certain fonts, depending on whether proportional spacing is on or off and what proportional fonts WordStar officially supports with spacing tables.

Fixed-width fonts present no problem at all, because WordStar doesn't have to worry about the different character sizes. For proportionally spaced fonts, however, WordStar has to maintain a table of spacing values for *each* font! That means, for example, three different tables for just 12 point Times Roman regular, bold, and italic.

The README file contains lists of the fonts that WordStar works with for each printer driver. One such listing, the HPLJ:Y cartridge, appears in Figure 26–1.

If the font you need is not on the list for your particular driver, try using it anyway. But don't be surprised if it doesn't print correctly! One major problem with nonsupported proportional fonts is that WordStar might not print the correct spaces between words. It may skip some spaces altogether! You may have to add extra spaces, or even binding spaces, to correct this problem.

This particular driver handles the Y cartridge, which has no proportional fonts, and the AC package of soft fonts, which has many. The x marks

```
Cartridge/
Soft font  .PS .CW              Font/Point Size    R B I  Landscape
--------------------------------------------------------------------
    Y        on   none available
             off    7 (0-11)   Line Printer 8.5   x           x
                   12 (12-30)  PC Courier 12      x x x

   AC*       on     5 (0-5)    Times Roman 6      x x x       x
                    7 (6-7)    Times Roman 8      x x x       x
                    9 (8-9)    Times Roman 10     x x x       x
                   11 (10-11)  Times Roman 12     x x x       x
                   13 (12-14)  Times Roman 14     x x x       x
                   16 (15-18)  Times Roman 18       x         x
                   20 (19-24)  Times Roman 24       x         x
                   25 (25-30)  Times Roman 30       x         x
             off    7 (0-11)   Line Printer 8.5   x           x (0-30)
                   12 (12-30)  Courier 12         x
     * Other .CW settings may access additional fonts if a
       cartridge is also installed.
```

Figure 26-1   Available Fonts for the HPLJ:Y Printer

designate the available spacing tables for *R*egular, *B*old, and *I*talic fonts in portrait orientation, and those in landscape orientation. Now, what in dickens do the **.CW** settings mean?

The Dual Role of the Character Width Command

Until the WordStar designers come up with a better plan (possibly in WordStar Release 5), you use the *same* **.CW** command to (1) select a specific font, and (2) determine the horizontal character width for that font. In other words, the **.CW** setting has a dual role—a "vertical role" to note the font size, and a "horizontal role" to determine the character width.

The **.CW** setting you'll use also depends on whether you've inserted a **.PS ON** command in the file. In Figure 26-1, you'll note that **.CW 12** can select different fixed-width and proportional fonts depending on the status of **.PS**.

Now for a bit of confusion. In the **.CW** column of the chart, you'll note *two* sets of figures. What do those figures in parentheses mean? They show the available horizontal character widths for the font listed. The standard setting is on the left.

For example, with proportional spacing on, the **.CW 13** setting selects the regular 14 point Times Roman font *and* sets the character width to 13 characters per horizontal inch. If you use a **.CW 12** or **.CW 14** setting, you change the horizontal character width for *the same* font size! That is, if the current **.CW** setting is already **12**, **13**, or **14**, then **.CW 12** or **.CW 13** or **.CW**

14 just change the horizontal character width. If the current **.CW** setting is anything else than **12** through **14**, a **.CW 12**, **13**, or **14** selects the font, too.

Alas, only experimentation will help you determine what character width setting works best for a particular font size. One final point: WordStar selects whatever is the *next lower* available setting when you insert a **.CW** command that isn't one of the listed settings. For example, on the HPLJ:Y driver with proportional spacing off if you insert a **.CW 10** setting in the file, WordStar uses the Line Printer 8.5 font (**.CW 7**). If you choose **.CW 12**, WordStar selects the PC Courier 12 font.

Switching Fonts from One Line to the Next

To change fonts from one line to the next is easy: just insert the correct **.CW** dot command on a separate line directly above the text that you want to print in the new font size.

Well, maybe things aren't *that* easy! You'll have to change the margin settings to accommodate different font sizes. You may also want to change the vertical pitch (with the **.LH** command). Examples later in the chapter show you typical changes. **Tip:** Check the table in WordStar's documentation under "Character Width" to determine the recommended right margin settings for each character width.

Still, if you work with only a few different fonts, you can set up format files or macros to make the changes for you. Remember to reinstate the previous font when you need it. If you have the bold and italic versions of a font available, then WordStar switches to them automatically when it sees the **^PB** and **^PY** commands, respectively.

Switching Fonts on the Same Line

Other than selecting bold and italic fonts, you have a bit of forethought when you want to switch fonts on the same line. You must set up the second font as the alternate character width—that is, the **^PA** command—and the first font as the normal character width—the **^PN** command.

You can only switch between two fixed-width fonts or two proportional fonts with this method. Of course, at any time you can change the two fonts that you intend to use by redefining the **^PA** and **^PN** keys. Here's an example:

```
.PS ON
.CW 11
^A
.CW 13
^N
```

The setup here is for the alternate font to be 14 point Times Roman and the normal font to be 12 point. Keep in mind that the ^PA has to be on a separate blank line. Often you can start your text on the same line as the ^PN command to avoid two blank lines, but you may also discover that WordStar won't justify a line correctly. In that case, leave the ^PN command on its own blank line.

When you switch fonts on the same line, the differing size of the alternate font affects the line length. As Figure 26–2 illustrates, you may also have to adjust the vertical pitch and line length to accommodate a larger font on the same line as a smaller font. Other settings, such as page offset, may also have to change.

Using the .LH command to set vertical pitch is thus the only way to change *leading* in WordStar. This typographer's term, which by the way rhymes with *bedding,* indicates the amount of blank space between lines. How much leading you'll need depends on the font size and style, how dense you want the printout, and your general sense of aesthetics.

In Figure 26–2, on the line that is longer than the others you would use ^OR to change the right margin to a smaller setting. Press **F7** to realign the paragraph and return the cursor to the same place. Move to do the next line, change the right margin back to its original setting, and realign the rest of the paragraph.

There is no easy way to switch between fixed-width and proportional fonts on the same line. You *can* do it, as one of the examples below will show you, but it involves using the overprint line command—frustrating!

"Wizzy Wig"

No matter what fonts you use with WordStar, you won't have what the desktop publishing industry refers to as *WYSIWYG*, pronounced "wizzy wig." This

This is a example of changing fonts in the middle of a line. The normal font is 12 point, while the alternate is 14 point. When one font is only a bit larger than the other, the resulting line is more or less acceptable.

This is a example of changing fonts in the middle of a line. This time the normal font is 12 point and the alternate is 18 point bold. Notice what happens if one font is **much larger** than the other!

The only way to rectify this unsightly situation is to increase the amount of space **between the lines.** That is, use a larger .LH setting. Here, the .LH setting is 9. In any case, you'd also have to adjust the right margin on the line containing the bigger font so that it doesn't "stick out" past the other lines.

Figure 26–2   What Happens When You Switch Fonts

term means "what you see is what you get." Unfortunately, the screen appearance of your file will often be substantially different from its final printout. That means, more than likely, printing many "dry runs" of a file before getting the results you want. **Tip:** Use the PRVIEW driver to print to disk to get at least an approximation of how the pages in a file will break.

You may also want to investigate certain "add-on" programs that work with WordStar and give it substantial desktop publishing capabilities. See Chapter 28.

Some Examples

Dear Reader: I can (alas!) present only a few examples of ways to work with WordStar and laser printers. I hope that they give you "food for thought" and the inspiration to pursue your own needs. None except the first is particularly easy, so take your time studying each example. Make sure you understand how I arrived at the commands I used. For more tips, look at the LASER1.DOC and LASER2.DOC files that are part of the WordStar package.

Envelopes Again!

On some printers it's difficult or almost impossible to print individual envelopes. On others you must insert the envelope through a special slot or from a particular location in the paper feeder. On the LaserJet Series II, there's an envelope slot on the paper bin that makes printing envelopes a cinch. The printer *first* tries to feed paper from the slot, so if there's something in the slot it goes into the printer. If not, the printer just feeds in the next sheet of paper from the tray.

You'll have to adjust the page formatting and paper orientation to print envelopes, depending on where they enter the printer. Here's a revised version of the E envelope file from Chapter 21 for the LaserJet Series II. Recall that this file prints an individual envelope after requesting the name and address information from the keyboard. The file uses the printer's internal Courier font.

```
.PR OR=L
.MT 12
.PO 15
.PF OFF
.LS 1
.OP
.AV line1
.AV line2
.AV line3
```

```
.AV line4
.AV line5
.AV line6
```
<Your return address here>

ten or twelve blank lines here

```
.PO 42
&line1&
&line2/o&
&line3/o&
&line4/o&
&line5/o&
&line6/o&
```

If you compare this setup with the original E file, you'll notice that the page length is still the default. Why? Because the laser printer "assumes" that whatever you feed into it is a standard page, no matter that the paper orientation is landscape (**.PR OR=L**). So you must adjust the top margin setting to print the return address down further on the page, because the envelope enters the printer in about the middle of the page. You may also have to finagle with the page offset so that the printer prints at the correct left margin of the page.

A Fancy Memo

In Chapter 16 I showed you how to create a standard memorandum format file. Now you'll get fancy and use your laser printer to jazz up that memo format. Believe me, although this example *looks* easy, it took me quite a while to get it exactly the way I wanted it!

Go to DOS and copy the following soft fonts to the printer: 12 point Times Roman regular, 12 point Times Roman bold, 12 point Times Roman italic, and 14 point Helvetica bold. If you have a cartridge containing these fonts, make sure it's in the printer. Then return to WordStar.

Press   **D** [open a document]

Type   `memo.las`

Press   **RETURN**

Type   **y**

because this is a new file.

Figure 26–3 presents a completed memo. Refer to it as you study the commands for the basic memo format. This format includes the heading, the *To:, From:, Re:,* and *Date:* lines, and the divider line. The entire format is:

```
.. Memo format for laser printer
.. uses the following proportional fonts:
..        12 point Times Roman regular - .CW 11
..        12 point Times Roman bold
..        12 point Times Roman italic
```

MEMORANDUM

To: Jaime Pescado, Director of Marketing

From: Randolph D. Sturgeon, Head Buyer

Re: Some Thoughts

Date: April 26, 1988

- -

I am *sick and tired* of being a big fish in a little pond! When are you going to realize my true potential by getting me out of this rathole and into a job with more bite? As you know, I have repeatedly broached the subject of the company's marketing plans with you. Here are some more ideas to show some of my great potential.

It seems that the Felt Platypus chain is suffering from what I call the *ho-hum syndrome.* Diners are bored by our menus and would rather eat at the golden arches. I suggest the following two ad campaigns to get the FP back into the swing of things.

First, the broadside: **Dine with a Platypus Tonight**. How's that for a catchy title? Then the more subtle approach: **Is There a Platypus in Your Future?** Both would feature Pete the Platypus, our company mascot.

You owe it to yourself and to the company to get me involved with marketing, where I *really* belong.

Figure 26–3   A Fancy Memo

```
..              14 point Helvetica bold - .CW 13
.OP
.LH 7
.MT 6
.MB 6
.PO 10
.LS 1
.OJ OFF
.CW 12
.PS ON
.CW 13
.RM 60
                    M E M O R A N D U M



.CW 11
.RM 82
To:        ^@

From:      ^@

Re:        ^@

Date:      ^@


.PS OFF
--------------------------------------------------------------------


.LH 8
.PS ON
```

In all examples I've included nonprinting message lines to remind myself what fonts this memo uses and their corresponding **.CW** commands as listed in the README file. WordStar will switch to the bold and italic fonts when it sees the corresponding print codes in the text.

The next set of commands determines the page formatting. Notice that I'm using a slightly condensed vertical pitch setting, **.LH 7**, which I change later to **.LH 8** for the actual text of the memo. If you want to see the difference just one digit makes, try printing the memo *without* the **.LH 8** setting. The text lines are more "squeezed together."

The **.CW 12** setting determines the *general* horizontal character width. Notice that it's above the **.PS ON** command, so at this point WordStar is using a fixed character width.

With the **.PS ON** command in place, further **.CW** commands tell WordStar to choose the appropriate proportional font. The first one, **.CW 13**, selects the 14 point Helvetica bold for the title. Looking in the WordStar manual under "Character Width," I determine by the process of experiment that the right margin setting for this character width is **.RM 60**. I type the heading with its spaces between letters and then center it with the **^OC (SHIFT F2** or **ESC C)** command. There are four blank lines between the title and the next section.

So, even though WordStar doesn't technically support any Helvetica fonts from the AC package, I can still use them in many situations, provided they don't interfere with any Times Roman fonts.

The **.CW 11** command selects the 12 point Times Roman font. Because this font prints more characters per line, again by a process of experimentation I discover that a **.RM 82** setting is about right. At first I used a **.RM 80** setting, but WordStar didn't print the lines evenly, even when I turned hyphen help on and tried to hyphenate some words. Just changing the right margin to 82 made quite a difference in the printout!

In the *To:* section, notice the use of the **^P@** command on each line at column 11. This command, as you know, ensures that text prints at the *absolute* column represented by the command. No matter how long the beginning text of each line is, then, the tabbed text that you supply later always prints at column 11.

There are three blank lines below this section and the divider line of hyphens. Here I've employed a little trick. I've temporarily turned proportional spacing off so that I get fixed-character hyphens. The **.CW** setting is still **11**, by the way. After a bit of experimentation once again I determine that I need 70 hyphens for this line.

Then I just add three more blank lines, change the vertical pitch, and return to proportional spacing for the text of the memo. There should be a hard return at the end of the **.PS ON** command.

When you're finished typing the format file, press **^KD (F10)** to save the file. Then open a new file called MEMO.3, press **^KR**, type MEMO.LAS, and press **RETURN** to insert the format file. Fill in the information for the *To:* section and complete the memo as you see it in Figure 26–3. Notice the use of italics (**^PY**). The word *ho-hum,* by the way, contains a hard hyphen.

Press **^KD (F10)** to save the new memo when you're finished.

Creating Your Own Letterhead

The next example illustrates how to create your own "typeset-looking" letterhead and save printing costs. The example includes several tricks to cajole your laser printer into doing what *you* want it to do. This is a very complicated setup, so be careful!

For this example, I've turned off my printer to clear its memory of the previous fonts, then loaded the following soft fonts: 10 point Times Roman regular, 12 point Times Roman italic, 14 point Times Roman bold, and 18 point Times Roman bold. You can also use a cartridge with the same fonts. I then returned to WordStar and opened the letterhead setup file:

Press   **D** [open a document]

Type   `ltrhead`

Press   **RETURN**

Type   `y`

because this is a new file.

Figure 26–4 shows the letterhead you'll create. This is a fictitious company, so please don't try contacting them, even if you *are* a cat lover!

Now, what's the big deal about this letterhead? It's that you're using different fonts of widely different sizes on *what appears to be the same lines.* As it turns out, that's where the tricks come into play: you set up the middle section *first,* and then you go back and do the two side sections. But how?

Dear Reader, do you remember the sub/superscript roll command, **.SR**? And how about the overprint line command, **^P RETURN**? Put those little gray cells into action, as Hercule Poirot would say, and try to figure out what I'm getting at.

Casa de Gato

A Boarding Hotel for Felines
11000 Venture Boulevard
Studio City, CA 91605
(818) 222-5555

R. Ramos, President
M. Ramos, Vice President
Y. Ramos, Treasurer

We Accept:
MasterCard, Visa,
American Express

"If It Meows, We Like It"

19 May 1987

Dr. Vincent Alfieri
4118 Loony Tunes Boulevard
Los Angeles, CA 90027

Dear Dr. Alfieri:

    Blah, blah, blah ...

Figure 26–4   A Sample Letterhead

Stumped? Okay, take a look at the entire format for the letterhead and see if your gray cells have a brainstorm. *Hint:* Note the **^PT** superscript commands that appear in the file as ^T. What do they do?

```
.. Format file for letterhead
.. uses the following proportional fonts:
..              10 point Times Roman regular - .CW 9
..              12 point Times Roman italic  - .CW 11
..              14 point Times Roman bold    - .CW 13
..              18 point Times Roman bold    - .CW 16
.LH 8
.OP
.PO 8
.LS 1
.OJ OFF
.PS ON
.CW 16
.RM 52

                Casa de Gato


.CW 13
.RM 67


                A Boarding Hotel for Felines
                 11000 Venture Boulevard
                 Studio City, CA 91605
                    (818) 222-5555


.CW 11
.RM 80

                    "If It Meows, We Like It"
.LH 4
.SR 32
.RM 160
.CW 9
.. The first two lines that begin with a superscript command, ^T,
.. end with a overprint line command, ^P RETURN
^TR. Ramos, President                              We Accept:^T
.SR 24
^TM. Ramos, Vice President                    MasterCard, Visa,^T
.SR 16
^TY. Ramos, Treasurer                        American Express^T
.SR 8
.LH 8
.RM 65
.PS OFF
.CW 12
```

```
.. End here: the rest is just example!
                                            19 May 1988



Dr. Vincent Alfieri
4118 Loony Tunes Boulevard
Los Angeles, CA 90027
```

Make sure you type the extra blank lines for spacing between *Casa de Gato* and the address and elsewhere. I've deliberately included the default **.LH 8** command to emphasize that later I'm using a more compressed vertical pitch setting for the side sections of the letterhead.

I think you understand how I've set up the 18 point and 14 point fonts for the company name and address in the middle section. But what about that italic font for the phrase, *"If It Meows, We Like It"*? Because there is no 12 point regular font available, you can't just use the ^PY italic command. Instead, you must explicitly instruct WordStar to switch to the 12 point font, which happens to be italic.

The biggest problem I had with the middle section was getting the lines centered correctly on the page. You'll notice that I include a different right margin setting for each font, but none of the settings worked exactly right! After *a long period* of trial-and-error printouts I gave up attempting to center each title according to the margins. I merely adjusted the lines so that they begin at the following columns (none of which is the center position):

Casa de Gato	Column 20
A Boarding . . .	Column 20
11000 Venture . . .	Column 22
Studio City . . .	Column 22
(818) . . .	Column 26
"If . . .	Column 27

The dot commands that begin with the **.LH 4** line are the ones that involve the trick I told you about. The **.LH 4** command just changes the vertical pitch to "squeeze" the lines together, but what does the **.SR 32** line do? Recall that the default sub/superscript roll is three ticks, and that there are *eight* ticks in a full line. By setting the roll to 32, you're instructing WordStar to move up or down *four full lines!* That is, $4 \times 8 = 32$. Remember that the **.SR** command governs both the subscript roll and the superscript roll.

So, if you now issue the ^PT (superscript) command, WordStar shifts the printhead up *four* lines. That's exactly what you do: you insert a ^PT command (it appears as ^T) and then the text of the first line. I'll discuss the text on the right side of the line in a moment. At the very end of the line, you issue another **^PT** command to toggle the superscript off and return the print head to where it was before you started the line.

Wait, there's more! Now you want to shift up *three* lines instead of four for the *next line of the side text*. To do this, you must end the first line with an overprint line command, **^P RETURN**. WordStar shows a hyphen (-) in the flag character display, but that's not visible in the figure. The overprint line command ensures that you start the next line exactly where you left off the previous one.

However, this time you set the sub/superscript roll to 24, that is, a roll of three lines. Issue the **^PT** command and type the second line, which WordStar rolls up. At the end of the line, issue another **^PT** command and another **^P RETURN** command. For the third line you want to go up only two lines, so the **.SR 16** command does the trick. Press **^PT** and type the line, ending it with another **^PT**. This time, however, press **RETURN** to start a new line, because you're finished with the side sections that have to be "superscripted up."

Now for the flush right lines on the right side of the letterhead: it took me much trial and error to arrive at the correct column locations. Why? Because of the different character widths in a proportional font. Here's where the lines start (the figure text is not "to scale"):

We Accept . . .	Column 146
MasterCard . . .	Column 132
American . . .	Column 135

Finally, you set up the rest of the letter to be for a standard page and the standard fixed-width font, because you want the letter to look "typed." The **.PS OFF** command turns proportional spacing off, but because the previous **.CW 9** command is still in effect, you have to insert the correct **.CW 12** command to access the standard 12 point Courier font.

Notice I've included just a few sample lines from the letter itself to show the difference in fonts, but don't type them in the letterhead file. Just end a few blank lines down from the last dot command. That way, you can insert this file whenever you want to start a new letter.

When you're finished typing the file, press **^KD (F10)** to save it.

Whew! That took a lot of work and even more experimenting. If you have access to a laser printer, I strongly urge you to try this example and make sure you understand how it works. If you don't have the exact same fonts, use fonts of similar size and adjust the formatting accordingly.

Fixed-Width and Proportional Fonts Together

The only way to print fixed-width and proportional fonts on the same line without going completely insane is to use the overprint line command, **^P**

RETURN. When I submitted the manuscript for this book to my publisher, that's exactly what I had to do to get the "Type" lines correct.

You may have noticed that what you type is shown in a fixed-width font to imitate what you'll see on the screen. But the word *Type* itself is in a proportional font. Figure 26–5 shows how part of the manuscript looked.

What I had to do to get this effect took me hours to figure out because of the numbering scheme for the fonts I was using. For the standard proportional text font, 12 point Times Roman, I used the **.CW 11** setting, as the README file suggests. However, when I switched proportional spacing off, WordStar would print in the small, Line Printer 8.5 font. I couldn't for the life of me get WordStar to use the 12 point Courier font, even if I inserted a **.CW 12** command in the file.

As it turned out, all I had to do was designate the 12 point Courier font as the alternate character width! But the file itself used the **.CW 12** setting to determine the general horizontal character width. As strange as it may seem, when I used the *same* setting twice, it worked! Here, then, are the commands that I inserted at the top of the file:

```
.CW 12
^A
.CW 12
^N
.PS ON
.CW 11
```

The first **.CW 12** command, as I mentioned, sets the horizontal character width for the entire file. The second **.CW 12** setting determines the alternate character width (**^PA**). *Then* I turned proportional spacing on for the main font setting, **.CW 11**.

But I wasn't through yet. I still had to use the overprint line command, the **^P@** command to set the absolute column location, and the **.PS OFF** and

Press	D [open a document]
Type	burbank.1e
Press	RETURN
Type	y

because this is a new file.

Figure 26–5   Mixing Fixed-Width and Proportional Fonts

.PS ON commands where necessary. Here's how the lines finally appeared in the file:

```
Press           ^@^BD^B [open a document]


Type                                                              -
.PS OFF
                ^@^Aburbank.1e^N
.PS ON


Press           ^@^BRETURN^B


Type                                                              -
.PS OFF
                ^@^Ay^N
.PS ON


because this is a new file.
```

Notice that each *Type* line ends with a overprint line command, the hyphen in the flag character display. To get WordStar to print in the 12 point fixed-width font, I had to turn off proportional spacing and then use the **^PA** command to select the alternate character width. Then I had to turn proportional spacing back on to continue. Sheesh!

WordStar Goes Scholarly!

The last example seemed easy when I thought about it, but it turned out to be the hardest to do. Most of the problems I had related to aesthetics, that is, how to get the printout to look as pleasing as possible—or at least as pleasing *to me*. Whether *you* like the result is another matter: "You can't argue about taste." In any case, the final section in the chapter outlines some helpful design tips.

The entire example is in Figure 26–6. It's the first page of a chapter in a "scholarly" book. Of interest to the discussion at hand are the following: (1) how to print superscripted footnote reference numbers in a smaller font, (2) what to consider when you're doing indented sections, and (3) other page formatting issues, such as headers and footers, in relationship to proportional fonts.

You don't have to type the example, but do take a look at how I set up the formatting for each section. Here are the main formatting commands at the top of the file:

Chapter 1

Descriptive Imagery and Metaphor

As a writer representative of his century, Charles Dickens filled his novels with a great deal of descriptive imagery. The author "sets the scene" not only to give the reader an idea of where the action is to take place, but also to present a feeling for the mood of the work. No example illustrates this more clearly than the opening pages of *Bleak House*.[1] The fog that is certainly part of many a London day becomes a metaphor for the obfuscating world of the law and of Chancery, the subjects of the novel:

> Fog everywhere. Fog up the river, where it flows among green aits and meadows; fog down the river, where it rolls defiled among the tiers of shipping and the waterside pollutions of a great (and dirty) city. ... Fog in the eyes and throats of ancient Greenwich pensioners, wheezing by the firesides of their wards; fog in the stem and bowl of the afternoon pipe of the wrathful skipper, down in his close cabin; fog cruelly pinching the toes and fingers of his shivering little 'prentice boy on deck. ... *(p. 17)*
>
> The raw afternoon is rawest, and the dense fog is densest, and the muddy streets are muddiest near that leaden-headed old obstruction, appropriate ornament for the threshold of a leaden-headed old corporation, Temple Bar. And hard by Temple Bar, in Lincoln's Inn Hall, at the very heart of the fog, sits the Lord High Chancellor in his High Court of Chancery. *(p. 18)*

Dickens starts with a Typical "mood" description of the London fog and slowly, but perceptibly, elaborates upon it until it becomes symbolic of the High Court of Chancery itself. Dickens, thus, starts with a general phenomenon and gradually gives it a specific meaning. And in so doing he sets the stage for the entire novel, because *Bleak House* deals almost entirely with the "fog" of Chancery, how this fog "envelopes" the lives of many people and usually overcomes them.

---

1. All page references are to the paperback edition of *Bleak House* published by The New American Library (New York, 1964).

- 1 -

Figure 26–6   WordStar Goes Scholarly

```
.. This file uses the following proportional fonts:
..
..              8 point Times Roman regular - .CW 7
..             10 point Times Roman regular - .CW 9
..             10 point Times Roman italic
```

```
..                12 point Times Roman regular - .CW 10
..                12 point Times Roman italic
.LH 7
.MT 6
.MB 6
.PS ON
.CW 10
.LS 2
.OJ ON
.RM 80
.FO                                    - # -
.FM 3
^A
.CW 7
^N
```

I'll use the 8 point font for the superscripted footnote numbers. After the standard period of trial-and-error, I discovered that a **.RM 80** setting works best with the main text lines in 12 point. The **.LH 7** command gives the main text lines a less "spaced out" appearance.

Take special notice of the *position* of the footer command, which centers the page numbers and encloses them in hyphens. If I had put the **.FO** line *above* the **.PS ON** line, WordStar would have printed the footer in the fixed-width Courier font! Always be careful about where your formatting commands are in relation to the **.PS ON** command. (Notice, too, that I've changed the footer margin.)

To have WordStar print superscripted footnote reference numbers in the smaller font, I've set up that font as the alternate character width. In this example, I can begin the actual text of the file *(Chapter 1)* on the same line as the **^PN** command. If, however, the file began with a paragraph on the same line, WordStar would not have aligned the first line of the paragraph correctly. So I would need to insert the **^PN** command on its own separate blank line.

The footnote reference number at the end of the third sentence in the first paragraph is worth noting. Here's how the end of that sentence appears with the print codes turned on:

```
... ^YBleak House.^Y^A^T1^T^N
```

The placement of print codes is important. You first *end* the italics, then you instruct WordStar to begin using the alternate font, then you insert the superscript command. Make sure you end all toggles correctly!

The indented sections, in the 10 point Times Roman font (regular and italic), required more trial-and-error on my part to determine the correct margins. I finally settled on the following commands for this section:

```
.CW 9
.LM 10
.RM 80
.LS 1
.LH 6
```

Again, I've squeezed the lines together a bit with the **.LH 6** command to make them appear more like real printing. Make sure you insert the correct number of blank lines between the main text and the indented sections. The commands to return to the main format are:

```
.LH 7
.CW 10
.LM 1
.RM 80
.LS 2
```

Finally, here are the commands for the footnote, which is also in the 10 point font. I discovered that I needed two blank lines between the divider (40 underlines) and the note. I'm also using a shorter line length for footnote text.

```
.LH 6
.LS 1
.CW 9
.LM 6
.PM 1
.RM 70
```

Dear Reader: The proof of the pudding is in the printout. With laser printers you'll have to spend considerably more time than usual to get the formatting correct, but once you do the results are great!

A Few Design Tips

Laser printers are either going to bring out the artist in us all or supply the psychiatrists and psychologists of this world with patients for years! It takes someone with a good eye to compose a page that is visually appealing to the reader. What was the old adage about silk purses and sows' ears?

Still, there are some easy design do's and don'ts that can help you create aesthetically pleasing laser-generated printouts. I'll close this long and complicated chapter with them as an inspiration to you to continue where I'm leaving off.

- First and foremost, do *keep things simple.* Don't go overboard with a zillion fonts and sizes, graphics, and other doodahs. Simplicity doesn't mean superficiality.

- Do stick to one font family as much as possible. Rely on variations of the *same* family—such as different point sizes, boldface, or italics—instead of a different font family to vary the look of the page.

- Do use a lot of "white space." That is, set up a good sized blank margin on all four sides of the page and adequate spacing between sections. Don't squeeze too many characters on a line. Maintain an adequate amount of leading—blank space—between printed lines. Too much type on the page is difficult to read!

- Don't go to extremes. It looks awful when a page has a wide range of point sizes. Stay within a limited range of font sizes, such as 12 to 18 points.

- Do show your printouts to others. Get a second opinion about how things look.

- Similarly, do take a look at what others have done. Open any book and try to determine what makes it visually appealing or unappealing.

- Do consider printing in a large typesize and then photomechanically *reducing* the printout. This method produces a near typeset quality look.

- With the above considerations in mind, don't be afraid to experiment. Nothing ventured, nothing gained, you know.

And, oh yes, save scrap paper. You'll need it for the seemingly endless number of trial-and-error printings you'll have to do before you get that project "just right." Good luck!

Have It Your Way!

Dear Reader: I've mentioned this chapter often. Well, you're finally here, and it's time to learn how to *customize* WordStar for your own needs. One of the nicest features of the program is that you can change virtually every default setting to create, as it were, your own "personal WordStar." This chapter shows you how.

    Note: To customize WordStar, you should be at the DOS prompt, so—

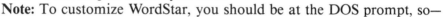

DON'T DO WARM-UP

The WSCHANGE Program

As you know, the program WINSTALL.EXE *installs* WordStar for your computer system and printer. Although you can run WINSTALL as many times as you want, it only handles the basic installation. To customize all WordStar's settings, you call on the services of another program, WSCHANGE.EXE. (WSCHANGE actually comprises *two* files, the program file WSCHANGE.EXE and an overlay file WSCHANGE.OVR.)

    Because WSCHANGE is a separate program, you can run it from DOS. Below are the "warm-up" instructions for starting WSCHANGE on either floppy disk or hard disk computers. Follow these steps before you continue with the rest of this chapter.

    Tip: It might be a good idea to *copy* the WS.EXE file to a temporary file, such as WST.EXE. Then use WSCHANGE to change WS.EXE. That way, you can test your changes to make sure they're correct. If not, you still have the original file to fall back on.

Starting WSCHANGE on Floppy Disk Computers

Insert the disk containing WSCHANGE.EXE (it should be on the "Installation" disk) in the A—top or left—drive and the WordStar program disk in the B—bottom or right—drive; close both drive doors. Then:

Type   **a:**

Press   **RETURN**

to select the A drive as the current drive.

Type   **wschange b:ws**

Press   **RETURN**

This loads WSCHANGE and tells it that you want to change the standard WordStar program, stored in a file called WS.EXE. If you've renamed the WordStar program file, use its current name without the .EXE extension instead of **ws** . For example, I've set up a version of WordStar with "book" formatting defaults as WSB.EXE.

Starting WSCHANGE on Hard Disk Computers

The WSCHANGE program files should be in the same directory as WordStar. Make sure that that is the current directory by first issuing the CD command to select that directory (such as CD \WS4 to select the WS4 directory). Then:

Type   **wschange ws**

Press   **RETURN**

This loads WSCHANGE and tells it that you want to change the standard WS.EXE program. If you've renamed the WordStar program file, use its current name without the .EXE extension instead of **ws** .

Supplying a File Name and Canceling WSCHANGE

You'll then briefly see the WSCHANGE sign-on screen, followed by the *Main Installation Menu.* If you don't supply a file name when you load WSCHANGE, it asks you for one:

```
What file do you want to install? (normally WS)

Type the filename and press RETURN...
```

You can *cancel* WSCHANGE and return to the DOS prompt at any time by pressing ^C (^**SCROLL LOCK**) without making any changes to WordStar.

The Main Installation Menu

The Main Installation Menu presents the five general change areas: (a) Console, (b) Printer, (c) Computer, (d) WordStar, and (e) Patching. Of course, even though choice D says *WordStar,* all the changes are to WordStar! Choice D refers to WordStar's standard editing defaults.

You'll find that there is a certain amount of duplication in some of the menus. That is, you can change several settings in two *or more* different places. WSCHANGE will always show you the current setting after any changes you've made.

Although the five categories seem straightforward enough, at times there doesn't appear to be any rhyme or reason to the order of changes in the menus. Most changes that you are likely to make are in the first four categories. The fifth category, *Patching,* only contains a couple useful changes and is generally best left to experienced computer users.

To move from the Main Installation Menu to submenus, press the letter for your choice. Do *not* press **RETURN**. When you make changes, follow the prompts on the screen. To back up to the previous menu, you generally press **X**. **Tip:** To avoid backing up through many levels of menus when you just want to exit WSCHANGE quickly, press ^**X**.

Whenever you see the prompt ? Help you can press **?** (**SHIFT /**) to get information about the current screen, what the changes do, or how to make the changes. In fact, there is some information in WSCHANGE's help screens that you won't find anywhere else!

Finding the Change You Want

The rest of this chapter outlines the changes by *topic.* That is, under the heading "Computer Hardware Settings" you'll find subheadings listing the most common hardware-related changes. For example, the function keys are part of the computer's hardware, as is the monitor. There's a separate section for printer settings.

Therefore, scan the chapter subheadings first to locate the change you want. If you don't find it, check the index. Unfortunately, I can only touch upon the most standard or common changes. At some point you may want to investigate WSCHANGE more thoroughly by viewing each menu and submenu.

For each change, I instruct you how to reach the screen or menu that governs that change *from the Main Installation Menu.* For example, to change the function key arrangements: I tell you:

Press   **A** [Console] **B** [Function keys]

That means press the letter **a** and then the letter **b**. The labels in square brackets are the menu names. **Caution:** WordStar releases after Release 4 may use different letters in the WSCHANGE menus.

Saving Your Changes

When you're finished making all your changes, press ^X to back up quickly through all menus. You'll see this message:

```
Are you through making changes? (Y/N)
```

If you type any letter except **y** for "yes," WSCHANGE returns to the Main Installation Menu. If you type **y**, WSCHANGE saves the changes to the WordStar program. **Caution:** Make a backup copy of the changed WordStar program *immediately* so you don't have to go through the steps again!

Computer Hardware Settings

Type of Monitor

Most monitors work with the default setting: "IBM Compatible using video RAM directly." If you have a monitor that displays "snow" on the screen during scrolling—and many color monitors have this defect—do this:

Press   **A** [Console] **A** [Monitor] **A** [Monitor selection]

Press   **B** [IBM Compatible using ROM BIOS calls only]

Note: You may also have to use the "ROM BIOS calls only" selection if you want to run WordStar in a special *window* under a multitasking program.

The Compatibility Issue

If your computer is not 100 percent compatible with the IBM PC, you may have to change one or two WordStar installation settings. First, try changing the monitor to choice **B** [IBM Compatible using ROM BIOS calls only], as outlined in the previous section. Second, change the FILES=20 line of your CONFIG.SYS file to FILES=30. Use WordStar nondocument mode to open this file. **Note:** You must reboot your computer after you change the CONFIG.SYS file. To do this without turning off your machine, from the DOS prompt press **CTRL ALT DEL**.

Number of Text Lines Shown on the Screen

Standard monitors show 25 text lines on the screen, but the EGA type monitor can display 43. To use this monitor with WordStar,

Press   A [Console] A [Monitor] A [Monitor selection]

Press   C [Use IBM EGA ...]

To *reduce* the number of text lines on your monitor:

Press   A [Console] A [Monitor] C [Screen sizing]

and change the A [Height] setting to a number less than 25.

Function Key Labels

To remove the function key labels from the screen and thus have WordStar display more text:

Press   A [Console] B [Function keys]

Press   L

Press   X

to finish.
      You can also turn the labels off like this:

Press   D [WordStar] B [Editing settings] A [Edit screen, help level]

Press   J [On-screen function key labels]

and type y for "yes" to change the setting from on to off.
      To turn the labels back on, repeat the procedure. See below on how to change the function key definitions and label text.

Horizontal Scrolling

To change the number of columns WordStar scrolls the screen horizontally when the cursor reaches the edge of the screen:

Press   A [Console] A [Monitor] C [Screen sizing]

and change the C [Horizontal scroll width] setting.

Display of Print Attributes and Screen Colors

You can modify the colors that WordStar displays for normal text, the status line, menus, function key labels, the ruler line, and many print enhancements such as boldface or underlining.

Press   **A** [Console] **C** [Video attributes]

Follow the guide at the top of the screen for selecting colors by pressing the appropriate function key. Press **X** to finish or **ESC** to cancel your changes.

Function Key Definitions

You can change the definitions of *40* different function keys: the function keys alone or the CTRL, SHIFT, or ALT function keys.

Press   **A** [Console] **B** [Function keys]

Use the cursor movement keys to select the key combination that you want to change. For example, suppose you want SHIFT F1 to be ^OP:

Press   **^D** or **RIGHT ARROW** twice

to select Shift+F1.

Press   **RETURN**

WordStar shows the current definition and asks if you want to change it.

Type   **y**

Press   **^OP**

Press **DEL** *instead of* BACKSPACE to erase mistakes and make corrections. To save the new definition:

Press   **END**

WordStar displays the regular and SHIFT function key labels and positions the cursor on the key label for the key you just changed, SHIFT F1. Type a new label using whatever mix of uppercase and lowercase you want, but notice that labels are at most *seven* characters in length. Press **END** to save the new label.

You can define function keys to type text, too, or a combination of text and WordStar commands.

When you've made all changes,

Press   X

to finish.

See also "Using Your Settings Again" at the end of the chapter.

The BACKSPACE and DEL Keys

You can have the **BACKSPACE** key (or ^H) just move the cursor to the previous character (like ^S or **LEFT ARROW**), and the **DEL** key delete the previous character (instead of the **BACKSPACE** key or ^H):

Press   **D** [WordStar] **B** [Editing settings] **H** [WordStar 3.3 compatibility]

Number of Disk Drives, Including Your RAM Disk

WordStar has to know the *total* number of disk drives on your system, including any drive you use for a RAM disk (Chapter 28). Also be sure you tell WordStar which is the default drive.

Press   **C** [Computer] **A** [Disk drives] **A** [Valid disk drives]

To change the setup, type y and follow the prompts. The first drive you specify is the default drive. Include the RAM disk drive as any other, for example, the D drive for the RAM disk and the C drive for the real hard disk.

Local Area Networks

If WordStar is running on a local area network, or LAN, you must tell WordStar that it's on a multiuser system and determine the status of file locking. *File locking* means that other users can't view a file that someone else is editing.

Press   **C** [Computer] **B** [Operating system]

Press   **B** [Multiuser or network system]

WordStar asks:

```
If 2 people try to edit the same document, should the second user
be able to browse through it (without making changes)? (Y/N)
```

Type n to turn on file locking or y to leave file locking off. In either case, only one person at a time (the *first* person who opens a file) can edit the file.

You may also want to select the *device* to which a workstation on the network sends output for printing. To do this:

Press   **B** [Printer] **F** [Printer interface] **A** [Printer port selection]

Change the **O** setting [Redirection device or file] to include the device name.

Printer Settings

Printing Defaults

By far the most common changes you'll want to make are to the default responses to the print options questions and other standard printing defaults.

Press   **B** [Printer] **E** [Printing defaults]

Here are the changes you can make from this menu:

1. Choice **A** [Pause between pages] instructs WordStar to pause between pages automatically so you can insert a new sheet of paper without having to answer this print option explicitly. The default is OFF.

2. Choice **B** [Use form feeds] tells WordStar to send a form feed to the printer at the end of each page. This is necessary for laser printers and some sheet feeder setups. The default is OFF.

3. Choice **C** [Print nondocument as default] prints nondocuments instead of the normal documents as the default file type. Recall that WordStar will "pretty print" nondocuments with document-type page formatting.

4. Choice **D** [Bidirectional printing] turns on bidirectional printing, just like the **.BP ON** command.

5. Choice **E** [Letter quality printing (NLQ)] turns on near letter quality printing, the **.LQ ON** command.

6. Choice **F** [Microjustification] turns on microjustification, like the **.UJ ON** command.

7. Choice **G** [Underline blanks] underlines blanks in a phrase, the **.UL ON** command.

8. The next choice, **H** [Proportional spacing], turns on proportional spacing, the **.PS ON** command.

9. Choice **I** [Strike-out character] changes the character that ^**PX** uses to overstrike a phrase. The default is the hyphen, but you may want something else, such as a slash.

10. To change what WordStar considers the normal character width (^**PN**)—by default a **.CW 12** setting—use choice **J** [Normal char width (120ths)].

11. To change what WordStar considers the alternate character width (^**PA**)—by default a **.CW 10** setting—use choice **K** [Alternate char width (120ths)].

12. The **L** choice [Line height (48ths)] changes the vertical pitch command, **.LH** (the default is **.LH 8**).

13. To change the sub/superscript roll, the **.SR** command (the default is **.SR 3**), use choice **M** [Sub/superscript roll (48ths)].

14. Finally, choice **N** [Print page numbers] turns off the automatic printing of page numbers, the **.OP** command. The default is for WordStar *to* print page numbers.

Note: You'll see many of the same settings in other menus in the **D** [WordStar] section, for instance, **I** [Printing defaults].

Primary and Secondary Printers and Ports

To select your primary printer from a list,

Press   **B** [Printer] **A** [Printer choices] **A** [Printer selection]

If the printer you want isn't on the first menu, press **2**, **3**, or **4** for the other menus. You can change the name that WordStar displays with the **B** [Printer name] choice.

To use as the default printer a new printer driver file that's not on the list:

Press   **B** [Printer] **A** [Printer choices] **C** [Default printer driver]

Set up the *printer port* like this:

Press   **B** [Printer] **F** [Printer interface] **A** [Printer port selection]

Choose the letter representing the port you need. **Note:** If you have a serial printer, more than likely you'll have to change the port to COM1 or COM2.

If you have *two* printers connected to your computer and you want to designate the *secondary* printer, change the "Alternate printer output:" selection to that printer's port. Whenever you choose the secondary printer's driver from the list, WordStar will send the output out the alternate port. If you have only one printer, make sure that both outputs are the same port.

Sheet Feeders

To select a sheet feeder:

Press   B [Printer] B [Sheet feeders]

and choose the letter from either menu 1 or 2.
   Note: You may also have to change the printing defaults and the page formatting defaults depending on your sheet feeder settings. Consult the README file for more information.

Background Printing and Printing Speed

Normally, WordStar prints in the background so you can continue editing. If you want to turn background printing off, thus printing faster but not allowing editing while printing:

Press   B [Printer] F [Printer interface] D [Background printing]

Change the A choice [Concurrent printing] to off.
   To alter the default speed with which WordStar sends characters to the primary and alternate printers, change choices B [Primary print speed] and C [Alternate print speed], respectively. If you establish a primary speed that's not full speed, you'd then have to use the F [print at full speed] choice from the Printing menu to access the printer's full speed.

Reducing the Number of Printer Drivers

If you're working with WordStar on floppy disks, you might not have enough room to maintain all the printer drivers on the program disk. You can reduce the number of printer drivers in the WSPRINT.OVR files to only those you need.

Press   B [Printer] C [Printer driver lib] B [Create smaller library]

Type the *numbers* next to the drivers you want to retain, and separate each number by a comma. You can also type a *range* of numbers separated by a dash. For example, to keep numbers 1, 3, and 5–7:

Type   1,3,5-7

Press   **RETURN**

It takes WordStar a few seconds to extract the drivers you want and copy them to the new WSPRINT.OVR file. WordStar then tells you that the old printer driver file now has the extension .BAK. That means it's WSPRINT.BAK. Press any key to return to the previous menu. If you wish, you can rename the smaller WSPRINT.OVR file and tell WordStar that you want to use the new file name:

Press   **B** [Printer] **C** [Printer driver lib] **A** [Select library file]

Supply the new file name and press **RETURN**. Then rename the WSPRINT.BAK file to WSPRINT.OVR to keep the complete printer driver file. You'll need the entire library if you later want to change the drivers, because WordStar just shows the drivers in the current file. Once you've reduced the printer library file, WordStar doesn't show all drivers unless you use the complete library.

Caution: If you plan to generate tables of contents or indexes, make sure you include the special $TOC and $INDEX printer drivers in your new driver file. Also include in your smaller printer driver file the special printer drivers, ASCII, PRVIEW, and XTRACT, if you use these drivers as much as I do!

General WordStar Program Settings

This section outlines changes that apply to the WordStar program as a whole. Next are changes that affect the Opening menu, and then changes to editing settings.

WordStar Entirely in Memory

If you want WordStar to run faster, or if you'd like to *remove* the WordStar program disk after you've loaded the program, you can have WordStar copied entirely into memory during each session. This means that the various *overlay* files that WordStar uses are in memory, too, so WordStar doesn't have to "look" for them on the disk when it needs them.

Caution: You must have at least 256 kilobytes of system memory to use this option. The WordStar help screens will, however, *not* be available.

Press   **C** [Computer] **C** [Memory usage]

Change the **B** choice [WordStar RAM resident] to "yes." Notice that, as a compromise, you can have just the *default* printer driver in RAM, choice **A**, but then you can't select any special drivers.

Directory Containing WordStar Program Files

If you've installed WordStar on a hard disk, the program "assumes" that its files are in a directory called WS4. You can put WordStar in any directory and tell it to use that directory instead of WS4. You must change the *file search path*.

Press   **C** [Computer] **D** [WordStar files]

Press   **A** [File search path]

WordStar tells you the current path and gives you information about how to change it. For example, suppose you want to change the path to \WS:

Type   **y**

because you want to change the path.

Type   **\WS**

Press   **RETURN**

You can't change the default drive in this menu, only the file search path. See "Number of Disk Drives, Including Your RAM Disk," above, to set a new default drive.

Delays, Menus, and Prompts

There are three kinds of delays: (1) long delays, such as during sign-on; (2) medium delays, when WordStar displays a menu; and (3) short delays, for instance, those during paragraph alignment. You can change the length of all three delays:

Press   **D** [WordStar] **C** [Other features] **F** [Miscellaneous]

You'll have to experiment with the settings for choices **C** [Longest delay], **D** [Medium delay], and **F** [Short delay]. For example, if you make the medium delay longer, then WordStar won't display the Help (^J), Block & Save (^K), Onscreen Format (^O), Print Controls (^Q), or Quick (^Q) menus too quickly, thus giving you more time to complete a double letter command.

In the same menu, change choice **B** [Require RETURN after Y/N answer] to ON if you want WordStar to wait for a press of the RETURN key in response to yes/no prompts (the default is OFF).

Dealing with .BAK Files!

Ever since WordStar appeared, there have been two camps: users who like backup files, and those who don't. I must say that when I was working on floppy disks those .BAK files seemed a nuisance, because they took up so much precious disk space. But now that I have a hard disk, I'm not as opposed to them. They've saved my skin many a time!

Press   **C** [Computer] **D** [WordStar files]

Answer "no" to the **L** choice [Make backup files when saving]. You can also change the .BAK extension to something else with the **M** choice [Backup file type].

Tip: Instead of instructing WordStar *not* to create .BAK files, I've set up a DOS *batch file* (Chapter 28) that deletes all the unnecessary .BAK files with two keystrokes. It just issues the DOS command **DEL *.BAK**. That way, I can have my cake and eat it, too.

Opening Menu Settings

The Directory Display

You can control whether WordStar displays a file directory at the Opening menu, the order in which it displays files, what file types it shows and those it excludes, and how it displays file size.

Press   **C** [Computer] **E** [Directory display]

Choice **A** [Display file directory] is the same as the **F** [file directory] command on the Opening menu. That is, it determines whether the directory displays at all. Choice **B** [Directory in alphabetical order] determines whether WordStar sorts the files in alphabetical order *by name,* or whether they appear in the random order that WordStar "sees" them on the disk.

Normally, WordStar excludes file types that you can't edit, such as .COM and .EXE files. With choice **C** [File types excluded from directory], you can change the list of excluded files.

If you want to display only files with a certain name or extension, press choice **D** [File names that are shown] to limit the display. Use the standard DOS wildcards, * and ?, to distinguish files. For example, to show only files with the name CH, no matter what the extension, supply CH.* as the file name.

Choice **F** [Show space remaining on disk] lets you turn off the display of bytes available.

Initial Work Directory

You can select a specific directory as your initial work directory when you load WordStar. That is, you can have the WordStar program files in one directory, but after you load the program it automatically changes to your work directory, which contains your document files.

Press   C [Computer] E [Directory display] E [Initial directory log on]

Type the initial directory path and press **RETURN**.

Default Editing and Printing Mode: Document or Nondocument

WordStar "assumes" that you're editing a document when you open a file at the same time as you load the program. For example, if you type ws text.doc from the DOS prompt, WordStar opens TEXT.DOC as a document file. If you type ws text.doc p, WordStar prints TEXT.DOC as a document.
       You can change the default mode from document to nondocument so that WordStar opens a nondocument from the DOS prompt:

Press   D [WordStar] C [Other features] B [Nondocument mode]

Change choice **A** [Nondoc file when in command line] to ON.
       From the same menu, change choice **B** [Print nondocument as default] to ON if you work mostly with nondocuments.

Document Mode Editing Settings

Here are the real "meat and potatoes" settings that you'll change the most. They involve virtually all the editing and formatting defaults and how WordStar displays the status bar, ruler line, and messages while you're working in a file.

Help Level, Status Line, Ruler Line, Soft Spaces, Preview Mode, Screen Updating

You have almost complete control over the screen display and help level.

Press   D [WordStar] B [Editing settings] A [Edit screen, help level]

Use this menu to change the following:

1. Choice **A** [Help level] changes the help level from the default of 3 to 0, 1, or 2. This is the in-file **^JJ** command.

2. Choice **B** [Status line] turns the status line on or off. A help level of 0 also turns off the status line.

3. Choice **C** [Status line filler character] lets you substitute another character, such as a hyphen, for the spaces on the status line.

4. Choice **D** [Soft space display] turns the default from off to on (the **^OB** command), while choice **E** [Soft space character] lets you substitute another character for the bullet. When you type the character, WordStar shows it (along with its ASCII code in hexadecimal if it's an extended character).

5. Choice **F** [Normally show print controls] determines the status of the **^OD** command, while choice **G** [Normally show text in preview mode] controls the *protected* status of a document. If you change this to ON, WordStar opens all documents in preview mode.

6. Choice **H** [Ruler line] governs the **^OT** toggle.

If you're a fast typist, you can prevent WordStar from updating the screen until you pause:

Press   **D** [WordStar] **B** [Editing settings] **B** [Typing]

Change the delays for choices **C** [Fast typing display holdoff delay] and **D** [Fast typing page/line/column delay]. The former delay doesn't update the line until you pause, while the latter waits to update the status line.

Default Ruler Line for Next File

Unlike earlier versions of the program, WordStar Professional Release 4 automatically uses the default ruler line every time you save one file and open another. That is, it doesn't retain the ruler line settings from the previously edited file. To have WordStar use the previous defaults,

Press   **D** [WordStar] **B** [Editing settings] **A** [Edit screen, help level]

Change choice **I** [New ruler each edit session] from ON to OFF.

Insert Mode and Wordwrap

To turn insert mode (**^V** or **INS**) or wordwrap (**^OW**) on or off by default:

Press   **D** [WordStar] **B** [Editing settings] **B** [Typing]

If you turn wordwrap off, WordStar will *beep* at you when the cursor reaches the end of the line—just like a typewriter!

Line Formatting: Margins, Tabs, Line Spacing, Justification

To change the default left margin (**.LM**), right margin (**.RM**), and paragraph margin (**.PM**):

Press   **D** [WordStar] **A** [Page layout] **A** [Page sizing and margins]

Use choices **G**, **H**, and **I**. Notice that the default **0** setting disables the paragraph margin. The lowest left margin setting is **1**, while the highest right margin setting is **255**.

To change the default regular tab settings or add default settings for *decimal* tabs:

Press   **D** [WordStar] **A** [Page layout] **C** [Tabs]

Then press **A** [Regular tab stops] or **B** [Decimal tab stops]. Type y to clear the previous settings. Type the new tab stop column numbers that you want, one by one, pressing **RETURN** after *each*. You can enter the new tab stops in any order. Press **RETURN** alone to finish. For nondocument fixed tabs (the **^PI** command), see "Nondocument Mode Tab Stops and Auto Indent."

To alter the line spacing or right-margin justification settings:

Press   **D** [WordStar] **B** [Editing settings] **C** [Paragraph alignment]

If you don't like the way WordStar Release 4 adds a combination of soft and hard returns for double or triple line spacing, you can have it insert only hard returns. Do this by reverting to WordStar 3.3 compatibility:

Press   **D** [WordStar] **B** [Editing settings] **H** [WordStar 3.3 compatibility]

Page Formatting

To change the default page length (**.PL**), top margin (**.MT**), bottom margin (**.MB**), or page offset (**.PO**):

Press   **D** [WordStar] **A** [Page layout] **A** [Page sizing and margins]

Pagination, Headers, and Footers

To turn off the automatic printing of page numbers (**.OP**), change the page number column position (**.PC**), or alter the initial page number (**.PN**):

Press   **D** [WordStar] **A** [Page layout] **B** [Headers and footers]

    Use the **A** [Max line length] to change the maximum size of each header or footer line; the default is 100 characters. Recall that you can have up to three header lines and three footer lines. (You make the same change from **C** [Computer] **C** [Memory usage].)

Unerasing

    WordStar normally can hold up to 500 characters in its "undo" buffer. You can restore these characters with ^U (**F2**). To increase or decrease the size of the buffer:

Press   **D** [WordStar] **B** [Editing settings] **E** [Erase and unerase]

    Change the **A** choice [Max characters that can be unerased], but keep in mind that the larger the unerase buffer, the less memory for regular editing.

    By the way, if you want the ^U (**F2**) command to unerase *single* characters, change the **B** choice [Unerase single character erasures].

Column Modes and Block Markers

    You can change whether column mode (^**KN**) and column replace mode (^**KI**) are on by default. You can also modify the beginning and ending block markers, say, to **B** and **E** or **BB** and **BE**:

Press   **D** [WordStar] **B** [Editing settings] **D** [Blocks]

    If you modify the block markers, make sure you include all characters you want in the marker. For example, to change the ending marker from <K> to <E>, supply the left and right brackets, too.

    If you don't like the way WordStar Release 4 handles cursor movement when you block a line starting at column 1, you can revert to WordStar 3.3. compatibility:

Press   **D** [WordStar] **B** [Editing settings] **H** [WordStar 3.3 compatibility]

Hyphenation

    You can turn hyphen help (^**OH**) on by default, or determine the minimum size of hyphenated words:

Press   **D** [WordStar] **B** [Editing settings] **C** [Paragraph alignment]

The **C** [Hyphen help] choice determines whether hyphen help is ON or OFF. The **D** choice [Characters before hyphen help] sets the *minimum* number of characters that a word must contain before WordStar stops to hyphenate it at the end of a line. The default is five characters.

Find and Find and Replace Options

Normally, WordStar does not "assume" any of the special options for find (^QF) or find and replace (^QA). You must type the options yourself. If you use certain options all the time, you can have them as defaults:

Press   **D** [WordStar] **B** [Editing settings] **G** [Find and replace]

Press   **A** [Default find and replace options]

You can enter up to *six* default options. Even if you do set up default options, you can override the defaults whenever you issue a find or find and replace command by typing in other options. To use no options when you've set up some as the default, press the SPACEBAR and then RETURN in answer to the options prompt.

Number of Dot Command Characters in Memory

The maximum number of dot command characters that WordStar stores in memory is 500. If you use a lot of different ruler lines (**.RR**), WordStar has to store all characters in the ruler line as the cursor passes over them. Later, if you return to that section of the file governed by that ruler line, WordStar can adjust the formats. You can supply a higher memory allocation for dot command lines:

Press   **C** [Computer] **C** [Memory usage]

Change choice **J** [Dot command buffer], but keep in mind that you're taking up memory that WordStar normally uses for editing files. You need only do this if you see a Dot-Limit warning on the status line.

What WordStar Considers a "Word"

You may have noticed that WordStar doesn't skip over certain characters in a "word" when your press ^F (^**RIGHT ARROW**) or ^A (^**LEFT ARROW**), or when you delete the word with ^T (F6). You can change the characters that WordStar includes in a "word":

Press   **D** [WordStar] **B** [Editing settings] **F** [Lines and characters]

Change choice **L** [Characters for moving across words]. Follow the prompts to amend the table that WordStar displays on the screen. Note that you must enter the character's hexadecimal code as listed on the table. (There's a separate word table for determining which words to index and which to spell-check.)

Accent Marks and Foreign Characters

If you type a specific accent mark (such as ˜) often, you know that you must press **^PH** to backspace the printer to print the mark over another character. You can instruct WordStar to backspace *automatically* when it "sees" the accent mark character.

Press   **D** [WordStar] **B** [Editing settings] **B** [Typing]

Change choice **F** [Automatic backspace characters] and supply the one character.

You can instruct WordStar about what the codes are for uppercase equivalents of lowercase foreign letters, such as ö and Ö:

Press   **D** [WordStar] **B** [Editing settings] **F** [Lines and characters]

Press the **M** choice [Upper/lowercase conversion table] and follow the prompts.

Merge Printing Settings

Field Separator in Data Files

To change the default field separator (the comma) in merge printing data files to another character:

Press   **D** [WordStar] **C** [Other features] **E** [Merge printing]

Change choice **A** [Separator between data items].

Date and Time Formats

 From the same menu as above, use choices **B** [Date format for &@& variable] and **C** [Time format for &!& variable] to change either or both formats. **Note:** When you change these formats here, the corresponding formats for the shorthand keys **ESC @** and **ESC !** also change.

CorrectStar Settings

Spelling Check Options

You can tell WordStar the name of the overlay file containing the CorrectStar program instructions, determine whether to align paragraphs after the correction of a word, and even turn off the spelling check "permanently," thus freeing memory for editing.

Press   D [WordStar] C [Other features] A [Spelling checks]

Notice, for instance, choice I [Align paragraph after correction]. If you want auto-align to be off by default, change this choice. See the next two sections for information about other choices.

What Constitutes a "Word" to Check

CorrectStar bypasses words that contain certain characters, such as numbers. To change what these characters are:

Press   D [WordStar] B [Editing settings] F [Lines and characters]

Change choice K [Characters that are part of a word], following the instructions on the screen. See also "What WordStar Considers a 'Word'."
To change the size of the *smallest* word that CorrectStar will check:

Press   D [WordStar] C [Other features] A [Spelling checks]

Change choice H [Smallest word checked].

Dealing with Dictionaries

Take a look at the main spelling check menu:

Press   D [WordStar] C [Other features] A [Spelling checks]

Choices B through D let you supply different file names for the default dictionary files. Now do this:

Press   E [Dictionary usage]

As the screen message notes, choices A [Swap dictionary/program disk] and C [Personal dict on program disk] are for those of you with floppy disk systems. You'd change both these choices to ON. Using choice F [Always ask for personal dictionary] set to ON, you can easily specify a different personal dictionary than the default whenever you begin CorrectStar.

Shorthand Settings

To change the settings listed in this section:

Press   **D** [WordStar] **C** [Other features] **D** [Shorthand (key macros)]

Shorthand Definitions File Name

WordStar normally looks for its shorthand definitions in a file called WSSHORT.OVR. To supply a new file name, change choice **A** [Shorthand storage file].

Amount of Shorthand Storage

From the same menu as above, select choice **B** [Shorthand buffer size (records)] to enlarge the amount of storage used for shorthand definitions. Supply the number of 128-byte records you want (the default is 4 records or 512 bytes).

Date, Time, and Dollar Amount Formats

From the same menu as above, select choice **C** [Format for today's date], **D** [Format for current time], or **E** [Dollar format for numbers] to change the format for the **ESC @**, **ESC !**, and **ESC $** shorthand macros, respectively. **Note:** Any changes you make to the date or time formats also affect the merge printing variables, **&@&** and **&!&**. In addition, even though one is called "date" and the other "time," either format can contain any combination of date and time. You could, for example, set up **ESC !** as an alternative date format instead of the time format. I never use the time format, so it's convenient for me to have two date formats from which to choose.

Indexing Settings

You can change the name of the file containing the exclusion list (normally, WSINDEX.XCL), or you can alter whether WordStar will automatically index every word in a file (normally, this is off):

Press   **D** [WordStar] **C** [Other features] **C** [Indexing]

Nondocument Mode Tab Stops and Auto Indent

You can have different tab settings and turn the auto-indent feature on or off in nondocuments, depending on file extension. For example, you can set up a different editing environment for Pascal files (extension .PAS), C files (extension .C), and dBASE program files (extension .PRG). Each time you open a file with one of these extensions in nondocument mode, WordStar uses the format you've specified.

Press   **D** [WordStar] **C** [Other features] **B** [Nondocument mode]

Select **D** [Tabs and auto-indent by file type] and follow the prompts.
From the same menu you can set the tab stops for nondocument fixed tabs, the **^PI** command, with the **E** choice [Tab stops if variable tabs enabled]. The tab stops you set up will work in document mode also.

Using Your Settings Again

Instead of going through all your changes again, you can save the settings to a nondocument file that you can then use again.

Press   **E** [Patching] **B** [Save settings]

Supply a file name and press **RETURN**. Then type y to save the entire user area. To use the file name containing the patches another time,

Press   **E** [Patching] **A** [Auto patcher]

and supply the file name.
The auto patcher file need not contain changes to all possible settings. For instance, there's a file called WS3KEYS.PAT that sets up the function keys and labels as they were in Release 3.3. This file doesn't make any other changes to WordStar Release 4.
Now for my parting shot: a rainy day diversion for all you WordStar hackers out there in Readerland. In Chapter 1, I mentioned that you can change the commands mapped to the numeric keypad keys such as HOME or END. To learn how, you'll need a copy of a file called PATCH.LST. It should be on the "Installation" disk.
Open the PATCH.LST file as a nondocument and find the string "Edit Menu Function Keys." You'll see the default key settings. It's a simple matter

to change the defaults by merely replacing the current settings with new ones. Edit and save PATCH.LST, then use it as the auto patcher file in WSCHANGE. (If you want to be really brave, try configuring the function keys to issue different commands at the Opening menu and within a file—there *is* a way to do it!)

WordStar and the
Wide, Wide World

In this chapter you'll learn the following new commands:

File Command

^Q~   Avoid "flushing" the typeahead buffer when you use certain terminate and stay resident programs

DOS Commands

ATTRIB	Change the file attribute (transient)
CLS	Clear the screen (resident)
COMP	Compare two files (transient)
DISKCOMP	Compare two disks (transient)
ECHO	Control the display of commands on the screen (resident)
FC	List the differences between two files (transient)
MORE	Display command output one screen at a time (transient)
PATH	Set up the file search path (resident)
PAUSE	Pause, display a message, and wait for the user to press a key (resident)
PROMPT	Change the DOS prompt (resident)
RECOVER	Recover files (transient)
SORT	Sort the contents of a file or the file directory (transient)

more . . .

> **Other DOS Features**
>
> <   Redirect the input to a command
>
> \>   Redirect the output from a command
>
> | Pipe information from one program to another
>
> \+   Concatenate (join) copied files
>
> **NUL**   "Null" device

To paraphrase John Donne: no software product is an island unto itself. In Chapters 12 and 13 you learned how to work with the disk operating system from within WordStar or from the DOS prompt. This chapter takes a brief look at other DOS commands and features, including the very useful DOS batch files. You'll even learn the secret of restoring accidentally deleted files!

Note: The DOS commands discussed in this chapter may be different from those of the new OS/2 operating system that will be available sometime in 1988. When in doubt, check your manual.

Even though all programs on your computer operate under DOS, each program deals with data differently. There have to be ways to *exchange* information so you don't have to retype it. This chapter explores common methods for moving information out of WordStar files to other "foreign" programs and from other programs into WordStar format.

Finally, I'll present some of my favorite add-on programs that enrich the WordStar environment. I'll also discuss a few other useful topics, such as how to use WordStar on a RAM disk and what you need to know when you transfer WordStar files over the telephone.

DOS Revisited

This section describes a few more useful DOS commands and features. You can issue the DOS commands from within WordStar by first going to DOS with **R** [run a DOS program] from the Opening menu or ^KF from within a file. There are many other DOS commands, so one of these days take the time to *skim through* your DOS documentation. You'll be glad you did! At the end of this section is discussion of a particularly useful DOS feature: batch files.

Comparisons and Differences

You can compare individual files or entire disks to see if they are the same or different. To compare files, use the COMP command. To compare two disks, use DISKCOMP. DOS will merely tell you whether the two files or disks you specified are the same or different. To *list* the textual differences between two files, use the FC command. All are transient commands: COMP.COM, DISKCOMP.COM, and FC.EXE.

Remember that DOS doesn't "know" about WordStar's use of the eighth bit, so FC will list text using the extended ASCII codes, just as TYPE does. Here's an example of how to use the FC command:

```
C> fc file.1 file.2
```

This command lists the textual differences between FILE.1 and FILE.2. Check your DOS manual for information about the various FC switches.

Joining Files Together

The + symbol is the *concatenation* operator. Use it with the DOS COPY command to copy several files and in the process join them together to create a new file. For example:

```
C> copy file.1+file.2+file.3 file.4
```

This command copies the first three files and joins them in the order you specify to create the fourth file, FILE.4. Spaces aren't necessary around the plus symbols, but you need at least one space between the copied file names and the new file name. If you don't specify a new file name, DOS copies and concatenates to the *first* name you list:

```
C> copy old+new
```

Here you're copying NEW to the end of the present contents of OLD. **Caution:** DOS doesn't tell you that you're copying over the original contents of OLD with itself plus NEW. Be careful!

Tip: Concatenating files in DOS is much faster than opening a file in WordStar, positioning the cursor at the end of the file, pressing ^KR to insert the file, and so on. Learn how to concatenate!

The File Search Path

A very useful DOS command is PATH. This command sets up the *file search path* so that if DOS can't find a command file in the current directory, it looks at the directories you've listed in the PATH statement. It continues to look in each directory in turn until it finds the command. For example,

```
C> PATH=C:\;C:\WS4;C:\D;C:\INSTANT;C:\CL;C:\B
```

Here, DOS starts searching in the root directory, then the WS4 directory, the D directory, and so on. For example, if I'm in the INSTANT directory, I can still load WordStar because it's in one of the other directories in the PATH statement. The Opening menu displays the files in the current directory, that is, INSTANT. So I don't have to have multiple copies of WordStar in each directory, or use the **L** [change logged drive/directory] command too often.

Changing the DOS Prompt

The PROMPT command changes the prompt that DOS displays so that you can customize DOS. The command—

```
C> prompt Hello!
```

—changes the prompt to the string Hello!. There are a variety of special PROMPT symbols, each represented by a question mark and letter combination, such as **$g** to display a >.

Below is an example of how to change the DOS prompt to include some fancy graphics. To try the example, you must include this line in the CONFIG.SYS file:

```
DEVICE=ANSI.SYS
```

You can edit the CONFIG.SYS file using the **N** [open a nondocument] command from the Opening menu. **Caution:** Don't delete the line FILES= 20; it must be in the CONFIG.SYS file for WordStar to operate correctly. In addition, a copy of the file ANSI.SYS, which is on the DOS disk, must be in the *root* directory of your startup disk.

The ANSI "escape sequences" that begin with **$e[** are weird (they're listed somewhere in the DOS manual). Here's that fancy example of a prompt (I found it in a computer magazine):

```
C> prompt $e[s$e[24A$e[1D$e[K$e[7m$p     $t$h$h$h     $d$e[m$e[uVince-$g $e[m
```

This line changes the prompt so that it displays the current drive and directory, the time, the day of the week, and the date, all highlighted. Below that appear my name (Vince) and an arrow pointing to the command line. If you try this example, make sure you issue the commands *exactly* as you see them with the same spaces and in the same case. Substitute your name for Vince.

Redirecting the Output

Normally DOS displays the output of commands on the screen. This is the "standard output," or STDOUT. You can *redirect* the output of a command to a file or to a device such as the printer instead of to the screen. The > symbol redirects the output. Here are a couple examples of output redirection.

Saving the File Listing in a File. You can direct the file directory listing to a file that you can later edit or even sort. For example:

```
C> dir > files
```

This command saves the file directory in a file called FILES. You can then edit or print the file as any other from within WordStar or at the DOS prompt. That is . . .

Copying a File to the Printer. You can redirect the output of a COPY operation to your printer, thus printing it. Make sure the printer is on.

```
C> copy text lpt1:
```

This command copies the contents of the file TEXT to the first parallel port, where your printer connects to your computer. Because to DOS LPT1: is a known device, you don't have to use the > redirection symbol.

Redirecting Input: Sorting a File

Normally DOS assumes that its "standard input" (STDIN) is the keyboard. You can redirect the input for a DOS command from a file by using the < symbol. A practical example of input redirection is sorting the contents of a file.

Guess what the command to sort files is. Right! It's SORT, in the program file SORT.EXE. This is a transient command, so make sure you have a copy of SORT.EXE on the disk. If you don't supply an output file, SORT displays the sorted result *on the screen,* the standard output. That is probably not what you want because you'd more than likely need to save the sorted file. So use the output redirection symbol, too.

For example, to sort an index exclusion file called WORDS to a file called WORDS.XCL:

```
C> sort < words > words.xcl
```

You'll be happy to know that SORT disregards the difference between uppercase and lowercase letters. If SORT used the ASCII coding scheme, it would sort words beginning with uppercase letters *before* words beginning with lowercase letters. That's because the ASCII code numbers for uppercase are in the range 65–90, while the codes for lowercase are higher: 97–122.

Try sorting your PERSONAL.DCT file to a new file. Use the **N** [open a nondocument] command from the Opening menu to look at the new file. If you want to make *it* your personal dictionary, delete the original PER-SONAL.DCT file and rename the new file.

Pipes: Sorting the File Directory

Besides redirecting output, you can also *filter* the output through another command with a *pipe*. The pipe symbol is a vertical bar (¦). DOS takes the output from the command to the left of the pipe and filters it through the command to the right of the pipe. A good use of pipes is the SORT command again. This time, you'll pipe the standard directory listing through the SORT command.

As you know, WordStar displays the file listing in alphabetical order, although you can have WordStar list files in the order they're on the disk. From DOS you have other ways to sort the file listing: by name, extension, size, date, or even the time you last saved them. What's more, you can sort in *descending* order instead of ascending order, say, if you want to display the files sorted with the largest first down to the smallest.

SORT doesn't physically *rearrange* the files on the disk; it merely sorts their names. How you use SORT with the file directory is slightly tricky, so pay close attention. Unless you tell it otherwise, SORT uses the information in the *left-most* column as the basis for the sorting. For example, Figure 28-1 shows a typical DOS file directory listing. Drive D is a *RAM disk* that I use with WordStar (see "WordStar and RAM Disks," below). The left-most column contains the file names.

If you want to sort by file extension, size, date, or time, you must tell DOS the *column offset number.* Just count the number of columns to the position you want. In fact, I've done all the work for you! Here are the column numbers: for extension it's *9,* for size it's *14,* for date it's *24,* and for time it's *33.*

You supply the column number as a special SORT *switch.* Begin the switch with a / character, followed by a plus sign (+), and finally the column offset. You can even have multiple sorts. To perform a descending sort, use the **/R** switch. Here are some examples of sorting the file directory:

```
C> dir ¦ sort
```

```
    Volume in drive D has no label
    Directory of  D:\

COMMAND  COM     23322   8-05-86    2:02p
WSD      EXE     78208   5-21-87    1:45p
WSPRINT  OVR    134784   2-14-87   12:00p
WSBSHORT OVR       512   5-27-87   12:00p
WSMSGS   OVR     43668   2-14-87   12:00p
WSSPELL  OVR     23520   2-14-87   12:00p
CC       BAT        50   2-24-87    2:26p
WD       BAT        63   4-29-87    8:11a
SORT     EXE      1664   3-17-85   12:00a
B        1       52096   5-27-87   11:59a
B        28      34304   5-27-87   12:21p
B        BAK     53504   5-26-87   11:03p
B        8       53632   5-27-87   12:29p
B        25      58368   5-27-87   12:27p
     16 File(s)   1232896 bytes free
```

Figure 28–1   A DOS File Directory Listing

This command sorts the file listing alphabetically by file name.

C> dir ¦ sort /+14

This command sorts the file listing numerically by file size, from smallest to largest.

C> dir ¦ sort /+14/r

This command sorts the file listing numerically by file size, but in descending order, from largest to smallest. Notice you must repeat the switch designator (/).

C> dir ch.* ¦ sort /+24/+9 > chapters

This command sorts only those files that begin with CH, no matter what their extension. It first sorts these files by date, from earliest to latest, and then by extension. It redirects the results of the sort to a file called CHAPTERS. By the way, if several files have the same date, SORT arranges them according to the time.

The MORE pipe in the file MORE.COM is useful because it displays one screenful of information at a time. It's like using the /P option of the DIR command. For example:

```
C> dir | sort /+14/+9 | more
```

This command sorts the directory first by size and then by extension. It pipes the sorted output through MORE to pause after each screenful and display the message --More--. Just press any one key to continue.

Dealing with Bad Sectors

DOS divvies up a disk into *tracks* and *sectors*. The information in a file may be spread out over many sectors. Sometimes a sector goes bad (its surface becomes damaged), and DOS can't read the information there. You can still *recover* part of the file with the DOS RECOVER command. Although you can use this command to recover the good sectors on an entire disk, it's better to recover individual files. That way, you don't scramble together the information in all the files on the disk.

Tip: The best way to avoid bad sectors in the first place is to issue the CHKDSK command often. If CHKDSK reports bad sectors on a floppy disk, copy the files to another disk and reformat the disk with bad sectors. If there are still some bad sectors, discard the disk. To block out and thus make bad sectors harmless on a hard disk, use the *Norton Utilities* (see below).

Changing a File's "Attributes"

It's now time to learn what is happening behind the scenes when you *protect* a file with the **C** choice from the Opening menu. DOS maintains certain *attributes* for each file, among these whether a file is *read only* or *read write*. Usually files are read write so that anyone can read, that is open, and write, that is edit and save, them. Read only files are the ones you've protected from editing *and* accidental deletion.

You can change a file's *read write* attribute with the transient ATTRIB command, in the file ATTRIB.EXE. Use the +**R** switch after the command and *before* the file name to turn read only status on and protect the file. Use -**R** to turn read only status off, thus making the file read write. To check whether a file is read only, issue ATTRIB with just the file name after the command. For example:

```
C> attrib +r file.1
```

This command tells DOS to make FILE.1 read only. If you open this file in WordStar, you'll note the word Prtect on the status line.

```
C> attrib -r file.1
```

This command turns the read only status off, so you can now edit the file.

```
C> attrib file.1
```

This command displays the read only status of FILE.1. If the file is read only, an R appears at the left column. If the file is read-write, no R appears.

Caution: Never change the attribute of a file that's currently open. That is, don't use the go to DOS command in WordStar, run ATTRIB, and change an open file from read-write to read only.

Batch Files: Your DOS Amanuensis

A DOS *batch file* is a special file that contains a "batch" of commands that you want DOS to type for you in a certain order. The advantage to batch files is that you don't have to type the commands every time you want to issue them. You set up a batch file once. Then whenever you want to run the commands in the batch file, type the file name and press **RETURN**. They represent your own personal DOS amanuensis!

Batch files are straight ASCII text files, and they must have the extension .BAT. You can create batch files using the **N** [open a nondocument] choice from the Opening menu. Do *not* use the **D** choice! Type each command on a separate line ending in a hard return. For example, the batch file D.BAT contains one line:

```
DEL *.BAK
```

To issue this command, I type just **d** at the DOS prompt and press **RETURN**—I don't type the .BAT extension—and DOS deletes all WordStar backup files! Here's another example:

```
ECHO=OFF
CLS
ECHO Insert the "project" backup disk in drive B
PAUSE
COPY PROJECT B:
```

Normally, the ECHO command repeats (echoes) other commands on the screen. The line **ECHO=OFF** turns off the repeating. The CLS command clears the screen. The next line just displays the message Insert the "project" backup disk in drive B on the screen (the word ECHO doesn't appear because ECHO is OFF!). The PAUSE command displays the message Strike a key when ready ... and waits for you to press any *one* key. The last command copies the file PROJECT to the B drive.

Note: To cancel a batch file, press ^C or ^**SCROLL LOCK**.

The most important batch file is the *automatic executing file.* DOS always looks for this file for when you turn on or reboot your computer. Its name *must* be AUTOEXEC.BAT, and it must be in the *root* directory. If it exists, DOS executes the commands therein, thus saving you many keystrokes for those setup operations that you perform daily.

An AUTOEXEC.BAT file might look like this:

```
ECHO=OFF
CLS
PROMPT $e[s$e[24A$e[1D$e[K$e[7m$p     $t$h$h$h       $d$e[m$e[uVince-$g $e[m
PATH=C:\;C:\WS4;C:\D;C:\INSTANT;C:\CL;C:\B
DATE
TIME
VERIFY ON
DOSEDIT
FASTDSK
KEY C.PRO /ML
SK
WF
CD \WS4
CLS
```

I've already explained the first four commands. The next two just request the date and time. The VERIFY ON command turns on the verification of all copying. The next few commands issue various terminate and stay resident programs that I use. Notice the command to load the Word Finder thesaurus. Finally, the batch file changes to the WS4 directory and clears the screen before going to the DOS prompt.

Restoring Deleted Files

Neither DOS nor WordStar has a facility for unerasing deleted files, but you can do this seemingly impossible task with a program called a *DOS utility.* My favorite DOS utility package is the *Norton Utilities,* a collection of very useful little programs that can really help you out of a jam! Contact: Peter Norton Computing, Inc., 2210 Wilshire Boulevard, Santa Monica, CA 90403.

Restoring deleted files isn't magic. When you delete a file, DOS just removes the file's name from the directory listing. It hasn't deleted the *contents* of the file at all! What it *has* done is freed up the space that that file occupies, which means that sooner or later DOS will overwrite the file with another.

The secret to restoring files, then, is to do the operation *as soon as you can* after accidentally deleting the file. As long as DOS hasn't written to the disk, your chances of restoring the file intact are very good. Follow the directions supplied with the DOS utility to restore deleted files.

WordStar and RAM Disks

A *RAM disk* is a section of random access memory (RAM) that you pretend is a disk. Because RAM is instantly available, a RAM disk speeds operations up quite a bit, and WordStar really flies! However, when you turn off your machine everything in RAM *disappears,* so you have to take one precaution when you use a RAM disk. That precaution is, of course: *save your work to a real disk, and save it often.*

Before you can set up a RAM disk, you might have to set the *hardware switches* on your computer to tell it the total number of drives. For example, I have two floppy disk drives (A and B), a hard disk (C), and a ram disk (D). I set my computer switches for four disks, even though I may not use the RAM disk all the time.

You also have to use WINSTALL or WSCHANGE to tell WordStar the total number of drives on your system. As you know, the first drive you specify is the default drive. WordStar displays an asterisk (*) next to that drive. In my example, the drives display as C* D A B .

Some versions of DOS include a driver called VDISK.SYS that sets aside part of available memory as a RAM disk. You include reference to VDISK.SYS in your CONFIG.SYS file. There are scores of similar RAM disk programs, some even free! If you've set up a RAM disk, use a batch file to copy the WordStar files to the RAM disk, load WordStar, and copy the file you're editing *back* to the real disk. Here's an example that I call FAST.BAT that uses drive D as the RAM disk drive:

```
ECHO=OFF
CLS
COPY %1 D: > NUL
COPY WS.EXE D: > NUL
COPY WSPRINT.OVR D: > NUL
COPY WSSHORT.OVR D: > NUL
COPY WSMSGS.OVR D: > NUL
COPY WSSPELL.OVR D: > NUL
D:
WS %1
COPY %1 C:
```

There are a couple interesting new features in this batch file. First, the **%1** sets up a *substitution* from the command line. When I start this batch file, I include the name of the file I want to edit in WordStar. For example, if I type—

C> fast ch.7

—the batch file substitutes "ch.7" wherever it sees the **%1**. So, it *copies* that file to the RAM disk, drive D, copies the necessary WordStar program and overlay files, changes to drive D, and then loads WordStar and opens the file (**WS %1**). When I exit WordStar the same batch file copies the edited file back to the C drive (**COPY %1 C:**) lest I forget to do it myself. This is one way to avoid losing your work when you're using a RAM disk. Unfortunately, if there's a power outage you may lose the entire RAM disk.

What does > **NUL** mean? NUL is a special DOS device that literally means nothing! When you redirect the copy command to the "null" device, all you're doing is not displaying the command's messages. For instance, **COPY WS.EXE D: > NUL** just copies the WS.EXE file to the D drive without echoing the command's response on the screen. (Other devices you've seen are LPT1:, the first parallel port, and COM1:, the first serial port.)

You could have included the commands that copy the necessary WordStar files to the RAM disk in your AUTOEXEC.BAT file. That way, WordStar is always ready to go on the RAM disk. Notice that FAST.BAT only copies the *first* file that you typed when you started the batch. If you stay in WordStar and edit other files, remember to copy them from your RAM disk to a real disk, too.

Tip: To avoid the potential loss of data due to power problems like brownouts, use the go to DOS command in WordStar and copy your files to a real drive *often!* Why not create a macro to do this?

WordStar and "Foreign" Programs

In the early days of microcomputers, only 128 ASCII codes were generally available. As you know, many codes represent the 52 upper- and lowercase letters of the alphabet, the nine digits and zero, and the standard punctuation marks. The remaining 30 or so codes have different jobs in different programs. That is, WordStar uses these codes for formatting and special printing effects, while a foreign spreadsheet program like Lotus 1-2-3 uses them for totally different purposes.

Even with the advent of the 128 extended ASCII codes, there aren't enough codes to deal with all the different tasks that computers can do. So, the process of moving information from one program format to another usually involves *stripping* the ASCII codes that can change and *leaving* the ones that represent the standard text elements.

How you *convert* a WordStar file to or from another file format depends on several factors:

- Whether the file you're converting to or from is a WordStar document or nondocument

- What kind of program you're converting to or from

- How you plan to use the converted information in the foreign program or in WordStar

Most of the time, you'll work with text files that are in straight ASCII format. That is, you'll strip out all nontext control codes and extended ASCII codes and make sure that each line ends with a *hard* carriage return. As you know, straight ASCII files are the same as WordStar nondocument files.

Often the conversion requires a certain amount of *massaging* to get the converted file into the proper format. For example, to convert an ASCII file into WordStar document format, you must change some—but not all—hard returns to soft returns.

Some foreign programs, notably word processors, have *conversion utilities* to convert WordStar files to their own format. I won't discuss them here, but you may want to check whether a conversion utility can handle the *new* commands and features of WordStar Professional Release 4. If it can't, you might be better off doing the conversion yourself.

Most other programs have some means of converting files to straight ASCII format. Many programs, such as Lotus 1-2-3, print to a disk file, in a similar fashion to WordStar's ASCII printer driver. Others, such as dBASE III PLUS, require a specific command option to copy a file into ASCII format. Check the foreign program's documentation under *text files* or *ASCII files* to determine the correct method.

Dealing with Print Controls

If you want to retain special printing effects, such as italics or boldface, you may have to find and replace the WordStar print controls with *text codes*. For example, replace the ^Y italic code with \i\, or another text string. After you've converted the file and called it up in the foreign program, do another find and replace to replace the text strings with the appropriate printing commands.

WordStar Document Format to ASCII

There are two ways to convert WordStar documents files to ASCII format:

1. Open the file as a nondocument. Then press ^QU to remove all high order bits in the entire file (Chapter 11). Save the file. Depending on the size of the file, this may take some time.

2. Print the file to a disk file using the special ASCII printer driver. Recall that if you don't supply a file name, WordStar gives the disk file the name ASCII.WS. Make sure you rename the file before printing to disk again. This is by far the faster method of the two.

Besides the time factor, there is another possible disadvantage to method 1. The ^QU command doesn't remove print controls, extended ASCII characters, or dot commands. They may get in the way of the foreign file. However, this disadvantage could be an advantage if you *want* to retain the codes for "massaging" later. Method 2 always removes print codes.

Tip: To retain the dot commands when you print using the ASCII printer driver, answer **y** for "yes" to the print option, Nondocument (Y/N)? .

ASCII to WordStar Document Format

There are, again, two ways to convert ASCII files to WordStar *document* format:

1. Open the file as a document and press ^6 to change hard returns to soft returns *except* at the ends of paragraphs. Then return to the top of the file and press ^QU to realign the entire file, or ^B to realign individual paragraphs. Depending on the size of the file, this may take *a lot* of time and require many keystrokes.

2. Use a find and replace trick that old-time WordStar fans have known about for years.

Method 2 looks complicated, but it isn't. Once you learn and understand it, it can be much faster than method 1 when you're converting large files. There is just one easy rule to follow *before* you convert: Make sure the ASCII file is single spaced and that there are *two* hard returns between paragraphs. Use the foreign program to massage the file into this format before you convert it to WordStar. Then follow these steps:

1. Open the file as a WordStar *non*document (that's right!).

2. Press ^QA (^F2) to begin find and replace. Press ^N *twice* and then **RETURN** to find all double hard returns, that is, the ends of paragraphs. WordStar shows the string as ^M^J^M^J.

3. Choose an unusual character or string of characters as the replacement. For example, type \\ and press **RETURN**.

4. For the find and replace options, type **gn** and press **RETURN**. Then *immediately* press an **ARROW** key to prevent the screen display from updating for each replacement.

5. When find and replace has finished, repeat the procedure, but this time find all *single* hard returns (^N) and replace them with *nothing—* just press **RETURN** as the replacement string. Use the same options. At this point there are *no* carriage returns at all in the file, and everything is a mess!

6. Repeat the find and replace, this time finding the \\ characters, or whatever you used, and replacing them with *two* hard returns, ^N^N (they'll again appear as ^M^J^M^J on the screen). You've reinstated the hard returns at the ends of the paragraphs.

7. Save the file with ^KD (**F10**), then *reopen* the file as a document. Press ^QU to realign the entire file. Save the file again. Voilà!

Exchanging Merge Printing Data Files

As you know, merge printing data files are nondocuments, but the data is in a specific format. There are commas or other characters separating fields, quotation marks around fields containing commas, and hard returns at the ends of records.

Some foreign programs, such as dBASE III PLUS, can read this information directly during conversion once you've told them what the field separator is. With other programs, you may have to arrange the information in columns before the foreign program can read in the information. Similarly, some foreign programs can convert their data into the correct WordStar merge printing data file format, while others cannot.

Lotus 1-2-3 to WordStar Document Files

I don't recommend even *attempting* to copy information from any WordStar file into Lotus 1-2-3 format: it's a difficult and frustrating experience! However, you *can* copy information from a Lotus 1-2-3 worksheet into a file that WordStar can then read directly. This involves printing the range of the worksheet that you want to an *unformatted* disk file.

After retrieving the worksheet file in Lotus 1-2-3, press / and select **Print File**. Lotus 1-2-3 asks for a file name of up to eight characters. Type the name, including drive and directory, and press **RETURN**. Lotus 1-2-3 then requests the range. Stipulate the range by typing or pointing and press **RETURN**. Then select **Options Other Unformatted** to set up the unformatted disk file. Select **Quit** and **Go** to print. Finally, select **Quit** to leave the Print menu and return to the worksheet.

Lotus 1-2-3 prints each column from the worksheet range as a separate column in the disk file. It also appends the file extension .PRN to the name of the disk file. After you've opened a WordStar document into which you want to read the file with **^KR**, make sure you include the .PRN extension when you supply the file name.

dBASE III PLUS and WordStar

As a *database management system,* dBASE III PLUS can sort and arrange structured information in many ways. WordStar, as you know, has no sorting capabilities, but its formatting and merge printing features run rings around dBASE III PLUS. Here's how to exchange information between the two programs. I'm using as an example a simple dBASE III PLUS database that contains information about music lovers. The fields in the database are: FIRST, LAST, STREET, CITY, ZIP, AGE, SEX, and HAIR_COLOR.

To WordStar Documents. Use the dBASE III PLUS **COPY** command with the **SDF** option. This stands for "system data file," in other words a file that any program on the system (DOS) can read. Supply the correct *scope* in the command. For example, you want to copy out records for all teenage boys in Hollywood who have purple hair (quite a lot these days!) to a file called NEW. The dBASE III PLUS command at the "dot prompt" would be: COPY TO NEW FOR CITY = "Hollywood" .AND. SEX = "M" .AND. (AGE > 12 .AND. AGE < 20) .AND. HAIR_COLOR = "Purple" SDF.

dBASE III PLUS copies the information that fits the various stated conditions to a file called NEW.TXT. dBASE III PLUS always appends the file extension .TXT to system data files. Then you could open a document file in WordStar and use **^KR** to insert NEW.TXT. Notice that dBASE III PLUS has set up the fields in columns, each column width being the same as the width of the fields in the dBASE III PLUS database.

You can also create a text file from a dBASE III PLUS report and then use **^KR** to read the file into a WordStar document. For example, suppose you've created a report form called NAMES and you want to save the report to an ASCII text file called NTEXT. After opening the data file and index file that the report uses, type REPORT FORM NAMES TO FILE NTEXT. dBASE III PLUS appends the extension .TXT to the new NTEXT file. Include the PLAIN and NOEJECT options to make as "vanilla" a report as possible, if you wish. You'll note that dBASE III PLUS still inserts form feeds between pages in the new text file. You can find and delete these form feeds later in WordStar.

From WordStar Documents. To copy information from a WordStar document into a dBASE III PLUS database is more difficult. First, the field information in WordStar must be in columns, each column representing a separate field. Second, the WordStar file must be a nondocument, so convert the document into a nondocument before going into dBASE III PLUS. Third, make sure the nondocument file has the extension .TXT.

Finally, you must have created a dBASE III PLUS database, and the *field structure* of the database must match the column widths *exactly.* That is, if a column containing first name information is 12 characters wide in the

WordStar file, the corresponding FIRST field in the dBASE III PLUS database must be 12 characters wide.

After you've made sure that you've followed these rules to the letter, you can *append* the WordStar information into dBASE III PLUS. Suppose the WordStar file is called NAMES.TXT. In dBASE III PLUS you'd type: `APPEND FROM NAMES SDF`. Once again, the **SDF** tells dBASE III PLUS that the NAMES.TXT file is a system data file, not a regular dBASE III PLUS file.

To WordStar Merge Printing Data Files. This is much easier, because dBASE III PLUS can copy information to the exact merge printing data file format that WordStar requires. Merely use the **DELIMITED** option with the **COPY** command. You *don't* have to include the **SDF** option because a "delimited" file is by nature a system data file.

dBASE III PLUS "assumes" the comma as the default delimiter, so to copy the same records to a merge printing data file called NEW, type this: `COPY TO NEW FOR CITY = "Hollywood" .AND. SEX = "M" .AND. (AGE > 12 .AND. AGE < 20) .AND. HAIR_COLOR = "Purple" DELIMITED`. Once again, dBASE III PLUS adds the .TXT extension to the file name. The NEW.TXT file will contain commas as field separators, but *each* field will be enclosed in quotation marks. No problem! WordStar can handle that easily.

From WordStar Merge Printing Data Files. Similarly, use the **DELIMITED** option to tell dBASE III PLUS that the fields are separated by commas in the WordStar file. dBASE III PLUS appends the information in the first field in the WordStar data file to the first field in the dBASE III PLUS database, and so on. To append records to an existing dBASE III PLUS database from a WordStar data file, a typical command would be: `APPEND FROM NAMES DELIMITED`. dBASE III PLUS "assumes" that NAMES is, again, NAMES.TXT.

Sending WordStar Files over the Phone or to Another Computer

Suppose you want to send WordStar files over the phone to a friend. You'll need a *modem* (*mod*ulator/*de*modulator), a hardware device that connects to a serial port and converts the computer and telephone signals correctly. You'll also need *communications* software to handle the process.

If you're sending WordStar nondocument files over the phone, there's no big problem because they're straight ASCII. However, if you want to transfer WordStar document files and retain all the formatting codes, you must set the communications software so that it sends *all eight bits of each byte*. Normally, these programs only deal with the first seven bits, so check the documentation to ascertain how to send all eight bits. Both ends of the connection should be using the same communications program.

To transfer files between computers, you'll need a *null modem cable* that connects the two machines through their serial ports. Check with a printer "guru" for help in making this simple cable. Then use a *file transfer program* such as the excellent—and free!—*Kermit* program from my alma mater, Columbia University. Both ends of the connection should be using the same file transfer software. (Kermit also works over the telephone lines, by the way.)

For more information about Kermit, contact your users' group or: Kermit Distribution, Columbia University Center for Computing Activities, 612 West 115th Street, New York, NY 10025. I've written an article, "A Practical Guide to Kermit," that appeared in the May 1987 issue of Heath/Zenith's *REMark* magazine, pages 27–31.

The Add-On Phenomenon

There are a host of separate programs that work either directly with WordStar or with WordStar files. These *add-on* products enrich WordStar's capabilities and increase your productivity. Many add-ons are terminate and stay resident programs, so you can access them quickly from within WordStar. Below I discuss a few of my favorites that you, too, might find handy.

One significant benefit of add-ons is that they work with *other* programs, too, so they're not restricted to just WordStar. Additionally, because WordStar isn't overblown with a lot of features that you may never need, it still runs fast and lean!

The above-mentioned *Norton Utilities* tops my list of indispensable programs. Besides the file undelete feature, this package has a wonderful text search program that runs rings around the DOS FIND command. It also lets you take care of bad sectors so that they don't interfere with your work, change screen colors, list subdirectories graphically, and even hide a file, among other things. No *serious* computer user should be without this product.

Even when a future release of WordStar *does* have the capability to "do" windows, you'll find *Sidekick* a helful companion. Besides having a WordStar-like pop-up editor that gives you a window for notes and other files, Sidekick also offers a calculator, appointment calendar, and phone dialer. You can also quickly cut-and-paste text from one program into WordStar—and *vice versa*—through Sidekick. Contact: Borland International, 4585 Scotts Valley Drive, Scotts Valley, CA 95066.

WordStar's shorthand macro feature only works with the ESC key and the 36 alphanumeric keys. If you want to customize other key combinations, such as ALT G, you should investigate the benefits of a *keyboard enhancer program.* These programs are terminate and stay resident: they intercept your keystrokes and act on them before sending them on to WordStar. My favorite is *SuperKey,* also from Borland International. With SuperKey you can customize any key combination and you have virtually no limit to the number of keystrokes you can "record" or "play back." You can even have SuperKey type lengthy text blocks for you.

For instance, I use SuperKey to change the default cursor movement keys on the numeric keypad: the HOME key issues the cursor to left side of line command (^QS), while the END key issues the cursor to right side of line, ^QD, command. I think these two commands are far more useful than ^QE and ^QX. You say you'd rather press ALT B to begin a block? That's no problem if you have SuperKey.

A program to read your text and correct your style? Well, not exactly, but *Grammatik II, The Writing Analyst* comes close. Similar to a spelling checker, Grammatik II, The Writing Analyst contains a list of improper, arcane, or incorrect usages against which it compares your text. It will stop at an "offending" word or phrase, offer suggestions, and mark locations that you can later edit in WordStar. This program provides a good way to pinpoint areas that need work—every writer has them! Grammatik II, The Writing Analyst also does a commendable job at catching that most annoying of all bugbears: passive voice constructions. Highly recommended. Contact: Reference Software, 330 Townsend Street, Suite 135, San Francisco, CA 94107.

By far one of the best ideas to come around in a long time is *MemoryMate,* originally *Instant Recall,* a free-form database program that lets you keep track of notes, lists, telephone numbers, ideas, or *anything* you want. You don't have to create a container or structure for your data: just enter it and save it. Later, retrieve it quickly by keyword. There's practically no limit to ways you can use this program. It's substantially reduced the number of sticky paper notes on the desk and walls in the Alfieri household! You can use MemoryMate with WordStar as a terminate and stay resident program, or as a stand alone. Contact: Broderbund Software, Inc., 17 Paul Drive, San Rafael, CA 94903.

If you need the discipline and structure of an outline to arrange your thoughts, look no further than to a "semifree" program called *PC-Outline.* You can get a free but limited version to try out. Just contact any users' group in your area. Then if you like the program—and I'm sure you will—you can pay for the complete version, which includes substantial documentation. This interesting software marketing concept is known as *shareware.*

PC-Outline is an *outline processor* program. It maintains the indentation, arrangement, and numbering of your outlines for you. For instance, you can hide the subsections of an outline and only look at the overall picture, or expand parts of the outline or the entire outline to see it all at once. When you move or delete outline sections, PC-Outline renumbers the entire outline automatically. Neat! Later, you can copy the outline into a WordStar file for prettying up. You can even have PC-Outline resident in RAM and jump back and forth between it and WordStar with a few keystrokes. Contact: Brown Bag Software, 2155 South Bascom Avenue, Campbell, CA 95008.

Because PC-Outline is available under the shareware system, you're expected to buy the software eventually if you plan to use it. There are also hundreds of programs that are in the *public domain.* That means they're absolutely free! One extremely useful free program is DOSEDIT. I don't know who wrote this gem or where you are, but my hat is off to you! DOSEDIT "remembers" all the DOS commands you type, so you can scroll back through them and repeat a command by pressing RETURN. You don't have to type the command again! Contact your users' group for this program. While you're at it, try to get VIEW.COM, a program that displays WordStar files on the screen without the funny eighth bit. This is what the TYPE command in DOS *should* have been!

As Chapter 26 has shown, the world of laser printers and desktop publishing can be a confusing one. A variety of add-on programs can help you produce even better-quality laser output with your WordStar files than just WordStar alone can produce. You can thus approximate the features of a true desktop publishing program without having to learn an entirely new setup! These add-on programs, for instance, have the ability to print text and graphics on the same page, but you'll need a certain amount of extra memory in your laser printer. All of these programs use special codes that you insert into WordStar files. Here are my favorites.

Polaris PrintMerge has far more features than WordStar for accessing the power of laser printers, including the ability to draw lines, boxes, and other graphics symbols easier than in WordStar. One distinct advantage to this product is that it uses WordStar-like dot commands for formatting, so learning the product is relatively easy for WordStar users. Many dot commands are the same in both WordStar and Polaris PrintMerge. However, some of the WordStar Release 4 commands are not the same, because PrintMerge appeared before Release 4. Contact: Polaris Software, 613 West Valley Parkway, Suite 323, Escondido, CA 92025.

Another interesting product, *LaserWare, The Resident Publisher,* works specifically with the Hewlett-Packard LaserJet printers. It's very similar in power to Polaris PrintMerge, but its command structure is different. One unique advantage to this product is that it is a terminate and stay resident program (TSR), so you can call it up at any time. Indeed, it works with most other programs, not just WordStar. That means you can produce very high-quality laser printouts from, say, Lotus 1-2-3 or dBASE III PLUS, too. A companion product, *Glyphix,* lets you create or change your own soft fonts. Contact: SWFTE International, Ltd., Box 219, Rockland, DE 19732.

Billing itself as "automatic desktop publishing software," *PowerText Formatter* may be all you need to enter the new and exciting world of desktop publishing. Its price is far more reasonable than the hundreds you would spend for other desktop programs, yet it has a great deal of power. Scholars will love the ability to generate bibliographies as well as tables of contents or indices. Although not a true WYSIWYG program, PowerText Formatter does let you display on the screen an approximation of your printed file. Contact: Beaman Porter, Inc., 417 Halstead Avenue, Harrison, NY 10528.

Don't let the name *Fancy Font* mislead you. Although you can create your own fonts and symbols with this program, you can do much more. In fact, Fancy Font has extensive formatting and typesetting capabilities that can produce almost any type of document—newsletters, forms, books. If you own a dot-matrix printer, you have access to those fancy fonts that you thought were available only on laser printers. If you own a laser printer, you can mix and match your printer's internal and cartridge fonts with Fancy Font's. For proof of this product's power, look at its beautiful documentation: it was printed entirely with Fancy Font. Be forewarned, though, that this isn't an easy program to learn. Contact: SoftCraft, Inc., 16 North Carroll Street, Suite 500, Madison, WI 53703.

Finally, there's *Inset 2,* the "graphics and text integrator." With Inset 2 you specify where pictures and other graphics elements are to appear in WordStar files, then merge these elements with the text during printing. You can preview the final result on the screen before printing and create "clip art" files of images that you use often. Inset 2 works with a large variety of dot-matrix and laser printers. It has also become more or less of a *de facto* standard for producing "screen dumps" (Chapter 3) that you can save in disk files and print later. Contact: Inset Systems, Inc., 12 Mill Plain Road, Danbury, CT 06811.

Flash! Just as this book was going to press, I discovered a tremendous program that can make your computing life much more productive. It's called *DESQview,* and what it does is let your computer run many programs simultaneously. For example, you can have Lotus 1-2-3, dBASE III PLUS, and WordStar all working at the same time and then switch among them by pressing just two keys. Why, you can run *many* copies of WordStar and edit a different file in each! DESQview offers macros and will even "learn" a series of keystrokes automatically. You can transfer information between different file types, too. Although this isn't an easy program to master either, once you've set up DESQview for your particular needs you'll be amazed at how useful it can be. Very highly recommended. Contact: Quarterdeck Office Systems, 150 Pico Boulevard, Santa Monica, CA 90405.

The ^Q~ Command

For the sake of completeness, I'd like to mention one last, *very* esoteric WordStar command that you'll probably never need: ^Q~. Indeed, this command only makes sense when it's issued by certain terminate and stay resident programs (TSRs). If you're a TSR programmer, you may want to read this section. Otherwise, skip it!

When you type rapidly, your computer keeps the keystrokes in a *typeahead buffer* until the program you're using can get around to dealing with them. However, when you issue certain deleting commands very quickly—for example ^G (**DEL**) to delete a character—you'd want WordStar to stop deleting as soon as you lift your fingers off the keys. So WordStar flushes the typeahead buffer of any extra keystrokes, that is, extra ^G's.

Some TSR programs respond to fast typing and delete characters very quickly. In this case, it may be beneficial for WordStar *not* to flush the typeahead buffer so that the TSR program can handle all the characters in the buffer. Thus, the TSR issues the ^Q~ command to WordStar. The command also instructs WordStar to turn insert mode on, whether it's on or not. The Word Finder thesaurus, for example, uses the ^Q~ command before it inserts a synonym into a WordStar file.

Later, when the typeahead buffer is completely empty (the TSR has dealt with all characters in the buffer), WordStar automatically starts flushing the buffer again and restores the insert mode status (on or off). The point of all this is that if you're using a TSR that doesn't seem to work well with WordStar, it's probably reacting adversely to that flushed typeahead buffer.

Note: You can use WSCHANGE to tell WordStar not to flush the typeahead buffer: press **D** [WordStar] **C** [Other features] **F** [Miscellaneous] and take a look at choice **F** [Erasing & cursor type ahead]. If you do make this change, however, when you lift your fingers off the keyboard you'll sometimes get a "run-on" of some commands.

Dear Reader: You've completed your journey through the world of WordStar. I hope it's been a pleasant one and that you're now ready to get serious with WordStar. Happy word processing!

Appendixes

Appendix

A

The Files Created in This Book

File Name	Created in Chapter	Used or Changed in Chapter
ARREARS.DTA	24	
ARREARS.LET	24	
BIB	21	
BURBANK.1	19	20, 22
BURBANK.1E	20	21
BURBANK.1L	20	
BURBANK.1L2	20	
BURBANK.1L3	23	
BURBANK.R1	23	
BURBANK.RR	23	
BURBANK.DTA	19	20, 22, 23
BURBANK.FRM	21	
BURBANK.LST	20	
BURBANK.STK	21	
CALHOUN.LTR	5	
CH.27	9	10, 15, 25
COMPUTER	10	14
CONTRACT	6	8, 9, 14
CONTRACT.7	23	
DATES	9	
DF	10	
DRAFT	22	
E	21	22

File Name	Created in Chapter	Used or Changed in Chapter
EFFECTS	17	
EX	21	22
EXPENSES.JAN	9	11, 18
EXPENSES.FEB	11	
F.7	25	
FLEA.LTR	24	
FN	25	
FORM	15	16
FORM.2	16	
GRID	21	
HUNTPECK	6	
INT	5	
INVOICE	24	
JONES.LTR	4	
LET	5	
LTRHEAD	26	
MACTEST	7	
MATH.EX	18	
MEETING.APR	9	
MEMO.1	9	
MEMO.2	9	
MEMO.3	26	
MEMO.LAS	26	
NUMBERS.TST	24	
ORDERED	21	
PARIS	11	
PECAN.PIE	9	
PERKINS.LTR	4	5
PIES	9	
PROPOSAL	22	
PUBLISH.DTA	22	
REPLY	23	
REPORT.1	23	
RULER	11	
SALES.1M	24	
SALES.1Q	18	

File Name	Created in Chapter	Used or Changed in Chapter
SALES.DTA	24	
SCRIPT	16	
SIGLINES	5	
SMITH.ANS	16	
SMITH.DEP	16	
SPACE	3	
STOCK.1	22	
STOCK.2	22	
STORY	1	2, 3, 5
STORY.COL	11	
STORY.ELT	10	
STORY.LA	5	6, 8, 10, 11, 14
TEMP	5	

Appendix

B

WordStar Quick Reference Guide

Here is a list of commands and features for quick reference. The number or name in square brackets following a command description indicates the chapter in which I *first* discuss a particular command or feature, so you can turn to that chapter to learn the command.

An asterisk (*) designates a new command or a new implementation of an old command in WordStar Professional Release 4. Where only part of the command implementation is new, that part appears in parentheses.

There is also a separate listing of commands from earlier WordStar versions that don't appear in WordStar Release 4, as well as those DOS commands that I discuss in this book.

As noted, some in-file WordStar commands work only in document or nondocument mode, some print commands are toggle switches, and certain dot commands work only with merge printing.

Options for Loading WordStar [Intro]

WS <filename>	Loads WordStar and opens <filename> as a document file
WS <filename> N	Loads WordStar and opens <filename> as a nondocument file*
WS <filename> D	Loads WordStar and opens <filename> as a document file (only if the default file mode is nondocument)*
WS <filename> P	Loads WordStar, prints <filename>, and then displays the Opening menu*
WS <filename> PX	Loads WordStar, prints <filename>, and then exits back to the operating system*

Opening Menu Commands

Command	In-File Equivalent	Description
^\	^\	Clear the screen* [11]
?		Check WordStar's memory allocation* [13]
C		Protect a file (toggle)* [13]
D		Open a document [1]
E	^KE	Rename a file [5]
ESC	ESC	Shorthand menu* [7]
F		Turn the file display on/off (toggle) (or restrict the file listing with wildcards)* [12]
I		Index a file* [25]
J	^J	Help* [1]
L	^KL	Change the current drive (or directory)* [7]
M	^KP	Merge print a file* (display printing screen if printing or merge printing is in progress)* [19]
N		Open a nondocument [8]
O	^KO	Copy a file [5]
P	^KP	Print a file [1], (display printing screen if printing or merge printing is in progress [3])*
R	^KF	Run a DOS command [12]
T		Create a table of contents* [25]
^W	^W	Scroll up through file listing [1]
X		Exit WordStar and return to DOS [1]
Y	^KJ	Delete a file [2]
^Z	^Z	Scroll down through file listing [1]

In-File Commands

Single-Letter Commands

Command	IBM PC Keyboard Alternate	Description
^PRT SC		Save and print a file* [3]
^\		Clear the screen* [11]
^6	SHIFT ^6	Change a hard return to a soft return (document mode)* [11]
		Turn auto indent on/off (toggle) (nondocument mode)* [11]
^A	^LEFT ARROW	Cursor to the previous word [1]
^B		Align a paragraph (document mode) [1]
		Turn the eighth bits off on all words on a line (nondocument mode)* [11]
^C	PG DN	Scroll through a file down by screenful [1]
^D	RIGHT ARROW	Cursor right one character [1]
^E	UP ARROW	Cursor up one line [1]
^F	^RIGHT ARROW	Cursor to the next word [1]
^G	DEL	Delete the character at the cursor [1]
^H	BACKSPACE	Backspace the cursor and delete the previous character* [1]
^I	TAB	Tab [1]
^J	F1	Help [1]
^K		Block & Save menu [5]
^L	^F3	Repeat the last find or find and replace [6]
^M	RETURN	End a paragraph or insert a blank line [1]
^N		Insert a blank line without moving the cursor [2]
^O		Onscreen Format menu (document mode) [2]
		Set the fixed tab interval (nondocument mode)* [11]
^P		Print Controls menu [3]

^Q		Quick menu [1]
^R	PG UP	Scroll through a file up by screenful [1]
^S	LEFT ARROW	Cursor left one character [1]
^T	F6	Delete a word [1]
^U	F2	Cancel a command or ("unerase" the previously deleted text)* [1]
		Cancel printing or merge printing [3]
^V	INS	Turn insert mode on/off (toggle switch) [1]
^W	^PG UP	Scroll through a file up by line [1]
^X	DOWN ARROW	Cursor down one line [1]
^Y	F5	Delete a line [1]
^Z	^PG DN	Scroll through a file down by line [1]

Double-Letter Commands

ESC (Shorthand) Commands

ESC	Shorthand menu* [7]
ESC ^J	Display help for shorthand* [7]
ESC =	Insert the result of last math operation into the file* [18]
ESC $	Insert the dollar formatted result of the last math operation into the file* [18]
ESC #	Insert the last equation into the file* [18]
ESC @	Insert today's date* [4]
ESC !	Insert the current time* [7]
ESC ?	Display the shorthand definitions screen* [7]
ESC C	Center a line* [2]

ESC P		Cursor to the previous paragraph* [2]
ESC T		Transpose the word at the cursor with the next word* [2]

Help Commands

^J?	**F1 ?**	Help with WordStar editing screen layout* [2]
^J.	**F1 .**	Help with dot commands* [2]
^JJ	**F1 ^J**	Change the help level* [2]

Block & Save Commands

^K'		Change a block to lowercase* [11]
^K"		Change a block to uppercase* [11]
^K0–9		Set place marker 0–9 (toggle) [7]
^KB	**SHIFT F9**	Mark the beginning of a block [5]
^KC	**SHIFT F8**	Copy a block [5]
^KD	**F10**	Save the file and return to the Opening menu [1]
^KE		Rename a file [12]
^KF		Run a DOS command* [12]
^KH	**SHIFT F6**	Hide a block (toggle) [5]
^KI		Turn column replace mode on/off (toggle)* [11]
^KJ		Delete a file [12]
^KK	**SHIFT F10**	Mark the end of a block [5]
^KL		Change the current drive (or directory)* [12]
^KM		Total the numbers in a marked block* [18]
^KN		Turn column mode on/off (toggle) [11]
^KO		Copy a file [12]
^KP		Print a file from within a file (display printing screen if printing is in progress)* [3], (or merge print a file from within a file [19])*
^KQ		Quit the current edit without saving any changes [2]
^KR		Read (insert) a file into the current file [5]

669

^KS	**F9**	Save the file and stay in the file [1]
^KV	**SHIFT F7**	Move a block [5]
^KW		Write a block to a file [5]
^KX		Save the file and exit to DOS [5]
^KY	**SHIFT F5**	Delete a block [5]

Onscreen Format Commands

^OB		Turn the soft space display on/off* [2]
^OC	**SHIFT F2** **ESC C**	Center a line [2]
^OD	**SHIFT F1**	Turn the print controls display on/off (toggle) [3]
^OE		Enter a soft hyphen from the keyboard* [8]
^OF		Set the ruler line from a file line [4]
^OG		Paragraph tab [9]
^OH		Turn hyphen help on/off (toggle) [8]
^OI		Set a tab [4]
^OJ		Turn justification on/off (toggle) [4]
^OL		Set the left margin [4]
^ON		Clear a tab or all tabs [4]
^OO	**F8**	Insert the current ruler line in the file* [4]
^OP		Turn preview on/off (toggle)* [4]
^OR		Set the right margin [4]
^OS		Set the line spacing [4]
^OT		Turn the ruler line on/off (toggle) [2]
^OW		Turn wordwrap on/off (toggle) [9]
^OX		Turn margin release on/off (toggle) [9]

Print Controls Commands

^P@		Print the following text at a fixed column* [17]
^PA		Turn the alternate character width on [17]

^PB	F4	Turn boldface print on/off (toggle) [3]
^PC		Pause printer from within a file [3]
^PD		Turn doublestrike print on/off (toggle) [3]
^PE		User-defined print code [17]
^PF		Phantom space [17]
^PG		Phantom rubout [17]
^PH		Backspace and overprint a character with the next character [17]
^PI		Insert a nondocument fixed tab in a document file* [17]
^PJ		Insert a line feed [17]
^PK		Suppress blanks in the header or footer text (for alternating text) on odd-numbered pages [14]
		Enclose file text as an index reference (toggle)* [25]
^PL		Insert a form feed [17]
^PM	^P RETURN	Overprint a line with the next line [11]
^PN		Turn normal print on [17]
^PO		Binding (nonbreak) space [3]
^PQ		User-defined print code [17]
^PR		User-defined print code [17]
^PS	F3	Turn underlining on/off (toggle) [3]
^PT		Turn superscript on/off (toggle) [17]
^PV		Turn subscript on/off (toggle) [17]
^PW		User-defined print code [17]
^PX		Turn strikeout on/off (toggle) [3]
^PY		Change ribbon color (or turn italics on/off)* (toggle)* [3]

Quick Commands

^Q?		Display the character count from the beginning of the file to the cursor location* [13]

^Q~		Avoid "flushing" the type-ahead buffer when using certain terminate and stay resident programs* [28]
^Q0–9		Cursor to place marker 0–9 [7]
^Q DEL		Delete to the left side of the line [2]
^QA	^F2	Find and replace [6]
^QB		Cursor to the beginning of a block [5]
^QC	^END	Cursor to the end of the file [1]
^QD	^F10	Cursor to the right side of the line [1]
^QE	HOME	Cursor to the top left side of the current screen* [1]
^QF	^F1	Find [6]
^QG		Cursor forward to a character* [2]
^QH		Cursor backward to a character* [2]
^QI	^F4	Cursor to page number (document mode)* [2]
		Cursor to line number (nondocument mode)* [11]
^QK		Cursor to the end of a block [5]
^QL	SHIFT F3	Check the spelling of the rest of the file* [8]
^QM		Turn on the calculator* [18]
^QN	SHIFT F4	Check the spelling of the word at the cursor* [8]
^QO		Check the spelling of the next word you type* [8]
^QP		Cursor to the previous position [1]
^QQ		Repeat the next command or keystroke [7]
^QR	^HOME	Cursor to the beginning of the file [1]
^QS	^F9	Cursor to the left side of the line [1]
^QT		Delete forward to a character* [2]
^QU		Align the rest of the file (document mode)* [2]

		Turn the eighth bits off in an entire file (nondocument mode)* [11]
^QV		Cursor to the previous block location [5]
		Cursor to the last find or find and replace location [6]
^QW		Scroll continuously up [7]
^QX	END	Cursor to the bottom line of the current screen* [1]
^QY		Delete to the right side of the line [2]
^QZ		Scroll continuously down [7]

Dot Commands

..	Nonprinting comment line [4]
.AV	Ask for a variable from the keyboard (merge printing) [21]
.AW ON/OFF	Turn paragraph align on/off* [9]
.BN	Select a sheet feeder bin* [17]
.BP ON/OFF	Turn bidirectional printing on/off [17]
.CP	Conditional page break [15]
.CS	Clear the screen of messages (or display optional message)* (during printing)* or merge printing [16]
.CW	Change the horizontal character width [10]
.DF	Define the data file (merge printing) [19]
.DM	Display a message (during printing)* or merge printing [16]
.EI	End a condition (merge printing)* [22]
.EL	Begin a conditional alternative (merge printing)* [22]
.FI	Insert a file (during printing)* or merge printing [16]
.FM	Footer margin [14]
.F1 or .FO	First footer line* [14]

.F2		Second footer line* [14]
.F3		Third footer line* [14]
.GO TOP/BOTTOM		Go to the top or bottom of the file and continue (merge printing)* [22]
.H1 or .HE		First header line* [14]
.H2		Second header line* [14]
.H3		Third header line* [14]
.HM		Header margin [14]
.IF		Begin a condition (merge printing) [22]
.IG		Nonprinting comment line [4]
.IX		Insert an index reference* [25]
.LH		Set the vertical line height [15]
.LM	^F5	Set the left margin* [4]
.LQ ON/OFF		Turn letter quality printing on/off* [17]
.LS		Set the line spacing* [4]
.MA		Define a math equation variable (merge printing)* [24]
.MB		Set the bottom margin [4]
.MT		Set the top margin [4]
.OJ ON/OFF		Turn right margin justification on/off* [4]
.OP		Omit printing of page numbers [4]
.PA	^F8	Unconditional page break [15]
.PC		Page number column position [14]
.PF ON/OFF/DIS		Turn the print time line former on/off/discretionary* [16]
.PG		Restore page numbers* [14]
.PL		Set the page length [15]
.PM	^F7	Set the paragraph margin* [9]
.PN		Change the page number [14]
.PO		Set the page offset [4]
.PR OR=P/L		Change the laser printer paper orientation* [26]
.PS ON/OFF		Turn proportional spacing on/off* [17]
.RM	^F6	Set the right margin* [4]

.RP	Repeat printing* [16]
.RR	Insert a ruler line* [4]
.RV	Read the name and order of variables in the date file (merge printing) [19]
.SR	Set sub/superscript roll [17]
.SV	Define the data (or format)* for a variable (merge printing) [23]
.TC	Insert a table of contents reference* [25]
.TC1–9	Insert an alternate (list) reference* [25]
.UJ ON/OFF/DIS	Turn microjustification on/off (or discretionary)* [17]
.UL ON/OFF	Turn the underlining of spaces in a phrase on/off* [4]
.XE	Define the ^PE command string* [17]
.XL	Define the form feed string* [17]
.XQ	Define the ^PQ command string* [17]
.XR	Define the ^PR command string* [17]
.XW	Define the ^PW command string* [17]

Miscellaneous Commands and Features

F7	Align a paragraph (^B) and return the cursor to the previous position (^QP)* [2]
ALT 1	Look up the word at the cursor in the Word Finder thesaurus* [8]
ALT F1 through **ALT F10**	Line and box drawing characters* [17]
!	Tab stop on an embedded ruler line [9]
#	Indicate a decimal tab stop [9]
	Page number in a header or footer [14]

$	Substitute a digit in a numeric format assigned with a **.SV** dot command, with a dollar sign to left of first digit (merge printing)* [24]
&	Variable field delimiter (merge printing) [19]
&@&	Insert today's date (merge printing)* [19]
&!&	Insert the current time (merge printing)* [20]
&#&	Insert the current page number (merge printing)* [20]
&_&	Insert the current line number (merge printing)* [20]
( )	Enclose a negative number in parentheses in a numeric format assigned with a **.SV** dot command (merge printing)* [24]
*	Substitute a digit in a numeric format assigned with a **.SV** dot command, or an asterisk if there is no digit (merge printing)* [24]
	Wildcard to match any character in file names* [12]
-	Column on embedded ruler line
	Substitute a digit in a numeric format assigned with a **.SV** dot command, with a minus sign to left of first digit (merge printing)* [24]
	Indicate an index cross-reference* [25]
+	Indicate an index primary reference* [25]
,	Field delimiter in data files (merge printing) [19]
	Insert a comma in a numeric format assigned with a **.SV** dot command (merge printing)* [24]
	Separate an index subreference from its reference* [25]
.	Insert a decimal point in a numeric format assigned with a **.SV** dot command (merge printing)* [24]

?	Wildcard option for find or find and replace* [6]
	Substitute a digit in a numeric format assigned with a **.SV** dot command, or a zero if there is no digit (merge printing)* [24]
	Wildcard to match one character in file names* [12]
\	Print the next character literally in a header or footer [14] (or table of contents [25])*
/	Assign a format to a variable (merge printing)* [23]
/O	Omit a variable entry without leaving a blank line (merge printing) [19]
\<number\>	Find the nth occurrence (represented by \<number\>) of a string, or replace the string \<number\> times in a find and replace [6]
9	Substitute a digit in a numeric variable assigned with a **.SV** dot command, or a zero if there is no digit (merge printing)* [24]
0–9	Change the repetition speed for **^QQ** [7]
A	Align paragraph option for find and replace* [6]
	Add word to personal dictionary during a spelling check [8]
B	Print or merge print from background* [3]
	Backward search option for find or find and replace [6]
	Bypass one occurrence of word during a spelling check [8]
C	Continue printing or merge printing after a pause* [3]
	Centered string format assigned with a **.SV** dot command (merge printing)* [23]
CHANGE or **C**	Change the disk during printing or merge printing* [16]

E	Enter correction of word into file during a spelling check [8]
ESC	Repeat the last file name and complete a command* [1]
F	Print or merge print at full speed* [3]
G	Move to the beginning or end of the file before a find or find and replace* [6]
	Turn global replace on/off during a spelling check (toggle)* [8]
I	Ignore word during a spelling check [8]
L	Left margin position on an embedded ruler line [9]
	Left-justified string format assigned with a .SV dot command (merge printing)* [23]
M	Display more suggested corrections during a spelling check* [8]
N	Nonstop find and replace option [6]
P	Paragraph margin position on an embedded ruler line* [9]
	Pause printer during printing or merge printing [3]
^P	Prefix for all commands in shorthand macros* [7]
^P SHIFT -	Find or find and replace code for a soft hyphen at the end of the line* [8]
^P SHIFT 6	Find or find and replace code for a soft hyphen in the middle of the line* [8]
R	Right margin position on an embedded ruler line [9]
	Search through rest of file from cursor position in find and replace* [6]
	Right-justified string format assigned with a .SV dot command (merge printing)* [23]
^R	Repeat last file name in file operations [2]

	Repeat the last find or find and replace string [6]
	Restore the last equation in the calculator* [18]
T	Turn auto-align on/off during a spelling check* [8]
U	Ignore case option for find or find and replace [6]
V	Position of paragraph tab on ruler line* [11]
W	Whole word option for find or find and replace [6]
WC	Display the character, word, and line count of selected files (separate program: issue from the DOS prompt) [13]
Z	Substitute a digit in a numeric format assigned with a **.SV** dot command, or a space if there is no digit (merge printing)* [24]

Conditional Merge Printing Operators [22]

=	Is the same as alphabetically
<	Comes before alphabetically
>	Comes after alphabetically
<=	Comes before or is the same as alphabetically
>=	Comes after or is the same as alphabetically
<>	Is not the same as alphabetically
#=	Is equal to numerically
#>	Is greater than numerically
#<	Is less than numerically
#>=	Is greater than or equal to numerically
#<=	Is less than or equal to numerically
#<>	Is not equal to numerically

Commands No Longer Available in WordStar Release 4

Opening Menu Commands

H	Set help level
S	Run SpellStar or CorrectStar (use ^QL, ^QN, or ^QO in a file)
T	Run TelMerge

In-File Commands

^JH	Change the help level (use ^JJ)
^KF	Display the file directory (toggle) (use any file command)
^OE	Turn soft hyphen entry on/off (toggle) (see new ^OE)
^OP	Page break display on/off (toggle)
^OV	Turn variable tabs on/off (toggle) (see ^PI)
^P-	Enter a hard hyphen when soft hyphen entry is on (use a regular hyphen)
^Q-	Delete the character to the left of the cursor (use ^Q DEL)
^QL	Cursor to first marked misspelling (see new ^QL)

Dot Commands and Other Features

.AND.	Conditional "and" (merge printing) (use nested conditions)
.EF	End of conditional "if" (merge printing) (use .EI)
.EX	Conditional "except" (merge printing) (use nested conditions)
GOTO	Conditional "go to" label (merge printing) (use .GO TOP/ BOTTOM)

| .IJ | Turn input justification on/off (merge printing) |
| .OR. | Conditional "or" (merge printing) (use nested conditions) |

DOS Commands and Features Discussed in This Book

^NUM LOCK (^S)	Stop scrolling temporarily [12]
^PRT SC	Send the screen display to the printer [12]
ATTRIB	Change the file attribute (transient) [28]
BACKUP	Back up files for archive purposes (transient) [13]
^BREAK (^C)	Cancel a DOS command [12]
CD or CHDIR	Change the current directory (resident) [12]
CHKDSK	Check the disk space and available memory (transient) [13]
CLS	Clear the screen (resident) [28]
COMMAND	Run the DOS command processor (resident) [12]
COMP	Compare two files (transient) [28]
COPY	Copy files (resident) [13]
DATE	View or change the current date (resident) [12]
DEL or ERASE	Delete files (resident) [13]
DIR	Display the files on a drive or in a directory (resident) [12]
DISKCOMP	Compare two disks (transient) [28]
DISKCOPY	Copy an entire floppy disk (transient) [13]
ECHO	Control the display of commands on the screen (resident) [28]
EXIT	Return to the previous level (resident) [12]
FC	List the differences between two files (transient) [28]

FIND	Search files for a text string (transient) [12]
FORMAT	Format (initialize) a disk (transient) [12]
LABEL	Create or change the volume label (DOS 3.0 and higher, transient) [12]
MD or **MKDIR**	Make a new directory (resident) [12]
MORE	Display command output one screen at a time (transient) [28]
PATH	Set up the file search path (resident) [28]
PAUSE	Pause, display a message, and wait for user to press a key (resident) [28]
PROMPT	Change the DOS prompt (resident) [28]
RD or **RMDIR**	Remove (delete) an empty directory (resident) [12]
RECOVER	Recover files (transient) [28]
REN or **RENAME**	Rename files (resident) [13]
RESTORE	Restore files archived with BACKUP (transient) [13]
SEARCH	Locate specific files (transient) [12]
SORT	Sort the contents of a file or the file directory (transient) [28]
TIME	View or change the current time (resident) [12]
TREE	Display all directories (transient) [12]
TYPE	Display the contents of a text file (resident) [12]
VERIFY	Verify a copy (resident) [13]
VOL	Display the volume label (resident) [12]
..	Parent directory [12]
\	Path designator [12]
/	Switch designator [12]
*	Wildcard to match any characters [12]

?	Wildcard to match one character [12]
<	Redirect the input to a command [28]
>	Redirect the output from a command [28]
¦	Pipe information from one program to another [28]
+	Concatenate (join) copied files [28]
COM1	First serial printer port [Intro]
LPT1	Default printer port [Intro]
NUL	"Null" device [28]

Index

Symbols (in ASCII order)

running multiple versions of WordStar
works best if WordStar is configured
for, 307–8
shared printers for, 81
WSCHANGE settings required for,
619–20
Newsletters, WordStar unable to handle
multiple columns for, 262
NewWord, xxv
Nodes, 81
Noise words defined, 567
Nonbreak space. *See* Binding space
Nondocument Edit menu, 189
Nondocument file(s), 254–57
auto indent turned on with ^6 in, 256
converting WordStar documents to,
80–81, 254, 255
defined, xxi
hard returns removed with ^6 or SHIFT
^6 when you create a document file
from a, 252–54
merge printing data files as, 432–35, 448
PERSONAL.DCT as a, 189–90
printing, 74, 257
^QI or ^F4 to move the cursor to a
specific line number of a, 256–57
^QU or ^B to turn off eighth bits in a,
255
suppressing dot commands by
temporarily treating files as, 106
tab stops, 255–56, 404
WS <filename> N to load WordStar and
open a, 9
WSCHANGE to make the default
printing, 620, 626
Nondocument mode
no wordwrap in the, 252
tab stops, 634
for writing and editing programs, 43
Norton Utilities
to block out bad sectors, 644
to restore deleted files, 646–47
text search program of, 654
Null device, 648
Numeric keypad, 3
ALT key and ASCII character code to

insert extended characters from the,
391
Numerical conditional operators
equal to, #=, 479
greater than, #>, 479
greater than of equal to, #>=, 480
less than, #<, 479
less than or equal to, #<=, 480
not equal to, #<>, 480

O

Odd pages, printing only, 74
Onscreen formatting commands (^O), 84–85
to change formats "on the fly," 103
dot commands preferable to, 85, 97
quick reference to the, 670
using, 97–103
Onscreen Format menu, 43
Opening a document with D, 14–15
Opening menu, 13
bypassing the, 8–9
closing a file and returning to the, 32–33
commands, quick reference to the, 666
directory display, WSCHANGE to
change the, 625
initial work directory customizable to
load from the, 626
SPACEBAR pressed as WordStar loads to
quickly display the, 8
WSCHANGE to change default settings
of the, 625–26
Operators
alphabetical. *See* Alphabetical conditional
operators
conditional, 479–80, 481
math, 408
merge printing. *See* Merge printing
numerical. *See* numerical conditional
operators
order of precedence for, 410–11
scientific, 409–10
Order of precedence
in equations that are merge printed,
535–36
in the Math menu, 410–11
Orphan as ending line of paragraph printed
at top of page, 338–40